TEACHING COMMUNICATION
Theory, Research,
and Methods

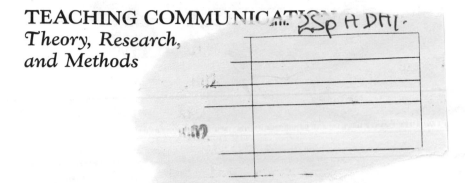

COMMUNICATION TEXTBOOK SERIES

Jennings Bryant—Editor

Instructional, Reading, Written Communication
John Daly—Advisor

DALY/FRIEDRICH/VANGELISTI • Teaching
Communication: Theory, Research,
and Methods

TEACHING COMMUNICATION:
Theory, Research, and Methods

Edited by

John A. Daly
University of Texas

Gustav W. Friedrich
University of Oklahoma

Anita L. Vangelisti
University of Iowa

LEA LAWRENCE ERLBAUM ASSOCIATES, PUBLISHERS
1990   Hillsdale, New Jersey   Hove and London

Lawrence Erlbaum Associates, Inc., Publishers
365 Broadway
Hillsdale, New Jersey 07642

Library of Congress Cataloging-in-Publication Data
Teaching communication : theory, research, and methods / edited by
John A. Daly, Gustav W. Friedrich, Anita L. Vangelisti.
    p.   cm. — (Communication textbook series)
Includes index.
ISBN 0-8058-0645-8
ISBN 0-8058-0162-6(p)
    1. Communication—Study and teaching (Higher) I.Daly, John A.
(John Augustine), 1952- . II. Friedrich, Gustav W.
III. Vangelisti, Anita L. IV. Series: Communication (Hillsdale, N.J.)
P91.3.T43 1990
302.2′071′1—dc20

89-12038
CIP

Printed in the United States of America
10 9 8 7 6 5 4 3 2 1

Contents

PART III ORGANIZING THE INSTRUCTIONAL CONTEXT

Introduction

The field of communication was founded, in part, because of a felt need to make people better communicators. That meant teaching them how to communicate more effectively, whether it be in public settings (e.g., public address, groups) or in private (e.g., interpersonal). Most of that teaching has happened within the classroom and many professionals have spent their lives instructing others on various aspects of communication. Yet, in all the 70 years or so that the field of communication has existed, very little integrated attention has been paid to the methods involved in teaching communication. While there have been journal articles on techniques, as well as classes on instruction in communication there have been few attempts to integrate the many issues and concerns that face teachers. This book attempts to do that.

Who is this book for? Many readers should find it especially useful when they start out their careers as communication educators. One of the toughest parts of graduate school is moving from one side of the desk to another with little or no preparation or guidance. There are few fields of endeavor where people expect so much quality so quickly yet provide so few resources. At best, most beginning graduate students are hired to teach undergraduate courses (at paultry rates) and receive a single 3-hour course in teaching. Many times these beginning teachers don't even receive credit for the course and are forced to fit that course in with more, so-called "substantive" courses. This book is for them. One of the prime motivators for doing this book was to provide a useful reference for beginning teachers in communication—whether they be graduate students or, perhaps, beginning faculty members who have not yet faced an audience of 20, 30, or even 500 inquiring, demanding pupils.

Another audience for this book is the individual teacher who has, perhaps for many years, taught communication. The editors of this book often find themselves sharing and listening to stories about teaching. Learning to teach isn't a one-time effort. It is a continuing, growing experience. Good teaching requires more than knowledge about the topic area. It demands an understanding of instructional processes, of learning, and constant refining of skills. Hopefully, this book will offer new insight and fresh perspective for even the most experienced of teachers.

Who also might use this book? Aside from Gus' son, Anita's mother, and John's children, we hope that department chairs and deans will offer it to new faculty members in both 2-year and 4-year colleges, directors of basic courses and multisection courses will give it to instructors who they supervise, and directors of graduate studies and/or instructors of courses in communication education make regular use of it in their classes.

In thinking about the organization of this book, the editors identified six major concerns that face any communication educator and asked some of the best people in the discipline to write chapters elaborating these concerns.

The first issues addressed in this book, examined in Part I, focus on the goals of communication education. In four chapters, authors describe the nature of the communication discipline and the goals for communication instruction that derive from it. Having identified the goals of communication education, Part II focuses on the preparation of specific communication courses. Rather than examining every potential course that could be developed, this section offers descriptions of a smaller sample of traditional topics and provides hints from experts on how to prepare course materials on topics such as public speaking, persuasion, and intercultural communication. Both page limitations and the timing of the preparation of this manuscript precluded the inclusion of equally important subjects (e.g., interpretation, political communication, language). Hopefully, even if a reader's favorite course is left unmentioned, he or she may be able to garner ideas and perspectives from other course areas. Part III assists the instructor in organizing the instructional context. Within this section, the emphasis is on classroom roles of teachers and students, classroom management, and organizing the first day of a class. Part IV, then, focuses on using specific instructional strategies and tools. This section is concerned with both global issues (e.g., the choices of an instructional model) and more specific tools (e.g., using writing, case study, and games and simulations). In addition to describing various instructional tools and criteria for their selection, the chapters in this section also offer ideas on evaluating both the processes and the products of instruction. In Part V the focus is on unique teaching assignments that readers of this book may sometimes encounter. For instance, it is not uncommon for new assistant professors to direct a basic course, whether it be "the" basic course or multiple sections of the basic public speaking course. Nor is it uncommon to be asked to prepare instructional material for continuing education. Each of these assignments require particular skills. Two additional assignments discussed in this section are teaching in the 2-year college and directing forensic programs. The final section of this book, Part VI, explores important professional issues that face both the new and experienced communication instructor. One chapter involves ethical concerns—issues connected to both day to day instructor student interaction (e.g., plagiarism) and issues that relate to the content of communication instruction (e.g., freedom of speech). A second chapter is concerned with political and ethical issues that may arise as instructors join a department. Finally, the last chapter focuses on how one grows as a professional—an issue that includes, among other things, the relative emphasis one should place on teaching, research, and service activities.

The publication of this book marks a turning point for the field of communication. Most mature disciplines have books on teaching their respective contents. Yet, for many years, people interesting in garnering knowledge about teaching communication have been forced to turn to other fields to find information about teaching. No integrated text existed that specified the conceptual, as well as the practical issues related to communication instruction. We hope this book does just that.

I

THINKING ABOUT THE GOALS OF COMMUNICATION EDUCATION

1

The Communication Discipline

Gustav W. Friedrich
University of Oklahoma

Don M. Boileau
George Mason University

THE BEGINNINGS

Giles Wilkeson Gray (1949) persuasively argued the case for studying the history of communication education in America:

> a more complete examination of the route we have traveled in coming from our beginning . . . to our present position is well worth the undertaking. . . . It will give us a still deeper understanding and appreciation of that position, in the same way that any study of history may provide the basis for a better orientation as an aid in determining the direction we should proceed. (p. 156)

Based on Gray's premise, and the need to provide a context for understanding the diversity of tasks that face the communication educator, this chapter surveys the development of the communication discipline in America and then explores its current status in terms of goals and structure.

The starting point for the field of communication in this nation was 1636, 16 years after the Pilgrims landed in America, with the founding of Harvard University by the Massachusetts legislature. Because Harvard's mission, as was true of other New England colleges soon to follow, was to train ministers of the gospel with a curriculum modeled on medieval universities, instruction in the practical discipline of communication (Craig, 1989) was needed.

An important goal of ministerial schooling was to produce clerics who were able to defend the church with well-crafted arguments. Because Latin was the language of educated people, the pedagogy for developing presentational and dialectical skills was the Latin syllogistic disputation. A tutor (usually the college president) selected a student to defend the "truthful" side of a question from one of the arts or sciences taught in the college. This student, utilizing a format specified by the divisions and dicotomies of Ramistic logic, opened the disputation by reading a carefully worded Latin discourse that: (a) stated the thesis, (b) defined and delimited the question, and (c) used the format of a syllogism to present the arguments supporting the thesis. At the conclusion of this presentation, the other students in the class raised objections, also in syllogistic format, by either disagreeing with the definitions or by denying the major or minor premises. As objections were raised, the disputation's author was provided the opportunity to reestablish the original arguments. During this whole process, of course, the tutor actively assisted students who experienced difficulty in the use of either Latin or logic (Potter, 1954).

As the mission of higher education expanded to include other professions, English replaced Latin, and students received instruction in persuasion in addition to argumentation. As this happened, college presidents and tutors were replaced by specialists in rhetoric, elocution, and speech as providers of communication instruction.

EMERGENCE OF DEPARTMENTS

Although communication instruction was a part of higher education from the beginning, separate departments of communication were not the original providers of training in the subject. In fact, as recently as 1900, there was no such entity as a department of communication. In his description of the origin and development of departments of speech, Smith (1954) pointed out the college departments, as we know them, did not exist until late in the 19th century, when the structure of higher education responded to tremendous expansion. Smith identified four interrelated pressures that produced a departmental structuring of higher education: (a) a flood of new knowledge; (b) the development of specialization within numerous and narrowly defined segments of the curriculum; (c) the inclusion of useful and practical knowledge (e.g., agriculture and engineering) within the college curriculum; and (d) college enrollments that more than doubled in the last quarter of the 19th century. In short:

> The modern college department . . . was born out of the pressures of new knowledge, specialization, new utilitarian concepts of the functions of education, and swelling enrollments. It judged the fitness of course offerings, the relationships of courses to one another; it set up prerequisites, and programs for majors and minors; it cultivated the expansion of knowledge in its own segment of the academic globe, and looked anxiously to unoccupied territory between itself and neighboring departments; it sought money and equipment, and made recommendations for appointments, promotions, and salary changes. (p. 449)

The departmentalization of American higher education proceeded rapidly between 1860 and 1900. Although it was possible to form autonomous departments of communication during this period, and this occurred in some institutions, the general trend saw departments of English language and literature take responsibility for most communication instruction. Smith believes that this occurred for two reasons: (a) the fact that both communication and English literature trace their historical roots to the study of rhetoric, which, with its traditional concern for the arts of both oral and written discourse, has been an established part of the curriculum since medieval times, and (b) "a certain lack of independent vitality within the area of rhetoric" (p. 451). In short, "neither the practice of rhetoric nor the practice of elocution, as it was conceived in the colleges in the last half of the nineteenth century seems to have possessed the status necessary for the general emergence of a department separate from English literature" (p. 453).

The bonds between communication instruction and the English department, however, were from the beginning very fragile. Smith identified four pressures that provided early impetus for the establishment of independent communication departments:

1. Pressure created by the specialization of interest within English. As English developed as an academic speciality, it defined its uniqueness and academic respectability in terms of intensive literary study and linguistics—a move that left little room for teachers of speaking and writing.

2. The outspoken discontent of speech teachers working in departments of English. Individuals who believed strongly in the importance of providing instruction in the practical skills of discourse were quickly disillusioned by their location in a department whose budget was controlled by individuals with different enthusiasms. The first important public demand for the separation of speech and English came on March 25, 1913, at the Public Speaking Conference of the New England and North Atlantic States.

3. The claims of distinctiveness in subject matter—claims that had their origins in two sources. First, teachers of public speaking asserted that their subject matter possessed a heritage (the rhetorical tradition) that was equally as classical as that of literature. Second, they argued that the modern sciences, and particularly psychology, provided them with new knowledge that was both foreign to the interests of English departments and worthy of independent departmental status.

4. The demand of students. The influence of student interest and pressure on the formation of communication departments is illustrated by the following editorial in *The University of Oklahoma Magazine* (Great need, 1912):

> At the time we are writing our editorials it is rumored that a movement is on foot, backed by some one hundred and fifty students of the University who are members of literary societies to petition the State Board of Education to establish a Department of Public Speaking with a full-paid professor with special training in that line in charge. It is hoped that the Board will give the matter very careful consideration, as the need for such a department here is extremely urgent.
>
> It is not enough to have a student as a debating coach, giving in addition one or two courses in public speaking. Such a plan does not meet the needs at all. During the past two years we have had Paul Walker at the head of this work. The Board will have to look a long time before it will find a man with Walker's qualifications willing to work for what Walker has been working for. He could afford to do it because he wanted to study law and the work afforded him the opportunity. He had had previous training in the work and he was specially fitted for the job. But even the work he has been able to do has not met the need. The need requires the full time of a trained professor.
>
> There are about one hundred and fifty students in the University who are engaged in active literary society work. Every one of them would like to have some training in public speaking. Most of them consider it a waste of time to enter classes taught by one of their fellow students. Teaching public speaking is not like any other teaching. After one has studied well a subject in mathematics, or geology, or some kindred subject, where the accumulation of facts, rules, laws, etc., is the main thing, all of which can be done in one year's application to a given course, any student ought to be qualified to teach that subject. But in public speaking the ability to teach it cannot be learned by merely studying a text book, nor can one teach it by merely knowing a few rules, or laws, or facts. A good teacher of public speaking must be a good speaker himself.
>
> Ever since we have been at the University we have heard the complaint frequently made that not enough attention is given to public speaking. The English Department gives some courses in debating, which is only one phase of public speaking. The debating coach gives a course each semester in debating. Aside from the training given by the expression department

that is the extent of instruction the University offers at present in public speaking. The training in the expression department does not properly come under what we are discussing. Someone has said: "Whistle to a dog and he comes—that's oratory; speak to him and he runs away—that's elocution." Well, it's the whistling that we're discussing.

If a student wants training in how to be at ease on the stage, or how to hold his hands (not her's), or how to make a graceful appearance, or how to control his gestures so as to make them effective, or how to train his voice so as to make his speech smooth and eloquent—his only resource is the downtown preachers, and some of them need a little of that training themselves. In the Kansas–Oklahoma debate this year our boys clearly excelled in argument, but the Kansas boys had been trained in these things; our boys showed that they had not. Now suppose that Kansas had put up as good an argument as our boys did they would have won the debate in spite of everything, because they were better speakers than our boys were.

One hundred and fifty students asking for a strong Public Speaking Department ought to be sufficient to warrant the Board in giving it to us. Now is a good time to ask for it, too, for a new coach will have to be selected for next year to take Paul Walker's place, and why not just have a full-time man who can give us a little more than training in debating. There are other phases of public speaking that are just as important—indeed, if not more so. (pp. 17–18)

As a result of the pressures just described, independent communication departments began to emerge in significant numbers shortly after the turn of this century. Although the titles of these departments were varied, a common one was Department of Public Speaking. This title began to change to Department of Speech after 1920, to Department of Speech Communication in the 1960s, and, most recently, to Department of Communication.

In the beginning, departments focused their instructional efforts on developing the skills of formal, public discourse through courses with such labels as Forensics, Declamation, Elocution, Oratory, Logic, Rhetoric, Extemporaneous Speaking, Debate, Dramatic Interpretation, and Public Speaking. Coursework in drama was present from the beginning; theater production courses were added in the 1920s; the addition of speech science and training for speech therapists developed after 1920; and coursework in radio developed after 1935. During the 1950s, departments began to develop coursework in less formal modes of discourse as the field started to expand the focus of investigations. Haiman's *Group Leadership and Democratic Action,* published in 1951, was the first book to focus on the concepts, developments, and research findings in group dynamics, leadership, and interpersonal communication. The first text to focus completely on interpersonal communication was Wiseman and Barker's *Speech—Interpersonal Communication,* published in 1967.

As this discussion suggests, departments of communication were founded to serve utilitarian and pedagogical ends. Although our founding fathers called for research (as a means for achieving academic respectability), much of the early research was directed toward pedagogical ends. This changed rapidly, however, as scholars "rediscovered" the classical and modern rhetorical traditions and as they explored the applicability of social scientific research methods to communication phenomena. For excellent treatments of the history of our research traditions, see Cohen (1985), Delia (1987), and Pearce (1985).

CURRENT STATUS

Currently, the field of communication is both broad and diverse—encompassing teacher/scholars housed in departments with varied titles (e.g., Communication, Speech Communication, Mass Communication, Journalism) that are, in turn, located in various colleges (e.g., Arts & Sciences, Humanities, Social Sciences, Fine Arts, Communication). It is possible, therefore, to define the communication discipline in multiple ways. This chapter adopts (with minor exceptions) a position articulated by Craig (1989). Craig has argued that communication is best conceived as a practical discipline whose essential purpose is to cultivate communication as a practical art through critical study. For Craig (1989), and for us, the defining characteristic of the communication discipline is "the intimate tie that exists between the discipline's work and practical communicative activities" (p. 2). As such, the communication discipline views communicative behavior as basic to human activity—to individual development, to interpersonal and social relationships, and to the functioning of political, economic, cultural, and social institutions. Thus, communication professionals study communicative behavior with the dual goal of (a) understanding the structure, patterns, and effects of human communication and (b) facilitating a higher quality of communication both for individuals and for society.

Across a diversity of level and focus, communication professionals share three key assumptions that are reflected in the nature of the courses we teach and in the nature of our scholarly research.

The first assumption is a belief that communication is an individual's most distinctive and significant behavior and the basic building block of literacy. It is through the multisensory process of symbolic interaction that we define both ourselves and our environment; and it is through communication that we are able to link ourselves to that environment. Without it, it would be impossible to develop the complexity of thought that sets us apart from the other creatures on this planet. In addition to providing the foundation for higher learning, communication is also central to the functioning of political, economic, and social institutions. Thus, in the words of Theodore Gross, Dean of Humanities at New York City College (1978):

> Communication should be a course of study as important to a young person's education as sociology or political science or foreign languages and should be integrated into the liberal arts curriculum. One does not justify the study of literature, history, or philosophy in terms of careers; one should not defend [the study of] communication only on the grounds of popular appeal or the number of jobs available. One must understand its sociology and history and technology and art and literature because it is the subject of our time and of the future. (p. 39)

The second assumption is a belief that continuity of instruction in communication is crucial. The improvement of speaking and listening skills is a lifelong project that must start with the earliest years of life and that does not stop when basic speech and language skills are in place. Rather, our abilities must be continually modified through learning new vocabulary, developing distinctive patterns of speaking, and—most importantly—learning means by which talk can be used to achieve goals. As relationships with others come and go, and as our roles in society change, opportunities for learning and modifying communication strategies are presented. Thus, systematic instruction and supervised practice yield positive returns at any stage in an individual's communication development. For this reason, communication professionals seek to improve individuals' abilities for such communication functions as public speaking, handling informal conversations, interacting with individuals from other cultures, solving problems in groups, coping with an organization's power structure, and becoming more effective producers and/or consumers of artistic performances and the outpourings of the mass media.

The third assumption is a belief that the improvement of speaking and listening skills is both a concern of the total educational community and an area where the communication discipline is uniquely qualified to make important contributions. We concur with Ernest Boyer, President of the Carnegie Foundation for the Advancement of Teaching, when he argued that speaking and listening are so central to education that they deserve both specialized training and emphasis in all classrooms (Scully, 1981). Therefore, in addition to providing coursework in communication, communication professionals are also involved in training parents to enhance the communication development of their preschool children and with providing teachers in all disciplines and at all academic levels with strategies that they can utilize to facilitate the development of communication competence for students in their classrooms. Whatever the level (preschool through graduate school) or content area (art, music, history, science, or math), communication professionals consider it their responsibility to help teachers maximize the communication activities and training of every student.

In addition, however, communication professionals are trained to tailor specialized coursework in communication to the social and cognitive development of individual students. Communication professionals are trained not only to diagnose the nature of the communication difficulties, but—more important—to provide an approach to cope with them. Whereas all teachers can, for example, observe that a student's message appears disorganized or that a student is not involved in class discussion, communication professionals have been trained to discover whether this difficulty is caused by (a) a conscious and rational decision to reduce involvement in the situation, (b) fear or anxiety about participation, (c) a physical disability or other skill deficit, or (d) a faulty perception of the requirements of the situation. Then, depending on the cause of the difficulty, communication professionals can identify and implement an instructional approach that is appropriate for the situation (e.g., perhaps a motivational session if the source of the difficulty is conscious choice, systematic desensitization to reduce fear or anxiety, the use of speech models to cope with a skill deficit, or cognitive restructuring to remedy a faulty perception). In addition to helping individuals directly, communication professionals can help other teachers diagnose and solve communication problems. It is important to know, for example, that someone who suffers from shyness or anxiety is likely to be harmed, rather than helped, by being subjected to a regimen restricted solely to additional practice.

It should also be noted that basic communication competency training, as important as it is, is not the sole or even major emphasis of communication professionals. As a discipline concerned broadly with the study of the nature, processes, and effects of human symbolic interaction, it is home to individuals who specialize in such diverse areas as:

- code systems (e.g., studying the uses of verbal and nonverbal symbols and signs in human communication)
- family communication (e.g., studying communication practices among members in a family unit)
- health communication (e.g., studying doctor–patient and other communication in health care settings)
- intercultural communication (e.g., studying communication among individuals of different cultural backgrounds)
- instructional communication (e.g., studying communication in the classroom and other pedagogical contexts)

- interpersonal communication (e.g., studying interaction occurring in person-to-person and small group situations)
- mass communication (e.g., studying uses and effects of radio and television)
- organizational communication (e.g., studying interrelated behaviors, technologies, and systems functioning in the workplace)
- oral interpretation (e.g., studying literature through performance)
- political communication (e.g., studying communication within local, state, and national political campaigns)
- pragmatic communication (e.g., studying debate, argumentation, and public speaking as they influence or facilitate decision making)
- public address (e.g., studying speakers and speeches, including the historical and social context of platforms, campaigns, and movements)
- theater and drama (e.g., studying dramatic literature through performance)
- rhetorical and communication theory (e.g., studying the principles that account for human communicative experiences and behavior)
- speech and hearing science (e.g., studying the physiological and acoustical correlates of speech and hearing behavior).

These areas of communication involve research and teaching efforts that manifest themselves professionally in various ways. Some areas gather enough agreement and appeal that journals are developed (e.g., *Critical Studies in Mass Communication, Text and Performance,* and *Journal of Applied Communication Research*) to provide a research outlet. Other areas attract such interest that initial interest groups develop their own professional association (e.g., the American Speech-Hearing-Language Association), which in turn develop their own professional outlets.

The teaching of communication, which provides the basic rationale for employment of most communication professionals, currently is largely reserved for postsecondary education. Nonetheless, the level of instruction provides yet another perspective for understanding the growth of the discipline.

K–12 CURRICULUM

Although the K–12 curriculum reserves focus on the discipline to junior high and high school, communication at the elementary level has an indirect focus on language development and experiencing communication. In addition, specialists (speech therapists) help students with problems. Courses in speech at the secondary level are generally electives. A study by Book and Pappas (1981) sampled speech communication education in 15 states (Georgia, Indiana, Kentucky, Maryland, Massachusetts, Michigan, Minnesota, Nebraska, North Dakota, Ohio, Oklahoma, Pennsylvania, Texas, Washington, and Wisconsin). Of 8,362 schools contacted, 4,341—or approximately 52%—responded. Seventy-six percent of the respondents offer a speech course or program, and 32% of these (range by state = 2.2% to 58.9%) require the course for graduation. Thus, if 76% of the schools surveyed offer speech and 32% of those require it, the number of students required to take a speech course is less than 25%. Additionally, because schools that do not offer a speech course are more likely to be in the 48% of schools that did not respond to the survey, the percentage of students required to take a speech course is, no doubt, significantly less than 25%.

What is the nature of the basic course? Book and Pappas (1981) summarized:

> The basic course was described as a semester long, offered only once each year to a combination of ninth or tenth through twelfth graders. The average section had twenty students and was generally fifty-five minutes in length. While a number of topics were taught in the basic course, public speaking dominated. The most frequently cited textbooks were published in the 1960s, and teachers used a combination of both oral and written work to evaluate their students. Finally, the speech course was usually taught as a separate course, but when combined, was most frequently taught with English. (p. 203)

Many schools, of course, offer advanced courses in addition to the basic course. In terms of frequency of offering, they include drama (59.5%), advanced speech (30.3%), debate (26.5%), radio/television and mass media (18.5%), oral interpretation (14.9%), film (11.2%), discussion (7.6%), and interpersonal communication (7.0%). Some schools also offer cocurricular speech activities: theater, the most common (78.2%), is followed by forensics (53.5%), debate (39.6%), and discussion/student congress (17.5%). Book and Pappas (1981) concluded:

> The offerings of speech communication curricula in high schools across the United States have not changed much in the past fifteen years: the same number of courses are being offered, although fewer are being required; the major focus of speech programs in the curriculum continues to be public speaking; and theater continue to be the most frequent extracurricular offering. (p. 206)

High school courses emphasize the performance aspects of skill development. The 90 or 180 periods of a course allows time for numerous performances. The challenge at the college level combines the university goal of theoretical studies with fewer days for instruction.

COLLEGE CURRICULUM

What happens when high school students move on to colleges and universities? Their most likely exposure to communication education is in an introductory or basic course. Gibson and several of his colleagues have conducted four studies of instructional practices in the basic communication course (Gibson, Gruner, Brooks, & Petrie, 1970; Gibson, Gruner, Hanna, Smythe, & Hayes, 1980; Gibson, Hanna, & Huddleston, 1985; Gibson, Kline, & Gruner, 1974). For their most recent study, 2,078 questionnaires were mailed in August, 1983 to junior/community colleges, senior colleges, and graduate schools listed in the Speech Communication Association Directory. They received 581 usable responses for a return rate of approximately 28%.

The authors (Gibson et al., 1985) concluded that "the basic course in speech remains a vital component of American higher education in the mid 1980's, reflecting a societal trend to prepare students for skilled oral presentation of ideas in a competitive society" (p. 290). They found enrollments in the course to be "increasing or holding steady in 92% of responding schools during the past five year period" (p. 283). "Nearly a third of the schools report the basic course increasing in enrollment faster than the institution itself with less than 10% reporting a rate of growth less than that of the school itself" (p. 290). Although the course is not a universal requirement for college and university students, 53% of the colleges of education, 45% of the arts and sciences colleges, and 50.3% of the business schools require their majors to take the basic course.

In terms of approach to the course, 54% report a public speaking orientation, whereas 34% report a combination of public, interpersonal, and group communication. Less than 10% report an interpersonal (6%), communication theory (4%), or group communication (2%) approach. Consistent with this finding, 80% of the courses require from 4 to 10 performances. To accommodate this load, average class size is within the range of 18 to 30. Organizationally, 85% of the instructors teach sections of the course intact rather than in a large-lecture, small-lab format, and 71% of the teaching is done by graduate assistants or junior faculty in a 3-semester-hour or 4 or 5 quarter-hour format. Although undergraduates from all 4 years of college take the course, the majority are freshmen and sophomores.

Most of the 2,028 departments in the Gibson survey, of course, offer courses beyond the basic one. In addition, the 1,579 academic units (housed in 1,034 institutions) listed in the 1987 SCA Directory as offering a major in one or more of the communication arts and sciences offer a diverse array of skill development and theory courses. For a recent survey, Wilson & Gray (1983) drew a random sample of 200 departments in 4-year institutions that were listed in the 1980 SCA directory. Their return rate was 25% (50 departments). In terms of departmental emphasis, the authors found that:

> 40% of the departments have a communication studies emphasis, 36% report an education emphasis, 36% a broadcasting emphasis, and 30% a traditional rhetoric emphasis (some offer more than one emphasis). Mentioned less were theater (26%), organizational (26%), public relations (26%), mass communication (20%), speech pathology (18%), oral interpretation (18%), journalism (16%), group process/pre-law (10% each), and business, consulting, political communication, instructional media (approximately 5% each). Several others were indicated only once. When respondents were asked where enrollments were increasing, they said the greatest increases were in: broadcasting (30%), public relations (22%), organizational communication (14%), theater and mass communication (12% each) and communication studies and general speech (10% each). Conversely, declining enrollments were noted in speech education (22%), rhetoric (16%), and oral interpretation, general communication, and theater (about 10% each). (p. 33)

EMPLOYMENT OPPORTUNITIES

Additional hints about the future can be gained via an examination of employment opportunities in the discipline. Using listings of the SCA Placement Service (the only full-range placement service for the profession), Clavier, Clevenger, Khair, and Khair (1979) examined the 12-year period from August, 1966 through July, 1978. Using a 28-category coding scheme to label areas of specialization, the authors explored yearly as well as 6-year, 9-year, and 12-year trends. Areas with the largest growth in terms of advertised positions were, in rough order of frequency: interpersonal communication, broadcasting, mass communication, and organizational communication. Though the percentages were somewhat smaller, other growth areas were special speech (e.g., speech for special groups such as business and professional people, teachers, health professionals), small group communication, research design, persuasion, nonverbal communication, journalism, intercultural communication, and advertising. Some areas, of course, witnessed less growth. Among the areas advertising fewer positions were theater, rhetoric, Black studies, speech education, debate, oral interpretation, and voice and diction. Such trends indicate both general movement of the field and wave-like spurts. At the 1988 SCA convention in New Orleans, job postings reflected an increased demand in rhetoric/public address, debate/forensics, and interpersonal communication

GRADUATE EDUCATION

A final area of communication education is that of graduate school. The 1986–1987 Directory of Graduate Programs in Communication Arts and Sciences (Hall, 1987) identifies 278 Departments, located in 194 institutions, that offer a graduate degree—79 at the PhD level. A faculty of 4,030 (2,578 with doctorates) are helping 10,636 masters students and 1,984 doctoral students to attain a degree. A feel for the nature of their offerings can be gained by examining the areas of concentration that they list for graduate study:

Code Systems: listed by 11 programs at the MA level; 8 at PhD
Intercultural Communication: MA = 46; PhD = 17
Interpersonal Communication: MA = 107; PhD = 35
Organizational Communication: MA = 111; PhD = 33
Oral Interpretation: MA = 34; PhD = 10
Pragmatic Communication: MA = 23; PhD = 7
Public Address: MA = 72; PhD = 23
Rhetorical and Communication Theory: MA = 119; PhD = 33
Speech Communication Education: MA = 60; PhD = 13
Speech and Hearing Science: MA = 57; PhD = 22
Theater: MA = 94; PhD = 20
Radio/TV/Film: MA = 94; PhD = 19
Journalism/Mass Comm: MA = 82; PhD = 19
Misc. Titles: MA = 50; PhD = 10

Putting the preceding figures into the context of higher education, Eadie (1979) compared the number of earned degrees in communication studies between 1960 and 1976 with several cognate areas:

Communication Studies: MA = 75,786; PhD = 6,694
Psychology: MA = 65,650; PhD = 24,633

Sociology: MA = 23,219; PhD = 6,993
Philosophy: MA = 9,920; PhD = 4,534
History: MA = 65,881; PhD = 12,832
English: MA = 106,992; PhD = 16,131
All Fields: MA = 3,055,701; PhD = 379,610

PROFESSIONAL ASSOCIATIONS

Departments of communication, of course, do not operate in isolation.
They are influenced both by factors within their local environment (e.g.,
the institution and the community) and by events at the state, regional,
and national levels. With the switch from the perception of being a faculty member at a college to being a faculty member *in a department* at a
college came the growth of professional associations. Faculty members
with specific research interests wanted to meet with faculty members of
similar interests. Professional associations followed with conventions (a
way to meet other teachers) and publications (a way to learn what was
being discovered). The growth of oral communication in English departments meant an identifiable group of people with strong interests in
nonliterature issues. This group of people, belonging to the National
Council of Teachers of English (NCTE) felt a need for "autonomy in
courses and department organization" (Rarig & Greaves, 1954, p. 501).
The feeling that public speaking was different from oral English
spawned the National Association of Academic Teachers of Public Speaking (now the Speech Communication Association, SCA) at the 1914
NCTE convention. James O'Neill became the first president as well as
the editor of the *Quarterly Journal of Public Speaking,* the association's
first academic journal.

Two major directions defined the field over the next 75 years. One
direction, following the origins of the SCA, involved splintering off and
forming new associations. The American Theater Association and the
American Speech-Hearing-Language Association represent this trend.
These groups have developed separate questions, publications, and departments. The second trend involved forming subgroups to reflect specific interests *within* the context of the Speech Communication Association. Groups such as the American Forensic Association, the Commission
on American Parliamentary Practice, the International Society for the
History of Rhetoric, and the Religious Speech Communication Association, for example, hold their annual meetings at the same time and same
place as the SCA. Although other groups such as the International Communication Association and the International Listening Association hold

separate meetings, most of their members are located in communication departments.

The essence of professional associations spring from meetings (conventions, workshops, institutes) and publications (journals, books, monographs, teaching guides, and professional standards). Thus, professional associations create a network that links together people in departments in different parts of the world. Annual national (or state, regional, or international) conventions provide: (a) programs for sharing current discoveries and beliefs, (b) meetings for understanding the decisions that the field must make, and (c) the opportunity for individual networking through social events, interviewing for jobs, school alumni gatherings, and so on. According to Wilmot and Nussbaum (1983), almost two thirds of convention participants attend programs (p. 291). A survey at the Western Speech Communication Association convention indicates that people attend programs because of an "appreciation for the topic and for new ideas and information" (Nyquist & Wilson, 1984, p. 449).

CONCLUSION

As we have discovered, the field of communication is both broad and diverse—and professionals within it have many interests. The theme that ties this diversity of communication professionals together is a common interest in understanding communication as a practical art (Craig, 1989). In the remainder of this book, we explore the research, theory, and methods relevant to communication instruction that allow us to exploit our diversity for practical, pedagogical ends.

REFERENCES

Book, C. L., & Pappas, E. J. (1981). The status of speech communication in secondary schools in the United States: An update. *Communication Education, 30,* 199–208.

Clavier, D., Clevenger, T., Jr., Khair, S. E., & Khair, M. M. (1979). Twelve-year employment trends for speech communication graduates. *Communication Education, 28,* 306–313.

Cohen, H. (1985). The development of research in speech communication: A historical perspective. In T. W. Benson (Ed.), *Speech communication in the 20th century* (pp. 282–298). Carbondale, IL: Southern Illinois University Press.

Craig, R. T. (1989). Communication as a practical discipline. In B. Dervin, L. Grossberg, B. O'Keefe, & E. Wartella (Eds.), *Paradigm dialogues in communication; Vol. I: Issues* (pp. 97–122). Beverly Hills, CA: Sage.

Delia, J. G. (1987). Communication research: A history. In C. R. Berger & S. H. Chaffee (Eds.), *Handbook of communication science* (pp. 20–98). Beverly Hills, CA: Sage.

Eadie, W. F. (1979). Earned degree trends in communication studies, 1960–1976. *Communication Education, 28,* 294–300.

Gibson, J. W., Gruner, C. R., Brooks, W. D., & Petrie, C. R., Jr. (1970). The first course in speech: A survey of U.S. colleges and universities. *Speech Teacher, 19,* 13–20.

Gibson, J. W., Gruner, C. R., Hanna, M. S., Smythe, M., & Hayes, M. T. (1980). The basic course in speech at U.S. colleges and universities: III. *Communication Education, 29,* 1–9.

Gibson, J. W., Hanna, M. S., & Huddleston, B. M. (1985). The basic speech course at U.S. colleges and universities: IV. *Communication Education, 34,* 282–291.

Gibson, J. W., Kline, J. A., & Gruner, C. R. (1974). A re-examination of the first course in speech at U.S. colleges and universities. *Speech Teacher, 22,* 206–214.

Gray, G. W. (1949). Research in the history of speech education. *Quarterly Journal of Speech, 35,* 156–163.

Great need for public speaking department. (1912, June). *The University of Oklahoma Magazine,* pp. 17–18.

Gross, T. L. (1978). The organic teacher. *Change,* June/July, p. 39.

Haiman, F. (1951). *Group leadership and democratic action.* Boston, MA: Houghton Mifflin.

Hall, R. N. (Ed.). (1987). *Directory of graduate programs: Communication arts and sciences 1986–1987.* Annandale, VA: Speech Communication Association.

Nyquist, J. D., & Wilson, C. E. (1984). Participant reactions to the 55th annual WSCA convention. *Western Journal of Speech Communication, 48,* 441–451.

Pearce, W. B. (1985). Scientific research methods in communication studies and their implications for theory and research. In T. W. Benson (Ed.), *Speech communication in the 20th century* (pp. 255–281). Carbondale, IL: Southern Illinois University Press.

Potter, D. (1954). The literary society. In K. R. Wallace (Ed.), *History of speech education in America: Background studies* (pp. 238–258). New York: Appleton-Century-Crofts.

Rarig, F. M., & Greaves, H. S. (1954). National speech organizations and speech education. In K. R. Wallace (Ed.), *History of speech education in America: Background studies* (pp. 490–517). New York: Appleton-Century-Crofts.

Scully, M. G. (1981, April 13). General education called a "disaster area" by Carnegie officials: Need for revival seen. *Chronicle for Higher Education,* p. 1.

Smith, D. K. (1954). Origin and development of departments of speech. In K. R. Wallace (Ed.), *A history of speech education in America: Background studies* (pp. 447–470). New York: Appleton-Century-Crofts.

Wilmot, W. W., & Nussbaum, J. N. (1983). Participant reactions to the 54th annual WSCA convention. *Western Journal of Speech Communication, 47,* 288–301.

Wilson, G. L., & Gray, P. A. (1983). A survey of practices and strategies for marketing communication majors. *ACA Bulletin, 45,* 32–35.

Wiseman, G., & Barker, L. (1967). *Speech—Interpersonal communication.* San Francisco: Chandler Publishing Company.

2

The Goals of Communication Education

Jo Sprague
San Jose State University

There is no need to ask whether a teacher has goals. If, as philosophers tell us, any complex human activity presupposes a *telos,* some direction or end toward which it strives, then certainly all teaching reflects an underlying purpose. All teachers have goals, but all are not equally aware of their goals or equally able to articulate them.

This chapter is based on the assumption that goal setting is an important prerequisite to every instructional decision that a teacher makes. Whenever you decide to use a certain text, make an assignment, or lecture on a topic, you are choosing these options over other alternatives. Choices imply criteria and criteria imply goals. If a decision is better, then it is better to some end. Despite the compelling logic of this view, teachers tend to rush through goal setting or to skip over this step altogether. New teachers are so worried about finding materials and planning activities that they start off on their trip without knowing their destination. Experienced teachers rarely seem to find the time for contemplation and for rethinking their instructional goals. The three sections that follow survey some of the general goals of education, relate these to the unique goals of communication instruction, and lead you through the steps that you can follow as you translate your general educational goals into specific objectives for a particular course.

GENERAL GOALS OF EDUCATION

Most college teachers approach the classroom without formal training in educational theory. The end of education is one of the questions most discussed by philosophers over the ages. You will be richer for exploring the ideas of Plato, St. Thomas Aquinas, Rousseau, Locke, Hutchins, Dewey, and Whitehead. These great thinkers have struggled with the same issues that you and I worry about as educators. At the very least, their writings will help you frame your questions. At best, they may even provide some answers. Read a basic survey of education thought for a start (for example, Bowyer, 1970; Brown, 1970) and complete the inventory offered by Briggs and Pinola (1985) to see if your present approach to communication education is classified as idealism, realism, neothomism, experimentalism, or existentialism.

Extending the timeless themes of educational philosophy, each era generates its own lively debate about the purposes of education. It is these current controversies, cast in contemporary vocabulary, that you are most likely to encounter as you plan your course. Why do we have formal institutions of higher education? Here are four of the most common answers to that question.

Transmitting Cultural Knowledge

This view presupposes that there are certain important ideas, great works of art and literature, and significant scientific discoveries that a liberally educated person should be familiar with. The purpose of this sort of education is not to create an elite class but simply to ensure entry into mainstream national culture. E. D. Hirsch, Jr. (1987) has claimed that, without such knowledge, an individual can be well trained in phonics, word recognition, and other decoding skills but still be culturally illiterate. This is due to the fact that most books and newspapers ". . . assume a 'common reader,' a person who knows the things known by other literate persons in the culture. . . . Any reader who doesn't possess the knowledge assumed in a piece he or she reads will in fact be illiterate with respect to that particular piece of writing" (p. 14).

Beyond the individual benefits of liberal arts education lies a belief that our collective survival demands that the best ideas of the past be kept alive, not in a few museums or libraries, but in the consciousness of a large segment of society. "[Education] has to do with the perpetuation of positive values of inherited culture by embodying them in the dispositions of individuals who are to transmit culture into the future" (Dewey, cited in Brown, 1970, p. 53). Alarm over the technological thrust of our society and the superficiality of popular culture may well have motivated the calls of educational leaders for a renewed commitment to the humanities (Association of American Colleges, 1985; Bennett, 1984; Boyer & Levine, 1981; Carnegie Foundation, 1977; National Institute of Education, 1984). Allen Bloom (1987) is concerned about the moral bankruptcy of a generation that has no familiarity with the wisdom and virtues embodied in the finest products of cultural tradition. In the name of openness, students have embraced a mindless relativism, concluding that all ideas, lifestyles, and ideologies are equally moral.

Developing Students' Intellectual Skills

The emphasis here is not so much on what students learn as on how they learn; that is, on the processes they perfect through their educational experiences. This approach is sometimes likened to treating the mind as a sort of intellectual muscle that needs to be strengthened and exercised. The most fundamental skills are those of basic literacy, and the discovery that many college students are deficient in those skills has led to the recent Back to Basics movement. Teachers of all disciplines are urged to incorporate skills training in reading, writing, speaking, and listening into their instruction. At a less remedial level, the intellectual skills approach centers on critical thinking skills. To survive in a changing world and to participate effectively in a democratic society, students must be prepared to critically analyze and evaluate ideas (Adler, 1983; Dressel & Mayhew, 1954; Young, 1980). The interest in lifelong learning has spawned new interest in the questions of learning how to learn (Rogers, 1969; Smith, 1982). During their brief years in the formal educational system, students learn techniques of research, inquiry, and problem solving that they can apply to new topics throughout their lives.

Providing Students With Career Skills

The university can be seen as a provider of specific vocational credentials, a role that has traditionally been assigned to trade schools or to graduate and professional schools. Following the launching of Sputnik, the American educational system was charged to produce more scientists. Universities have been expected to respond to cyclical demands since that time for teachers, computer engineers, business managers, or health care workers. From this perspective, the test of curriculum is its responsiveness to the needs of the workplace. It is a position that has few advocates among educational theorists. One well-known statement of this position is *The Saber-Tooth Curriculum* (Peddiwell, 1939), a charming satirical fable of a neolithic society that persists in teaching the "classical" subjects of fish grabbing, wooly horse clubbing, and saber-toothed tiger scaring long after they have become irrelevant to survival. The scarcity of philosophical support for the view of vocationalism as the *primary* purpose of higher education has not restricted its general popularity. If you ask students why they attend college, or ask parents, alumni, and legislators why they fund higher education, the answer will very often have to do with careers. In fact, one 15-year study of undergraduates found that, over that period of time (1969–1984), the goal of training and skills for a job went from last to first place on their list of reasons for seeking a college education ("Philosopher hurls," 1987, p. 11).

Reshaping the Values of Society

Not all educational theorists assume that the purpose of the schools is to socialize or enculturate students. If one sees society as flawed at best, or evil and repressive at worst, then why should students learn to fit in? They should be taught instead to critique and transform their world. One such radical educational philosophy was developed by Brazilian educator Paulo Friere (1972) in his now classic work *Pedagogy of the Oppressed.* In developing a program of education for literacy in Latin America, he came to recognize the ways that traditional education has the ideological intent of preserving existing power relationships and indoctrinating students to adapt to the world of oppression (p. 65). One ongoing strand of educational thought has recapitulated Aristotle's position that *theoria,* or scientific knowledge, only takes on meaningfulness through *praxis,* or the application of ideas to the problems of living. In this view, education finds its *telos* in the emancipation of the human spirit, an end that is ideally pursued through various techniques of dialectic, consciousness raising, and critical analysis (Giroux, 1988; McLaren, 1989).

It is evident that these four positions of the goals of higher education are neither exhaustive nor mutually exclusive. Countless other goals have been posited—worthwhile ends, such as the development of character or the preparation for citizenship—that cross the boundaries of the four goals discussed here. Most educators see value in several goals. They aim, for example, to provide career training within a liberal arts education or to help students to develop intellectual skills that may lead to a transformation of society. Because time and energy are finite, however, and because the underlying premises of some systems are contradictory, educators cannot stress all of these goals as *primary.* A clear sense of the relative priorities of your own goals for education is essential as you go about making daily decisions as an educator.

UNIQUE GOALS FOR
COMMUNICATION INSTRUCTION

Having reviewed some of the purposes of all higher education, we can now look at how our own field has approached the problem of determining the purpose of instruction. Identifying our goals is made especially challenging due to the nature of what we teach. Communication is not just another content area for students to master or even just another academic skill. Nor is ours a subject that is new to students. We must recognize that when we say we are going to teach people to communicate, we are "teaching" them something they have been doing rather successfully for most of their lives. The ways that they presently communicate are closely tied to their individual attitudes, values, and self-concepts. It is both our strength and our weakness that we change not just what people know, or even what they can do, but who they are.

Setting goals for instruction in communication is further complicated by the fact that we are such a diverse and eclectic discipline. We draw on different intellectual heritages and resonate with the language of different academic orientations ranging from the social sciences to the humanities to applied studies. Without a personal vision of the overarching purpose of our field, those who teach courses across different subareas will tend toward schizophrenia or rigid intellectual compartmentalization.

The Four Goals of Education
Applied to Communication

All of the purposes discussed in the previous section, justifying education in general, have been advanced as reasons for studying communication in particular. Let us revisit these orientations noting how the rationale for each approach takes a form that is distinctive to our discipline.

Transmitting Cultural Knowledge. The study of communication is often justified in terms of its contribution to a liberal education (For example, Blankenship, 1981; Bradley, 1979; Dance, 1980; Dearin, 1980; Emmert, 1985; Hostettler, 1980; Hunt, 1955). In its more modest form, this means keeping alive the great works about communication and the great examples of communication. A large part of the world's literary tradition is found in speeches, debates, and dialogues that are important both because of the timeless issues they address and because of their eloquence of expression.

A stronger statement of our field's role in the liberal arts positions communication as the central process by which a culture develops and survives. One version of the argument goes like this: To understand historical events like wars and revolutions, one must grasp the ideas and values that drove people to action. Yet of all the ideas that are written in books and discussed among philosophers, only a few capture the popular imagination and actually change the world. The study of those ideas— how and why they had such impact—is the key to understanding human experience. Thus, in a sense, the history of the world is actually the history of rhetoric.

Besides exposing our students to the works of rhetorical significance, there is a body of cultural knowledge within our field. Without a grasp of certain terminology and basic content, students cannot proceed to advanced study of small group communication or media studies or intercultural communication. Socializing students to communication scholarship is a major goal for some educators.

Developing Students' Intellectual Skills. The skills rationale for education takes a special form in our discipline. We go beyond defending the practical importance of speaking, listening, discussing, debating, and relating in our students' lives. We argue that the communication skills we teach are essential to gaining other knowledge. Students must be able to analyze, organize, refute, and defend ideas if they are to become educated in any field of study (Boyer, 1978; Hopper & Daly, 1979; Modaff & Hopper, 1984). Indeed, many scholars have gone even further; they claim that it is only through communication that knowledge is created (Dance, 1980; Scott, 1967; Gadamar cited in Howard, 1982; Ong, 1982). Ideas come into being through speech process; there is no "truth" to be apprehended until that truth takes form in language and is processed interpersonally.

The skills approach to communication study seems to be enjoying renewed popularity. The most recent survey of the basic course reflects an emphasis on public speaking skills (Gibson, Hanna, & Huddleston, 1985). The goal of teaching critical thinking gained importance following World War II with the need to understand techniques of propaganda analysis (Sproule, 1987). Traditional methods of dialectic, debate, and discussion long central to communication instruction have been supplemented by a more sophisticated understanding of the cognitive processes involved in critical thinking. (Fritz & Weaver, 1986; Katula & Martin, 1984). Even an area like interpersonal communication, often approached as either a matter of insight and personal growth or as a subject for analytic study, has received wide treatment as a set of specific skills to be mastered (e.g., Glaser & Eblen, 1986).

Developing Students' Career Skills. Speech and communication educators have traditionally taken pride in the practical applications of our field of study. The sophists in ancient Greece responded to a need for citizens to defend themselves in court. Later, rhetorical theories were directed to the needs of statesmen or the clergy. Today, we frequently tailor our instruction to be of the most practical benefit to managers, engineers, attorneys, or health care professionals (e.g., DiSalvo, Larsen, & Backus, 1986; Jamieson & Wolvin, 1976; Johnson & Johnson, 1982; Matlon, 1982). When we apply our theories to various workplaces, we are more likely to stay grounded in reality. Constantly adapting our content helps us remain flexible and avoid taking ourselves too seriously. The danger of this approach, of course, comes when it is seen as anti-intellectual or as serving the interests of particular institutions outside the academy. Also, students who are overly specialized in their preparation may not be well educated for a changing world as those who have learned the more universal principles of communication.

Reshaping the Values of Society. This approach also has a long heritage in our field. Since Plato's attack on the sophists, scholars have pondered the relationship among rhetoric, truth, and justice. Those who challenge the position that communication can ever be value-free insist that students be taught to examine the connection of language to social reality. The general semantics movement and the encounter movement, in different ways, contested dualistic and hierarchical assumptions reflected in everyday communication. More recently we have discovered that European critical theory has much to say about communication. Jurgen Habermas described language itself as a kind of sedimented ideology that must be critiqued so that the corrupt forms residing in its usage can be detected (Howard, 1982, p. 155). Michel Foucault urged that the study of communication be used to "discover the power relations in a culture and to give voice to those who have no power" (Foss, Foss, & Trapp, 1985, p. 246). From these perspectives, communication instruction may have as its goal the identification of sexism in language, the exposure of ideological assumptions in media, and the empowering of individuals to resist subtle intimidation in interpersonal encounters. Students learn to look beyond what is said. They ask also "What is *not* said? Why? Who profits from keeping communication the way it is now? How could changing communication patterns change social reality?"

Hart (1986) exposed the potential political impact of our instruction when he suggested that if "rhetorical power becomes decentralized, then it becomes infinitely more difficult for certain power blocs in society to continue to practice economic, social and political hegemony" (p. 7. See also Hart, 1985). In the area of organizational communication, where Hart claimed that some courses might as well be retitled Corporate Toadying 301, critical theory has recently had a major impact on the goals of instruction. Redding (1985) urged that we stop training students to be compliant middle managers and instead teach them when to function as boat-rockers and whistle blowers. Understanding the role that communication plays in perpetuating power relationships in the workplace can form the basis of a critique aimed toward humanizing organizations and liberating workers (Deetz & Kersten, 1983).

Tensions in Goal Setting

These four perspectives on the goals of communication instruction reflect the general philosophical orientations identified in the preceding section. When communication educators talk about goals there are other related themes that emerge in the form of recurring intellectual tensions.

The Tension Between Theory and Skill. The debate is also cast as a discussion of competence versus performance (Spitzberg, 1983). In setting goals, teachers have to decide how much stress to place on knowing about communication and how much to place on being able to communicate effectively. The two are not the same. Some students will have a superb grasp of principles but not be able to apply them. Others seem to perform effectively with no idea of what they are doing or why it works (McCroskey, 1982). Based on the revered notion that there is nothing as practical as a good theory, some teachers decide that it is best to emphasize the universal principles that students can put to use throughout their lives. (See for example, Mehrley & Backes, 1972). It can also be convincingly argued, however, that students need direct practical experiences more than they need abstract principles (Phillips, 1984). The issue is made even more troublesome by the fact that being overly aware of how communication works can sometimes even hinder performance (Andersen, 1986).

The Tension Between Process Goals and Product Goals. In any instruction, we ask students to create certain products—speeches, papers, answers to test questions,—and we hope that those products measure up to our standards. Yet, is our *goal* really for them to produce a beautiful outline, or rather to learn how to organize ideas? Products are easier to evaluate, but processes are what students will reuse after the class is over. Think about the balance of product and process goals you set for your course. Too much emphasis on the former can trivialize instruction (Conville, 1977; Sprague, 1974; Tucker, 1973); too much on the latter can leave you with no sound basis for designing instruction or evaluation (Kibler, Barker, & Cegala, 1970).

The Tension Between Content Goals and Presentation Goals. Whenever a course involves student presentations, we must confront the problem of the relative importance of content or delivery. Deep in the genetic memory of every speech teacher is the sting of Plato's attack on the sophists. In our insistence that we are not engaged in "mere cookery," technique devoid of substance, we seem to need to dissociate ourselves completely from the elocutionists of the 19th century and the Dale Carnegies and Toastmasters of the 20th century. Those who favor a content orientation can justify the centrality of invention in the communication process (Kneupper & Anderson, 1980). Many teachers have privately wondered if we even *want* to make articulate speakers out of students who have nothing of substance to say, no research to support it, and no sense of responsibility for its impact. Yet, people still look to us for advice about delivery and style—advice we are qualified to give with results that can make their lives better (Hart, 1985; Phillips, 1984). Moreover, too much emphasis on teaching students what to say, rather than how to say it, effectively may smack of a violation of their freedom of expression (Brummet, 1986).

The Tension Between Goals for Senders and Goals for Receivers of Communication. Historically, our pedagogical concern has been with developing competent speakers, debaters, leaders of discussions, and initiators of interpersonal contact. But successful communication also requires good listeners, critics, followers, and respondents. People spend more time listening than speaking. Those who are skilled listeners are valued in business (Hunt & Cusella, 1983). They have successful interpersonal relationships and are discerning citizens (Wolvin & Coakley, 1985). For instruction to most accurately reflect the way communication functions, what ratio of sending goals and receiving goals seems most appropriate?

This brief review of the unique goals of communication education was not designed to have you select any one of the four goals of instruction or to resolve any of the tensions. Throughout your career, you will be attracted to these and other goals, frustrated by these and other tensions. More realistic than looking for final resolutions is a commitment to stay involved in the dialogue. You must be conscious of where you currently stand, or at least where you lean, as you begin the process of establishing goals and objectives for any class you will teach.

PREPARING OBJECTIVES FOR A COURSE

If I were to start jotting down at random my goals for a public speaking course, I might come up with a list like the following. I want my students to:

Be ethical in the use of evidence
Never say "nucular" for "nuclear"
Know the difference between induction and deduction
Feel more confident about speaking

It is evident that this list is far *too* random to be of much use in course planning. Some of these objectives are very important, whereas others are trivial. Some deal with what I want students to do, some with what I want them to know, and some with how I want them to feel. Clearly, translating general goals of instruction into specific course objectives demands some system for organizing and prioritizing outcomes. In the domains of learning and the taxonomies of skills we find the basis of such a system.

Classifying the Outcomes of Instruction

Educators usually divide the types of learning into three domains: cognitive, affective, and psychomotor. The cognitive domain concerns knowledge and the development of intellectual skills. The affective domain is made up of attitudes, interests, values, and feelings. The psychomotor domain deals with manipulative or motor-skill activities. Most academic disciplines at the college level emphasize the cognitive domain, and communication is no exception. However, instructional goals from the other two domains are evident throughout our curricula.

The psychomotor goals encountered most often have to do with the effective production of speech, such as speaking audibly and distinctly, and the nonverbal skills, such as maintaining eye contact and controlling physical movements and gestures. A few mechanical skills may be among minor course goals, such as operating video equipment.

The affective goals of communication instruction are more numerous and challenging. The reduction of communication apprehension is a nearly universal goal in courses that require oral presentations, one that is usually operationalized by the student's own self-reported *feeling* of comfort or discomfort. Many classes in rhetoric, public address, oral interpretation, and media studies aim to increase students' appreciation of effective communication. Attempts to instill ethical values in speakers fall into the affective domain as do teachers' efforts to have their students be more rhetorically sensitive, to remain open minded in group discussions, and to respect the freedom of speech of others. (Notice that most of the affective objectives illustrated previously are general and non-controversial. We might consider them metagoals, in that they are necessary to preserve dialogue and inquiry so that the study of communication itself can continue. Though professors will profess, they should not indoctrinate. Attempts to force students to accept the instructor's specific attitudes and values are particularly insidious when the goals are not explicitly stated to students, or worse yet, not even consciously acknowledged by the teacher.)

The third domain is best illustrated by introducing Bloom's (1956) taxonomy of educational objectives for the cognitive domain. It will be apparent that most of the instruction in our communication classes can be subsumed under the following categories.

Knowledge Level. Remembering, memorizing, recognizing. What terminology, facts, and basic information do you want students to be able to recall?

Comprehension Level. Translating, interpretating, extrapolating. What concepts and information should they be able to state in their own words or transform into different formats?

Application Level. Making use of previously learned information. What material do you expect students to transfer to new situations to solve new problems?

Analysis Level. Breaking an idea or topic down to reveal its component parts and identify its underlying structure. When should students be able to get beneath the surface to find relationships and connections and to make these explicit?

Synthesis Level. Arranging and combining elements in such a way as to create a unique product. What complex outcomes do you expect students to produce by putting ideas together in original patterns that clearly did not exist before?

Evaluation Level. Making quantitative and qualitative judgments about the value of ideas, objects, or conditions? In what areas do you expect students to establish criteria for appraisal and apply those standards to particular cases?

The usefulness of this taxonomy is in explicating the hierarchical nature of learning. We see the need to organize goals, instruction, and evaluation around intellectual processes rather than around global topics. Use of this taxonomy will help you avoid three of the most common instructional errors: teaching exclusively at lower levels of cognitive instruction, teaching high-level skills without being sure that students have mastered the prerequisite knowledge and skills at lower cognitive levels, and centering instruction at one band of the hierarchy and then evaluating a different level.

Bloom's taxonomy and the comparable lists for the affective and psychomotor domains (Harrow, 1972; Krathwohl, Bloom, & Masia, 1956) are the most widely used, perhaps because they were developed by educational practitioners based primarily on classroom experiences (Snelbecker, 1985, p. 460.) Other useful taxonomies come from alternate perspectives. A psychologically based system was proposed by Gagné (1970), who described eight types of learning drawn from laboratory research paradigms. A more philosophically oriented schema is Perry's (1969) four-phase description of intellectual and ethical development. Besides the other taxonomies and classification schema developed by educators (e.g., Harvey, Hunt, & Schroder, 1967; Hunt, 1971; Kohlberg, 1981; Loevinger, 1966), our own literature suggests several ways of organizing communication learning. Feezel (1985) has proposed a taxonomy that combines the three domains of learning. There are various classifications of competencies (Rubin, 1982) and a taxonomy of functional communication outcomes (Allen & Brown, 1976). Becoming familiar with several systems will give you a number of ways to classify your objectives. You can select the one that is the best fit for a particular course.

Using Behavioral Objectives

Any discussion of educational goal setting must explore the controversy over the specificity of objectives. Though the task analysis models of planning originated earlier in this century (Tyler, 1949), Robert Mager's brief programmed text *Preparing Instructional Objectives* (1962) has most influenced our field. Mager (see also 1984) made a case for specifying the goals of instruction as measurable outcomes observable in overt behaviors of learners. He attacked the fuzziness of most educational goals, such as "the student will know the principles of discussion leadership" or "the students will appreciate the style of great orators." What exactly is the student *doing* when he is knowing? How is she *behaving* when she is appreciating? To increase the specificity of instructional objectives, Mager recommended that each objective meet these three criteria:

1. The objective must be stated in terms of the student's terminal behavior. Thus, behavioral objectives should use concrete verbs. Words

like "list," "identify," "name," and "distinguish" replace words like "understand," "grasp," and "relate to."

2. The object must specify the conditions under which the behavior will be performed. The context in which acts are performed affects how they are evaluated; therefore, teachers should clearly state which information, tools, equipment, and sources the student may and may not use in demonstrating terminal behavior (Kibler, Cegala, Barker, & Miles, 1974, p. 38).

3. The objective must specify the criterion level to be attained in order to say that an objective has been achieved. This can take the form of stating a minimum number, a percent or proportion, the tolerable departure from a fixed standard, or the distinguishing features of successful performance (Kibler et al., 1974, p. 40).

The following examples of behavioral objectives illustrate the presence of the three conditions. The behavioral outcome is enclosed in brackets, the conditions of performance are placed in parentheses, and the criterion level is underlined.

(Using the textbook and the supplemental readings listed in the bibliography,) [the student will prepare and present a 10- to 15-minute oral report on a small group communication variable approved in advance by the instructor.] *The report must receive an instructor rating of seven or higher on each of five criteria—research, analysis, clarity, organization, and delivery—explained in more detail on the attached rating sheet.*

(Without the aid of notes,) [the student will list, define, and provide original examples of] *at least five of eight* [fallacies discussed in lecture.] *The names and definitions must correspond directly with those presented in class, and the examples must be valid ones in the instructor's judgment.*

(Following a semester course in oral communication,) *at least 80% of the students* [will report significant reductions of communication apprehension from that which they reported at the beginning of the course] *as measured by a drop of at least five points on the PRCA.*

The behavioral objective movement gained popularity in the late 1960s and early 1970s and was widely advocated as an instructional practice in speech communication (Cegala, Kibler, Barker, & Miles, 1972; Haynes, 1973; Kibler et al., 1970; Tucker, 1973). Stating objectives in behavioral terms has distinct advantages. The process of articulating objectives precisely causes instructors to discipline their thinking, to separate the measurable from the unmeasurable, and to isolate the most important aspects of each course. The inclusion of criteria for evaluation makes it more likely that teachers will grade on what they actually taught. Subjectivity is minimized. When students know exactly what is expected of them, they can put their efforts into achieving the objectives instead of trying to guess what the teacher really wants them to do. Clearly stated objectives help educators to communicate to each other exactly what each class covers so that overall curricular planning can be more coherent.

Not all educators were enthusiastic about the movement to specify all instructional objectives in behavioral terms. The evidence on their effectiveness was not conclusive (Kibler et al., 1974, pp. 5–8). The lower-level skills, such as knowledge and comprehension, lend themselves well to the formula for writing behavioral objectives. When higher-level objectives dealing with synthesis or evaluation were written, subjectivity often slipped back into the phrasing with such criterion statements as "in the instructor's opinion." Humanist educators were sometimes uncomfortable with the mechanistic language and flow chart mentality of the behavioral approaches to goal setting. Critics challenged the behaviorist notion that "If you can't measure it, it doesn't exist" (e.g., Conville, 1977; Sprague, 1974). Claiming that often the most important outcomes of instruction are intangible, they cautioned that the preoccupation with terminal behaviors would lead to undue focus on communication products that could be standardized rather than on the processes that are unique to individuals and contexts. It might be asked, do we really want our students to be more alike at the end of a course? Or do we hope that they will be more different from each other? The most serious fear was that the behavioral objectives movement might cause educators to set their sights too low. The sincere concern for specifying minimal standards of performance could gradually lead to settling for mere competence instead of hoping for excellence. A fuller summary and analysis of the arguments for and against behavioral objectives can be found in Popham (in Kibler et al., 1974, pp. 9–17) and Findley and Nye (1973).

How to Write Goals for a Course

1. *Begin by Considering the Educational Mission of the Institution and the Department.*   You might look at this step as conducting an analysis of the organizational culture that will set the context for your instruction. How does the institution define itself? I have a colleague who sometimes teaches the same class at a community college, a large state university, and a small, private, church-related college. Even with the same text, the same assignments, and the same personal philosophy, his classes differ somewhat. The differences are not due just to demographics and academic skill levels at the three schools; they largely reflect the philosophy of each campus. Communication instruction is seen to fit into the overall education of students in varying ways.

Academic departments also have diverse missions and emphases. A communication department could have a liberal arts orientation or a social science orientation. Programs may exist primarily to provide service courses for other disciplines, to equip students for certain careers, or to prepare majors for graduate school. Some departments have drafted mission statements that reflect a clear vision of what the faculty hopes to achieve. One such statement that I find particularly eloquent discusses the education of the mind, the education of the heart, and the education of the voice. Helping each student to "understand and have confidence in what s/he alone can communication" (Department Goals and Objectives, pp. 1–2) provides a touchstone against which to check educational decisions. Other things being equal, teachers in that department would choose those assignments that developed each student's heart and voice as well as mind. Not all departments have such a clear statement of philosophy, but usually there is a set of guiding assumptions that you can discover.

2. Become Familiar With Any Agreements That Guide the Course Content. Catalogue descriptions are frequently limited to 40 words, and they provide only the roughest guide of the parameters within which you will plan a course. Often, departments have on file more elaborate statements of the minimal requirements for a class. If a course is a prerequisite for others, there are certain areas that must be covered. Service courses must meet the expectations of the client population. In multisection courses, textbooks and materials may be prescribed. Even within the constraints imposed by campus and department, you will still have many choices left to you as an instructor.

3. Establish Course Goals. Select a handful of important outcomes that you value deeply and really wish for your students. State these in terms of their ultimate usefulness. Is it really your goal for students to give an 8-minute persuasive speech using the motivated sequence? Or is that a means to the end of being able to arrange persuasive arguments for maximum effectiveness? To keep yourself focused on the essential, rather than the merely important, ask yourself questions like these: If the students only learn one thing this term, what should it be? What do I hope they remember from this course 10 years from now?

4. Establish Intermediate Goals for Units of Instruction or Key Assignments. For each course goal, determine what more specific goals will contribute to the achievement of those outcomes. When in doubt, select the ones that are prerequisite to other important goals, that are most generalizable to a variety of situations, and most realistic to accomplish in your course.

5. *For Each Goal, Write a Series of Behavioral Objectives.* Follow the preceding guidelines and include the terminal behavior, the conditions of performance, and the criterion level. You will find that there are some objectives that can't be measured. Obviously, these cannot be given substantial weight in evaluation of students. However, do not be too quick to eliminate them from your course if they fall into either of the following categories. First, there may be some affective objectives related to intangible but important values or attitudes. You can keep these goals and try to attain them as long as they do not enter into evaluation. Second, there may be some activities that you are certain will be educational for your students to experience, regardless of the outcome. These have been labeled "exploratory objectives" or "experiential objectives" (Houston & Howsam, 1972, p. 30). Goals of this sort can enter into evaluation in a minor way, such as giving pass/fail credit for participation in certain exercises or extra credit for selecting enrichment options.

6. *Rewrite the Objectives Appropriately for the Various Audiences that They Will Serve.* Behavioral objectives are technical tools stripped to minimalist language for analytic purposes. We must remember, though, that objectives serve an important communicative purpose and should be presented for top rhetorical impact. This resembles the task of turning a syllogism into an enthymeme. Only a certain class of academic administrator will respond favorably to the three-part objectives like those just illustrated. Students have been shown to respond more favorably to more personal and informal language (Civikly, 1976). Replace the Prussian sounding "the student will" with "we will be studying. . ." or "each of you will be asked to. . . ." Objectives written for student syllabi and assignment sheets might well include some clause of motivation as well, such as "in order to help you critically evaluate the media. . . ." Objectives written to communicate with your colleagues should stress curricular links, such as "In order to prepare students to conduct independent research in advanced courses, ..." For other teachers of the same class, it is helpful to mention the conditions of learning so they can use some of your ideas if they choose to. "By having each student bring to class an editorial in which he or she has identified the warrant, claim, and data of an argument. . . ."

This chapter has invited you to ask a series of important questions: Why should students pursue higher education? Why should they study communication? What should they accomplish in each course? How do you want your students to have changed when your class is finished?

Realize that these are questions that you will answer over and over throughout your teaching career. An educational philosophy is not static. Neil Postman, in *Teaching as a Conserving Activity* (1980), suggested that schools should serve a thermostatic function, constantly changing and adapting to emphasize whatever society seems to be ignoring at a given time. Educational goals should reflect the needs of society, the nature of students, the content of our discipline, and the teachers' own values. Stay alert to all of these factors. As they change and reconfigure, your educational goals will necessarily change too. Enjoy the process of discovering and refining your goals; welcome the challenge of finding new ways to meet them.

REFERENCES

Adler, M. (1983). *How to speak, how to listen.* New York: Macmillan.

Allen, R. R., & Brown, K. L. (1976). *Developing communication competence in children.* Skokie, IL: National Textbook Company.

Andersen, P. A. (1986). Consciousness, cognition and communication. *Western Journal of Speech Communication, 50,* 87–101.

Association of American Colleges. (1985). Integrity in the college curriculum: A report to the academic community. *The Chronicle of Higher Education, 29,* 12–30.

Bennett, W. J. (1984). *To reclaim a legacy: A report on the humanities in higher education.* Washington: National Endowment for the Humanities.

Blankenship, J. (1981). The liberal arts in and out of academe: Some questions about ends and means. *Association for Communication Administration Bulletin, 36,* 63–67.

Bloom, A. D. (1987). *The closing of the American mind: How higher education has failed democracy and impoverished the souls of today's students.* New York: Simon and Schuster.

Bloom, B. (Ed.). (1956). *Taxonomy of educational objectives: The classification of educational goals. Handbook I: Cognitive domain.* New York: David McKay.

Bowyer, C. H. (1970). *Philosophical perspectives for education.* Glenview, IL: Scott Foresman.

Boyer, E. L. (1978). Redefining literacy and basics communication: Message senders and receivers. *Communication Education, 27,* 271–276.

Boyer, E. L., & Levine, A. (1981). *A quest for common learning: The aims of general education.* New York: The Carnegie Foundation for the Advancement of Teaching.

Bradley, B. E. (1979). Speech communication and liberal education. *The Southern Speech Communication Journal, 45,* 1–11.

Briggs, N., & Pinola, M. (1985). A consideration of five traditional educational philosophies for speech communication. *Central States Speech Journal, 36,* 305–314.

Brown, L. M. (Ed.). (1970). *Aims of education.* New York: Teacher's College Press.

Brummett, B. (1986). Absolutist and relativist stances toward the problem of difference: A model for student growth in public speaking education. *Communication Education, 35,* 269–274.

Carnegie Foundation for the Advancement of Teaching. (1977). *Missions of the college curriculum: A contemporary review with suggestions.* San Francisco: Jossey-Bass.

Cegala, D. J., Kibler, R. J., Barker, L. L., & Miles, D. T. (1972). Writing behavioral objectives: A programmed article. *The Speech Teacher, 21,* 151–168.

Civikly, J. M. (1976). A case for humanizing behavioral objectives. *Communication Education, 25,* 231–236.

Conville, R. L. (1977). Cognitive goals in communicating learning. *Communication Education, 26,* 113–120.

Dance, F. E. X. (1980). Speech communication as a liberal arts discipline. *Communication Education, 29,* 328–331.

Dearin, R. D. (1980). Public address history as part of the speech communication discipline. *Communication Education, 29,* 348–356.

Deetz, S. A., & Kersten, A. (1983). Critical models of interpretive research. In L. Putnam & M. Pacanowsky (Eds.), *Communication and organizations: An interpretive approach* (pp. 147–171). Beverly Hills, CA: Sage.

Department Goals and Objectives. (1987). Department of communication, Santa Clara University Santa Clara, CA.

DiSalvo, V. S., Larsen, J. K., & Backus, D. K. (1986). The health care communicator: An identification of skills and problems. *Communication Education, 35,* 231–242.

Dressel, P. L., & Mayhew, L. B. (1954). *General education: Explorations in evaluation.* Washington, DC: American Council on Education.

Emmert, P. (1985). Liberal arts education and the communication arts and sciences discipline. *Association of Communication Administrators Bulletin, 53,* 29–31.

Feezel, J. D. (1985). Toward a confluent taxonomy of cognitive, affective and psychomotor abilities in communication. *Communication Education, 34,* 1–11.

Findley, C. A., & Nye, R. A. (1973). ERIC Reports: Behavioral objectives and speech instruction. *The Speech Teacher, 22,* 257–262.

Foss, S. K., Foss, K. A., & Trapp, R. (1985). *Contemporary perspectives on rhetoric.* Prospect Heights, IL: Waveland.

Freire, P. (1972). *Pedagogy of the oppressed.* (M. B. Ramos, Trans.). New York: Herder and Herder. (Original work published 1970)

Fritz, P. A., & Weaver, R. L. III. (1986). Teaching critical thinking skills in the public speaking course. *Communication Education, 35,* 174–181.

Gagné, R. M. (1970). *The conditions of learning* (2nd ed.) New York: Holt, Rinehart & Winston.

Gibson, J. W., Hanna, M. S., & Huddleston, B. M. (1985). The basic speech course at U.S. colleges and universities: IV. *Communication Education, 34,* 281–291.

Giroux, H. A. (1988). *Teachers as intellectuals: Toward a critical pedagogy of learning.* Granby, MA: Bergin and Garvey.

Glaser, S. R., & Eblen, A. (1986). *Toward communication competency: Developing interpersonal skills* (2nd ed.). New York: Holt, Rinehart & Winston.

Harrow, A. (1972). *A taxonomy of the psychomotor domain.* New York: David McKay.

Hart, R. P. (1985). The politics of communication studies: An address to undergraduates. *Communication Education, 34,* 162–164.

Hart, R. P. (1986, February). *Sex, drugs, rock'n roll and speech: Why we're in Tucson.* Address presented at the meeting of the Western Speech Communication Association, Tucson, AZ.

Harvey, O. J., Hunt, D. E., & Schroder, H. M. (1961). *Conceptual systems and personality organization.* New York: Wiley.

Haynes, J. L. (1973). Improving instruction in speech-communication skills through learning hierarchies: An application to organization. *The Speech Teacher, 22,* 237–243.

Hirsch, E. D., Jr. (1987). *Cultural literacy: What every American needs to know.* Boston: Houghton Mifflin.

Hopper, R., & Daly, J. A. (1979). Oral communication as a basic skill: Some preliminary issues. *Association for Communication Administration Bulletin, 27,* 22–25.

Hostettler, G. F. (1980). Speech as a liberal study II. *Communication Education, 29,* 332–347.

Houston, W. R., & Howsam, R. B. (1972). *Competency-based teacher education.* Chicago: Science Research Associates.

Howard, R. J. (1982). *Three faces of hermeneutics.* Berkeley: University of California Press.

Hunt, D. (1971). *Matching models in education.* Toronto: Ontario Institute for Studies in Education.

Hunt, E. L. (1955). Rhetoric as humane study. *Quarterly Journal of Speech, 53,* 285–289.

Hunt, G. T., & Cusella, L. P. (1983). A field study of listening needs in organizations. *Communication Education, 32,* 393–410.

Jamieson, K. M., & Wolvin, A. D. (1976). Non-teaching careers in communication: Implications for the speech communication curriculum. *Communication Education, 25,* 283–291.

Johnson, J. R., & Johnson, S. H. (1982). Assessing the human communication needs of practicing engineers. *Association for Communication Administration Bulletin, 40,* 56–60.

Katula, R. A., & Martin, C. A. (1984). Teaching critical thinking in the speech communication classroom. *Communication Education, 33,* 160–167.

Kibler, R. J., Barker, L. L., & Cegala, D. J. (1970). A rationale for using behavioral objectives in speech communication instruction. *The Speech Teacher, 19,* 245–256.

Kibler, R. J., Cegala, D. J., Barker, L. L., & Miles, D. T. (1974). *Objectives for instruction and evaluation.* New York: Allyn and Bacon.

Kneupper, C. W., & Anderson, F. D. (1980). Uniting wisdom and eloquence: The need for rhetorical invention. *Quarterly Journal of Speech, 66,* 313–326.

Kohlberg, L. (1981). *Essays on moral development Vol. I: The philosophy of moral development.* New York: Harper and Row.

Krathwohl, D. R., Bloom, B. S., & Masia, B. B. (1956). *Taxonomy of educational objectives, Handbook II: Affective domain.* New York: David McKay.

Loevinger, J. (1976). *Ego development: Conceptions and theories.* San Francisco: Jossey-Bass.

Mager, R. F. (1962). *Preparing instructional objectives.* Belmont, CA: Fearon.

Mager, R. F. (1984). *Goal analysis* (2nd ed.). Belmont, CA: Pitman.

Matlon, R. J. (1982). Bridging the gap between communication education and legal education. *Communication Education, 31,*39–53.

McCroskey, J. C., (1982). Communication competence and performance: A research and pedagogical perspective. *Communication Education, 31,* 1–7.

McLaren, P. (1989). *Life in schools: An introduction to critical pedagogy in the foundations of education.* New York: Longman.

Mehrley, R. S., & Backes, J. G. (1972). The first course in speech: A call for revolution. *The Speech Teacher, 21,* 205–211.

Modaff, J., & Hopper, R. (1984). Why speech is "basic." *Communication Education, 33,* 38–42.

National Institute of Education. (1984). *Involvement in learning: Realizing the potential of American higher education.* Washington: U.S. Department of Education.

Ong, W. (1982). *Orality and literacy: The technologizing of the word.* London: Metheun.

Peddiwell, J. A. (1939). *The saber-tooth curriculum.* New York: McGraw-Hill.

Perry, W. G. (1969). *Forms of intellectual and ethical development during the college years.* New York: Holt, Rinehart & Winston.

Phillips, G. M. (1984). A competent view of "competence." *Communication Education, 33,* 25–36.

A philosopher hurls down a stinging moral gauntlet. (1987, May 11). *The Washington Times, Insight Section,* pp. 10–11.

Postman, N. (1980). *Teaching as a conserving activity.* New York: Delta.

Redding, W. C. (1985). Rocking boats, blowing whistles, and teaching speech communication. *Communication Education, 34,* 245–258.

Rogers, C. R. (1969). *Freedom to learn: A view of what education might become.* Columbus: OH: C. E. Merrill.

Rubin, R. B. (1982). Assessing speaking and listening competence at the college level: The communication competence assessment instrument. *Communication Education, 31,* 19–23.

Scott, R. (1967). On viewing rhetoric as epistemic. *Central States Speech Journal, 18,* 9–17.

Smith, R. M. (1982). *Learning how to learn: Applied theory for adults.* Chicago: Follett.

Snelbecker, G. E. (1985). *Learning theory, instructional theory, and psychoeducational design.* Lanham, MD: University Press of America.

Spitzberg, B. H. (1983). Communication competence as knowledge, skill and impression. *Communication Education, 32, 323 329.*

Sprague, J. (1974). Cognitive aspects and teaching for mastery in teacher education in speech communication. In P. J. Newcomb & R. R. Allen (Eds.), *New horizons for teacher education in speech communication* (pp. 74–96). Skokie, IL: National Textbook Company.

Sproule, J. M. (1087). Whose ethics in the classroom? An historical overview. *Communication Education, 36,* 317–326.

Tucker, C. O. (1973). Toward facilitation of behavioral objectives in speech communication. *The Speech Teacher, 22,* 231–236.

Tyler, R. W. (1949). *Basic principles of curriculum and instruction.* Chicago: University of Chicago Press.

Wolvin, A. D., & Coakley, C. G. (1985). *Listening* (2nd ed.). Dubuque, IA: W. E. Brown.

Young, R. E. (Ed.). (1980). *Fostering critical thinking: New directions for teaching and learning.* San Francisco: Jossey-Bass.

3

An Ecological Perspective on College/University Teaching

Ann Q. Staton
University of Washington

Colleges and universities in American society are social institutions that serve two primary functions: (a) to teach a manifest curriculum, comprised largely of academic content, and (b) to teach a hidden curriculum, comprised largely of social content. Most new instructors are hired because of their expertise in a particular body of academic content, and preparation for college/university teaching focuses largely on the subject matter to be taught. Although the hidden curriculum is widely considered important, there is typically little or no training for college/university teaching that addresses the social content. This chapter deals with that social content—the hidden curriculum.

A major component of the social content is the teaching environment. In order to understand this environment, it is necessary to focus on several dimensions: (a) the classroom context, (b) the institutional context, and (c) the societal context. As these contexts and their relationships are examined, the interdependence of the academic and social goals becomes clear.

The purpose of this chapter is to examine the college/university teaching environment and the socialization processes that occur within it. The approach taken is ecological, that is, it is based on the relationship among individuals, their immediate settings, and "the larger contexts in which the settings are embedded" (Bronfenbrenner, 1979, p. 21). The chapter is grounded in four assumptions, set forth by Hamilton (1983):

1. Interactions between persons and their environment are important. Both the physical setting of classrooms and the social atmosphere are critical aspects that influence and are influenced by students and teachers.

2. Teaching and learning are viewed as continuously interactive processes, rather than as causally related. In order to understand life in classrooms, it is important to take a wholistic view of interaction and not to isolate segments of behavior.

3. Person–environment interactions, typically examined within the immediate classroom and school environment, must also be viewed with respect to external forces, such as the family, community, and socioeconomic system. Classrooms are systems nested within larger institutional systems and even larger societal ones.

4. The attitudes and perceptions of the participants—teachers, students, and administrators—provide important data about classrooms and schools. To gain a depth of understanding, it is necessary to have the perspectives of insiders about events and their importance.

The first section of this chapter identifies the classroom, institutional, and societal environments and discusses their importance in understanding college/university teaching. The second section focuses on the socialization process by which teachers and students accomplish their transition into new classroom and institutional environments.

ENVIRONMENTS FOR COLLEGE/UNIVERSITY TEACHING

The Classroom Context

The college/university classroom generally consists of a group of students and a single instructor, typically a professor or a graduate teaching assistant (GTA). These participants come together in a specific physical setting and interact for a particular duration of time, usually an academic semester or quarter. The class meets at regular intervals each week for a specified length of time. As the instructor and students interact within the physical environment, a social atmosphere, or climate, emerges. Norms for appropriate verbal and nonverbal behavior develop, constituting a classroom culture.

Physical Setting. A number of different dimensions constitute the physical environment of the classroom (Weinstein, 1979). Included are such aspects as the size and configuration of the room, whether the chairs are fixed or moveable, the seating arrangement, the level of attractiveness of the room, the location of the chalkboard, the availability of resource equipment (e.g., overhead projector, slide projector, video monitors, etc.), the duration of the class, the time of day the class meets, and the number of students enrolled. Each of these factors contributes to the overall environment.

Anyone who has ever sat in a college or university classroom knows that the size and shape of the room make a difference in the communication that occurs and often in the atmosphere that develops. Contrast, for example, a large lecture room with fixed chairs that seats 250 students with a moderate-sized classroom with moveable desks that accommodates 35 students. In the large room, the instructor is at the center and must look up to tiers of students. The instructor typically uses a microphone to be heard by all and, unless blessed with extraordinary vision, is unlikely to be able to see clearly the faces of all students.

The mode of instruction is almost dictated by the constraints and confines of the room. A highly interactive class session, with students doing most of the talking, is difficult to facilitate because the size of the room makes it impossible for all students to hear one another. Because the desks do not move, it is not easy for an instructor to assign the class to work in small groups. Thus, most instructors of large classes rely on the lecture method. In fact, the room itself is often referred to as a lecture hall. In a moderate-sized classroom with considerably fewer students, an instructor has many more instructional options. The lecture format is possible, but so also are the small group format and the large group discussion.

Just as the size of the room constrains the type of instruction that occurs, the seating arrangement is also influential. A variety of research (Smith, 1979; Sommer, 1969; Totusek & Staton-Spicer, 1982; Woolfolk & Brooks, 1983) indicates that students seated in the first row across the front of the classroom and those seated in a vertical column down the center of the room are the ones who are most likely to participate. What is not clear is whether it is the seating arrangement that causes students to participate or whether seating choice by students is a function of their personalities or desire to participate. Whatever the case, it has been demonstrated that teachers maintain eye contact most readily and most often with those students seated in what has come to be termed "the action zone." Similarly, in an alternative seating arrangement such as a circular one, there tends to be increased eye contact and interaction among the classroom participants.

Other important physical dimensions include temporal aspects—the time of day the class is taught and the duration of the session. Students (as well as instructors) know what it is like to attend a class at 8:00 in the morning, when neither the body nor the mind is fully awake. Similarly, it is uncomfortable for many students to attend a class immediately after the lunch hour; they find themselves nodding to sleep even when genuinely interested in the class. And any instructor who has tried to teach to students who are dozing knows the difficulty of the task and how disconfirming it can be. It is also a challenge to maintain the attention and focus of students when the class meets for a long period of time. Many students and instructors prefer classes that meet for only 1 hour, or even 50 minutes.

Finally, the general attractiveness of the classroom can influence the atmosphere and the interaction that occurs. In the classic study of Maslow and Mintz (1956), researchers found that students in a neutral or unattractive classroom had less energy and were less motivated to complete instructional tasks than were students place in a room judged to be attractive. Similarly, Franzolino (1977) had college students engage in an instructional-type task in rooms designated as beautiful, average, and ugly. Individual and group scores on the task were higher for students in the beautiful and average rooms than for those in the ugly room. Thus, both of these studies lend support to the importance of the physical environment of the classroom.

Social Atmosphere. "The cultures of teaching are shaped by the contexts of teaching" (Feiman-Nemser & Floden, 1986, p. 515). Both instructors and students bring with them to the classroom certain expectations for the kind of speech that should and should not occur, for the kind of behavior that is and is not appropriate, and for the roles that the instructor and students should and should not take. Each person brings in values and assumptions about classroom norms, some of which will usually be shared by class members but others of which will likely conflict. Within the constraints of the physical setting previously discussed, patterns for communication will develop in the classroom. From the beginning of class, the instructor and students engage in a process of negotiation about classroom norms and patterns, including norms for interrupting, joking, noise level, terms of address, degree of familiarity, and amount and type of classroom interaction. Adaptation by the class members occurs in the process of achieving some degree of harmony. The communication norms and patterns that emerge constitute the culture of the particular classroom (Condon, 1986).

The Institutional Context

The institutional context refers to the particular type of organization or school (including the physical facilities as well as structural properties) and the social atmosphere or culture.

Physical Setting. The physical environment of a college or university encompasses such dimensions as the location of the particular department on campus, whether needed resources are housed within the department or must be obtained from outside, the structural arrangement of space within the department, and the allocation of time.

If an academic department is housed in a building that is at the center of campus, for example, the likelihood is increased that students will stop in for unscheduled visits. If most resources for faculty and GTAs are located within the building (e.g., computer terminals, area library, media center), then there is little need for contact with others outside of the department. In these situations, instructors can become isolated from other units on campus.

The structural arrangement of space within the department also influences the interaction that occurs. The placement of faculty and GTA offices, for example, and their proximity to classrooms can have an effect on the frequency of student visits. If students have to check in with a secretary before seeing an instructor, they are less likely to drop in than if they have direct access to instructor offices. If the department has a student-faculty lounge or some other central gathering area, this will increase the interaction between faculty and students. This is in contrast to facilities that are segregated according to rank, which serve to decrease interaction. Another spatial dimension has to do with a closed-versus open-door policy. Instructors who leave their office door open invite students to stop in, whereas it requires more assertiveness on the part of a student to knock on a door that is closed. The placement of a faculty desk is often a spatial factor that can affect interaction. Zweigenhaft (1976) found differences between faculty whose desks served as a barricade between themselves and students and those faculty who were "unbarricaded." Students perceived the "unbarricaded professors" as more willing to give individual attention and more encouraging of different viewpoints.

Finally, just as the temporal dimension is an important one in the classroom environment, it is also important in the institutional environment. The time allotted for office hours by faculty and GTAs is a major factor affecting communication. The sheer numbers of students that an instructor can see, as well as the amount of time given to each one, is often dictated by the number of office hours each week. Instructors who announce to students that they can stop by only during office hours discourage spontaneous visits. This is in contrast to a policy of "come see me whenever I am in the office."

Social Atmosphere. As Geertz (1973) defined cultural patterns, they are "historically created systems of meaning in terms of which we give form, order, point, and direction to our lives" (p. 52). Increasingly in recent years, organizations have been viewed as having cultures. From the list of best sellers (e.g., Deal & Kennedy, *Corporate Cultures,* 1982) to academic books and journals (e.g., Barley, 1983; Frost, Moore, Louis, Lundberg, & Martin, 1985), cultural perspectives of organizations are advocated.

Colleges and universities, as organizations, have their own cultures, or "shared assumptions, priorities, meanings, and values—with patterns of beliefs among people" (Frost et al., 1985, p. 17). A variety of dimensions contribute to the overall culture: whether the school is primarily a teaching or a research institution, whether the school is public or private, religious or secular, the nature of the student population, whether the particular department is considered a humanities or a social science department, and the political clout of the department.

A school that defines itself as a major research institution sets forth priorities that differ from a college or university whose primary mission is the education of undergraduates. Such differences are likely to be manifested in the allocation of resources and in the reward structure for faculty, for example. Similarly, public and private (religious and secular) institutions differ in the values that are espoused and the atmosphere that permeates the campus. In many Protestant institutions, for example, Christian ideals are proclaimed in public discourse and are made the basis for many of the rules and codes of conduct for faculty and students. The student population generally varies in accord with the culture of the school, as well as serving to constitute the culture.

On a more microscopic organizational level, the department can also be considered as having a culture of its own. As Snow (1959) argued some three decades ago, a sharp cultural distinction can be made between the humanities and the sciences. These divisions are more prevalent on some campuses than others and have different implications with respect to teaching and research activities as well as to the status, prestige, and influence of a department.

Regardless of the culture that typifies a particular college or university, the pervasive values and norms are critical aspects of the overall environment and, thus, are influential in the teaching environment. Instructors need an understanding of the institutional culture as well as the physical context.

Societal Context

The societal context includes both the physical location of the institution and the cultural values and norms.

Physical Setting. With the founding of Harvard College in 1636, higher education in the United States was launched. Although the curriculum was European in flavor, the setting was New England and the time was colonial (Boyer, 1987). These physical dimensions influenced the structure and character of the educational system. As the years progressed, American colleges and universities developed in concert with the changing times. Schools located in different regions of the country took on distinct characteristics of the locale. Traditionally, for example, people have spoken of ivy league schools in the northeastern United States as centers of liberal political thought in contrast to more conservative institutions in the south.

Social Atmosphere. Because the values of society are reflected in its colleges and universities, American institutions of higher education are uniquely "American." Although distinctly "American" in their norms and values, this does not mean that there is cultural consistency across colleges and universities. Indeed, as Hirsch (1987) has argued, "American national culture is neither coherent nor monolithic, and no convincing attempt fully to define its character has even appeared . . ." (p. 102). He went on to note that the "politics, customs, technologies, and legends that define and determine our current attitudes and actions and our institutions . . ." are in a state of "constant change, growth, [and] conflict" (p. 103).

Despite continual societal change, there are those who have characterized a culture in American higher education. Bloom (1987) wrote of the values of openness and relativism that permeate American education. And Boyer (1987) identified two essential goals of American colleges that are consonant with the longstanding, traditional values of individuality and community:

> The individual preferences of each student must be served. But beyond diversity, the college has an obligation to give students a sense of passage toward a more coherent view of knowledge and a more integrated life. . . . Just as we search culturally to maintain the necessary balance between private and public obligations, in education we seek the same end. . . . Through an effective college education, students should become personally empowered and also committed to the common good. (pp. 68–69)

Regardless of whether one agrees with a particular view of American culture, the colleges and universities in this country are undeniably "American".

SOCIALIZATION INTO COLLEGE/UNIVERSITY ENVIRONMENTS

When students and instructors come together in new situations and in new environments, both of them embark on a socialization experience.

Socialization, a process by which "people selectively acquire the values and attitudes, the interests, skills and knowledge—in short the culture—current in groups to which they are, or seek to become, a member" (Merton, Reader, & Kendall, 1957, p. 287) is an ongoing and recurrent phenomenon that people experience each time they contemplate and then actually encounter new situations. Berger and Luckmann (1966) referred to this repeated process as *secondary socialization,* a "process that inducts an already socialized individual into new sectors of the objective world of his society" (p. 130).

Types of Socialization

There are two types of secondary socialization: (a) occupational or role socialization and (b) organizational or cultural socialization. Occupational or role socialization involves individuals learning necessary skills and knowledge to fulfill a particular role (Wanous, 1977). They begin to acquire attitudes and values that resemble those of others in the same role or occupation. Thus, a new college/university student must learn how to act, how to function as a student of higher education, and how being a college student differs from being a high-school student. Similarly, a new instructor must learn what it means to be a teacher, must understand how being a teacher differs from being a student, and must take on the trappings of the new role.

In contrast, organizational or cultural socialization is "the process by which a person learns the values, norms and required behaviors which permit him to participate as a member of the organization" (Van Maanen, 1976, p. 67). The emphasis is not on the role, but on the particular organization or institution. A student who transfers from a large, public institution to a small, conservative, religious university will need to adapt to the differences in cultures and to understand that the same behaviors are probably not appropriate in the two contexts. Similarly, an instructor who takes a position at this small, private university must learn what it means to be a faculty member in the culture and must adapt to the different expectations that students, administrators, and the local community have for faculty.

Considered from an ecological perspective, a new GTA or instructor is undergoing an ecological transition that includes changes in role and context as a function of a person's development, maturation, and life cycle (Bronfenbrenner, 1977).

Phases of Socialization

There are three widely discussed phases of organizational socialization (Van Maanen, 1976) that are also applicable to occupational or role socialization. *Anticipatory socialization* refers to the choice phase, or selection process during which an individual makes the decision to join a particular organization or begin a new profession. For students, this may involve an initial decision to go to college and become a student, followed by a second decision to attend a certain school. As these decisions are made, the student develops expectations about what it will be like to be a student as well as what it will be like to be a student at a specific university. For instructors, a decision must be made to become an academic instructor, then an institution must be selected.

A second phase is that of *entry* (or encounter), during which the newcomer experiences the new situation—either the occupation or the organization—for the first time. A common experience during this entry phase is what is known as "reality shock" (Veenman, 1984). A student confronted with the first week of college classes and the enormous time demands and pressures may realize that the actual experience does not at all match the expectations. The same feeling is also frequently felt by a new instructor facing the job realities for the first time. Differences between the new environment and a previous one may be readily apparent.

The third phase of socialization is that of *continuance* (or adaptation), during which the newcomer makes whatever changes are necessary in order to remain in the role and/or in the organization. For students this may involve an altered set of expectations for the time that will be spent studying or, for example, an acceptance that they will dress more formally for the classes of certain professors in order to be accepted. A new instructor may, after discussion with the departmental chair, decide to continue to teach using somewhat unorthodox methods, but realize the impact that this approach to teaching will have on some students as well as some faculty members.

Dialectical Model of Socialization

Contrasting with a functionalist conception of socialization (Parsons, 1951) is a model of socialization as a dialectical process (Zeichner, 1980). Considered from an ecological perspective, this model is one that focuses on the interaction between people and the environments in which they interact. Unlike the functionalist view, in which the environment dominates the individual, who is merely a passive recipient, the individual in the dialectical model is an initiator who actively influences the environment. The focus is on "the constant interplay between individuals and the institutions into which they are socialized" (Zeichner, 1980, p. 2). The implication of this model for student and teacher socialization into the school environment is that the process is a dynamic one in which individuals must face the constraints of the environment but are not controlled by, and do not necessarily acquiesce to, the environmental demands.

Student Socialization

Recent research has begun to examine the process of student socialization into schools, with much of the research focusing on the perspective of students. It is important for teachers to have an understanding of students' views as they make transitions into new environments. Although little of the research has investigated college/university student socialization, certain of the issues and themes from research on students at other levels may have relevance to higher education.

Staton (in press) conducted a case study of new kindergarteners and discovered that part of learning to be a student involves making sense of a new environment laced with inconsistencies and contradictions. Similarly, Oseroff-Varnell and Staton-Spicer (1987), in a study of a group of third graders who were new to their grade level and school, found that socialization includes several dimensions: academic, procedural, and social. Students have to adapt to increasingly difficult academic content, adjust to new procedures for classroom work, and learn about and enter into a complex social environment.

A study of student socialization into the high school environment indicated that students have to make sense of two domains, an academic one and a social one. Cavanaugh and Staton-Spicer (1986) surveyed 200 new high-school freshmen and found that three of the dimensions are socially related (activities, making friends, talking with friends) and one is academically related (academics). These students perceive the academic dimension as more important than any of the social dimensions.

Although similar studies of the socialization of college/university students have not been forthcoming, research has demonstrated that there are differences across school environments and that students face various socialization challenges. In a comparison of freshmen orientation programs at four universities in a metropolitan area, Green (1988) discovered different themes and values articulated across the settings.

Teacher Socialization

A wealth of research has examined teacher socialization from both functionalist and dialectical perspectives (Staton-Spicer & Darling, 1987), with most of the studies conducted with teachers at the K–12-grade levels. Functionalist studies have focused on identifying various *outcomes* of socialization (such as attitude changes and conformity) and *agents* of socialization (such as cooperating teachers and university supervisors). Dialectical studies, in contrast, have focused more on the *process* of socialization (Staton-Spicer & Darling, 1986).

What emerges from these bodies of research is the conclusion that neophyte teachers face an array of new situations, ranging from learning the teaching role to interacting with a new set of people to adapting in a new environment. Increasingly, teachers are viewed as active agents who interact with school environments in creative, assertive ways in order to achieve their goals.

Graduate Teaching Assistant Socialization

Because GTAs at some universities take responsibility for up to half of all undergraduate instruction, they are clearly important to the college/university teaching environment (Smock & Menges, 1985). Their socialization experiences are unique, in that often a GTA must socialize simultaneously to the instructor role and to the graduate student role (Darling & Staton, in press; Staton & Darling, in press). According to Darling (1987), most of the research on GTA socialization can be classified into two categories: (a) the training and development of effective teachers, and (b) changes in the academic orientation of graduate students. Although informative, such research has not been particularly helpful in illuminating the process of GTA socialization.

In a recent study, however, Darling (1986) examined the actual socialization experiences of three GTAs in one department during their first year of graduate study. Among other findings, she reported the importance of the physical environment. In one department, faculty and GTA offices were physically separated—with faculty on the first floor near the mail room, main office, and classrooms and GTAs on the fourth floor with immediate access only to one another. The physical location of the offices affected interaction and information-seeking behavior, with GTAs talking primarily among themselves and seeking assistance from faculty only rarely.

In a related study, Darling and Staton-Spicer (1986) examined the formal orientation program designed by an academic department to socialize new GTAs. Consistent with the ecological perspective of this chapter, their research was guided by a view of the department as a culture. Analysis of the discourse during the orientation week revealed a culturally meaningful description of "TA," and the conclusion was drawn that "different themes and metaphors would emerge as a product of similar research in other departments/cultures" (p. 24).

A subsequent study by Darling (1987) focused on the socialization of a group of five GTAs in three academic departments during their first term. Their experience was multifaceted, involving socialization into the role of graduate student, into the role of teaching assistant, and into the particular department at the specific institution. The interplay among the GTA's personal goals, the department's standards, and the role of the university as a research institution lends support to the importance of an ecological perspective.

SUMMARY AND CONCLUSIONS

Three contexts must be understood in order to make sense of the college/university teaching environment: the classroom context, the institutional context, and the societal context. To understand college/university teaching, it is not enough to be familiar with the academic content or manifest curriculum; one must also have an awareness of the hidden curriculum. This chapter has presented an ecological perspective in which the focus is on the interaction between people (students and instructors) and their environment (classroom, college/university, societal). A brief discussion has been provided of the physical aspects of each of the three environments, as well as the social atmosphere or culture of each.

In the second part of the chapter, the process of socialization into new school environments was discussed. New faculty or GTAs are typically involved in both learning a new role and learning to make sense of a new organization. To be an effective instructor requires more than knowledge of content; it demands successful socialization into the classroom, institution, and perhaps society as well.

Although this chapter has not drawn from research conducted specifically on faculty and GTAs in communication, the applications are relevant. Because the discipline of communication deals with a process-oriented subject matter (i.e., human communication), an understanding of an ecological approach to college/university teaching may be even more critical than for educators in other disciplines.

REFERENCES

Barley, S. R. (1983). Semiotics and the study of occupational and organizational cultures. *Administrative Science Quarterly, 28,* 393–413.

Berger, P. L., & Luckmann, T. (1966). *The social construction of reality.* New York: Doubleday.

Bloom, A. (1987). *The closing of the American mind.* New York: Simon and Schuster.

Boyer, E. L. (1987). *College: The undergraduate experience in America.* New York: Harper & Row.

Bronfenbrenner, U. (1977). Toward an experimental ecology of human development. *American Psychologist, 32*, 513–531.

Bronfenbrenner, U. (1979). *The ecology of human development.* Cambridge: Harvard University Press.

Cavanaugh, P. D., & Staton-Spicer, A. Q. (1986, November). *So now you're a freshman: Communication in the socialization of high school freshmen.* Paper presented at the annual meeting of the Speech Communication Association, Chicago.

Condon, J. C. (1986). The ethnocentric classroom. In J. M. Civikly (Ed.), *Communicating in college classrooms* (pp. 11–20). San Francisco: Jossey-Bass.

Darling, A. L. (1986, November). *On becoming a graduate student: An examination of communication in the socialization process.* Paper presented at the annual meeting of the Speech Communication Association, Chicago.

Darling, A. L. (1987). *Interaction in the socialization process of graduate teaching assistants.* Unpublished doctoral dissertation, University of Washington, Seattle.

Darling, A. L., & Staton, A. Q. (in press). Socialization of graduate teaching assistants. A case study in an American university. *International Journal of Qualitative Studies in Education.*

Darling, A. L., & Staton-Spicer, A. Q. (1986, April). *Communication in the socialization of graduate T.A.'s: An ethnographic study.* Paper presented at the annual meeting of the American Educational Research Association, San Francisco.

Deal, T. E., & Kennedy, A. A. (1982). *Corporate cultures.* Reading, MA: Addison-Wesley.

Feiman-Nemser, S., & Floden, R. E. (1986). The cultures of teaching. In M. C. Wittrock (Ed.), *Handbook of research on teaching* (3rd ed., pp. 505–526). New York: Macmillan.

Franzolino, P. L. (1977). *Effect of aesthetic environment on individual and group task performance.* Unpublished manuscript, Department of Speech Communication, University of Texas at Austin, TX.

Frost, P. J., Moore, L. F., Louis, M. R., Lundberg, C. C., & Martin, J. (1985). *Organizational culture.* Beverly Hills, CA: Sage.

Geertz, C. (1973). *The interpretation of cultures.* New York: Basic Books.

Green, K. (1988, May). *Socialization messages during university freshman orientation.* Paper presented at the annual meeting of the International Communication Association, New Orleans, LA.

Hamilton, S. F. (1983). The social side of schooling: Ecological studies of classrooms and schools. *The Elementary School Journal, 83*, 313–333.

Hirsch, E. D. Jr., (1987). *Cultural literacy: What America needs to know.* Boston: Houghton Mifflin.

Maslow, A. H., & Mintz, N. L. (1956). Effects of esthetic surroundings: I. Initial effects of three esthetic conditions upon perceiving "energy" and "well being" in faces. *Journal of Psychology, 41*, 247–254.

Merton, R., Reader, G., & Kendall, P. (1957). *The student physician.* Cambridge: Harvard University Press.

Oseroff-Varnell, D., & Staton-Spicer, A. Q. (1987, November). *Communication in the socialization of elementary school students.* Paper presented at the annual meeting of the Speech Communication Association, Boston.

Parsons, T. (1951). *The social system.* London: Routledge & Kegan Paul.

Smith, H. A. (1979). Nonverbal communication in teaching. *Review of Educational Research, 49*, 631–672.

Smock, R., & Menges, R. (1985). Programs for TAs in the context of campus policies and priorities. In J. D. W. Andrews (Ed.), *Strengthening the teaching assistant faculty* (pp. 21–33). San Francisco: Jossey-Bass.

Snow, C. P. (1959). *The two cultures: And a second look—An expanded version of the two cultures and the scientific revolution.* Cambridge: Cambridge University Press. (Part II added 1964).

Sommer, R. (1969). *Personal space.* Englewood Cliffs, NJ: Prentice-Hall.

Staton, A. Q., (in press). *Communication and student socialization.* Norwood, NJ: Ablex.

Staton, A. Q., & Darling, A. L. (in press). Socialization of teaching assistants. In J. D. Nyquist, R. D. Abbott, & D. H. Wulff (Eds.), *The training of teaching assistants.* San Francisco: Jossey-Bass.

Staton-Spicer, A. Q., & Darling, A. L. (1986). Communication in the socialization of preservice teachers. *Communication Education, 35,* 215–230.

Staton-Spicer, A. Q., & Darling, A. L. (1987). A communication perspective on teacher socialization. *Journal of Thought, 22,* 12–19.

Totusek, P. F., & Staton-Spicer, A. Q. (1982). Classroom seating preference as a function of student personality. *Journal of Experimental Education, 50,* 159–163.

Van Maanen, J. (1976). Breaking in: Socialization to work. In R. Dubin (Ed.), *Handbook of work, organization, and society* (pp. 67–130). Chicago: Rand McNally.

Veenman, S. (1984). Perceived problems of beginning teachers. *Review of Educational Research, 54,* 143–178.

Wanous, J. P. (1977). Organizational entry: Newcomers moving from outside to inside. *Psychological Bulletin, 84,* 601–618.

Weinstein, C. S. (1979). The physical environment of the school: A review of the research. *Review of Educational Research, 49,* 577–610.

Woolfolk, A. E., & Brooks, D. M. (1983). Nonverbal communication in teaching. In E. W. Gordon (Ed.), *Review of research in education* (Vol. 10, pp. 103–150). Washington, DC: American Educational Research Association.

Zeichner, K. M. (1980, April). *Key processes in the socialization of student teachers: Limitations and consequences of over-socialized conceptions of teacher socialization.* Paper presented at the annual meeting of the American Educational Research Association, Boston.

Zweigenhaft, R. (1976). Personal space in the faculty office: Desk placement and the student—faculty interaction. *Journal of Applied Psychology, 61,* 529–532.

4

Creating a New Course

Jean M. Civikly
University of New Mexico

Consider the start of any new project or production—an architectural design, a scientific experiment, a theatrical performance, a musical score, a journal article, a book chapter, a new college course. Each of these projects has any number of possibilities and approaches. Just how does the genesis of a specific work—in our case, a college course in communication—come about? *M&Ms* may not be the response you expected, but there is a good amount of *method* and a touch of *mystery* involved in the process of creating a new course.

Most models of curricular development typically include at least four components: learners' pre-entry skills, objectives, strategies, and evaluation (Darling, chapter 20, this volume; Kibler, Barker, & Miles, 1970). In this chapter, a pragmatic extension of these models, a five-plan method of instructional design (Civikly, 1987) is presented: (a) the organizational plan, (b) the motivational plan, (c) the communication/interaction plan, (d) the props plan, and (e) the timing plan. So, *methods* do exist: Instructional development is a series of plans that answers the question: "What do I want to do and accomplish in this new course?".

But what about the *mystery* of creating a course? Often, the development of a new course is accomplished in the solitude of one's mind and workplace. Sometimes, it is an outcome of group interaction. But, although we can see the *product* of that creative endeavor, we are usually not privy to the actual *process* and thus have few models for learning how to create a new course.

The intention of this chapter is to take you "behind the scenes" of the creative and critical thinking processes involved in designing a new course. The sources of the information presented include both *print* (published research and text information) and *people* (student and teacher feedback about course successes and failures that was purposely solicited in writing and conversation or gratefully overheard in hallway and campus chats). As we begin, be assured that we are not starting from scratch—we are all experienced students and participant-observers in the process of learning.

WHERE TO BEGIN?

News that you will be teaching a new course may elicit feelings of joy and excitement, a sense of challenge, and a touch of terror or anxiety. Where do you begin? How do you prepare? I have posed these questions to groups of teaching assistants participating in workshops on instructional training, and the response has been consistent, albeit narrow: Learn the content. The deception hidden in this response is the belief that knowledge of the content alone is sufficient for effective teaching. In actuality, *knowing the content* is just the beginning and, in some cases, research by the new teacher about what comprises even the content must be undertaken.

But, before we jump too far ahead, two questions need to be addressed. The first is "What is a new course?". In its most narrow form, a new course is defined as one that has not been offered previously by a department and for which the department has no file of syllabi, assignments, or tests. In a more broad sense, a new course may be one that *you* are teaching for the first time. Although course materials used by others are available, your handling of the course has your distinctive signature. In either case, the possibilities for approaching the new course are as diverse as the individuals developing the course.

The second question is "How does a new course take shape?". Ideas for new courses (or parts thereof) may come from any number of opportunities that are presented to us. How many of the following situations have you experienced: learners' unmet needs; your own dissatisfactions with an established course; informal conversations with students, colleagues, and friends; quiet time and personal reflection; an evolving body of new research and publications; discussions at professional conferences and seminars; colleagues' (and your own) new interests and research; perceived gaps in the department's curriculum; personal reading (fiction, nonfiction, magazines); insights from media (television, radio, film); insights from the performing arts (theater, music); needs of specific learner populations; needs for specific contexts and professions (law, medicine, counseling, business); new technologies; and interdisciplinary moves for curricular cooperation and team teaching?

Examples of new courses often appear as "special topics" and include such titles as: Communication in Marriage; Humor and Communication; Communication Technologies and the 21st Century; Practicing What is Preached: Successful Communication Behaviors; and Communication for Global Coexistence. The generation of ideas for new courses is limited only by your openness to be curious and to wonder, question, and seek new learning and discovery.

RESEARCHING THE IDEA

Once an idea is selected and approved for development, the search for resources can begin in earnest. Depending on the topic, this search might include textbooks and chapters, professional journals, conference papers, media reports, visits with experts, contacts with individuals on campus and in the community, and correspondence and teleconferences with experts outside the local community.

Resources that may be particularly useful in developing the course materials include newspaper articles, editorials, articles from popular magazines, political cartoons, comic strips, television programs (soap operas, situation comedies, talk-show formats), films and videotapes, commercially produced instructional tapes, courtroom proceedings, congressional hearings, literary passages and dialogues, music lyrics, advertisements, texts of speeches, quotations, and observations of selected interactions (labor negotiations; family, work, and teacher–student interactions; conversations; interviews).

When these resources have been collected and studied, the extent of course content can be estimated. Is there sufficient information that is relevant to the course topic and concepts? Is the information distinctive to communication principles? Can a case be made for its substance and need? Presuming you have positive responses to these questions and support from the necessary departmental and university committees, let's move on to the "nuts and bolts" of course development.

DEVELOPING THE COURSE

Now that resources for the course have been reviewed adequately, you can proceed to arrange the topics into groups (units) that go together and that appear to follow from each other. Look for natural groupings of topics. Some common progressions include (a) History, Theory, Research,

Applications, Implications; (b) Levels of Communication: Cultural, Sociological, and Psychological; and (c) Communication Settings: Home, School, Work, Community.

The topic groupings will form the basis for *units of instruction* in the course; that is, the clusters of topics usually covered in 2 to 5 weeks, depending on the topic. Your creativity again is evident as you develop relationships among the possible topics. The number of units for a course (usually between four and eight) depends on such factors as number of weeks and class sessions, holidays, length of class sessions, coverage within each topic, and projected class activities (individual/group interactions, class reports, reviews for exams, exams, assignment descriptions, feedback about learner performance, course evaluations, guest speakers, films, and so forth).

To determine the fit of your topics within the constraints of the course, develop a preliminary worksheet of the course units and each class session. Be prepared to rework this sheet several times, for it is likely that new ideas, rescheduling, and different arrangements may come to mind during this process. A list of headings with a few entries is provided in Fig. 4.1 to help you get started.

After you complete your worksheet, see if you can explain the course to a colleague and/or student. It is helpful to audiotape these conversations, as it is likely that you will express certain assumptions you are making about the course that may need to be made more explicit in your printed information.

At this point, you have now successfully tackled the preparation of the course content. But, effective instruction goes beyond content competence and must address issues of communication competence (Civikly, 1986a). In other words, now that you know *what* you are going to teach, it's time to consider *how* you are going to teach. The five-plan framework (Fig. 4.2) is designed to guide you through this second dimension of course development.

Development of a course (the macro level) and of each class session (the micro level) can be clarified by taking into account five plans: (a) the organizational plan, (b) the motivational plan, (c) the communication/interaction plan, (d) the props plan, and (e) the timing plan. A brief description of each plan and its uses for course development and class sessions follows.

The Organizational Plan

This plan builds directly on your knowledge of the course content. Common organizational structures are chronological, problem–solution, cause–effect, topical, and advantages–disadvantages. At the *macro* level

Date	Topic	Readings and Assignments Due
Jan 15, 17	Course Introduction	McGuire, Chapter 1
	First Name Basis (exercise)	
	UNIT ONE: PRINCIPLES OF COMMUNICATION	
Jan 22, 24	Definitions of Communication	McGuire, Chapters 3, 4
	Models of Communication	
Jan 29, 31	Communication Ethics	McGuire, Chapter 9
	Cultural Dimensions	Model of Communication Due
Feb 5, 7	Verbal Messages	McGuire, Chapter 5
	Language and Behavior	
Feb 12, 14	Nonverbal Messages	McGuire, Chapter 6
Feb 19, 21	Listening	McGuire, Chapter 7
	Feedback	
Feb 20, 20	Review Session and Exam I	Exam I - February 28th
	UNIT TWO: INTERPERSONAL & SMALL GROUP COMMUNICATION	
Mar 5, 7	Communication Climates	McGuire, Chapter 8
	Supportive & Defensive	Case Analysis I Due
	Communication	
Mar 19, 21	Self-Disclosure	McGuire, Chapter 11
Mar 26, 28	Relationship Development	McGuire, Chapter 10
	Relationship Dissolution	
Apr 2, 4	Small Group Communication	McGuire, Chapter 12
Apr 9, 11	Problem Solving, Review Session	McGuire, Chapter 13
	Exam II	Exam II - April 11th
	UNIT THREE: PUBLIC COMMUNICATION	
Apr 9, 11	Public Communication Contexts	McGuire, Chapter 14
	Preparing a Presentation	Case Analysis II Due
Apr 16, 18	Message Organization	McGuire, Chapter 15
	Message Delivery	
Apr 23, 25	Evidence/Supporting Materials	McGuire, Chapter 16
	Evaluating Presentations	
Apr 30,	Review Session	
May 2	Conclusions and Visions	
May 8	Exam III	Exam III - May 8th

FIG. 4.1.   Daily class schedule.

of organizing a course, it is important to plan and specify the number of sessions needed for introducing the course, covering each unit, and providing closure to the course. Introductions and closures for each unit should also be planned, along with transitions that indicate the connections between units.

At the *micro* level of organizing a class session, introductions and conclusions are also part of the plan. Distinctions between "covering the day's material" and doing so with finesse and polish can be attributed in part to the attention given to three aspects of organization: planned in-

Topic of Class Session/Unit/Course: _____

Organizational Plan	Motivational Plan	Communication/ Interaction Plan	Props Plan	Timing Plan
Introduction	Students' Attitudes and Physiological Needs			
Part I				
Part 2	Students' Emotions and Stimulation Needs			
Part 3				
Part 4				
Conclusion/Closure	Students' Competence and Reinforcement Needs			

FIG. 4.2. Five-plan framework.

troductions, clear transitions, and crisp conclusions. Students have reported that visible use of introductions, transitions, and conclusions helps them understand the relationship of the course units without losing sight of the focus of the course as a whole.

The Motivational Plan

Traditionally, motivation has been prescribed as something teachers should do at the start of the course or the class session, and thereafter it becomes the sole task of the learner to maintain it. In his book *Enhancing Adult Motivation to Learn,* Raymond Wlodkowski (1986) discussed the need for motivational planning at three junctures of instruction: beginning, during, and ending. At each of these junctures, the motivational plan should emphasize certain learner qualities. For example, Wlodkowski recommended addressing the learners' attitudes and needs at the beginning, their emotions and stimulation needs in the middle period of instruction, and their competence and reinforcement needs towards the end. For these three time frames, Wlodkowski identified 68 motivational strategies to achieve the specified purposes. The implication of this motivational model is that teachers need to develop a motivational plan for the three junctures of the course, the units of instruction, and each class session.

The Communication/Interaction Plan

Preparation of a new course needs to include a plan for how the teacher anticipates interacting with the class members. How does the course provide for individual, dyadic, group, and/or presentational interactions? In what ways are learners given opportunities for viewing models of performance, for practice, feedback, group interaction, and class participation? The communication/interaction plan is likely to vary according to the objectives of different units of instruction and class sessions. Instructional strategies that can be used for your communication/ interaction plan are extensive: group discussion, brainstorming, case studies for discussion and analysis, simulations, symposia, role playing, individual and group reports, problem-solving tasks, cooperative learning groups (Johnson, Johnson, & Holubec, 1986; Kohn, 1986), experiments, question generation by learners, journals, debates, dramatic performances, writing tasks (Ruggiero, 1988), and use of film, videotapes, television programs, print media, computers, and guest speakers.

Perhaps the most pervasive aspect of your communication/interaction plan is the preparation you make for a supportive learning climate (Darling & Civikly, 1986–7; Gibb, 1961). Classroom behaviors that adult learners have identified as supportive and conducive to learning include:

1. Teachers treat learners as intelligent and empowered individuals who are partners in learning.
2. Teachers make and take time to listen to learners' concerns and questions.
3. Teachers use learners' names and can distinguish individual learners rather than group all in the role of "student."
4. Learners are told what is expected of them and when.
5. Learners are given choices for how to demonstrate their learning and progress.
6. Learners are not victims in the classroom—they feel safe and not threatened by the teacher.
7. Learners are not put in embarrassing situations or subjected to teacher sarcasm or putdowns.

Fortunately, much has been written about developing supportive learning climates, and, unfortunately, space limitations curtail detailed discussion here. Works by the following individuals are recommended for your reading and reflection: Andersen (1986), Civikly (1986b), DeVito (1986), and Jones (1986).

The Props Plan

My use of the term *props* is deliberate. The term refers to the assortment of materials, equipment, and arrangements for demonstrating and clarifying the concepts and objectives of instruction. Props include any paper materials such as textbooks, readings on library reserve, course syllabi, newsprint pads, and class handouts (worksheets, inventories, outlines). Even the board is a prop, and as such, it helps to plan if and how you will use the board. Props also refer to computers and other audiovisual equipment (videotapes, audiotapes, slides, photographs, films, opaque and overhead projectors). Finally, props include arrangements for visits to libraries, laboratories, museums, community organizations and businesses, and special events and exhibits. Props usually require advance preparation that involves selection, creation, and often some mechanical form of reproduction (photocopying, collating). Arrangement for delivery and operation of equipment also requires planning. Identifying and following your props plan can alleviate last-minute frustrations for both learners and teachers.

The Timing Plan

The final plan to include in your course developments is the timing plan. At the macro level, this plan outlines the number of sessions for each unit of the course. At the micro level, this plan identifies the amount of time anticipated for activities in each class session. The intent of the timing plan is not to strap a teacher to a stopwatch, but rather to provide guidelines on how the class objectives can best be managed and covered.

PULLING IT TOGETHER:
THE COURSE SYLLABUS

Perhaps the single best vehicle for describing a course is the course syllabus. There are three primary functions of a course syllabus: to inform students of the *scope* of the work, to identify the *sequence* that the work will follow, and to describe the *tasks* by which attainment or success will be determined (Saunders, 1978). Teacher use of course syllabi runs the gamut from no use at all to verbal accounts to printed handouts ranging from a half-page to 10 pages. Syllabi for my own courses tend to run eight pages and are presented to the students as a "course reference manual" designed for use throughout the term. I have found the course syllabus to be extremely useful in helping to establish the tone of the class, share views about learning and teaching, and provide students with straight-forward and explicit instructions for course readings, written assign-ments, and exams. The course syllabus enables students to determine on the first day of class the nature of the class, expectations for participa-tion, written work (including due dates), class procedures and policies, and a sense of the person who is the teacher.

It may be helpful to summarize the contents of an extended syllabus and discuss the benefits of this approach:

p. 1:   Course number and title, meeting days/place/time, instruc-tor's name, office location and hours, department and office phone numbers, one to two paragraphs providing an over-view of the course including the general goals and a descrip-tion of a "typical" day in class, complete citations for re-quired readings and information on reserve readings at the library.

p. 2:   Evaluation and grading system, one-paragraph descriptions of evaluated work (class participation, written assignments, speeches, etc.), a table outlining each assignment and noting due dates, percentage of course grade, space for students to record their grades, and directions on how to calculate the final course grade.

p. 3:   A weekly class schedule (see Fig. 4.1) that lists date, topic, readings to have completed, assignments and due dates, and exam dates.

pp. 4–6: One-page descriptions for each class assignment, and criteria for evaluating each.

pp. 7–8: Specific study/test guidelines for exams that identify infor-mation from text chapters, class readings, and class handouts.

p. 9:   Recommended readings, additional research topics, applica-tions of the course content.

The time it takes to develop a thorough syllabus has many payoffs. The most important of them is the reduction of student uncertainty and anx-iety about the course and expectations for successful performance. An-other benefit is the all-in-one-place reference manual approach—students rarely misplace or lose these information packets. The inclusion of de-tails on dates, criteria for assignments, and topic suggestions also serves to cut down on the number of factual questions posed during class discus-sions of upcoming assignments and allows for discussion of higher level issues pertinent to the objectives of each assignment. Finally, based on the course syllabus, it appears that students develop a positive view of the teacher's investment of time and energy in the course.

YOUR HOMEWORK ASSIGNMENTS

The creation of a new course is an excellent opportunity to practice your creative and critical thinking skills. Both of these skills are called into play when determining course content, objectives, activities, teaching strategies, responses to student questions and comments, evaluation alternatives, review sessions, and student assignments and projects.

As you can see, we have covered extensive territory in this adventure known as instructional development. It is now time for you to take charge of the adventure and to apply this information to your own courses. Accordingly, four homework assignments are in order:

1. Extend your background and knowledge base of course development research. Helpful sources include Brookfield's *Understanding and Facilitating Adult Learning* (1986), Civikly's *Communicating in College Classrooms* (1986a), Lowman's *Mastering the Techniques of Teaching* (1984), Raudsepp's *How Creative Are You?* (1981), Ruggiero's *Teaching Thinking Across the Curriculum* (1988), Smith's *Helping Adults Learn How to Learn* (1983), and Wlodkowski's *Enhancing Adult Motivation to Learn* (1986).

2. At least once a week, talk with at least one colleague about ideas you have for teaching a class or a concept. Share your enthusiasm and energies. Ask for feedback and extensions on your ideas.

3. Set a teaching goal for yourself: to continue developing and polishing your skills at seeking student feedback about course development and refinements. Learners frequently know how they can be their best in a particular course. Many, however, are not challenged, encouraged, asked, or allowed to do so. Develop a climate in which learners have the opportunity, safety, and encouragement to be and do their best.

4. Enjoy your courses, enjoy your teaching, enjoy the students, and enjoy the opportunities for learning that come with each new class group.

If the goals of this chapter have been achieved, then you now have a better sense of the "behind the scenes" processes involved in creating a new course. It is challenging and exciting work! Welcome the challenge! When your efforts at creating, researching, and following the five-plan framework are complete, it will be time for rehearsals, time for the "critics'" reviews, time to refine, and time to shine!

REFERENCES

Andersen, J. F. (1986). Instructor nonverbal communication: Listening to our silent messages. In J. M. Civikly (Ed.), *Communicating in college classrooms* (pp. 41–49). San Francisco: Jossey-Bass.

Brookfield, S. (1986). *Understanding and facilitating adult learning.* San Francisco: Jossey-Bass.

Civikly, J. M. (Ed.). (1986a). *Communicating in college classrooms.* San Francisco: Jossey-Bass.

Civikly, J. M. (1986b). Humor and the enjoyment of college teaching. In J. M. Civikly (Ed.), *Communicating in college classrooms* (pp. 61–70). San Francisco: Jossey-Bass.

Civikly, J. M., (1987). *Instructional training manual for pediatric residents.* Unpublished manuscript, Department of Communication, University of New Mexico Albuquerque, NM.

Darling, A. L., & Civikly, J. M. (1986–87). The effect of teacher humor on student perceptions of classroom climate. *Journal of Classroom Interaction, 22* (1), 24–30.

DeVito, J. A. (1986). Teaching as relational development. In J. M. Civikly (Ed.), *Communicating in college classrooms* (pp. 51–59). San Francisco: Jossey-Bass.

Gibb, J. R. (1961). Defensive communication. *Journal of communication, 11,* 141–148.

Johnson, D. W., Johnson, R. T., & Holubec, E. J. (1986). *Circles of learning: Cooperation in the classroom.* Edina, MN: Interaction Book Co.

Jones, J. M. (1986). The art of teaching: An act of love. In J. M. Civikly (Ed.), *Communicating in college classrooms* (pp. 83–91). San Francisco: Jossey-Bass.

Kibler, R. J., Barker, L. L., & Miles, D. T. (1970). *Behavioral objectives and instruction.* Boston: Allyn and Bacon.

Kohn, A. (1986). *No contest: The case against competition.* Boston: Houghton Mifflin.

Lowman, J. (1984). *Mastering the techniques of teaching.* San Francisco: Jossey-Bass.

Raudsepp, E. (1981). *How creative are you?* New York: G. P. Putnam's Sons.

Ruggiero, V. R. (1988). *Teaching thinking across the curriculum.* New York: Harper and Row.

Saunders, P. (Ed.). (1978). *Resource manual for teacher training programs in economics.* New York: Joint Council on Economic Education.

Smith, R. M. (Ed.). (1983). *Helping adults learn how to learn.* San Francisco: Jossey-Bass.

Wlodkowski, R. J. (1986). *Enhancing adult motivation to learn.* San Francisco: Jossey-Bass.

II

PREPARING SPECIFIC COMMUNICATION COURSES

5

Teaching Public Speaking

Stephen E. Lucas
University of Wisconsin

Public speaking is the bedrock of the undergraduate curriculum in most departments of speech and communication. It occupies roughly the same place in relation to historical, critical, and theoretical inquiry in rhetoric and communication research as does written composition in relation to the study of literature in departments of English. It is also a subject of exceedingly rich lineage. Taught more or less continuously in Western civilization since the days of ancient Greece, it has engaged the energies of such thinkers as Aristotle, Plato, Isocrates, Cicero, Quintilian, Saint Augustine, Francis Bacon, Hugh Blair, Richard Whately, James Rush, and Edward Channing.

Although this is not the place to trace the development of rhetorical theory during the past 2,500 years, it is important to view public speaking within the context of its intellectual heritage. Once that is done, we can see that there is no single correct approach to teaching public speaking. Whether it be Plato and Aristotle versus the Sophists, neoclassicists versus the disciples of Peter Ramus, or the psychological school of speech education versus proponents of elocution, the teaching of public speaking has long been marked by diverse perspectives, methods, and premises. Moreover, what works splendidly for one teacher or one group of students might fail miserably with another teacher or a different set of students. What follows, then, should be seen as one approach to a subject that has provoked debate among scholars and teachers for the past 25 centuries.

OBJECTIVES AND SIGNIFICANCE
OF A COURSE IN PUBLIC SPEAKING

The first step in teaching public speaking is to have a clear vision of what the course is designed to accomplish. At most schools, public speaking is regarded as a skills course. Its purpose is to teach students how to prepare and present effective public speeches. It also has a certain theoretical component. Most of the principles of effective speechmaking are based on broad theoretical insights derived from centuries of practical experience and confirmed by modern research. In this sense, the materials of a public speaking class are inescapably grounded in theory.

The course, however, is not preeminently concerned with theory. One of the most crucial requirements for teaching any subject effectively is to essentialize—to fasten sharply on what is vital to achieving a given set of educational objectives and to pare down all material that is extraneous to those objectives. Understanding Aristotle's concept of the enthymeme, exploring the dimensions of cognitive dissonance, knowing the major concepts of archetypal metaphor, making fine distinctions among attitudes, values and beliefs—these are all important to communication study at some level, but they are seldom essential to the introductory course in public speaking. At best, that course can provide an exposure to the basic principles of speechmaking and some opportunity for students to begin to develop their own skills. It cannot turn college freshmen and sophomores into polished orators or sophisticated rhetorical critics any more than it can instill in them a detailed understanding of rhetorical theory or of communication research.

This is not to demean the course or to say that it lacks intellectual content—quite the contrary. It is, rather, to recognize the complexity of public speaking and the wide range of cognitive abilities and practical skills involved in creating and presenting effective oral discourse. Think for a moment about what a public speaking class requires of students. It requires that they learn how to choose and narrow a topic, how to determine a central idea and main points, how to analyze and adapt to an audience, how to gather information by conducting library research and personal interviews, how to employ supporting materials soundly, clearly, and persuasively, how to organize ideas strategically for a specific audience and occasion, how to use language accurately, clearly, vividly, and appropriately, and how to control their voice and body so as to deliver a message fluently and convincingly. This is a lot to learn in one academic quarter or semester without also trying to master a great deal of theory at the same time.

Moreover, with the exception of speech delivery, almost all of the skills taught in a typical public speaking class are integrally connected with critical thinking. The process of speech composition is not much different—and is certainly no less demanding—than that of composing a written essay. We need not apologize for the intellectual content of public speaking courses any more than teachers of English composition apologize for the intellectual content of their courses. Given the inextricable relationship between thought and language, between cognition and expression, there can be no gainsaying the intellectual substance of a well-taught course in public speaking. As we teach students how to choose and develop topics, how to organize their speeches, how to assess evidence and reasoning, and how to employ language clearly and concisely, we are, at the same time, dealing with the invention of discourse, the structure of thought, the validity of claims, and the meaning of ideas. In the process of instructing students how to construct speeches with accuracy, order, and rigor, we are also teaching them how to think with accuracy, order, and rigor.

In short, although introductory public speaking is properly a skills course, it should not be characterized as "just" a skills course. By helping students become capable, responsible speakers, it also helps them become capable, responsible thinkers. In this respect it remains today, as it has been through much of Western civilization, a vital part of humanistic education and democratic citizenship.

PEDAGOGICAL PRINCIPLES: AN INCREMENTAL, EXPERIENCE-BASED APPROACH

In addition to understanding the objectives and significance of a course in public speaking, teachers should have an equally clear sense of the pedagogical principles underlying a skills course. One of those principles is that people acquire skills incrementally. This is especially true when the subject is as complex and demanding as public speaking. Students have a great deal to learn in a public speaking class, and they cannot learn it all at once. Even if it were feasible to have students read the entire textbook or memorize all of the basic principles of effective speechmaking before their first graded speech, it would not enhance their performance appreciably on that speech or accelerate the rate at which they progress on subsequent speeches.

A more fruitful approach is to break the course into several units, each of which takes students through a series of reading, homework, and speaking assignments that build systematically upon one another so students can develop their skills cumulatively throughout the quarter or semester. If, for example, the first unit deals with informative speaking, it might concentrate on such matters as choosing a topic, framing a specific purpose and central idea, organizing and outlining the speech, creating introductions and conclusions, and working on basic delivery skills. These constitute the foundation of successful speechmaking at any level. Once they are in place, students are ready to move on to more complex matters such as determining the target audience, building credibility, handling emotional appeals, and using reasoning and evidence. These might be handled in a unit on persuasive speaking, which would follow the unit on informative speaking.

After dealing with speaking to inform and speaking to persuade, students will have been exposed to a wide range of conceptual and practical materials. Building upon these two units, a third unit might deal with something like commemorative speaking, after-dinner speaking, or speaking to entertain. Because these kinds of speaking depend so much on the resourceful use of language, this would be a good time to focus explicitly on style. Impromptu speaking might be another possibility for this unit—or for a fourth unit—because it would allow students to deal with a new aspect of speech delivery while continuing to build upon skills introduced earlier in the course.

By this point, students will have taken up all the major skills of speechmaking. A concluding unit, in which students prepare and present their final speech, gives them an opportunity to strengthen their command of those skills. Such a speech might be informative or persuasive, depending on the instructor's preference, or it might be a more specialized speech, such as a rhetorical criticism or a report on a famous speaker, both of which can work nicely as a capstone assignment. In any event, the final speech should require a fairly comprehensive application of the principles of speechmaking dealt with throughout the course.

There are, of course, other ways to structure a course in public speaking, and there are several alternatives to the speeches discussed above. Yet regardless of how the course is organized and of what specific speeches are assigned, the principle of teaching skills in incremental units remains the soundest pedagogical approach, for it follows the natural process by which most people internalize knowledge and solidify skills.

It is also consistent with the tenet that learning skills is an experiential process that requires extensive practice and repetition. Although many speech teachers shy away from regular, graded, written homework assignments, such assignments are a valuable way for students to apply the principles discussed in the textbook. Rather than rehashing the reading in lecture, the teacher can use the homework assignment as the basis for class discussion. This has several advantages. The first is that students are more likely to learn the types of reasoning or the methods of organization by working with them rather than merely by reading about them or hearing the instructor talk about them. The second advantage is that students are more likely to complete the reading assignment if they have to turn in a written assignment based on it. The third advantage, which derives from the second, is that the quality of class discussion usually improves dramatically when students have prepared written work in advance. Rather than sitting on their hands with nothing to say about material they have not read carefully (if at all), they often get surprisingly involved in presenting and defending their answers to the homework assignment.

These written assignments can be based on chapter exercises in the textbook or on exercises devised by the instructor or course director. They need not be lengthy or onerous, nor need they require extensive evaluation. In most circumstances, a simple plus or minus, or a check mark for satisfactory completion, is all the grade they require. The purpose is not to make work for either the class or the instructor, but to enhance learning by requiring that students actively deal with the concepts, materials, and techniques of speechmaking on an everyday basis.

If this approach is to be successful, students must be given adequate time between speech assignments to learn the specific principles and skills that are appropriate to each unit of the course. Rather than rushing hastily over the textbook and trying to squeeze in six or seven graded speeches in a single quarter or semester, it often works better to schedule four major speeches and give students more time to prepare each. Not only does this produce better quality speeches, it also gives students greater opportunity to internalize the materials of the course. If students want more work on delivery, it can be provided by an impromptu speech assignment, or by a brief one-point speech on a personal topic (my hometown, my most embarrassing moment, my biggest complaint, etc.) that can be prepared overnight without interfering with other work in the class.

Finally, the incremental approach to teaching public speaking requires that instructors have a clear sense of what they hope to accomplish with each daily assignment. Because one third to one half of the total class time over a full quarter or semester is taken up with the presentation of speeches, teachers of public speaking have far fewer class sessions available for instruction than do teachers in most courses. As a result, they need to make sure every daily assignment is clearly formulated to achieve a precise purpose in relation to the overall objectives of the course.

Suppose, for example, that one day in the unit on informative speaking is devoted to analyzing sample speeches. The teacher should focus class discussion on those aspects of the speeches—formulating a specific purpose and central idea, developing introductions and conclusions, outlining the speech, and so forth—that are most central to the unit on informative speaking. This may require slighting other aspects—such as style or reasoning—but these can be taken up in later units of the course when students are better prepared to deal with them. Students cannot assimilate all the principles of public speaking simultaneously. In the long run they will learn more if each class session is strategically designed to deal sharply and systematically with particular increments of the public speaking process.

COMMUNICATION APPREHENSION, GRADES, AND OTHER PRACTICAL MATTERS

Questions of pedagogical philosophy and course structure aside, teachers of public speaking face a number of practical concerns such as dealing with communication apprehension, developing standards for grading, preparing speech critiques, encouraging attendance and participation, and maintaining a positive classroom atmosphere. Dealing productively with these matters will go a long way toward ensuring success as a teacher.

There are two types of communication apprehension. The first, and more serious, is known as trait apprehension. People who suffer from trait apprehension experience fear or anxiety in a wide range of communication transactions, from interpersonal exchanges to group discussions to public speeches. Students with high trait apprehension are so fearful about the prospect of speaking before a group that they cannot do so without severe emotional stress. Although as many as 20% of American college students may experience high trait apprehension, most of those will do all they can to avoid taking a public speaking class. Even so, almost everyone who teaches public speaking will periodically confront students with severe trait apprehension.

Although some students are very open about their fear of speaking, others try to disguise it as long as possible—often by concocting a string of excuses for not completing speech assignments on time. Teachers who suspect that a student's poor work may be caused by trait apprehension should raise the issue with the student and, perhaps, may wish to administer one of the diagnostic tests that measure public speaking anxiety. Treatment, however, should not be approached casually. Some departments offer special classes for students who exhibit high trait apprehension, whereas others have individualized programs to help particular students. Because the most extreme cases can require the attention of a professional therapist, the best advice for beginning teachers is to consult the course supervisor or a more experienced instructor whenever they suspect that a student is experiencing severe trait apprehension.

The second type of communication apprehension is known as state apprehension. Corresponding to what is commonly called "stage fright," it is the normal anxiety that people experience when called upon to communicate orally in a specific setting in which they will be observed and evaluated by other people. Although even the most accomplished orators suffer from this variety of communication apprehension (indeed, many regard it as essential if they are to be properly "psyched up" before taking the floor), it can be devastating for novice speakers if it is not controlled. Fortunately, unlike trait apprehension, which is often aggravated by the required presentations of a public speaking course, state apprehension usually diminishes in severity as students acquire speaking experience. Its negative effects can also be curtailed by following such traditional bromides as being fully prepared for each speech, concentrating on communicating with the audience rather than thinking about being nervous, using a good introduction to build confidence for the rest of the speech, and recognizing that listeners seldom perceive how nervous a speaker really is.

Dealing sensitively and sympathetically with stage fright is especially crucial at the beginning of a public speaking course. Unless students have prior experience in speechmaking, they typically approach the course with a different set of attitudes than they would bring to, say, a course in history, engineering, or accounting. The teacher's task is to ease their initial anxiety by creating an environment in which they can begin to acquire speaking experience with a minimum of perceived risk. Most instructors accomplish this with a brief, nongraded speech assignment. Although there are many approaches to this assignment, one that works particularly well is a 2-minute speech introducing a classmate. In preparation, students should be paired off the first or second day of class so they can interview one another and compose speeches based on the interview. Not only does this speech avoid the awkwardness that affects many students in speeches of self-introduction, it also helps to create bonds among members of the class—especially among those who have interviewed one another—and to promote a healthy psychological climate for the graded speeches to follow.

No matter how healthy that climate may be at the time of the introductory speeches, however, there is no guarantee it will endure once the graded assignments begin. Students take their grades very seriously, and if they believe they are being evaluated unfairly or criticized too harshly, they can quickly develop a deeply negative perception of the teacher and of the course in general. Worse, their self-confidence can be seriously damaged if the teacher is insensitive to their need for encouragement and positive reinforcement. Yet teachers also have an obligation to assess students objectively on the quality of work they produce. They cannot give students higher grades than they deserve just to maintain good feelings in the class. Striking a balance between the psychological needs of the students and the integrity of the grading system is one of the most difficult challenges facing a teacher of public speaking.

This challenge can be particularly severe in the case of graduate students who are teaching the course for the first time. Not only do they lack an established repertoire of instructional methods to guide them, but they often have less initial credibility than older, more experienced teachers. As a result, students may be more inclined to question their expertise and to challenge their judgment on grades. New instructors should be aware that everything they say and do in the classroom—their personal appearance, their command of the material, their tone of voice, their reactions to questions, their handling of speech critiques, and so forth—will affect their credibility and the respect they receive from students. The ideal, of course, is to maintain an open, trusting classroom atmosphere in which students provide psychological support for one another, feel free to take the risks necessary to develop their speaking skills, and respect the teacher's evaluation with regard to grades.

Although there is no substitute for experience when it comes to grading speeches, there are some steps you can take, if you are a new instructor, to enhance your evaluative skills. One, of course, is to talk about grading with an experienced teacher who is willing to share his or her philosophy, methods, and criteria. Another is to view a number of student speeches—either on videotape or in other sections—and see how your assessments of them stack up against those of veteran teachers. Yet another is to have a more seasoned instructor visit your class on a day when students are giving speeches. By comparing the grades you assigned with those the other instructor would have assigned had it been his or her class, you can get a good sense of whether you need to make adjustments in either your criteria or your methods of evaluation.

No matter how grades are assigned, it is extremely important that students receive formal evaluations of their speeches. Because such evaluations are usually the major channel of feedback from the instructor about the speeches, they need to be handled with great care. Evaluation forms should indicate clearly the elements of the speech on which the student is being assessed. They should also allow room for written comments. Such comments should usually start with discussing positive features of the speech—even if that means praising something as basic as the choice of topic (no matter how badly it may have been developed) or the fact that the student has a pleasant speaking voice (regardless of how well the student used his or her voice). It is not necessary, when discussing weaknesses of the speech, to compose a high-powered rhetorical analysis. A better approach is to point out three or four specific items that the student needs to work on in the next speech. Above all, it is crucial that teachers avoid the temptation to come down too hard on students. Evaluations should be realistic in appraising the speech, but they should be written in a kind, optimistic tone that provides hope and encouragement for future speeches.

Another useful practice is to have students prepare evaluations of their peers' speeches. This can be done by assigning particular students as critics for each day's speeches. These students should fill out an evaluation form for every speech delivered that day. By the end of the unit, each student in the class should have served as a critic for one day. This can be arranged by assigning students to critique speeches in the class session after they have delivered their own speeches, except, of course, for the last group of speakers, who should be assigned to critique the first group of speeches. Thus if a class contains four speaking groups—groups A, B, C, and D—group D will critique the speeches of group A, group A will critique group B, group B will critique group C, and group C will critique group D. Not only does this arrangement encourage the development of listening skills, it also helps curb the perennial tendency of students to skip class the day after delivering their speeches.

It is particularly important that students attend class on days when they are assigned to speak. Public speaking classes typically run on an extremely tight schedule. If students habitually skip class when they are supposed to speak, the syllabus for the entire course will be quickly thrown off. Perhaps the best way around this is to allow students to choose their own speaking dates. Even that, however, may not solve the problem entirely. Many instructors, therefore, assign an automatic grade penalty to any student who fails to deliver a speech on the specified day because of an unexcused absence. Many also limit students to a maximum of two or three absences for the entire course, with excessive absences resulting in a reduction of the student's final grade. Whatever a teacher's attendance policy, it should be stated clearly on the syllabus, so students will be aware of it from the start of the course.

One of the best ways to encourage strong voluntary attendance on a regular basis is to arrange the syllabus so students are required to turn in work, or to complete work in class, on most days. If a homework exercise is due, an advance speech outline is to be handed in, or a chapter quiz is being given, students are more likely to get in the habit of attending class—partly because a portion of their grade is at stake, but also, as we have seen, because class time is usually spent more profitably when students have completed some kind of written work beforehand. Incorrigible as some students may be, most are inclined to attend regularly when they find the class sessions interesting and productive.

In addition to everything we have discussed, there are several basic guidelines for teachers of public speaking to keep in mind:

1. Be thoroughly prepared for every class session.
2. Maintain a professional demeanor at all times in the classroom.
3. Return student work—speech outlines, critiques, written assignments, exams—as quickly as possible, preferably at the next class session.
4. Explain speech assignments clearly and notify students of their speaking dates well in advance.
5. Avoid anything that might be interpreted as favoritism toward individual students or groups of students.
6. Treat students' ideas with respect—no matter how ludicrous they may seem—and do not ridicule or put down a student in class.
7. No matter what your private feelings, do not make negative comments to students about the course, the textbook, the assignments, or other instructors. Such comments undermine your own position, as well as the credibility of the course in general.
8. Seek consistently to accentuate the positive. Remember, much of public speaking is a matter of self-confidence. Do all you can to get your students to believe in themselves.

Finally, it is essential to believe in yourself. Be sure of what you know, but never be afraid to admit you don't know something. There is no quick-and-easy formula for being a good teacher any more than there is a surefire set of rules for being an effective public speaker. Both require creativity, commitment, enthusiasm, and lots of hard work. If you bring those qualities to your teaching, you stand a much better chance of instilling the same qualities in your students.

6

Teaching Interpersonal and Small-Group Communication

Gerald R. Miller
Michigan State University

Two crucial initial steps in teaching anything are to define the boundaries of pedagogical concern and to decide on some broad approach, or plan of attack. Some experts in instructional communication would say that even here I am ahead of myself, because these two steps should be preceded by careful articulation of educational objectives and desired behavioral outcomes. Though I do not quarrel with the importance and possible primacy of this goal-setting step, I sense a potential "hen–egg" controversy that I would just as soon avoid, for how can teachers identify sought-after educational objectives and behavioral outcomes without a clear map of the instructional terrain? Hence, I eschew extended discussion of objectives and outcomes and move immediately to my thoughts about the broad approaches that currently dominate the teaching of interpersonal and small-group communication and to my views about the conceptualization of these two communicative species. Interwoven in my remarks are implicit assumptions and explicit statements about the relationships between particular approaches and conceptualizations, on one hand, and specific educational objectives and behavioral outcomes, on the other.

One disclaimer seems mandatory. I am duly impressed with the credentials of the authors appearing in this volume, and I am quick to grant that my expertise in instructional communication pales by comparison. What I know—or more accurately, what I *think* I know—about teaching courses in interpersonal or small-group communication rests principally on my own experiences. I have taught graduate and undergraduate courses in interpersonal communication fairly continuously for about 20 years, as well as taking occasional stabs at teaching courses in small-group communication. I have coauthored an interpersonal text (Miller & Steinberg, 1975), and I am one of two contributors to perhaps the longest running uncompleted manuscript on small-group communication in our field's history (Miller & Boster, in preparation). Naturally I have both picked the brains of and taken issue with colleagues who share these instructional interests. From this amalgam of experiences emerges my argument concerning important issues and factors in application. Indeed, as readers will shortly see, I have elected to craft this chapter in the same way as I would craft a course in interpersonal or small-group communication.

THREE BROAD INSTRUCTIONAL APPROACHES

The Learning-By-Doing Approach

As the name implies, this approach emphasizes experiential, activity-centered instruction; put somewhat more formally, it is skills-oriented. This approach rests on two key assumptions: (a) that through involvement in communicative activities, students will acquire and sharpen the skills needed to make them more effective communicators in real-world interpersonal and small-group encounters, and (b) that the meaning and significance of important concepts can be gleaned experientially by participating in activities relating to such concepts—for example, by falling and relying on a classmate to break the fall, students can acquire meaning and understanding of the concept of trust. This is not to say that content is completely ignored, but rather that content mastery plays second fiddle to participation in communicative activities.

If one subscribes to the view that the primary goal of courses in interpersonal and small-group communication is to maximize student involvement in communicative exchanges, the learning-by-doing approach has much to recommend it. Proponents contend that the mere ability of students to define key concepts and to summarize relevant research findings does not ensure their capacity to communicate effectively in interpersonal and small-group settings. In its broadest sense, this contention rings convincingly; knowledge about theory and research is no guarantee of effective practice: To borrow a metaphor from one of my mentors, Donald C. Bryant, that humans are better judges of an omelet than any chicken does not endow them with the capacity to lay eggs.

Notwithstanding this fact, two notes of caution should be sounded. First, no substantial body of evidence reveals that communicative attitudes and behaviors polished and honed in instructional surroundings are generalized to the varied communicative encounters experienced by students in everyday life. To the contrary, good grounds exist for skepticism regarding this issue. Just as communication researchers have questioned the ecological validity of role-playing procedures in the laboratory, communication instructors should be wary of the generalizability of role-playing activities in the classroom. Moreover, even activities lacking the "let's pretend" aura fostered by role playing are constrained by the assumptions and expectations that students bring to formal, stylized educational settings. To return to my convenient poultry metaphor, although it is pragmatically acceptable for hens to lay all their eggs in one barnyard, the value of the learning-by-doing approach relies heavily on the ability of students to use their acquired skills in varied, diverse communicative barnyards.

Though my second cautionary note does not concern a tendency inherent to the learning-by-doing approach, it does relate to a potential occupational hazard frequently observed among proponents of this viewpoint: Specifically, much advice and counsel centers on the ways that people *ought to* communicate—that is, on the attitudes and practices that supposedly characterize ethical, morally defensible communicators—rather than on skills that are likely to yield pragmatic communicative returns. This tendency is reflected by expressions of concern about openness and being "an authentic person," or by singing the praises of indiscriminate, unbounded self-disclosure. Indeed, such messianic pronouncements probably account, at least in part, for the "touchy-feely" label pinned on this approach by some detractors.

Lest I am misunderstood, I am not advocating an amoral stance that brands ethical questions associated with interpersonal and small-group communication as irrelevant. What does worry me is that the value preferences proffered by some advocates of the learning-by-doing approach are far from open-and-shut cases. For example, achieving a desirable ethical posture about the place of self-disclosure in daily communicative commerce is not as simple as some learning-by-doing advocates imply. Frequently, the consequences of self-disclosing messages are negative for disclosers, disclosees, or both. Moreover, as Miller and Steinberg (1975) have stressed, apparent self-disclosure can be used to manipulate and to achieve power over relational partners. Given these complexities, the zeal of some learning-by-doing proponents in championing simplistic ethical prescriptions about communication is a serious cause for concern.

The Laundry List Approach

Contrasted to learning-by-doing, this approach to interpersonal and small-group instruction relies more heavily on content drawn from communication and related fields. The guiding assumption is that wide-spread exposure to the ideas of communication scholars results in more effective interpersonal and small-group communicators. Or alternatively, to be as fair as possible, the assumption may sometimes be that skills development is tangential, with the most important outcome being to familiarize students with a hearty portion of the basic theoretical and research writings—in the words of my overworked poultry metaphor, judging omelets is deemed more important than laying eggs.

To achieve this aim, students are typically introduced to several different conceptualizations and/or models of interpersonal or small-group communication, exposed to various treatments of concepts such as meaning, learning, and perception, and acquainted with motivational schemes ranging from nonspecific arousal models to Maslow's need hierarchy—to mention but a few possible topics. In some cases, content coverage is supplemented by skills training; in others, the course is almost entirely content-centered. Although laundry list proponents sometimes express preferences for particular positions, students often are left to sort through the numerous viewpoints and to reach their own conclusions about fitting things together.

The laundry list approach strikes me as particularly appropriate for broad survey courses in interpersonal and small-group communication designed for advanced undergraduate and beginning graduate students. In introductory courses, where most students are primarily concerned with using information to improve their communicative competence, laundry list teaching lacks focus and leaves many students confused about "what it all means." Stated differently, beginning students usually lack the needed sophistication to synthesize the material covered into a coherent scheme for analyzing and improving their own interpersonal or small-group communicative skills: They are not only unable to lay eggs, they are faced with the task of judging scrambled eggs rather than omelets.

The Know-It-All Approach

The know-it-all approach, the perspective I favor, avoids the problem of overwhelming students with a barrage of content while still providing them with a conceptual foundation for analyzing and improving their communicative activities. The know-it-all format focuses on an extended argument concerning the most useful—or at least, *a* useful—way to define and to conceptualize interpersonal and/or small-group communication. Considerable time is spent initially developing crucial definitional and conceptual points, followed by examination of the important implications of the conceptual stance for communicating interpersonally. For example, the first 3 weeks of my course center on a guiding conceptualization of interpersonal communication; the next 3 explore its implications for certain individual communicator variables, and the last 4 extend the analysis to particular relational variables. As suggested by the descriptive label for this approach, class time is devoted primarily to advancing my own position, but some attention also is given to comparing and contrasting it with other viewpoints.

The know-it-all perspective capitalizes on two principal potential advantages. First, students are afforded a single coherent analytic framework that can be applied to a wide variety of interpersonal and/or small-group settings, rather than being asked to sort and evaluate various treatments of isolated aspects of the communicative process or to practice numerous skills and activities with but a shadowy understanding of underlying conceptual and theoretical foundations. Testimony from my students reveals their belief in the pragmatic values of such a unifying framework. Recently, one student waxed enthusiastically about the virtues of *Between People* (Miller & Steinberg, 1975). When queried as to the source of his enthusiasm, he said that he was employed in face-to-face sales. Before reading the book, he had experienced average success; after reading it, his sales had increased dramatically. Though I suspected at least a mild attack of *post hoc ergo propter hoc,* I said nothing to disabuse the student of his exuberance, partly because I was relishing the rare experience of landing a disciple and partly because I believed his faith in the book was at least modestly justified, albeit overzealous.

The second advantage of the know-it-all approach is that it provides the best forum for identifying the unique characteristics of interpersonal and/or small-group communication. Put differently, the conceptual arguments advanced by know-it-all proponents typically stress some crucial feature, or features, that differentiate these two areas from other communicative transactions. To be sure, mere identification of unique processes and concepts is of limited interest and utility unless they are helpful to scholars and practitioners: The proof of the pudding is in the theoretical and social significance of the conceptualization. Furthermore, there is no in-principle reason why such distinguishing characteristics cannot surface in learning-by-doing or laundry list classrooms; my modest contention holds only that the logic and the structure of the know-it-all perspective provide the most effective means for airing such distinctions. Being that the sorts of definitional and conceptual moves to which I allude are probably ambiguous and murky, I next consider my views of some useful ways of differentiating interpersonal and small-group communication from other kinds of communicative transactions.

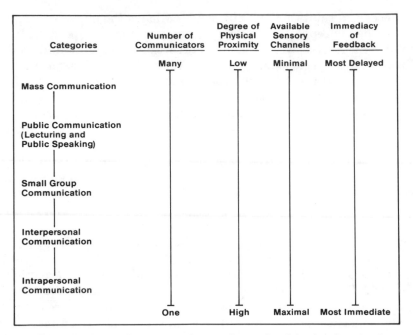

Categories	Number of Communicators	Degree of Physical Proximity	Available Sensory Channels	Immediacy of Feedback
	Many	Low	Minimal	Most Delayed
Mass Communication				
Public Communication (Lecturing and Public Speaking)				
Small Group Communication				
Interpersonal Communication				
Intrapersonal Communication				
	One	High	Maximal	Most Immediate

FIG. 6.1. A set of categories frequently employed in the situational approach to distinguishing interpersonal communication. From Miller (1978, p. 165), reprinted with permission of the International Communication Association.

UNIQUE PEDAGOGICAL ASPECTS OF INTERPERSONAL AND SMALL-GROUP COMMUNICATION

Typically, distinctions among various communicative transactions using labels such as "interpersonal," "small-group," "public," and "mass communication" are rooted in a *situationist* perspective (Miller, 1978). The situationist view (Fig. 6.1) differentiates types of communicative encounters in terms of selected contextual, or situational criteria. Though these criteria vary from one writer to the next, those listed in Fig. 6.1 are broadly representative. Thus, to contrast two relative extremes of the continuum, mass communication is contextually characterized by its many communicators, reliance on mediated messages, restricted availability of sensory channels, and delayed feedback mechanisms. Conversely, interpersonal communication is situationally defined by its relatively small number of communicators, eyeball-to-eyeball message exchanges, potential availability of the entire gamut of sensory channels, and immediate feedback mechanisms. As Fig. 6.1 indicates, small-group communication is more situationally akin to interpersonal than to mass communication.

In themselves, these contextual variations reveal little about important differences in communicative relationships and exchanges: *It is what they auger for the qualitative nature and potential of communication that is important.* Stated simply, communicative transactions involving several million transactants are not only quantitatively but also qualitatively different from communicative transactions involving several transactants. In attempting to isolate relatively unique dimensions of interpersonal and small-group communication, I focus on two such qualitative differences.

Opportunity for Differentiation and Individuation

Conceptual Considerations. Despite well-meaning advice to the contrary, cursory analysis quickly reveals that it is often impossible to relate to other communicators as individuals. The large number of transactants involved in public and mass communication settings ensures that participants will be perceived as undifferentiated cultural members or role occupants, not as individuals.

Consider, for example, the evening network news conceived of as a 30-minute communicative transaction involving a large staff of news employees, headed by an anchorperson, and a viewing audience of millions of news consumers. When selecting the tiny subset of news items to be included (contrary to slogans present and past, consumers are not afforded "all the news that's fit to print," nor are they made privy to "the way it is" on any given evening), network communicators must rely on cultural and sociological generalizations to fix priorities. Thus, while writing this chapter, a local restaurant where my son works was robbed and two employees were slain. As *individuals,* members of my family place an extremely high priority on information relating to this event. We can confidently predict, however, that nothing about it will appear on network news, because for uninvolved consumers, it is a run-of-the-mill murder (callous as this label may sound) replicated dozens of times nationally. By contrast, the Arkansas murder of 14 family members and several outsiders is nationally newsworthy; hence, it is currently receiving much attention on all the networks.

The same situation pertains when choosing the persuasive strategies and content to be employed in the program's advertising messages. Because network and advertising agency communicators cannot begin to know the millions of viewers as individuals, persuasive messages are crafted to conform with cultural and sociological generalizations about the needs, motivations, and preferences of most viewers. Whether the product is annuities, antacids, or automobiles, the issue remains one of persuading the *greatest number* of viewers, not one of persuading *a particular* viewer.

Finally, this process of viewer undifferentiation and deindividuation guides selection of key network communicators, especially the anchorperson. Does the anchor look like and sound like the kind of person *most viewers* would perceive as highly credible? (Recall, for instance, that during the period when CBS reigned supreme in the news ratings, a survey revealed that Walter Cronkite was considered the most credible person in America.) Is the anchorperson free of any idiosyncratic features that might be responded to negatively by the "mainstream" viewing audience? Indeed, this personal sanitization process is deemed so important that a popular commentator once hypothesized that men had monopolized tho anchor positions because their typically "solid, middle-American" first names—"Dan," "Tom," "David," "Walter," for example—appealed to most viewers, whereas women newscasters were plagued by esoteric, unpopular first names—"Leslie," "Meredith," "Jessica," "Lea," and so on. Though probably oversimplistic, there is enough truth in the hypothesis to justify the predictions that (a) network anchors with names like "Slick" or "Shifty" are unlikely to be encountered soon, and (b) that an anchor position will probably continue to elude Roger *Mudd*.

As revealed in Fig. 6.2, this same depersonalized posture exists when two strangers or casual acquaintances communicate in interpersonal or small-group settings. During initial interactions, communicators relate as cultural entities and/or role occupants, rather than as individuals. Unlike mass and public contexts, however, greater individuation and personalization can emerge as the relationship unfolds over time: *If the communicators are motivated to expend the effort, and if they possess the needed skills, they may begin to relate to one another as persons (individuals) instead of undifferentiated cultural and/or sociological beings.*

As Fig. 6.2 indicates, greater individuation in interpersonal and/or small-group settings is not inevitable. Many casual acquaintanceships involve little or no differentiation simply because the relationship functions smoothly without it. For that matter, some supposedly intimate relationships suffer from a lack of individuation because one or both parties lack the attitudes and skills to achieve it. The crucial point remains that differentiation and individuation are logically and behaviorally possible in interpersonal and small-group communication, but not in communicative contexts featuring large numbers of communicators.

If greater individuation evolves over time, it acts as both a cause and an effect of certain qualitative changes in the relationship. During the early stages, relational parties pursue a path of mutual uncertainty reduction (e.g., Berger, 1979; Berger & Calabrese, 1975); that is, they seek

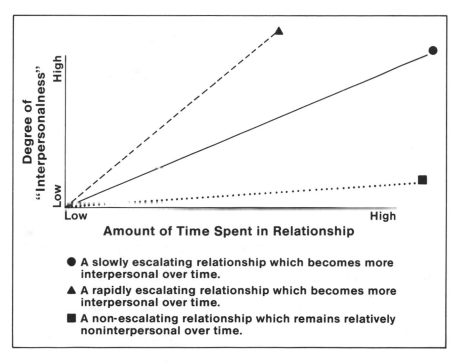

FIG. 6.2. Continuum of relational development showing several possible alternatives. From Miller (1978, p. 168), reprinted with permission of the International Communication Association.

to define and to acquire more and more social knowledge about each other. Most initial information consists of available and inferred cultural and sociological data (Miller & Steinberg, 1975). These data are inherently low in differentiation and individuation, because they contribute to uncertainty reduction by centering on *similarities* between the relational partner and other members of his or her cultural and sociological groups. Syllogistically, social reasoning takes the following form:

1. This relative stranger is a Catholic (U.S. citizen, woman, professor, etc.).
2. Most Catholics (U.S. citizens, women, professors, etc.) think (behave) in this way.
3. Therefore, this relative stranger will think (behave) in this way.

As the relationship unfolds, sufficiently motivated and skilled partners begin to accumulate, either directly or indirectly, data that permit increased individuation. Such psychological information (Miller & Steinberg, 1975) focuses on *differences* between the relational partner and other cultural and sociological group counterparts. As a result, the partner becomes an exception to the syllogistic rule: Whereas most members of the group can be expected to think or behave in this way, this relational partner cannot. Thus, as more predictions about the partner are grounded in psychological as opposed to cultural and sociological information, differentiation increases and partners relate to each other as individuals rather than undifferentiated cultural members or role occupants.

Other qualitative relational changes associated with greater individuation include an evolution in the levels of "knowing" relational partners (Berger, Gardner, Parks, Schulman, & Miller, 1976) and a shift in the primary locus of rules governing the relationship (Miller & Steinberg, 1975). In the early stages of relationships, participants "know" each other at only the *descriptive* and, at best, *predictive* levels; that is, they can physically distinguish the relational partner from other people, and they may be able to predict a few of the partner's beliefs and/or behaviors. As the relationship progresses, participants may begin to "know" each other at the *explanatory* level; that is, they not only can predict the ways the partner believes and behaves, they also feel they can explain the reasons *why* she or he believes and behaves in these ways. At the same time, the relational partners may be engaged in the process of defining and negotiating idiosyncratic rules to supplement or to replace the externally imposed cultural and sociological rules that initially guided their relationship. These moves toward greater individuation, and others like them, mark a fundamental shift in psychological and relational dynamics, as well as signalling a very different communicative process. Moreover, as emphasized earlier, the changes themselves are endemic to interpersonal and small-group communication.

Practical Applications.   Acceptance of the possibility of increasing individuation as a relatively unique characteristic of interpersonal and small-group communication suggests several instructional priorities. Included among these are attention to strategies for gathering information and strategies and processes for reinterpreting and debiasing messages, concern for the process and outcomes of self-disclosure, and, because much useful differentiating information is not provided voluntarily, careful examination of how to process and interpret nonverbal information. Finally, because greater individuation is not easily achieved, discussion about the importance of establishing relational priorities is also appropriate.

Conflict Between Autonomy and Community Needs

Conceptual Considerations.   In our uncompleted small-group communication text, Boster and I (in preparation) argue that all persons confront a fundamental and persistent dilemma of reconciling, or balancing, the potentially conflicting needs for *community* and for *autonomy*. "The need for community centers on the notion of collective togetherness, assigning priority to the common characteristics and aspirations shared by groups of people. The need for autonomy focuses on the idea of individual freedom, placing emphasis on the unique traits and objectives of particular persons" (ms. p. 7).

The idea that people experience these two fundamental needs is certainly not new. Furthermore, the potentially conflictful nature of the two needs is evident. On the one hand, people are counseled to work harmoniously with others, subordinating their egos for the achievement of collective goals; on the other, they are urged to "be individuals," to think independently and act autonomously, and to place individual excellence, achievement, and need satisfaction above the group demands. My contention here is simple: Although the potential for conflict between community and autonomy needs exists in any communicative setting, strain between the two needs is felt most keenly in the small-group context, with the interpersonal context a reasonably close second.

This claim can best be redeemed by first considering the objectives of most public and mass communication messages. Typically, such messages emphasize the primacy of community needs by extolling audience members to work collectively in behalf of some social cause or political candidate. In addition, as noted earlier, message strategies are rooted in cultural and sociological generalizations rather than data about individual message recipients. Even supposed appeals to individuality, so common in such areas as media advertising, are, in fact, founded on cultural generalizations stressing the ideological power of an individual ethic; paradoxical as it may seem, media appeals to "be an individual" and "think (or purchase) for yourself" rely on the culturally shared values of individuality and freedom of choice.

To explore this point in greater detail, I state my argument as a common-sense proposition: *The greater the number of persons involved in a communicative transaction, the greater the degree of deindividuation.* Several factors contribute to the validity of this proposition. First, as collectivities grow larger, it becomes increasingly difficult for each person to interact with all others, and as groups become extremely large, such interaction becomes impossible. Picture someone trying to interact with all members of the Democratic or Republican Parties, the Methodist or Roman Catholic Churches, the National Chamber of Commerce, the Americans for Democratic Action, or the National Rifle Association—to mention but a few extremely large collectivities. Obviously, such an undertaking would be doomed to failure.

Of course, members of these groups are privy to common messages, disseminated by the organization's leadership. These messages stress the common goals of group members, rather than seeking to adapt to the many unique characteristics of individual members. A presidential aspirant's campaign speeches invariably dwell on objectives shared by all, or at least most members of the party, and they contain numerous reassurances that these objectives will be realized, or at least furthered under the candidate's administration. Moreover, the candidate strives to project an image that is consistent with widely shared perceptions about what constitutes an attractive, credible candidate.

The closest the candidate ever comes to face-to-face interaction with party members—save for political dignitaries and members of the party's power structure—is in the ritualistic "pressing of the flesh." When shaking the hand of a faceless member of the group, the candidate is greeting a "good party member" or a "political supporter;" the handshake reinforces common community ties, not the recipient's individuality. In fact, it is easy to imagine a movie scene from a Woody Allen-type comedy where the candidate, ringed by Secret Service personnel, stops at each member of the milling throng and pursues a long dialogue aimed at discovering the person's unique traits and characteristics. Such a course of action would not only be hazardous, it would be ludicrous and role-discrepant.

Thus, a personal commitment to a very large group usually entails subordination of autonomy needs to a greater common cause. In such cases, individuals are assisted in repressing autonomy needs by their relative anonymity. Anonymity stems from lack of concern for individuation; instead of teasing out numerous dimensions of each person's personality, a limited number of dimensions that bind group members together are stressed. As a consequence, individuals may express support for specific group norms or actions—or at a minimum, withhold criticism—with little fear that others will know they do not actually subscribe to the group position. Or conversely, the size of the group enables individuals to register disapproval of particular norms or policies with relative social immunity. In either case, group size results in a deindividuated state where the self is less open to public scrutiny.

By contrast, the structure and functions of small groups are more likely to produce conflict between autonomy and community needs. First of all, the individual's reasons for group affiliation are usually less clear-cut than in the case of larger collectivities. People join the national Democratic Party to lend a small hand in furthering community goals sought by all Democrats; people join the Membership Committee of the Ingham County Democratic Party primarily to further these same party goals, to make some friends, to demonstrate group leadership qualities, or for yet other reasons. Because the likelihood of mixed membership motives is greater, conflicting motivations to conform with group norms, as opposed to "expressing oneself," are more keenly felt.

Second, no small group can be entirely promotively interdependent; that is, groups cannot always focus on collective goals that reward all members equally. Even when the entire group seeks a common end, the importance of individual contributions differs. One inevitable outgrowth of these disparities is role specialization: Groups not only assign varying roles to members, they also assign differing values to these roles. Some roles are so mundane that all members of the group can perform them, whereas others require unique traits or skills. The latter roles confer higher status, because the role occupant's unique abilities are vital to the achievement of community goals. Of course, this same situation exists in larger collectivities; indeed, role specialization is even more essential to a group's effectiveness. What differ sharply are the expectations and aspirations of individual members, whereas most people resign themselves to secondary roles in large collectivities, the belief that one can "rise to the top" is more pervasive in small groups. Thus, although I do not assume that I could ever be the Democratic candidate for president, I do harbor the belief that I could become the chairperson of the Ingham County Democratic Party Membership Committee. And although realization of this latter goal would undoubtedly require allegiance to group community needs, it would also require actions aimed at impressing members with my unique skills.

Last, and perhaps most crucial, the communicative dynamics of the small group are conducive to conflict between community and autonomy needs. High levels of face-to-face interaction among group members produce greater individuation. This increased familiarity, along with the sharp reduction in group size, reduces anonymity. If members are pressured into accepting group decisions or actions that they do not endorse, discrepancy between public behavior and private acceptance is more readily apparent to other group members; consequently, to avoid the stigma of being labeled "conformist," "weak-willed," or even "hypocrite," members will be more strongly motivated to assert independence by defying the group's mandate. Conversely, such defiance usually entails greater personal risks and consequences in small groups than in larger collectivities, because deviations can be more readily observed and sanctioned by other group members. In either case, the individual is caught squarely on the horns of the community–autonomy dilemma.

Finally, a few words as to why community and autonomy needs are likely to conflict less sharply in interpersonal relationships. Most frequently, such relationships involve two parties, and opportunities for negotiation and accommodation are greater in dyads than in groups of three or more members. After all, dyadic group norms are bilaterally shared views negotiated by the two participants. With the addition of even a third party, the opportunity for coalitions and for majority rule arises; the odd person out may face the dilemma of either accepting a community demand imposed by the other two group members or following the dictates of autonomy needs and deviating from community expectations. Furthermore, opportunities for dyadic relationships are relatively abundant; hence, if conflict between autonomy and community needs becomes acute, members are relatively free to seek other relationships. By contrast, the limited availability of multiperson small groups restricts people's latitude to move from group to group. Thus, the only alternative to striking a balance between autonomy and community needs—or at minimum, learning to tolerate imbalance between the two sets of needs—may be the unattractive option of foregoing group membership entirely.

Practical Applications. As in the case of the idea of differences in indi viduation, the preceding conceptual distinction suggests several instructional priorities. To prepare students for the conflicting tugs of community and autonomy needs, close attention should be paid to developing an understanding of the processes of cooperation and competition as they function in small-group and interpersonal contexts. Because conflict is virtually inevitable, students should gain an appreciation for ways of coping creatively with it. Finally, although I am generally wary of such concepts as *values clarification,* the attitudinal aspects of the community versus autonomy needs dilemma mandate concern for arriving at a sound and functional value position regarding the relative importance of these needs.

A FINAL WORD

Hopefully, the various approaches to instruction and the several conceptual distinctions explored in this chapter will aid teachers of interpersonal and small-group communication. As stressed at the outset, the position sketched here is but one of several alternatives. Though readers may not choose to swallow my viewpoint hook, line, and sinker, I retain my modest belief that it is at least worth a pedagogical nibble.

REFERENCES

Berger, C. R. (1979). Beyond initial interaction: Uncertainty, understanding, and the development of interpersonal relationships. In H. Giles & R. St. Clair (Eds.), *Language and social psychology* (pp. 122–144). Oxford: Blackwell.
Berger, C. R., & Calabrese, R. J. (1975). Some explorations in initial interaction and beyond: Toward a developmental theory of interpersonal communication. *Human Communication Research, 1,* 99–112.

Berger, C. R., Gardner, R. R., Parks, M. R., Schulman, L., & Miller, G. R. (1976). Interpersonal epistemology and interpersonal communication. In G. R. Miller (Ed.), *Explorations in interpersonal communication* (pp. 149–171). Newbury Park, CA: Sage.

Miller, G. R. (1978). The current status of theory and research in interpersonal communication. *Human Communication Research, 4,* 164–178.

Miller, G. R., & Boster, F. J. (in preparation). *Communicating in the small group: The eternal dilemma.*

Miller, G. R., & Steinberg, M. (1975). *Between people: A new analysis of interpersonal communication.* Chicago: Science Research Associates.

7

Teaching Rhetorical Studies

Bruce E. Gronbeck
University of Iowa

To be interested in rhetorical studies in the last decade of the 20th century is to be committed, usually, to a series of philosophical, social, psychological, and even (for some) ethical propositions:

1. Human beings are symbol-using animals. Among all of the things that characterize humans, most determinative of the qualities of their individual and collective lives is their ability to create and manipulate symbols (e.g., Burke, 1962). The power of symbolization is the power to infuse sense-data and experience with *meaning*—their significations, interpretations, and evaluations. Symbols allow humans to construct personal and public meaning-structures, and to control the ways in which "reality" is perceived, ordered, and assessed. Although reality, the *Dasein* ("out-there"), assuredly has existence independent of human thought, it is meaningless to humanity independent of symbolization.

2. Human beings are social actors. We are purposive creatures who both reflect behaviorally standards of action fostered by collectivities and follow prescribed forms of rituals when seeking to express particular ideas and motives in the presence of others. We are actors because, through socialization processes, we are acculturated to follow "social rules" in our public behavior in order to be understood and in order to avoid public sanction or ostracism.

3. As actors, persons are acculturated to play certain roles in certain situations. For most situations we face, there are preoutlined script-like

formulas we are expected to follow as we play those roles. To be sure, different persons play those roles differently, for there are gaps or inde- terminacies in the role expectations fostered in given situations; and so, a variety of role performances can be counted as "proper" or "competent" when people function as parent, friend, teacher, or president of the United States. Yet, there probably are only a limited number of such formulas available in most situations and only a finite number of perfor- mance styles deemed suitable for them (Combs, 1980).

4. By implication, then, the social order is negotiated. As we share meanings with each other via symbols, we together negotiate commonly articulated ideas, commonly understood behavior patterns, and com- monly agreed-on evaluations of those ideas and behaviors. Although there are ideas and behaviors meaningful only to individuals, and al- though there assuredly is a *Dasein,* our lives as social beings occur within "social reality," that is, within the descriptions, interpretations, and eval- uations of the "out there" that we develop together.

5. Such negotiation processes are best studied rhetorically. Histor- ically, rhetoric has comprised the theoretical and critical-pedagogical ex- amination of discursive practices. Although Western rhetoricians at vari- ous times have emphasized theoretical ruminations, critical reflections, and technique, rhetoric always has been centered on affective or prag- matic discourse—on discourse that defines the mutual perceptions of, mediates differences between, and aligns the political or ethical behav- iors of human beings. Rhetoric always has been concerned with the con- versations of cultures, with public negotiations taking place between socially and historically situated actors.

"Rhetorical studies," thus, in our time represents the collective efforts of various scholars to describe, account for, and evaluate public talk about matters of shared importance—political processes, economic and political influences, social relations, sacred and secular myths and ide- ologies, and inter- and trans-cultural exchanges. In the phraseology of our time, the adjective "rhetorical" is recognition of the importance of dealing with publicly accessible symbol systems in our search for insight into social processes, and the noun "studies" privileges humane investi- gations. Rhetorical studies are humane researches into the pragmatic operations of public symbol systems. They represent a theoretical, histor- ical, and critical area of study within general communication studies.

Rhetorical studies often are divided, these days, into subfields: *Rhe- torical theory,* "the rationale of the informative and the suasory in dis- course" (Bryant 1973, p. 14); *rhetorical criticism,* the interpretive and evaluative examination of practical discourse; *rhetorical history,* exam- ination of the rationales for and effects of practical discourse in earlier epochs; and *rhetorical pedagogy,* the assumptions guiding attempts to improve individuals' rhetorical performances. The focus of this chapter, therefore, is on ways we can teach rhetorical theory, rhetorical criticism, rhetorical history, and rhetorical pedagogy in our undergraduate curricula. It focuses on the instructional goals, strategies, resources, and evaluation processes that, ideally, should accompany undergraduate rhetorical studies.

INSTRUCTIONAL GOALS IN RHETORICAL STUDIES

As may be obvious through everything noted so far, the instructional goals of rhetorical studies are those of liberal arts education in general: description, contextualization, and judgment.

Description

A foundational aim of liberal education is the instillation of technical or in other ways precise language that enables its users to talk more accurately and usefully about the world. With the act of naming, as Burke has noted (1962, intro.), comes the abilities to assume perspectives on and to express attitudes toward the world. Just as the apprentice carpenter learns to ask for the "mitre box" instead of the "watchamacallit for cutting corners," so the student of all disciplines, including rhetoric, must learn technical talk.

The language of rhetoric is the language of: (a) communication in general (sender/receiver/channels/verbal and nonverbal messages/encoding/decoding/feedback); (b) persuasion (audience analysis/targeting/segmentation/fear appeals/credibility/motivational appeals/narratives/figure—ground relationships); (c) argument (data/warrant/claims/fallacies/refutation and rebuttal/syllogisms/enthymemes); (d) political process (ideology/hegemony/legitimation/power/demographics/party/primaries/conventions/general elections/spots and advertising/negative campaigning/announcement, nomination, acceptance, concession speeches/*topoi* and slogans); and (e) rhetorical theory (Platonic/Aristotelian/Isocratean/Ramistic/Port Royalist/empirical/belletristic/elocutionary/Burkean/epistemic). In these and many other concepts and conceptualizations are to be found the ways of identifying and discussing rhetorical theory, history, criticism, and pedagogy from the 5th century B.C. to the present.

A technical vocabulary is more, of course, than simply the mark of an educated person; it also is a tool to discovery, insight, communication, and both individual and shared pleasures. To discover, say, the "ancient" and "modern" formulas for sermons is to gain insight into the Puritan revolution in 16th- and 17th-century England, to learn a way to discuss differences between today's homilies (ancient) and sermons proper (modern), and to better appreciate a well-prepared talk from a local pulpit. A technical vocabulary affects our understanding of the world, discussions about it, and self-satisfactions and shared experiences.

Contextualizations

A second goal of a liberal education is to help people see their world in perspective—to put it into contexts so as to better reflect upon its significance. To "put something in context" is to articulate a set of relationships between it and other elements, forces, ideas, or institutions that we think form or account for it. Rhetorical studies seek to put our public communication habits and processes into such contexts. There are many ways to discuss rhetorical contexts for or perspectives on communication processes, as follows.

Pragmatic Context. One can be interested in the pragmatics of rhetoric—its effects on the world. The first logographers (speech writers) of the 6th century B.C. were concerned primarily with pragmatics—with constructing speeches for their clients that would win the day in court. "Rhetorical effect" has been a staple study area since then.

Psychological Context. Two sorts of psychological contexts for rhetorical messages are worth study: (a) The rhetor's state of mind has been studied. What sorts of people construct radically conservative discourses (Hart, 1971)? Do liberal and conservative rhetors see the world in different ways (Weaver, 1953)? How do people's youthful experiences affect their mature rhetorical habits (Maloney, 1955)? (b) The audience's predispositions and tendencies likewise have been looked at by scholars. Will a truly hostile audience ever come hear a speaker (Bauer, 1964)? In what ways must rhetors adapt specific lines of argument to subaudiences with special interests (Cox, 1974)?

Generic Context. Some types of talks are given often enough that people expect them to possess similar characteristics; a *genre* of discourse is a family of texts with similar features. Aristotle (1954) identified three genres of rhetorical discourse: political, legal, and ceremonial. Such genres even have species; so, we know that in political campaigns we are likely to hear announcement speeches, policy speeches, keynote addresses, nomination speeches, acceptance speeches, debates (joint appearances), *ad hominem* attacks, self-defenses (apologia), victory speeches, and concessions. To learn about genres of rhetoric is to be in touch with important rules of talk, with matters of "rhetorical manners" or appropriateness.

Sociocultural Context. Also interesting to examine are the "social rules"—the guides to prudential public behavior—underlying social and political rhetorical processes. For example, what kinds of rhetorical behavior do we expect from presidential candidates? What sorts of things do we expect them to say prior to announcing, during primaries, while giving convention speeches, in the middle of debates, and on the stump during the general election? Presidential elections are usefully examined dramaturgically, as choreographed acts and counteracts that come together as sociodramas scripted through unwritten social rules—cultural myths and rituals (Gronbeck 1984, 1985). Other kinds of rhetorical behavior (e.g., routines for justifying one's conduct when publicly attacked, the outlines of college commencement addresses, ritualized fights between labor and management) can be examined equally well from a sociocultural perspective.

Ethical Context. Public talk is powerful enough to make many worry about its morality. Plato (1962) worried that rhetors would pretend to talk about "justice" without knowing what is just and unjust, and that worry has followed rhetoric through its Western history. By what ethics should rhetoric be judged—by absolute standards of "right" and "wrong," by situational standards, by a kind of "majority rule" public vote (the principles of democracy) of what is correct or not, or by standards for action built into language itself? Ethical perspectives dominate public discussions of advertising, politics, and corporate messages (especially after product defects or accidents are discovered).

These and other perspectives (e.g., linguistic, psychoanalytical, technical) are available to students of rhetoric. Each perspective is a way of looking at rhetoric. Each way of looking is a way of seeing; with sight comes insight, and with insight comes the knowledge one needs to function as a thoughtful, informed member of a citizenry. Contextualization, therefore, is part of the burden of liberal arts education because it helps create fully rounded citizens.

Judgment

If we better understand something from a variety of vantage points, then presumably we ought to be more prepared to assess its beauty or defects, rightness or wrongness, effectiveness or ineffectiveness. Making aesthetic, moral, and pragmatic judgments about people, objects, and processes in informed ways is the mark of a well-educated person. Teaching under-graduates to make knowledgeable, subtle, reasoned judgments is a diffi-cult task, generally, and teaching them to make rhetorical judgments seems especially difficult, because the object of judgment is so ephemeral, yet complex, and because standards of judgment too often appear to work at cross purposes.

Regarding emphemerality, much rhetorical discourse comes at us au-rally. "Public speech" has been the central rhetorical practice through all of its history. "Speech," as contrasted with written discourse, is spoken and then lost into the air forever. It can be taken down shorthand or recorded and then transcribed, but, technically, once written or recorded for mechanical reproduction, it no longer *is* speech; it is a record of speech, but not speech per se. Speech is oral interchange: Its reputed powers undoubtedly are related to the facts that it occurs face-to-face, that it eminates directly from one person's body and "flows into" another person's, that feedback makes it explicitly and always a two-way commu-nication process. These and other characteristics (Ong, 1982, chap. 3) of orality make it an ancient practice yet one that it is difficult to analyze; analysis demands, often, inspection and then reexamination—something impossible to do with oral events. Most of the time, our rhetorical judg-ments must be based upon some record or memory of oral events.

Variability in rhetorical standards, likewise, complicates the judgmen-tal process. Five judgmental criteria often are applied to rhetorical exchanges:

1. Rhetorical effect. Did the speech "work"? Did it accomplish the aims articulated by the rhetor? Such a standard seems to come right from the core of rhetoric understood as affective or pragmatic discourse (Hoch-muth, 1955).

2. Rhetorical artistry or effectiveness. Was the speech strategically sound? Situations may be such that a speaker is doomed from the start by opposing votes or other circumstances, yet it still is possible that the speech could be adjudged a great one, artistically. It might be thought "effective" even if it did not achieve its primary aims (Parrish, 1968), as some think happened, for example, when Edmund Burke attacked Amer-ican taxation in 1774.

3. Ethicality. As already has been suggested, speeches can be assessed on moral grounds: One can use ethical standards derived from democratic principles (Wallace, 1963), pragmatism (or effects; Haiman, 1958), situa-tional ethics (Rogge, 1959), the speaker's own words (Campbell, 1972), or understandings of human dignity (Wander, 1984) to assess the moral worth of rhetorical discourse.

4. Fittingness. Lloyd Bitzer (1968) has suggested that we also can judge speeches by the degree to which they respond to situational exigencies in a fitting way. Bitzer would ask: Has the rhetorical discourse removed an imperfection from some situation so that people can return to their normal routines and activities? If it does, Bitzer would identify it as fitting.

5. Rhetorical competency. To ask if someone has spoken ("performed") competently is to inquire whether he or she has observed the social rules that govern talk in a particular situation. Just as "linguistic competency" is a standard for assessing the grammatical use of language, so is "rhetorical competency" a standard for evaluating its rhetorical use. "Competent" speakers may not always win, but they demonstrate understanding of social expectations and situational constraints (Gronbeck, 1987).

These judgments, of course, can conflict. A speech might "work" (effects judgment) and yet seem to suppress the rights of minorities (ethical judgment, pragmatic criterion); or, the speaker might tell the truth (ethical judgment, absolutist criterion) yet violate the expectations that listeners have for a situation (competency judgment). In such cases, critics must *argue for the relevance of their judgmental criteria*. Put another way, students must be taught that judgments are more than matters of personal preference or taste; they are *propositions* demanding articulation, support, and refutation of countering propositions before others can be expected to accept them. Part of the burden of liberal arts education—including rhetorical education—is instruction in the argumentative defense of one's positions.

INSTRUCTIONAL STRATEGIES AND RESOURCES IN RHETORICAL STUDIES

Let us next consider instructional strategies and resources together, because the resources that one uses in providing rhetorical training tend to determine, in many ways, one's instructional strategies. For the sake of illustration, consider briefly the following three sorts of resources.

Published Rhetorical Texts and Textbooks

Because rhetorical studies have been identified with oratory in communication departments, we commonly teach with anthologies of speeches, collections of rhetorical theories or essays on theorists, textbooks on rhetorical criticism, and anthologies of critical essays. Samples of such resources include: *Vital Speeches of the Day;* Linkugel, Allen, and Johannesen's *Contemporary American Speeches* (1982); new works emerging from Waveland Press, including Ryan's *American Rhetoric from Roosevelt to Reagan* (1987); collections of classical orations, among others Freeman (1963); and collections of the great British orators, such as Bryant, Arnold, Haberman, Murphy, and Wallace's *An Historical Anthology of Select British Speeches* (1967).

Published rhetorical texts—including collections of political pamphlets (e.g., Bailyn, 1965)—are normally taught in lecture–discussion formats. As noted, students must be taught to be careful and systematic observers of rhetorical detail. Taking them through speeches paragraph by paragraph, even word by word in the case of elaborate metaphors, demands that lectures be used, at first, to demonstrate critical analysis. Such texts also provide good resources for in-class discussions of varied approaches to criticism. A common practice among teachers of criticism is to select a specimen speech (e.g., Martin Luther King, Jr.'s "I Have Dream") and to ask students to critique it variously, doing, say, a Bitzerian situational analysis (Bitzer, 1968), a metaphoric analysis a la Osborn (1976), a look at mode of address in the manner of Duncan (1968, pp. 81–110), or a generic analysis of its formal characteristics. Model critical essays also can be read: a course on presidential rhetoric might well use both Windt's anthology (1987) and Windt and Ingold's collection of critical essays (1983). A problem here, however, is that undergraduates can be overwhelmed by scholarly essays; both the thought and the research that goes into them are too much. If they are asked to read sample critical essays, start them on those with simpler methods and the clearest writing, and only later move to intense and technical criticisms.

Prepared Audiovisual Materials

Available on audiotape (e.g., National Public Radio, 1984) and videotape (e.g., Educational Video Group, 1987) are great speeches, from Franklin Roosevelt through Geraldine Ferraro. Reels of the *CLIO Award Winning Television Commercials* (1973, 1978) and kinescopes of *Television's Classic Commercials 1948–1958* (Diamant, 1971) are in many audiovisual centers, as are films and videotapes showing techniques used in commercial and political ads. For teaching discussion and evaluation skills, the classic *Protest!* (1970) series of trigger films on social unrest contains useful films (that also provide students with historical overviews of 20th-century social movements).

Such audiovisual materials can be used like other texts, as specimens for analysis; the difference here, of course, is that one also can add analyses of nonverbal, iconic, and other visually oriented languages or codes.

Instructional strategies change somewhat when we begin using audiovisual materials; the shift from print to electronic media is really, as Ong (1982) has noted, a shift in ways of conception and even reaction, and hence modes of analysis often change. So, traditional rhetorical analyses—whether neoAristotelian (Thonssen & Baird, 1948) or contemporary (Andrews, 1983)—are strongly oriented to words, or verbalized symbol systems. As Barthes has demonstrated (1967, 1972, 1977), we ask different questions, usually, of visual symbol systems—about visuality and the representation–signification tension, about visual codes and underlying myths and ideologies. Adding paralinguistic, iconic, and other audiovisual languages to one's critical object multiplies the facets of rhetoric to be analyzed. That means teachers probably have to change their instructional strategy: They probably have to do close, intense, teacher-generated analyses of short scenes and even single frames from visual material, using such model criticism to teach students the subtleties of multimedia rhetorical study.

Student-Generated Materials

At the other extreme, teaches can turn over the onus for learning to the students. They can be sent to the streets to find and analyze the rhetoric of popular culture—billboards, tee shirts, bumperstickers, store logos and shelf arrangements, cafe decor, architecture (the difference between a federal building and an earth home, for example). Asking students to answer a single question, "In what ways are your expectations, attitudes, and beliefs influenced by X?", after some instruction in code breaking, can produce creative studies of environmental rhetorical discourse; "discourses", after all, are not only verbal—they can also include a wide variety of representations that make and circulate a set of meanings (Fiske, 1987, p. 14). In this sort of case, one's pedagogical assumption is that "texts" get created in reader-viewers, who have been acculturated to negotiate meanings in their environments; not everyone will "read" those discourses in precisely the same way, but all certainly have the wherewithal to create and use texts for their purposes. "Rhetoric," in this conception, has its broadest possible definition—the ways in which meanings are created and used by "reading groups" (subcultures) in societies.

The point of all this is that teachers of rhetorical studies must decide (a) how to broadly define "rhetoric" when theorizing and exemplifying rhetoric at work in society, and (b) to then adopt a series of pedagogical strategies, from traditional lecture to nontraditional observation projects, that are consistent with that definition.

IN CONCLUSION: EVALUATION PROCESSES

This chapter should conclude with the question: How can teachers know if they have taught rhetorical studies well? For some kinds of communication studies, that question can be answered directly, through technical examinations of speech texts delivered, films or videotapes produced, or poems interpreted. When it comes to the liberal arts portions of our studies, however, that question produces answers that are given well after college is completed. Engaging in rhetorical studies is learning to talk critically about that with which one has been surrounded mundanely for all of one's life. One's very culture is created and maintained through words; the political processes that perpetuate or replace leadership grind away, whether or not you are attuned to them; and hegemonic relationships between the ruler and the ruled almost by definition remain embedded in common sense ("Well, that's just the way we do things here."). Such a statement signals the presence of a culturally based, rhetorically maintained hegemony that deserves analysis and evaluation.

Ultimately, the cliché is true; Rhetorical training is education for life. Social relations are constructed, regulated, and changed through rhetorical discourse. Public meaning-making and society-making are all but identical processes. And hence, we cannot really assess the degree to which our instruction in rhetoric takes root until students make their way through the adult worlds of work, leisure, and sociality. When adults use the rhetorical words we taught them to assume perspectives on sociopolitical situations in which they find themselves, and to make both personal and collective decisions and judgments, then we may discover if we taught them well.

REFERENCES

Andrews, J. R. (1983). *The practice of rhetorical criticism*. New York: Macmillan.

Aristotle (1954). *Rhetoric; Poetics*. New York: Modern Library.

Bailyn, B. (Ed.). (1965). *Pamphlets of the American Revolution 1750–1776: Vol. 1: 1750–1765*. Cambridge, MA: Belknap Press of Harvard University Press.

Barthes, R. (1967). *Elements of semiology* (A. Lavers & C. Smith, Trans.). New York: Hill and Wang. (Original work published 1964)

Barthes, R. (1972). *Mythologies* (A. Lavers, Trans.). New York: Hill and Wang. (Original work published 1957)

Barthes, R. (1977). *Image-music-text* (S. Heath, Ed. & Trans.). London: Fantana.

Bauer, R. A. (1964). The obstinate audience: The influence process from the point of view of social communication. *American Psychologist, 19,* 319–328.

Bitzer, L. (1968). The rhetorical situation. *Philosophy & Rhetoric, 1,* 1–14.

Bryant, D. C. (1973). *Rhetorical dimensions in criticism*. Baton Rouge: Louisiana State University Press.

Bryant, D. C., Arnold, C. C., Haberman, F. W., Murphy, R., & Wallace, K. R. (Eds.). (1967). *An historical anthology of select British speeches.* New York: Ronald Press.

Burke, K. (1962). *A grammar of motives and a rhetoric of motives.* Cleveland: Word Publishing. (Original works published 1945 and 1950)

Campbell, K. K. (1972). *Critiques of contemporary rhetoric.* Belmont, CA: Wadsworth.

CLIO. (1973, 1978). *CLIO award winning television commercials: Educational reels* [Films]. N.P.: ATV-CLIO.

Combs, J. E. (1980). *Dimensions of political drama.* Santa Monica: Goodyear.

Cox, J. R. (1974). The rhetoric of child labor reform: An efficacy-utility analysis. *Quarterly Journal of Speech, 60,* 359–370.

Diamant, L. (1971). *Television's classic commercials; The golden years 1948–1958.* New York: Hastings House. (From the Celia Nachatovitz Diamant Memorial Library of Classical Television Commercials, Brooklyn College of CUNY.)

Duncan, H. D. (1968). *Symbols in society.* New York: Oxford University Press.

Educational Video Group. (1987). *Great speeches, Vols. 1–4* [Film]. Accompanying text: L. Rohler & R. Cook (Eds.), *Great speeches for criticism & analysis.* Greenwood, IN: Allistair Press.

Fiske, J. (1987). *Television culture.* London: Methuen.

Freeman, K. (Ed.). (1963). *The murder of Herodes and other trials from the Athenian law courts.* New York: W. W. Norton.

Gronbeck, B. E. (1984). Functional and dramaturgical theories of presidential campaigning. *Presidential Studies Quarterly, 14,* 486–499.

Gronbeck, B. E. (1985). The presidential campaign dramas of 1984. *Presidential Studies Quarterly, 15,* 386–393.

Gronbeck, B. E. (1987). Ronald Reagan's enactment of the presidency in 1981. In H. W. Simons & A. A. Aghazarian (Eds.), *Forms, genres, and the study of political discourse* (pp. 226–245). Columbia SC: University of South Carolina Press.

Haiman, F. S. (1958). Democratic ethics and the hidden persuaders. *Quarterly Journal of Speech, 44,* 385–392.

Hart, R. P. (1971). The rhetoric of the true believer. *Speech [Communication] Monographs, 38,* 249–261.

Hochmuth, M. K. (1955). The criticism of rhetoric. In M. K. Hockmuth (Ed.), *A history and criticism of American public address* (pp. 1–23). New York: Longmans.

Linkugel, W. A., Allen, R. R., & Johannesen, R. L. (Eds.). (1982). *Contemporary American Speeches* (5th ed.). Dubuque, IA: Kendall/Hunt.

Maloney, M. (1955). Clarence Darrow. In M. K. Hochmuth (Ed.), *A history and criticism of American public address* (pp. 262–312). New York: Longmans.

National Public Radio (1984). *Audiotapes of great speeches.* Washington, DC: Author.

Ong, W. J. (1982). *Orality and literacy; The technologizing of the word.* London: Methuen.

Osborn, M. (1976). *Orientations to rhetorical style.* Chicago: Science Research Associates.

Parrish, W. M. (1968). The study of speeches. In W. A. Lindsey (Ed.), *Speech criticism: Methods and materials* (pp. 76–98). Dubuque, IA: Wm. C. Brown.

Plato. (1962). *Gorgias* (W. C. Helmbold, Trans.). Indianapolis: Bobbs-Merrill.

Protest! series (1970). *Protest films.* N.P.: PFI.

Rogge, E. (1959). Evaluating the ethics of a speaker in a democracy. *Quarterly Journal of Speech, 45,* 419–425.

Ryan, H. R. (1987). *American rhetoric from Roosevelt to Reagan* (2nd ed.). Prospect Heights, IL: Waveland Press.

Thonssen, L., & Baird, A. C. (1948). *Speech criticism: The development of standards for rhetorical appraisal.* New York: Ronald Press.

Wallace, K. R. (1963). The substance of rhetoric: Good reasons. *Quarterly Journal of Speech, 49,* 239–249.

Wander, P. (1984). The third persona: An ideological turn in rhetorical theory. *Central States Speech Journal, 35,* 197–211.

Weaver, R. M. (1953). *The ethics of rhetoric.* Chicago: Henry Regnery.

Windt, T. (Ed.). (1987). *Presidential rhetoric (1961 to the present)* (4th ed.). Dubuque, IA: Kendall/Hunt.

Windt, T., & Ingold, B. (Eds.). (1983). *Essays in presidential rhetoric* (rev. printing). Dubuque, IA: Kendall/Hunt.

8

Teaching Persuasion

Roderick P. Hart
University of Texas at Austin

I have taught an undergraduate course entitled "Principles of Persuasion" for the last 18 years. This course is my passion as an undergraduate teacher. Securing the right to teach it was one of only two demands that I made during my first job interview in 1970. A guarantee to teach an eventual graduate course in rhetorical criticism was the second. At the time, it did not occur to me to demand an annual salary as well. Luckily, I was hired by a kindly gentleman who, fearing for my family's welfare, also promised to pay me. Needless to say, I was more sophisticated by the time of my second job interview in 1979. Then, after securing the right to teach the undergraduate persuasion course and the graduate course in criticism, I *immediately* initiated a salary discussion. No longer was teaching the persuasion course merely an opiate for me and my people. By 1979 I had learned the essential Marxian couplet: Power is good; pay is better.

Still, there is something empowering about teaching persuasion. It is, I feel, the most liberating course in the modern communication curriculum. On the first day of class, I observe to my students that all persuaders ask to borrow just a bit of their minds, for just a little while. Persuaders promise to do no damage when borrowing the values essential to their purposes ("Friends, we all like to save money, so. . .") and they also promise, irresistibly, that that which people give most easily—their attention—is a munificence that costs them nothing. Brashly, perhaps, I tell my students that my course will return their minds to them. I tell them that the cupsfull of themselves that they willingly loan out to teachers and preachers and cheerleaders in the bleachers can lead to an empty emotional cupboard. I tell them that if they keep giving portions of themselves away there will be nothing left when they need themselves most— when they are confused, frightened, uninformed, or pressured for a decision. I tell them that persuasion is a science that moves by increments, that it happens most powerfully when it least seems to happen at all. I tell them that the persuaders from afar (advertisers, propagandists, lawyers, politicians) must be understood if one is to lead a self-directed life. I also tell them, however, that the persuaders close at hand, such as lovers, parents, friends, and neighbors, must also be watched like hawks, because persuasion is most effective when it is defined as something else: concern, affection, advice, gossip. And I tell them about other exempted persuasions, such as the "guidance" of the local physician, the "selections" of the corner librarian, the "facts" of the nightly newscaster, and the "rules" of the imperious bureaucrat, emphasizing that persuasion by any other name is precisely what persuasion most wishes to be. I try to instill a kind of arrogant humility in my students, a mindset that gives them the courage to disassemble rhetoric but also the wisdom never to underestimate it. This is a tall order.

Middle age is a special time of reckoning in one's life. Perhaps because I now find myself in that exquisitely deplorable condition, I have used the occasion of this essay to explore why the undergraduate course in persuasion is important. During my career, I have had many reasons for teaching this course, and I explore each of these reasons here; but at the present time I seem to have only one such purpose, a purpose that I find myself phrasing in frighteningly grandiose terms. The great sin of youth—impetuosity—and the great sin of old age—banality—seem rather venial compared to that wondrous excess of middle age, grandiosity, and I earnestly anticipate the day when my grandiosity begins to slide irreversibly into the banal. Until then, I will tell my students that the persuasion course is the most important course they will take in college. I will tell them this because it is true. It is true, first, because persuasion deals with human motives, and there is nothing harder to understand—nor more important to understand—than human motives. It is true, also, because the persuasion course taps a variety of social scientific traditions and concentrates their insights on a single, central problematic: how symbolic action is transformed into social action. It is true, third, because persuasion always involves choices made by people, which is to say it involves the religion of the humanities—ethics. It is true, fourth, because the persuasion course deals with the socially inevitable; one needs biology to be a physician, thermodynamics to be an engineer, and economics to be an industrialist, but one must only breathe to need to know something of persuasion. It is true, fifth, because unlike other communication practices (choral reading, informal conversation, group conferencing, job interviewing, etc.), persuasion emanates from and results in *policy choices,* choices that often become instantiated in highly public, and hence massively constraining, ways. And it is true, last, because the undergraduate persuasion course does something that many college courses do not do—it makes a difference in students' lives. In this sense, the persuasion course bears the markings of its parent discipline (communication studies or rhetoric) and thus represents the essential Deweyan endstate: practical knowledge for the practical business of living.

My feeling is that there are at least three legitimate motives for teaching an undergraduate course in persuasion. At various times, I have been motivated by each.

The Practitioner's Motive

This motive is perhaps the most dominant of the three, no doubt because it springs directly from the rhetorical tradition itself. It treats the persuasion class as a more advanced and more specific version of the basic course in communication skills. In such a persuasion course, students not only learn the principles of persuasion, they also test them out in the laboratory of the college classroom by preparing and delivering speeches, by assembling audiovisual presentations, by redrafting extant persuasive messages, and so on. This version of the persuasion course represents the Isocratean ideal: Knowledge utilized is knowledge retained. Often, the students attracted to such a course are the sorts of people who will eventually persuade for a living—business majors, prelaw students, would-be politicians, and those sensing that they have a ministerial vocation. Such students have long been attracted to communication courses, and for good reason—rhetorical engagement is an ageless bridge across the chasm of human misunderstanding. More important, persuasion is a *non-coercive* method for securing public cooperation and therefore has ample attractions from a societal perspective. After all, even when they seek "public cooperation" in behalf of making Cheetos the snack food of choice, or Jesse Helms a favored legislator, or salvationism a county mandate, persuaders are doing what they have a right to do, and, given the options, their work simply must be encouraged. A course that increases the number of able persuaders in the world might also add to the world's supply of eloquence, a not-unpleasant eventuality. The highest calling of such a course, however, is to make coercion an increasingly remote possibility in human affairs, a good semester's work indeed for a teacher of persuasion.

The Scientist's Motive

This motive for teaching the undergraduate persuasion course best captures the Aristotelian ideal of rhetorical education: studying human influence patterns so that interpersonal psychology can be better understood. This has been a powerful motive since the 1950s in the United States, no doubt paralleling the rise in social scientific studies of human behavior. On many campuses, the persuasion course has become a course in applied social psychology, and every persuasion textbook on the market, without exception, borrows heavily from this research tradition. Most often, communication researchers are interested in what social psychologists call the "message variable" in the persuasion process, and this message orientation heavily flavors many undergraduate persuasion courses taught today. Instructors inspired by the Scientist's motive tend to teach their classes dispassionately, covering such topics as audience behavior, source credibility, models of attitude change, media penetration, the psychology of language, and so on. As social scientific research methods have improved in sophistication, the Scientist's motive has become increasingly dominant in certain quarters, even though the third- and fourth-generation laboratory studies produced in support of this model have become increasingly arcane. Moreover, the Brobdignaggian list of qualifications impressed upon a persuasion teacher by the partiality of these research findings makes pedagogy increasingly difficult. After patiently explaining to students that recency effects obtain only under certain hard-to-specify, not-invariant, methodologically contaminated conditions, the intellectual bang of an instructor's lecture is too often reduced to a professorial whimper. "Alas," the persuasion teacher says to the students seated in the lecture hall, "real life is often not a tidy thing." To such remarks, college students often respond with a chorus of noisy, pained silences.

The Consumerist's Motive

There is a sense in which the Practitioner's motive "features" the speaker in the persuasion process and a corresponding sense in which the Scientist's motive features the message. In sharp contrast, the Consumerist's motive features the audience: The teacher inspired by such a motive teases out the strategies used by persuaders on persuadees, thereby equipping students with the intellectual resources needed to ward off unwanted influences. To teach with such a rationale is clearly to play defense. This motive best represents the Platonic approach to rhetoric, an approach that decries the utilitarianism of the Isocratean model and the remoteness of the Aristotelian quest. In many senses, Plato was the ultimate Consumerist, decrying the sophists of his day for using cookery to distract citizens from the "manifestly true." The modern persuasion teacher is normally less sure what such truth looks like (and is often ill-equipped to launch a search for it during a 16-week semester), but the Platonic spirit of critique still remains in many communication departments and still inspires the Consumerist's teaching *against* persuasion (as opposed to the Practitioner's teaching *of* persuasion and the Scientist's teaching *about* persuasion). Typically, the Consumerist makes four central arguments in a persuasion class: (a) there is a great deal of rhetoric in the everyday world, more than most people notice and probably more than is good for them; (b) the most fundamental persuasive move made by persuaders is to declare themselves nonpersuaders; (c) a given piece of persuasion achieves its greatest social utility when persuadees accept it knowingly; and (d) the only right more fundamental in a democracy than the freedom to persuade is the freedom not to be persuaded. The Consumerist tends to fetishize this latter proposition, often becoming hortatory in class when warning students about the beguiling rhetorics of the day. Normally, students smile pleasantly at such hectoring, tacitly appreciating the storm warnings being signalled but also faintly resenting the avuncular tones in which they may have been cast.

The three motives I have presented here are not mutually incompatible, and many undergraduate persuasion courses are inspired by a mix of them. But most courses tend to *emphasize* one of these motives, and the resulting course profiles differ considerably. Put reductionistically, the Practitioner becomes something of a coach, the Scientist something of an oracle, and the Consumerist something of a crybaby. It is this latter persona that has walked into the lecture hall with me during the last decade or so. I did not summon it up intentionally. Rather, it emerged as I matured as a teacher and, I suppose, as I aged as a person; but I can fix its onset even more precisely. The Scientist's motive waned within me when Jim Jones persuaded more than 900 persons to their deaths in November of 1978. Reading accounts of that incident, I quickly discovered that many of these slaughtered innocents had graduated from American colleges and universities. It became apparent to me that "having an education," or "being generally informed," provided no antidote to the poison of crazed charismatics. Rather, the Jones incident made me existentially aware that it took a particular *kind* of knowledge, rhetorical knowledge, to keep such maniacs at bay and that it took certain *kinds* of instincts, rhetorical instincts, to fight off such maniacs when they could be kept at bay no longer. All of this sounds rather melodramatic, I suppose, and too maudlin for we sophisticates of the Academy. But middle age causes one to cast about for some "grand purpose," and keeping my students out of the clutches of the next Jim Jones gave me mine. Naturally, it gives me pause to share such personal thoughts in a professional publication (and I am not unaware that they could be parodied as some sort of ersatz born-again experience). Still, the Jim Jones incident showed me that source credibility could no longer be treated as a mere variable in some elegant stochastic equation. At least, it could not be treated thusly in *my* classroom.

My rejection of the Practitioner's motive had both practical and political roots. For one thing, it dawned on me that the typical communication department already taught productivity skills in many of its courses and that it only rarely taught receptivity skills. Isocrates was handsomely accorded his due in the curriculum, whereas the critical faculties championed by Plato and Augustine were given short shrift. Communication students could speak cleverly, it was clear, but what did they listen to, I asked, and did they do so cleverly? They listened to little, I concluded, and when they did listen, they listened awkwardly. I also concluded that any *academic* discipline teaching an art as powerful as rhetoric also had an obligation to teach techniques for falsifying that art. That is, by analogy, if professors of nuclear engineering are responsible for the building of nuclear power plants, then so must they be responsible for inventing safe methods of nuclear waste disposal. The analogy is an imperfect one, as are all analogies, but if communication courses give aid and comfort *and skill* to tomorrow's corporate scions (or to its established prelates or the look-alikes in U.S. politics or those whose advocacy skills protect the affluent in court), then so must such courses educate the listeners who must sort out the lies, near-lies, and not-lies of these spellbinders. Power tends to collect around rhetoric, after all, and money collects there also. At least in Western democracies, strategic cleverness often belongs to the comfortably walled in, rather than to the painfully walled out. Moreover, even the most elementary sort of arithmetic will reveal that there are very few speakers speaking these days and that they are doing so for a limited number of institutionally entrenched reasons. At the same time, there are many, many listeners in the world, and their listening is largely untrained; also, these listeners have a panorama of personal, cultural, and economic needs that typically go unmet when they listen. Must the field of communication serve only the few, the speakers? No. It must also educate the many, the audiences, I have concluded.

For a variety of reasons, then, I found myself becoming a Consumerist many years after Ralph Nader did so with Chevrolets. I adopted this posture tentatively, knowing that my students must be given the freedom to become better Practitioners (and better informed Scientists) and knowing, too, that in my zeal to expose the vagaries of persuasion, I must not become so zealous that I myself become a target for my students' newly developed deconstructive urges. Classroom cant is merely an upscale sort of cant, after all, and thus the persuasion teacher's truest ally in the lecture hall is a healthy sense of self-doubt, a willingness to question all orthodoxies, even the most personal. More positively stated, the undergraduate persuasion course might best be thought of as a place for showing students that life is a blank canvas for *their* artistry and not merely a cramped place filled with the etchings of The Wise and The Powerful. Helping students learn to listen critically is, therefore, a high calling for the undergraduate teacher of persuasion. To wrest intellectual and emotional power from persuaders and to offer these gifts instead to students is at once a depowering act and an empowering act. Conceivably, upon reflection, these same students may choose to return this power to traditional persuaders. But if they do so *upon reflection,* the teacher of persuasion will have done his or her job well.

Other than idiosyncratic preference, is there one good reason to prefer the Consumerist model? In fact, there are two.

Technological Reasons To Be a Consumerist. The United States is almost single-handedly responsible for pioneering the most sophisticated methods for creating and delivering persuasive messages known to humankind. Buoyed by such traditions as political rabble-rousing and pamphleteering in the 18th century, religious evangelism and popular lecturing in the 19th century, and mass entrepreneurism and social mobilization in the 20th century, the United States has always been a hotbed for vigorous rhetorical exchange. Many of its institutions—Congress, the marketplace, the mass media—have become shrines to the persuasive arts. In a free society, of course, all of this is permitted—indeed, encouraged. In a free society, people cannot be made to hear. But in a free society, people can be made to listen—if persuaders are clever enough to understand human susceptibilities. For that reason, if no other, the persuasion teacher must stand as a bulwark against flackery. Surely, any society that has pioneered the 20-second political spot, the computerized telephone solicitation, the personalized mass mailer, the product-centered cartoon show, the socially relevant sitcom, the corporate-cozy theme park, or the selling of kitchenware-cum-conviviality also has a responsibility for defending its citizenry against these unseen persuasions. It might even be said that teaching people how to consume persuasion intelligently is something of a patriotic obligation. But perhaps that would sound too much like rhetoric.

Humanistic Reasons To Be a Consumerist. I resurrect an argument here that I made a decade ago when asked to comment on new directions in the teaching of human communication. At that time, enrollments in communication classes were beginning to burgeon nationally, and students were simultaneously turning away from traditional studies in the humanities. Too loftily, perhaps, I warned that a New Philistinism was stalking the college campus and that that placed special burdens on all teachers in the field (Hart, 1981):

> If speech communication teachers are to fill the gap created by the New Philistinism, they must become more vigorous in teaching the principles of human reasoning because their students are not taking sufficient course work in logic. Teachers of speech communication must demand that their students write, rewrite, and write again because these students are not taking advanced courses in English either. Teachers of speech communication must expose their students to the world of political controversy, to the techniques of problem-solving through discussion, and to the infinite diversity of human auditors because these students are surely not taking extensive work in political science, philosophy, or anthropology. . . . It is quite possible that my students' inability to understand subtle rhetoric when they see it results from their lack of knowledge of the complex human motivations depicted in that unread Shakespearean play or from their unfamiliarity with such historical personages as Joe McCarthy and Huey Long. Their untutored critical sensibilities, dulled by a pablum of mediated extravaganzas, surely are part of the problem as well. (pp. 40–41)

As the 1990s unfold, I see no essential change in these enrollment patterns. Today's students are still woefully uninformed about history and, thus, are susceptible to the next Adolph Hitler appearing among them. Today's students still do not understand the subtleties of human language, so they can be seduced by the practiced evasions of an Oliver North. Today's students are still ignorant of foreign tongues and international affairs, so they find appeal in the provincialism of a Pat Robertson. As a college teacher of the undergraduate course in persuasion, I therefore find myself trying to do in one semester what the nation's school systems have not been doing for my students for the last 20 years (and for what they have not been doing for themselves either). I choose not to bemoan this fate. My students, at least, know that they do not know, and that normally makes teaching them a pleasure. But imagining what my students would have if they had more of the humanistic heritage tends to make one wistful in the odd moment.

There are perhaps other good reasons to adopt the Consumerist model in the persuasion classroom, but these two reasons are sufficient for me. They are not sufficient for everyone. Some teachers still feel the weight of tradition in these matters, arguing that their only legitimate role in the classroom is that of Practitioner's assistant. Having emerged from that same tradition, I have great respect for this viewpoint, even though it is no longer my own—at least not when I am in the undergraduate persuasion class. I also respect the Scientist's pedagogical motives and hope that I have not veered so far to the left that I have lost sight of a center that holds intellectually. In any event, although I have listened to these alternatives respectfully, I am still resolved to make unhappy little consumers out of my students.

A colleague at another institution recently warned me, however, of a subtle, yet grave, danger in the Consumerist model, and it is a danger that bothers me not a little. Such a model, she argued, could quickly usher in a post-Nietzchean era in which distrust reigns supreme, an era in which no idea is allowed preeminence and hence an era in which *any* idea—even subhuman ideas—would suffice. She warned me that what I am here calling Consumerism undermines trust in trust itself, breeds a dissatisfied quiescence in people, and thereby deenergizes social change. She argued that education should build ideas, not destroy them, and that a teacher who leaves nothing standing at the end of a semester leaves his or her students unprotected against the cold blasts of nihilism. From what I have been able to observe, my colleague operates as something of an Activist/Practitioner in the classroom, teaching students the technique of rhetorical influence so that *they,* perversely, can turn the tables on those who now control the rhetorical establishment.

I greatly admire the verve of this particular colleague, a person who blends scholarly excellence and pedagogical commitment as well as anyone I know. As a result, her critique of consumerism gives me special pause. Finally, however, her model cannot be my model. In many senses, our friendly argument parallels the more acrimonious disputes waged between the deconstructionists and the Marxists. The former have raised semantic suspicion to an art form, asserting that the weight of all messages, all ideologies, and all certainties cannot ultimately be supported by the frail linguistic foundations underpinning them. As critics, their goal is to show the *aporia* in human meaning, to make a reader content with discontentedness, and to demonstrate that no political, religious, or social dialogue can ever be a completed dialogue. The deconstructionist is therefore a searcher.

The Marxists deplore such nonsense and are concerned to show how certain exploitative belief systems work their ways into human affairs (and into human locutions in particular), thereby reestablishing certain establishments and restabilizing what are often completely arbitrary stabilities. As critics (and presumably as teachers), the Marxists' job is to replace such corruptions with more socially enlightened modes of thought and action. Marxists use their insights to undermine both repressive ideas and repressive political systems. The Marxist is, therefore, a savior.

All of this may seem rather far afield from the humble little undergraduate course in persuasion. My argument, however, is that a dose of deconstruction might not be an altogether inappropriate medicine for what ails today's undergraduates. And what ails them is this: excessive respect for formal authorities, insufficient curiosity about language forms, heightened regard for scientized solutions, too much reverence for traditional orthodoxies—in short, too much believing and too little knowing. My students' intellectual health would be especially improved by a helping of the deconstructionists' critical playfulness and an extra helping of their faith that all "isms"—*nihilism included*—will ultimately betray themselves. Thus, I continue to pop my students' balloons, knowing that, no matter what I say to them, they will work out their own ideologies later in life; as their teacher, I only insist that they do not announce any final versions of these ideologies during their semester with me. And for the moment, at least, I do not worry about a post-Nietzchean universe developing on the University of Texas campus because of my persuasion course. Rather, I trust my students' natural inclinations to disagree with one another. I also trust in the stimulative value of a rigorous skepticism—and of the respect for the ironic and the tolerance of the absurd that it entails. Above all, I trust in the critical mind's wondrous capacity to call a spade a spade and a rhetoric a rhetoric, to depuff puffery and make mortals out of gods, and to maintain a tenacious resolve that we shall not all fall, lemming-like, into the sea.

REFERENCE

Hart, R. P. (1981). Speech communication as the new humanities. In G. Friedrich (Ed.), *Education in the 80s: Speech communication*. Washington DC: National Education Association.

9

Teaching Organizational Communication

Linda L. Putnam
Purdue University

Leigh Ford
Western Michigan University

Organizational communication is a relative newcomer to the discipline. As an outgrowth of public address, interpersonal communication, small group discussion, and organizational behavior, the pedagogy of organizational communication has evolved into a broad-based cadre of courses that encompasses business and professional speaking, communication training and development, and business writing, as well as ones that center primarily on the study of communicative behavior in organizations. Organizational communication, then, is often associated with an applied approach to communication, specifically with the "training" and development of communication skills for managers. Recent texts and course syllabi, however, have moved beyond training specific skills to teaching students how to understand and manage the complexities of organizational environments. This shift emanates from a concomitant change in the assumptions that underlie organizational communication.

Early pedagogy in organizational communication focused primarily on the fidelity of downwardly directed communication, particularly newsletters and other forms of written communication (Sexton & Staudt, 1959). This emphasis on the tangible aspects of messages followed the lead of organizational theorists who cast organizations as static containers structured by physical hierarchies, boundaries between departments, and written rules and regulations. Definitions of communication stressed the accuracy and clarity of transmitting messages across organizational

115

levels that are constrained by differences in status and authority and by formal rules and regulations.

Current perspectives have moved beyond explicit and concrete messages to the study of information processing, interaction patterns, symbol systems, and message interpretations (Putnam & Cheney, 1985). By centering on the dynamic qualities of "communicating" and "organizing," this approach places communication at the forefront of organizing and makes it central to the enactment of most concepts in organizational behavior. Thus, the uniqueness that organizational communication brings to communication pedagogy is the merger of communication theory with organizational theory, an alliance that extends beyond simply adding communication to organizational principles and practices (Redding, 1972). The fusion of these two domains recasts *both communication theory* and *organizational behavior*. Hence, organizational communication is not simply the study of public speaking in organizations or interpersonal communication in a collectivity; rather, it is the study of how communication processes fuse with, shape, and reshape the activities of organizing within and between institutions.

Organizations are typically characterized by such components as common goals or purposes, interdependence, division of labor, hierarchical structure, formal policies, and regulations (Redding, 1989). The integration of organizational behavior with communication theory suggests that interaction processes both constitute and are constituted by these characteristics. That is, organizational designers develop charts that illustrate the chain of command or hierarchical structure of the organization. This blueprint of "who reports to whom" may reflect, as well as influence, the direction, amount, and type of communication that occurs in organizations. The simultaneity of interactions across organizational units; the multiple perspectives represented by the wide range of positions, backgrounds, and personalities in organizations; and the numerous and often conflicting interpretations of organizational events support the assumption that communication problems and "breakdowns" are inevitable in this context.

MISGUIDED ASSUMPTIONS ABOUT ORGANIZATIONAL COMMUNICATION

Helping students understand the fusion between organization behavior and communication theory is difficult, because many students have limited organizational experiences. Although a number of students hold part-time jobs in high school and college, they typically have only a modicum of information about the larger repertoires of organizational communication (Jablin, 1987). In fact, many students with part-time jobs have very distant communication relationships with their coworkers and their supervisors (Greenberger, Steinberg, Vaux, & McAuliffe, 1980). Thus, one of the challenges in teaching organizational communication is finding ways to help students conceptualize the dynamics and complexities of organizations. In effect, students must be trained to bring a "communication mindset" to bear on organizational components, principles, and theories.

With limited experience as full-time organizational members, students cling to a number of naive expectations and assumptions about communication in organizations. Students typically seek prescriptions, or "five easy steps," to address complex organizational issues. Although teachers can generate guidelines, suggestions, and options for effective communication, variations in organizational cultures and environmental constraints make it difficult to prescribe communicative behaviors. For instance, research suggests that effective supervisors display openness and candor with their subordinates (Redding, 1972), but circumstances arise in which effective supervisors have to be strategically ambiguous with their employees or be secretive in discussing policies that have direct implications for their subordinates (Sitkin, in press).

Students also assume that communication is a panacea for solving organizational ills. For example, they might think that the marketing and production departments can reduce their long-standing conflicts of interest through frequent and open communication. More communication, however, typically exacerbates, rather than lessens, deep-seated conflicts. The panacea of "more communication" is particularly problematic in organizations because of the shear volume of information flow, the use of authority and status differences, and the need to understand how and what is communicated at a particular point in time. A similar naive notion is that good ideas will get adopted and disseminated if communication channels are open and frequently used. Good ideas can get lost en route to the proper source, amidst managerial overload and subsequent inertia, or be blocked because of political expediency. Although students recognize that power and politics play a key role in organizational decision making, they tend to minimize the pervasiveness of the political factions that influence daily interactions.

In addition to naive assumptions about communication in organizations, students tend to blame individuals for complex problems. Even though personalities and individual competences play key roles in shaping organizational events, complex dilemmas typically penetrate into multiple levels and work units. Organizational problem solving, then, entails disentangling message patterns and events, rather than simply disciplining or firing a "troublemaker." Finally, students typically hold an orthodox view of authority in organizations. Issuing legitimate challenges, questioning ethical and moral issues of organizational life, and adopting a proactive rather than a submissive attitude toward authority is unconscionable for most students. Thus, in addition to helping students understand the way communication shapes and is shaped by organizational processes, instructors must challenge these assumptions, heighten organizational awareness, and develop maturity in solving complex problems.

GOALS AND INSTRUCTIONAL STRATEGIES

Goals and strategies for teaching organizational communication range from developing interpersonal competencies to designing formal communication systems. Most courses begin with a general introduction to communication and move into a review of organizational theories (classical management/human relations/decision theorists/systems theory/ecological theory), the contributions of major organizational theorists (Taylor/Fayol/Weber/Barnard/Simon/Weick), and the communication concepts and principles embedded in these theoretical perspectives (formal and informal structures/information flow/message distortion/network patterns/conflict management/leadership/climate/feedback/motivation/group dynamics/decision making). From this theoretical grounding, courses typically evolve into one or a combination of four approaches, depending on instructional goals.

One approach centers on managerial communication and general communication competencies (e.g., see Hawkins & Preston, 1981; Redding, 1984; Shockley-Zalabak, 1988). A second approach follows a career track and accentuates the skills needed for training-development and human resource positions, for instance, communication pedagogy, communication audits, and organizational development (e.g., see Goldhaber, 1986; Pace, 1983). A third approach aims at the design and control of communication systems in organizations through understanding organizational environments, internal–external communication, information technologies, change and innovation (e.g., Daniels & Spiker, 1987; Farace, Monge, & Russell, 1977; Rogers & Agarwala-Rogers, 1976). A fourth direction adopts a process or cultural-rhetorical view of organizations, often exposing the nonrational side of bureaucracies. Topics such as power and politics, conflict management, cognitive maps, equivocality, stress and burnout, and organizational deviance surface in teaching this perspective (e.g., Conrad, 1985; Johnson, 1977; Kreps, 1986). Although the specific objectives and exact content of courses vary, most organizational communication classes espouse three general instructional goals—organizational awareness, problem analysis, and communication skills development.

Organizational Awareness

One key objective in studying organizational communication is to make students aware of the ubiquitous nature of communication in organizational life. Communication is not simply invoked when managers send messages to subordinates or when employees use the telephone or write a memo. Knowledge of the intersection of communication theory and organizational behavior helps students understand the role of communication in forming effective work relationships, in matching self-interests with organizational needs, and in creating shared perspectives (Conrad, 1985). In effect, communication underlies every domain of organizational life, including coordinating tasks, planning strategies, making decisions, enacting power relationships, managing conflicts, developing and enforcing formal and informal norms, assimilating newcomers, and providing social support.

Gaining awareness of the complex and omnipotent nature of organizational communication helps employees take actions to minimize communication problems by choosing appropriate behaviors. For example, the study of directional flow helps students see that messages sent to middle and upper managers are frequently filtered to reduce information overload. This filtering, however, distorts the picture that a manager receives of task performance by screening out "bad news" and accentuating "good news." If a manager understands this inevitability, he or she can take overt steps to provide for the transmission of bad news up the channel (for instance, initiate formal and informal gripe sessions, befriend the chronic complainer, etc.) while delegating and filtering out other types of messages to reduce excessive overload.

Problem Analysis

Once students acquire some understanding of how an organization functions, they need to develop skills in analyzing complicated situations. Organizational communication theory, then, becomes a diagnostic tool for problem solving (Elsea, 1980). Learning how to decipher and make sense of organizational events requires perspective taking and interpersonal sensitivity; an assessment of how organizational systems impact on the individuals involved; an understanding of organizational structures, norms, and political activity; and knowledge of environmental factors that currently impinge on the organization. Analysis occurs (a) prior to making choices for strategic action (Conrad, 1985), (b) while monitoring ongoing communication activities, and (c) during diagnosis of communication problems after interaction occurs. Hence, organizational analysis forms the basis for planned interactions, it accompanies choice of communicative behaviors, and it aids in unraveling communication problems in organizations.

Training in organizational analysis typically begins with providing students with organizational situations and then asking them to identify the relevant factors that contribute to the events, to determine communicative choices that are (or should be) made, and to evaluate the outcomes of these choices. Although these steps replicate the traditional problem solving model, in this context students must wrestle with the criteria for deciphering problems and making appropriate organizational choices.

Communication Skills

To implement action strategies in organizations, students need basic communication skills. These skills entail effective speaking and writing; interviewing; listening, seeking and giving feedback; conducting meetings; persuasion; empathy, information search, acquisition, interpretation, and transmission; critical thinking; management of organizational symbols; and sense making. Hence, a central goal in teaching organizational communication is the development of communication competencies (Staley & Shockley-Zalabak, 1985). These competencies, while similar to those taught in interpersonal communication and public speaking, center on the organizational exigencies and constraints that call for particular skills. For example, in reprimanding employees or when delivering bad news, managers need to employ interpersonal skills grounded not only in sensitivity and face-saving gestures but also in directness and organizational authenticity (Shockley-Zalabak, 1988). Hence, developing skills in organizational communication classes touches on the topics that are frequently covered in other communication courses, but centers on the uniqueness of these skills in the organizational environment.

INSTRUCTIONAL RESOURCES AND EVALUATION

To heighten organizational awareness, resources for teaching organizational communication typically combine cognitive and experiential learning (Pace, 1977). Textbook material, guest lectures, films, and popular books are used to facilitate cognitive learning, whereas field research, case studies, role playing, and simulations provide experiences for developing analytical and communication skills. Evaluating cognitive and experiential learning in organizational communication is often difficult to determine. Most courses reflect a ratio of 60% cognitive evaluation (from exams, papers, and book reports) and 40% experiential learning (Pace & Ross, 1983). Even though examinations are valuable assessment tools, they typically tap only part of the learning experience in organizational communication classes. Through evaluating student performance in activities that provide experiential learning, teachers reaffirm the goals of integrating organizational and communication theory and of applying theoretical knowledge to organizational events.

Instructional resources vary in the degree of student involvement entailed in an activity. Films, lectures, and television aim to enhance cognitive learning while providing only a modicum of experiential involvement. In case studies and field research, students participate as outside observers who are removed from the organization, whereas in role playing and simulations, students assume predetermined roles to act out organizational situations.

Films, Popular Media, and Guest Lectures

Through visual media, organizational complexities become vividly dramatized, and routine behaviors take on heightened sensory awareness. A number of award-winning informational and dramatic films exist on such topics as power and authority, conflict management, performance appraisal, active listening, creative problem solving, leadership, and groupthink (see, for example, the Visions of '80 Series, 1972–1978). Each of these entail direct or implicit links to organizational communication. Moreover, a number of high-quality, short, impressionistic films (8 to 15 minutes) are available on topics such as communication dilemmas of middle managers and admitting error in organizations (see Stephen Bosustow, the Mitt Mittle Series, 1975). Prior to showing films, instructors should highlight relevant organizational communication concepts or perhaps provide students with film outlines so that students can concentrate on the dramatizations of organizational experiences.

Popular books such as *In Search of Excellence* (Peters & Waterman, 1982), *Getting to Yes* (Fisher & Ury, 1981), *Men and Women of the Corporation* (Kanter, 1977), and *Working* (Terkel, 1972) provide provocative and even controversial examples of organizational communication. Two of these books, *In Search of Excellence* and *Working,* are highlighted in documentary films produced by the Public Broadcasting Station. The controversy engendered by the research reported in *In Search of Excel-*

lence (the companies listed as excellent and the attributes linked to excellent corporations) provide the gist of a lively classroom debate (see, e.g., Aupperle, Acar, & Booth, 1986, and "Who's Excellent Now?", 1984). Guest speakers from the corporate world can provide exciting, first-hand accounts of communication situations in organizations. Corporate leaders, human resource personnel, and employees in the rank and file might serve as speakers. Students might conduct a "Meet the Press"-type interview with guest panelists. Because guest speakers are typically unfamiliar with course content, teachers need to maintain direct control of the lecture topic and nature of class discussions.

Case Studies

In case studies, students assume the roles of detached observers who identify and diagnose problems, generate alternatives, assess consequences of these actions, and recommend a specific alternative (Kreps & Lederman, 1985). A case study is any description or account of a sequence of events that confronts an individual, work unit, or organizational system as a whole (Apple, 1986). A typical case summarizes an organizational situation, depicts the actions of the key players, explains their perceptions, describes the sequence of events leading up to the situation, and identifies reactions to the situation. The case description should provide enough clues about the events to make meaningful judgments about communication patterns. The case method provides a low-threat form of experiential learning that applies theory to practice and that shows how communication patterns are constrained and influenced by organizational contingencies (Apple, 1986; Kreps, 1986; Kreps & Lederman, 1985; Mier, 1982).

Cases are often included in teacher's manuals, organizational communication textbooks, and/or in such supplementary books as *Case Studies in Organizational Communication* (Sypher, in press), *Organizational Reality: Reports from the Firing Line* (Frost, Mitchell, & Nord, 1985), *Organizational Theory: Cases and Application* (Daft & Dahlen, 1984), and *Case Studies in Organizational Communication* (case studies, 1975). Less conventional sources (such as newspapers, magazines, short stories, novels, and television) can provide excellent cases and case comparisons that have an added advantage of being current and generally familiar to students. Novels and narrative accounts—such as *The Soul of a New Machine* (Kidder, 1981), *Something Happened* (Heller, 1975), *Catch-22* (Heller, 1962), and *The Death of a Salesman* (Miller, 1976)—encapsule samples of organizational texts for students to analyze and interpret. *The Ropes to Skip and the Ropes to Know* (Ritti & Funkhouser, 1977) follows the experiences of a newcomer in the organization and illustrates text material on communication and assimilation. Episodes of such television series as "St. Elsewhere" and "Hill Street Blues" dramatize organizational life, thereby providing exemplars of how the media shapes expectations of organizational communication while simultaneously illuminating key course concepts (see Ekdom & Trujillo, 1989).

Case analysis sessions vary from instructor-led discussions to small group problem solving. The instructor draws attention to neglected information and insights about the case by questioning student recommendations for a particular course of action and by emphasizing the crucial role of theory in analysis (Kreps & Lederman, 1985). Individual performance can be evaluated through a presentational model in which each student is responsible for outlining the case and leading class discussions. Students might also provide a written case analysis or participate in group projects in which members debate other groups on their analyses and recommendations for solving case problems. Controversy over policy issues stimulates as well as simulates.

Field Research

In field research (unlike case studies), students assume the role of detached observers but gain first-hand, rather than vicarious, insights about organizational situations. Field research is typically conducted as part of a class project (Jablin, 1983; James & Smilowitz, 1984). Students gain experience in administering, analyzing, interpreting, and reporting data collected to examine specific concepts or to audit an organization's communication patterns (Husband & Helmer, 1984). Through interviews, questionnaires, and/or participant observation, students apply theory and course concepts to obtain data on organizational events. This project typically leads to several assignments that teachers can evaluate, including a research report that triangulates the various methods. The instructor could also evaluate written reports produced for the organization, oral presentations to the class on research results, and student evaluations of the research experience (Jablin, 1983).

Although the value of this activity is clear, a teacher might weigh his or her commitment and responsibility to external organizations against the students' knowledge of organizational communication and their research competencies. Practical considerations (such as anonymity of participants, confidentiality of results, financial responsibility, and the scope of the project) must be negotiated with the participating companies. Also, the instructor must be prepared to serve as an intermediary, consultant, public relations agent, sounding board, or any other role that is needed to facilitate the research process and to maintain community goodwill for the department and the university.

Role Playing

Unlike case studies and field research, role-playing exercises require students to enact organizational situations within specific guidelines and persona; hence, students dramatize a specific organizational incident (Falcione, 1977). Even though the roles and circumstances of the incidents are structured, the interaction between the participants emerges spontaneously. Role-playing exercises serve three primary functions.

1. They give students an opportunity to practice specific organizational communication skills not typically encountered in classrooms. For example, in enacting performance appraisal interviews, students adapt interviewing techniques to a company's evaluation procedures.

2. Role-playing exercises can be used to demonstrate effective or appropriate communicative behaviors in organizations.

3. Role-playing exercises provide concrete exemplars of abstract concepts. Enacting a job assignment conflict between a superior and his or her subordinate helps class members identify messages that exemplify influence strategies.

Samples of role-playing exercises are available in organizational communication textbooks, in teacher's manuals, and in such supplementary texts as *The Role-Play Technique* (Maier, Solem, Maier, 1975) and *Role-playing in Business and Industry* (Corsini, Shaw, & Blake, 1961). Supplementary texts also provide guidelines for planning the exercise, orienting participants to their role, enacting the scenes, and conducting feedback discussions.

The success of a role-playing activity is dependent, in part, on a student's ability to enact the role effectively. Instructor sensitivity to the interpersonal skills of class members aids in matching participants to role-playing demands, thus promoting a successful performance. Repeated practice also reduces the tendency to overact, as well as the anxiety of performing. In evaluating role playing, teachers tend to focus on a student's performance, which often has little relationship to the ultimate goal of the exercise. Rather than center on performance, the instructor might ask students to write reaction papers that apply course concepts to the appropriateness of the interaction. In addition, several students might observe and record communicative behaviors and make presentations on their findings to the class.

Simulations

Organizational simulations increase the complexity, sophistication, and involvement of students by immersing them in an organization-like setting. In a simulation, unlike in role playing, the entire organization is created in the classroom; students are assigned to particular organizational positions and asked to execute routine tasks. Students receive job descriptions, but they do not enact a scenario as they do in role playing. Role occupants bring their own personalities and capabilities to the organizational setting.

Organizational simulations may be highly structured, such as HI FLI FIREWORKS (Pacanowsky, Faraco, Monge, & Russell, 1977) and SIM-CORP (Lederman & Stewart, 1983), or they may rely on participants to create the structure, job functions, job design, rules, regulations, and evaluation process, as exemplified in THE INSTITUTE FOR COMMU-NICATION IMPROVEMENT (James & Smilowitz, 1984) and in GROUP DYNAMICS INCORPORATED (Bormann, 1975). The types of organizations simulated by classes range from product-based manufacturing firms (Pacanowsky et al., 1977) to providing products and services for real-world clients (for example, producing Christmas stockings stuffed with candy for a YMCA bazaar) to teaching the communication class (Baxter & Clark, 1982; Bormann, 1975). Simulations require varying amounts of theoretical background and class time. For example, HI FLI FIREWORKS may run for as short as 90 minutes and begin in the third or fourth week of the semester. In contrast, SIMCORP is designed for advanced students who participate in the simulation for the entire semester or for at least 8 weeks.

Students find the initial stages of the simulation confusing and anxiety-ridden. As they negotiate their roles and learn what fellow employees expect of them, anxiety is reduced and commitment to the organization increases. Commitment typically reaches its peak when an organizational crisis occurs or a conflict breaks out between work units or departments. Simulations require instructors to commit considerable time and effort before the activity begins, but while the simulation is running, the instructor typically assumes a passive role, allowing events to unfold naturally. In the debriefing, the instructor must manage emotional reactions triggered by the simulation, keep discussions of member behaviors at a descriptive rather than an evaluative level, guide discussions to the source of problems, and analyze the strengths and weaknesses of the corporation by applying course concepts.

Evaluation of student involvement in the simulation should be commensurate with the time and effort devoted to the project. Many simulations culminate with a major research paper that applies course concepts to organizational events. Students might also keep dairies or daily logs as a resource for class discussions and preparation of papers (Elsea, 1980). In some instances, the organizational performance of each student is evaluated. For example, in SIMCORP, supervisors and employees conduct routine and summary performance appraisals in addition to the teacher keeping a separate record of student contributions to the simulation (Lederman & Stewart, 1983).

Even though the work involved in conducting an organizational simulation is great, students receive invaluable learning through sharing common experiences, becoming aware of the complexities and subtleties of organizing, wedding communication and organizational theory to practice, and improving critical thinking and communication skills. Simulations also offer opportunities for students to experiment with different communication strategies and to examine dyadic and small group communication within an organizational framework (Lederman & Stewart, 1983).

CONCLUSION

Approximately 80% of our adult lives is spent working in and interfacing with organizations. Whether we are in positions of management or are managed by others, communication is vital to member satisfaction and organizational effectiveness. An organization is not some mysterious entity that acts in a uniform manner; it consists of the coordinated activities of its members. These activities are defined by the messages, information processing, symbols, and communication patterns of its participants. Communication, then, is not only vital to managerial effectiveness and organizational productivity, it is also the basis for understanding how individuals form a collectivity.

As teachers of organizational communication, we have the responsibility to incorporate broad-based views of communication in organizations and to provide students with diverse ways of observing organizational reality. Through applying theory and concepts to experiential activities, instructors create a learning environment in which multiple perspectives of organizational reality emerge. Courses in organizational communication, then, should help students understand "how [communication] creates and solves problems, how it makes some situations occur and prevents others [from taking place], how it makes some outcomes more probable and others" less ostensible (Conrad, 1985, p. 5).

REFERENCES

Apple, C. (1986, April) *The case study method of instruction: Achieving competency in the organizational communication classroom.* Paper presented at the annual convention of the Central States Speech Association, Cincinnati, OH.
Aupperle, K. E., Acar, W., & Booth, D. E. (1986). An empirical critique of *In Search of*

Excellence: How excellent are the excellent companies? *Journal of Management, 12,* 499–512.

Baxter, C., & Clark, T. D. (1982). My favorite assignment: Putting organizational and interpersonal communication theory into practice: Classroom committees. *American Business Communication Association Bulletin, 45*(3), 38–41.

Bormann, E. G. (1975). *Discussion and group methods: Theory and practice* (2nd ed.). New York: Harper & Row.

Bosustow, S. (Producer). (1975). *The Mitt Mittle Series: Films for managers, supervisors & trainers* [Film]. Santa Monica, CA: Stephen Bosustow Productions.

Case studies in organizational communication. (1975). New York: Industrial Communication Council and Towers, Perrin, Forster & Crosby.

Conrad, C. (1985). *Strategic organizational communication: Cultures, situations, and adaptation.* New York: Holt, Rinehart & Winston.

Corsini, R. J. Shaw M. E. & Blake. R. R. (1961). *Roleplaying in business and industry.* Glencoe, IL: Free Press.

Daft, R. L., & Dahlen, K. M. (1984). *Organizational theory: Cases and application.* St. Paul, MN: West.

Daniels, T. D., & Spiker, B. K. (1987). *Perspectives on organizational communication.* Dubuque, IA: William C. Brown.

Ekdom, L. V., & Trujillo, N. (1989). *Organizational life on television.* Norwood, NJ: Ablex.

Elsea, K. J. (1980, November). *Doing communication in the "real world": Strategies for teaching non-traditional students.* Paper presented at the annual convention of the Speech Communication Association, New York.

Falcione, R. L. (1977). Some instructional strategies in the teaching of organizational communication. *Journal of Business Communication, 14,* 22–34.

Farace, R. V., Monge, P. R., & Russell, H. M. (1977). *Communicating and organizing.* Reading, MA: Addison-Wesley.

Fisher, R., & Ury, W. (1981). *Getting to yes.* New York: Penguin Books.

Frost, P. J., Mitchell, Y. F., & Nord, W. R. (Eds.). (1985). *Organizational reality: Reports from the firing line* (3rd ed.). Glenview, IL: Scott, Foresman.

Goldhaber, G. M. (1986). *Organizational communication* (4th ed.). Dubuque, IA: William C. Brown.

Greenberger, E., Steinberg, L. D., Vaux, A., & McAuliffe, S. (1980). Adolescents who work: Effects of part-time employment on family and peer relations. *Journal of Youth and Adolescence, 9,* 189–202.

Hawkins, B. L., & Preston, P. (1981). *Managerial communication.* Santa Monica, CA: Goodyear Publishing.

Heller, J. (1962). *Catch-22.* New York: Ballantine.

Heller, J. (1975). *Something happened.* New York: Ballantine.

Husband, R. L., & Helmer, J. E. (1984, November). *Building a context of experience: Communication audits to teach communication concepts.* Paper presented at the annual convention of the Speech Communication Association, Chicago.

Jablin, F. M. (1983, May). *Teaching the undergraduate organizational communication course.* Paper presented at the annual convention of the International Communication Association, Dallas TX.

Jablin, F. M. (1987). Organizational entry, assimilation, and exit. In F. M. Jablin, L. L. Putnam, K. H. Roberts, & L. W. Porter (Eds.), *Handbook of organizational communication: An interdisciplinary perspective* (pp. 679–740). Newbury Park, CA: Sage.

James, A., & Smilowitz, M. (1984, May). *Organizational communication theory and practice: Courses in the undergraduate curriculum.* Paper presented at the annual convention of the International Communication Association, San Francisco CA.

Johnson, B. M. (1977). *Communication: The process of organizing.* Boston: Allyn and Bacon.

Kanter, R. M. (1977). *Men and women of the corporation.* New York: Basic Books.

Kreps, G. L. (1986). *Organizational communication: Theory and practice.* New York: Longman.

Kreps, G. L., & Lederman, L. C. (1985). Using the case method in organizational communication education: Developing students' insight, knowledge, and creativity through experience-based learning and systematic debriefing. *Communication Education, 34,* 358–364.

Kidder, T. (1981). *The soul of a new machine.* New York: Avon Books.

Lederman, L. C., & Stewart, L. P. (1983). *The SIMCORP SIMULATION participant's manual.* Princeton, NJ: Total Research Corporation.

Maier, N. R. F., Solem, A. R., & Maier, A. A. (1975). *The role-play technique: A handbook for management and leadership practice.* La Jolla, CA: University Associates.

Mier, D. R. (1982). From concepts to practice: Student case study work in organizational communication. *Communication Education, 31,* 151–154.

Miller, A. (1976). *Death of a salesman.* New York: Penguin Books.

Pacanowsky, M., Farace, R. V., Monge, P. R., & Russell, H. M. (1977). *Instructor's guide to accompany communicating and organizing.* Reading, MA: Addison-Wesley.

Pace, R. W. (1977). Experiential approach to teaching organizational communication. *Journal of Business Communication, 14,* 37–47.

Pace, R. W. (1983). *Organizational communication: Foundations for human resource development.* Englewood Cliffs, NJ: Prentice-Hall.

Pace, R. W., & Ross, R. F. (1983). The basic course in organizational communication. *Communication Education, 32,* 402–412.

Peters, T. J., & Waterman, R. H. (1982). *In search of excellence.* New York: Harper & Row.

Putnam, L. L., & Cheney, G. (1985). Organizational communication: Historical development and future directions. In T. W. Benson (Ed.), *Speech communication in the 20th Century* (pp. 130–156). Carbondale, IL: Southern Illinois University Press.

Redding, W. C. (1972). *Communication within the organization: An interpretive review of theory and research.* New York: Industrial Communication Council.

Redding, W. C. (1984). *The corporate manager's guide to better communication.* Glenview, IL: Scott, Foresman.

Redding, W. C. (1989). Organizational communication. In E. Barnouw (Ed.), *International encyclopedia of communications* (Vol. 3, pp. 236–239). New York: Oxford University Press.

Ritti, R. R., & Funkhouser, G. R. (1977). *The ropes to skip and the ropes to know.* Columbus, OH: Grid.

Rogers, E. M., & Agarwala-Rogers, R. (1976). *Communication in organizations.* New York: Free Press.

Sexton, R., & Staudt, V. (1959). Business communication: A survey of the literature. *Journal of Social Psychology, 50,* 101–118.

Shockley-Zalabak, P. (1988). *Fundamentals of organizational communication.* New York: Longman.

Sitkin, S. B. (in press). Secrecy norms in organizational settings. In L. D. Browning (Ed.), *Conceptual frontiers in organizational communication.* White Plains, NY: Longview.

Staley, C. C., & Shockley-Zalabak, P. (1985). Identifying communication competencies for the undergraduate organizational communication series. *Communication Education, 34,* 156–161.

Sypher, B. D. (in press). *Case studies in organizational communication.* New York: Guilford.

Terkel, S. (1972). *Working.* New York: Avon.

Visions '80 Series [film] (1972–1978). Del Mar, CA: CRM/McGraw Hill.

Who's excellent now? (1984, November 5). *Business Week,* pp. 76–86.

10

Teaching Nonverbal Communication

Mark L. Knapp
University of Texas at Austin

When Julius Fast's bestseller *Body Language* hit America's bookstores in 1970, you could count on one hand the number of college and university courses entirely devoted to the subject of nonverbal communication.[1] In less than 20 years, this course has become a staple curricular offering in most departments of communication. Similar courses are frequently offered in anthropology, linguistics, and psychology. Today, textbooks written for the introductory or basic courses in the field of communication—especially those in interpersonal communication—routinely include at least one chapter on nonverbal communication that can be used as the foundation for several class periods devoted to the subject. Thus, in today's communication curriculum, it is common for students—particularly communication majors—who take semester-long courses in nonverbal communication to enter it with some basic understandings and exposure to the area. Nonverbal communication is so integral to modern communication education, it is hard to imagine that time, not so long ago, when such courses did not exist.

---

[1]As Harrison, Cohen, Crouch, Genova, and Steinberg (1972) noted, there was a dramatic increase in the published literature about nonverbal communication during the early 1970s—in the popular marketplace, in professional books, and in textbooks. Fast's book was only one source of influence that predated the rapid growth of courses devoted to nonverbal communication. Because it was a bestseller, however, it no doubt had a significant effect on public recognition and demand—often an important requirement for rapid course growth.

I remember it vividly. I had been teaching a survey course called "Approaches to the Study of Communication" for several years in the late 1960s. It was an ancestor of what we now call "interpersonal communication" and was guided by the literature of that time, which focused primarily on psychological constructs and verbal behavior. In response to the research findings I presented in my lectures, students regularly raised questions based on the logic and experience of their everyday living: "Wouldn't the effect of feedback change depending on the speaker's tone of voice?" "Doesn't the way a person dresses have as much influence on credibility as what the person says?" My standard reply to these and other questions was: "Yes, well, you may be right, but I'm not sure anyone has studied that specific question. I'll see if I can find anything." These student inquiries resulted in my accumulating a sufficiently large body of scholarly literature to publish a textbook (Knapp, 1972) that summarized the literature and served as a resource for teachers who wanted to design a separate course in nonverbal communication.

I provide the preceding historical account of the origins of my own professional interest in this area because I believe it serves as an important reminder that it was questions about verbal behavior that eventually led to the development of my separate course focusing on nonverbal communication. Thus, I repeatedly remind my students that a separate course in nonverbal communication should not discourage questions about how verbal behavior interrelates with nonverbal behavior. And I incorporate this perspective into my lectures. I describe myself as a student of human communication, not merely a student of nonverbal communication. There is probably pedagogical value in studying pieces of the process of human interaction separately, but this value is lost if it discourages students from trying to restore the parts of the whole during their development in this course.

GOALS

Like any course, there are many ways to teach nonverbal communication. I try herein to point out options and alternatives, but because *I* was asked to write this chapter, my own biases predominate. One of the first considerations for an instructor in this course is to carefully identify the nature of the subject matter to be covered in the course. The term *nonverbal* attracts students who have a wide range of expectations for course content. To the speech pathology major, a nonverbal child is one who does not have the ability to use any meaningful oral language (Cole & Cole, 1981, see chap. 6). Broadcasting students may be interested in learning about nonverbal messages related to camera angles, whereas marketing and advertising students may be seeking a greater understanding of color and packaging for print media (Hecker & Stewart, 1988). Some students will ask whether you intend to cover animal communication (Sebeok, 1968). The nonverbal literature is equally diverse—ranging from the study of movement in dance (Hutchinson, 1970) to an analysis of Nazi marching (Bosmajian, 1971). As a rule, I do not deal with any of the preceding areas in the class—although I often try to find sources for students who want to read in an area not covered in the course.

My course in nonverbal communication focuses on "normal" human beings (usually adult) and the process of human interaction (usually face-to-face). There are many goals appropriate to this course, but the following five are especially important for the course as I teach it:

1. Students should leave the course with an understanding of the history of nonverbal study (Davis, 1979; Harrison & Knapp, 1972; Knapp, 1978). For many students, this is the only course they will ever take in this area. As such, they should know how the area developed and who are the key figures associated with the major theoretical formulations and research areas.

2. Students should leave the course with an understanding of the major theoretical perspectives associated with nonverbal studies, as well as facts derived from research associated with these perspectives.

3. Students should leave the course with an understanding of how nonverbal communication functions with verbal communication. As noted earlier, I try to emphasize these interrelationships throughout the course (e.g., Aguilera, 1967; Furnham, Trevethan, & Gaskell, 1981; Kendon, 1983; Krauss, Apple, Morency, Wenzel, & Winton, 1981; Leathers, 1979; Scherer, 1980).

4. Students should leave the course with an understanding of how research knowledge can be applied to various spheres of everyday living—for example, the judicial process (Pryor & Buchanan, 1984; Starr & McCormick, 1985, chaps. 11, 12, & 13); management, sales, and business operations (Cooper, 1979; Heilman & Saruwatari, 1979; McCaskey, 1979); the classroom (Galloway, 1979; Woolfolk & Brooks, 1983); the political process (Tiemens, 1978); and the development of relationships (Knapp, 1983).

5. Students should leave the course with an understanding of how to analyze their own nonverbal skills and those of others. Although my course does not emphasize skill development, it is not ignored. Throughout the course, opportunities are provided for working on encoding and decoding skills. Most of these are nongraded exercises, but one of my exams requires students to accurately decode slides that depict various posed facial expressions of emotion.

SETTING EXPECTATIONS IN OPENING SESSIONS

The opening sessions of any course try to address expected student questions and set the expectations for the course. Topics covered, assignments, grading policy, classroom procedures, time apportioned for lectures and discussion, and various "bookkeeping" matters (such as office hours) are common. There are six additional concerns that are particularly important for instructors of courses in nonverbal communication to address:

1. Normally, the first session of a course is a time when instructors can introduce themselves—indicating what kind of teacher they will be. For the nonverbal course, students will be assessing the instructor in ways that are related to the course—for example, does the instructor show a sensitivity to his or her own nonverbal signals? Is the instructor sensitive to student nonverbal messages? Can I learn anything by imitating my instructor? In short, is the instructor a credible source in this area? There are many ways to address this issue the first day—using your own nonverbal behavior as examples to discuss, talking about the classroom environment as it may affect learning, and so on. Although the first days are crucial in setting initial expectations for the instructor's abilities in this area, the process continues throughout the duration of the course.

2. The opening sessions of this course should also address the issue of *importance*. Although this is a standard topic for many courses, it is especially critical for nonverbal communication, because the "importance" may not be as obvious for this course as it is for other areas. When describing communication events, it is common for the participants to focus on the verbal transaction. The subtlety and indirect nature of many nonverbal signals often masks their importance. Therefore, I use the Two Men Talking exercise described in Harrison's *Beyond Words* (1974). This exercise shows students not only how many decisions they make about others based on nonverbal signals, but how the important these decisions are. With this exercise, the instructor can elicit student perceptions of honesty, confidence, trust, liking, and status, based wholly on nonverbal signals. These judgments are the substance of interpersonal life, and they help to determine not only how we get along, but also whether we even get together with other people.

3. I also use the Two Men Talking exercise to make another point that represents a crucial perspective for the entire course—the multimeaning capacity of nonverbal signals. Students tend to assume that a particular nonverbal signal means one thing and one thing only. When I ask students to write down *the* meaning of the word "fast," many start to write and then look up and ask me *which* meaning I want; when students are

asked to write down what it means when somebody doesn't look at you, many of them will not ask for a context to clarify the meaning I am seeking. Instructors have to use particular caution in this area. For example, if you report a study in which liars tended to look away from their questioners more than when telling the truth, some students will interpret this to mean that in conditions where telling the truth is salient, "looking away" can *only* mean the person is lying. Or, when an instructor tells a student to look at his or her interaction partner because it shows attention, the student may assume that looking at a person means attention—regardless of other contextual and co-occurring signals. Just like verbal behavior, nonverbal behavior has the potential to "mean" anything   depending on the configuration of behaviors, people, and circumstances. Although it is important to emphasize the multimeaning capacity of nonverbal signals early in the course, it is an issue that will raise its ugly head many times throughout the course.

Another "meaning" issue that commonly arises during the course concerns stereotyped meaning versus idiosyncratic meanings. Much research in this area focuses on public settings and people who do not know each other well. As a result, many of the findings do not account for the specialized meanings that people in close relationships and in private settings may attribute to similar behaviors. For example, students usually point out that the cluster of nonverbal signals associated with "liking" (Mehrabian, 1972) may or may not appear when communicating "liking" in close relationships (Anderson, 1985; Knapp, 1983).

4. The first days of class are also good times to explain to students the potential problems involved in using nontechnical language to explain the nature of nonverbal signals. At present, we don't have an adequate technical vocabulary for all the behaviors that will be discussed in this course, but this should not prevent instructors from using more precise language to distinguish smile$_1$ from smile$_2$ and glance$_1$ from glance$_2$, and so on. Although this kind of precision may seem tedious, it helps to ensure a referent that students and instructor share while simultaneously communicating the complexity involved in perceiving and analyzing nonverbal behavior.

5. Most textbooks for this course point out that the research findings reported in the book are limited to the United States—unless specifically stated otherwise. This qualification is most appropriate, but what these books don't usually say, and what instructors would be well advised to point out early in the course, is that it is equally dangerous to assume that the research findings recounted in their text are applicable to everyone in the United States. The group to which these research findings have the most applicability is White, middle-class, college students attending the country's larger universities. And, as I indicated earlier, the

findings apply primarily to interactions between people from this group who do not have very close relationships. There are, of course, other age groups (Blurton-Jones, 1972; Carmichael & Knapp, 1988; Feldman, 1982; McGrew, 1972) and ethnic groups (Halberstadt, 1985) and relationships (Knapp, 1983) studied, but the resources are not plentiful, and instructors need to be careful not to overgeneralize and to be open to student input concerning other patterns of behavior that may be typical of other groups within this culture.

6. There are two student attitudes about the controllability of nonverbal behavior that instructors should try to defuse early in the course. In both cases, students believe that we have very little control over our own nonverbal behavior. In the first instance, students are highly motivated to learn how to "read" another person's nonverbal signals because it will give them power. It is *the* key to success, because nobody can fool you. Students with this orientation (and there are many) will typically come up after the first day of class and ask how I am able to deal with this ability to know what everyone is thinking. The questioners are understandably nervous and awkward when asking the question, because they believe that I am somehow looking into their very soul as we talk. For these students, I point out that in any learning endeavor, the knowledge gained is inevitably incomplete. In the nonverbal area, this occurs for a variety of reasons, including: (a) assuming our senses could pick up all information desired, the nature of human interaction is such that it places constraints on what information is available to us; (b) we probably don't want to process some information so we deliberately shut it out; and (c) our interaction partners may also not want us to pick up certain information, so they try to hide or mask it.

In response to the "nonverbal behavior tells all" perspective, I point out that in recent years behavioral scientists have spent a lot of time and energy trying to identify the behaviors exhibited by liars (Ekman, 1985), but once this information is made public and brought to the awareness of liars, they'd have to be crazy not to try to change their behavior. And if that isn't enough, I point out that we've been studying persuasion for over 2,000 years, but even the best persuaders don't know how to get others to do what they want all the time. Similarly, there are some people who are better communicators because they have developed their skills in sending and receiving nonverbal signals—but even these people are not capable, not interested in, reading everything about another person. Finally, to encourage them, I point out that once they have improved their skill level and knowledge, they will not have total power over others but they will have the option of using some skills they don't currently have—skills that can make a significant difference in their lives.

The other student attitude associated with the controllability of nonverbal signals assumes that it is futile to try to learn anything about them because they can't be changed. This student typically views the course as "nothing new" or "common sense," but his or her common sense is often not sufficient to get a passing grade in the course. Unlike the other students, who eagerly come up to talk about your prowess in this area, these students do not identify themselves, and, thus, it is difficult to disarm these perceptions. In the absence of individual contact, instructors should make a point of using examples early in the course that are clearly not common sense and examples of people who have, with difficulty, changed nonverbal behavior for their benefit.

INSTRUCTIONAL STRATEGIES

Organization and Sequencing

One of the primary decisions about the organization of this course has to do with whether it will be organized around how nonverbal signals function in achieving several common outcomes sought by communicators (e.g., communicating identity; communicating our relationship to others; achieving accuracy/understanding; managing the interaction; influencing others and ourself; and communicating feelings and emotions) or whether it should be organized around the various signalling systems themselves (e.g., eye gaze behavior; vocal behavior, touching behavior; gestural behavior; etc.) Nonverbal textbooks and nonverbal research were originally classified by body parts, but now most textbooks try to combine both orientations.

I try to combine both approaches in my course. The first part of the semester is spent examining the theory and research associated with various individual "channels" of communication, and the second half of the semester covers the outcomes that have received the most multichannel research attention. Specifically, the course is composed of six units— as shown in Fig. 10.1.

The first unit introduces students to concepts such as classifications, history, importance, and conflicting cues and helps prepare students for observational assignments by examining the process of observing. The second unit addresses environmental factors that may affect the communication situation. The third unit looks specifically at the communicators per se—generally emphasizing nonmovement matters like physical appearance, dress, and color. The next unit, the longest, examines communicator behavior in various forms: proxemics, facial expressions, touching behavior, eye gaze, nodding, and vocal signals. The fifth unit focuses on multichannel perspectives. Topics may vary, but identity issues are

NONVERBAL COMMUNICATION

Professor's Name   Semester
TA's Name   Course Number
                                                                        Time & Location
Textbook:

AN INTRODUCTION TO THE STUDY OF NONVERBAL COMMUNICATION: UNIT I

Week 1-   Orientation; Plan of the Course; Assignments; First-Day Rituals; Overhead
           Surprise; Films Introducing the Area.
Week 2-   Basic Perspectives: Concepts, Definitions, Classifications, History.
Week 3   Basic Perspectives. Interrelationships of Verbal and Nonverbal Communication;
           Conflicting Cues; The Process of Observation.

THE COMMUNICATION ENVIRONMENT: UNIT II

Week 4-   Environmental Factors

THE COMMUNICATORS: UNIT III

Week 5-   Physical Appearance, Odor, & Dress

THE COMMUNICATOR'S BEHAVIOR: UNIT IV

Week 6-   Proxemics: Film, "Invisible Walls"
Week 7-   Examination #1; Facial Expressions of Emotion; Slides, Diagnostic Test; Film:
           "What's In a Face?"
Week 8-   Touching Behavior; Nodding Behavior
Week 9-   Eye Behavior
Week 10-   Vocal Signals; Examination #2

THE COMMUNICATOR'S BEHAVIOR: MULTICHANNEL PERSPECTIVES: UNIT V

Week 11-   Body Movement & Gestures: Lying & Deception; Relationship Development &
           Equilibrium theory
Week 12-   Body Movement & Gestures: Turn-Taking; Gender Signals

ACQUIRING & USING NONVERBAL BEHAVIOR: UNIT VI

Week 13-   Developmental Perspectives; Phylogeny and Ontogeny
Week 14-   Ability to Send and Receive Nonverbal Signals: Your Social Intelligence Quotient;
           Emotional Charades
Week 15-   Examination #3

FIG. 10.1.   Sample syllabus for a course in nonverbal communication.

covered during periods devoted to gender; interaction management specifically focuses on turn-taking; at least one session deals with how we
communicate our relationship to others; and I use lying and deception as
a topic relevant to the goal of influencing others and self. Achieving
accuracy and understanding is emphasized earlier in the course during
the session on incongruent cues, whereas communicating emotions is the
focus of the class periods devoted to analysis of facial expressions. The
last unit of the course deals with the process of developing nonverbal
behaviors and the process of refining skills.

Size of Class

There is nothing inherent in the subject matter that would determine class size. I regularly teach the course with nearly 300 students, but I have taught it with 30 students as well. The differences are differences associated with any large or small class: With classes over 100, you should have an auditorium with the capacity to show slides, films, videotapes, and so on, which are easily and clearly visible to all students; a teaching assistant may be needed to grade papers and to share the student counseling load; the exams in the large class are more likely to be limited to "objective" tests; the assignments are more likely to be those that can be easily graded; and the class exercises will have to be altered. It is still possible, though more difficult, to obtain quality comments and class interaction in a large class, and this depends largely on the talents, experience, and subject matter knowledge of the instructor. New instructors should be encouraged to teach smaller classes if possible.

Outside Assignments

I normally have three types of outside class assignments: term papers, group reports, and guided observation reports. Term papers and group reports are more likely to be assigned when class size is smaller; outside observation assignments can be done with any size class. Each assignment, however, should include some observation. This helps the student blend library research with actual data collection and to learn the analytic thinking involved in understanding methods of gathering data and reporting results. Topics for term papers may go beyond the topics discussed in class, but group reports are normally used to give students a chance to learn and present material that would otherwise be presented by the instructor—material central to the course. I sometimes chide students by telling them that this is their chance to show me how teaching should be done.

For my class of 300, I normally have four outside observation exercises that are designed to provide each class member with some data that is pertinent to the theory and research in my lecture for that day. Although each student has done the same assignment, there are many differences in what they observed. These differences in observations provide an excellent foundation for discussing why such differences occurred. These observation assignments are effective in providing active participation in a relevant, "real-life" learning experience. Assignments I have used in recent years include: turn-taking, touching, eye behavior, the environment, and nodding. Because it is impossible for the instructor to grade these assignments on "correctness," they are instead graded on com-

OUTSIDE ASSIGNMENT #3   Instructor
NONVERBAL COMMUNICATION: Eye Behavior   Course Number

1. Due Date
2. During a conversation with another person, look directly at them (do not look away) <u>for two
    minutes</u>. If the other person looks away, just continue looking at their head so when they
    return their eyes toward you, your eyes will be looking directly at their eyes. Otherwise, try to
    conduct the conversation as you normally would. Describe what happened.
    a. Your reactions and behavior:
    b. Your partner's reactions and behavior:
3. During a conversation with another person (not the same person you talked to in #2 above) avoid
    looking at the person <u>for two minutes</u>. If the other person tries to look at you, continue to look away.
    Otherwise, try to conduct the conversation as you normally would. Describe what happened.
    a. Your reactions and behavior:
    b. Your partner's reactions and behavior:
4. Watch people's eye behavior in conversation. When you find someone who seems to be looking
    more than you consider normal, try to find out why. You may talk to the person if you think it
    would help clarify things.
5. Watch people's eye behavior in conversation. When you find someone who seems to be avoiding
    eye contact more than you would consider normal, try to find out why. You may talk to the
    person if you think it would help clarify things.

Observer's Name: _____
                                    (print)

FIG. 10.2.   Example of an outside observation assignment dealing with eye behavior.

pleteness and whether they are turned in on time. Figure 10.2 provides
an example of an outside observation assignment dealing with eye
behavior.

Readings

Most readings in my course are from the textbook. With smaller classes,
however, extra readings can be assigned if desired. These readings will
vary with each instructor's needs, but the main issues regarding selection
revolve around technical quality and interest factors. Readings that are
interesting as well as technically accurate are, of course, first priority.
There is plenty of popular literature in this area that is misleading and
inaccurate but easy and fun to read; similarly, there are some exquisitely
precise studies of microscopic behavior that don't do a very good job of
holding the attention of undergraduate students. Like any course, the
readings selected for the course become a part of the course image—for
both students and outsiders.

In-Class Exercises

Fortunately, instructor's manuals for the textbooks on nonverbal communication have many exercises to choose from. These exercises are de-

signed to illustrate a point and provide a memorable learning experience while at the same time keeping the focus on the substance, not the activity itself. Generally, I try not to have too many exercises, because I think it may detract from the intellectual focus of the course. There are eight in-class exercises that I've found to be very useful for illustrating concepts. Three of these exercises are found in the instructor's manual for my textbook, *Nonverbal Communication in Human Interaction* (Knapp, 1978) and are called: "Back Me Up If You Can" (proxemics); "The Unusual Interview" (eye behavior); and "Emotional Charades" (sending and receiving ability). Harrison's (1974) "Two Men Talking" is also in my instructor's manual as well as in Harrison's book. This is the "Overhead Surprise" listed earlier in Fig. 10.1 (during week 1). For the session on "lying" behavior, I have students reenact the old television show "To Tell the Truth," in which four panelists are quizzed about something they all claim to have done, but that only one has actually done. The entire class then votes on who they think is telling the truth, and the discussion centers around the reasons for everyone's choice. The gender lecture is preceded by a panel discussion between four students who are all blindfolded. Prior to the discussion, however, one male student is asked to engage in nonverbal behavior which is stereotypical of females; one female student is asked to portray stereotypical male nonverbal behavior. Each of the role players is seated next to a person who is told only to act naturally. Thus, observers can look for similarities and contrasts between what the students think the other gender does and what at least one member of that gender, on this occasion, actually does. This leads to a sometimes animated discussion of gender stereotypes and provides a worthwhile foundation for a lecture on research and theory in this area. For the session on vocal signals, I play standardized recordings of people ranging in age from 22 to 92 and ask students to guess the person's age; I also have people from five different occupations (one male and one female) count to 10 and then I ask students to guess their occupation. The Social Intelligence Quotient (SIQ) is a videotape that I use in the "skills" unit to provide students with an opportunity to practice what they have learned without the threat of being graded (see Audio-Visual Materials, following).

Resources

Resources for instructors of this course include published articles and books as well as audio-visual materials. It would be impossible to list all important publications in this area, so the focus is on those resources of most value to new instructors—textbooks and summaries of the literature.

Textbooks.   There are, no doubt, other textbooks available for courses in nonverbal communication, but the following list provides a wide range of choices. I tried to select those that seem to be specifically directed at the undergraduate market.

Argyle, M. (1975). *Bodily communication.* New York: International Universities Press.
Benson, T. W., & Frandsen, K. D. (1976). *An orientation to nonverbal communication.* Chicago: Science Research Associates.
Burgoon, J. K., Buller, D. B., & Woodall, W. G. (1989). *Nonverbal communication: The unspoken dialogue.* New York: Harper & Row.
Eisenberg, A. E., & Smith, R. R. (1971). *Nonverbal communication.* Indianapolis: Bobbs-Merrill.
Harrison, R. P. (1974). *Beyond words.* Englewood Cliffs, NJ: Prentice-Hall.
Heslin, R., & Patterson, M. (1982). *Nonverbal behavior and social psychology.* New York: Plenum Press.
Hickson, M. L., & Stacks, D. W. (1985). *Nonverbal communication.* Dubuque, IA: Brown.
Katz, A. M., & Katz, V. T. (Eds.). (1983). *Foundations of nonverbal communication.* Carbondale, IL: Southern Illinois University Press.
Knapp, M. L. (1978). *Nonverbal communication in human interaction.* New York: Holt, Rinehart & Winston.
Knapp, M. L. (1980). *Essentials of nonverbal communication.* New York: Holt, Rinehart & Winston.
LaFrance, M., & Mayo, C. (1978). *Moving bodies.* Monterey, CA: Brooks/Cole.
Leathers, D. G. (1976). *Nonverbal communication systems.* Boston: Allyn & Bacon.
Leathers, D. G. (1986). *Successful nonverbal communication.* New York: Macmillan.
Malandro, L. A., & Barker, L. L. (1983). *Nonverbal communication.* New York: Random House.
Mehrabian, A. (1981). *Silent messages.* Belmont, CA: Wadsworth.
Rosenfeld, L. B., & Civikly, J. M. (1976). *With words unspoken.* New York: Holt, Rinehart & Winston.

Reviews, Summaries, Literature Surveys.   Some of these books could be used as textbooks, but these resources are, with a few exceptions, written for professors and not for undergraduate students.

Burgoon, J. K. (1980). Nonverbal communication research in the 1970s: An Overview. In D. Nimmo (Ed.), *Communication yearbook 4* (pp. 179–197). New Brunswick, NJ: Transaction.
Burgoon, J. K. (1985). Nonverbal signals. In M. L. Knapp & G. R. Miller (Eds.), *Handbook of interpersonal communication* (pp. 344–390). Beverly Hills, CA: Sage.
Bull, P. (1983). *Body movement and interpersonal communication.* New York: Wiley.
Davis, F. (1971). *Inside intuition.* New York: McGraw-Hill.
Druckman, D., Rozelle, R. M., & Baxter, J. C. (1982). *Nonverbal communication: Survey, theory, & research.* Beverly Hills, CA: Sage.
Harper, R. G., Weins, A. N., & Matarazzo, N. J. (1978). *Nonverbal communication: State of the art.* New York: Wiley.
Hinde, R. A. (Ed.). (1972). *Non-verbal communication.* London: Cambridge University Press.
Kendon, A. (Ed.). (1981). *Nonverbal communication, interaction, and gesture.* The Hague: Mouton.

Knapp, M. L., Wiemann, J. M., & Daly, J. A. (1978). Nonverbal communication: Issues and appraisal. *Human Communication Research, 4,* 271–280.

Morris, D. (1985). *Body watching.* New York: Crown.

Morris, D. (1977). *Manwatching.* New York: Abrams.

Morris, D., Collett, P., Marsh, P., & O'Shaughnessy, M. (1983). *Gestures.* New York: Stein & Day.

Patterson, M. (1983). *Nonverbal behavior: A functional perspective.* New York: Springer-Verlag.

Ruesch, J., & Kees, W. (1956). *Nonverbal communication; Notes on the visual perception of human relations.* Berkeley & Los Angeles: University of California Press.

Scherer, K. R., & Ekman, P. (Eds.). (1982). *Handbook of methods in nonverbal behavior research.* New York: Cambridge University Press.

Sebeok, T. W., Hayes, A. S., & Bateson, M. C. (Eds). (1964). *Approaches to semiotics.* The Hague: Mouton

Siegman, A. W., & Feldstein, S. (Eds.). (1985). *Multichannel integrations of nonverbal behavior.* Hillsdale, NJ: Lawrence Erlbaum Associates.

Siegman, A. W., & Feldstein, S. (Eds.). (1978). *Nonverbal behavior and communication.* Hillsdale, NJ: Lawrence Erlbaum Associates.

von Cranach, M., & Vine, I. (Eds.). (1973). *Social communication and movement.* New York: Academic Press.

Weitz, S. (Ed.). (1979). *Nonverbal communication: Readings with commentary.* New York: Oxford University Press.

Wiemann, J. M., & Harrison, R. P. (Eds.). (1983). *Nonverbal interaction.* Beverly Hills, CA: Sage.

Wolfgang, A. (Ed.). (1979). *Nonverbal behavior: Applications and cultural implications.* New York: Academic Press.

Wolfgang, A. (Ed.). (1984). *Nonverbal behavior: Perspectives, applications, and intercultural insights.* New York: Hogrefe.

Instructors of this course will also be able to keep abreast of the field by examining the *Journal of Nonverbal Behavior* as well as journals dealing with anthropology, linguistics, psychology, and communication. Sometimes, special issues are entirely devoted to nonverbal communication—such as the *Journal of Communication,* vol. 22, number 4, December, 1972. The field is gradually becoming more and more specialized, so each subarea of the field may also have books that summarize the literature.

Audio-Visual Materials. In a course so heavily focused on the senses, it is critical that optimum use of audio and visual resources be made. With the availability of video cameras, many instructors will soon be able to make their own visual aids. These videos will be able to show movement—a limitation of slides. Audio tapes are especially useful during discussions of vocal signals. For those who wish to use extant visual aids, I recommend the following. It should be said that these are only a few of the many films and videotapes available for such a course. Useful slides can sometimes be made by taking pictures of photos in books—for example, Ekman & Friesen's *Unmasking the Face* or Morris' *Manwatching.*

*"Invisible Walls" 16mm. 12 minutes. Black & White. (1969). University of California Extension Media Center, Berkeley, CA 94720. Proxemics.

*"Nonverbal Communication." 16mm. 22 minutes. Color. (1976). Harper & Row Media, 2350 Virginia Ave., Hagerstown, MD 21740. Introductory.

*"Communication: The Nonverbal Agenda." 16mm. 30 minutes. Color. (1975). McGraw Hill, CRM, 1221 Avenue of the Americas, New York, NY 10020. Introductory.

*"What's in a Face?" 16mm. 52 minutes. Color. (1974). Time-Life Video, 100 Eisenhower Drive, P.O. Box 644, Parmus, NJ 07652. Facial Expressions.

*"Interpersonal Perception Task (IPT)" Videotape. 35 minutes. 30 video scenes and 30 multiple choice answers. Written and produced by Dane Archer and Mark A. Costanzo. Distributed by the University of California, Santa Cruz, Extension Media Center, Santa Cruz, CA 95604. This is a videotape that can be used for research or as a diagnostic test in class—acting as a foundation for discussing skills in perceiving nonverbal signals. As an adjunct to this videotape, teachers may wish to consult the book that addresses many of the same issues: Archer (1980), which deals with many of the same issues as the videotape.

CONCLUSION

I teach this course every semester, and I eagerly look forward to it every time. Part of it has to do with the interest that students bring to the course. There is something inherently interesting about the subject matter—these subtleties of human interaction—that makes many students eager to learn. When students are eager to learn, professors are eager to provide learning experiences. Another factor that makes this course a favorite of mine is related to the often hidden or subtle nature of the subject matter. There are many times during the course when these little-noticed actions are identified and discussed and an instructor can actually see the "aha" learning experience take place. Seeing that you are having an effect on student learning is the kind of feedback that spurs instructors on. For a variety of reasons, then, this can be a very satisfying course to teach.

The course in nonverbal communication, like some other courses, is also affected by the "teaching–learning paradox." The more we learn about nonverbal communication, the more we need a single course to cover the range and complexity of the information accumulating; but, the more we learn about nonverbal communication, the more we realize how misleading it is to talk about nonverbal behavior without discussing other co-occurring stimuli and responses that are critical to understanding the act of human communication. We deal with this paradox in today's curriculum by showing how nonverbal communication fits into the process during introductory courses and providing students the option to explore the subject in greater depth in a more advance course. My emphasis here has been on the course devoted entirely to nonverbal communication. This information, however, can be used to construct shorter units or to creatively design the course of the future—perhaps a two-semester course that integrates verbal and nonverbal perspectives throughout.

REFERENCES

Aguilera, D. C. (1967). Relationships between physical contact and verbal interaction between nurses and patients. *Journal of Psychiatric Nursing, 5*, 5–21.

Anderson, P. A. (1985). Nonverbal immediacy in interpersonal communication. In A. W. Siegman & S. Feldstein (Eds.), *Multichannel integrations of nonverbal behavior* (pp. 1–36). Hillsdale, NJ: Lawrence Erlbaum Associates.

Archer, D. (1980). *How to expand your SIQ (social intelligence quotient)*. New York: Evans.

Blurton-Jones, N. G. (Ed.). (1972). *Ethological studies of child behavior*. Cambridge: Cambridge University Press.

Bosmajian, H. (Ed.). (1971). *The rhetoric of nonverbal communication*. Glenview, IL: Scott-Foresman.

Burgoon, J. K., Buller, D. B., & Woodall, W. G. (1989). *Nonverbal communication: The unspoken dialogue*. New York: Harper & Row.

Carmichael, C. W., & Knapp, M. L. (1988). Nonverbal aspects of communication and aging. In C. W. Carmichael, C. H. Botan, & R. Hawkins (Eds.), *Human communication and the aging process* (pp. 111–128). Prospect Heights, IL: Waveland Press.

Cole, M. L., & Cole, J. T. (1981). *Effective intervention with the language impaired child*. Rockville, MD: Aspen.

Cooper, K. (1979). *Nonverbal communication for business success*. New York: Amacom.

Davis, M. (1979). The state of the art: Past and present trends in body movement research. In A. Wolfgang (Ed.), *Nonverbal behavior: Applications and cultural implications* (pp. 51–66). New York: Academic Press.

Ekman, P. (1985). *Telling lies*. New York: Norton.

Ekman, P., & Friesen, W. V. (1975). *Unmasking the face*. Englewood Cliffs, NJ: Prentice-Hall.

Fast, J. (1970). *Body language*. New York: Evans.

Feldman, R. S. (Ed.). (1982). *Development of nonverbal behavior in children*. New York: Springer-Verlag.

Furnham, A., Trevethan, R., & Gaskell, G. (1981). The relative contribution of verbal, vocal, and visual channels to person perception: Experiment and critique. *Semiotica, 37*, 39–57.

Galloway, C. M. (1979). Teaching and nonverbal behavior. In A. Wolfgang (Ed.), *Nonverbal behavior: Applications and cultural implications* (pp. 197–207). New York: Academic Press.

Halberstadt, A. G. (1985). Race, socioeconomic status and nonverbal behavior. In A. W. Siegman & S. Feldstein (Eds.), *Multichannel integrations of nonverbal behavior* (pp. 227–266). Hillsdale, NJ: Lawrence Erlbaum Associates.

Harrison, R. P. (1974). *Beyond words*. Englewood Cliffs, NJ: Prentice-Hall.

Harrison, R. P., & Knapp, M. L. (1972). Toward an understanding of nonverbal communication systems. *Journal of Communication, 22*, 339–352.

Harrison, R. P., Cohen, A. A., Crouch, W. W., Genova, B. K. L., & Steinberg, M. (1972). The nonverbal communication literature. *Journal of Communication, 22*, 460–76.

Hecker, S., & Stewart, D. W. (Eds.). (1988). *Nonverbal communication in advertising*. Lexington, MA: Lexington/D. C. Heath.

Heilman, M. E., & Saruwatari, L. F. (1979). When beauty is beastly: The effects of appearance and sex on evaluations of job applicants for managerial and nonmanagerial jobs. *Organizational Behavior and Human Performance, 22*, 360–372.

Hutchinson, A. (1970). *Labanotation: The system of analyzing and recording movement.* New York: Theatre Arts Books.

Kendon, A. (1983). Gesture and speech: How they interact. In J. M. Wiemann & R. P. Harrison (Eds.), *Nonverbal interaction* (pp. 13–45). Beverly Hills, CA: Sage.

Knapp, M. L. (1972). *Nonverbal communication in human interaction.* New York: Holt, Rinehart & Winston.

Knapp, M. L. (1978). *Nonverbal communication in human interaction* (2nd ed.). New York: Holt, Rinehart & Winston.

Knapp, M. L. (1980). *Essentials of nonverbal communication.* New York: Holt, Rinehart & Winston.

Knapp, M. L. (1983). Dyadic relationship development. In J. M. Wiemann & R. P. Harrison (Eds.), *Nonverbal interaction.* Beverly Hills, CA: Sage.

Krauss, R. M., Apple, W., Morency, N., Wenzel, C., & Winton, W. (1981). Verbal, vocal, and visible factors in judgments of another's affect. *Journal of Personality and Social Psychology, 40*, 312–320.

Leathers, D. G. (1979). The impact of multichannel message inconsistency on verbal and nonverbal decoding behaviors. *Communication Monographs, 46*, 88–100.

McCaskey, M. B. (1979). The hidden messages managers send. *Harvard Business Review,* November–December, 137–48.

McGrew, W. C. (1972). *An ethological study of children's behavior.* New York: Academic Press.

Mehrabian, A. (1972). *Nonverbal communication.* Chicago: Aldine.

Morris, D. (1977). *Manwatching.* New York: Abrams.

Pryor, B., & Buchanan, R. W. (1984). The effects of a defendant's demeanor on juror perceptions of credibility and guilt. *Journal of Communication, 34*, 92–99.

Scherer, K. R. (1980). The functions of nonverbal signs in conversation. In R. N. St. Clair & H. Giles (Eds.), *The social and psychological contexts of language.* Hillsdale, NJ: Lawrence Erlbaum Associates.

Sebeok, T. A. (Ed.). (1968). *Animal communication.* Bloomington, IN: Indiana University Press.

Starr, V. H., & McCormick, M. (1985). *Jury selection: An attorney's guide to jury law and methods.* Boston: Little, Brown.

Tiemens, R. K. (1978). Television's portrayal of the 1976 presidential debates: An analysis of visual content. *Communication Monographs, 45*, 362–270.

Woolfolk, A. E., & Brooks, D. M. (1983). Nonverbal communication in teaching. In E. W. Gordon (Ed.), *Review of research in education* (Vol. 10, pp. 103–149). Washington, DC: American Educational Research Association.

11

Teaching Intercultural Communication

Young Yun Kim
University of Oklahoma

William B. Gudykunst
California State University, Fullerton

No two individuals are alike. Differences between people compel them to communicate in the first place and make their communication simultaneously challenging and rewarding. As individuals attempt to communicate, they are faced with the inherent problem of interpersonal discrepancy in expressing and understanding. They are encouraged to "fill in" each other's meaning from their respective reservoirs of information. It is only by means of this filling-in activity that they are able to understand each other's messages.

If they have been raised within the same culture, they are likely to share many common denominators that will help them interpret the messages. They may differ or even argue about preferences, but they do understand each other with at least minimum accuracy. Comparatively, individuals from different cultures are faced with a potentially greater problem of understanding each other. Recognition of verbal and nonverbal codes and interpretation of the hidden assumptions underlying the behaviors are likely to be difficult. The common denominator by which they can understand each other's behavior is limited.

From this communication perspective, the significant intercultural differences can be identified as differences in verbal and nonverbal codes, behaviors, and meaning systems. Essentially, the culturally based differences between communicators in codes, behaviors, and meaning systems provide a special context of communication. Here, culture is not limited to the life patterns of conventionally recognizable groups (such as national, ethnic, or racial groups), but is open to all levels of group memberships (e.g., age, gender, occupation, and socioeconomic status) whose life patterns discernibly influence individual behavior and meaning systems. Underlying this perspective is the understanding that all communication is intercultural, and the degree of "interculturalness" of a given communication encounter depends on the degree of heterogeneity between the experiential backgrounds of the participants (cf. Gudykunst & Kim, 1984a; Sarbaugh, 1988/1979).

INTERCULTURAL COMMUNICATION AS AN AREA OF STUDY

Awareness of intercultural differences is growing in the United States and in all parts of the world. The need for creative pluralism across and within nations and for promoting peace among linguistic, religious, racial, ethnic, and political groups is intensifying. This need reflects the increasing connectedness of human groups and the necessity to promote peace and ease tension among groups as they daily confront each other's assumptions, ideas, and actions.

The intercultural reality of world societies has elevated intercultural communication to a topic of significant academic merit. Intercultural communication began to grow as an area of study in the 1960s and 1970s. It was, and still is, the need to meet practical intercultural problems that generated many educational programs. Training courses have been developed, for example, to provide answers to problems of intercultural encounters of overseas government agencies, business persons, international students, Peace Corps volunteers, immigrants, missionaries, and individuals of minority groups within societies.

Initial research activities in intercultural communication ranged from reports of highly personalized experiences and observations of limited aspects of communication patterns in different cultures to narrowly focused "fact-finding" pieces of empirical research that were primarily descriptive and atheoretical. Many such studies relied on the formulation of other disciplines, particularly cultural anthropology and cross-cultural psychology. The bulk of the time and energy of intercultural communication researchers was directed toward "intracultural" or "cross-cultural" issues that focused on communication patterns in specific cultures and on cross-cultural comparisons of communication-related phenomena.

As the area of intercultural communication matured and expanded, it moved toward increasing crystallization of its central focus on communication (rather than culture). The pragmatic, problem-oriented beginning grew into a developmental stage that featured conceptual consolidation. A greater emphasis is placed on the importance of viewing intercultural communication as a process that is NOT unique in kind from intracultural communication. This new conceptualization regards the former as differing from the latter only in the degree of heterogeneity of the backgrounds of communicators and, thus, greater unfamiliarity and uncertainty in predicting each other's communication behavior (Gudykunst & Kim, 1984a; Sarbaugh, 1988/1979).

We have also witnessed an increasing depth and integration in theorizing and research activities. The number of publications, research activities, and conference programs within the discipline of communication has grown significantly. Foundations for major research paradigms have been advanced (cf. Gudykunst, 1983; Gudykunst & Kim, 1984b; Kim & Gudykunst, 1988) and a greater emphasis is placed on the interdisciplinary and international integration of studies of intercultural communication. The study of intercultural communication has crossed the boundaries of several of the social sciences as well as the boundaries of many societies. Recent anthologies, such as *Intergroup Communication* (Gudykunst, 1986), *Theories in Intercultural Communication* (Kim & Gudykunst, 1988), *Analyzing Intercultural Communication* (Knapp, Enninger, & Knapp-Potthoff, 1987), and the *Handbook of Intercultural and Development Communication* (Asante & Gudykunst, in press), reflect this interdisciplinary, international integration.

In addition, specialized research topics in intercultural communication have been explored in depth and presented in such books as *Communication, Culture, and Organizational Processes* (Gudykunst, Stewart, & Ting-Toomey, 1985), *Interethnic Communication* (Kim, 1986), *Communication and Cross-Cultural Adaptation: An Integrative Theory* (Kim, 1988), *Cross-Cultural Adaptation: Current Approaches* (Kim & Gudykunst, 1987), and *Culture and Interpersonal Communication* (Gudykunst & Ting-Toomey, in press).

Each of these publications integrate intercultural communication as a solid member of communication science, not an esoteric collection of pieces of information. These efforts, individually and collectively, "push" the field forward in the direction of greater coherence, depth, and rigor. Together, they align the intellectual core of the area of study with the theoretical mainstream of the field of communication at large, while integrating research interests in related social sciences.

ORGANIZING AN INTRODUCTORY COURSE: A MODEL

Intercultural communication has achieved a clear visibility within the study of human behavior, particularly in the field of communication. Accordingly, an increasing number of introductory-level college textbooks (or books used as texts) have become available in recent years (e.g., Brislin, 1981; Condon & Yousef, 1975; Dodd, 1987; Gudykunst & Kim, 1984a; Harrison, 1983; Klopf, 1987; Prosser, 1978/1985; Samovar & Porter, 1976/1988; Samovar, Porter, & Jain, 1981; Sarbaugh, 1979/1988; Singer, 1987). In addition, an increasing number of resource books focus on specific cultures (e.g., Almaney & Alwan, 1982; Asante, 1988; Condon, 1985; Harrison, 1983; Hutchison & Poznanski, 1987; Kapp, 1983; Nydell, 1987; Phillips-Martinsson, 1981), or present theoretical frameworks for comparing many cultures (e.g., Gudykunst & Ting-Toomey, in press; Hall, 1976; Hofstede, 1984).

Because of the complex, interdisciplinary nature of intercultural communication, textbooks vary in specific topics that are introduced and covered. They also vary in the degree to which they utilize empirical research findings and in their theoretical/conceptual groundings for topic selection and organization. Some textbooks take an anthropological approach, placing primary attention on culture and cultural variables without linking them directly to the communication process itself (e.g., Condon & Yousef, 1975; Prosser, 1985/1978). Other textbooks emphasize the role of communication in the process of social/cultural change in "developing" countries (e.g., Dodd, 1987), and some textbooks show a practical or experiential bent (e.g., Klopf, 1987; Singer, 1987).

Finally, there are textbooks that combine a communication focus with an interdisciplinary integration of concepts and research findings (e.g., Gudykunst & Kim, 1984a), extending interpersonal communication theory by taking into consideration cultural and subcultural differences between communicators. This last approach reflects the present authors' approach, and is presented in detail in the following section.

Given the diversity of approaches to teaching, what should an introductory course on intercultural communication cover? We propose here a model for an introductory course by listing key topics and their organization. This model reflects recent trends in the area of intercultural communication discussed previously: (a) the merging of theory, research, and practice, (b) the communication focus, and (c) the interdisciplinary integration. This model closely parallels the organization of the materials presented in the book *Communicating with Strangers: An Approach to Intercultural Communication* (Gudykunst & Kim, 1984a), and, to a lesser extent, *Intercultural Communication: A Reader* (Samovar & Porter, 1988/1976).

Instructional Goal

The model projects an instructional goal that consists of three interrelated dimensions: (a) cognitive learning, (b) affective orientation, and (c) behavioral development. This three-dimensional goal emphasizes a balanced enhancement of students' conceptual understanding of intercultural communication, their attitudes toward cultural differences, and skills required to manage such differences in face-to-face encounters.

Specifically, the cognitive dimension involves increasing students' intellectual knowledge of how the intercultural communication process works, how cultural differences (along with other sources of difference) influence the process, what significant differences exist across cultures (in worldviews, beliefs, values, norms, and verbal and nonverbal communication behaviors), the factors that facilitate or impede intercultural communication effectiveness, and the outcomes of intercultural communication experiences. The affective dimension stresses the importance of heightened sensitivity, empathy, and motivation to facilitate intercultural communication effectiveness. Students are encouraged to accept, and not make hasty ethnocentric value judgments about, different cultural systems (including their own). In this dimension, students are further encouraged to participate emotionally in the experiences of culturally different individuals and to appreciate cultural differences as each culture exhibits unique merits that serve as sources of learning for other cultures. The behavioral dimension attempts to increase student skills for managing interactions with individuals from different cultures. Students learn to adapt their verbal and nonverbal behaviors in a way that maximizes interpersonal understanding, effectiveness, and relationship development.

This threefold instructional approach to intercultural communication provides an opportunity for instructors to lead students beyond a functional, or utilitarian, goal toward personal enrichment and growth (cf. Saral, 1980). Through understanding the process of intercultural communication, students come to realize that there is no absolute "truth" or "untruth"; there are multitudes of ways for approaching and defining human experience.

Conceptual Grounding

In the communication approach to teaching intercultural communication, human communication activities are viewed as transactional, symbolic activities that involve predictions and uncertainty reduction. High uncertainty exists when communicating with strangers—those who are unknown and unfamiliar. Intercultural communication is a special case of communication between strangers only in the sense that many of the unknown and unfamiliar qualities of strangers are culturally based.

Conceptualizing intercultural communication as communication between strangers provides several advantages over frameworks used in

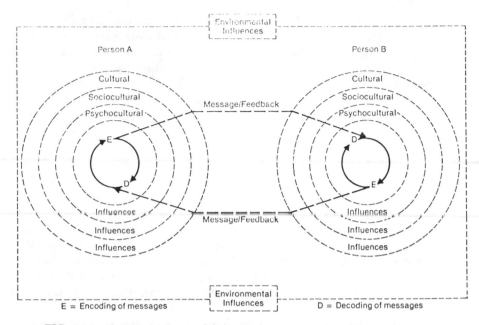

FIG. 11.1. An organizing model for studying intercultural communication (from Gudykunst & Kim, 1984, p. 30).

other intercultural texts. The major advantage is that the course focuses primarily on the study of communication, rather than on culture or cultural anthropology. Also, this perspective asks students to view intercultural communication as a phenomenon that is not unique, but that reflects the same basic underlying process of any interpersonal communication event.

This conceptualization, in turn, enables students to consider all other sources of interpersonal differences, including sociocultural, psychocultural, and environmental influences (see Fig. 11.1). It also points to the importance of recognizing that no two individuals from the same culture are alike in their behavioral and meaning systems, and that not every communication environment brings about the same outcomes.

Topics

Based on this conceptualization of intercultural communication, our course begins with a historical overview that sets the groundwork for the course. Following the explication of the perspective, each of the "levels" of influence on the process of communication between strangers—cultural, sociocultural, psychocultural, and environmental—is examined in detail. Also, variations in verbal and nonverbal communication behavior across cultures are analyzed, with an examination of the dynamics of culture and communication behavior based on the work of Hall (1976). Because intercultural communication presupposes, and deals with, cultural differences between the communicators, such cultural characteristics must be understood. Students also learn that beneath the differences that set peoples apart are profound commonalities in basic needs, concerns, and aspirations, as well as communication patterns.

The course then moves to an examination of the process of communication between strangers. This part begins with a discussion of intercultural communication effectiveness, interpersonal relationship development between cultural strangers, adaptation to a new cultural environment, and personal growth vís à vís prolonged intercultural communication experiences. The development of interpersonal relationships between strangers requires that individuals have some understanding of each other's cultural, sociocultural, and psychocultural patterns.

As strangers' relationships become more meaningful, they proceed through a gradual process of adaptation to each other's culture. Because encounters with strangers pose surprises and uncertainties (in varying degrees, depending on the severity of cultural differences), the concept of "culture shock" is examined. Students learn that the adaptation process is characterized by a stress-adaptation-growth dynamic that is present in the intercultural communication experiences and that acts as a "mover" of individual minds toward increasing interculturalness—toward psychic growth beyond their respective original cultural parameters. The course ends by exploring intercultural personhood as a model for personal growth in today's intercultural world.

The outline of course content is summarized in the following list of 16 main topics, which can be covered within the period of an academic semester or quarter.

I. CONCEPTUAL FOUNDATIONS

    1. Conceptualizing communication
    2. Conceptualizing culture
    3. The concept of the stranger
    4. An organizing model for studying communication with strangers

II. INFLUENCES ON THE PROCESS OF COMMUNICATING WITH STRANGERS

    5. Cultural influences
    6. Sociocultural influences
    7. Psychocultural influences
    8. Environmental influences

III. COMMUNICATION PATTERNS ACROSS CULTURES

    9. Cultural variations in message decoding
    10. Cultural variations in verbal behavior
    11. Cultural variations in nonverbal behavior
    12. Universals of communication

IV. INTERACTION WITH STRANGERS

    13. Developing interpersonal relationships with strangers
    14. Effectiveness in communicating with strangers
    15. Adapting to new cultures
    16. Becoming intercultural

Instructional Methods

By and large, an introductory course on intercultural communication does not require instructional methods that are much different from other introductory-level communication courses. Through **lectures,** instructors help students to understand the course content. Utilizing available **audiovisual aids** (such as films, videotapes, slides) and effective **group discussions,** instructors help students participate in the learning process and personalize the concepts and ideas presented.

Also, **case studies** can be utilized to develop students' abilities to apply the concepts and ideas to various international and domestic issues and events. Newspapers, magazines, TV programs, and movies can present such cases for classroom use. Case studies of organizational practices (cf. Smith, 1982) can help students link intercultural communication theories and concepts to policy issues in international and domestic organizations in their practices of communication with multicultural work forces and social environments. Additional instructional methods, such as **exercises, role plays,** and **simulations,** can be utilized to enhance students' affective (motivation and attitude) and behavioral (skill) learning. (For various ideas for experiential methods of instruction, see Batchelder & Warner, 1977; Brislin, Cushner, Cherrie, & Young, 1986; Harris & Moran, 1979; Landis & Brislin, 1983; Moran & Harris, 1982; Seelye, 1987; Seelye & Tyler, 1977. Also, the Society for Intercultural Education, Research, and Training provides help in locating available resources for intercultural training and education.)

Students' affective and behavioral learning is further enhanced through **field experiences,** in which they engage in the task of communicating and building a relationship with a person (or persons) who is distinctly different from the student in cultural/ethnic membership. In carrying out field experiences, students can be asked to keep diaries that examine and evaluate their own internal reactions and communication effectiveness. An additional method, which has been found to be effective in solidifying students' commitment to intercultural communication effectiveness, is an **essay presentation** (or **essay contest,** if students are competitively inclined) at the end of the course. Students are instructed to prepare and deliver a persuasive speech on a general topic such as "Intercultural communication: A personal point of view." In preparing and seeing themselves persuading others, students often persuade themselves and clarify their own philosophical views on intercultural communication.

CONCLUSION

In this chapter, we reviewed recent developments in the area of intercultural communication and identified (a) the trend toward an increased focus on communication, (b) a balance of theory, research, and practice, and (c) an interdisciplinary integration. Based on these emphases, we proposed a model for organizing an introductory college course on intercultural communication. The goal of this course is threefold—cognitive, affective, and behavioral. The course is designed to enhance students' understanding of the process of intercultural communication, promote open and affirmative attitudes toward cultural differences, and develop skills to manage intercultural encounters and cultivate intercultural relationships.

REFERENCES

Almaney, A. J., & Alwan, A. J. (1982). *Communicating with the Arabs: A handbook for the business executive.* Prospect Heights, IL: Waveland Press.

Asante, M. K. (1988). *The Afrocentric idea.* Philadelphia, PA: Temple University Press.

Asante, M. K., & Gudykunst, W. B. (Eds.). (in press). *Handbook of intercultural and development communication.* Newbury Park, CA: Sage.

Batchelder, D., & Warner, E. G. (Eds.). (1977). *Beyond experience: The experiential approach to cross-cultural education.* Brattleboro, VT: The Experiment Press.

Brislin, R. W. (1981). *Cross-cultural encounters: Face-to-face interaction.* New York: Pergamon.

Brislin, R. W., Cushner, K. C., Cherrie, C., & Young, M. (1986). *Intercultural interactions: A practical guide.* Newbury Park, CA: Sage.

Condon, J. C. (1985). *Good neighbors: Communicating with Mexicans.* Yarmouth, ME: Intercultural Press.

Condon, J. C., & Yousef, F. (1975). *An introduction to intercultural communication.* Indianapolis, IN: Bobbs-Merrill.

Dodd, C. H. (1987).*Dynamics of intercultural communication.* Dubuque, IA: Wm. C. Brown.

Gudykunst, W. B. (Ed.). (1983). *Intercultural communication theory.* Newbury Park, CA: Sage.

Gudykunst, W. B. (Ed.). (1986). *Intergroup communication.* London: Edward Arnold.

Gudykunst, W. B., & Kim, Y. Y. (1984a). *Communicating with strangers: An approach to intercultural communication*. New York: Random House.

Gudykunst, W. B., & Kim, Y. Y. (1984b). *Methods for intercultural communication research*. Newbury Park, CA: Sage.

Gudykunst, W. B., Stewart, L. P., & Ting-Toomey, S. (Eds.). (1985). *Communication, culture, and organizational processes*. Newbury Park, CA: Sage.

Gudykunst, W. B., & Ting-Toomey, S. (1988). *Culture and interpersonal communication*. Newbury Park, CA: Sage.

Hall, E. T. (1976). *Beyond culture*. Garden City, NY: Anchor Books.

Harris, P. R., & Moran, R. T. (1979). *Managing cultural differences*. Houston, TX: Gulf.

Harrison, P. A. (1983). *Behaving Brazilian: A comparison of Brazilian and North American social behavior*. Rowley, MA: Newbury House.

Hofstede, G. (1984). *Culture's consequences: International differences in work-related values*. Newbury Park, CA: Sage.

Hutchison, W. R., & Poznanski, C. A. (1987). *Living in Columbia: A guide for foreigners*. Yarmouth, ME: Intercultural Press.

Kapp, R. A. (Ed.). (1983). *Communicating with China*. Yarmouth, VT: Intercultural Press.

Kim, Y. Y. (Ed.). (1986). *Interethnic communication: Current research*. Newbury Park, CA: Sage.

Kim, Y. Y. (1988). *Cross-cultural adaptation: An integrative theory*. Avon, England: Multilingual Matters.

Kim, Y. Y., & Gudykunst, W. B. (Eds.). (1987). *Cross-cultural adaptation: Current approaches*. Newbury Park, CA: Sage.

Kim, Y. Y., & Gudykunst, W. B. (Eds.). (1988). *Theories in intercultural communication*. Newbury Park, CA: Sage.

Klopf, D. W. (1987). *Intercultural encounters: The fundamentals of intercultural communications*. Englewood, CO: Morton.

Knapp, K., Enninger, W., & Knapp-Potthoff, A. E. (Eds.). (1987). *Analyzing intercultural communication*. Berlin, West Germany: Mouton de Gruyter.

Landis, D., & Brislin, R. W. (Eds.). (1983). *Handbook of intercultural training* (Vols. I–III). New York: Pergamon.

Moran, R. T., & Harris, P. R. (1982). *Managing cultural synergy*. Houston, TX: Gulf.

Nydell, M. K. (1987).*Understanding Arabs: A guide for Westerners*. Yarmouth, ME: Intercultural Press.

Phillips-Martinsson, J. (1981). *Swedes as others see them: Facts, myths or a communication complex?* Yarmouth, ME: Intercultural Press.

Prosser, M. H. (1985). *The cultural dialogue: An introduction to intercultural communication*. Washington, DC: SIETAR International. (Originally published 1978)

Samovar, L. A., & Porter, R. E. (1988). *Intercultural communication: A reader* (5th ed.). Belmont, CA: Wadsworth. (Originally published 1976)

Samovar, L. A., Porter, R. E., & Jain, N. C. (1981). *Understanding intercultural communication*. Belmont, CA: Wadsworth.

Saral, T. B. (1980). The scope, content and process of intercultural communication education. In M. H. Prosser (Ed.), *Intercultural communication in an interdependent world*. Washington, DC: International Communication Agency.

Sarbaugh, L. E. (1988). *Intercultural communication*. New Brunswick, NJ: Transaction Books. (Originally published 1979)

Seelye, H. N. (1987). *Teaching culture: Strategies for intercultural communication*. Lincolnwood, IL: National Textbook Co.

Seelye, H. N., & Tyler, V. L. (Eds.). (1977). *Intercultural communication resources*. Provo, UT: Brigham Young University Language and Intercultural Research Center.

Singer, M. R. (1987). *Intercultural communication: A perceptual approach.* Englewood Cliffs, NJ: Prentice-Hall.

Smith, A. G. (1982). Content decisions in intercultural communication. *Southern Speech Communication Journal, 47* (3), 252–262.

12

Teaching Interviewing

Charles J. Stewart
Purdue University

In the mid-1960s, a mere handful of interviewing courses existed in American colleges and universities, and few textbooks treated interviewing from a communication perspective or dealt with more than one type of interview (e.g., survey research, counseling, or employee selection). Today, hundreds of interviewing courses are taught in a variety of departments at colleges and universities throughout the United States; instructors have numerous books, booklets, and project texts to choose from; and there is a growing body of research into all aspects and types of interviews (Arvey & Campion, 1982; Doyle, 1982; Goodall, Wilson, & Waagen, 1986; Schleifer, 1986; Zakus, Hutter, Dungy, Moore, & Ott, 1976).

Unfortunately, the popularity of interviewing courses often thrusts inexperienced instructors into classes with little preparation. Too often, instructors view the interviewing course as merely an "interpersonal communication" course, assign their favorite readings in interpersonal theory and research, and spend several days each on a variety of theoretical concepts (language, nonverbal communication, listening, and relational dimensions); "interviewing" becomes a minor preoccupation. Students, on the other hand, often enroll in interviewing courses expecting to be transformed quickly and easily into effective job applicants. They yearn for simple steps and correct answers to frequently asked questions and are eager to get into interviews with little or no reading of principles and "theory" that is not "real world." Students firmly believe that "practice makes perfect," even when they do not know what they are (or should be) practicing.

The interviewing course must be more than an interpersonal theory or job preparation course, and it must be an appropriate blend of principles and practice. Make no apology for teaching an interviewing skills course, but also be sure to introduce students to the relevant theory and research so you teach a bona fide university course, not a skills workshop.

UNIT 1: AN INTRODUCTION TO THE INTERVIEWING PROCESS

Begin by formulating a working definition that sets the interview apart from other interpersonal forms and identifies its essential ingredients. For example, you may define the interview as a "process of dyadic, relational communication with a predetermined and serious purpose designed to interchange behavior and involving the asking and answering of questions" (Stewart & Cash, 1988, p. 3). A definition such as this emphasizes the interaction of many variables (process), the unique form of interpersonal communication (dyadic), the interpersonal connection between interview parties (relational), the distinction between conversation and interviewing (predetermined and serious purpose), the sharing of speaking–listening roles (interchanging behavior), and the primary forms of interaction (asking and answering questions). Discussion of a complete working definition makes students aware, first, that the interview involves more than appearance, a firm handshake, or a few clever answers and, second, that its forms are many: information giving, information getting, employee selection, counseling, grievance, problem solving, and persuasive.

The Ingredients in the Process

Once students understand what is and is not an interview, make them aware of the many ingredients that interact in the complex interview process. They need to understand the nature and importance of relational dimensions (such as inclusion, control, and affection) between the two parties, the problems of *upward* and *downward communication* inherent in many interviews (employee–supervisor, applicant–recruiter, student–teacher, professor–dean, vice president–president), perceptions (of self, the other party, and the situation), verbal and nonverbal interactions, listening, feedback, the two fundamental approaches to interviewing (directive and nondirective), and situational variables (location, seating, events before and after the interview, rules governing the interview, and time of day or week). Students are eager to jump into interviews, and they become impatient with discussions of vaguely relevant communication theory, so place all interpersonal principles into an interview context. Provide real-life examples of a variety of interview types and settings to counteract perceptions that interviewing is confined to applicants and recruiters, journalists and politicians, or survey takers and respondents. Make students aware that they take part in interviews virtually every day, not just occasionally in their professions or when changing careers.

The use of **models** is an old and effective instructional strategy for teaching the interviewing process. Require students first to *read about* the ingredients of the process and then *apply* these insights to a sample interview that has built-in strengths and weaknesses. Unlike the perfect model that students should emulate, an imperfect model challenges them to distinguish the good from the bad and to offer suggestions for improvements and alternative means that the interviewer and interviewee might have employed. Ask questions such as the following to lead class discussion: What relationship existed between the interview parties? How willing was each to take part? How was control shared? How much did they like one another? How did their relationship appear to affect the interview? What perceptions did each party have, and how did these perceptions appear to influence the interview? How did the parties share the roles of interviewer and interviewee? Was the interviewer's approach directive, nondirective, or a combination? How did situational variables influence the interview? What problems resulted from poor use of language? How did nonverbal communication affect the interview? How effective were the parties as listeners (Stewart & Cash, 1988, pp. 9, 34)? The model approach immerses students in an interview, helps them to see the relevance of the theory and research they have been reading about, emphasizes both interviewer and interviewee, and enables students to be perceptive and critical of interviewing principles and practices.

Structuring the Interview

Once students know what an interview is, understand that they are involved in a variety of interviews on a daily basis, and appreciate its many interacting ingredients, emphasize the importance of structuring interviews effectively. A good textbook will discuss the importance of the opening, body, and closing and present a variety of techniques; so do not waste class time merely repeating textbook material (Gottlieb, 1986; Hunt & Eadie, 1987; Stewart & Cash, 1988).

The Opening. Emphasize the importance of the opening to the entire interview that follows, the tone it sets for the interactions that take place, and its effects on disclosure of feelings as well as information (Krivonos & Knapp, 1975). Continue to use a model approach. Have students analyze a variety of sample interview openings, considering such questions as: How appropriate was the opening for the situation? How appropriate was the opening for the relationship that existed between the parties? How might other techniques have affected the interview? Stress the necessity for interviewers to select from among a variety of opening techniques the one or ones best suited for a given interview situation and relationship. Students want simple formulas and rules: Always do X in Y situation. Show, through several sample interviews or openings, why interviewers must know (a) the techniques and options available to them and (b) how to select and adapt these tools to specific situations and interviewees.

The Body. Students come to interviewing classes with the impression that interviewers merely jot down a few questions in advance and then "wing it" during interviews; success results from lots of practice rather than thorough preparation. Counteract this impression by first introducing them to interview guides (careful outlines of topics and subtopics to be covered in interviews). The traditional guide of journalists (who, what, when, where, how, and why) and samples from insurance claims adjusters, survey takers, and recruiters show that professionals prepare guides. Remind students of simple outline techniques and how these will help in the construction of a well-organized interview and minimize the chances of failing to cover important topics or issues.

When students understand what a guide is and how it may be used prior to and during interviews, introduce them to interview **schedules** in which the outline of topics and subtopics becomes an outline of primary and secondary questions. The thoroughness of preparation may range from a nonscheduled interview in which the interviewer operates from a guide, to a moderately scheduled interview with all primary questions and some secondary questions written out, to a highly scheduled interview in which all primary and all secondary questions are prepared and asked in the same wording from interview to interview, to a highly scheduled standardized interview that includes all questions and answer options from which an interviewee must select (Gorden, 1980). The interviewer must select the option that is most appropriate for his or her skill level, the amount of time available for preparation, the degree of control necessary for the interview, the breadth and depth of information needed, the necessity to adapt to a particular party or individuals, and the degree of precision, reproducibility, or reliability required to achieve a particular goal. Review sample interviews with students and have them reconstruct the guides or schedules employed. Use hypothetical interview situations to see if students can determine which schedule or combination of schedules would be most appropriate for each situation and why.

The Closing. Emphasize the importance of the closing in maintaining the relationship and trust established during the interview and for future interactions between interview parties. Discuss common nonverbal signals that the "leave-taking" stage of the interview is commencing (Knapp, Hart, Friedrich, & Shulman, 1973). Use a model approach in which students analyze a variety of interview closings, considering questions such as: How appropriate was the closing for the situation and the interchanges that had taken place? How appropriate was the closing for the relationship between the parties? What other closing techniques might the interviewer have used, and how might these have affected the next interview between these parties? Emphasize the importance of selecting from among a variety of closing techniques the one or ones best suited for each interview situation and party. Remind students that the interview "is not over until it's over." As long as interviewer and interviewee are within sight and sound of one another, the interview has not ended, because the parties will continue to note what each does and does not do, says and does not say.

Types and Uses of Questions

Although questions are the "tools of the trade," students feel that "A question is merely a sentence with a question mark, and no big deal" (Payne, 1951). Quiz the students over a wide variety of questions to emphasize the importance of questions in interviews for both interviewer and interviewee, to point out why it is essential to understand the types of questions available, and to illustrate what each is designed to accomplish.

Types of Questions. Spend a class period in which students identify a variety of questions in four ways: open or closed, primary or secondary, neutral or leading, and a special tool such as nudging probe, bipolar, loaded, clearinghouse, reflective, or mirror (Stewart, 1988, pp. 5–6). Emphasize, for example, that interviewers who know and understand question tools ask bipolar questions only when they want interviewees to select between two choices such as agree or disagree, important or unimportant, yes or no; ask closed questions only when they want brief answers and open questions only when they want lengthy answers; ask leading or loaded questions only when they want to influence how interviewees respond; and ask reflective probing questions only when they want to clarify or verify answers.

As you proceed through a variety of questions, take opportunities to discuss how choices of options might affect answers, self-disclosure, relationships, cooperation, and accurate transmission of information. Explain, for instance, what a reflective probe, nudging probe, or clearinghouse question can do for an interviewee or interviewer. Compare and contrast question types to show how they are similar and different and their unique functions in interviews. Students begin to learn how question tools are designed to get information efficiently and effectively and to see the interview as a two-way process in which both parties use questions for a variety of purposes. By the end of the hour, the question uppermost on many students' minds at the beginning of the hour should be answered: "Why should we know all of these labels for questions?"

Probing Questions. Most interviews are nonscheduled or moderately scheduled, and probing skills are critical because answers are often vague, suggestible, incorrect, incomplete, superficial, or irrelevant. An interviewer or interviewee might remain silent rather than respond. The skilled interview participant must be able, within fractions of a second, to determine (a) if a response is unsatisfactory or seems to contain clues (about feelings, attitudes, disclosure, or information available) and (b) how to phrase an appropriate secondary or probing question. Spend a class period in which students supply probing questions in sequences such as the following:

Interviewer: What kind of person was your coach?
Interviewee: Enthusiastic.
Interviewer:

Students must identify the inadequacy of the answer, the possible cause of the inadequacy (including a poorly phrased question), identify the question tool they would use, and then phrase the probing question. Insist that students ask a probing question and not a primary question that delves into a different area of inquiry. The following is a typical example of this error:

Interviewer: Who do you plan to vote for in the presidential election?
Interviewee: Oh, I don't know.
Interviewer: Which candidate do you feel has the best grasp of foreign policy?

This probing question does not get closer to *the* candidate for whom the interviewee plans to vote. Discuss a variety of probing questions best suited for each interaction, once again emphasizing *options* available to interviewers and interviewees.

Phrasing Questions.   More problems result from poor question phrasing than from any other factor in interviews, so spend part of a class period analyzing sample questions that illustrate common problems. Focus on factors such as language, relevance, information level, complexity (length, complicated answer options, or double-barrelled), and accessibility (questions that involve social, psychological, or situational constraints). Ask students to identify the problem or problems with a question and then rephrase the question to make it effective and efficient (Stewart, 1988, pp. 9–11). Emphasize how a single poorly selected word may lead to a vague, inaccurate, or incomplete answer. Cover 20 or more questions in this exercise so a wide variety of problems and solutions are illustrated.

Question Sequences.   Students tend to think that interviewers merely write down a list of questions that come to mind prior to interviews. The earlier discussion of interview guides and schedules helps to reduce this perception, but students also need to understand that a skilled interviewer may employ one or more question sequences: funnel, inverted funnel, tunnel, or quintamensional design (Stewart & Cash, 1988, pp. 74–77). Spend part of a class period in which students identify the question sequence or sequences apparent in a number of sample interviews to help them understand the uniquenesses of different sequences and how they are used in interviews. Pose several hypothetical situations and ask students to explain which sequence or sequences they would recommend and why.

The First Oral Exercise

End the introductory unit of the course with a nongraded, nonthreatening oral exercise that allows students to practice and observe the principles discussed throughout the unit. For example, simple 10-minute biographical interviews in which students attempt to find out everything they can about interviewees require only part of one class period (Stewart, 1988, p. 11–12). Divide students into triads (A = interviewer, B = interviewee, and C = observer-critic), and switch roles within the trios every 10 minutes. Provide discussion questions such as: Why did interviewers cover certain topics and avoid others? How did the relationship between the parties affect the interviews? Which levels of communication were reached and why? How often and when did interviewers and interviewees switch roles? How did the parties communicate nonverbally? What types of questions dominated the interviews? This simple exercise is an effective way to summarize and integrate the many principles learned in the introductory unit.

The First Unit Test

Use a mixture of objective and essay questions. Multiple-choice questions are effective in assessing student knowledge of principles, theories, and research findings. Essay questions (in which students critique openings, closings, and questions; create guides, schedules, and sequences; and discuss uses of interviewing approaches and techniques) are effective in assessing student skills in applying principles, theories, and research findings.

UNIT 2: INFORMATIONAL INTERVIEWING

The second unit of the course should delve into both information-giving and information-getting interviews—building upon the topics covered in Unit 1 and introducing students to principles and skills necessary for more specialized types of interviews, such as employee selection, performance appraisal, counseling, and health care.

Information-Giving Interviews

Most of us are involved in giving information and instructions nearly every day, but we rarely question the nature or success of our techniques (Golden & Johnson, 1970; Ley, 1966). We assume that what we do often we do well, so devote a class period to problems encountered when transmitting information orally and the means of improving accurate transmission and retention of information. A simple "parlor" exercise is fun and illustrates dramatically how information is omitted, added, changed, and distorted when passed from person to person. Send five or six students out of the room; call one in and read a paragraph-length message; call a second student in and have the first student repeat the message from memory; repeat the transmission until all have heard and repeated the now distorted message (Stewart, 1976, pp. 22–24; Stewart, 1988, pp. 13–14). Repeat this exercise two or three times with different messages, and have seated students keep record of the problems encountered. When several students have tried their best, discuss why information is lost or distorted (even in simple interactions), and show a variety of ways to improve information giving.

Survey Interviews

Because we are involved frequently in surveys and polls as both interviewers and interviewees, spend two class periods discussing and illustrating survey principles and techniques. During the first period, act as a person who needs expert advice on how to prepare and conduct a survey on a topic of interest to your students. Pose questions that require them to consider options and determine which one or ones are best for your purpose and limitations (such as money and time in which to create and conduct the survey and report the results). Ask: What research should you do? Should you conduct a *cross-sectional* or *longitudinal* study? What is your *population* or *target group?* How many people should you interview? How should you select these people? How accurate should your results be? How advisable would it be to conduct all or part of your interviews over the telephone? How should you open the interview? What topics should you cover (Stewart, 1988, p. 27)? Questions such as these allow students to "apply" the principles and techniques discussed in their textbooks. During the second class period, focus on question strategies and scales first by identifying and evaluating a variety of sample questions and then by analyzing a *model* survey interview.

The Probing Interview

Devote the remainder of Unit 2 to *probing* interview principles and skills that are essential for many types of interviewers, including recruiters, police officers, counselors, journalists, health care professionals, and supervisors. Emphasize (through samples and models) preparation, selection of interviewees and interviewers, probing questions, common question pitfalls to avoid, note taking and tape recording, handling difficult situations and interviewees, and interviewee skills.

The Second Oral Exercise

The second oral exercise, and the first to be graded, should provide students with an experience in preparing moderately scheduled interviews that forces them to ask open questions, to listen carefully to answers, to detect clues or problems in answers, and to ask appropriate probing questions, including nudging probes, reflective probes, mirror questions, and clearinghouse questions (Stewart, 1988, pp. 15–16; Stewart, 1976, pp. 24–25). Interviewees should be reticent (answer yes–no questions with yes or no, closed questions with a bit of information, and open questions with a sentence or two); so, to force students to exhibit patience as well as listening and probing skills but not mislead them, instructors often play the role of interviewee in this exercise. They are more able to maintain the right degree of reticence and to rescue interviewers who find it difficult to handle this demanding assignment. Because students tend to see units of courses as separate rather than cumulative, remind them to review earlier readings and discussions on the process, structure, and questions in order to adapt to interviewees and situations, to open and close the interviews effectively, and to use the correct question tools to gain information efficiently and accurately.

SELECTING ADDITIONAL UNITS OF STUDY

The first two units will have introduced students to principles, research, and techniques that are applicable to most interviews. Subsequent units should present principles, research, and techniques that are unique to specific types of interviews. Select units most appropriate for the purpose of your course, the students your course attracts, and the role your course plays in the curriculum. If, for instance, your course is designed to serve all communication majors as well as students from a wide variety of majors at your school, subsequent units may be employee selection, counseling, and persuasive. If the course is an integral part of an organizational communication program and attracts management majors, it may include employee selection, performance appraisal, and disciplinary interviews.

CONCLUSION

Regardless of the units covered in your course, focus discussions, analyses, and practice on *interviewing* principles, theories, and research. It should not be merely a course in interpersonal communication, nor should it be a management, counseling, or sales course. Introduce students to the approaches, structural techniques, and question tools available to interviewers, and teach them how to select the best ones for each interview. Address instruction and practice to the role of recruiter as well as applicant, counselee as well as counselor, persuadee as well as persuader, patient as well as health care professional.

REFERENCES

Arvey, R. D., & Campion, J. E. (1982). The employment interview: A summary and review of recent research. *Personnel Psychology, 35,* 281–321.

Doyle, R. E. (1982). The counselor's role, communication skills, or the roles counselors play: A conceptual model. *Counselor Education and Supervision, 22,* 123–131.

Golden, J., & Johnson, G. D. (1970). Problems of distortion in doctor–patient communication. *Psychiatry in Medicine, 1,* 127–149.

Goodall, H. L., Jr., Wilson, G. L., & Waagen, C. L. (1986). The performance appraisal interview: An interpretive reassessment. *Quarterly Journal of Speech, 72,* 74–87.

Gorden, R. (1980). *Interviewing: Strategy, techniques, and tactics.* Homewood, IL: The Dorsey Press.

Gottlieb, M. (1986). *Interview.* New York: Longman.

Hunt, G. T., & Eadie, W. F. (1987). *Interviewing: A communication approach.* Englewood Cliffs, NJ: Prentice-Hall.

Knapp, M. L., Hart, R. P., Friedrich, G. W., & Shulman, G. M. (1973). The rhetoric of goodbye: Verbal and nonverbal correlates of human leave-taking. *Speech Monographs, 40,* 182–198.

Krivonos, P. D., & Knapp, M. L. (1975). Initiating communication: What do you say when you say hello? *Central States Speech Journal, 26,* 115–125.

Ley, P. (1966). What the patient doesn't remember. *Medical Opinion Review, 1,* 69–73.

Payne, S. L. (1951). *The art of asking questions.* Princeton, NJ: Princeton University Press.

Schleifer, S. (1986). Trends in attitudes toward and participation in survey research. *Public Opinion Quarterly, 50,* 17–26.

Stewart, C. J. (1976). *Teaching interviewing for career preparation.* Falls Church, VA: Speech Communication Association.

Stewart, C. J. (1988). *Interviewing principles and practices: A project text.* Dubuque, IA: Kendall/Hunt.

Stewart, C. J., & Cash, W. B., Jr. (1988). *Interviewing: Principles and practices.* Dubuque, IA: William C. Brown.

Zakus, S. E., Hutter, M. J., Dungy, C. I., Moore, V. M., & Ott, J. E. (1976). Teaching interviewing for pediatrics. *Journal of Medical Education, 51,* 325–331.

13

Teaching Mass Communication and Telecommunication

Thomas A. McCain
The Ohio State University

$\mathbf{A}$pproaches to the study of mass communication, the media, and telecommunication are increasing in complexity. Where once the media studies teacher had to deal only with wandering minstrels, cave painters, smoke signalers, and royal censors, the modern educator must deal with issues of new technology and social organization that blur distinctions that were made about telecommunication and mass communication only a decade ago. The purposes of this chapter are to suggest some of the unique aspects of mass communication processes, to discuss several approaches to instruction as they apply to teaching media topics, and to present a smorgasbord of learning activities for students.

Mass communication courses are exciting for both teachers and students. They are about phenomena with which everyone has experience and an opinion. There are myths to dispel and controversial issues to discuss, all cloaked in a Hollywood-like aura of fame and fortunes, power and politics. People talk about television more than they discuss any other topic, including the weather, sex, sports, or family. It is part of nearly everyone's reality.

DEFINITIONS

A variety of terms are used to capture the phenomena of mass communication. The correctness of varying definitions is significantly less important than that the central concepts be understood. For purposes of this chapter, the *Mass Media* are organizations that engage in the production and/or distribution of messages designed for public consumption by large audiences (television, radio, newspapers). *Telecommunication* organizations are those that traditionally have engaged in activities of distribution, transformation, and storage of nonpublic information, but not in the production of content (telephone, satellite, computer networks). New media technologies blur these distinctions (videotext, cable, Integrated Services Digital Networks). *Mass Communication* is used here as an umbrella term to refer to the variety of processes that account for these organizations' activities and the uses, effects, and/or consequences of mass media and telecommunication.

MASS COMMUNICATION ENCODING AND DECODING

The two issues that are central to understanding mass communication phenomena are the rather separate processes of encoding and decoding. Most courses and curricula need to address: (a) the processes and practices of organizations that produce, store, distribute, and transform information into mass communication messages and (b) the uses, consequences, or effects of this message content for individuals, groups, societies, and culture. Imbedded in both encoding and decoding processes is the problem of defining message content. A third issue, producing a theory that accounts for the encoding and decoding process in some kind of comprehensive fashion, is one of the elusive phenomena of mass communication, although there are several excellent summaries (Becker, 1987; DeFleur & Ball-Rokeach, 1982).

DIFFERENTIATING MASS COMMUNICATION

The relationships between source and receiver in mass communication are seldom interactional, because receivers have essentially no functional control over the activities of sources. Mass communication sources are involved in exchange processes whereby they sell or trade in audience attention. In the United States, media sources "sell" audiences to advertisers. Mass communication sources are groups or organizations, not individuals.

Messages are publicly transmitted, rapidly diffused, and transiently consumed (Wright, 1975). In fact, mass media messages are manufactured and multiplied; they are the product of group effort, the media social system, and society norms and values. They are also constrained by technology of storage, transformation, and transmission. Each medium's potential to manipulate sensory stimuli is inherently limited by technological potential. The sound of things is not available for manipulation to the newspaper source, just as manipulation of the shape, color, or feel of things is not transmittable directly on radio. Newspapers manipulate visual/verbal and visual/nonverbal stimuli; radio sources manipulate audio/verbal and audio/nonverbal stimuli; television and film have the potential to utilize both audio and visual message forms. None of the mass media have been very successful in utilizing touch, smell, or taste, except for the occasional "scratch and sniff." Mass media, then, are limited by the sensory integration potential of their technology (Avery & McCain, 1982).

COMMUNICATION PROCESSES

In other communication contexts, transactional and interactional models of communication are prevalent and of high currency. These approaches are of little use in mass communication, however, because the messages created by media industries have a time and space dimension that is quite different from interpersonal or public speaking situations. Most media messages are not alterable by audiences once they have been encoded by a source. For the study of mass communication, it is typical to examine messages as residing in a time and space of their own, having been created by an organization and designed for consumption by a public audience. Channel capacity, technology, and message form are more important for understanding aspects of the mass communication processes than they are in other contexts.

The process is also highly impersonal and, in many respects, "nonmoral" and manipulative, in the sense that the sender usually takes no moral responsibility for specific consequences for individuals (McQuail, 1987). The impersonal aspects of mass communication are related to the public nature of the activity, which, in some respects, makes normative the issues of neutrality, detachment, and "objectivity." Yet, mass communication audiences are apt to consume media in private. There is also a differential power relationship between source and receiver, partly due to the perceived resources, expertise, prestige, and authority of senders.

The mass communication receiver, on the other hand, is part of a large, heterogeneous and anonymous audience, having little formal power except for sharing experiences with others. Mass communication audiences tend to react in predictable and patterned ways to the messages produced by media sources.

Mass communication typically involves a single source (organization) providing contact with a multitude of receivers simultaneously. The exigencies of this phenomenon are awesome for policy makers, program makers, and those with ideas, goods, and services for sale. They are equally awesome for parents, consumers, voters, and viewers. The one-to-many situation allows for immediate reactions by huge numbers of people. Although there are hundreds of studies that show that the effects of mass communicated messages are not direct, the media continue to wield enormous influence. The uniformity of impact for mass communication is apt to be less variable than that of a slower, sequential, gossip network by individuals.

The focus of most research in mass communication has been on the decoding process—"What are the effects?" Wanting to understand the audience has resulted from both commercial interests as well as the media's potential to subterfuge or undermine existing values and sources of influence in society. As the mass media and telecommunication became important sources of value information for individuals and society, the institutions responsible for teaching and monitoring information and values became alarmed. In a relatively short period of historical time, media became an institution of potential influence similar to the family, church, business, government, and education. The mass media serve a variety of functions as institutions: surveillance of the environment (news), correlation with other phenomena of importance (editorial), socialization with existing norms and values (education), and entertainment for the non-work-related needs of society (Lasswell, 1948, Wright, 1975). The media can also be viewed as a storytelling machine, communicating the myths and heros of the culture that controls it.

For individuals, the media are used in a variety of ways, often unrelated to the content of the programs. Television is used for information, for guidance, as a social lubricant, and as a social avoidance vehicle. It is used for background noise and as a source for parasocial interaction. The uses and gratifications that people derive from telephones and television are related to: the salience of their needs, their age cohort, the range of options available for need satisfaction, and a host of other contextual variables (Dimmick, McCain & Bolton, 1979, Rosengren, Palmgreen, & Wenner, 1985). Individuals are affected by media messages through a host of selectivity filters, including selective exposure, attention, perception, and recall (Zillmann & Bryant, 1985).

Students of media need to be skilled in describing potential and existing audiences for media messages. They must also be able to identify factors and forces that influence the impact and uses of the media for individuals, groups, societies, and cultures. Both quantitative and qualitative research methods are used in describing these audiences and their interaction with media messages. The sooner students have these research tools in their bag of critical thinking skills, the sooner they will be able to evaluate the interdependencies between media, content, and social life.

PURPOSES FOR STUDYING
MASS COMMUNICATION

The choice of mass communication education within a curriculum needs to be made within the context of a variety of options available. There are several possible general approaches or goals, including (a) preparing students for the world of work and careers, (b) helping students to understand generally the physical, artistic, and social world in which people live, (c) teaching students how to think and solve problems, (d) learning about the accumulation of knowledge in a particular field or speciality, and (e) teaching and learning about values and the valuing process of societies and individuals. The emphasis that teachers place on these approaches varies within the faculty of any one school and between curricula of different schools. It is important, nonetheless, that mass communication course objectives be understood in light of the varying possible orientations to instruction and that they be consistent with the general objectives or orientations of other departmental offerings. There are excellent programs and courses in all areas of mass communication that facilitate accomplishing each of the varying philosophical approaches to education. Television production, for example, can be taught as: (a) an important career skill, (b) an art form, (c) a planning and problem-solving enterprise, (d) a building block for visual literacy, or (e) an aid to understanding how credibility is nonverbally manipulated. It is important for teachers to be aware of their individual goals for students and to insure that their approaches to teaching mass communication are complimentary with other aspects of the curriculum. It is equally important to recognize that students may take courses to meet personal objectives that are not the same as the course objectives.

The theory versus practice or professional versus critical issues are alive and well in mass communication education. Mass communication study is newer than most other areas of communication; it remains close to its applied roots.

APPLIED ISSUES

The practical and applied approaches to studying radio, television, and electronic media are quite popular. Students need to learn about the language of visualization, sound, display, and format. For all students of communication, some technical skill with communication media seems desirable. It is ironic that people spend years studying the form and function of words and books, yet almost none with cameras, microphones, or television programs. People spend an inordinate amount of their lives watching television and using the mass media. Just as reading skills are taught by writing, so too viewing skills should be taught by program production courses. This hands-on approach is involving and relevant for the learner, educator, and the media industry. Care should be taken not to equate professional approaches to mass communication with skills training in mass communication.

A variety of technical skills and information is required to engage in the production of mediated messages. The practice of making radio programs, music videos, student newspapers, and the like allows students to gain these skills in simulated real-world environments. Students need to explore and test the possibilities within a medium's technical potentials. They also need to be familiar with the rules of media industries, for these rules set standards of appropriate practice. At the same time, students need to develop a critical ability to question and challenge the taken-for-granted practices of media and telecommunication industries with which they disagree. Learning and practicing media skills is critical for all students of mass communication; preparing for professional careers in media industries is not.

By way of contrast, most journalism schools are accredited by the professional association that determines the appropriateness of their curricula and courses. The results of having completed such a course of study renders the student a "professional journalist." Some broadcasting educators favor a similar approach to media curricula. Professional approaches *are* important for some schools with unique histories and resources, particularly for colleges with close links to certain media industries and for a few schools located in large metropolitan areas, like New York and Los Angeles, where there are demands for professionally trained personnel of a particular type. By and large, however, most communication departments will find such a professional approach inappropriate for their students.

What is important to note is that the applied nature of mass communication practice should be part of the curriculum, but its emphasis must be tempered by other issues regarding resources and philosophy. This applied orientation should be understood in the broader context of the importance of the mass media as they operate in contemporary societies.

THEORETICAL ISSUES

The theoretical issues that demand attention in studying mass communication revolve around politics, economics, ethics, and social and psychological impact. Although there are technological imperatives of tremendous importance, much of the structure and content of the media are shaped by accidents and forces of history. The political, economic, and social pressures that transpired at the time a particular communication technology developed shaped for generations the content and format of a medium *within its culture.* Although there are similarities in radio and newspapers from country to country, there are profound differences as well. If television were just a technology, then what is broadcast in the United States should be the same as what is broadcast in Nicaragua, for example; but it isn't. There should be no differences in the newspapers of the United Kingdom and Sweden, or the USSR and India; but there are. Students need to be able to identify concrete examples of how social, political, and economic factors influence the institutions of telecommunication and mass media.

Globalization and Localism

The rapid diffusion and change in communication technology is part of a change in the structure of modern societies—simultaneous and seemingly contradictory movements toward localism and globalization. The internationalization of economies (along with cross-national political and social alliances) makes mass communication policy issues of incredible relevance for today's media student. While international interdependence gets nearly daily coverage in the press, another social movement is also occurring across the industrialized world. It is a return to local communities and individuals "cocooning" themselves to home. Both globalization and localism are phenomena that parallel rapid growth in available communication technology and media. There is a return to more personal and local societies even within the burgeoning metropolitan areas of the world. At the same time, there is increased interdependence between people and nations of the world. There is now a global economy, and there are enormous changes in levels of information and kinds of exchanges among peoples of the world. Students of mass communication, no matter where they study the topic, must consider the social, political, and economic forces that influence the shape of media and society.

ENCODING PROCESSES—THE SHAPE OF MEDIA ORGANIZATIONS

In order to understand the dynamic processes of mass communication, particularly new communication technologies, students must be able to identify how particular technologies become a communication medium of a particular type serving a particular function and purpose. They need to study the history of the local ownership of newspapers and radio and television stations, as well as the background of the cable operators and other telecommunication and media personnel. Why do people have to call so many companies to get a telephone these days? What business were most video rental distributors in 20 years ago? Who controls what movies play in town? Who calls the shots concerning what music plays on the local radio stations? Researching answers to these kinds of questions helps students understand the linkages between media institutions and society.

The reason why the media and telecommunication are the way they are in each country, as well as in each town and state, has to do with the interaction between (a) what is technologically possible, what it costs, and who's in control and (b) what constitutes the critical social issues of the day. The possibilities for debates and discussions should lead to lively times in and out of the classroom. Both applied and theoretical issues are necessary purviews of mass communication study.

DECODING PROCESSES—AUDIENCE USES AND EFFECTS

The issues related to society and the media that have received the most attention from parents, politicians, social critics, media personnel, educators, and religious leaders parallel the topics that have been most widely researched by mass communication scholars. They include: racism and stereotyping; role models and stereotypes; effects on beliefs, attitudes, and opinions; media portrayals of violence; arousal and pornography; effects on the political process; the electronic church; advertising; cultural imperialism and the flow of information and technology; development and mass communication; and specific effects on children (Jeffries, 1986). Student research papers and class discussions can bring these controversial and lively topics to the floor.

STUDENT LEARNING ACTIVITIES

Interviewing

One way to discover aspects of both encoding and decoding processes in media and telecommunication is to have students interview a variety of senders and receivers of mass communication. There are professionals who write, produce, engineer, film, distribute, fund, and create media messages everywhere. There are telephone personnel and satellite distributors who are able and willing to talk with students. Politicians and newsmakers, as well as sponsors and cable installers, all consider media and telecommunication part of their daily routines. It is important that students understand that just plain folk, engaged in largely mundane activities, are the people of mass media and telecommunications. Regular interviewing and discussions with such personnel (both in and out of the classroom) helps to contextualize the mass communication encoding process.

Students might also interview people of different ages regarding their media experiences and dependencies. Student interaction with the elderly and with children about their television reality can be a particularly useful way of understanding the variety of meanings and uses that the media have for others.

Production and Performance

Nothing can make the process of mass communication as vivid as the production of programs, newspapers, magazines, videos, and the like. The organizational experience of group effort, deadlines, strict format requirements, targeting audiences, and planning for the use of expensive equipment and time, as well as aesthetic principles of audio and visual production, helps students to understand a variety of communication principles. Whenever possible, the practice of communication principles should be a foundational experience.

Critiques and Evaluation

Part of every mass communication course should be a critical evaluation of media messages or telecommunication services. It is particularly important that programs and content be understood not only for their social meaning, but also in terms of their commercial intent. Students can describe advertisements that are shown during a television program, and determine the "needed audience" for the show based on the likely purchasers of the products in the spots. With this in mind, the program's themes, characters, use of comedy, and conflict can be evaluated in terms of how they would be received by such a needed audience. Exercises like these help to contextualize the content of both the encoding and decoding processes in American media.

Media Use Exercises

Helping students become aware of their own complicated uses of the media and telecommunication facilitates understanding the ubiquity of the media and the relationships between audience need, audience use, content, and habit. One approach is to have a "cold turkey day"; a day where students avoid all media and telecommunication while monitoring and logging their behavior. This can be extended to 2 days, but probably no more. Another method is to have students log their daily diet of media and telecommunication over a period of several days to a week. This log can be analyzed in a paper and interpreted in light of the audience uses and effects literature. A third approach is to focus on the varying uses and needs of students and to log their media and nonmedia activity in light of these needs. It is important to have students analyze, write about, and discuss their reactions to these activities.

Simulations

There are a variety of mass communication processes for which direct observation or production is impossible given limited resources and time. Simulating media pressures for deadlines or specific audience delivery works well. Likewise, creating situations where students must role-play reactions to particular mass communication phenomena from a variety of perspectives is very useful for stimulating thinking and class discussion. Students can listen across the dial of the radio and analyze the impact that programming variety might bring to different people. Some of the liveliest times in a class on international communication, for example, occur when students must assume the role of first-, second- and third-world countries and debate the effects of importation of American television programming and technology, or discuss the concepts of freedom, censorship, and ownership from these various perspectives.

Reading, Writing, and Research

Students should be encouraged to read, analyze, write about, and discuss the media at every opportunity. Discussions are greatly improved when students have prepared even a mini research report prior to class. Critical reading is improved if written reports or evaluations are part of the process. Writing to telecommunication and media companies with praise or complaints will usually reap a reply, because these companies seldom hear from their users. The heart of every media production is good writing. Experiences with creative and analytic writing for media should be part of every course.

As the world swirls into the year 2000, part and parcel of the everyday will be media and telecommunication. Mixtures of old and new media are part of a changing view of human interdependence. Students and teachers of communication have two choices to this inevitability. They can react or proact. Jointly, all interested in human communication must deal with the phenomena in a meaningful way. Hopefully, school administrators, educators, politicians, business persons, and the general public will insure that the salient issues of the new information age are introduced and discussed in the communication classroom.

REFERENCES

Avery, R. K., & McCain, T. A. (1982). Interpersonal and mediated encounters: A reorientation to the mass communication process. In G. Gumpert & R. Cathcart (Eds.), *Intermedia. Interpersonal communication in a media world* (2nd ed.) New York: Oxford University Press.

Becker, S. (1987). *Discovering mass communication* (2nd ed.). Glenview, IL: Scott, Foresman.

DeFleur, M. L., & Ball-Rokeach, S. (1982). *Theories of mass communication* (4th ed.). New York: Longman.

Dimmick, J. W., McCain, T. A., & Bolton, W. T. (1979). Media use and the life span. *American Behavioral Scientist, 23*(1), 7–31.

Jeffries, L. W. (1986). *Mass media processes and effects*. Prospect Heights, IL: Waveland Press.

Lasswell, H. (1948). The structure and function of communications in society. In L. Bryson (Ed.), *The communication of ideas*. New York: Harper.

McQuail, D. (1987). *Mass communication theory: An introduction* (2nd ed.). London: Sage.

Rosengren, K. E., Palmgreen, P., & Wenner, L. (1985). *Media gratification research: Current perspectives*. Beverly Hills, CA: Sage.

Wright, C. R. (1975). *Mass communication: A sociological perspective* (2nd ed.). New York: Random House.

Zillmann, D., & Bryant, J. (Eds.). (1985). *Selective exposure to communication*. Hillsdale, NJ: Lawrence Erlbaum Associates.

14

Teaching Research Methods

Ruth Anne Clark
University of Illinois

As a doctoral student, one of the most exciting courses I took was an introduction to empirical research; and as an instructor, one of the most exciting courses I have taught is an introduction to empirical research. The source of the excitement in both instances is the same: learning methods for the discovery of new ideas.

Not all students come eagerly to the basic course in research methods, whether restricted to empirical approaches or defined more broadly. In fact, some students are more apprehensive about this course than any other that they take within the communication curriculum. Most commonly, this apprehension is rooted in the belief that any course that encompasses empirical methodology requires a solid background in mathematics, and some students in communication are skeptical about their skills in this area. This apprehension can be dispelled quickly, however, by emphasizing from the outset that the focus will be on basic thought processes, not statistics, and that any sensible person is capable of mastering the fundamental concepts of the course.

PURPOSE OF THE COURSE

The purpose of an introductory research methods course should be to facilitate an understanding of modes of inquiry. The focus at this level should not be to further specific skills, such as the ability to locate source material or to perform statistical manipulations; rather, the course should enable students to understand the thought processes involved in the research enterprise. At least four specific objectives can be served by the basic course in research methods:

1. Facilitating an understanding of the fundamental steps in any research project.

2. Providing insight into the variety of major approaches available to pursuing a specific research question and helping emphasize the array of specific alternatives within each major approach.

3. Engendering appreciation for the extent to which selection of the major approach and specific decisions at each step of the process influence the outcome of the project.

4. Developing criteria for evaluating the research product.

The instructor hopes, of course, that working toward these objectives will generate respect and enthusiasm for the research enterprise and direct students toward the more specialized training necessary to their becoming independent researchers.

STRUCTURE AND PRINCIPLES
UNDERLYING THE COURSE

There are, of course, a variety of ways of structuring a course on research methods. The one suggested here provides a framework for emphasizing what seem to be important principles underlying the diverse methods of research that prevail in our discipline. Four sections are included: the nature of research, general methodologies used within the discipline, phases of the research process, and evaluation of the research project.

The Nature of Research

1. Research investigates questions of fact, not questions of value or policy. It is not possible to ask what the "best" persuasive appeal might be, for a value such as "best" may mean quite different things to different individuals. For instance, "best persuasive appeal" might mean the appeal that is most likely to gain compliance to one individual, but to another it might mean the one that gives the recipient of the appeal greatest freedom of choice.

2. Research is a creative, not formulary, activity. There is no set formula to follow in answering a specific research question. In fact, there

are literally an infinite number of ways to pursue the same question. One could ask which of two specified persuasive appeals is more likely to gain immediate compliance by studying a rhetorical movement, conducting an experiment that compares two types of appeal, or engaging in naturalistic observation (e.g., identifying instances of the two types of appeal under question and noting their apparent impact). These alternatives do not, of course, exhaust the options available.

3. The answer to any research question in a given investigation is influenced by the specific method used to pursue the question. Any investigation must be conducted within a specific environment, using particular methods and instruments, and is subject to influence from unsuspected sources.

4. The answer to a research question, then, gains credence when based on multiple investigations, particularly when they employ diverse methodologies and are conducted under varying specific contexts.

5. Research raises questions, as well as answers them. The observant researcher becomes aware of the relevance of additional variables, for instance, by noting that some cases behaved differently than others. Consequently, productive scholarship typically occurs within a systematic research program that probes a general issue over an extended period of time.

Types of Research Methodologies

Types of research may be classified in a variety of ways. Within our discipline, perhaps because of its eclectic nature and diverse interests, types of research characteristically are classified on the basis of the kinds of questions asked and the nature of the data used to answer them. The category system introduced by J. Jeffrey Auer (1959), in the first comprehensive research methods book published in our field, has endured with only minor modifications in similar works published up through the current decade. Auer identified three fundamental research methodologies: historical/critical, descriptive, and experimental.

Historical/Critical Methods. Rubin, Rubin, and Piele (1986) described historical research as locating and evaluating observations of past events and critical research as the selection and application of appropriate criteria for judgment. The scope of such research may range from concern with a single event to investigation of an entire social movement, or even to comparison of movements. The researcher's own background and assumptions guides his or her definition of what counts as evidence and how it should be interpreted and, thereby, influences the conclusions reached.

The conclusions reached from critical research quite naturally differ with the set of criteria applied to the phenomenon. No one critical stance is inherently superior to another. The value of a critical approach in a given instance must be determined by the particular function that the criticism is designed to serve.

Descriptive Research.   Rubin, Rubin, and Piele (1986) characterized descriptive research as seeking "to describe or explain *what is,* rather than *what was*." Thus, the primary distinction between historical and descriptive research is that the investigator *generates* evidence or data in descriptive research rather than discovering and systematizing it, as is done in historical research. The two most common forms of descriptive research identified are observational and survey research.

With either observation or survey methods, the researcher must abstract from the phenomenon of interest a restricted range of variables to be described. For example, if the research is interested in interactional patterns during children's play, observation may be constrained to identification of which child apparently initiates a change in the general direction of the interaction, and even this concern will be restricted to a small number of identifiable cues. This abstractive process influences the conclusions the research yields.

Descriptive methodology, perhaps even more than the other two approaches, has the potential to produce serendipitous findings. For instance, the researcher might assume that changing the direction of an interaction is viewed as leadership by children but discover that it is thought to be disruptive instead.

Experimental Methodology.   Experimental methodology seeks to describe generalizations about the relationship among two or more variables by controlling for the impact of other relevant variables. Conditions of one or more variables (designated the independent variables) are manipulated in order to observe the impact of this manipulation on another variable (labeled the dependent variable). A key feature of an experiment is the attempt to control for the impact of additional variables that are potentially relevant to fluctuations in the dependent variable.

This control sometimes forces the researcher to narrow the scope of the project more than would be required with descriptive methodology. However, the researcher typically has greater confidence that whatever relationship is found among the variables of concern is genuine; that is, not an artifact of other relevant variables.

Phases of the Research Process

Regardless of the type of research selected, four steps are involved in any research enterprise: clarifying the research question, collecting data, analyzing data, and reporting the project.

Clarifying the Question. The success of the research project frequently hinges on the clarity of the question or hypothesis before data collection begins. The researcher must have a clear understanding of what is meant by each key concept involved in the research question. For instance, "ego involvement" may refer to the extent to which a belief or attitude has concrete implications for the individual, the extent to which it is directly related to other beliefs and attitudes, and so on.

In addition, concepts must be amenable to operationalization. That is, the investigator must be able either to manipulate or measure each key concept in such a way that it does not distort the meaning of the concept. Clearly, the researcher cannot capture all facets of meaning of a central concept, but the particular operationalization used in the study must fairly reflect the central meaning of the concept.

The scope of the question must also be clarified. The researcher should be as specific as possible about the conditions under which relationships described in the research question are expected to obtain. Consider the hypothesis "People evidence more attitude change when they receive a message from a highly credible source than from a lowly credible source." Based on numerous investigations, the claim appears to be true only within a very short time after receipt of the message and only for issues in which the message recipient has little at stake.

Finally, when possible, the extent of any purported relationship should be specified. Rather than simply indicting that a highly credible source produced more attitude change than a lowly credible one, it would be helpful to know *how much* more. This degree of precision is frequently difficult to obtain in communication research, however, because we do not have an absolute scale to measure many variables of interest to our discipline.

Collecting Data. An introductory course in research methods cannot hope to describe all or even most of the factors involved in data collection. The principles that should be stressed, therefore, should center on the importance of *anticipating* how the data will be used in planning the collection procedure.

The researcher should anticipate as specifically as possible the manner in which data will be analyzed before collecting any information, because the mode of analysis will influence the form in which data ought to be collected. Suppose the investigation centers on the question of whether women offer more support than do men to others who introduce new ideas in a discussion. If the researcher later decides to include as one index of support the extent of eye gaze from others while an individual introduces a new idea, it would be very helpful to have video tapes available to code this measure. If this decision had not been reached prior to data collection, video tapes might not exist.

The researcher should attempt to maximize the explanatory power of the data. For instance, video tapes might reveal that women expressed more verbal agreement than did men with individuals introducing a new idea. But the researcher might have had participants in the discussion review the video tape and indicate each time they spoke what the purpose of their utterance had been. This procedure of probing the reasons for the utterance might yield direct confirmation from women that they felt a need to support an individual introducing a new idea, or it might reveal that the women simply were more convinced than men that the new idea was a good one.

Before collecting data, the researcher should anticipate any potential questions concerning the reliability and/or validity of the data, and make an effort to preclude such questions. If a measure is not reliable (replicable) and valid (reflects the concept it is designed to measure), then no conclusion that relies on this measure can be defended. Thus, if the investigator were planning to use a method of direct observation, and they anticipated that serious questions could be raised about the reliability of this approach in the given case, multiple observers might have been used if a method such as videotaping did not seem appropriate or practical.

Analyzing Data.   At least three general principles apply to the analysis of data, regardless of the type of methodology employed:

1. The primary analysis should attempt to straightforwardly and unequivocally respond to the question that motivated the project. Sometimes, a researcher will become mired in a mass of data and begin presenting so many analyses that the reader finishes a research report without being certain whether the research question was supported.

2. The investigator may find it useful to perform subsidiary analyses designed to refute alternative explanations. For instance, a positive relationship has been demonstrated repeatedly between perspective taking and use of communication strategies that accommodate to the needs of others. One counterargument to the claim of a direct relationship between these variables is that both characteristics increase with age, and

if subjects with a wide age span are included in the study, the results may reflect nothing other than the correlation of both these variables with age. Statistical techniques have been used, however, to hold constant the impact of age, and to document the relationship between perspective taking and listener accommodation directly.

3. Data analysis serves the function of discovering answers to questions, but it also serves the function of yielding evidence to support the conclusions the researcher has reached. Thus, the investigator should attempt to find the clearest and most persuasive way of presenting this evidence.

Reporting the Research Project.   The basic steps in the research report outlined next are those typically used in reporting empirical work. Historical and critical studies follow essentially the same pattern, although in these cases the results are more elaborated because there are not brief, quantitative summaries of the findings.

1. The introduction should provide a rationale for conducting the study. The introduction should not review all relevant literature but should present an argument for the contribution that the study has to offer. The argument may justify both investigating the general area and indicating the specific contribution of this particular study. The introduction also serves to introduce and clarify the specific research question(s).

2. The methods used in the study need to be described in enough detail and with sufficient precision that the study could be replicated.

3. Similarly, the results must be presented in sufficient detail to make clear the degree to which the research question was supported.

4. The function of the discussion is to indicate the value and limitations of the study. Thus, any features of the design or its execution that may have influenced results ought to be identified. The investigator should also explain *why* the results were obtained. Finally, the discussion section should indicate the way the results of the current study support, contradict, or refine thinking in the area under investigation.

Evaluation of Research

Three criteria can be applied to evaluate the worth of any research project: the value, or significance, of the question itself, the internal validity (i.e., the extent to which the data support the conclusions reached), and the external validity or generalizability of the results.

Value of the Question.   Although any research project may yield some useful information, resources are finite, including the time of both the researcher and consumers of the research. Thus, it is useful to evaluate the comparative worth of questions that might be pursued:

1. Questions of broader scope seem to be of greater value. Early research in persuasion, for instance, was frequently criticized for concentrating primarily on issues in which individuals had little personal investment. The research questions would have been more useful if they had pursued issues related to a broader range of human behavior.

2. The greater the explanatory power of the question, the more useful it is likely to be. Research in differences in communication patterns between men and women, for example, has become more useful since the focus has shifted from simple differences in gender to underlying factors that account for the differences, such as the desire for power.

3. Questions are of greater value if they contribute to an understanding of phenomena that we consider to be significant in their own right, such as variables that account for success in the business world, ones that account for interpersonal attractiveness, or variables that are related to openness of expression. Although we might not reach perfect agreement about the relative importance of these areas, most would consider all three of these variables more important than use of an indefinite versus a definite article first in a sentence.

Internal Validity.   A research project has internal validity to the extent that the conclusions reached concerning relationships among the variables investigated actually exist. Without internal validity, the results of a study are not meaningful.

A major factor affecting internal validity is whether the operational definitions of the variables (i.e., the manner in which they are manipulated or assessed) actually reflect the core meaning of the variables. If the operational definitions fail to adequately reflect the concepts they represent, then the results cannot be taken as support for a relationship among variables under investigation.

It is possible for variables other than those that the researcher intends to study to influence the relationship of the variables under investigation. For example, in early empirical work in communication, the claim emerged that oral and written communication from the same individual differed on a number of features, such as sentence length, diversity of vocabulary, and so on. Later scrutiny suggested, however, that perhaps the difference was due simply to amount of preparation time rather than mode of encoding. Thus, preparation time was a contaminating variable, diminishing the internal validity of the study.

External Validity.   A research project is externally valid to the extent that its results generalize to a wide range of situations. A large number of factors can affect the generalizability of a study, so only the most common are mentioned here:

1. If the operational definition of a variable is not typical of the way it functions in general, then the results cannot generalize to the kinds of cases normally represented by the variable. For instance, if an instrument designed to measure attitude toward a speech actually measures interest in the speech instead, then no valid conclusions can be drawn about how the variable affects attitudes.

2. All variables are embedded in a specific context (e.g., fear appeals exist in speeches, not in a vacuum). The more typical the context, the more generalizable the results will be.

3. Similarly, the individuals used as subjects should be representative of the group to whom the results are intended to apply.

Ethical Procedures. Attention to use of ethical procedures may not influence the results, but it does influence the overall evaluation of the project. It is almost impossible to catalogue all the issues that must be considered in proceeding in an ethical fashion. Perhaps the most sensible criterion to be stressed, therefore, is that researchers should follow the same guidelines they would in their other behavior. We consider it unethical to deceive others, humiliate them, inflict pain on them, and so on. Thus, the researcher should abide by the same constraints we place on all of our dealings with fellow humans.

SUGGESTIONS FOR INSTRUCTION

As is typically true in teaching any course, success is contingent, in part, upon selection of appropriate illustrations, assignments that enable students to apply what they are studying, and readings and resource material that is comprehensible and useful. Accordingly, suggestions are offered in each of these areas.

Illustrating Basic Principles

When students are first becoming familiar with basic types of research and the stages necessary to produce research, principles should be illustrated with simple, uncluttered designs that involve few variables. Much contemporary research requires the ability to understand relationships among multiple variables simultaneously and a fairly sophisticated understanding of statistics to appreciate the design. Studies that involve few variables are less likely to confuse the novice. Work of earlier decades might be used at the beginning of the course until students understand basic features of designs. As students gain a better grasp of the principles of design, the instructor can introduce studies with obvious flaws for students to identify and suggest alternative means of avoiding the problems.

Sample Assignments

In an introductory course that encompasses a variety of methodologies, the instructor is always frustrated by the lack of time to develop skills in depth. The assignments suggested hereafter are ones that can be truncated or abbreviated as the instructor sees fit, but are intended to reinforce the principles and strategies outlined earlier in this chapter.

1. Abstract a research report within each major methodology. Be sure to highlight the basic design and research choices that were made.

2. Critique a research report within each major methodology using the categories for evaluation outlined earlier.

3. Write a research proposal (the student should select the research question and basic methodology). Justify each major design decision.

4. Conduct, as a group, a very limited research project (each student should write an individual report of the project). Class discussions should emphasize the options available at various stages of the project, and the class should justify the choices that they make. Writing individual reports ensures that each student has an understanding of the basic decisions reached and essential features of the design.

SUPPLEMENTARY READING

Because the introductory course in research methods cannot treat any one method in detail, it may be useful to use a text that provides an overview of all the methods described earlier.

Anderson, J. A. (1987). *Communication research: Issues and methods.* New York: McGraw-Hill.
Auer, J. J. (1959). *An introduction to research in speech.* New York: Harper & Brothers.
Bowers, J. W., & Courtwright, J. A. (1984). *Communication research methods.* Glenview, IL: Scott, Foresman.
Rubin, R. B., Rubin, A. M., & Piele, L. J. (1986). *Communication research: Strategies and sources.* Belmont, CA: Wadsworth.
Smith, M. J. (1988). *Contemporary communication research methods.* Belmont, CA: Wadsworth.
Tucker, R. K., Weaver, R. L., & Berryman-Fink, C. (1981). *Research in speech communication.* Englewood Cliffs, NJ: Prentice-Hall.

REFERENCES

Auer, J. J. (1959). *An introduction to research in speech*. New York: Harper & Brothers.

Rubin, R. B., Rubin, A. M., & Piele, L. J. (1986). *Communication research: Strategies and sources*. Belmont, CA: Wadsworth.

III

ORGANIZING THE INSTRUCTIONAL CONTEXT

15

Classroom Roles
of the Teacher

Kathleen M. Galvin
Northwestern University

Teaching is a word that describes a multifaceted relationship. As you find yourself wearing the label "teacher," you will ask yourself: "Who am I for these students in this classroom?" and "How are they changing my life?" The label "teacher" seems to imply a singular entity—a teacher is a person who performs the act of teaching. Yet, the more time you spend in classrooms, the more you recognize the complexity of the teaching–learning process. A focus on classroom roles provides one lens for examining this complexity. Through this examination one quickly discovers the many aspects of life as a teacher—the many parts of the role of teacher.

What are roles? Are they parts one plays or are they masks one puts on for an hour or a term? Some current writers view the college classroom from a dramatistic perspective, drawing parallels between acting and teaching (Homan, 1985, Timpson & Tobin, 1982). These authors maintain that both acts exercise one's capacity to learn: Both are problem solving activities, and both involve playing roles in order to communicate. This dramatistic perspective may, however, reduce teachers to actors, playing a part that is removed from their actual person. Other literature on teaching describes teachers as playing such roles as supporter, evaluator, disciplinarian, expert, facilitator, socializing agent, formal authority, ego ideal, or person. (Friedrich, Galvin, & Book, 1976; Mann et al., 1970; Timpson & Tobin, 1982). These labels provide a partial understanding of how roles function in classrooms.

Historically, roles have been conceived of as "positions"—a static view that describes a series of expectations for an occupant of a given position, such as "teacher" or "student." These expectations carry beliefs about how a role can and should be enacted no matter what the circumstances (Linton, 1945). According to this traditional view, the label "teacher" implies the performance of a list of behaviors, such as: (a) teachers come to class prepared, (b) teachers treat students equally, and (c) teachers evaluate student learning. This one-dimensional approach ignores the effects that other parts of the instructional classroom have on teacher performance.

In recent years, roles have been viewed from an interactive perspective, emphasizing the emerging aspects of roles and the behavioral regularities that develop out of social interaction. Classroom roles are viewed as repetitive patterns of behavior by which classroom members (teachers and students) fulfill classroom functions. This approach captures the transactional nature of encounters experienced by persons with labels such as teacher or student.

A transactional view of communication describes each party in an interaction as simultaneously involved. Such a view of classroom interaction implies that teachers and students are engaged in a constant mutual influence process with each simultaneously affecting how the other communicates. Hart (1986) captured the essence of this process: "Teachers act. They act on people. And they are acted upon in return. This is the physics of educating" (p. 5).

THREE DIMENSIONS OF INTERACTIVE ROLES

Viewing roles as interactive requires a description of three dimensions: (a) the personality and background of the person who occupies a position, (b) the relationships that the person is involved in while holding the position, and (c) the system expectations and feedback. It requires a consideration of teacher–student interaction as well as the influence of outside forces (such as the administration or department's position on how the classroom members assume their roles). Assume that you are teaching an introductory survey course to see how each of the three dimensions affects your classroom life.

Personality and Background

Your personal characteristics and previous experience affect classroom behavior. If you are a very organized and analytical individual, you will critique points of organization or reasoning in a speech that someone else might miss. If you attended schools with a homogeneous religious, ethnic, or socioeconomic student body, you may base your expectations on this experience. If you went to an undergraduate school that emphasized an experimental approach to interpersonal communication, you will bring different expectations about how class time should be spent than a colleague who heard only theoretical lectures on the subject.

In addition to your personal characteristics and experiences, your students' personalities and backgrounds influence class learning. If you have an extroverted student with a strong debate background in your rhetorical analysis class, you may create opportunities for that student to do an in-depth speech analysis for the class. In addition, you may ask that student to work individually with certain anxious speakers before their presentations.

Relationships

Your relationships with students, faculty, and administration will also influence your role. Students who challenge your every comment may bring out your well-veiled argumentative nature. The students who pay attention only when you discuss the business application of communication skills may lead you to discuss applications frequently. Your colleagues may share their class materials, providing you with new approaches. In some cases, you may find yourself team teaching and negotiating each lesson plan with a dissimilar colleague.

System Expectation and Feedback

Institutional expectations directly affect your teaching. If you are expected to administer a departmental exam at the end of the quarter, you cannot ask students to design their own learning evaluation measure. If you receive feedback from your department chair that your persuasion unit is too difficult for freshmen, you may change your material for the next term. You will maintain required office hours and teach required units.

As these examples demonstrate, roles are inextricably bound to the communication process. Teacher and student roles are developed and maintained through communication. In order to understand how roles operate in the speech classroom, one must look at role development, role functions, and role conflicts. Although this chapter approaches roles from an interactive perspective, greater attention is devoted to teachers than to students.

ROLE DEVELOPMENT

Classroom roles emerge through a complex two-fold process that involves (a) role expectation and (b) role performance. In both cases, personal background, relationships with significant others, and system expectations and feedback affect development.

Role Expectations

Much of your life has been spent in classrooms—evaluating subjects and teachers and developing implicit expectations about teaching. As you considered a career in teaching, you may have resolved to challenge fine writers, as your sophomore-year English teachers did, or you may have decided never to mimic poor performers, as your junior-year drama teacher did. You may have found cross-cultural communication or oral history to be so fascinating that you planned to incorporate such issues in many of your classes.

Your experience with teachers and speech-related courses helped set your expectations. You may have studied with one professor for three or four classes, resolving to "teach like Professor Griffin someday." Your positive experiences in small discussion classes set expectations for creating similar classroom dynamics. If you enjoyed small group work, you are likely to use small groups in your teaching.

The comments of significant others (fellow students or other faculty) may set expectations about how good teachers act. Their criticism or praise of teachers influences how you view "good" or "bad" classroom behavior. The hours spent drinking soft drinks or coffee and comparing teachers set strong expectations for future behavior.

Finally, messages from the educational system influence expectations. As a student, you may have learned that good teachers are rewarded by the educational system. Or you may have learned that only research articles matter to administrators. While job hunting, faculty may inform you that students at their college are brilliant and highly self-motivated. This information establishes very specific expectations for classroom behavior. It is in these ways that beliefs and background, significant others, and the general system expectations influence role expectations.

Role Performance

In classrooms, things don't always happen as expected. Your capacities affect how you assume your role. For example, although you may wish to hold open-ended discussions, your personal anxiety surfaces whenever students raise unpredictable ideas and, in order to keep control, you may return to lecturing. Although you wish to use simulations, you may find that your lack of experience keeps you from being comfortable with this approach. Surprises occur when expectations do not meet reality. A teacher who expects to lecture regularly may feel drawn to a less-structured small group approach. Another teacher who expects to be satisfied only with graduate seminars may look forward to freshman class assignments.

Significant others also influence how you play a role. A close colleague may say, "I refuse to support your move to develop a competency test for the basic course." Another may say, "Here are my unit plans for the language unit. You can get some ideas from them." The most important significant others (your students) influence what is possible in a classroom. For example, you may wish to act as a facilitator but encounter students who refuse to take responsibility for their own learning. In contrast, you may prepare to rely on the introductory textbook and discover that the students demand more rigorous content. Students from very different religious, ethnic, or socioeconomic backgrounds than your own may present you with unanticipated issues or concerns.

A recent study of college classrooms reports a frequent mismatch between faculty and student expectations, a gap that leaves both parties unfulfilled. The faculty (concerned with scholarship) wanted to share ideas with appreciative students. "'Intellectually-meek' students wanted everything spelled out and were willing to conform for the sake of grades" (Boyer, 1987, pp. 140–141).

Finally, the institutional system influences performance. For example, you may receive a notice from the dean's office stressing the need to teach writing within the speech course or requiring X number of office hours a week. The basic course committee may decide to drop the rhetorical analysis assignment and replace it with an interviewing experience. You may wait for years to teach your favorite subject because another professor or department "controls" the course.

Whatever your current state of role development, be assured it will be different in 5 years and in 25 years. Personal changes will be reflected in your classroom expectations and performance. Societal and school changes will be reflected in the students and systems.

ROLE FUNCTIONS

Role functions provide a means for examining classroom life. The image of a system as a mobile can be used to visualize the various role functions within a classroom that affect the balance of the institutional system.

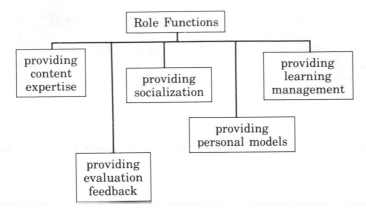

FIG. 15.1.   The various role functions within the classroom.

Figure 15.1 pictures a mobile containing the various role functions needed to keep the system operating and balanced. From a transactional perspective, teachers, students, and significant others may perform as part of each role function. The primary role functions are: (a) providing content expertise, (b) providing learning management, (c) providing evaluative feedback, (d) providing socialization, and (e) providing personal models.

Providing Content Expertise

The finest teachers care passionately about their subject. They find joy in talking about the field of study that pervades their lives. These people are committed to creating a change in their students through thoughtful structuring of content that connects to their students' lives. Teachers of communication experience countless opportunities to excite students. Some of the most memorable teachers are those who use the classroom as a communication laboratory. There are those who use the previous night's presidential address as an example of a rhetorical device or who describe family systems theory at work in a new film. Communication becomes part of one's intellectual life, rather than an isolated academic responsibility. Students contribute to this process through questions, challenges, individual knowledge, and personal research. Individual students may contribute content expertise as a result of past experiences. Such classrooms reflect a sense of intellectual heritage as well as recognition of current thought.

Although content expertise may result partly from graduate school training, over time it depends on a teacher's willingness to (a) keep abreast of his or her chosen area and (b) explore the complexities of the communication field and its related areas. Today's courses in political communication, family communication, oral history, and performance art were originally exploratory offerings taught by persons exploring interconnections of theories and research perspectives.

Managing Learning

Not only must teachers know their subjects; they must communicate them effectively with learners. In his study of master college teachers, Epstein (1981) concluded:

> There is many a tried, but no true method for doing this: Socratic teaching, sonorous lecturing, sympathetic discussion, passionate argument, witty exposition, dramatics and other parts of derring-do; plain power of personal example, main force of intellect, and sometimes even bullying. (p. xii)

The teacher creates, alone or with student involvement, the specific learning process, including diagnosis, objective setting, selection of strategies, and evaluation. Effective teachers demonstrate an ability to use a wide range of methods or strategies (such as discussion, lecture, higher order questioning, role playing), selecting the appropriate one based on perception of student needs. Throughout the term, the teacher uses learner feedback to modify original goals and plans.

The establishment of policies, rules, deadlines, and disciplinary structures occur within the management function. These may be established through vertical communication from the instructor or through a more horizontal approach involving student input.

Management includes the creation of a classroom climate designed to support a particular type of learning. For example, teachers of performance or discussion-oriented classes work to establish a safe and supportive climate for performance and the sharing of opinions. Rules and disciplinary policies are developed as an intrinsic means of supporting the desired learning climate.

Providing Evaluation/Feedback

Most educational institutions require a formal evaluation upon the completion of a specified unit of study. Often, the function of evaluation serves to demonstrate a separation of teachers and students on the basis of power. It could, however, serve to engage them in a cooperative development of evaluation measures. According to Fuhrmann and Grasha (1983, see pp. 182–183), assigning grades may be perceived as negative if grades allow faculty to exercise superiority and unnecessary control over students who view the grade solely as an academic end. Grades may be perceived as valuable if they are used to motivate, reward student accomplishment, or provide feedback. The use of the evaluation function interacts significantly with the management of learning.

The nature of the communication field necessitates that classroom members develop skills in critiquing or delivering feedback of oral performance. Students must receive carefully created critiques designed to foster continued improvement. Such feedback may be given by the teacher, other students, or both. A review of research on providing feedback suggests that teachers need to be knowledgeable about the effects of various types of feedback and should consciously provide appropriate criticism to student speakers. In addition, the research indicates that students can be trained to give helpful feedback to peers (Book, 1985).

Providing Socialization

Classrooms are the settings for academic socialization to an entire field and to ways of thinking. Teachers are gatekeepers to a world that represents their field and the values, assumptions, and types of intellectual life that characterize their discipline. As a representative of an academic field and an academic way of life, a teacher discusses his or her intellectual positions, research interests, and the process of intellectual growth. Students question, react, and contribute positions learned elsewhere.

A teacher's classroom behavior may include lectures and anecdotes describing positions taken by members of the field and reasons for these positions. In addition, a teacher may describe his or her academic background, past professional positions, current research interests, and intellectual struggles. Out-of-class behaviors may include personal conversations on choices of graduate schools and future careers.

Classrooms are also the scene of more personal socialization as teachers exert influence regarding societal values. In Hart's (1986) words, teachers are revolutionaries, insurgents, and liberators as "they make people better than they thought they could be" (p. 4). He has claimed, "As teachers of speech communication, then you and I peddle freedom. And it is the best source of freedom of all: Our students become all that they can imagine becoming" (p. 6). Communication courses speak directly to values that support democratic and cultural citizenship, interpersonal growth, or political awareness.

Although student–teacher relationships are normally affected by forces such as length of terms or graduation, in unusual cases a teacher may evolve into a mentor for one or more specific students. The mentor, a trusted counselor, serves as a guide to life in the academic world of communication. Issues of sensitivity to students, a scholar's curiosity, academic ethics and values, publication directions, and personal boundaries may be explored over time between mentor and student, a relationship that enhances both parties (McGovern, 1980).

Providing Personal Models

Teachers teach *who* they are as well as *what* they believe intellectually. From the first moments in a classroom, students begin to build a persona for an instructor. Although some instructors deliberately cloak themselves in distance or mystery, most portray many sides of their nature, engaging students in mutually rewarding relationships. Teachers and students are interested in having themselves validated within the relationship that develops in the classroom. Teachers share personal anecdotes, family stories, or feelings about certain significant moments in the class. Students refer to family and work experiences, as well as to their developing values and intellectual positions. As stated by Friedrich et al. (1976), when teachers participate as persons in the class, ". . . the interaction is not limited to the course content, but deals with relational messages and personal feelings, attitudes and values out of a sense of interpersonal awareness, respect and trust" (p. 42). This relationship may continue outside of classroom boundaries as students seek personal guidance about family, romantic, or personal growth issues.

For some students, a teacher serves as a role model—an adult who appears to have reached a desired level of intellectual and personal development. Within the communication field, students expect to view a teacher as a model of personal communication competence as well as a communication scholar.

Students may serve as peer role models, demonstrating their excitement and capability in intellectual pursuits or their performance competence in theatre, interpretation, media, or speechmaking. Graduate students often find themselves serving as realistic and intellectually stimulating personal models for undergraduates.

The preceding five role functions could be expanded to include additional categories. Whatever the categories, they will reflect the interactive nature of the functions—teachers act on people, and they are acted upon in return.

As you already know, this interaction may not occur smoothly or predictably. The final section addresses some of the conflicts that may occur as teachers and students together attempt to create a learning environment.

ROLE CONFLICT

Teaching has been described ideally as two persons sitting on both ends of a log and talking. At key moments, teaching is that dialogue—an interlocking of two minds. A fine teacher struggles to confront and understand concerns that surface as one's being (background, beliefs, experience, values) come into contact with those of another person or system. Conflicts may occur over differences in the priority of role functions or the choices within role functions. This section briefly addresses interpersonal and intrapersonal conflicts related to role development and role functions.

Interpersonal Conflicts

When role expectations or performances of significant others collide with the teacher's or students' expectations or performance, role conflicts develop. For example, you may wish to share your content expertise in a large group lecture, with little one-to-one time devoted to feedback on papers or performances. Students, colleagues, or administrators, however, may pressure you to hold longer office hours or to be more available for student conferences. You may plan to manage classroom learning as a facilitator, forcing students to take responsibility for extensive independent work. The class, however, may resist this approach by consistently arriving unprepared or confused, forcing you to confront the issue directly. Department or school administrators may send messages that your good work in teaching is "fine," but you should not spend too much time on it—thus neglecting your research. These admonitions may run counter to your personal values. Your position within the system may contribute to role conflict. If you are a graduate student, you may find yourself constantly negotiating the boundaries of a system. You struggle with questions such as, "To what extent am I a full-fledged teacher and to what extent am I still a student? Will undergraduates treat me differently than they would a full-time faculty member?" The ambiguous "in between" status may leave you open to more conflictual experiences and situations than those faced by full-time faculty.

Background experiences provide you with role expectations for interpersonal conflict style. Hocker (1986) described this well: "If one had as models professors who were imperious and demanding but rigorous and fair, one might try to emulate that style in class" (p. 75). On the other hand, she suggested, if one learned from professors who were empathetic and concerned about the personal growth of their students, a different style of conflict resolution might be adopted. The conflict style you develop will reflect your expectations and experiences in the performance of classroom confrontation.

Intrapersonal Conflicts

When teachers experience incongruity between role expectation and performance, internal conflict arises. On occasion, such conflict serves the productive function of driving one to meet a desired expectation. In other situations, you may realistically or reluctantly revise your expectations, and you may rely on the feedback of significant others, students, colleagues, and/or administrators to check out your perception of effectiveness. Students experience similar types of internal conflict when their expectations do not match the feedback given to their performance.

Finally, classroom members face a special type of internal conflict when confronting interface issues. An educational myth suggests that teachers can and should treat everyone equally. Yet reality tells you that you connect easily or positively with one student, whereas your contact with another is negative or distant. In some cases, this linkage or lack of linkage is so powerful that it can interface with clarity or fairness in the classroom. Interface issues arise when a strong internal psychological concern is triggered by another classroom member.

A brash, confrontive student may remind you of your immature teenage self or your overpowering parent and evoke feelings of anger or disgust. A shy student may cause feelings to surface regarding your own reticence and cause you to be overprotective toward this student. These powerful, emotional reactions to a student signal an internal conflict and a need to consider whether the problem lies in the student or in oneself.

Conflicts are less likely to arise when all parties believe they are engaged in meaningful work. The effective functioning of a classroom system depends on the cooperative attitude and intellectual curiosity of all members. If faculty and students do not see themselves as having important business to do together, prospects for effective learning are diminished (Boyer, 1987, p. 141).

The teaching–learning process is enhanced when members of the classroom community can make explicit and can negotiate, if necessary, their role expectations and performance of role functions. When all persons involved in learning enrich each other, sparks fly. Or, in the words of Epstein (1981):

> Everywhere the task of teaching is the same—this lighting of sparks, this setting aflame—and everywhere it is carried differently. This is the inherent fascination of the subject. (p. xviii)

REFERENCES

Boyer, E. (1987). *College: The undergraduate experience in America.* New York: Harper & Row.

Book, C. (1985). Providing feedback: The research on effective oral and written feedback strategies. *Central States Speech Journal, 36,* 14–23.

Epstein, J. (Ed.). (1981). *Masters: Portraits of great teachers.* New York: Basic Books.

Friedrich, G., Galvin, K., & Book, C. (1976). *Growing together: Classroom communication.* Columbus, OH: Charles Merrill.

Fuhrmann, B., & Grasha, A. (1983). *A practical handbook for college teachers.* Boston: Little/Brown.

Hart, R. (1986, February). *Sex, drugs, rock 'n roll and speech: Why we're in Tucson.* Speech delivered at the meeting of the Western Speech Communication Association, Tucson, AZ.

Hocker, J. (1986). Teacher–student confrontations. In J. Civikly (Ed.), *Communicating in college classrooms. New directions for teaching and learning* (pp. 71–02). San Francisco. Jossey-Bass.

Homan, S. (1985). The classroom as theater. In J. Katz (Ed.), *Teaching as though students mattered: New directions for teaching and learning* (pp. 69–78). San Francisco: Jossey-Bass.

Linton, R. (1945). *The cultural background of personality.* New York: Appleton-Century-Crofts.

Mann, R., Arnold, S., Binder, J., Cytrynbaum, S., Newman, B., Ringwald, B., Ringwald, J., & Rosenwein, R. (1970). *The college classroom: Conflict, change and learning.* New York: Wiley.

McGovern, T. (1980). The dynamics of mentoring. In J. Noonan (Ed.), *Learning about teaching: New directions for teaching and learning* (pp. 53–62). San Francisco: Jossey Bass.

Timpson, W., & Tobin, D. (1982). *Teaching as performing.* Englewood Cliffs, NJ: Prentice-Hall.

16

Individual Differences in Classroom Dynamics

Joan Gorham
West Virginia University

If a teacher talks in the woods—perhaps next to the proverbial tree that has just fallen—and no one hears, has he or she taught? Probably not. Teaching–learning transactions are interactive. Effective instructional communication is receiver-centered; it is done *with* students, not *to* them. It is not uncommon, however, to find perfectly normal teachers and administrators, with well-managed classrooms and schools, who perceive themselves as principal players and their students as generic extras ("Call Central Casting. We need a few more student-types to balance the set.")

This chapter is organized around four philosophical tenets that have emerged from research as well as experience on both sides of the teacher's desk:

1. If you don't know where you're going, you won't know when you get there;
2. There is more than one route to Chicago;
3. Learning doesn't have to hurt; and
4. Education and learning are not necessarily synonymous.

IF YOU DON'T KNOW WHERE YOU'RE GOING, YOU WON'T KNOW WHEN YOU GET THERE

In his *Basic Principles of Curriculum and Instruction* (1949), Ralph Tyler (the father of the instructional objective) noted that there are four fundamental questions that must be answered in developing any curriculum or plan of instruction:

1. What outcomes should the school (course, unit) seek to attain?
2. What experiences can be provided that are likely to attain these outcomes?
3. How can these experiences be effectively organized?
4. How can we determine whether these outcomes are being attained?

The first question concerns objectives; the other three questions cannot be addressed until the objectives are clarified.

Tyler further noted that there are two kinds of "needs" that must be considered when formulating objectives. The first kind of need represents the gap between where students are and where we would like them to be. Assessing needs of this type can be compared to a travel agent's planning a client's trip: Before an itinerary can be established, the agent must know where the client is starting from and where he or she would like to end up. The second kind of need represents physical, social and integrative priorities. Using the same analogy, the travel agent's planning will be further influenced by his or her knowledge of whether the client can drive 4, 8, or 12 hours a day before exhaustion sets in, whether smoking or nonsmoking airline seats are required, whether an isolated beach or a Club Med atmosphere is preferred, and whether a tightly planned itinerary or one with more flexibility is appropriate.

Both kinds of needs are likely to differ among individual students. Both must be considered prior to planning and organizing the activities in which students will engage, and the means by which they will be evaluated. For example, foreign students who have a relatively unsophisticated command of the English language are at an immediate disadvantage in a competitively evaluated public speaking class. Insofar as their success in the American educational system—and beyond, should they plan to remain in this country—is likely to be influenced by their ability to communicate effectively, the objective of improving their public communication skills in English is appropriate. The concepts we teach them are no different than those that we teach the native students: organization, simplification, redundancy, visual aids, and interest. The applied product will probably be different, with more emphasis on, for example, visual aids to clarify words and points that may be unclear in the verbal/vocal delivery and less emphasis on humor, drama, and other verbal skills. Foreign students are also more likely to assume a passive learner role in the classroom, in part because of lack of confidence in their ability to express ideas in a second language and in part because they are likely to be accustomed to more formal teacher–student roles and less classroom interaction than that desired by many American communication teachers. Any student who is new to the American culture and educational system is likely to have different social and integrative needs than do native students. Teachers can choose to evaluate their participation differently or to work specifically toward teaching the skills of and providing practice in "active studenting." In either case, the objectives should be clear to both teacher and students.

Adult students (those who are older than the traditional student and who are likely to be juggling student, spouse, parent, and employee roles) can also have social and integrative needs that are different from those of traditional students. They are likely to have their own objectives for applying what they learn, particularly in the case of practical commu nication concepts and skills, to their personal experience base. Some adult students have a good deal of sophisticated first-hand experience, the kind that can be intimidating to an instructor who is considerably younger and not particularly confident in his or her expert power base. These students often have a great many preoccupations outside of the learning situation. Some are organized, some impatient, some overwhelmed: most of them have a strong need for some sense of control over both learning and grade outcomes. Setting objectives *with* rather than *for* adult students often fosters a sense of "joint ownership" that is comfortable to both instructor and student.

The needs of traditional students will also differ within a high school or college classroom. It is important to remember that instructional objectives can (and should) target cognitive, affective, and psychomotor outcomes. Cognitive learning objectives focus on the transfer of knowledge and can be directed toward lower order outcomes (such as recall and comprehension) or higher order outcomes (such as application, synthesis, analysis, and evaluation). Affective objectives focus on changes in student attitudes, beliefs, and values. Psychomotor objectives focus on improving performance of observable skills. Communication teachers will enhance their effectiveness if they clearly articulate and explicitly acknowledge their goals in each of the learning domains. Test questions tend to evaluate, and reward, only lower order cognitive learning through the use of closed questions with specific right or wrong answers. Application, analysis, synthesis, and evaluation goals can be encouraged through the use of open questions (e.g., How does this fit? What could you do with this? What do you think of this? What questions could you ask regarding this approach or topic?) These can be test questions (evaluated on reasoning rather than opinion) or the topics of short response papers, journal entries, or directed small group discussions.

Public speaking classes may focus on performance outcomes at the expense of affective outcomes, rewarding students who liked speaking to begin with and causing students who disliked or feared speaking at the outset to dislike or fear it more as they are judged in comparison to others in the class. In nonperformance communication classes, students who see value in the concepts discussed and who believe that they have real-world application will be more likely to use what they learn outside the class-room. If we believe that the study of communication is a practical endeav-or (that argument is used to defend the inclusion of required communica-tion courses in secondary and higher education degree programs), we cannot ignore the centrality of affective objectives. We also cannot ignore the fact that many students who take communication courses to meet graduation requirements do not expect to like the course, do not initially believe that the concepts or skills addressed are useful, and do not expect any value beyond the credit hours earned. In bridging the gap between where students are and where we would like them to be, we must consider the differing affective, cognitive, and psychomotor baselines of indi-vidual classes and students; which leads to the second tenet.

THERE IS MORE THAN ONE ROUTE TO CHICAGO

There is no reason why everyone must take the same route to Chicago (or anywhere). One route may be faster but cost more in tolls; one may be more scenic; one may allow a stopover a little off the track to take in a once-in-a-lifetime exhibition. A thoughtful travel agent will often pro-vide alternative plans, allowing clients the luxury of informed choice with the assurance that following any of several options will eventually lead to Chicago.

Students deserve to know a teacher's objectives, what they are ulti-mately expected to do or know or think or feel, and how the attainment of those objectives will be approached and evaluated. Some students will choose to go only part of the way. Some will encounter breakdowns and make wrong turns. If a curriculum is geared toward objectives, rather than routes and timing, however, a teacher will be more likely to adapt to such situational anomalies.

With objective-based teaching, there is no reason why every student—from term to term or even among sections of the same course in the same term—needs to have the same set of experiences in the same order *if the objectives are met*. As Tyler (1949) has noted, "Learning takes place through the active behavior of the student; it is what *he* does that he learns, not what the teacher does. It is possible for two students to be in the same class and for them to be having two different experiences" (p. 63). This is one reason why there can be such tremendous variation among students' evaluations of the same class. Some like it, and some don't; some feel the teaching is direct and clear, and some are continually confused; some want more, whereas some drop out. Students who are afforded an opportunity to make choices regarding their approaches to course objectives benefit from the sense of shared power and control. They are also more likely to receive courses that accommodate their individual learning styles.

Learning styles have been defined by Keefe (1982) as the "cognitive, affective, and physiological traits that serve as relatively stable indicators of how learners perceive, interact with, and respond to learning environments" (p. 43). Style elements may be conditions under which an individual is most comfortable and prefers to learn or factors that must be considered for information to be processed and stored. They may refer to cognitive processing; to affective or motivational concerns; to visual, auditory, or manipulative information-processing strengths; or to structural/environmental preferences. Regardless of the focus of assessment, conclusions and recommendations throughout the learning style literature reflect several common themes: different individuals prefer to learn in different ways; individual learning styles are identifiable; teachers and institutions should consider style in instructional delivery; students' recognition of their own learning styles can help them make useful decisions regarding their approaches to selecting and modifying information; and matching or mismatching learning style and instructional technique has significant implications for both cognitive and affective learning (Gorham, 1986, p. 411).

Curry's (1983) analysis of various learning style models led her to suggest that style elements can be likened to the layers of an onion, with the inner layers more stable than the outer layers. "Cognitive personality" elements are at the core of the onion. Probably the most widely researched example of cognitive personality is Witkin's field dependence–independence continuum (Witkin, Dyk, Oltman, Raskin, & Karp, 1971). Field independent (FI) persons use predominantly internal cues when making judgments; they are "splitters" who have little difficulty learning separate parts of a whole out of context. Field dependent (FD) persons are "lumpers" who use predominantly external cues and learn best once they have "the big picture." FIs tend to do better in traditional classrooms and are thus more likely to become teachers who continue to teach the way they learn best, by splitting concepts and skills into small units and systematically working toward pulling them together. FDs learn best with models and practice. They appear to depend more on *impression* than on *expression;* they are better able to "feel" their way through various public speaking opportunities (developing a gestalt sense of what works and what does not work along the way) than they are able to pull together the lessons of separate units for demonstration in one or two final performances.

In any classroom we are likely to find students who range from highly field dependent to highly field independent. In some classrooms, such as those in programs serving educationally disadvantaged students from low socioeconomic backgrounds, the majority of students may tend toward field dependence (Gorham & Self, 1987). Insofar as the development of communication competencies is regarded as a stepping stone to successful competition in academic, employment, and social environments, communication teachers should be aware that differences in cognitive processing may make traditional instructional techniques, which are geared toward FIs, difficult for some students. Several points should be considered in working with FD students:

1. FDs are likely to take their cues from the immediate environment and compare their performance to immediately available models rather than to an abstract ideal. Good students hired as tutors for subsequent terms can provide peer models, as can taped student performances. FD students who experience only poor models will have difficulty analyzing problems in what they observe, despite discussion of effective communication strategies; their performance baseline tends to be drawn from their experience.

2. FDs use a holistic problem-solving approach and have difficulty drawing disconnected concepts out of a large body of information. FD students may do well on speaking assignments but experience difficulty articulating the concepts they used in creating the speech in an outline or on a test. The learning curve of FDs tends to show a sharp rise at the end of a course or unit, when all the pieces are in place. Grades averaged over the course of a term may not reflect end-point competencies; a succession of low grades might also undermine motivation before synthesis occurs.

3. FD students tend to be less competitive, to need more feedback, and to be more responsive to extrinsic motivation and to authority. This situation presents a strong case for cooperative, mastery learning models with shorter intervals between feedback opportunities and specific clarification and reinforcement of objectives.

4. FD students may have trouble in structuring independent time, a problem in adjusting to the flexibility of a university schedule. They are also less able to see the relevance of skills outside of context; thus, assignments that transfer skills to "real" situations within the university and beyond are suggested.

5. FD students may have a history of frustration in FI-oriented classrooms. This can lead to lower performance expectations and adoption of a

passive learner role, particularly in a competitive system. Sharing information on learning styles as differences, rather than deficiencies, has proven to be effective. Taught as receiver-centered information processing strengths, this concept is clearly related to other concepts that are regularly taught in communication courses.

6. FDs are particularly attentive to nonverbal cues and strongly influenced by their emotional responses to material. Their teachers should be aware of nonverbal immediacy cues and their demonstrated relationship to affective learning (Gorham & Self, 1987).

The middle layers of Curry's "onion" represent *information processing style,* an individual's intellectual approach to assimilating information. The outer layers represent *instructional preferences,* such as lecture versus group discussion. Information processing differences among individuals represent an interaction between cognitive personality traits and instructional preferences. A number of assessment approaches have been suggested (see Cornett, 1983; Gorham, 1986; Kirby, 1979; National Association of Secondary School Principles, 1979, 1982). McCarthy (1981) and Kolb (1976), for example, have developed learning style assessment inventories that classify learners as one of four types based on the degree to which they prefer concrete versus abstract and active versus reflective learning. Figure 16.1 illustrates the resulting four information processing styles.

Type One learners perceive information concretely and process it reflectively. They are innovative, imaginative, and concerned with personal

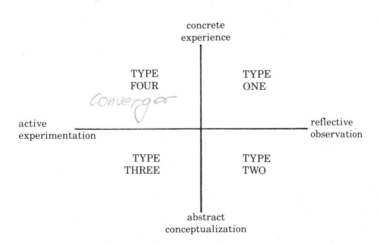

FIG. 16.1.   Information processing styles.

relevance; they need to clarify the ways in which a new concept or area of study links with previous experiences before they are receptive to learning it. They learn best through methods that encourage brainstorming and empathy.

Type Two learners perceive information abstractly and process it reflectively. Schools are traditionally designed for these learners, who value sequential thinking, details, and expert opinion. They are data collectors, more interested in ideas than applications, and they learn best with teachers who assume the role of information giver.

Type Three learners perceive information abstractly and process it actively. They seek utility and enjoy solving problems that test theories against common sense. They resent being given answers, and they have a limited tolerance for "fuzzy" ideas that cannot be applied practically. They learn best with teachers who act as coaches while facilitating hands-on experience.

Type Four learners perceive information concretely and process it actively. They learn well by trial and error, with teachers who serve as evaluators and remediators but who encourage self-discovery. They are dynamic learners with a very practical orientation; they prefer to teach themselves and then share what they have learned with others.

McCarthy's study of 17- and 18-year-old high school students categorized 35% as Type One, 22% as Type Two, 18% as Type Three, and 25% as Type Four learners. She subsequently suggested that teachers develop instructional units that move through the four quadrants, addressing each student's information processing style in the process (McCarthy, 1981). A unit on speech introductions, for example, might begin with students reading or listening to speeches with and without effective introductions and discussing their reactions. The class might then break into discussion groups to analyze their impressions of the purposes of a speech introduction (Type One). The instructor would then teach the concept, explaining the objectives of and techniques for gaining attention and previewing information as they are detailed in any public speaking text (Type Two). Students could then, on their own or in groups, formulate three or four different introductions for the same speech, decide which they like best, and explain why (Type Three). They might later be asked to prepare an outline for a speech they will give and to write two or three possible introductions on a separate page. Dyads could then exchange outlines, clarify the content as needed, and write two or three possible introductions for their partner's topic. Students would then evaluate the various possibilities, as well as discuss similarities and differences between speaker-generated and partner-generated ideas (Type Four). A unit on nonverbal communication might begin with the instructor asking his or her students to participate in several illustrative activities (e.g., "Pick a partner. Look him or her in the eyes. Now slowly move forward, maintaining eye contact, until your noses touch."), proceed through a lecture on theory and related research, continue with students trying and reporting on the responses to some nonverbal norm-breaking attempts outside of class, and end with groups designing simple studies that address questions of interest.

Instructional planning of this type is likely to also accommodate visual, auditory, and manipulative learners at various points. The redundancy is instructionally sound; the instructor may "cover" fewer concepts in a course, but a greater percentage of students will understand those that are presented. We have long taught that personalized examples, visual aids, and audience participation add interest to a speaker's presentation and thus contribute to retention and/or action. Perhaps these effects are related to variations in information processing style among audience members. At any rate, knowledge of learning styles gives communication teachers an added reason to practice what they preach.

LEARNING DOESN'T HAVE TO HURT

Social psychologist Elliot Aronson (cited in Kohn, 1986a) has observed that "The American mind in particular has been trained to equate success with victory, to equate doing well with beating someone" (p. 22). One need only read about "normal" grade distributions and pre-med students sabotaging their peers' experiments to be reminded how pervasive this philosophy is within the educational system. A very large body of research, however, has consistently shown that competition interferes with learning and that a cooperative approach yields far superior results, regardless of subject matter or age group (Kohn, 1986a, 1986b, 1987). Competition is often a cause of anxiety. In the words of Kohn (1986a), "Even if the tangible stakes—money, job, trophy, grades—are not always high when people compete, the psychological stakes invariably are. The possibility of losing makes for an emotional state that interferes with performance" (p. 27).

David and Roger Johnson, professors of education at the University of Minnesota, have completed more than 80 original studies (and reviewed hundreds of others), matching cooperative learning against competitive and individualistic models of instruction (Johnson & Johnson, 1987). In 21 of 26 controlled studies of achievement, cooperation clearly led to superior outcomes (two studies had mixed results and the other three yielded nonsignificant results). In 35 of 37 studies of interpersonal attraction, the Johnsons found that students tended to like each other more when they worked cooperatively. When some of the students were handicapped or of different ethnic backgrounds, prejudice declined and ridicule practically disappeared. Students who learned cooperatively had a higher regard for the subject, the teacher, and school in general. They also developed greater self-confidence. Removing the emphasis on competition, then, is likely to improve both cognitive and affective learning outcomes.

As Kohn (1986a) pointed out, motivational theory provides a framework for understanding why trying to do well and trying to beat out others work at cross-purposes. Extrinsic motivators do not make people perform as well as intrinsic motivators. In fact, several studies have shown that people judged high in achievement motivation do not perform well unless extrinsic motivation has been minimized. Psychologist Edward Deci of the University of Rochester, a leading investigator of extrinsic and intrinsic motivation, has noted that competition works just like any other extrinsic motivator: The activity itself is not the reward; the consequence of beating someone else is.

When we consider the goals of teaching communication, these findings are particularly salient. We do want our students to learn *about* communication; we also want them to come away from our classes with enhanced communication skills. This is true not only in the obvious context of public speaking courses; it should be an outcome of the study of other areas of communication as well. We know that students enter our classes with different abilities and needs. If we fail to assess and address these differences, we are likely to reward those students who already have a more sophisticated background, better writing skills, less communication apprehension, and greater interpersonal awareness. We are likely to lose students who lack precisely the abilities we are supposed to be developing.

Anxiety can inhibit learning. In highly stressful situations, individuals undergo physiological changes and adaptive responses that hinder the ability to manage the situation. Thus, test anxiety or communication apprehension can result in students' responding so strongly to the stress that they cannot respond appropriately to the demands of the task.

Communication-apprehensive students are those who experience a high level of fear or anxiety in response to real or anticipated communication with another person or persons. Richmond and McCroskey (1989) noted that approximately 20% of the population falls into each of the extreme high or low communication apprehension (CA) categories. Low CAs may not experience anxiety in situations where they should; high CAs experience apprehension in virtually all oral communication situations, even where there is no rational reason for such anxiety. People who are in the "normal" range may respond differently to different situations; for example, they may be quite comfortable in dyadic or small group situations but more anxious in highly evaluative situations, such as a job interview or giving a speech.

High CAs are likely to favor larger, lecture-type classes with few opportunities for student–student or student–teacher interaction. They will often drop a class with high communication requirements. One study found that over 50% of high CAs dropped a required public speaking course during the first 3 weeks, just before the first speech was due. Other studies have shown that high CAs are very likely to be absent on days when they are scheduled for presentations, that they sit in the back and along the sides of classrooms to avoid recognition, and that they almost never volunteer to participate, even when they know the right answer. In some instances, high CAs will knowingly give wrong answers to reduce their chances of being called on again. Recent research with college students demonstrated that high CA students who were told that they would be asked to participate in class by recalling information given in lecture for another classmate lost approximately 20% of the information. Their recall dropped sharply in contrast with high CA students in other classes who were not told they would have to communicate later (Richmond & McCroskey, 1989, pp. 52–54).

Communication classes are likely to place value on communicative behavior, even when they are not strictly performance classes. When they are performance classes, particularly required performance classes, teachers must be aware that approximately one in five students will experience anxiety that goes beyond simple stage fright. Treatments such as systematic desensitization and cognitive restructuring can reduce CA. They require training to administer and are most appropriately used in situations where high CAs have been identified and offered specialized help. Skills training itself may improve communication behavior and result in modest reductions in CA. A student who becomes confident in his or her knowledge of how to give an effective speech may perform better and feel less anxious as a result; however, such effects are usually related to the degree to which high CAs recognize skill deficiencies as a problem and voluntarily commit themselves to improving them, and to the degree to which the goals of the skills training are narrowly and specifically defined.

Knowledge of CA has obvious administrative and curricular implications. If the development of basic oral communication skills is perceived as a desired goal for an educational program, and if requiring a basic communication course is perceived as a fitting means to that end, then the existence of a single, generic "Speech 1" is clearly insufficient. Many instructors, however, find themselves teaching in precisely that situation. For them, CA must be recognized as a salient difference among individual students. Skill objectives must be narrowly and specifically defined, affective objectives explicitly recognized, and learning (or behavioral change) evaluated against an attainable standard.

Simply put, it is not fair to evaluate students on skills or abilities that we have not taught them. This does not mean that we should not have standards for evaluation; rather, that we need to develop instructional models that give all students an opportunity to achieve those standards. If we are going to grade students on their ability to write papers, we should be willing to provide formative feedback and an opportunity to rewrite for those who aren't as skilled at writing papers. If we are going to grade students on their ability to give speeches, we should be willing to provide help in dealing with the communication apprehension that will affect the performance of some students. A cooperative classroom model operates on the support group principle, encouraging communication among students and from student to teacher, as well as from teacher to student. Some students will have to work harder than others, and in the real world (this is important to remember), some will choose not to do so. The "match," however, is with an achievement standard rather than with other students' abilities.

EDUCATION AND LEARNING ARE NOT NECESSARILY SYNONYMOUS

Anyone who has "done time" in educational institutions, as a student or a teacher, knows that educational models and learning models are sometimes at odds. Learning models are concerned with student needs, individual achievement, cognitive and affective changes. They are process–product models that focus on learning outcomes. Educational models are input–output models. They are concerned with head counts, credit hours generated, G.P.A.s, faculty–student ratios, availability of rooms, and sacrosanct time slots. Educational systems generally report grades as indicants of learning; however, teachers quickly learn that good grades and good learning represent different motivations.

Milton, Pollio, and Eison (1986) have suggested that students are characterized by both learning and grade orientations. Learning-oriented (LO) students view the classroom as a context in which they expect to encounter new information and ideas that will be both personally and professionally significant. Grade-oriented (GO) students view the educational experience as a crucible in which they are tested and graded and that is endured as a necessary evil on the way to getting a degree or becoming certified in a profession.

We would expect students who are both grade and learning oriented to be a teacher's ideal, to become involved in class discussions, ask pithy questions, show obvious (and genuine) interest, *and* conscientiously meet whatever requirements are proposed by the instructor. They are, in reality, often less able students for whom the educational institution is perceived as a stressful and chancy environment. They are interested in learning but need the reassuring anchor provided by grades to let them know they are doing alright as students. Milton et al. (1986) found that High LO/High GO students tended to earn the lowest test scores of any LO/GO group, perhaps because of their pointedly high test anxiety. They may "make" Cs but we want to "give" them Bs to reward their concern and protect their esteem.

Students who are neither learning nor grade oriented may be in school because their parents sent them, to have a good time, or to avoid getting a job. Whatever their reason for being enrolled in our classes, they are disinterested, often absent, and likely to do just enough work to earn the credit. Low LO/Low GO students "earn" their Ds. New teachers (who rarely were Low LO/Low GOs themselves) sometimes have difficulty understanding that their motivation is outside the context of learning and grades.

Students who are learning oriented but *not* grade oriented are likely to be involved students who challenge their teachers and who take courses related to things they want to know even if they aren't sure how well they will do in them. They may also fail to meet requirements that do not fulfill their own goals. They may turn in thought-provoking 5-page or 25-page papers when the assignment requested 10; they may present captivating speeches that cannot be evaluated by the criteria presented for a particular assignment; they may choose not to rewrite a paper or retake a test if they think they met their own objectives the first time. High LO/Low GO students impress their instructors as intellectually and emotionally able. We hope they don't bend the rules too far to "make" the grade we feel they "earned."

Students who are grade oriented but *not* learning oriented view all aspects of the classroom in terms of their effects on the course grade. Instructional procedures and policies that make getting a good grade easy are valued; activities not related to grades are seen as a waste of time and may be ignored. Low LO/High GO students are more likely than other students to drop or audit classes for fear of getting a poor grade. They are also more likely to cheat (Milton et al., 1986). These students may frustrate their instructors, who find themselves spending a great deal of time policing compliance with policies and requirements that contribute little to assessing learning.

Most of us who teach do so within educational institutions. We will inevitably encounter some students who play the system and some who refuse to play it. We will also have to recognize and work within certain constraints imposed by the institution. There is no easy formula for handling evaluation and grading quandaries; however, it is important that a need to assign grades does not become the primary consideration in organizing courses. To run full circle to the first philosophical tenet proposed in this chapter, we need to maintain a focus on *learning* objectives in making instructional decisions. Clearly articulated objectives (cognitive, affective, and psychomotor) provide a means for answering accountability questions to supervisors, administrators, students, and—most importantly—ourselves.

CONCLUSION

There is no such thing as a generic student. Students are active, co-creators of the classroom environment. They have different orientations, learning styles, abilities, and needs. Just as physicians and pharmacists have learned that the same dose of a drug has different effects on different individuals, and that alternative prescriptions are often indicated, we need to recognize that there are alternative approaches to achieving our instructional objectives. If our goal in teaching communication classes is to enhance students' interpersonal and public communication skills, we must be adaptable enough to recognize their needs and respond to their strengths. This understanding does not necessarily imply radical changes in educational and institutional policies; it does imply an interactive teacher–student relationship in which feedback is solicited and used to continually assess and modify the pace and direction of approaching objectives.

REFERENCES

Cornett, C. E. (1983). *What you should know about teaching and learning styles*. Bloomington, IN: Phi Delta Kappa Educational Foundation.

Curry, L. (1983, April). *An organization of learning styles theory and constructs*. Paper presented at the annual meeting of the American Educational Research Association, Montreal. (ERIC Document Reproduction Service No. ED 235 185).

Gorham, J. (1986). Assessment, classification and implications of learning styles in instructional interactions. *Communication Education, 35,* 411–417.

Gorham, J., & Self, L. (1987). Developing communication skills: Learning style and the educationally disadvantaged student. *Communication Research Reports, 4,* 38–46.

Johnson, D. W., & Johnson, R. T. (1987). *Learning together and alone: Cooperative, competitive and individualistic learning*. Englewood Cliffs, NJ: Prentice-Hall.

Keefe, J. W. (1982). Assessing student learning styles. In *Student learning styles and brain behavior* (pp. 43–53). Reston, VA: National Association of Secondary School Principals.

Kirby, P. (1979). *Cognitive style, learning style, and transfer skill acquisition*. Columbus, OH: National Center for Research in Vocational Education.

Kohn, A. (1986a, September). How to succeed without even vying. *Psychology Today,* pp. 22–28.

Kohn, A. (1986b). *No contest: The case against competition.* Boston, MA: Houghton Mifflin.

Kohn, A. (1987, October). It's hard to get left out of a pair. *Psychology Today,* pp. 53–57.

Kolb, D. (1976). *Learning styles inventory.* Boston, MA: McBer and Co.

McCarthy, B. (1981). *The 4Mat system: Teaching to learning styles with right/left mode techniques.* Oak Brook, IL: EXCEL.

Milton, O., Pollio, H. R., & Eison, J. A. (1986). *Making sense of college grades.* San Francisco: Jossey-Bass.

National Association of Secondary School Principles. (1979). *Student learning styles: Diagnosing and prescribing programs.* Reston, VA: Author.

National Association of Secondary School Principles. (1982). *Student learning styles and brain behavior: Programs, instrumentation, research.* Reston, VA: Author.

Richmond, V. P., & McCroskey, J. C. (1989). *Communication apprehension, avoidance, and effectiveness* (2nd ed.). Scottsdale, AZ: Gorsuch Scarisbrick.

Tyler, R. W. (1949). *Basic principles of curriculum and instruction.* Chicago, IL: University of Chicago Press.

Witkin, H. A., Dyke, R., Oltman, P. K., Raskin, E., & Karp, S. A. (1971). *A manual for the embedded figures tests.* Palo Alto, CA: Consulting Psychologists Press.

17

Classroom Management: Structuring the Classroom for Work

Timothy G. Plax
Patricia Kearney
California State University, Long Beach

A frustration that is common to all beginning teachers is the realization that many students are reluctant to assume a conciliatory, cooperative student role. Anxious to please, stimulate, and educate like no teacher before them, new teachers can become confused, angry, and disenchanted when students fail to appreciate their efforts (Kearney, 1987). Attempting to adjust to the realities of the classroom, beginning teachers become socialized into a "we–they" culture. The resulting teacher–student alienation is expressed in teachers' complaints as they sigh among themselves and worry about the future of education. ("I work hard on my lessons; how dare they criticize me?" "Students don't care about learning; all they care about is getting the degree.") Importantly, none of these complaints suggest strategies to assist in structuring learning environments in ways that teachers will *Want* to teach and students will *Want* to learn.

This chapter overviews issues that are pertinent to classroom control and focuses on techniques that can make the task of teaching easier. While reading this chapter, keep in mind that knowing the content you are supposed to teach is not a sufficient condition for teaching. New teachers often spend an inordinate amount of time preparing to teach by learning and relearning the content. Comparatively little time is spent on those activities that set up a climate that is conducive for disseminating that content; yet, we know that content competencies constitute only a small part of teaching preparation. To be effective teachers, we must go beyond the subject matter. Specifically, we need to ask ourselves, "What should we do to teach what we know in a way that students will be open and responsive to learning?"

The most common response to this question has, in the past, focused on discipline. Defined by Wlodkowski (1982) as "student acceptance of or submission to teacher authority" (p. 2), *discipline* is construed as a panacea for all learning-related problems. Proponents argue that all formal training in a content area is useless without a well-disciplined classroom. In other words, no matter how well you, as the teacher, know the subject matter, students may still challenge your credibility, dislike your personality, or prefer to engage in what they believe to be "more meaningful" activities.

Demands for disciplined and obedient students are part of our culture. The public continues to clamor for more classroom discipline, claiming that uncontrolled students are the number one problem facing our schools (Gallup, 1982). Educators are evaluated, retained, and tenured on their abilities to *make* students learn. Good teaching, in many schools, is equated with student control. In fact, administrators are quick to reprimand beginning teachers for their tendency to be too permissive in the classroom.

Ironically, however, discipline alone may actually work against learning. Classrooms that are highly disciplined fail to stimulate greater learning and are often associated with increased disruption. *No* research evidence exists to suggest that more discipline, in and of itself, leads to greater teacher effectiveness. On the contrary, teachers who employ frequent discipline tend to find their classrooms problematic and hard to manage. More rules, harsher penalties, and "get tough" policies fail to gain student compliance (Wlodkowski, 1982).

Nevertheless, schools have traditionally been conceived as despotic structures where teachers "ruled" and students were regarded as "subjects to be civilized" (Boocock, 1983, p. 402). This longstanding characterization is still reflected in a contemporary *custodial* orientation toward education. Custodial teachers emphasize autocracy, dominance, rigidly defined teacher/student role hierarchies, and strict unilateral teacher control. Although novice teachers typically enter the classroom with a more *humanistic,* permissive control ideology, they are encouraged to shed such idealism and adopt a custodial model (Hoy, 1968).

Contemporary educators can ill afford to demand student submission as a function of teacher authority. "Education for education's sake" holds little meaning for today's youth. Although formal education may have been equated with political, social, and economic opportunities in the past, students question the relative value of education today. Students no longer believe that a college degree will ensure them of either professional opportunities or the training that is necessary for on-the-job performance. Additionally, students may view school as a holding place, where they wait until employment becomes available to them (Boocock, 1983). The declining value granted education inevitably leads to a loss of teacher authority. In other words, students will not do what you want them to simply because you are the teacher. The current reality is that student resistance is common across elementary, secondary, and college classrooms.

COLLEGE STUDENT MISBEHAVIORS

It is often assumed that college teaching is easier because we do not have the discipline problems teachers have to deal with at lower grade levels. This is not so. Because the problems often differ from those in elementary and high school classrooms, misbehaviors confronted in the college classroom may be infinitely more difficult to handle. Teachers of adult students cannot easily "call parents" for support, threaten expulsion, require detention, or establish more positive means of control by fostering personal, long-term teacher–student relationships.

In a recent survey (Plax, Kearney, & Hays, 1988) college students reported engaging in both active and passive forms of misbehavior and/or resistance. *Active* misbehaviors, that is, overt attempts to disrupt learning, include cheating, asking counterproductive questions, challenging the teacher's authority, diverting classroom talk from the lesson, interrupting, leaving class early (or walking in late), and talking with friends. On the other hand, *passive,* or covert, misbehaviors include inattention to teacher, lack of attendance, turning in assignments late (or not at all), sleeping through class, and reading the newspaper or doing other "more important" homework in class.

For teachers who are unprepared for such misbehaviors, two primary reactions result. Many beginning teachers are too permissive in their control orientation. That is, they find themselves "giving in" to student resistance. Although it might seem reasonable to allow Mary or John extra time to type a paper, others in the class may resent this exception. Other new teachers are guilty of being too custodial or heavy-handed. Having been told "not to smile before Christmas," teachers wind up taking themselves and their rules far too seriously. For example, Mary may be going through a very real crisis and, as a result, should be given the opportunity to turn in her paper late. After all, these are adult students who suffer from adult problems. A loss of a parent, divorce in the family, pregnancy, car accidents, and rape all constitute adult problems that are not infrequent.

Recognizing that adult students can and do misbehave in the college classroom is but the first step in dealing with misbehaviors. Understanding why students misbehave is crucial for coping with or managing students when they engage in resistance. Although it is a natural tendency to attribute blame to *students* for problems in the classroom, we feel that it is important to work first from attributions about *teacher* behavior when students fail to respond to instruction the way we would like.

The position we take is that students misbehave largely because their teachers do. For instance, we all know a professor or two (not us, of course) who bores his or her students. Students may have had the content already and, thus, perceive the lecture material as redundant. (How many times have you been taught the definition of communication?) Worse, the teacher may be less than inspiring. Regardless of whether the source of boredom is the teacher's style of communication or the material itself, the teacher in this situation is misbehaving.

On the surface, of course, some teacher "misbehaviors" may not appear to be misbehaviors at all. We have all known a professor who took great delight in boasting that students rarely receive A's from him or her. Students have to "work" in his or her classes, and if they cannot master the material, then they obviously aren't working hard enough. Although sometimes students do *not* work hard enough, an alternative explanation may reside with the teacher. Perhaps the content is too hard and prerequisite material is needed, or perhaps the standards for mastery are unrealistically high. Although we have no problem with standards, a continually skewed distribution of low grades does not say much for this professor's effectiveness as a teacher.

Students expect to do well when they work hard at learning. When their efforts to learn the content are continually punished (low grades, confusion), students are likely to attack the teacher. Teachers who take pride in punishing students by systematically overloading them with content or imposing unattainable objectives are teachers who want their students to fail. The term "professoritis" is often used to label teachers who engage in misbehaviors of content overload and unrealistic learning expectations.

Miscalls are another type of teacher misbehavior. Miscalls are the misclassification of student problems as disciplinary problems when, in fact, they are not. This major source of teacher misbehavior involves the labeling of educational problems, guidance problems, or teacher's hurt feelings as discipline problems (Seeman, 1988). One common example of a miscall occurs when a teacher reprimands a student in class for quietly working alone on other homework. This student's behavior does not disrupt others' learning and does not interfere with instruction. Even though a teacher might argue that the student is missing out on the lesson, such behavior constitutes an educational, not a disciplinary, problem. As such, no disciplinary action is required. Other examples of mis-calls include (a) personality clashes with students who irritate you, for whatever reason, (b) intolerance of those who fail to give you their un-divided attention at *all* times, (c) reprimanding students who don't appre-ciate your humor, (d) responding impatiently to those who complain that they still don't understand what you mean, and (e) holding a grudge against someone who angered you a week before (Seeman, 1988).

Teacher misbehaviors are potential antecedents to a number of conse-quent student misbehaviors. When the teacher lacks vocalic variation (monotone!) and other indices of nonverbal expressiveness, the conse-quent effect is student boredom. When assignments are too vague, or the homework is unreasonably difficult, students may require physiological release via crying, screaming, or pushing. When favorite students are isolated for special treatment, or the teacher is perceived as "unfair," students may attempt to gain revenge by "tattling" to the teacher's supe-rior or giving negative teacher evaluations.

Occasionally, students misbehave because of uncertainty. Teachers who are unclear or who change the requirements for the final course grade may cause students to complain openly about course policies. Ob-viously, students may misbehave in an effort to get the teacher's or oth-ers' attention. The class clown and the constant talker are but two types of students who attempt to make themselves known and sometimes liked. Finally, students misbehave because they model the teacher's (or others') misbehaviors. Teachers who arrive late to class can expect their students to do the same. Teachers who come to class unprepared can expect their students to come to class without having read the assignment. Teachers who regularly pass out materials with misspellings and grammatical errors can expect their students to turn in sloppy work.

Not all students misbehaviors, of course, are a direct result of teacher misbehaviors. Students bring with them a history of classroom experi-ences that impact their current behaviors. Check first to determine if you might be the source of their misbehavior. Only as a last resort should you consider other student-related factors (e.g., student lacks essential pre-requisites or is learning disabled; suffers from psychological problems). When considering student factors, however, attempt to provide teacher solutions. Often, a student's communication anxieties can be eased, for instance, by omitting "student participation during class" as a major requirement for the final course grade. We do not suggest, however, that all student problems become your problems. Sometimes, there just aren't solutions you can or should enact. Sometimes, students must learn to adapt or cope by themselves.

Generally, then, college teaching is not without its share of discipline problems. Not unlike elementary and secondary students, college students engage in both active and passive forms of resistance to teacher authority. Moreover, college student misbehaviors may be more difficult to manage simply because the "controls" are either inoperative or non-meaningful. Understanding the source of student misbehavior is helpful, particularly when we recognize that teacher misbehaviors are a major cause of student disruptions in the classroom. An examination of those behaviors that we can change (our own!) is the first and sometimes final step in altering others' behaviors.

CLASSROOM MANAGEMENT

Teachers who choose to "own" the problem of student misbehavior will find support in a contemporary approach to discipline. Within this newer tradition of classroom management, discipline loses its name, meaning, and pervasive emphasis. Rather than forcing students to learn, the teacher creates and manages a classroom where techniques are employed to influence students to *want* to learn. Specifically, classroom management refers to teacher behaviors that "produce high levels of student involvement in classroom activities, minimal amounts of student behaviors that interfere with the teacher's or students' work, and efficient use of instructional time" (Emmer & Evertson, 1981, p. 342). Rather than focusing attention on student misbehavior, this alternative implies a preventative stance toward discipline. Don't wait for problems to occur; prevent them from happening in the first place!

The appeal of classroom management has its roots in a line of research that demonstrates that the single best predictor of learning is "academic engagement time" (Woolfolk, 1987). Although a variety of teacher and student behaviors are also associated with student achievement, the amount of active time spent on specific academic tasks consistently results in higher achievement gains. The strongest link between teacher instruction and student achievement is student task engagement. Teachers who keep their students motivated and involved in mastering objectives are more likely to be effective in helping students learn (Woolfolk, 1987). This fundamental principle has led researchers to identify those teacher behaviors that influence students' academic engagement time.

"With-it-ness"

Teachers who are "with it" are those who are keenly aware of what's going on in their classroom at all times (Kounin, 1970). They notice when a student in the back yawns and another student on the sideline initiates talk with a peer. We have all known teachers who did not have a clue of what was going on in class. Students openly cheated; hidden jokes were directed toward the teacher; and a whole lot of socializing occurred right under the teacher's nose! In contrast, not much is missed by "with it" teachers. "With-it-ness" skills allow teachers to notice discrepancies in the classroom early and put a stop to them before they spread throughout the class. Such ripple effects suggest that misbehaviors are highly contagious and have a way of infecting other students unless they are checked early.

Overlapping

Being able to deal with more than one task at a time is another characteristic of effective classroom managers (Kounin, 1970). For example, in the middle of your lecture, you might notice that someone looks confused. At the same time, another student walks in late. While finishing your thought aloud with the class, you make a mental note to anticipate questions about a point you made earlier and hand the attendance sign-up sheet to the late student. All three activities are completed without missing a beat. Teachers without overlapping skills are likely to interrupt the lesson frequently and attend to those peripheral activities that trigger others to stray from the task.

Momentum

Momentum is measured by the presence or absence of down times or slow downs (Kounin, 1970). The point here is that the teacher is in charge of "pacing." At no time during instruction should lengthy pause time be evident. Students should have no reason for abandoning their attention toward the teacher (or the instruction). When down times or slow downs occur, students are likely to find other, more entertaining activities to engage in. We often observe lack of momentum when an inexperienced teacher assigns students to small group activities and then requires that *all* the students wait patiently until *every* small group is finished with the task. Students who must wait are likely to become impatient, frustrated, and bored.

Changing or maintaining a given activity in the classroom is determined by two factors: work completion rates and estimates of students' attention span (Doyle, 1986). "Completion rates" refers to a criterion group. That is, students between the 10th and 25th percentiles in class ability should be the referent for maintaining momentum. Although this estimate may be more suitable for elementary or secondary classrooms, the issue to keep in mind is that changing pace or establishing momentum requires the class to move ahead even when some students may not be finished with the task. Students' attention span should be considered as well. An exercise or film that the teacher thought was interesting may not be perceived similarly by the class. If that's the case, then it's wise to quickly abandon the plan and move on to something else.

Establishing Reasonable Rules

Effective classroom managers establish explicit, reasonable rules early in the term (Biehler & Snowman, 1986). Unfortunately, many of us are guilty of imposing a rule *after* we see an instance of the violation. Be sure your rules are communicated clearly and frequently until all students have "learned" them. Reasonableness is a key to rule planning. An "unreasonable" rule of one of the authors was pointed out to her while she taught a unit on *Rules*. She no longer uses the arbitrary rule of "stapling your papers together." Instead, she brings a stapler with her to class and passes it around before student papers are turned in. We recognize that all rules are potentially reasonable; however, classroom rules should be *educationally* based. Stapled papers may keep you more organized and reduce the possibility of losing loose pages, but stapled papers do not enhance learning in the classroom. Other examples of arbitrary rules include chewing gum, the use of pencil or pen, lined versus unlined paper, assigned seating, and participation requirements.

Consistent Application of Rules

Effective classroom managers typically have fewer rules than ineffective managers. At the same time, good managers regularly enforce the rules they do have (Emmer, Evertson, Sanford, Clements, & Worsham, 1984; Evertson, Emmer, Clements, Sanford, & Worsham, 1984). It is wise, therefore, to keep the list of rules brief. The more rules a teacher has, the harder it is to scrutinize and apply consequences to every rule violation. Consistency is essential to rule imposition, because teacher consistency provides students with reliable expectations of teacher behavior. As a result, students learn to depend on predictable teacher responses to regulate their own behavior. When a rule is explicitly stated, students "learn" what behaviors are expected and what consequences will be applied should they fail to deliver. When a teacher imposes a rule irregularly, then students become confused about what the teacher really wants or expects from them. Without consistent rule application, some students will follow the rule, whereas others will not.

Other classroom management techniques are discussed in detail by

Emmer et al. (1984) and Evertson et al. (1984). Differentiating effective from ineffective classroom managers, these researchers have reported that positive questioning techniques, use of motivational messages (cues and prompts), attending more often to positive than negative student behaviors, providing students with good role models, giving frequent feedback, holding students accountable, and planning success-oriented learning experiences are all strategies that good managers employ regularly. The end result is that effective managers increase students' time spent on-task. Other research indicates that students at all aptitude levels spend more time engaged and achieve more when taught by teachers who are competent in classroom management.

COMPLIANCE-GAINING STRATEGIES

Even the most well-managed classroom is likely to be disrupted occasionally. Instructional communication researchers argue that classroom management sometimes demands that we "persuade" our students that learning is important, enjoyable, and beneficial to their overall well-being (Kearney, 1987). Early studies on this type of classroom influence were framed within French and Raven's (1959) concept of power. "Power in the classroom" refers to the teacher's ability to influence students to do something they would not have done had they not been influenced. Thus, the teacher's ability to strategically employ different types of power can impact the potential success of his or her classroom management.

Within this research tradition, the first two studies (McCroskey & Richmond, 1983; Richmond & McCroskey, 1984) relied on general descriptions of five power bases: reward, coercive, referent, legitimate, and expert. The results of that research provide indirect support for more contemporary beliefs about discipline in the classroom. Teacher authority and discipline in the traditional sense have little or no meaning in today's classroom. That is, legitimate or assigned power ("Do it because I'm the teacher!") as well as coercive or punishment power ("If you don't, you'll get an F!") were both negatively associated with cognitive and affective learning. Both types of power closely resemble notions of teacher authority and discipline.

Recognizing the limitations of relying on general descriptions of power, subsequent studies derived an extended typology of power-based teacher influence strategies (Kearney, Plax, Richmond, & McCroskey, 1984, 1985). Based on responses from teachers themselves, 22 "Behavior Alteration Techniques" (BATs) resulted. Unlike the bases of power explicated in the early studies, these BATs demonstrate that teacher power is often indirect. In other words, power need not be restricted to direct appeals. BATs that teachers report frequently using are "student-centered," referencing inherent student benefits through compliance ("Try it, you'll like it!"). Teachers also rely on "student audience effect" techniques, or those strategies that appeal to students' peers and reference groups for compliance ("The rest of the class is doing it"). Asked which of the techniques were most and least effective for influencing student behavior, teachers consistently identified the more prosocial, reward-type strategies as effective, whereas antisocial or punishment-based BATs were perceived as ineffective.

Similarly, students' perceptions of BATs used in the classroom showed that prosocial-type BATs were positively associated with cognitive and/or affective learning, whereas antisocial BATs were negatively related to both learning outcomes (McCroskey, Richmond, Plax, & Kearney, 1985; Plax, Kearney, McCroskey, & Richmond, 1986; Richmond, McCroskey, Kearney, & Plax, 1987). If we equate learning with effectiveness, then we can conclude that teachers and students agree on the preferred use of prosocial compliance-gaining techniques.

Knowing that prosocial strategies are the method of choice for optimizing classroom managerial skills, why is it that some teachers continue to use antisocial means of control? Unfortunately, many teachers initially try to employ a prosocial management approach, but are unsuccessful and give up. Moreover, training teachers to adopt and tactically employ prosocial *verbal* messages of control overlooks the essential contributions of *nonverbal* messages that underscore meaning; *how* teachers communicate may be more critical than *what* is actually said to obtain student compliance.

Accordingly, the interaction between teachers' nonverbal immediacy behaviors and the use of either prosocial or antisocial BATs on students' resistance was tested (Kearney, Plax, Smith, & Sorensen, 1988). Four groups of college students were presented with descriptions of four types of teachers. The first group was presented with the image of a friendly, nonverbally immediate teacher (smiling, positive head nods, vocally expressive, purposeful gestures, relaxed and open body position) who requests that the student come to class more prepared from now on. This immediate teacher was described as using a prosocial BAT ("Because it will help you later on in life" or "You'll find it a rewarding and meaningful experience"). To the second sample of students, the same immediate teacher description was used, except that instead of a prosocial technique, antisocial BATs were inserted in the scenario ("Because I told you to" or "I'll lower your grade if you don't"). The third and fourth sets of students received descriptions of a nonimmmediate, aloof instructor (tense, reserved, vocally unexpressive, seldom smiles, avoids looking at students) who used either the prosocial or the antisocial techniques, respectively.

Students who were presented with the immediate teacher scenarios, regardless of the BAT employed, reported greater likelihood of compliance than did those students who imagined themselves with the nonimmediate teachers. The overwhelming contributor to student compliance, then, was nonverbal behaviors of the teacher as opposed to the relative pro- or antisocialness of the technique type. Given the two immediacy conditions, however, students reported greater compliance tendencies with the immediate teacher who used prosocial, rather than antisocial, techniques. Curiously, students who were exposed to the nonimmediate teachers reported slightly greater compliance when the nonimmediate teacher employed antisocial, as opposed to prosocial, strategies.

Additional analysis revealed that students distorted or selectively perceived the strategy type employed in the immediacy/nonimmediacy scenarios. When students were asked to indicate the relative prosocial or antisocialness of the BATs employed, students in both of the immediate teacher conditions perceived the teacher to be using "prosocial" techniques, even when the antisocial BATs were used. Similarly, for the nonimmediacy conditions, students believed both teachers to use "antisocial" strategies. Consequently, we recommend that teachers be trained first in the nonverbal behaviors of immediacy. Without exception, the research on teacher nonverbal immediacy and student affect has demonstrated a substantial, positive association. In short, students like their more nonverbally immediate teachers and, as a result, are more willing to comply with such teachers' requests and/or demands.

Correspondingly, new teachers should be exposed to the variety of available prosocial techniques that can assist them in their influence attempts. After examining preteachers' and experienced teachers' perceptions of the techniques they would use to gain the compliance of particular types of misbehaving students, it is imminently clear that preteachers limit their alternatives to only one or two techniques. In contrast, experienced teachers are much more likely to avail themselves of a diversity of prosocial BAT types (Kearney & Plax, 1987; Kearney, Plax, Sorensen, & Smith, 1988; Plax, Kearney, & Downs, 1986; Plax, Kearney, & Tucker, 1986).

SUMMARY

Removing the expectation that students will occupy roles of submission as a function of teacher authority is prerequisite to successfully managing the classroom. Alternatively, preparing and maintaining a learning environment that enhances on-task student behaviors can minimize the need to impose discipline. Assuming a stance of classroom manager, rather than disciplinarian, then, requires a change in emphasis. Teacher as disciplinarian will enter the classroom looking for (and finding) off-task student misbehaviors. Teacher as manager will enter that same classroom looking for (and finding) on-task student behaviors. The disciplinarian will spend an inordinate amount of time correcting (or attempting to correct) student misbehaviors. The manager will spend similar time orchestrating those activities that maintain momentum. The disciplinarian will complain that students just aren't like they used to be. The manager knows teachers often aren't who they should be.

This change in emphasis requires a change in teacher behavior. Effectively managing the classroom requires that teachers employ monitoring skills that include both "with-it-ness" and overlapping. Good classroom managers also pace their instructional activities to maintain a level of momentum that continually alerts students to the task. The consistent application of reasonable, as opposed to arbitrary, rules defines for both the manager and students expectations (and consequences) for behavior. Engaging in these and other classroom management behaviors is likely to result in positive learning experiences.

Communicating persuasively is also an important supplement to classroom management. Recognizing the need to convince students that task engagement is essential for learning, experienced teachers are likely to draw upon a variety of behavior alteration techniques. Even in well-managed classrooms, a student may be reluctant to participate; another may choose not to attend regularly. Eliciting cooperation from these students may require more than proper pacing or establishing a rule. Such students may need further motivation. The use of prosocial messages can provide students with positive incentives for task engagement. However, prosocial messages must be communicated within the framework of positive nonverbal behaviors. Establishing an immediate, approachable relationship with students will help students perceive that your influence attempts are in their best interest.

In this chapter, we have taken the position that structuring the classroom for work need not rely on trial and error. Moreover, we maintain that students need not be blamed for our confusion and alienation when students balk at our attempts to create an optimal learning environment. Instead, the research on classroom management and compliance-gaining provides us with a systematic approach to maximizing students' academic engagement time. In other words, the use of strategic management skills and influence techniques maximizes students' learning outcomes and, at the same time, increases our satisfaction with the process and product of teaching.

REFERENCES

Biehler, R. F., & Snowman, J. (1986). *Psychology applied to teaching* (5th ed.). Boston, MA: Houghton Mifflin.

Boocock, S. (1983). Public schools and education. In M. L. DeFleur (Ed.), *Social problems in American society* (pp. 386–419). Boston, MA: Houghton Mifflin.

Doyle, W. (1986). Classroom organization and management. In M. C. Wittrock (Ed.), *Handbook of research on teaching* (3rd ed., pp. 392–431). New York: MacMillan.

Emmer, E. T., Evertson, C. M. (1981). Synthesis of research on classroom management, *Educational Leadership, 38,* 342–347.

Emmer, E. T., & Evertson, C. M., Sanford, J. P., Clements, B. S., & Worsham, M. E. (1984). *Classroom management for secondary teachers.* Englewood Cliffs, NJ: Prentice-Hall.

Evertson, C. M., Emmer, E. T., Clements, B. S., Sanford, J. P., & Worsham, M. E. (1984). *Classroom management for elementary teachers.* Englewood Cliffs, NJ: Prentice-Hall.

French, J. R. P., Jr., & Raven, B. H. (1959). The bases of social power. In D. Cartwright (Ed.), *Studies in social power* (pp. 150–167). Ann Arbor: University of Michigan Press.

Gallup, G. H. (1982). Gallup poll of the public's attitudes toward the public schools. *Phi Delta Kappan, 64,* 37–50.

Hoy, W. K. (1968). The influence of experience on the beginning teacher. *School Review, 76,* 312–323.

Kearney, P. (1987). Power in the classroom. *Journal of Thought, 22,* 45–50.

Kearney, P., & Plax, T. G. (1987). Situational and individual determinants of teachers' reported use of behavior alteration techniques. *Human Communication Research, 14,* 145–166.

Kearney, P., Plax, T. G., Richmond, V. P., & McCroskey, J. C. (1984). Power in the classroom IV: Teacher communication techniques as alternatives to discipline. In R. Bostrom (Ed.), *Communication yearbook 8* (pp. 724–746). Beverly Hills, CA: Sage.

Kearney, P., Plax, T. G., Richmond, V. P., & McCroskey, J. C. (1985). Power in the classroom III: Teacher communication techniques and messages. *Communication Education, 34,* 19–28.

Kearney, P., Plax, T. G., Smith, V. R., & Sorensen, G. (1988). Effects of teacher immediacy and strategy type on college student resistance to on-task demands. *Communication Education, 37,* 54–67.

Kearney, P., Plax, T. G., Sorensen, G., & Smith, V. R. (1988). Experienced and prospective teachers' selections of compliance-gaining messages for "common" student misbehaviors. *Communication Education, 37,* 150–164.

Kounin, J. S. (1970). *Discipline and group management in classrooms.* New York: Holt, Rinehart, & Winston.

McCroskey, J. C., & Richmond, V. P. (1983). Power in the classroom I: Teacher and student perceptions. *Communication Education, 32,* 176–184.

McCroskey, J. C., Richmond, V. P., Plax, T. G., & Kearney, P. (1985). Power in the classroom V: Behavior alteration techniques, communication training, and learning. *Communication Education, 34,* 214–226.

Plax, T. G., Kearney, P., & Downs, T. M. (1986). Communicating control in the classroom and satisfaction with teaching and students. *Communication Education, 35,* 379–388.

Plax, T. G., Kearney, P., & Hays, E. R. (1988). *A survey of active and passive misbehaviors among college students.* Unpublished manuscript.

Plax, T. G., Kearney, P., McCroskey, J. C., & Richmond, V. P. (1986). Power in the classroom VI: Verbal control strategies, nonverbal immediacy and affective learning. *Communication Education, 35,* 43–55.

Plax, T. G., Kearney, P., & Tucker, L. (1986). Prospective teachers' use of behavior alteration techniques: Reactions to common student misbehaviors. *Communication Education, 35,* 32–42.

Richmond, V. P., & McCroskey, J. C. (1984). Power in the classroom II: Power and learning. *Communication Education, 33,* 125–136.

Richmond, V. P., McCroskey, J. C., Kearney, P., & Plax, T. G. (1987). Power in the classroom VII: Linking behavior alteration techniques to cognitive learning. *Communication Education, 36,* 1–12.

Seeman, H. (1988). *Preventing classroom discipline problems: A guide to educators.* Lancaster, PA: Technomic.

Wlodkowski, R. J. (1982). Discipline: The great false hope. (ERIC Document Reproduction Service No. ED 224 782)

Woolfolk, A. E. (1987). *Educational psychology* (3rd ed.). Englewood Cliffs, NJ: Prentice-Hall.

18

The First Day

Gustav W. Friedrich
University of Oklahoma

Pamela Cooper
Northwestern University

> *I can always tell on the first day of class whether it'll be a winner or a dud. If the teacher makes a good impression, it'll be great. If not, well . . . If it ain't good, then it ain't gonna get better. For me to know the class will be good, the teacher has to let me know that she is available for questions of any caliber concerning her topic. She also has to let me know that she is approachable.*

The first meeting of a class is much too important to be treated as something to be gotten over with as quickly as possible. Teachers who simply put in an appearance, see if all the students are there, make an assignment for the next time, and dismiss class early are missing an important opportunity. Not only does this approach send students away frustrated because they do not get their basic questions answered, the instructor misses an important opportunity to demonstrate his or her commitment to the course, to the students, and to the communication discipline. This chapter, therefore, describes strategies that can help teachers use the first session of a class productively.

Although both students and teacher, through their communication, jointly create "the class," the task of this chapter is to describe *teacher* choices and activities that are potentially useful for the successful launching of a class. Though the chapter is, therefore, by choice teacher-centered, the most logical beginning point is the student perspective: What is it that students attempt to learn from the opening session of a class? The framework for answering this question is provided by the socialization literature as it has been utilized and interpreted by Staton-Spicer and Darling (1986) and their colleagues.

Socialization, according to Merton, Reader, and Kendall (1957), is "the process by which people selectively acquire the values and attitudes, the interests, skills and knowledge—in short the culture—current in groups in which they are, or seek to become a member" (p. 287). Socialization is either primary (the process by which children become part of society) or secondary (the process by which already socialized individuals acquire new roles). The focus here is on the process of secondary socialization, whereby students acquire the knowledge and skills that are necessary to perform the role of student in a particular classroom. Van Maanen and Schein (1979) suggested that this process can be viewed as occurring in three phases: *anticipatory* (based on the catalog, other students, and campus folklore, students anticipate what the course will be like), *entry* (during the first days of the class, students judge the course based on first impressions), and *continuance* (as the course unfolds, students may modify their initial perceptions). This chapter focuses on the first two phases of the secondary socialization of students into a classroom.

As students take their seats for the first day of a class (entry phase of secondary socialization), there are a number of things that they want to know about the class. Although partial answers to their questions may have been obtained haphazardly from, for example, campus folklore, the questions still remain—and a major purpose of the first session of a course is to answer them. To summarize what our students told us when, over the past several semesters, we asked them what they hope to learn during the first class period, there are three categories of information that students wish to acquire:

1. Course coverage: What will the course cover? How will it relate to other work?
2. Course rules: How will the course be conducted? What will be the work load? What type of exams are given? How will grades be determined?
3. Teacher personality: What kind of person is the teacher going to be? Will the teacher be easily accessible? Easy to talk with?

How do students acquire this information? Staton-Spicer and Darling borrowed from Berger and Calabrese's (1975) uncertainty reduction theory (URT) a description of information-seeking strategies that are used in the process of secondary socialization. Within URT, Berger and Calabrese (1975) argued that "when strangers meet, their primary concern is one of uncertainty reduction or increasing predictability about the behavior of both themselves and others in the interaction" (p. 100). This analysis appears equally applicable to the process of secondary socialization of students as they enter a class for the first time. URT describes the communication strategies aimed at reducing uncertainty as passive, active, or interactive. With passive strategies, information is acquired by means of unobtrusive observation—the individual observes his or her environment and the individuals in it, and attempts to make sense of the situation without the help of others. Active strategies require the individual to interact with "third parties" to obtain information. Thus, rather than asking the teacher directly about the number of tests in the course, a student might ask another student. Interactive strategies are those employed when individuals directly interact with a primary source of information in order to reduce uncertainty (e.g., they ask the teacher, rather than a fellow student, about the teacher's policy concerning class absences).

In short, then, as students enter a class on the first day, their task is to begin the process of acquiring their new role as student by reducing uncertainty about (a) the nature of the course, (b) the course mechanics, and (c) the personality of the teacher. The strategies available to them for doing so are passive (e.g., sitting back and observing), active (e.g., asking questions of fellow students), or interactive (e.g., interacting directly with the teacher). Which strategies an individual student will actually use, of course, depends on a variety of factors, including the personalities of both student and teacher.

Having identified three categories of information that students hope to glean from the activities of the opening session of a class, this chapter turns now to teacher choices and strategies that are potentially relevant and useful for coping with student expectations within each category.

COURSE COVERAGE

As suggested earlier, there are at least two issues related to course coverage that students would like to see addressed during the opening session of a class: What will the course cover? How will it relate to other work?

Tackling the second issue first, it is perhaps best addressed orally at the beginning of the period. In doing so, the teacher has an opportunity to function in the role of socializing agent—familiarizing students with the language and viewpoints of the communication discipline. This can be accomplished by describing how the course fits within the curriculum of the department. For example: Why does the department offer this course? How long has it done so? Is the course an elective or a required one? What is the rationale for this status? How does the course relate to other courses offered by the department? Is the course theory-oriented, skill-oriented, or a blend of both? The discussion of these issues can productively incorporate highlights both of the history of the department and of the communication discipline.

The specific course content is ideally presented in the form of a printed course syllabus that can be handed out to the students at the first session of the class. At a minimum, this syllabus should spell out both the objectives for the course and the topics to be covered. In addition to obvious advantages for the students, preparing such a syllabus forces the teacher to carefully think through what he or she wishes to accomplish with the students during the term. It also serves as an aid to pacing the course so that all areas get covered. Without it, because some areas of a course are of greater interest to the teacher (and students) than others, it is easy to focus on interesting topics and suddenly discover that the course is far behind schedule.

Some teachers include on their syllabus the dates on which specific topics will be discussed. Others, because they wish flexibility should they get slightly behind or ahead, merely list the topics and their order of discussion. The advantage of this approach is that the student is not in a position to judge whether the teacher is "behind" or "ahead." In addition to listing topics, the syllabus can also list assignments and their due dates—a practice that minimizes the misunderstood assignment, the forgotten assignment, or the assignment that had to be given after the bell has rung.

COURSE MECHANICS

A syllabus can also be used to address many of the issues that relate to students' second area of concern: course mechanics—How will the course be conducted?

The syllabus can, for example, specify the number of assignments, the number of quizzes, tests, and so on that will be given during the term—and, perhaps more importantly, the weights that will be assigned to each in calculating the final grade. In developing these weights, Kohls (N.D.) has advised teachers to allow themselves 5% to 10% leeway in the total—telling their students that this percentage is allocated to the teacher for personal evaluation above and beyond the specific grades and is used to reward, for example, excellent participation, a positive trend in grades, or other circumstances that may develop concerning a specific student.

In addition to listing grade-related policies on the syllabus, a frank discussion about what it will take to receive a given final grade is warranted: What will it take to get an A? What will it take to flunk? Although such issues are awkward to discuss, our whole educational system makes students "grade oriented." It is, therefore, necessary to accept the fact that most students are going to be concerned about grades and then work hard to make the grading rules for the course as clear, public, and fair as it is possible to make them. Students can also be told to ask for clarification whenever they are in doubt about their standing in the class.

In addition to grading-related issues, the rules of the game for classroom and course behaviors should also be clearly specified. For example: What are the teacher's attitudes toward attendance, make-ups, and excuses? Is classroom participation important? Should students raise their hand and be called on before speaking? Will there be specific seating assignments? What are the expectations concerning cheating, plagarism, and outside help on assignments? How ought students address the teacher (Mr. or Ms.? Professor? Doctor?), and how will the teacher address them (first name? Mr. or Ms.?). Obviously, some instructors prefer to say many of the later things aloud, perhaps when they introduce themselves to their classes.

More important than the specific choice a teacher makes on such issues is the fact that the teacher makes and consistently enforces a choice. In his review of the research on classroom organization and management, Brophy (1983) pointed out that the key to a well-functioning classroom is to maintain a continuous academic focus for student attention and engagement. This is best accomplished by:

1. Carefully thinking through, well in advance of starting the class, the procedures and routines that possess the potential to work best.

2. Teaching and implementing the key classroom procedures and rules both early in the class and consistently.

3. Engaging in the following three major clusters of behaviors as the term progresses: (a) behaviors that convey purposefulness (e.g., strategies that show concern about maximizing the time available for instruction and about seeing that students learn the content—not just that they are well behaved); (b) behaviors that teach students how to behave appropriately (e.g., being clear about what teachers expect of students and teaching students how to do things when necessary); and (c) skills in diagnosing students' focus of attention (e.g., being sensitive to student concerns and continuously monitoring students for signs of confusion or inattention).

In short, as stated by Brophy (1983):

It is clear from this research that the key to effective management is prevention; effective managers are distinguished by their success in preventing problems from arising in the first place rather than by special skills for dealing with problems once they occur. Their success is not achieved through a few isolated techniques or gimmicks. Rather, it is the result of a systematic approach, which starts with preparation and planning before the school year begins, is implemented initially through systematic communication of expectations and establishment of procedures and routines at the beginning of the year, and is maintained throughout the year. The approach is maintained not only by consistency in following up on stated expectations but by continually presenting students with well-chosen and well-prepared academic activities that focus their attention during lessons and engage their concentrated efforts during independent work times. (p. 271)

Although Brophy's review summarizes classroom organization and management issues that arise over the course of a term, a substantial number of studies have directly addressed the issue of how teachers establish themselves with their students in the first few days or weeks of school. Most of these studies have focused on the elementary classroom, producing consistent findings: The effective teacher begins the year by setting up an efficient and smoothly running classroom where instruction, not management, is the major thrust. The first few days involve explicit statements of the teacher's expectations and rehearsals of the teacher's chosen routines. As these expectations and routines become internalized, the teacher is able to call up these routines with minimal cues to the students—thus minimizing time on management concerns and maximizing time for instruction.

Illustrative of this research is a study by Brooks (1985). He investigated the first day of school at the junior high level by videotaping and comparing first-year "brand new" teachers with veteran "superstar" teachers during their 1st, 2nd, 10th, and 28th days of school. He found the following behaviors to be most conducive to success:

1. Routinization: Similar tasks were accomplished daily in a similar manner—routinely and swiftly.

2. Visual scanning: "Superstars" maintained direct eye contact with the entire class in order to gauge the collective attitude of the group.

3. Businesslike tone of voice: A no-nonsense, "let's get to work" tone was used to create a businesslike attitude toward learning.

4. Behavioral and academic expectations: Effective junior high teachers stated daily reminders of behavioral and academic expectations. On the first day, the method of presenting rules consisted of (a) stating the rule, (b) providing a student-centered rationale for the rule, (c) explaining the consequences of breaking the rule, and (d) giving a good example of what the infraction looked like.

5. Anticipation of confusion: Effective junior high teachers anticipated areas of student confusion. For example, if most students made a similar error on homework assignments, effective teachers addressed this obvious confusion. Effective teachers also anticipated confusion by calling for questions before initiating the day's lesson.

Brooks (1985) concluded: ". . . good school years begin with well-planned and executed first days that permit the teacher to establish a cooperative learning environment and permit the students to find out what is expected in the classroom. Effective first day procedures meet teacher and student needs and increase the likelihood of an effective second day" (p. 78). The effective lesson opening on second and subsequent days, according to Brooks, will typically include a quick call to order in a businesslike tone of voice, fast-paced roll taking, an opening remark that includes behavioral and academic expectations for the students, an apparent anticipation of areas of confusion in the explanations given, and a call for questions.

TEACHER PERSONALITY

Perhaps the most important of the three categories of questions that students sitting in the classroom on the first day of class have in their minds is "What kind of person is this teacher going to be?" In many cases, teachers do not start the first day with a clean slate. Assuming that the teacher has taught before, campus folklore has already contributed to the students' data base. Teacher reputations start building with the first class taught on campus and continue to shape student perceptions over an individual's teaching career. How one builds on (or repairs) these initial impressions is the topic of an area of theory and research known as "impression management."

One of the major theorists who has discussed self-presentation is Erving Goffman (1959, 1963). Goffman has analyzed human behavior via a theatrical metaphor. According to him, people are actors, structuring their performances to make impressions on audiences. People in focused interaction take turns presenting dramas to one another. For example, when we teach, we take on that role (however we define it) and present that character—the teacher. We want students to form that impression of us. How we dress, arrange the learning environment, the language we use, and so on, all help students form an impression of us as a teacher.

These impressions are formed quickly. Ask students the question "What will this class be like?" after the first class meeting and they can tell you. The quote at the beginning of this chapter is from one of our students after the first class period. This student makes a decision about a class and the instructor after only 50 minutes.

In his discussion of teaching as relational development, DeVito (1986) indicated the importance of first impressions for the teaching–learning process:

> First, the impressions are inevitable and form despite attempts to avoid prejudging anyone. Second, they have a powerful effect on how the relationship progresses. Third, and perhaps most important, these impressions are resistant to change. The primacy effect (the tendency to give dispropor tionate weight to what is perceived first) operates like a filter through which later impressions pass. Confirmatory information, we know, is received more easily and retained longer than contradictory information. First impressions, then, are crucial for the student, the teacher, and the teacher–student relationship. (p. 54)

What type of impression, then, should a teacher want to create? The answer to this question, of course, varies greatly with such factors as teacher resources, teacher definition of role, course objectives, and student personalities. Whatever the nature of the answer, however, it is wise to recall that the goal of teaching is student learning. Thus, teachers not only want to create the impression of being warm and likeable, they also need to be perceived as knowledgeable, confident, and in control. How do teachers do this?

Burgoon and Saine (1978) provided a general analysis of what happens the first time individuals meet, which they summarized as "principles" of first impressions:

1. People develop evaluations of others from limited information. Since talk is frequently limited to social amenities and topics such as the weather, we rely heavily on nonverbal cues.
2. First impressions are based on stereotypes. Because of the bombardment of nonverbal information that assails our senses, we need some way to classify this abundance of information.
3. Initial impressions are formed by treating others as objects, judging them on the basis of outward appearances.
4. Many stereotypic judgments are relatively accurate. Intuition is nothing more than tuning in to all available information, and that information frequently steers us in the right direction. (pp. 145–148)

A variety of individuals have explored the communication variables that impact on perceptions of teacher competency. Programs of research include those on teacher immediacy and nonverbal expressiveness, educational humor, teacher communicator style, teacher clarity and instructional explicitness, and strategies for coping with student misbehavior.

Much of this research has been recently summarized by Civikly (1986), Cooper (1988), Rubin and Feezel (1985), and Staton-Spicer and Wulff (1984). These variables, plus others such as self-concept, self-disclosure, descriptiveness, owning feelings, empathy, listening, response styles, and behavioral flexibility are all important to the successful management of first impressions. The communication instructor who is familiar with this literature is able to make informed decisions about how best to manage impressions during the opening session of a class.

It must be remembered, of course, that an individual plays the teacher role within the constraints of his or her resources. Luckily, there is not a single script for the successful performance of the teacher role. Thus, for example, if you are not good at telling jokes, don't tell them; if you tell them well, use them to capture interest and make a point.

CONCLUSION

As we began this chapter, we suggested that the first session of a class is much too important to waste. As teachers and students first meet, both attempt to discover a comfortable mode of existence. For students, this means learning as much as possible about the teacher and the class, establishing their own identity, and gaining as much control over the situation as possible. Hopefully, this chapter has provided useful suggestions for productively coping with these first-day expectations of students.

ACKNOWLEDGMENT

Many of the ideas in this chapter owe a debt to the unpublished notes of R. L. Kohls, a professor of agricultural economics who for many years taught a seminar on college teaching at Purdue University.

REFERENCES

Berger, C. R., & Calabrese, R. J. (1975). Some explorations in initial interaction and beyond: Toward a developmental theory of interpersonal communication. *Human Communication Research, 1,* 99–112.

Brophy, J. E. (1983). Classroom organization and management. *The Elementary School Journal, 83,* 265–285.

Brooks, D. (1985). The first day of school. *Educational Leadership, 43,* 76–78.

Burgoon, J. K., & Saine, T. (1978). *The unspoken dialogue: An introduction to nonverbal communication.* Boston: Houghton Mifflin.

Civikly, J. (Ed.). (1986). *Communicating in college classrooms.* San Francisco: Jossey-Bass.

Cooper, P. (1988). *Speech communication for the classroom teacher.* Scottsdale, AZ: Gorsuch-Scarisbrick.

DeVito, J. (1986). Teaching as relational development. In J. Civikly (Ed.), *Communicating in college classrooms* (pp. 51–60). San Francisco: Jossey-Bass.

Goffman, E. (1959). *The presentation of self in everyday life.* Garden City, NY: Doubleday.

Goffman, E. (1963). *Behavior in public places.* New York: Free Press.

Kohls, R. L. (N.D.). *Do as I say; not as I do.* Unpublished manuscript.

Merton, R., Reader, G., & Kendall, P. (1957). *The student physician.* Cambridge: Harvard University Press.

Rubin, R. B., & Feezel, J. D. (1985). Teacher communication competence: Essential skills and assessment procedures. *The Central States Speech Journal, 36,* 4–13.

Staton-Spicer, A. Q., & Darling, A. (1986). Communication in the socialization of preservice teachers. *Communication Education, 35,* 215–230.

Staton-Spicer, A. Q., & Wulff, D. H. (1984). Research in communication and instruction: Categorization and synthesis. *Communication Education, 33,* 377–391.

Van Maanen, J., & Schein, E. H. (1979). Toward a theory of organizational socialization. *Research in Organizational Behavior, 1,* 209–264.

IV

SELECTING AND EVALUATING INSTRUCTIONAL STRATEGIES AND TOOLS

19

Instructional Tools

Donald H. Wulff
Jody D. Nyquist
University of Washington

Communication instructors employ various tools to assist students in learning communication content. In some form, most instructors use course syllabi, textbooks and other print materials and instructional technology. Each tool provides opportunities for student learning outside of class or, as in the case of instructional media applications, enables students to process knowledge in additional visual and auditory modes.

SYLLABI

Syllabi are course documents developed by instructors primarily to communicate to students the structure and procedures for courses. In the communication discipline, the syllabus is a commonly used instructional tool that serves a variety of functions in the communication between an instructor and the students. In some cases the course syllabus, by listing weekly topics and due dates, may serve as a general outline of a course or as a guide to prepare students for reading, assignments, and exams. In other instances, the syllabus may be a more thorough document that clarifies specific expectations for students by providing basic information about the course objectives, content, policies, and procedures, and, in some cases, not only a schedule of assigned reading but also the actual readings. A thorough, carefully planned syllabus can function as an advanced organizer for the students as well as a form of protection for the instructor if students miss class, fail to turn in assignments on time, or get caught cheating. Finally, a syllabus can communicate to students an overall positive impression of the course. It provides an opportunity for the instructor to show an investment in the class, a commitment to the course content, and a concern for student learning.

Although a syllabus is an important part of communication within the classroom, it can also fulfill other important functions. First, the use of a syllabus assists an instructor in planning of courses. Because determining the structure for a course requires careful thought and decision making before the class begins, the syllabus provides an impetus for the instructor to organize the class early. Typically, during the preplanning stages for a course, the teacher thinks about the course objectives and the overall structure and content necessary to achieve those objectives. In these initial stages the syllabus helps the instructor make decisions about how to achieve course objectives within the constraints imposed by the instructional context. In addition, if an instructor teaches the same course more than once, the syllabus functions as a reminder of the previous framework for the course and parts of the course that need to be restructured. Also, the syllabus serves as an important summary for students who may be considering enrolling in the class or for other instructors, chairpersons, or administrators, who, for a variety of reasons, may need a description of the course. An important first step, then, is for the instructor to determine the particular functions the syllabus for a specific course will serve.

The functions the instructor chooses to fulfill through the use of the syllabus will determine, of course, what should be included in the document. Within the communication discipline, syllabi vary in format and content. Typically, however, they begin with basic information about the quarter/semester and year, the course (title and number), the meeting time and place, the instructor's name, and the time and place for office hours. In varying degrees of specificity, the syllabus might also include references to textbooks and other major resources for the class, a list of major course objectives, a description of ways objectives will be achieved, a daily or weekly schedule for content areas and assignment due dates, a weighting of major assignments and tests for grading and evaluation purposes, and a description of course policies regarding attendance, late assignments, and cheating.

Regardless of the general functions the syllabus will serve, it is important for the instructor to consider carefully how to develop the document to meet the needs for a particular course. The following considerations are especially relevant for instructors developing course syllabi.

Colleagues as Resources

Before preparing a syllabus, an instructor can ask colleagues for sample copies of their syllabi. This process allows the instructor to see the diversity in format and content used by colleagues as well as to raise questions about guidelines for use. It will also be an opportunity for the instructor to observe the variety of ways in which courses can be structured.

Policies and Procedures

Having course policies and procedures in writing is a way to avoid conflict with students. Before writing syllabi, however, instructors may want to check departmental and university policies that could affect their positions on attendance, testing, grading, and academic dishonesty. They may also want to confirm the dates of holidays that will affect scheduling during the term.

Specificity

The level of specificity in the syllabus will depend on what the instructor wishes to communicate to students about the particular course. The syllabus is a contract with students. Therefore, instructors do not want to promise any more or less than they intend to deliver. At the same time, they will want to balance some students' concern about ambiguity with other students' fear of structure. Although it is important that a carefully planned syllabus convey the instructor's investment in the course, the instructor also wants to allow students some sense of their responsibility for achieving the course objectives (McKeachie, 1986, p. 21).

Flexibility

A carefully planned syllabus allows flexibility. There may be a tendency, especially when instructors first develop a course, to include too much content and to schedule too heavily. Leaving an "open" day near midterm or the end of the term allows an instructor to address student overload as well as the problems that arise if the instructor misses class unexpectedly during the term. Flexibility is particularly important if the instructors are teaching courses for the first time and do not have a clear sense of student abilities or their own potential for moving through the content at a particular pace. Even though the use of a syllabus requires preplanning, some instructors prefer to do an initial needs assessment of their students during the first class period and then modify the syllabus before the students receive it during the second class meeting. This procedure can decrease the adjustments that have to be made during the term as the instructor moves through the syllabus for a new class the first time.

Whatever format instructors use to address these issues, they should know that students view the syllabus as valuable. They describe it as the "road map," organizational scheme, or "table of contents" for a course. Brief or extended, the syllabus sets expectations and serves as an important part of students' perceptions of the overall organization in a course.

TEXTBOOKS AND OTHER PRINT MATERIALS

The use of a textbook as an instructional aid is common in teaching communication, particularly in undergraduate courses. Although the specific ways in which instructors use textbooks in classes vary greatly, textbooks commonly fulfill two primary functions. Sometimes they function to provide the primary structure and content for a course; other times they may be used as a supplement to a course. Instructors must ask themselves, then, whether textbooks will provide the major structure and content for a course, with presentations highlighting important concepts and providing missing information and perspectives, or whether presentations will focus the course, with the textbook functioning as supplementary material. Answers to this question define the functions that textbooks will fulfill in a course.

Textbooks to Provide Course Structure

Instructors often use textbooks to provide the major information for a course, in some cases even the curriculum. When a major goal of a course is to impart large quantities of information quickly, one or more textbooks can function to make the information readily accessible. Typically, textbooks serve as the students' initial exposure to concepts, explanations, examples, and illustrations. During class time, instructors can then follow the structure of the textbook(s), focusing on important concepts or ideas and providing additional explanations or examples for particularly difficult concepts. This use of textbooks assures that the students have the major content for the course in written form where they can read, review, or refer to it as necessary. Using a textbook or textbooks as the primary source of information for a class is particularly common when a textbook presents the theoretical perspective, the framework, or the information that the instructor deems relevant for the course goals.

If instructors intend to use textbooks as major sources of structure or information for their courses, they will want to consider carefully the instructors' roles during class time. Success in the instructor's role depends not only on the balancing of content from the book with content brought in from other sources, but also on the processing of the two kinds of content. Although there are a number of ways to achieve such balance, in most cases instructors cannot simply repeat information from the textbook. Rather, they might devote a small part of class time to clarifying or supplementing textual material and the balance of the time to applying and amplifying text materials (Ehle, 1976, p. 87). If a goal is to use classroom interaction to stimulate learning related to the text, however, the instructor may spend less time clarifying and giving examples and more time facilitating discussion designed to get students to clarify, apply, and amplify the content.

Supplementary Textbooks and Print Materials

Most often, single textbooks cannot provide all the content, perspectives, or frameworks that an instructor deems appropriate for a particular class. In these cases, the instructor must decide whether to use the most appropriate text as it is or to integrate materials from a variety of sources. If the primary course goal is to provide a particular perspective or body of content that no textbook addresses appropriately, then textbooks might fulfill supplemental functions in the curriculum of the course while the instructor becomes responsible for providing perspectives, most of the content, and much of the integration and synthesis. Some instructors, for example, might provide the frameworks or theoretical perspectives for their classes, and even part of the content, based on their own synthesis of information. In these instances, the instructor might use a textbook or a portion of a textbook to provide additional information or contrasting views. In other instances, when available textbooks do not provide an appropriate structure or perspective for a class, the instructor may provide the overall framework or structure and use several different books, in some cases paperback editions, to provide the content that will achieve the objectives of the course.

Regardless of how instructors decide to use supplemental textbooks, it is helpful for them to remember that, for students, *the use* of such textbooks is a key issue. Students will be dissatisfied if they are required to read and take tests over supplemental material that is not carefully integrated into a course. Furthermore, students will complain, and rightfully so, if they are required to purchase supplemental textbooks that are ultimately not used in class. It is important, therefore, for instructors to clarify for students how supplemental readings fit into course structure and objectives.

Textbook Selection

Whether instructors want textbooks to function as primary sources of curriculum or as supplements to support specific perspectives and pro vide additional content, there are some general issues to consider in choosing a textbook for a communication course. First, the textbook is a tool for achieving course objectives. Therefore, before instructors select a textbook, they need to determine what the student outcomes for their course are and how those outcomes can best be achieved. If the course goals involve providing a specific body of information or a particular framework or perspective, instructors can select textbooks that are consistent with the approach that they intend to use in the course. If, on the other hand, their goals include presenting opposing points of view, instructors may want to select a textbook or textbooks that present appropriately opposing perspectives. It is important for instructors to remember, however, that students often express dissatisfaction when they do not understand the "overall picture" in the courses they take. Therefore, when the selection of textbooks is not completely consistent with the frameworks or perspectives presented in class, instructors can eliminate much frustration and confusion, particularly for undergraduate students, if they clarify how they are using textbooks to provide contrast.

It is important during initial stages of trying to match course objectives and textbooks that instructors consider not only whether the textbooks provide appropriate content or perspectives, but also whether the textbooks have presented accurate information, sequenced and developed at an appropriate level for the students. Particularly for upper division and graduate communication courses, instructors may conclude that there are no appropriate textbooks for achieving the course objectives. In these instances, instructors might develop a packet of readings that presents appropriate content, frameworks or perspectives. Such an approach allows instructors the flexibility of using current theoretical papers, research reports, and case studies that provide a variety of perspectives that enhance student interest. Typically, such packets consist of articles from journals or book chapters copied and made available to students through campus copy centers. Instructors must check copyright laws carefully, however, before making multiple copies.

Once instructors have determined that particular textbooks provide credible and appropriately sequenced content or perspectives for their

The following checklist provides a systematic guide for selecting a communication textbook. Score your assessment of the book on each item, and compute the average score for comparison.

Very Adequate — Very Inadequate

Very Adequate				Very Inadequate	
1	2	3	4	5	1. COPYRIGHT DATA: Are information and interpretation up-to-date?
1	2	3	4	5	2. AUTHOR: Is she or he credible in the field of communication?
1	2	3	4	5	3. REVIEWS: Have professional communication journal reviews been good?
1	2	3	4	5	4. TOPIC EMPHASIS: Do topics correspond to objectives of the course?
1	2	3	4	5	5. SEQUENCE: Are topics arranged in a desirable sequence or can they be adapted without disrupting the usefulness of the book?
1	2	3	4	5	6. CONTENT: Is it accurate? Is its point-of-view consistent with the current thinking in communication? Are recent communication developments included?
1	2	3	4	5	7. BIAS: Is it free of nationalistic, racist or sexual bias?
1	2	3	4	5	8. CONCEPTS: Are the important communication concepts clearly developed?
1	2	3	4	5	9. DETAIL: Is detail sufficient?
1	2	3	4	5	10. EXPLANATIONS: Are they clear and succinct?
1	2	3	4	5	11. READING LEVEL: Is it appropriate for the level of students in the class?
1	2	3	4	5	12. PRESUMED STUDENT EXPERIENCE: Have students had sufficient communication background to understand at the level assumed by the author?
1	2	3	4	5	13. TITLES, HEADINGS, SUBHEADINGS: Do these help the student visualize the organizing framework and the relationship among communication concepts?
1	2	3	4	5	14. SUMMARIES, REVIEW QUESTIONS: Are there study aids? Do they help the student generalize, apply, evaluate content, stimulate critical thinking, or require problem-solving?
1	2	3	4	5	15. TABLE OF CONTENTS, PREFACE, INDEX, APPENDICES: Are these adequate and useful?
1	2	3	4	5	16. SOURCES: Are these documented adequately?
1	2	3	4	5	17. ILLUSTRATIONS: Are these accurate, purposeful, properly captioned, and placed near the related text?
1	2	3	4	5	18. GRAPHS, TABLES, MAPS, CHARTS: Are these clear, pertinent, and carefully done?
1	2	3	4	5	19. DURABILITY: Is the book well constructed? Is the binding flexible?
1	2	3	4	5	20. TYPE: Is it clear and easily readable and large enough?
1	2	3	4	5	21. FORMAT: Do page size, column arrangement, margins, and white spaces contribute to communicating ideas? Do they allow for supplemental note taking?
1	2	3	4	5	22. PRICE: Is the price reasonable for the extent to which you will utilize the text for assignments?
1	2	3	4	5	23. SIZE AND WEIGHT: Will the text be easily carried to class? Is it too long, too detailed, too short, too sketchy?
1	2	3	4	5	24. INSTRUCTOR'S MANUAL: Are supplemental material, teaching aids, test questions, and suggested strategies for use included?
1	2	3	4	5	25. SUPPLEMENTAL WORKBOOK, COMPUTER SOFTWARE: Are related resource materials suitable for some or all students to purchase?
1	2	3	4	5	26. MEASUREMENTS FOR STUDENT ACHIEVEMENT: Are test items or other devices for assessment provided?

Average Overall Rating: _____

Author(s): _____

Textbook Title: _____

Publisher:_____Copyright Date: _____

FIG. 19.1. Checklist for communication textbooks.

courses, they can look more specifically at the ways in which information about communication is presented. Although such textbook assessment is at least partially influenced by the number and kinds of examples, illustrations, visual representations, and activities that instructors are able to develop on their own, it is influenced by the ways they feel course objectives can be fulfilled. If, for instance, an instructor wants students to read three chapters to acquire basic knowledge of interpersonal conflict but only intends to—or only has time to—emphasize the most important points in class, a major consideration will be whether the textbook provides sufficient detail, examples, and visual representations to assist students in understanding the basic information about interpersonal conflict. If, however, a major goal is to stimulate thinking about the content through class or small group discussion, then it might be important that the text raises issues or includes questions for further discussion.

Other considerations, and certainly pragmatic ones from the viewpoints of the students, are the size and the cost of textbooks. If the course goals are such that students need to bring the book to class for handy reference, then size may be a determining factor. If any one of several different communication textbooks can function successfully to fulfill course goals, then cost may be a factor. Because students are often reluctant to purchase expensive textbooks that are used only as secondary references, instructors have to weigh carefully the expense and size of textbooks in relation to perceived usefulness.

Textbooks and other print materials, when carefully selected and effectively used, provide a primary instructional strategy for the teaching of communication content. Therefore, as McKeachie (1986) pointed out, "There is no substitute for detailed review of competing texts for the course you are teaching. . . . one cannot adopt a textbook on the basis of the sales representative description any more than physicians should prescribe drugs on the advice of the drug company's detail men" (p. 12). The adaptation of a textbook checklist (Fig. 19.1) compiled by Wright (1987) is offered to assist instructors in the selection process.

INSTRUCTIONAL TECHNOLOGY

Instructional technology, or the use of equipment to deliver instruction, has become an essential strategy in many communication programs. Technological applications in the form of films, audio/videotapes, slide/tape programs, and computer software have been produced to present and supplement communication curricula. Purchased, prerecorded media, for example, make accessible historical and contemporary speeches— including the context in which they were delivered—and enable students to see and hear important personalities demonstrate communication skills that can be described or simulated for student imitation. Video/audio recording provides immediate playback for student and instructor critique and preserves communication events that are fleeting and perishable and otherwise unavailable for later study. Students can also make presentations utilizing media to supplement or enhance their oral messages. In addition, computer software development provides a valuable tool for teaching communication content. Although the use of instructional technology is dependent on the equipment and facilities available, it seems clear both that innovative applications of high technology enhance communication instruction and that the potential for its use is only beginning to be realized.

Instructional Media

The use of instructional media creates an act in the classroom that arouses interest (D'Angelo & Nyquist, 1973). According to Samuel Becker (1971), "Since the norms of those who work in television favor the showing of an act over the transmission of a word, one has a greater chance of being heard if he *does* something" (p. 30). At the very least, the use of media offers students an alternative learning experience that enriches perception of an event or situation by the increased number of cues presented. Instructors use media not only because it creates interest, but also because it can increase the possibilities for a clearer understanding of the message sent, provide audio and visual models of communication as they actually occur in our society, and decrease the lecture preparation time of instructors (D'Angelo & Nyquist, 1973).

Instructional media function in three distinct ways. First, instructors can use presentations in prerecorded form in the classroom to cover content, provide examples of concepts, give students access to experts in particular fields, and offer models for imitation. Media can also function as tools to record and play back classroom events and interactions, including student and instructor presentations, for subsequent review and critique. A third use of media actually enables students to control media to provide a piece of work as one would write a paper or produce a play. Student-produced audio and videotapes, films, and slide/tape programs become creative statements of student understanding of concepts and topics covered in a course.

Prerecorded Media. Prerecorded, purchased, media materials are available for every discipline. In communication, the videotape of great speeches (Rohler & Cook, 1987), which accompanies the Rohler and Cook text, brings real-life communication situations into the classroom in ways that instructors using conventional instructional strategies of lecture and discussion cannot.

Recording materials off the air provides another opportunity to access current communication events, such as presidential candidate speeches, critiques of candidate–press interactions, and even soap opera episodes that illustrate communication principles and failures. However, "off air pirating," even for educational purposes, raises serious ethical issues. Although W. E. Francoise (1980) has developed guidelines, legislation over these matters is still forthcoming, and the producers' rights will be litigated for some time to come. Making money from showing off air copies is not the issue. Whether an instructor is copying otherwise available materials, similar to full-scale photocopying of textbooks, to avoid paying a high purchase price presents one of the ethical dimensions of the problem. Certainly, film and radio and television broadcast materials, purchased or recorded, can add an important dimension to the classroom study of communication, but instructors must carefully observe the copyright laws.

Films produced specifically for the communication classroom are almost nonexistent, but access to films and other media produced for other purposes is easily attainable in most universities and videotape rental agencies. These materials, when repurposed, provide rich and illustrative examples for analysis in the communication classroom. Showing the videotape of "The Breakfast Club," a feature film targeted for the general populace that traces the activities of five teenagers who were placed in a Saturday detention program, can achieve several instructional goals. The students' escapades, poignant and sometimes hilarious, document the loss incurred when we judge people only on the basis of dress, social status, and so on, and fail to investigate the person's needs, desires, longings, successes, failures, and circumstances. Repurposed for showing in an interpersonal course, the film is illustrative of several key concepts: self concept, selective perception, negotiation of selves, self-disclosure, and conflict management, to name a few. Repurposed for a course on adolescent communication, the film becomes a study of adolescent interaction, age-appropriate and -inappropriate behavior, communication development and competence, adolescent–adult interaction, and other topics specific to course goals. Repurposed films and audio/video tapes often provide unique opportunities to use entire pieces or segments of multi-million-dollar Hollywood productions to illustrate communication concepts, strategies, difficulties, and effectiveness. Again, appropriate use depends on the goals for a course, the learning abilities of the students, and the observance of ethical standards.

Recording Media.   Using media, primarily audio and video, to record classroom events and student presentations has become a standard instructional tool in many colleges and universities. Student self-critique of segments of their own behavior often eliminates controversy about instructor feedback. Students and instructors benefit greatly from critiquing their own performances with the added opportunity to play and replay particular parts to analyze precisely what occurred versus what needed to occur and what changes can be made before the next presentation. Most learning theorists stress the importance of immediate feedback to skill development. Another application, the recording of guest speakers or instructor lectures, provides additional showings of otherwise real-time, single occurrences. Instructors can then use these one-time-only presenta tions in subsequent classes, enabling large numbers of students to share the experience. Audio and video recording and playback have become major instructional tools in most communication departments.

For those institutions that have been able to develop central distribution facilities, audio and videotaping between classrooms, laboratories, and large lecture rooms enhance the potential for effective and efficient instruction. Once all facilities are "patched" together, any number of instructional formats are possible. For example, the instructor can divide a class of 60 students in a group discussion course into four groups of seven to eight students who simultaneously participate in discussions occurring in rooms equipped with remote-controlled, wall-mounted cameras. By videotape, these discussions can be sent to the instructor and the other half of the class in the large lecture classroom. This process provides the capability of randomly selecting the interaction of the four groups and commenting on the groups' progress, pointing out examples of particularly useful individual contributions and group leader behaviors. Interviewing classes, organized in a similar fashion, make available to students the possibility of "sitting in" on interviews and learning through the modeling of others' interview strategies and approaches. Actual observation of interviews without the use of media can disrupt and make too contrived the simulated interview experience.

More sophisticated uses of media include (a) providing simultaneous audio feedback during student or instructor presentations (Nyquist & Wulff, 1982), particularly useful when intervention at critical moments is necessary; (b) simultaneous visual feedback processes, such as the ComEt system, which uses teleprompters to communicate with the speaker (Behnke & Beatty, 1977; Behnke & O'Hair, 1984); and (c) audience response systems, which allow listeners to communicate directly with the speaker (Behnke & O'Hair, 1984). Each of these situations provides the opportunity to coach the student during and immediately following a presentation.

Student Productions Using Media.   A third use of media requires students to control and experiment with a particular medium in order to communicate with class members or audiences other than classmates. It is amazing what students can produce in terms of media materials designed to explore certain communication concepts. Using video or slide/tape formats, student learning that occurs from defining the objective of a production, designing the audio and visual story lines, writing the script, shooting the visuals, recording the narration, combining the various elements into a coherent message, presenting the program, and evaluating its success is immense. In instances in which the students are producing for a real client (such as a nonprofit organization), working with clients adds the dimension of achieving effective client–student communication in order to get the task accomplished.

The use of media as an instructional strategy to teach communication content seems extremely efficacious. Prerecorded materials, usually repurposed, allow the instructor to add real-world experience to the academic classroom. Using audio or video recording to capture the communication act in various contexts for further study and analysis cannot help but result in increased student acquisition of effective communication skills and understandings. Finally, student productions using media provide opportunity for students to participate actively in constructing complex messages for specific audiences.

Instructional Computing

The use of instructional computing has exploded in many disciplines, becoming for some areas of study a primary way of acquiring competence. Computer simulations, for instance, are used extensively to teach business courses (Jandt, 1972; Nilsen, 1983), medicine, engineering, physics, biology, mathematics, and, of course, computer science. Recently, many professionals in the humanities and social sciences have become involved in developing materials to simulate performance situations such as: (a) dealing with people in times of disaster; (b) retrieving information in terms of the mastery of facts, principles, or understandings; and (c) dealing with "encounter" situations (Dennis, 1979). Surprisingly, although all three types of computer simulations have application for teaching communication concepts, King (1985) reported that, "One cannot find instructional computer simulations written by communication instructors for communication courses. If they exist, they do not appear in our literature" (p. 63). Hopefully, the development of simulation software in the area of communication is forthcoming, because the application is particularly appropriate for dynamic situations that offer alternative methods for solving problems. Clearly, communication study meets these criteria.

Communication instructors utilize computers for other instructional

purposes, of course, including the use of BIBLIO, created for the storage
and retrieval of articles in *Communication Education* (Williams & Edwards, 1983), computer modeling (Richmond, Groescher, Paterline, &
Springhorn, 1975), computerized criticism (Behnke & King, 1984), and
some computer-based instruction (Hemphill & Standerfer, 1987). Com
Serve's data base service now provides teaching materials, research instruments, calls for papers, funding announcements, and so on. Electronic
conferences are available in such topic areas as philosophy of communication, communication instruction, research methodology, communication
disorders, rhetoric, and interpersonal, mass, intercultural, organizational,
gender, and health communication.

Daily use of computers for word processing has become the norm, and
computer instruction in all research courses is essential. The use of microcomputer SPSS or Minitabs in quantitative methods courses allows
students to work at home or in department-based microcomputer laboratories and, thus, eliminates the difficulties sometimes associated with
access to main frame operations. If the data base requires main frame
capabilities, use of a microcomputer together with a modem provides a
convenient and accessible terminal for communicating with the larger
computer. Correlations, multiple regressions, factor analyses, and numerous statistical tests can all be handled using microcomputers. Relational data base programs, such as D-Base and R-Base, offer the potential
of handling large quantities of qualitative research data. Field notes and
interview data can be handled efficiently without compromising the
richness of the data.

With the integration of laser disc and computer technologies into "interactive video," computer based instruction (CBI) seems unlimited in its
potential to provide an active learning strategy, paced individually with
opportunity for re-teaching and exploration until the attainment of mastery. Students can ask questions and be provided with illustrations that
enable them to feel as if they are experiencing the subject of study.

The effect of combining still and motion visuals with frame-accurate
retrieval times of less than .5 seconds has revolutionized the delivery of
information. For instance, it is possible to store 108,000 frames, or 1 hour
of video, on one laser disc with the complete flexibility of calling up
different images in various sequences each time a presentation is given.
Entire collections of biological slides or works of art can be accessed by
pushing a single button. With the projection of these images on a large
screen, an instructor can provide students with visually supported lectures organized and reorganized to fit the curriculum and the level of the
class. Lecture aid utilities make it possible to catalog a videodisc, search
the catalog, and assemble the visuals found into an illustrated lecture
with a minimum of effort.

Use of Instructional Technology

Effective use of instructional technology depends, of course, on the match of instructors' instructional goals with the media or technology selected, establishment of student expectations and lines of inquiry to be pursued during the presentation or experience, and subsequent effective debriefing or processing procedures. As with any other instructional strategy, the use of instructional technology requires the instructor's careful planning and thoughtful implementation.

Selecting Technology. The first question of why an instructor should use technology is a critical one. Technology provides particular opportunities for simulations, real-world applications and evaluations, and the presentation of models; but an instructor must begin by determining that a technological approach is best suited for achieving a particular goal. For example, viewing via videotape Martin Luther King's "I Have a Dream" speech adds the nonverbal dimensions of King's delivery as well as the crowd response, environment, various commentaries, and so on, making the study a richer experience for students. If, on the other hand, the purpose is to enable students to become competent at the textual analysis of his speech including an exacting study of the language, word choice, phrasing, images, etcetera, the printed medium would be required and preferred. The key element is the matching of the technology to the goals for student achievement.

Establishing Student Expectations. An important step is preparing students for the technology. Making explicit the reasons for using a particular technology helps students to become more effective at learning. (Of course, this is true for all instructional strategies. See McKeachie, 1986, pp. 228–242, for further discussion of learning and cognition in the college classroom.) The establishment of pre-showing or computer use guidelines enables students to adopt appropriate expectations, to determine what ideas, issues, specific examples to look for, and to prepare for the subsequent discussion or response activity following the instructional technology experience.

Processing the Experience. Immediately following film, tape, slide/tape, or computer programs, it is helpful to process the experience. Students need to describe their experience, interpret the meaning of it, and transfer new insights or knowledge to other similar or dissimilar events or intellectual endeavors. Often, a discussion provides the most helpful opportunity for enabling students to practice interpreting and generalizing what they have learned.

As previously stated, effective use of technology depends on careful selection given the specific goal or purpose of the intended student learning; explicit explanations of three items: (a) choice of technology, (b) formulation of student expectations, and (c) establishment of anticipated outcomes as a result of the experience; and sufficient debriefing or processing of the particular instructional strategy. If the instructor omits any of these elements, the effect of the use of the technology diminishes.

SUMMARY

Although this short chapter cannot address all the instructional tools that instructors might use, it does provide the basis for an initial understanding of the ways tools might function in communication courses. It is clear, for instance, that a carefully designed syllabus is an important communication tool because it defines the direction for a course and aligns expectations of the students and the instructor. Textbooks and print materials that have been thoughtfully selected can provide organizational frameworks or information needed to supplement a course organization developed by the instructor. Instructional technology properly integrated into instructional activities can provide audio and visual stimuli that make important contributions to students' involvement in the content of the course. Regardless of the types of instructional tools available, however, it is important to consider course goals and the needs of the instructor and students in selecting such tools and to document the use of the tools so their effectiveness can be assessed before planning future courses.

REFERENCES

Becker, S. L. (1971). Rhetorical studies for the contemporary world. In L. Bitzer & E. Black (Eds.), *The prospect of rhetoric* (pp. 21–43). Englewood Cliffs NJ: Prentice-Hall.

Behnke, R. R., & Beatty, M. (1977). Critiquing speaker behavior through immediate video display. *Communication Education, 26*, 345–348.

Behnke, R. R., & King, P. E. (1984). Computerized speech criticism. *Communication Education, 33*, 173–177.

Behnke, R. R., & O'Hair, H. D. (1984). Applications of high technology to communication instruction. *Central States Speech Journal, 35*, 171–177.

D'Angelo, G., & Nyquist, J. (1973). Teaching strategies for large lecture courses: Use of multimedia and discussion groups. *The Speech Teacher, 22*, 310–317.

Dennis, J. R. (1979). *Computer simulation and its instructional uses* (Report No. 8e). The Illinois Series on Educational Application of Computers. (ERIC Document Reproduction Service No. ED183188)

Eble, K. E. (1976). *The craft of teaching: A guide to mastering the professor's art.* San Francisco: Jossey-Bass.

Francoise, W. E. (1980). Copyright law and videotaping of TV programs for classroom use. *Journalism Quarterly, 57,* 5–9.

Hemphill, M. R., & Standerfer, C. C. (1987). Enhancing computer-based lessons for effective speech education. *Communication Education, 36,* 272–276.

Jandt, F. E. (1972). Sources for computer utilization in interpersonal communication instruction and research. *Today's Speech, 20,* 25–29.

King, T. R. (1985). The status of computer simulation in speech communication. In H. W. Cummings (Ed.), *Microcomputing in speech communication: A report of the task force on use of computers* (pp. 59–67). Annandale, VA: Speech Communication Association.

McKeachie, W. J. (1986). *Teaching tips: A guidebook for the beginning college teacher* (8th ed.). Lexington, MA: D. C. Heath.

Nilsen, J. (1983). The games of BIG BUSINESS. *Classroom Computer News, 3*(3), 32–33.

Nyquist, J., & Wulff, D. (1982). The use of simultaneous feedback to alter teaching behaviors of university instructors. *Journal of Classroom Interaction, 18*(1), 11–17.

Richmond, V. P., Groescher, J. C., Paterline, E. J., & Springhorn, R. G. (1975). Computer modeling in the communication classroom: Follow up and extension. *Central States Speech Journal, 26,* 57–60.

Rohler, L., & Cook, R. (Producers). (1987). *Great speeches for criticism and analysis* [videotape, 4 vols.]. Greenwood, IN: The Educational Video Group.

Williams, M. L., & Edwards, R. (1983). Biblio: A computerized retrieval system for communication education. *Communication Education, 32,* 342–348.

Wright, D. (1987). Getting the most out of your textbook. *Teaching at UNL, 8*(3), 1–3.

SUPPLEMENTARY READING

Syllabi

Fuhrmann, B. S., & Grasha, A. F. (1983). *A practical handbook for college teachers* (pp. 248–278). Boston: Little, Brown.

Goldsmid, C. A., & Wilson, E. K. (1980). *Passing on sociology: The teaching of a discipline* (pp. 171–185). Belmont, CA: Wadsworth.

Lowman, J. (1984). *Mastering the techniques of teaching* (pp. 146–164). San Francisco, CA: Jossey-Bass.

Kozma, R. B., Belle, L. W., Williams, G. W. (1978). *Instructional techniques in higher education* (129–142). Englewood Cliffs, NJ: Educational Technology Publications.

Stark, J. S., Lowther, M. A., Ryan, M., Bomotti, S. S., Genthon, M., Martens, G., & Haven, C. L. (1988). *Reflections on course planning: Faculty and students consider influences and goals.* Ann Arbor, MI: The University of Michigan, National Center for Research to Improve Postsecondary Teaching and Learning, Tech. Rep. No. 88-C-002.0.

Textbooks and Other Print Materials

Doolittle, R. J. (1977). Conflicting views of conflict: An analysis of basic speech communication textbooks. *Communication Education, 26,* 121–127.

Dorris, J. M. (1981). Androgyny and pedagogy: An analysis of interpersonal textbooks, 1975–79. *Communication Education, 30,* 33–43.

Fuhrmann, B. S., & Grasha, A. F. (1983). *A practical handbook for college teachers* (pp. 228–233). Boston: Little, Brown and Co.

Goldsmid, C. A., & Wilson, E. K. (1980). *Passing on sociology: The teaching of a discipline* (pp. 185–199). Belmont, CA: Wadsworth.

Hubbard, R. C. (1983). The use of programmed speech communication textbooks as a means of meeting the needs of heterogeneous students in large class sections. *Communication Education, 32,* 9–13.

Kozma, R. B., Belle, L. W., & Williams, G. W. (1978). *Instructional techniques in higher education* (pp. 161–174). Englewood Cliffs, NJ: Educational Technology Publications.

Instructional Technology

Bush, J. D., Bitner, J. R., & Brooks, W. D. (1972). The effect of the video-tape recorder on levels of anxiety, exhibitionism, and reticence. *The Speech Teacher, 21,* 127–130.

Cummings, H. W. (Ed.) (1985) *Microcomputing in speech communication: A report of the Task Force on Use of Computers.* Annandale, VA: Speech Communication Association.

Gilkey, R. W. (1986). 16mm film, videotape, videodisc: Weighing the differences. *Media & Methods, 22* (4), 8–9.

Goldhaber, G. M., & Kline, J. A. (1972). Effects of videotape on attendance and attitude in the fundamentals of speech communication course. *The Speech Teacher, 21,* 93–98.

Gratz, R. D., & Salem, P. J. (1984). Technology and the crisis of self. *Communication Quarterly, 32,* 98–103.

Greenfield, P. M. (1987). Electronic technologies, education, and cognitive development. In D. E. Berger, K. Pezdek, & W. P. Banks (Eds.), *Applications of cognitive psychology: Problem solving, education, and computing* (pp. 17–32). Hillsdale, NJ: Lawrence Erlbaum Associates.

Hasselbring, T. S. (1986). Research on the effectiveness of computer-based instruction: A review. *International Review of Education, 31,* 313–323.

Hoglin, J. G. (1982). Video cassette instruction for the under-budgeted school program. *Communication Education, 31,* 357–360.

King, T. R. (1970). A multi-media approach to the beginning speech course. *Western Speech, 34,* 225–230.

Komoski, P. K. (1987). Beyond innovation: The systemic integration of technology into the curriculum. *Educational Technology, 27,* 21–25.

Kozma, R. B., & Bangert-Drowns, R. L. (1987). *Design in context: A conceptual framework for the study of computer software in higher education.* Ann Arbor, MI: The University of Michigan, National Center for Research to Improve Postsecondary Teaching and Learning.

Laybourne, K. (1975). The mirror image of classroom video. *Media & Methods, 12,* 54–63.

McCroskey, J. C., & Lashbrook, W. B. (1970). The effect of various methods of employing video-taped television playback in a course in public speaking. *The Speech Teacher, 19,* 199–210.

Porter, D. T., & King, G. W. (1972). The use of video-tape equipment in improving oral interpretation performance. *The Speech Teacher, 21,* 99–106.

Seiler, W. J. (1971). The conjunctive influence of source credibility and the use of visual materials on communicative effectiveness. *Southern Speech Journal, 37,* 174–185.

Seiler, W. J., Schuelke, L. D., & Lieb-Brilhart, B. (1984). *Communication for the contemporary classroom* (pp. 175–186). New York: Holt, Rinehart and Winston.

Shields, D. C., & Kidd, V. V. (1973). Teaching through popular film: A small group analysis of "The Poseidon Adventure." *The Speech Teacher, 22,* 201–207.

20

Instructional Models

Ann Darling
University of Illinois

So, you're going to teach communication. Among the many questions that you might be entertaining (e.g., "What am I going to say on the first day?") there is likely to be at least one "how" question: "How am I going to teach communication?" In response, you will probably think about the many excellent communication teachers that you've had; you might remember some terrific discussions, some stimulating lectures, and a few engaging role plays and think about incorporating those in your own instruction. Instructional strategies, or the classroom activities that a teacher uses to achieve educational goals, are a critical aspect of your teaching and, as such, warrant your attention.

Instructional models are systematic structures for teaching particular concepts, ideas, or processes (Joyce & Weil, 1986). As such, they provide guides within which a teacher can select, plan, and execute appropriate instructional strategies. Although there is a wide range of instructional models available for use in the classroom, this chapter focuses on two particular types that have received empirical attention and are especially relevant to communication instruction. *Information processing models* concentrate on the cognitive dimensions of learning. *Social models,* on the other hand, stress social interaction and human interdependence. Three specific examples of each type of model are discussed; selection of a specific model will be most effective when well informed by consideration of your educational goal(s), students' needs, and available resources.

267

INFORMATION PROCESSING MODELS

Information processing models focus on how learners sense and organize data, analyze problems, and generate solutions to problems (Joyce & Weil, 1986). These types of models share two fundamental assumptions about learning and teaching: first, that learning content matter is the primary purpose of instruction and, second, that effective instruction develops students' natural information-processing abilities (e.g., skills in observing, inferencing, and hypothesizing). Information processing models, then, are designed to help students acquire large bodies of information meaningfully and efficiently by triggering innate information-processing activities.

Three features help to further characterize these models. First, they focus on the cognitive, rather than the affective or behavioral, dimensions of learning. Further, efficiency of cognitive learning is a primary goal. Second, learners are presented with a stimulus that is designed by the teacher. In fact, the teacher's primary role in executing an information processing model is to present a carefully designed stimulus, the response to which will guide students to the desired cognitive learning. Third, learners are systematically moved through the process of drawing abstractions and/or generalizations. The learning process is not considered complete until the learner can generalize from the immediate experience to other similar experiences and/or apply the new information in different situations.

Research conducted by educational specialists reveals that information processing models enhance (a) short- and long-term memory, (b) retention of both simple and complex concepts, and (c) understanding of relationships among concepts (Ausubel, 1980; Barnes & Clawson, 1975). Bereiter and Kurland (1981) reviewed studies comparing programs that used information processing models with programs that did not. They reported strong and positive achievement gains in schools using the models. Further, the differences in achievement gains for the two groups of schools were statistically significant.

The most active debate over the usefulness of information processing models in communication instruction has centered on the use of advanced organizers (one application of an information processing model) in the form of instructional objectives. In a review of research, Kibler, Bassett, and Byers (1977) concluded that instructional objectives, when properly written and applied, facilitate cognitive learning in basic communication courses. The authors advised that instructional objectives should be clearly phrased and presented before instruction, and that students be taught how to use the objectives effectively.

Modifications of advanced organizers are frequently incorporated in our basic communication texts (e.g., Bradley, 1984; Stewart & D'Angelo, 1980) and are suggested by the people who design basic courses (e.g., Staton-Spicer & Bassett, 1980). Similarly, concept attainment and explanation generation (both products of information-processing activities) have been advised by those who discuss the content and function of basic communication courses (Deethardt, 1974; Hansen, 1982; Rushing, 1984). The following section presents a description of three different information processing models: advanced organizers, concept attainment, and Suchman inquiry.

Advanced Organizers

When Jan begins class on the first day, she presents an analogy of public speaking: She argues that any public speaking event is like an important conversation. In discussing that analogy, she addresses the components and complexities of both public speaking and important conversations, taking care to incorporate students in the discussion. Before closing her discussion, she informs her students that they will refer to the analogy throughout the course.

Jan is using an advanced organizer in her teaching. Her analogy of public speaking as conversation provides students with an orienting structure, or "intellectual scaffolding" (Joyce & Weil, 1986), to guide the learning process. David Ausubel (1963) is the primary architect of this model, which is formed around his theory of meaningful verbal learning. It is Ausubel's assumption that cognitive structures are organized deductively; therefore, learning is most efficient when instruction is presented in a similarly organized fashion: treating general ideas first, integrating new ideas with existing knowledge, and engaging the learner in a process of transforming the new information into a form that is compatible with his or her personal frame of reference. The focus of the model, then, concerns the presentation, organization, and internalization of information.

Using the Model. Presenting the advanced organizer is the first activity of the model, and the importance of this activity cannot be over estimated; a poorly conceptualized and/or inadequately presented advanced organizer will render the model useless (Joyce & Weil, 1986). The organizer should represent a clear and comprehensive abstraction of the targeted content. Analogies and metaphors make particularly potent advanced organizers (Ausubel, 1963). For advanced organizers to function effectively, however, students need to be taught how to use the strategy properly. For example, Jan took care to discuss her analogy (the advanced organizer), to embellish upon it, and to draw students into its complexities; she asked them to identify many ways in which public speaking was like an important conversation. At the end of her discussion, Jan informed her students that the analogy would be referred to and used to structure the entire course.

A learning stimulus follows the presentation of the advanced organizer. This learning stimulus can take a variety of forms: The teacher might *lecture* or provide a series of lectures on a given topic; students might be shown a *film* or be asked to *read* about the targeted information; or *discussions* might be organized, centering on a particular idea or concept. Regardless of the form that the stimulus takes, it is designed so that it will accomplish the following: capture and maintain student attention, make explicit the conceptual linkages between new and old information, and highlight relationships between the stimulus and the advanced organizer.

A discussion or writing assignment can be used to reinforce the new learning. Students might be asked to review the major concepts of the new material and to describe similarities and differences between the new concepts and those that have been previously addressed. Students can also be encouraged to provide additional examples of the new material and to examine it from a variety of perspectives. The primary purpose of this activity is to complete the internalization process and strengthen cognitive structures.

The Role of the Teacher.   In executing this model, the teacher's role is one of director and facilitator. He or she directs learning activities by structuring the advanced organizer, stimulus, and reinforcing exercise. The teacher also facilitates discussions in which students analyze and discuss the advanced organizer and relationships between new and more familiar information. Finally, the teacher also facilitates the process by which students transfer newly acquired information into other domains of their experience.

Concept Attainment

Dan begins the day by writing two scenarios on the board. The first describes an actual conflict (and is labeled "YES") and the second (labeled "NO") describes a potential one. He then tells the class that they will be given several of these paired examples and that their task is to identify and describe the concept that unifies all of the positive and none of the negative examples. Dan is using a concept attainment model.

The concept attainment model is based on inductive reasoning: Students are given specific information and asked to identify the general concept that unifies that information. Jerome Bruner (1966), whose theory of instruction asserts that individual concepts are the foundations of knowledge and that these are best learned when students are actively involved in their construction, is the person most responsible for the design and testing of the model. Its primary goals are to teach (a) individual concepts and (b) information-processing skills that are related to concept attainment.

The series of positive and negative exemplars that students are given and asked to correctly sort is a distinguishing feature of this model. A second key feature is the type of reflective process that the model encourages; students are asked to articulate and share the thinking processes that influenced their concept attainment decisions.

Using the Model. The primary activity of this model is the process of encountering and sorting data (the positive and negative exemplars). Exemplars are presented in a predetermined order until students feel confident that they can correctly name the concept and identify its distinguishing attributes. The paired exemplars should contrast important distinctions and/or features of the concept. Dan's exemplars, for example, focused on the distinguishing attributes of interpersonal conflict. Each exemplar should be clearly labeled "yes" (indicating a positive exemplar) or "no" (negative exemplar). As more exemplars are presented, finer distinctions among the distinguishing attributes are made.

Once students feel confident that they have correctly identified the concept, they are asked to test the inferences that have been made, by identifying additional examples of the concept and by generating their own positive and negative exemplars. Only after this final step does the teacher verify or deny the named concept.

A discussion of thought processes and decision making provides the necessary cognitive reinforcement. This discussion centers on the kinds of cues that were used to make decisions, how and why some cues were misleading, and what cues were critical for correct identification. Participation in the discussion allows students to compare and contrast various learning strategies, expand their repertoire of concept attainment skills, and strengthen information-processing abilities.

Role of the Teacher. Executing the model requires that the teacher act as a recorder and facilitator. He or she first records the attributes and emerging hypotheses as they are articulated by students. The teacher then facilitates information processing by prompting students to question and probe their observations and hypotheses. Finally, the teacher guides the closing discussion.

Suchman Inquiry

Lauren is teaching a unit on persuasion. At the beginning of a class, she presents the following problem to her students: "In the 1960s this country was heavily involved in peace corps programs. Millions of dollars and countless human hours were poured into programs to educate and train people of third-world countries. One of those programs was directed at reducing the birth rate. The birth rate was rising at alarming rates; food and resources were clearly not available to support the massive population. The efforts to educate and provide assistance in birth control were the least successful of all the programs advanced by the peace corps. Why?" Lauren is applying the Suchman inquiry model in her teaching.

The Suchman inquiry model, using a process of questioning, combines inductive and deductive reasoning skills. Richard Suchman is responsible for developing this model (cf. Suchman, 1964), which is based on the assumption that knowledge is tentative and developmental and that the proper goal of education is to develop independent learners. Specifically, the model is designed to teach skills in: (a) generating explanations and (b) scientific inquiry (Joyce & Weil, 1986).

The key feature of this model is the manner in which the learning stimulus is presented. Data, the learning stimuli, are generated by the students through a series of questions they develop in response to a perplexing problem posed by the teacher. The focus of the model, thus, is on the processes of questioning and deduction.

Using the Model. The teacher asks, in essence, why a particular problem exists and/or has evaded solution. In the preceding example, Lauren asked students to consider and explain why the peace corps efforts to persuade individuals to use birth control had continually failed. Student questioning, the centerpiece activity of the model, follows the presentation of the problem. These questions must be answerable by a "yes" or a "no." The teacher does not answer questions that require explanation or elaboration but asks, instead, that the question be rephrased. No constraints are placed on the number of questions asked by an individual student, and students are encouraged to work together to formulate questions and explanations.

When at least one student is fairly sure that he or she has an adequate explanation, the teacher asks the rest of the class if they are ready to advance and defend their explanations. Discussion then focuses on the relative strength and merit of the various hypotheses. Students are encouraged to ask additional questions in light of these generated hypotheses. The hypothesis that appears to be most reasonable and comprehensive is advanced as an adequate, but temporary, explanation of the perplexing problem.

The Role of the Teacher. The teacher's primary role is one of information source and catalyst. He or she provides information in the form of responses to legitimately phrased student questions. When appropriate, the teacher pushes students to articulate and critique hypotheses.

SOCIAL MODELS

Social models focus on social interaction and human interdependence and make two assumptions about teaching and learning. First, they assume that the primary responsibility of schools is to teach individuals how to operate in a social world. Second, they assume that learning is most productive when individuals construct their own learning experiences. These modes are designed, then, to engage students in interdependent activities and to make them responsible for their own learning.

The features that characterize these models reflect the basic assumptions. In social models, activities emphasize group problem solving and social responsibility. The teacher is cast in a role of facilitator an/or coinquirer, and students, in contrast, are cast as the chief advocates and directors of their own learning.

Johnson and Johnson (1974) and Slavin (1983) have conducted research to determine how shared tasks and reward structures affect individual learning outcomes. They have also examined whether or not students who participate in group endeavors learn to cooperate more effectively (share responsibilities, promote good feelings among participants, and acquire a sense of commitment to the group). The research indicates that these models are effective tools for teaching both problem-solving skills and prosocial behavior (Lew, Mesch, Johnson, & Johnson, 1986). Some social skills, especially the attitudes that are reflected in those skills, are better taught using a role play strategy. Shaftel and Shaftel (1982), for example, studied the effectiveness of role plays used to teach attitudes such as empathy and trust, and they concluded that learning about interpersonal conflict and interaction skill is more efficiently managed through role plays than through traditional lectures and/or discussions.

Applications of social models can be seen in a variety of communication journals and textbooks. Group projects are a frequently used strategy in interpersonal (Rowan, 1984), small group (Warnemunde, 1986), and intercultural (Beebe & Biggers, 1986) courses. Similarly, role plays are common tools used in interpersonal (Lederman & Ruben, 1984), intercultural (Broome, 1986), and interviewing (Seibold & Meyers, 1985) classes. Finally, the case study has become a prominent activity in organizational (Kreps & Lederman, 1985; Ray & Ray, 1986) and argumentation (Makau, 1985) curricula. In this section, three social models of teaching are described: group investigation, role playing, and jurisprudential inquiry.

Group Investigation

In his interpersonal communication class, Jeff requires his students to work in groups and conduct small-scale investigations. While students work on these projects, class does not meet regularly; Jeff is available for consultation but does not interfere with any individual group's activity. When the projects are completed, Jeff asks each student to write a short essay evaluating both the group's process and its product. Jeff is using a group investigation model.

The group investigation model is grounded in John Dewey's (1916) philosophy of education and, consequently, reflects several of his key assumptions about education and learning (Joyce & Weil, 1986). First, the model assumes that knowledge is a social phenomena. That is, it is the product of group efforts to acquire information and solve problems. Second, teaching group problem-solving skills and social responsibility are assumed to be the proper goals of education. Finally, learning the values and attitudes necessary for responsible participation in a democratic society is assumed to occur when individuals are required to analyze and reflect on their social experiences.

Using the Model.   Activity begins when students are given a task requiring investigation. Jeff, for example, asked his students to investigate the unique ways that particular occupations (e.g., law enforcement, sales, medicine, etc.) used communication in their work. Students were asked to work in groups to complete the task; typically resulting in a single product representing the entire group's efforts. Typically, the students are given a period of time during which class may be suspended and students can meet with their groups and pursue their investigative procedures.

Once completed, the groups' products are evaluated. Students are asked to identify and analyze instances of effective and ineffective group process, as well as examine the quality of their product in light of the original problem and the group's goals. This evaluation might take the form of an essay (as in Jeff's class) or a private discussion with the teacher.

The Role of the Teacher.   In this model, the teacher acts as academic counselor and consultant (Joyce & Weil, 1986). He or she is responsible for counseling groups during the various phases of the problem-solving process and advising students about the tools and procedures of inquiry. At all points beyond the presentation of the original stimulus, the teacher responds to, rather than directly orchestrates, student activity.

Role Playing

Mary asked her students what it felt like to disagree with someone they cared about. The class discussed their feelings about such situations, the typical issues that were involved, and the communication problems that often arose. Out of that discussion, the class designed a scenario in which a husband and wife disagreed about a particular aspect of child rearing: discipline. Mary was using a role play.

Role playing is designed to explore human relation problems (e.g., conflict management and perspective taking) through processes of action, reflection, and discussion (Shaftel & Shaftel, 1982). The model assumes that social life can be reproduced in the classroom context and that this reproduction and subsequent analysis can lead to substantive learning. The key feature of the model is the simulation of social and/or interpersonal problems.

Using the Model. Activity begins with a general discussion of the instructional value of role playing. This discussion is followed by the presentation of the stimulus (the situation to be enacted) and focuses students' attention on the attitudes, values, and feelings that will be examined in the role play.

A discussion of the roles to be enacted and the events that might transpire further stimulates the desired learning processes. Here, students talk about what particular actors might be feeling before, during, and after the focal situation. Similarly, students would discuss the actions and events that led to and might follow the focal situation. Before enacting the scene, a point at which to stop the role play (sometime after a sufficient amount of action has transpired but before frustration or confusion might occur) is agreed upon. Observers are then selected, and methods of observation are identified—what behaviors to observe, reasons for focusing on those particular behaviors, and how to record observations.

The class then moves through a cycle of enactment, discussion and analysis, and reenactment. After the role play is enacted, the class discusses that enactment, focusing on both the perspectives of the actors and those of the observers. During this analysis and discussion, the class revises roles and events to explore a variety of theoretical and/or conceptual interests. The situation is then reenacted, reflecting those revisions, and the reenactment is analyzed. In a final discussion, the class talks about the implications of the role play; they generalize to other people, circumstances, and situations.

The Role of the Teacher. The teacher is responsible for guiding discussions of the behaviors, values, attitudes, roles, and events illuminated in the focal situation. Throughout the activity, the teacher maintains an emotionally supportive environment; acknowledging and accepting all responses to the scenario as well as pushing students to examine the situation and feelings from a variety of perspectives.

Jursiprudential Inquiry

The state of Illinois is currently debating the issue of required AIDS testing for all marriage license applicants. Randy discusses this issue and the surrounding debate with his argumentation class. He then presents his students with the task of articulating and defending a personal position on the policy. Randy is using the jurisprudential inquiry model.

The basic assumptions of the model focus on the nature of society and the obligation of individuals to play a responsible part in that society (Oliver & Shaver, 1966). The model assumes, first, that a democratic society is characterized by differing viewpoints and, second, that the proper role of education is the preparation of citizens who are able to tolerate diversity and take responsible positions on public policy. The key feature of the model is the process of articulating and defending personal positions on public policy.

Using the Model. As was illustrated by Randy, after students are introduced to the facts and issues surrounding a particular controversial policy, they are required to research and analyze the pragmatic and value implications of the policy. Students can work in groups and are encouraged to consult the library and/or the variety of individuals who have expert knowledge on the policy under examination. The product of this research and analysis takes the form of a short speech in which students articulate a position.

After each presentation, students defend the positions taken. This is the most extensive, demanding, and critical aspect of the model. Much like a traditional Socratic dialogue, the teacher, through a series of questions, challenges each individual student. These questions are confrontational and designed to push the student's thinking about the social (i.e., moral, ethical, and ideological) implication of his or her position. Questioning continues until the teacher is satisfied with the student's analysis and defense or until the student indicates a need to reanalyze and perhaps revise his or her position.

The Role of the Teacher. The primary role of the teacher is that of adversary; he or she poses questions that are designed to force students to withstand the pressures of defense and to push them to investigate all complexities of an issue.

SUMMARY AND CONCLUSIONS

Each of the models described in this chapter is designed to focus on particular learning outcomes. Information processing models emphasize the efficiency of cognitive learning: The advanced organizer is useful for teaching the structure of a particular body of information; the concept attainment model facilitates in-depth and long-term comprehension of concepts; and the Suchman inquiry model develops skills in generating explanations.

Social models concentrate on social interaction and human interdependence. The models center on methods for teaching students to value and participate responsibly in society: Group investigation models emphasize cooperative and prosocial behaviors; role plays encourage students to explore feelings about human problems; and finally, the jurisprudential model engages students in an analysis and debate of the social implications of public policy.

Research on teacher effectiveness has made clear that there is no one best way to teach; rather, an effective teacher is able to apply a variety of strategies that are appropriate to the group of students, the teacher's skill and resources, and particular educational goals. Consistent with this information and advice, Joyce and Weil (1986) have suggested that teachers develop and use several models. Given that learning about communication is both a cognitive and social endeavor, models that reflect this diversity should be useful in our classrooms.

REFERENCES

Ausubel, D. P. (1963). *The psychology of meaningful verbal learning.* New York: Grune & Stratton.

Ausubel, D. P. (1980). Schemata, cognitive structure, and advanced organizers: A reply to Anderson, Spiro, and Anderson. *American Educational Research Journal, 17,* 400–404.

Barnes, B. R., & Clawson, E. U. (1975). Do advanced organizers facilitate learning? Recommendations for further research based on an analysis of 32 studies. *Review of Educational Research, 45,* 537–659.

Beebe, S. A., & Biggers, T. (1986). The status of the introductory intercultural communication course. *Communication Education, 35,* 56–60.

Bereiter, C., & Kurland, M. (1981). A constructive look at follow through results. *Interchange, 12,* 1–22.

Bloom, A. (1987). *The closing of the American mind.* New York: Simon and Schuster.

Bradley, B. E. (1984). *Fundamentals of speech communication* (4th ed.). Dubuque, IA: Wm. C. Brown.

Broome, B. J. (1986). A context based framework for teaching intercultural communication. *Communication Education, 35,* 296–306.

Bruner, J. B. (1966). *Toward a theory of instruction.* New York: W. W. Norton.

Deethardt, J. F. (1974). The use of questions in the speech communication classroom. *Communication Education, 23,* 15–20.

Dewey, J. (1916). *Democracy and education.* New York: Macmillan.

Hansen, S. P. (1982). Small is beautiful in the speech communication classroom. *Communication Education, 31,* 67–71.

Johnson, D., & Johnson, R. (1974). Instructional goal structure: Cooperative, competitive vs. individualized instruction on student prosocial behavior, attitudes toward learning and achievement. *Review of Educational Research, 44,* 213–240.

Joyce, B., & Weil, M. (1986). *Models of teaching* (3rd ed.). Englewood Cliffs, NJ: Prentice-Hall.

Kibler, R. J., Bassett, R. E., & Byers, J. P. (1977). Behavioral objectives and communication instruction. *Human Communication Research, 3,* 278–286.

Kreps, G. L., & Lederman, L. C. 91985). Using the case method in organizational communication education: Developing students' insight, knowledge, and creativity through experience-based learning and systematic debriefing. *Communication Education, 34,* 358–364.

Lederman, L. C., & Ruben, B. D. (1984). Systematic assessment of communication games and simulations: An applied framework. *Communication Education, 33,* 152–159.

Lew, M., Mesch, D., Johnson, D. W., & Johnson, R. (1986). Positive interdependence, academic and collaborative-skills group contingencies, and isolated students. *American Educational Research Journal, 23,* 476–488.

Makau, J. M. (1985). Adapting the judicial model of reasoning to the basic argumentation and debate course. *Communication Education, 34,* 227–234.

Oliver, D., & Shaver, J. P. (1966). *Teaching public issues in the high school.* Boston: Houghton Mifflin.

Ray, E. B., & Ray, G. B. (1986). Teaching conflict management skills in corporate training: A perspective taking approach. *Communication Education, 35,* 288–299.

Rowan, K. E. (1984). The implicit social scientist and the implicit rhetorician: An integrative framework for the introductory interpersonal course. *Communication Education, 33,* 351–360.

Rushing, J. H. (1984). Combining qualitative research with the teaching of interpersonal communication. *Communication Education, 33,* 361–370.

Seibold, D. R., & Meyers, R. A. (1985). Co-participant perceptions of information-gathering interviews: Implications for teaching interviewing skills. *Communication Education, 34,* 106–118.

Shaftel, F., & Shaftel, G. (1982). *Role playing in the curriculum.* Englewood Cliffs, NJ: Prentice-Hall.

Slavin, R. (1983). *Cooperative learning.* New York: Longman.

Staton-Spicer, A. Q., & Bassett, R. E. (1980). A mastery learning approach to competency-based education for public speaking instruction. *Communication Education, 29,* 171–182.

Stewart, J., & D'Angelo, G. (1980). *Together: Communicating interpersonally.* Reading, MA: Addison-Wesley.

Suchman, J. (1964). Studies in inquiry training. In R. Ripple & V. Rockcastle (Eds.), *Piaget rediscovered* (pp. 105–108). Ithaca, NY: Cornell University.

Warnemunde, D. E. (1986). The status of the introductory small group communication course. *Communication Education, 35,* 389–395.

21

Extended Discourse

Cassandra L. Book
Michigan State University

This chapter focuses on extended discourse, notably the lecture. Instructional strategies may be considered on various continua from teacher-controlled to student-controlled, from much to little student input, from expository to indirect, or from deductive to inductive. Lecturing tends to be on the one end of the continuum with most teacher control, least student input, most expository form, and most deductive mode of instruction. Although these characteristics are neither negative nor positive, they do help to define the lecture. Vladimir Sistek (1986) cited Michael Simpson as saying: "Sir Barcroft used to define a lecture as a process by which information is transferred from the notes of the lecturer to the notes of the student without going through the minds of either" (p. 1). Such a definition raises concern about the value of the lecture method. Chaudron and Richards (1985) stated that "the function of lectures is to instruct, by presenting information in such a way that a coherent body of information is presented, readily understood, and remembered" (p. 3). However, they recognize that not all lectures inherently function in these ways and, thus, they examine characteristics of lectures that make them more or less comprehensible to the listeners. These findings are reported later in this chapter.

One purpose of teaching is for students to gain and *retain* new knowledge and to be able to *transfer* it to other contexts. Use of the principles of learning enhances teachers' effectiveness and students' achievement. These principles of learning suggest that people learn best when they (a)

actively participate in the learning, (b) have knowledge (or specific feedback) of the results of their learning, (c) know what they are expected to
learn, (d) know the purpose of what they are learning, and (e) find the
learning to be meaningful to them. These principles of learning provide
guidelines for the development of effective instructional practice, including how one prepares, delivers, and follows-up a lecture.

People learn better when they are using as many senses as are appropriate. Lewis (1980) noted that "people retain about 10% of what they
hear, 30% of what they read, 50% of what they see and 90% of what they
do" (p. 27). The more actively involved people are in the learning process,
the better they learn. Given the limited involvement of the senses in the
lecture, the teacher who chooses to lecture needs to recognize the frailty
of the mode that relies solely on talking and should attempt to enhance or
reinforce the message with visual aids or other methods of instruction.

Cashin (1985) summarized the strengths of the lecture approach as
follows:

(1) Lectures can communicate the intrinsic interest of the subject matter;
(2) Lectures can cover material not otherwise available; (3) Lectures can
organize material in a special way; (4) Lectures can convey large amounts
of information; (5) Lectures can communicate to many listeners at the same
time; (6) Lecturers can model how professionals in a particular discipline
approach a question or problem; (7) Lectures permit maximum teacher
control; (8) Lectures permit minimum threat to the student; (9) Lectures
emphasize learning by listening. (p. 2)

Cashin described the weaknesses of the lecture approach as follows:

(1) Lectures lack feedback to the instructor about the students' learning; (2)
In lectures, the students are passive, at least they are more passive than the
lecturer; (3) Students' attention wanes quickly in 15 or 25 minutes according to studies; (4) Information learned in lectures tends to be forgotten
quickly; (5) Lectures presume that all students are learning at the same
pace and level of understanding; (6) Lectures are not well suited to higher
levels of learning—application, analysis, synthesis, influencing attitudes
or values, developing motor skills. Lecturing is best suited to the lower
levels of knowledge and understanding; (7) Lectures are not well suited to
complex, detailed, or abstract material; (8) Lectures require an effective
speaker; (9) Lectures emphasize learning by listening. (pp. 2–3)

In addition to the preceding strengths of lecturing, there are practical
reasons to lecture. Lectures require few materials or equipment (e.g.,
audio visual equipment), thus making it a teaching strategy that can be
adapted to a variety of settings on short notice or used by the itinerant
teacher who moves from classroom to classroom. The lecture provides

flexibility in content that can be altered spontaneously for different audiences and is not dependent on a particular size of audience to be successful. A good instructor will understand and weigh these characteristics of the lecture method when determining which instructional method to use in teaching for a particular goal.

In light of these characteristics, the effectiveness of the lecture method can be compared with other methods of instruction. The conclusions reached about the effectiveness of one teaching method over another must, of course, always be considered in terms of the objectives of instruction. McKeachie (1978) summarized a series of studies comparing lecture and discussion methods. When achievement was measured by factual tests, no significant differences between students' achievement in a discussion or a lecture class were found. However, when measures of delayed recall were taken, the discussion method was superior. In another study (McKeachie, 1978) "the lecture-demonstration method proved superior on a test of specific information, but the discussion method proved to be superior on measures of problem-solving and scientific attitude" (p. 27). Other studies reported by McKeachie demonstrate that students are more interested in courses taught via discussion or have more positive attitudinal outcomes in discussion courses as compared to lecture courses. As McKeachie (1978) has recommended, "In a course in which the instructor must not only give information but also develop concepts, the use of both lectures and discussion would thus seem to be a logical and popular choice" (p. 29).

Tatum and Lenel (1985) reported a comparison of self-paced and lecture/discussion teaching methods for a general psychology course:

> The results revealed little difference in course performance for the two teaching methods, except that the self-paced students performed better on the unit (chapter) tests. No differences were found between the two methods with respect to performance on the final exam, retention one year later, or average course grade. The results further revealed that the students were more satisfied with the self-paced courses than with the lecture/ discussion courses. (p. 2)

These authors noted that their "findings are consistent with other studies that have shown that self-pacing results in positive attitudes toward the course, despite the fact that there was little evidence for improved course performance" (p. 19), and reasoned that the students' greater sense of autonomy, greater opportunity to retake tests and achieve mastery of the material, and greater personal contact with the instructor during the self-paced course may help to explain their preference for the self-paced course.

According to Davis and Alexander (1977), the comparison of lecture with other methods of instruction indicates that "the lecture is generally as effective as other techniques when the objective is the transmission of information" (p. 15). However, they added, "Lectures are most appropriate for the transmission of information and less appropriate than discussion when the instructional objectives involve the application of information, the development of problem-solving skills, or the long-term modification of attitudes" (p. 15). Brock (1977) asserted that the lecture method is less effective than other methods "when students are average or below average in academic preparation or intelligence" (p. 2). Thus, the lecture method is a useful instructional strategy, but is limited in reaching some goals and some students.

CHARACTERISTICS OF A GOOD LECTURE

A good lecture is more than telling, for it involves arousing the students' interest and thinking about the content, it organizes and summarizes key ideas, and it provides a basis for the students to remember the new information and generate their own examples or applications of the content. The good lecture must have solid content, a logical structure, and ample and accurate examples. It should involve the principles of learning for maximum pedagogical effect. It should be delivered in an engaging and audible manner with effective use of eye contact, sincerity, movement, facial and vocal variety, and use of audiovisual aids.

At the center of a good lecture is the lecturer's coherent, thorough, and accurate knowledge of the content. The teacher of communication must know the facts, concepts, and principles of, for example, public speaking, interpersonal communication, and group discussion and must be able to present that subject matter in a meaningful way to the learners. Supplementary material, teachers' resource guides, and textbooks help to organize the content and the pedagogical content knowledge for the teacher, but they provide only one aspect of the curricular understanding needed by a teacher. A teacher cannot teach what he or she does not know, and the limitations of his or her knowledge become apparent in his or her ability to elaborate, define, and explain concepts, principles, and their relationships.

How much the teacher includes in the lecture and how he or she organizes the material can aid students' understanding and retention of the content. To begin with, the good lecturer should not attempt to cover too much within one lecture. The need for limiting lecture content has been reinforced by medical educators (Russell, Hendricson, & Herbert, 1984), who have cautioned:

. . . that the amount of information a student can learn within the span of a lecture is limited and the lecturer actually defeats the purpose by exceeding that limit. The data suggest that an instructor speaking at a rate of about four sentences per minute should introduce new material in only about 100 sentences during a 50-minute lecture. That would amount to approximately 50% of the total lecture time for an instructor speaking at an average rate. An equal period of time should then be devoted to reinforcement. (p. 887)

As to the part of the lecture that students in high and low density groups retained, the researchers reported that:

. . . all three lecture groups . . . performed best on questions from information presented in the final 15 minutes of the lecture. . . . After about 35 minutes of the high density lecture, the process of continually absorbing new information apparently caused students in this group to begin to forget what they learned earlier in the lecture. By contrast, the low density group demonstrated equal levels of retention during the beginning, middle and end of the lecture. (p. 888)

Thus, the good lecture will develop two or three key points with sufficient elaboration to make them meaningful, interesting, and memorable.

McKeachie (1978) made the point "that a high degree of organization does not seem to contribute to student learning" (p. 25), but Brock (1977) advocated "adopt[ing] some organizational scheme for each lecture (e.g., topical, problem–solution, chronological," "mak[ing] the organization of the lecture explicit," and "providing students with a lecture outline," pp. 9–10). Brock's recommendations are consistent with the principle that students learn better if they know what they are to learn. Apparently, students are aided when the structure of the content of the lecture is made evident to them and when connections among ideas are clarified. With non-native English-speaking students, Chaudron and Richards (1985) also found that "Macro markers, that is, the higher order discourse markers signalling major transitions and emphasis in the lectures [e.g., what I'm going to talk about today . . .] are more conducive to successful recall of the lecture than micro markers, that is, lower order markers of segmentation and interentential connections [e.g., because, then, well . . .]" (p. 16) Davis and Alexander (1977) recommended that the lecturer "summarize a lesson or part of a lesson so that students get a sense of completeness and structure" (p. 12). A summary may restate main points, review the lecture objective, and show how the parts of the lecture are related. Providing the overall structure, using language to show relationships, and emphasizing ideas all help students to understand and retain the lecture content.

In addition to solid content and a meaningful structure, the good lecturer should incorporate as many principles of learning into the lecture as possible. Specifically, after ensuring that students have the necessary prerequisite knowledge (e.g., through readings, study guides, previous lectures), the good lecturer will establish a "learning set." Davis and Alexander (1977) stated that "a learning set means attracting and focusing students' attention on materials to be covered, arousing their interest, and helping them direct their efforts toward achieving desired learning goals" (p. 5). Similar to the methods a speaker uses to introduce a speech, the good lecturer may ask provocative questions, pose a problem, tell a story, present a powerful quotation, give a demonstration, or use some activity that focuses attention on both the speaker and the subject. The good lecturer provides an "advanced organizer," or a guideline of what students are expected to learn. An "advanced organizer" previews the topics to be covered either orally or in writing. The lecturer may tell the students why the material is important to learn and how it is related to previously learned material. If the students are learning a skill or receiving instructions for an assignment, the specific procedures to be followed and the salient points to look for or include should be highlighted. Ensuring that the students have the prerequisite knowledge, are attending to the topic and the lecturer, and know what is to be learned and why it is worth learning are essential components of establishing the "learning set."

The next principle of learning that a good lecturer uses is to engage the students actively in the learning of the material. The caution is that teachers must be sure the content has been taught *before* asking students questions about it or asking them to practice using unlearned knowledge. Asking "guess-what's-in-my-head" questions or making assignments before teaching content does not give students correct or relevant knowledge and often gets in the way of the desired learning. Teachers should engage students in asking and answering questions about new content or have students summarize in their own words the new information as a means of *reinforcing* the content. When asking students questions, teachers should give students time to respond; *wait time* is a pedagogical technique that is underused. Most teachers wait only a few seconds for a student response before asking another question, turning to another student, or giving the answer themselves. Giving students ample opportunity to reflect on the new knowledge or to incorporate the new knowledge with prior knowledge is necessary for students to enhance their learning and their motivation to learn.

It is important for students to know if their answers are correct for more learning to occur. Thus, teachers should correct incorrect responses and recognize correct responses. This check on student comprehension provides feedback to the lecturer on how well his or her lecture was received and provides a reinforcement for students' learning. In addition, knowing that they will be held accountable for responding in class motivates students to attend to the lecture.

Finally, the effective lecture will be delivered in a stimulating manner. Generally, lectures that are delivered extemporaneously (using notes, but not read from a manuscript) are received best in the typical classroom. (Formal lectures may be read from prepared manuscripts when the occasion dictates it.) This extemporaneous style allows the lecturer to insert examples, adopt language that is appropriate to the specific class, reinforce points that are seemingly unclear, respond to questions from the students, and generally remain flexible. In this mode the teacher can maintain eye contact with students and more effectively manage the classroom. In addition to speaking in an audible tone and using clear articulation and correct pronunciation, the lecturer is advised to use a friendly, lively delivery style.

Although not specifically related to the lecture, Norton (1983) reported three studies on educators' communicative styles. Among the conclusions he reached are "The effective teacher is very animated and lively . . . the ineffective teacher is also significantly less friendly, dramatic, precise, and attentive" (p. 235). "In addition, the ineffective teacher is not very relaxed and does not use a dramatic style" (pp. 236, 238). He concluded that "getting others to fantasize, catching people up in stories, and being entertaining are strongly, positively associated with teacher effectiveness in an overall linear fashion" (p. 245). Norton (1986) recommended the development of a dramatic style for the teacher who wishes to be perceived by students as effective. Similarly, Brock (1977) listed factors (e.g., activity, novelty, humor, realism) that "influence a listener's attention, [but said] intensity or enthusiasm may be the central ingredient in motivating listeners. . ." He noted "that a positive relationship exists between the enthusiasm which students perceive that their lecturer exudes and their learning of the course material" key components. Clarity of explanation and use of humor are discussed hereafter.

MAKING THE LECTURE CLEAR

The importance of developing the concepts or ideas presented in a lecture cannot be overestimated. Such expansion of the lecture material is the heart of lecturing, for it makes the key points meaningful and memorable. As stated by Davis and Alexander (1977), explaining is "the skill of elaborating on a subject matter point (i.e., an idea, concept, or principle), so as to increase the student achievement of the relevant learning objectives. The process of explaining involves both the instructor and the student; it should not be limited to teacher talk" (p. 10). Research on teacher clarity, though not derived solely from lecture situations, can inform the lecturer concerning what can be done to increase the clarity of a lecture. The research on teacher clarity has consistently identified the importance of (a) defining the concept or idea, (b) supplying both accurate and sufficient numbers of both positive and negative examples highlighting the critical attributes, (c) explicating or elaborating on why the example is a positive or negative example of the concept, (d) checking on students' understanding, (e) using specific language (free of vagueness terms) and, (f) using connected discourse (free of mazes).

Several researchers (Cruickshank, Kennedy, Bush, & Meyers, 1979; Gage et al., 1968; McCaleb & White, 1980; Tennyson & Park, 1980) found support for teachers explaining the critical attributes of a concept and giving appropriate examples and nonexamples of the concepts. Recently, Hines, Cruickshank, and Kennedy (1985) found that the use of relevant examples during explanation is one of the teacher behaviors most strongly related to learner achievement and satisfaction. Gage et al. (1968) and Cruickshank et al. (1979) also found that students value teachers who provide examples and then explain them. Explication occurs when the teacher explains why the example illustrates the concept or definition and explicitly identifies the attributes in the examples that correspond with the general or abstract terms in the definitions. The value of teachers checking on student understanding (by use of questions or by having the students repeat back what has been taught) is discussed in research by Cruickshank et al. (1979), McCaleb and Rosenthal (1983), and Hines et al. (1985). Hines et al. (1985) found that asking questions to determine if students understand the information is strongly related to both learner achievement and satisfaction.

The effect of vagueness terms (e.g., "some," "a little," "perhaps," and "actually") on student achievement has been studied by Hiller, Fisher, and Kaess (1969); Smith (1977, 1985); and Smith and Land (1981). Both correlational and experimental data indicate that student learning is impeded by teacher language that features excessive use of vagueness terms. However, Book, McCaleb, and Meloth (1987) reported that vagueness terms expressed by teachers in a naturalistic classroom setting are not as excessive as those contrived in research and, thus, are not related to student awareness of the concepts taught. Another language variable studied by Hiller, Fisher, and Kaess (1969); Smith (1977); and Smith and Land (1981) is mazes, or "false starts or halts in speech, redundantly spoken words, and tangles of words" (p. 38). Although negative relationships between mazes and achievement were found, lessons were scripted to include an excessive amount of mazes.

Again, Book et al. (1987) did not find mazes to be significantly related to student awareness of what was taught, and they proposed that instances of mazes found in the naturalistic classroom setting are not excessive in number nor overly intrusive for the flow of thought. In addition, these authors proposed that problems with vagueness terms and mazes may be more related to the teacher content knowledge (or lack thereof) than to pedagogical knowledge or skill. They concluded that a focus on the positive aspects of clarity (e.g., inclusion of definition of terms, sufficient and accurate examples, explication of how the examples relate to the concepts taught, and confirmation or check on student learning) may enhance instruction more than mazes or vagueness terms detract from instruction. Thus, it is imperative for the lecturer to be knowledgeable of content, provide a variety of illustrations or examples that clearly illustrate the critical attributes of the definition or concept presented, and check on students understanding of those concepts. Although excessive use of mazes and vagueness terms should be avoided, the lecturer should be less concerned with the "ahs" and "ums" that may interrupt the flow of speech and should be more concerned with the content and explication of that content.

USING HUMOR IN THE LECTURE

A descriptive study by Bryant, Comisky, and Zillmann (1979) of 70 college class presentations noted that, on average, teachers made an attempt at humor about every 15 minutes and that "in general, most of the humor was conveyed through stories and brief comments" (p. 115). Similarly, Civikly (1985), focusing on teacher self-reports of uses of humor when teaching, concludes that "three humor types were consistently ranked high: (1) stories and anecdotes, (2) exaggeration, and (3) jokes on oneself. . . . The lowest ranked humor types included ethnic jokes, dirty jokes, putdowns, sexual jokes, and religious jokes" (p. 7). Although a wide variety of types of humor may be used, college teachers tend to use just a few.

Civikly (1985) reported that "five reasons were consistently reported as the reasons for using humor: (1) to make students feel comfortable, (2) relieve tension in the class, (3) create interest and maintain student attention, (4) relieve boredom in class, and (5) have a good time" (p. 7). In addition, Civikly (1986) cited earlier research with Darling to conclude that "the development of a relationship between teacher and student is critical to the student's accurate interpretation of teacher humor. Without some relational base, students are unsure of the teachers' motives" (p. 62). Although the reasons for using humor may seem appropriate to the instructor, it is important that students also share in the interpretation of humor as appropriate.

Student perceptions of teacher use of humor may affect their perception of the classroom climate and their evaluation of the teacher. Berlin (1978) found significant positive correlations (a) between teachers' intentional use of humor and students' perceptions of a positive classroom climate and (b) between students' perceptions of the humor as appropriate and positive ratings of the classroom climate. However, neither intentional nor appropriate humor used by the instructor was significantly related to student success in the class as measured by an over-all grade. Tamborini and Zillmann (1981) examined the comparative effect of no humor, sexual humor, other-disparaging humor, and self-disparaging humor on student perceptions of a lecturer's intelligence and appeal. They reported that "a speaker using self-disparaging humor is more appealing to members of the speakers' own sex than to members of the opposite sex," but "a speaker using [sexual] humor is likely to be more appealing to members of the opposite sex than to members of the same sex" (p. 431). They concluded that variations in humor have no effect on student perceptions of lecturers' intelligence.

In a further analysis of data on the relationship between college teachers' use of humor and students' evaluations of teachers, Bryant, Comisky, Crane, and Zillmann (1980) found that "male teachers who used funny stories frequently received more positive overall teaching evaluations . . . [and] . . . were perceived as more appealing and as having superior delivery . . ." (p. 516) and that "females that frequently used humor generally received lower evaluation scores on competence and delivery factors as well as on the measure of overall teaching effectiveness" (p. 518). These authors concluded that lecturers' usage of humor is recommended, but only for male teachers.

While the results of studies that examine the effect of humorous lectures and humorous examples on comprehension and retention are varied, in general they do not indicate that humor aids retention. Kaplan and Pascoe (1977) concluded that "the benefits of humor in the classroom are most clearly demonstrable for recall of humorous examples" and that "general comprehension and retention of a classroom message is not significantly improved by the use of humor" (pp. 64–65). Gruner and Freshley (1979) also found no difference in recall for either immediate or delayed testing of materials presented with humorous and nonhumorous exemplary materials. Finally, Desberg, Henschel, Marshall, and McGhee (1981) found that learning and memory are not facilitated by the use of related humor in a lecture. Although subjects find humorous presentations more enjoyable, they do not retain more of the information presented in a humor-related condition than in a repetition-controlled condition.

In effect, the authors found that "repetition whether or not through the use of humor enhances recall" (p. 4). Thus, although research supports the use of some forms of humor when it relates to the content taught (as a means of reinforcing concepts), caution is recommended in the use of humor.

CLASSROOM ENVIRONMENT

The physical arrangement of the room also requires the attention of the lecturer. Arranging the seats in a manner that either focuses students' attention on the speaker or on an overhead screen, or that prepares the class to engage in discussion (e.g., horseshoe or circle) can enhance the ease with which the purpose of the day's activities are fulfilled. In addition, the lecturer may need to close window blinds to shade the room from an outside glare, increase or decrease the heat in the room, or remove other physical distractions (e.g., writing on the chalkboard left from a previous class). In essence, the lecturer should attempt to make sure the environment does not distract and is as conducive to good listening or participation as possible.

SUMMARY

This chapter has emphasized the need to select the lecture method when it is most suitable for the objectives to be accomplished and the mix of student, teacher, and environmental characteristics. Once selected as the strategy, the lecturer needs to overcome weaknesses that are inherent in the method by incorporating content, structure, and style that utilize the principles of learning. Informing students why the information in the lecture is important and useful, and how it is related to other material that has been previously taught or will be subsequently taught is important. Students also need to know in advance what is being covered in the lecture, and they need verbal cues that show the relationships among and provide appropriate emphasis of key points. The lecture should be limited in information density to a few key points that are elaborated upon with multiple examples and reinforced visually or verbally and through students' illustrations.

The teacher needs to check on student understanding of the content by asking for summaries of key points, responding to questions, or giving students practice in using the concepts during the lecture period. Feedback regarding the accuracy of student understanding is also essential to enhance learning. Finally, a variety of stimuli, including, for example, use of humor, visual aids, or activities, is important to maintain students' attention and motivation to learn. There are many ways in which a lecturer can vary the lecture method (see Frederick, 1986, for examples). Regardless of the form, the lecturer must be certain that the content is accurate, thorough, and elaborated upon in a way that assists the learner in understanding, retaining, and transferring the information.

REFERENCES

Berlin, E. (1978). *The relationship of instructor humor to classroom climate and student success in the course.* Unpublished master's thesis, Michigan State University, East Lansing, MI.

Book, C. L., McCaleb, J. L., & Meloth, M. (1987). *Refining a teacher training program; Complementing content knowledge with pedagogical knowledge in clarity.* Unpublished manuscript, Michigan State University, College of Education, East Lansing, MI.

Brock, S. C. (1977). *Aspects of lecturing: A practical guide for IDEA users.* Manhattan, KS: University of Kansas, Center for Faculty Evaluation and Development in Higher Education.

Bryant, J., Comisky, P. W., Crane, J. S., & Zillmann, D. (1980). Relationship between college teachers' use of humor in the classroom and students' evaluations of their teachers. *Journal of Educational Psychology, 72,* 511–519.

Bryant, J., Comisky, P., & Zillmann, D. (1979). Teachers' humor in the college classroom. *Communication Education, 28,* 110–118.

Cashin, W. E. (1985). *Improving lectures* (Idea Paper No. 14). Manhattan: Kansas State University, Center for Faculty Evaluation and Development.

Chaudron, C., & Richards, J. C. (1985, April). *The effect of discourse markers on the comprehension of lectures.* Paper presented at the annual meeting of the Teachers of English to Speakers of Other Languages, New York.

Civikly, J. M. (1985, November). *Teachers' reports on their uses of humor when teaching.* Paper presented at annual meeting of the Speech Communication Association, Denver, CO.

Civikly, J. M. (1986). Humor and the enjoyment of college teaching. In J. M. Civikly (Ed.), *Communicating in college classrooms* (New Directions for Teaching and Learning No. 26) (pp. 61–69). San Francisco: Jossey-Bass.

Cruickshank, D. R., Kennedy, J. J., Bush, A. J., & Myers, B. (1979). Clear teaching: What is it? *British Journal of Teacher Education, 5,* 27–33.

Davis, R. H., & Alexander, L. T. (1977). *The lecture method: Guides for the improvement of instruction in higher education* (No. 5). East Lansing: Michigan State University, Instructional Media Center.

Desberg, P., Henschel, D., Marshall, C., & McGhee, P. (1981, August). *The effect of humor on retention of lecture material.* Paper presented at the annual meeting of the American Psychological Association, Los Angeles. (ERIC Document Reproduction Service No. ED 223 118)

Frederick, P. J. (1986). The lively lecture—8 variations, *College Teaching, 34*(2), 43–50.

Gage, N. L., Belgard, M., Dell, D., Hiller, J. E., Rosenshine, B., & Unruh, W. R. (1968). *Explorations of the teacher's effectiveness in explaining* (Tech. Rep. No. 4). Stanford: Stanford University, School of Education.

Gruner, C. R., & Freshley, D. L. (1979, November). *Retention of lecture items reinforced with humorous and non-humorous exemplary material.* Paper presented at the Speech Communication Association Convention, New York.

Hiller, J. E., Fisher, G. A., & Kaess, W. (1969). A computer investigation of verbal characteristics of effective classroom lecturing. *American Educational Research Journal, 6,* 661–675.

Hines, C. V., Cruickshank, D. R., & Kennedy, J. J. (1985). Teacher clarity and its relationship to student achievement and satisfaction. *American Educational Research Journal, 22,* 87–100.

Kaplan, R. M., & Pascoe, G. C. (1977). Humorous lectures and humorous examples: Some effects upon comprehension and retention. *Journal of Educational Psychology, 69,* 61–65.

Lewis, W. J. (1980). *Interpreting for park visitors.* Philadelphia: Eastern Acorn Press.

McCaleb, J. L., & Rosenthal, B. (1983). Relationships in teacher clarity between students' perceptions and observers' ratings. *Journal of Classroom Interaction, 19*(1), 15–21.

McCaleb, J. L., & White, J. A. (1980). Critical dimensions in evaluating teacher clarity. *Journal of Classroom Interaction, 15*(2), 27–30.

McKeachie, W. J. (1978). *Teaching tips: A guidebook for the beginning college teacher* (7th ed.). Lexington, MA: Heath.

Norton, R. (1983). *Communicator style: Theory, applications and measures.* Beverly Hills: Sage.

Norton, R. W. (1986). Communicator style in teaching: Giving good form to content. In J. M. Civikly (Ed.), *Communicating in college classrooms* (New Directions for Teaching and Learning No. 26) (pp. 33–40). San Francisco: Jossey-Bass.

Russell, I. J., Hendricson, W. D., & Herbert, R. J. (1984). Effects of lecture information density on medical student achievement. *Journal of Medical Education, 59,* 881–889.

Sistek, V. (1986, June). *How much do our students learn by attending lectures?* Paper presented at the annual conference of the Society for Teaching and Learning in Higher Education, Guelph, Ontario.

Smith, L. R. (1977). Aspects of teacher discourse and student achievement in mathematics. *Journal for Research in Mathematics Education, 8,* 195–204.

Smith, L. R. (1985). Teacher clarifying behaviors effect on student achievement and perceptions. *Journal of Experimental Education, 53,* 162–169.

Smith, L. R., & Land, M. L. (1981). Low inference verbal behaviors related to teacher clarity. *Journal of Classroom Interaction, 17*(1), 37–41.

Tamborini, R., & Zillmann, D. (1981). College students' perception of lecturers using humor. *Perceptual and Motor Skills, 52,* 427–432.

Tatum, B. C., & Lenel, J. C. (1985, August). *A comparison of self-paced and lecture/discussion teaching methods.* Paper presented at the annual meeting of the American Psychological Association, Los Angeles, CA.

Tennyson, R. R., & Park, O. (1980). The teaching of concepts: A review of instructional design research literature. *Review of Educational Research, 50,* 55–70.

22

Large Lecture Classes

Judy C. Pearson
Ohio University

Communication educators, like their peers in other disciplines, are discovering the role of the large section in higher education. Fewer dollars from state legislatures, tax repeals, and, in some cases, a shift toward the communication curriculum away from other, less marketable curricula have resulted in communication classes with higher enrollments. A number of authors have predicted that economic conditions will encourage the further development of large college courses (e.g., Adler, 1983; Gleason, 1986; McConnell & Sosin, 1984). Although alternatives such as personalized systems of instruction (Gray, Buerkel-Rothfuss, & Yerby, 1986; Seiler, 1983; Seiler & Fuss-Reineck, 1986), computer-assisted instruction (Pace, 1987), videotapes (Rosenkoetter, 1984), the use of undergraduates as teaching assistants (Baisinger, Peterson, & Spillman, 1984), and team teaching/learning (Krayer, 1986; Magnan, 1987) have been offered to solve economic problems, such approaches have not been as widely used as the large course.

Communication courses may be taught using a cognitive approach (Cronen, Pearce, & Harris, 1979), an experiential approach (Erickson & Erickson, 1979), or some combination of the two. All of these approaches can be achieved within the large course. The large course has been used for courses in fundamentals, public speaking, interpersonal communication, intercultural communication, mass communication, persuasion, argumentation, public relations, and even small group communication (Beebe & Biggers, 1986; Hazelton, 1986; Larson, 1986; Pearson, 1986; Semlak, 1986; Warnemunde, 1986; Weaver, 1986).

EFFECTIVE INSTRUCTIONAL PRACTICES

Although both communication theory and instructional development research suggest arguments against the large course, such arguments are often based on viewing the large course in a limiting and inflexible manner. A number of practices may lead to effectiveness in the large communication course and to student and instructor satisfaction. These recommendations are suggestive of a broader view of the large course than simply treating it as a lecture.

Use Active Participation in Learning

People learn better when they are actively involved than when they simply hear information (Bloom, 1976; Zayas-Baya, 1977–1978). Question asking and answering can be a useful way to encourage involvement. Questions can be asked of all students on the spur of the moment. They can also be asked in advance so that students have an opportunity to consider them in more detail.

Question asking can be particularly useful at the beginning of a class. Students can be asked about a particular concept; they can brainstorm information about the topic. For example, students can be asked to suggest what they believe to be true about leadership. Because brainstorming does not include evaluation, all ideas are written on the blackboard or on an overhead for later consideration. The specific ideas can be used to organize the lecture or to point out differences between misinformation and information about leadership.

Nelson (1986) encouraged teachers of the large section to consider covert student activity as well as overt behavior. He wrote, "Covert behavior is behavior that cannot be observed or seen but is nonetheless a form of active involvement. . . . It is possible that a student who appears passive may in fact be actively involved because he or she is intensely thinking about and mentally absorbing the information presented" (p. 316). He recommended that instructors ask more questions, allow sufficient time after asking a question for an overt response, and use stimulus words or phrases, such as "think about," "consider," "remember," "recall," "picture in your mind," "visualize," "mentally list," "what if," and "summarize to yourself" within the lecture. These techniques encourage covert activity.

To the extent that it is possible, the large course should be treated like the small one (Gleason, 1986). In the small section, students participate in experiential activities and written assignments. Students in the large course should be given the same opportunities to participate in games, exercises, experiential work, and writing. Erickson and Erickson (1979) demonstrated that most students prefer simulation and game exercises within the large section. Students can engage in dyadic and small-group work in class. Assistants can help the instructor to process such activities. Frederick (1987) suggested that small groups in large classes provide "energy and interaction" (p. 50). Class debates, simulations, and role-playing, which are familiar to smaller sections, can be used in the large class in an equally effective manner.

The use of quality control circles can also be adapted to the large course. Student volunteers (or appointed students) can meet regularly with the instructor to discuss the positive and negative features of the course. These students can provide the instructor with valuable information on how to improve. In addition, the instructor gains more personal contact with some of the students in the class; and students feel that the instructor cares both about the content of the course and relationships with the students.

Reward Positive Behavior

The simple act of taking attendance causes students to feel more involved and rewarded for positive behavior in the class. Students have reported that they feel more obligated to go to class when the instructor knows if they are present. Taking the attendance of a large class is difficult, of course, but creative methods may be instituted to take the roll of 1,000 people. A seating chart can be used, and an assistant can take the roll while the instructor is lecturing; students can sign "attendance cards" and someone can take roll after class. Alternatively, individual assistants or students can take the roll of a particular section of people. When large courses include smaller lab sections, the lab instructors can sit with their students, take roll, and interact with them. Students will also feel rewarded for attendance if they know that attendance correlates with scores on exams. After the validity and reliability of the exam is determined, the instructor may wish to modify the exam to improve such a relationship.

Positive behavior can be rewarded in other ways as well. The best speakers can be identified from one term and encouraged to become model speakers the next term. Excellent papers or essay answers can be read in class. Extra credit or some other form of reward for students who model particular communicative excellence can be provided.

Not all students may benefit from the preceding suggestions, but everyone can receive positive reinforcement if a "fill in the blank" lecture outline is used. Outlines of the lecture with missing words, phrases, percentages, and so forth can be distributed. As the instructor lectures, students can complete the lecture. Students gain a sense of satisfaction as they complete such handouts.

Create a Supportive Climate

Seating charts may help to create a supportive climate. A seating chart allows the instructor to quickly and easily call on at least some of the students by name. When the instructor demonstrates that he or she knows a few of the names of the people in the class, the students may generalize and believe that he or she knows all or most.

Gleason (1986) provided other specific suggestions. The instructor can announce the names of those students who did particularly well on an assignment or on an examination. They may be asked to stand when their name is read. If a student has asked a question outside of class, it can be brought up in the next class period as an example of an excellent question, the student who posed the question can be named, and then the question can be answered for the entire class. The large course does not have to be an impersonal entity. In a variety of ways, the instructor can demonstrate that he or she is accessible to students and that their questions and comments are encouraged.

Select a Competent Communicator as the Instructor

The instructor in the large communication course should be knowledgeable, credible, and highly dynamic. The level of dynamism, forcefulness, and energy is critical to effective instruction in this context; yet, because the large course is most frequently used in the beginning course, sometimes junior faculty or graduate assistants are given the assignment. This trend has been even more pronounced in recent times (Gibson, Gruner, Hanna, Smyth, & Hayes, 1980). The large course is the first place to put proven instructors rather than novices. The public speaking skills of the instructor become increasingly important as the audience becomes larger. Furthermore, it is essential that large numbers of students are provided with models of effective communication in communication courses if those courses are to maintain credibility.

The instructor should also be someone who is human. He or she should be viewed as a person, one of Mann's (1970) six relational dimensions for instructors. Although highly personal disclosures are inappropriate in the classroom, revelations of a personal nature encourage students to see the instructor as human (Gleason, 1986; Rosenkoetter, 1984). Self-denigration and humor are also helpful. Problems occur in the most highly planned class; when they do, we should laugh at them. The use of the "double-take" can be especially humorous.

Utilize Multiple-Channel Instruction

Individuals learn more when they both see and hear about a concept than when they only hear about it or when they only see it. Further, they are more likely to retain information when they are both shown and told something than when they are simply told about it or shown it (Zayas-Baya, 1977–1978). In general, people recall more information when they are exposed to two stimuli rather than to one, when the messages do not distract from each other (Gadzella & Whitehead, 1975).

In addition, different people learn best via different modes. Using multiple channels increases the opportunity of teaching a greater number of students. Use the written "fill-in-the-blank" for those who learn best in the written mode; television clips, movies, photographs, overheads, and other visual aids for those who learn best in the visual mode; and use a dynamic, organized oral presentation for those who listen best. Mediated forms of instruction can be highly useful; consider how technological advancements can be incorporated into the large course.

Frederick (1987) suggested that students' diverse learning styles require different strategies for teaching not only on different days, but within each class. He encouraged "energy shifts within a class about every twenty minutes by changing both the activity and the voice or voices that speak" (p. 46). One such alternating approach divides a 5-minute class into a 20-minute lecture, followed by 15 or 20 minutes of student participation, and concluded with a summary of important points and closure. Another approach is the problem-solving lecture, which begins with a problem to be solved, a mystery to be unraveled, a question to be answered, or a paradox to be revealed. The middle of the class may be spent in traditional lecture or in experiential activities. The answer, solution, or revelation is offered in the final 10 or 15 minutes of class.

Provide as Many Opportunities for Feedback as Possible

Microphones can be used, and the instructor can "walk the aisles." Students can be asked questions and allowed to ask the instructor about the material. Biology professors at the University of Nebraska creatively installed automatic telephone answering machines, which allowed students to ask questions at any time (Pardy & Mortensen, 1984). Although everyone does not have this technological sophistication, instructors can ask students to write down questions on the back of attendance forms in one class period and answer them at the beginning of the next period. They can recall questions that students have asked in previous terms to help students think of questions. "Participation areas" can be created, and students can be told that the instructor will call on people in that area. Students who wish to participate can choose a seat within that space (Gleason, 1986). A limited number of evaluation forms of the lecture can be distributed each time to different individuals. Systematic evaluation at the end of the term may be implemented.

Build Unity and Cohesiveness Among Members of the Class

Negative feelings about large courses sometimes result, particularly if the class is difficult. Some of this negative reaction may be offset if the instructor makes students feel involved and builds group cohesiveness. For instance, a problem that instructors in the large section format frequently experience is that they know so few students, yet so many know them. When the students and the instructor see each other on the street, the student does not know if she or he should initiate a conversation, and the faculty member does not recognize the student. An agreed-on greeting, like "Speech 75" or "InCo 101," can solve the uncomfortable feelings that are created and can also encourage a feeling of solidarity between the two.

Other methods of creating goodwill and positive feelings in the course are to allow students to entertain each other before classes begin. If the university includes people in the performing arts, students from the class who are in these fields can be asked to dance, sing, do a reading, portray a character, play a scene, or play an instrument in the time between classes. Alternatively, a phonograph or cassette player can be made available so students can bring their favorite music to share before class. Having excellent students from previous quarters model effective speaking in a variety of contexts—the public speech, an interview, a small group—also builds continuity and adds esprit de corps.

CONCLUSION

The large course is likely to become increasingly common in communication departments. Future research must continue to assess this delivery system. The importance of a supportive communication climate, perceptions of the teacher as immediate, homophilous, and credible, and students who are motivated to learn are acknowledged (Hurt, Scott, & McCroskey, 1978; Rosenfeld, 1983). The extent to which such essential features of the teaching–learning process can be incorporated into the large course is not known.

The large communication course can be viewed as an opportunity, rather than as a detriment to effective communication education. Instructional strategies must be considered and applied appropriately to this increasingly utilized format. To the extent that the variables in this communication context can be accurately assessed, improvement of the understanding of communicative behavior and the interactions among students may occur.

ACKNOWLEDGMENTS

The author wishes to express her appreciation to Anne M. Nicotera, who assisted in researching the topic, and to Patricia Cambridge, who typed the manuscript.

REFERENCES

Adler, K. (1983). Coping with administrative overload in large classes. *Communication Education, 32,* 339–341.

Baisinger, W. H., Peterson, G. L., & Spillman, B. (1984, January). Undergraduates as colleagues: Using undergraduates as teaching assistants in the basic course. *Association for Communication Administration Bulletin, 47,* 60–63.

Beebe, S. A., & Biggers, T. (1986). The status of the introductory intercultural communication course. *Communication Education, 35,* 56–60.

Bloom, B. S. (1976). *Human characteristics and school learning.* New York: McGraw-Hill.

Cronen, V. E., Pearce, W. B., & Harris, L. M. (1979). The logic of the coordinated management of meaning: A rules-based approach to the first course in interpersonal communication. *Communication Education, 28,* 23–38.

Erickson, K. V., & Erickson, M. T. (1979). Simulation and game exercises in large lecture classes. *Communication Education, 28,* 224–229.

Frederick, P. J. (1987). Student involvement: Active learning in large classes. In M. G. Weimer (Ed.), *Teaching large classes well* (pp. 45–56). San Francisco: Jossey-Bass.

Gadzella, B. M., & Whitehead, D. A. (1975). Effects of auditory and visual modalities in recall of words. *Perceptual and Motor Skills, 40,* 255–260.

Gibson, J. W., Gruner, C. R., Hanna, M. S., Smythe, M-J., & Hayes, M. T. (1980). The basic course in speech at U.S. colleges and universities: III. *Communication Education, 29,* 1–9.

Gleason, M. (1986). Better communication in large courses. *College Teaching, 34,* 20–24.

Gray, P. L., Buerkel-Rothfuss, N. L., & Yerby, J. (1986). A comparison between PSI-based and lecture-recitation formats of instruction in the introductory speech communication course. *Communication Education, 35,* 111–125.

Hazelton, V. (1986, November). *Teaching a large lecture public relations course.* Paper presented at the meeting of the Speech Communication Association, Chicago.

Hurt, H. T., Scott, M. D., & McCroskey, J. C. (1978). *Communication in the classroom.* Reading, MA: Addison-Wesley.

Krayer, K. J. (1986). Implementing team learning through participative methods in the classroom. *College Student Journal, 20,* 157–161.

Larson, C. U. (1986, November). *Teaching a large lecture persuasion course.* Paper presented at the meeting of the Speech Communication Association, Chicago.

Magnan, S. S. (1987). Teaming teachers and modifying class size: An experiment in first-year French. *The French Review, 60,* 454–465.

Mann, R. D. (1970). *The college classroom.* New York: Wiley.

McConnell, C. R., & Sosin, K. (1984). Some determinants of student attitudes toward large classes. *The Journal of Economic Education, 15,* 181–190.

Nelson, J. (1986). Improving the lecture through active participation. *College Student Journal, 20,* 315–320.

Pace, R. G. (1987). A commentary on computer-assisted instruction in speech communication. *Western Journal of Speech Communication, 51,* 136–141.

Pardy, R. L., & Mortensen, L. (1984). The biology hot line: Use of a telephone answering device in large classes. *Improving College and University Teaching, 32,* 188–190.

Pearson, J. C. (1986, November). *Teaching a large lecture interpersonal communication course.* Paper presented to the Speech Communication Association, Chicago, IL.

Rosenfeld, L. B. (1983). Communication climate and coping mechanisms in the college classroom. *Communication Education, 32,* 167–174.

Rosenkoetter, J. S. (1984). Teaching psychology to large classes: Videotapes, PSI and lecturing. *Teaching of Psychology, 11,* 85–87.

Seiler, W. J. (1983). PSI: An attractive alternative for the basic speech communication course. *Communication Education, 32,* 15–25.

Seiler, W. J., & Fuss-Reineck, M. (1986). Developing the personalized system of instruction for the basic speech communication course. *Communication Education, 35,* 126–133.

Semlak, W. D. (1986, November). *Teaching a large lecture mass communication course.* Paper presented at the meeting of the Speech Communication Association, Chicago.

Warnemunde, D. E. (1986). The status of the introductory small group communication course. *Communication Education, 35,* 389–396.

Weaver, R. L., II. (1986, November). *Teaching a large lecture introductory speech course.* Paper presented at the meeting of the Speech Communication Association, Chicago.

Zayas-Baya, E. P. (1977–1978). Instructional media in the total language picture. *International Journal of Instructional Media, 5,* 145–150.

23

Interaction Skills in Instructional Settings

Janis Andersen
San Diego State University

Jon Nussbaum
University of Oklahoma

Excellent classroom instructors are skilled at stimulating and sustaining relevant classroom discussion. Questions, opinions, shared contemplations, uttered insights, and lively exchanges are important components of well-functioning classrooms. Even a technical dissection of teaching skills highlights the importance of teacher ability to create interaction. For example, the microteaching clinic at Stanford University initially identified nine technical skills essential to effective teaching (Dunkin, 1987). Seven of those are directly related to classroom interaction: fluency in asking questions, reinforcing student participation, utilizing probing questions, utilizing higher order questions, facility with divergent questions, appropriate utilizing of nonverbal cues to reduce reliance on teacher talk, and utilizing interaction techniques to alleviate boredom and inattentiveness. In short, effective teaching is largely characterized by instructors who are competent interactants, skilled in interactional discourse. This chapter discusses interactional teaching techniques with a somewhat prescriptive orientation in the hope that exposure to verbal and nonverbal strategies for promoting classroom interaction will improve classroom experiences.

THE APPROPRIATE REALM

Instructional Goals

Interactive teaching is both an attitude and a set of skills. The first important attitudinal component of successful interactive teaching is a desire to *limit the use of interactional techniques to those instructional goals that are best met through classroom discussion.* Many individuals within the communication discipline hold an often subconscious bias regarding the importance and necessity of human interaction. Rather than assign interaction to its proper place in the universe, many hold misconceptions about its value, believing interaction to be a complete panacea. For example, until recently, communication textbooks failed to discuss potential negative outcomes in interpersonal relationships that can result from self-disclosure. Due to empirical and theoretical advances in relational communication, communication instructors no longer teach that self-disclosure, regardless of content and relational context, is competent communication. Similarly, instructional research documents interactive teaching as best suited for accomplishing some but not all instructional goals. The skilled instructor views interactional discourse as an essential instructional tool, choosing it when the instructional goals are compatible with the tool. In other words, effective instructors know when to nail down or saw apart, and they use a hammer only for the first task!

Classroom discussion is a preferred method of instruction for promoting critical thinking, problem-solving ability, higher level cognitive learning, attitude change, moral development, and communication skill development (Gall, 1987). Additionally, discussion strategies assist students' acceptance and belonging, and they create higher levels of classroom cohesion (Stanford & Stanford, 1969). In contrast, the lecture method is preferred for promoting direct acquisition of information, particularly new information (McKeachie & Kulik, 1975), whereas a personalized systems approach (PSI) is best for producing mastery learning of essential course material (Kulik, 1987). In their review of the empirical support for the effectiveness of discussion, McKeachie and Kulik (1975) argued that discussion is more effective for promoting retention of information and higher level thinking. It also better motivates students and creates more favorable student attitudes.

In his book on teaching tips for the beginning college teacher, McKeachie (1978) outlined eight specific instructional outcomes that are particularly appropriate for the discussion technique. The use of discussion is warranted when the instructor wants to:

1. use group members resources;
2. give students opportunities to formulate application of principles;
3. get prompt feedback on the attainment of instructional objectives;
4. help students practice thinking within the subject matter;
5. improve students ability to evaluate the evidence and logic of positions that they and others hold;

6. facilitate students' awareness of problems that necessitate additional information through further readings or lectures;
7. gain acceptance for information or theories counter to folklore or previous beliefs;
8. develop motivation for further learning.

In summary, in terms of instructional objectives, the discussion method is superior for achieving many higher level cognitive objectives (see Bloom, Englehart, Furst, Hill, & Krathwohl, 1956) and many affective objectives (see Krathwohl, Bloom, & Masia, 1956). Because classroom discussion is time consuming, it is highly inefficient for information transference goals. Thus, low level cognitive objectives are best met through alternative instructional strategies.

Interactional Skill

In addition to instructional objectives, a second limiting factor mitigating against the use of classroom discussion is the interactional skill of classroom members. A successful discussion requires interactional skill by both the instructor and the students (Cooper, 1984). Interactional skills are perhaps more developed in communication instructors—and certainly the development of student interactional skills is a more central instructional outcome for students of communication. Nevertheless, interactional skills are both a necessary prerequisite for successful discussions and an important byproduct of the process. With less skilled teachers and students, other teaching strategies will better facilitate immediate instructional objectives. Often, developing instructors must choose between a long-term goal of further enhancing instructional skills and a short-term goal of doing the best teaching possible at this point in time. Teachers who strive for excellence choose both alternatives some of the time.

Student Characteristics

The final issue that we address concerning the limits of classroom discussion involves characteristics of individual students and their optimal learning situations. A wide variety of student personality factors, psychological predispositions, cognitive styles and abilities, and cultural and gender differences have been examined for their impact on classroom outcomes (for brief overviews of these areas, see Bank, 1987; Debus, 1987; Dunkin & Doenau, 1987; Kahl, 1987; Sinclair, 1987). Inasmuch as an excellent classroom teacher creates a classroom situation that is most effective for resident students, student characteristics should be considered when deciding to use a discussion teaching strategy. The student characteristic most likely to predict a negative outcome with discussion techniques is high anxiety. Sinclair explained that high anxiety is not always debilitating in learning situations but is dependent on the features of the learning environment. For example, highly anxious students outperform low-anxiety students when task difficulty and ego involvement are low. Research suggests that from first grade to college, highly anxious students prefer and perform best in teacher-directed classrooms (Sinclair, 1987). High-anxiety students are superior achievers in lecture-oriented classrooms, whereas low-anxiety students perform best in classrooms with student-centered teaching methods, such as class discussion.

A particular type of anxiety labeled *communication apprehension* exerts similar instructional influence. McCroskey and Andersen (1976) found that although high-communication-apprehensive individuals "have lower academic achievement in traditional interaction-oriented educational systems" (p. 73), no similar relationship exists with academic achievement in a mass lecture communication class where communication is highly restricted. Although interaction is facilitative of many instructional goals for most students, it appears to be generally detrimental to the high communication apprehensive. Thus, Brophy and Good's (1986) general advice to "call on nonvolunteers frequently" (p. 363) sharply contrasts with McCroskey's (1977) specific admonition to wait for signs of volunteering before calling on the quiet, communicatively apprehensive students. An unusual classroom with only high-communication-apprehensive individuals would be taught best if discussion strategies were minimal or nonexistent. More usual classrooms with a mixture of students are taught most effectively with a mix of teaching strategies.

Similarly, field-dependent teachers and learners favor and prosper in interactive classrooms, whereas field-independent individuals prefer lecture approaches (Debus, 1987). Furthermore, Witkin, Moore, Goodenough, and Cox (1977) found a positive attraction for matching teacher–student cognitive styles. Once again, however, a mix of instructional strategies is considered best for all (Debus, 1987).

Research on the favorableness of discussion strategies for a particular sex or ethnic group is indirect. Discussion is a recommended strategy for changing attitudes and enhancing moral development—two relevant concerns with gender and ethnic prejudice. However, research suggests that teachers have differential interaction patterns with minority students (Dunkin & Doenau, 1987)—that is, teachers tend to have fewer positive and more negative interactions with minority students. Minority students are called upon less, respond less, and initiate teacher interaction less frequently. Teachers also have been found to direct different types of questions to minority students. Similarly, research suggests that teachers respond differently, particularly in terms of nonverbal cues (Bossert, 1981), to students of differing sexes. In terms of responding with an appropriate instructional strategy (based on ethnicity and gender), the admonition to classroom teachers is a challenge to use discussion methods within communication patterns that deny prejudicial bias. Discussion necessitates more frequent classroom interactions with this greater frequency creating the possibility of either diminishing or enhancing prejudicial messages.

RESPECTFUL ENVIRONMENTS

Moral Dispositions

Beyond consideration of the appropriate realm for classroom interaction, interactive teaching involves an overall approach to the classroom setting. The most effective class discussions are enacted in an *environment where participants share mutual respect and instructional responsibility*. Bridges (cited in Gall, 1987) delineated group norms, which he labeled "moral dispositions" and deemed necessary for good discussion:

> Participants should evidence: willingness to be reasonable and be influenced by others' evidence; peaceableness and conformance to such rules as "only one person talks at a time;" truthfulness in what one says; giving each person the freedom to speak his or her mind; the belief that participants are equal and that each one of them potentially has knowledge of relevance to the discussion; respect for all members of the discussion group . . . (p. 235)

Instructors who use discussion techniques should evidence these attitudes in their interactional styles and reinforce consistent student behaviors. Cooper (1984) suggested that the success of the discussion method requires a vow to let questions "live." Quoting from Frost (1974), she warned against killing a question: "It is a fragile thing. A good question deserves to live. One doesn't so much answer it as converse with it, or better yet, one lives with it" (Cooper, 1984, p. 117).

Supportive Climates

A supportive classroom climate is indicative that a mutual respect attitude is being promoted. Gibb (1961) suggested that defensive climates are created by evaluation, control, superiority, and a certainty orientation. On the other hand, supportive climates are fostered by description, spontaneity, equality, and provisionalism. Supportive climates encourage greater interaction, trust, participation, and involvement. Using Gibb's notion, Cooper (1984) outlined 12 pragmatic suggestions to help teachers create participative, supportive classroom climates:

1. Accept and develop students' ideas.
2. Accept and develop students' feelings.
3. Praise rather than criticize.
4. Encourage.
5. Insure a level of success for all students.
6. Listen.
7. Allow for pupil talk.
8. Abide by the rules for effective feedback.
9. Metacommunicate.
10. Accept pupil mistakes.
11. Don't seek instant closure.
12. Be authentic.

Student-Centered Teaching

This attitudinal profile of an effective classroom discussion leader was characterized by McKeachie (1978) as *student-centered* rather than *instructor-centered*. Although other names can be used to label this approach, they identify a classroom orientation that encourages greater student participation and breaks away from a traditional instructor-dominated approach. What many incorrectly label "classroom discussion" is really recitation. In recitation, the predominant classroom discourse pattern is teacher question–student response–teacher feedback–new teacher question. In contrast, true class discussions involve mutual influence among all group members with members directing remarks to the entire group. True classroom discussion will have many interactional sequences with student remark following student remark (Gall, 1987).

In a discussion mode, the instructor is not the sole information provider or organizational determiner; group members share in these functions. Instructor dependence is reduced, and group norms guide the interactional process. Incidentally, this can raise or lower achievement standards, depending on group expectations. In short, classroom discussion is optimized when an instructor relinquishes the instructor control and authority that are characteristic of a more teacher-dominated classroom.

In summary, interactive teaching begins with a set of attitudes. Effective instructors are cognizant of the instructional goals, interactional skills, and student characteristics that suggest reliance on discussion techniques. Furthermore, teachers who are effective classroom discussion leaders are student centered. They create mutually supportive classroom climates, and they model and reinforce appropriate discussion orientations. Interactive teachers willingly relinquish some teacher domination and control, trusting mutual influence processes to appropriately direct and sanction discussion behaviors.

Obviously, effective interactive teaching involves more than attitude or desire. Its successful accomplishment necessitates the competent enactment of discussion skills. In the next section some of these skills are delineated, and practical suggestions for their classroom use are provided.

DISCUSSION SKILLS

Questions

In their review of research on communication and instruction, Staton-Spicer and Wulff (1984) did not mention findings concerning the use of questions within the classroom. This seems more than strange, because any study of classroom communication is not complete without focusing on what many researchers believe to be the most common form of teacher speech—the question. In point of fact, Hoetker and Ahlbrand (1979) indicated that well over 70% of the average school day (across all classrooms) is taken up with questions. The reason Staton-Spicer and Wulff (1984) did not reference research on questions, of course, is the fact that since Deethardt's (1974) article addressing the use of questions in communication classrooms, no instructional communication researcher has been published that explores the use of questions as a speech phenomenon within the classroom.

Fortunately, the field of education has taken a different research path than the field of communication with regard to the use of questions within the classroom. Good and Brophy (1987) indicated that research investigating classroom questions remains one of the most popular areas of educational research. Countless studies have been conducted investigating every imaginable aspect of classroom questions. Many of these studies have used verbal coding schemes based on either Flander's (1970) count of teacher use of questions or on the more sophisticated schemes originating with Bloom's taxonomy of educational objectives.

The research generated within the field of education has not produced consistent findings. This lack of consistency tends to frustrate practitioners who wish to make simple, straightforward pronouncements that high-level or complex questions are better than low-level or simple questions and that thought questions are better than fact questions. In reality, most educational researchers find no evidence that type or level of question predicts positive learning by students (Brophy & Good, 1986; Good & Brophy, 1987). It appears that the usefulness of classroom questions is dependent on such factors as course content, student knowledge level, and teacher's ability to manage the classroom discussion from which the questions emerge.

Good and Brophy (1987) suggested that the only data that support a correlation between question use and academic achievement are investigations that study the frequency of question usage in the classroom. Frequent questions by the teacher are not only an indicant of active teaching (which has been linked to effective teaching within the communication literature; Norton & Nussbaum, 1980); they also present students with an opportunity to express themselves orally within the classroom. Thus, questions help to keep students on-task.

As was mentioned earlier, literally hundreds of articles have been published in the education literature that have attempted to link teacher questions to positive learning gains or effective teaching. Brophy and Good (1986) presented an excellent summary of these studies and recast this summary into practical suggestions.

Difficulty Level of Questions

When a teacher asks a question for the class to answer, how many students within the class should know the answer to that question? Research suggests that most questions asked by the teacher should elicit correct responses from the majority of students. At times, when the course content is complex, it may be useful for the teacher to pose questions that only a few students can answer correctly. Teachers should realize that higher level questions may raise the cognitive functioning ability of the students or it may turn the student "off" to the classroom discussion. Because a large portion of the content of basic communication courses centers on basic skill development, it may be wise for teachers to structure the level of questioning so that most students can answer the majority of questions. This reinforces student participation as well as maintains a high level of activity within the classroom.

Cognitive Level of Questions

Just because a question is difficult to answer does not mean that the question is asked at a high cognitive level. The research that reports on the benefits of asking students questions at higher cognitive levels is inconsistent. No consistent positive correlation exists between higher level cognitive questions and student learning gains. In fact, several research reports suggest that lower level questions actually increase student achievement—even on higher level objectives (Brophy & Good, 1986). Brophy and Good (1986) believe that "we should expect teachers to ask more lower-level than higher-level questions, even when dealing with higher-level content and seeking to promote higher-level objectives" (p. 363).

An important issue that has been ignored by researchers is question sequencing. It seems obvious that when a teacher is asking a series of questions, those questions need to move from lower level to higher level. This is easier said than done, however. Cooper (1984, p. 116) has provided a good example of question sequencing utilizing Bloom's taxonomy of cognitive learning.

Clarity of Questions

Grossier (1964) wrote that all good questions are clear, and research supports this claim (Rosenshine, 1968; Wright & Nuthall, 1970). An unclear question will cause confusion and anxiety on the part of the student. Thus, teachers should formulate and communicate clear questions to classrooms.

Post-Question Wait Time

Brophy and Good (1986) believe that after a question has been asked, the teacher should pause, allowing students to think before the teacher calls on them for answers. Cooper (1984) has warned teachers not to answer their own questions.

Although it may seem quite strange, teachers have a difficult time waiting for students to respond (Rowe, 1974a, 1974b). In a series of studies, longer wait times by teachers positively correlated with more active participation in the class and with higher quality participation (Rowe, 1986; Swift & Gooding, 1983; Tobin & Capie, 1982). Wait time becomes more important as the function of the question changes. As stated by Good and Brophy (1987), "If questions are intended to stimulate students to think about material and formulate original responses rather than merely to retrieve information from memory, it is important to allow time for these effects to occur" (p. 494).

Selecting the Respondent

Each teacher is faced with the problem of who to call on once a question is asked. The research on this issue is quite complex, depending on grade level, socioeconomic status, and the use of small-group assignments within the classroom. For the communication teacher, it may involve control of the assertive student to provide all students an opportunity to participate. Overt participation correlates positively with achievement for older students. Thus, the teacher must organize the class to permit a wide range of student participation—encouraging volunteering and inviting nonvolunteers in appropriate nonthreatening ways.

MISUSED QUESTIONS

Inasmuch as question research indicates an overall positive correlation between the frequent use of questions and positive classroom outcomes, a discussion of question types that can lead to unproductive student responses is warranted. Grossier (1964) has pointed to four types of questions that teachers should generally avoid: (a) yes–no questions, (b) tugging questions, (c) guessing questions, and (d) leading questions.

Yes–No Questions

Grossier (1964) and Good and Brophy (1987) have noted several dangers in yes–no questions. First, the yes–no question usually serves only as a warm-up for another question. For example, the teacher may ask, "Does Mark Knapp write about relationship stages?" After the student responds, the teacher says, "What are they?" Grossier (1964) has asserted that the first question was a waste of time.

A second danger of the yes–no question is that it encourages guessing. Because either answer has a 50% chance of being correct, students do not need to concentrate on learning but need only offer either answer to respond in some way. The third danger is that yes–no questions have low diagnostic power, in that responses to them do not permit evaluation by the teacher on how to proceed.

Tugging Questions

Good and Brophy (1987) wrote that "tugging questions or statements often follow a halting or incomplete student response ("well, come on" "Yes . . . ?")" (p. 488). The major difficulty with these questions is that the teacher provides no additional information to the student. It would be better for the teacher to give the student the answer rather than nagging or drawing the student out needlessly. This kind of nagging lowers student self-esteem and lowers classroom affect.

Guessing Questions

The field of communication has the perfect guessing question and every communication teacher asks it. The question is asked in many different ways but goes something like this: "How is communication defined?" The question requires students to reason and then to guess, because students often lack the required information to formulate a correct response (if, indeed, there is a correct response). According to Good and Brophy (1987), "Guessing questions are useful if they are related to teaching strategies that help students think rationally and systematically and if they are designed ultimately to elicit a thoughtful response" (p. 488). The major difficulty with guessing questions is that they may encourage impulsive or irrational thought, which can be self-defeating. To ask a student to define communication when there is no answer can lead to a useful discussion or it can turn students into very cynical consumers of communication content.

Leading Questions

Questions such as, "Don't you agree that self-disclosure is an important component of communication?" should not be used in the classroom. These leading questions reinforce student dependence on the teacher and nullify independent thought (Good & Brophy, 1987).

TEACHER RESPONSES

The interactive nature of the classroom depends as much on student answers to teacher questions and how the teacher responds to the answers as it does on questions asked by the teacher. Several scholars have offered suggestions concerning proper teacher reaction to student responses (Cooper, 1984; Good & Brophy, 1987).

Reacting to Correct Responses

When a student responds to a teacher's question incorrectly, the teacher should acknowledge the correct response in an overt fashion (anything from a head nod, e.g., to direct praise). The teacher must be careful not to praise in an inappropriate manner, because too much praise can be distracting or ingratiating. (See Brophy, 1981 for a review of teacher praise literature.)

Reacting to Partly Correct Responses

A common occurrence within the classroom is student answers that are only partly correct. It is important for the teacher to acknowledge the correct part of the response and then attempt to secure more information from the student. If the student cannot give additional correct information, the teacher should move on to another student or give the correct response.

Reacting to Incorrect Responses

An incorrect response from a student is be followed by a teacher statement that the response was not correct to prevent student confusion. Often the teacher can follow with an explanation of why the answer was incorrect and how the student can give a correct answer the next time he or she is called on. Teachers should subtly praise student attempts, however, if they wish to encourage future interaction.

Reacting to "No Response"

Perhaps the most frightening experience encountered by a teacher is to ask a student or the class a question and receive no response. When this occurs, it is best to wait an appropriate amount of time, attempt to rephrase the question, and then simply give the answer. Brophy and Good (1986) wrote that a teacher should train students to give an "I don't know" reply rather than respond with silence.

In summary, the effective use of questions is a major skill in interactive teaching. Good questions are moderately difficult or easy, are well sequenced, are at the appropriate cognitive level, and are clear. Good questions allow ample response time and appropriately spread interaction opportunities among many students. Effective questioners generally avoid yes–no questions, tugging questions, guessing questions, and leading questions.

NONVERBAL INTERACTION

Interactive teaching involves more than verbal interaction. Through nonverbal cues, the instructor creates the relational messages that encourage or discourage interaction. In this section, we describe the workings of some of these nonverbal cues.

Seating Arrangement

Relatively consistent research suggests a correspondence between student participation and classroom location. Students closer to the teacher (or those facing the teacher more directly) participate more. One question arising from classroom participation research is whether high verbalizers chose interactive seats or whether interactive locations create high verbalizers. Smith (1987) reported empirical support for a mutual influence. Thus, a U-shaped or a circular classroom arrangement is recommended for facilitating classroom discussion among the greatest number of students (Todd-Mancillas, 1982; Patterson, Kelley, Kondracki, & Wulf, 1979).

Teacher Immediacy

One cluster of teacher nonverbal behaviors that has been studied by communication researchers is teacher immediacy (see Andersen & Andersen, 1982, for a review of the immediacy construct). Immediacy behaviors include eye contact, head nods, smiles, gestural activity, vocal animation, open body postures, forward leaning posture, and other approach-oriented behaviors. They signal accessibility, involvement, arousal, and interest. Empirically, immediacy behaviors have been directly related to affective learning. Theoretical supposition and indirect evidence support a link to increased student classroom participation. Andersen and Andersen (1982) identified numerous experimental studies that found greater amounts of verbal interaction in more immediate laboratory conditions. Thus, higher levels of teacher immediacy are likely to result in greater student involvement and more overall classroom interaction.

Turn Taking

Classroom procedures often ritualize interaction and turn taking by having students raise hands to acquire the floor. Students are then recognized by the teacher for their speaking turn. Friedrich (1982) summarized this language "game" and its rules, suggesting that the rules have remained stable for more than 70 years. Friedrich pointed out that although 80% of classroom talk typically involves asking, answering, or reacting to questions, only 20% of the questions require student thinking. Sixty percent ask for recall of fact, and 20% are procedural (Gall, 1970).

This classroom ritual is antithetical to classroom discussion. Imagine how dinner conversation would change if all participants had to be recognized by the head of the family for their speaking turn. Even very large families have not typically resorted to a ritual this stifling. In group interaction, participants regulate conversation through eye contact, body leans, head nods, mouth opening, and gestural starts. These turn preparation cues signal an interest in and desire for interaction. More spontaneous systems like these can be adopted for classroom settings. If you feel that the classroom group is too large to be totally controlled by the nonverbal cues, a more spontaneous discussion would occur if the rules allowed the person speaking to call on the next person with a hand raised. (The teacher, as well as the students, would vie for the floor.) Additionally, a second turn taking rule might dictate that the next comment must have relevance to the previous one. This insures discussion continuity and progression without direct teacher interference, and it improves student interactional skill.

Teacher Reinforcements

Although verbal praise is an appropriate reinforcer for student participation, many nonverbal cues are more powerful, less disruptive, and judged more genuine. Teacher attention, eye contact, facial expression, and body orientation are powerful cues of acceptance and appreciation. In fact, it is possible to be verbally correcting of the content while being nonverbally appreciative of the interaction attempt. A reinforcing nonverbal demeanor will improve student participation and student affect.

In summary, attention to classroom arrangement and a greater reliance on nonverbal immediacy behaviors will enhance student involvement. Altered turn-taking rules can enhance spontaneous discussion. An appropriate use of nonverbal reinforcement messages will improve classroom interaction.

In conclusion, this chapter discusses the issue of interactive teaching. The authors have attempted to convince the reader(s) that interactive teaching is a powerful instructional strategy that, when used appropriately, can result in positive instructional outcomes. This strategy, like other ones, works best when used within an instructional arena that is best suited for it. Excellent classroom instructors remain flexible and choose instructional strategies to best accomplish instructional goals. Thus, interactive teaching is an essential but not sufficient instructional skill.

REFERENCES

Andersen, P. A., & Andersen, J. F. (1982). Nonverbal immediacy in instruction. In L. L. Barker (Ed.), *Communication in the classroom: Original essays*. Englewood Cliffs, NJ: Prentice-Hall.

Bank, B. J. (1987). Students sex. In M. J. Dunkin (Ed.), *The international encyclopedia of teaching and teacher education* (pp. 571–574). Oxford: Pergamon.

Bloom, B. S., Englehart, M. D., Furst, E. J., Hill, W. H., & Krathwohl, D. R. (1956). *Taxonomy of educational objectives. Handbook 1: Cognitive domain*. New York: David McKay.

Bossert, S. T. (1981). Understanding sex differences in children's classroom experiences. *Elementary School Journal, 81,* 255–266.

Brophy, J. (1981). Teacher praise: A functional analysis. *Review of Educational Research,* 51, 5–32.

Brophy, J., & Good, T. L. (1986). Teacher behavior and student achievement. In M. C. Wittrock (Ed.), *Handbook of research on teaching* (3rd ed., pp. 328–375). New York: MacMillan.

Cooper, P. J. (1984). *Speech communication for the classroom teacher*. Scottsdale, AZ: Gorsuch Scarisbrick.

Debus, R. L. (1987). Students' cognitive characteristics. In M. J. Dunkin (Ed.), *The international encyclopedia of teaching and teacher education* (pp. 564–568). Oxford: Pergamon.

Deethardt, J. F. (1974). The use of questions in the speech-communication classroom. *Speech Teacher, 23,* 15–20.

Dunkin, M. J. (1987). Technical skills of teaching. In M. J. Dunkin (Ed.), *The international encyclopedia of teaching and teacher education* (pp. 703–706). Oxford: Pergamon.

Dunkin, M. J., & Doenau, S. J. (1987). Students' ethnicity. In M. J. Dunkin (Ed.), *The international encyclopedia of teaching and teacher education* (pp. 568–571). Oxford: Pergamon.

Flanders, N. (1970). *Analyzing teacher behavior*. Reading, MA: Addison-Wesley.

Friedrich, G. W. (1982). Classroom interaction. In L. L. Barker (Ed.), *Communication in the classroom: Original essays* (pp. 55–56). Englewood Cliffs, NJ: Prentice-Hall.

Frost, G. E. (1974). *Bless my growing*. Minneapolis, MN: Augsburg Publishing.

Gall, M. D. (1970). The use of questions in teaching. *Review of Educational Research, 40,* 707–721.

Gall, M. D. (1987). Discussion methods. In M. J. Dunkin (Ed.), *The international encyclopedia of teaching and teacher education* (pp. 232–237). Oxford: Pergamon.

Gibb, J. (1961). Defensive communication. *Journal of Communication, 11,* 142–148.

Good, T. L., & Brophy, J. (1987). *Looking in classrooms* (4th ed.). New York: Harper & Row.

Grossier, P. (1964). *How to use the fine art of questioning*. New York: Teachers' Practical Press.

Hoetker, J., & Ahlbrand, W. P. (1979). The persistence of recitation. *American Educational Research Journal, 6,* 145–167.

Kahl, T. N. (1987). Students' social backgrounds. In M. J. Dunkin (Ed.), *The international encyclopedia of teaching and teacher education* (pp. 574–584). Oxford: Pergamon.

Krathwohl, D. R., Bloom, B. S., & Masia, B. B. (1956). *Taxonomy of educational objectives. Handbook 11: Affective domain*. New York: David McKay Co.

Kulik, J. A. (1987). Keller Plan: A personalized system of instruction. In M. J. Dunkin (Ed.), *The international encyclopedia of teaching and teacher education* (pp. 306–311). Oxford: Pergamon.

McCroskey, J. C. (1977). *Quiet children and the classroom teacher*. Urbana, IL: Eric Clearinghouse on Reading and Communication Skills (SCA publication).

315

McKeachie, W. J. (1978). *Teaching tips: A guidebook for the beginning college teacher* (7th ed.). Lexington, MA: Heath.

McKeachie, W. J., & Kulik, J. A. (1975). Effective college teaching. In F. N. Kerlinger (Ed.), *Review of research in education* (Vol. 3, pp. 165–209). Itasca, IL: F. E. Peacock.

Norton, R., & Nussbaum, J. (1980). Dramatic behaviors of the effective teacher. In D. Nimmo (Ed.), *Communication yearbook 4* (pp. 565–579). New Brunswick, NJ: Transaction.

Patterson, M. L., Kelley, C. E., Kondracki, B. A., & Wulf, L. J. (1979). Effects of seating on small group behavior. *Social Psychology Quarterly, 42,* 180–185.

Rosenshine, B. (1968). To explain: A review of research. *Educational Leadership, 26,* 275–280.

Rowe, M. (1974a). Science, silence, and sanctions. *Science and Children, 6,* 11–13.

Rowe, M. (1974b). Wait-time and rewards as instructional variables, their influence on language, logic, and fate control: Part 1—Wait time. *Journal of Research in Science Teaching, 11,* 81 84.

Rowe, M. (1986). Wait time: Slowing down may be a way of speeding up! *Journal of Teacher Education, 37,* 43–50.

Sinclair, K. E. (1987). Students' affective characteristics. In M. J. Dunkin (Ed.), *The international encyclopedia of teaching and teacher education* (pp. 559–564). Oxford: Pergamon.

Smith, H. A. (1987). Nonverbal communication. In M. J. Dunkin (Ed.), *The international encyclopedia of teaching and teacher education* (pp. 466–476). Oxford: Pergamon.

Stanford, G., & Stanford, B. D. (1969). *Learning discussion skills through games.* New York: Citation Press.

Staton-Spicer, A. Q., & Wulff, D. H. (1984). Research in communication and instruction: Categorization and synthesis. *Communication Education, 33,* 377–391.

Swift, J., & Gooding, C. (1983). Interaction of wait time feedback and questioning instruction on middle school science teaching. *Journal of Research in Science Teaching, 20,* 721–730.

Tobin, K., & Capie, W. (1982). Relationships between classroom process variables and middle school science achievement. *Journal of Educational Psychology, 74,* 441–454.

Todd-Mancillas, W. R. (1982). Classroom environments and nonverbal behavior. In L. L. Barker (Ed.), *Communications in the classroom: Original essays* (pp. 77–97). Englewood Cliffs, NJ: Prentice-Hall.

Witkin, H. A., Moore, G. A., Goodenaugh, D. R., & Cox, P. W. (1977). Field-dependent and field-independent cognitive styles and their educational implications. *Review of Educational Research, 47,* 1–64.

Wright, C., & Nuthall, G. (1970). The relationships between teacher behaviors and pupil achievement in three experimental elementary science lessons. *American Educational Research Journal, 7,* 477–492.

24

Individualized Approaches to Instruction

William J. Seiler
Chas McAliley
University of Nebraska, Lincoln

Gage and Berliner (1984) wrote that "individualized instruction occurs when the goals of instruction, learning materials, subject matter, or methods of instruction are specially chosen for a particular student or a small group of students with common characteristics" (pp. 521–522). It can not be assumed, however, that individualized instruction is carried out with only one individual at a time. Individualized instruction can occur in many different formats and, thus, it is our purpose in this chapter to discuss its rationale, its theoretical base, and several of its most predominant formats.

RATIONALE FOR INDIVIDUALIZED INSTRUCTION

Individualized approaches to instruction have gained in popularity during the past three decades and have become an attractive alternative to more traditional methods of instruction. A dissatisfaction with the conventional classroom, its basic assumptions, and, more importantly, its lack of effectiveness prompted many educators to reexamine traditional methods of instruction. This dissatisfaction arose from the inability of most conventional methods (e.g., lecture or discussion) to take into account individual differences. This concern surfaced as early as the 1920s with the beginning of intelligence testing. Testing revealed significant differences in intelligence among students and, thus, differences in ability to achieve in the typical classroom. Research continued to examine these differences, revealing that brighter students (who were capable of learning much more) were held back by those who were less able to achieve. These differences created controversy as well as complicated what teachers did in the classroom. For example, assignments that might be considered appropriate for some students were not appropriate for others. This often placed teaching and learning at odds.

During the 1950s, B. F. Skinner (1954) and other behavioral psychologists questioned the usefulness of traditional teaching methods (e.g., lecture and discussion) because they were inadequate for providing the proper individual reinforcement and motivation for students to learn. For example, one student might frequently respond to a teacher's directed questions because she continually received praise—"Great answer Jill!" Conversely, another student might rarely respond due to his inability or as a result of negative reinforcement cues from the teacher—"John, that answer was silly." These differences (along with student boredom, frustration, and resentment) were among the reasons for the failure of most large (and even small-group) approaches. It was concluded that any approach that assumes that every student is the same is bound to miss the mark for some students.

The obvious solution for Skinner and others was to develop new instructional techniques that would take into account individual differences. Thus, students would be able to work on tasks that were appropriate to their abilities and interests. Essentially, then, the position taken by Skinner and others was that each student would be given tasks appropriate to his or her abilities, backgrounds, and interests. The thrust of individual learning was based on the assumption that each student would learn and move ahead at his or her own pace.

THEORETICAL BASE FOR INDIVIDUALIZED INSTRUCTION

Since the work of B. F. Skinner, our view concerning learning and the conditions of its occurrence have changed dramatically. The change that has occurred is the result of a system that arose from the experimental analysis of behavior of both animals and humans—a system known as reinforcement theory. We know that punishment and reinforcement play significant roles in teacher and student interaction, and that much of student satisfaction is derived from reinforcement.

Punishment

Most present-day learning is based on punishment. A recent conversation of one of the authors with a colleague illustrates this very clearly. The conversation started out as follows (conversation edited and not recalled verbatim):

> "I just had a terrible class," he states. "Today was the first day of speeches and what a disaster. The first student got up to speak and with a big grin explained that she wasn't prepared to give her speech." He told her to sit down and hoped she'd be ready later in the period. The next speaker, according to the instructor, made it through the speech, but it wasn't very good. The third and fourth were also not prepared. In fact, the third speaker ran out of the room because she was nervous and felt sick. The instructor's explanation was, "Maybe I am too tough on them. But I am not going to be easy, either. Those who didn't get through the assignment will receive an F. What a heck of an environment to start out a speech assignment," he explained.

This instructor expressed two misconceptions about the learning that did not occur in his class: (a) demanding more of his students will increase learning and (b) punishment will make them try harder next time.

Punishment, according to Sherman (1974), has received a mixed reception by those in the classroom: "apparently we cannot teach with it, and we cannot teach without it" (p. 3). The effect of punishment can be rewarding to teachers who wish to have stern discipline in their classroom, but the use of punishment can also produce negative effects that lead to the broken will of some students and the destruction of confidence in others. Sherman concluded: it "kills the visions of nearly all" (p. 3).

Punishment usually leads to an environment of constant judgment and evaluation with no room for mistakes. The end result is an atmosphere of high tension and anxiety when punishment (whether by design or not) is the strategy.

Reinforcement

The general principles that underpin most individualized instruction are summarized by reinforcement theory. Some of these principles are:

1. Positive and negative human behaviors are learned by means of reinforcement.
2. A reduction in reinforcement can weaken previously or currently learned behavior.

3. Punishing a behavior will decrease the amount of times a behavior will occur.

4. Humans learn to generalize concepts to new and different situations.

5. Learning should occur in small continuous steps.

6. When learning has occurred it should receive immediate positive reinforcement.

7. A learned behavior can be weakened or eliminated by removing the reinforcer that created it.

8. There are secondary or generalized reinforcers (e.g., attention, approval, or affection) that can be meaningful even if a person has not been deprived of them (Scott & Young, 1976; Skinner, 1960).

These principles do not include all that is necessary for the learning of behavior, but they are important to the foundation and psychology of most individualized learning.

METHODS OF INDIVIDUALIZED INSTRUCTION

The most widely used methods of individualized instruction include: Personalized System of Instruction (PSI), mastery learning, tutoring, programmed instruction, and computer-assisted instruction (CAI).

Personalized System of Instruction

Fred Keller wrote in his diary, in March, 1963, that the Personalized System of Instruction (PSI) is "one of the most exciting and most radical (courses) ever given in a university setting" (Keller & Sherman, 1974, p. 7). A month later, Keller wrote:

> The Education program . . . represents a distillation of many things: the method of laboratory teaching at Columbia . . . the use of programmed instruction where possible; the treatment of textbooks, lectures, conferences, etc., as rewards for passing through various stages of individual study and experimentation; the use of lectures as inspirational rather than truly instructional; the measurement of progress by compilations of things that the student has successfully done, rather than by grades on examinations. (p. 7)

Little did Keller know at the time that the plan he described would bring about a renaissance of individualized instruction in colleges and university. It has been estimated that over 6,000 courses (in almost every discipline) have been organized around the Keller plan.

Using the theoretical principles of reinforcement theory, PSI is based on five defining features: (a) mastery learning, (b) self-pacing, (c) a stress on the written word, (d) proctors, and (e) the use of lectures to motivate rather than to supply essential information (Sherman, 1974).

The *mastery* feature requires that students in the PSI method be called upon to respond frequently and with responses that have consequences. The course's content is broken down into small units of instruction, and unless a student demonstrates mastery of a unit, he or she may not be allowed to move onto the next unit. The theoretical base of PSI suggests that if activities are to produce positive consequences for the learner, repeated testing must take place, with errors resulting in a program of remediation rather than in penalties.

It is important that success be rewarded (Scott & Young, 1976). Therefore, grades must reflect accomplishments, not the number of mistakes made along the way; an grading must be determined on absolute rather than on normative standards, which are competitive or comparative. A criterion is often set to determine success or when acceptable work has been done. This criterion can be set at any level, but most often is set at 80% to 90% correct.

The theory behind PSI suggests that if activities are to produce positive outcomes, learners must be allowed to learn at their own rate; learning should occur in small, sequential segments; and several trials should be allowed in order for students to obtain success. The traditional approach (and the instructors who use it) generally adheres to the notion of either success or failure, thereby allowing students only one opportunity to succeed. For example, in most traditional communication courses, students are given one opportunity to present an informative speech with evaluation almost always based on that one trial. If students succeed, that's great, but if they fail, that's too bad—the course must go on. This approach to instruction, according to Scott and Young (1976), is at odds with the process by which humans learn. They suggest that most learning requires several trials and is often characterized by a high rate of failure.

The mastery requirement (whether in part or in full) leads to the second feature, *self-pacing*. Given that PSI methods requires mastery, it must allow a go-at-your-own pace. Mastery cannot always be commanded on schedule, because individual differences must be taken into account. Some deadlines, however, are mandatory; for example, whatever is set as the minimum level criterion tasks must be completed within the time limits of the course—a semester, quarter, or whatever.

Given that not all learning can occur with one trial nor at the same rate, the PSI approach allows for repeated trials. Students can repeat activities or assignments several times with no penalties. Students are encouraged and often required to repeat activities until they are successful—that is, to learn from their mistakes rather than to be punished. The goal, therefore, of PSI is for the student to master content and skills in order to complete the course as well as to receive a grade according to ability and not according to others' successes or failures.

Units of information in the PSI method are deliberately small. Thus, students are not pressured to learn more than is practical at one time. Tests are used not only to evaluate students progress, but also to provide feedback on what students have learned and what they need to learn. Moreover, students are tested over shorter units of instruction, more frequently, and given immediate feedback.

The last three features follow directly from the first two. Because some self-pacing is required, a lock-step approach of disseminating information is impossible. *Written materials,* therefore, become the major informational source; they may be supplemented by other materials such as audiovisuals, video tapes, computer-assisted learning, and other innovations to aid student learning. A study guide is almost always required that states the objectives, offers suggestions concerning how to study, indicates relevant resources, contains assignments, and provides sample test items. The heavy reliance on the written word requires that the materials be written clearly and the objectives be specified.

Because the PSI method allows students to use repetitive testing, to work at different speeds, and to involve themselves in a wide range of materials, there must be a means to supplement and amplify the student–teacher contacts made by the instructor. This leads to the fourth feature—the use of *proctors* or tutors. Proctors are usually students who have previously taken the course. They are often selected on the basis of their academic success, personality, and interest in participating in the course. Proctors provide almost all of the individual attention to students. The proctor, according to Keller (1968), is not only an essential feature but may be the most valuable aspect of the PSI approach. As mentioned earlier, part of reinforcement is attention, approval, and personal concern for the well-being of the student. The proctor is able to provide all three. The same ratio of proctor to student (generally 1 to 10) allows for a great deal of interaction between proctor and student and provides an effective vehicle for student learning. Students find the proctors capable of answering most of their questions and often more willing to interact than a full-time faculty member. With training, proctors can learn to correct and grade tests, tutor, evaluate assignments, and record grades.

The use of *lectures,* the fifth feature, differs from that in the traditional classroom. Lecturing is not a major teacher commitment in the PSI method and is used to supplement and motivate. Thus, the teacher becomes a creator of classroom materials and a manager of a learning system.

PSI has many different variations. Boylan (1980) found that approximately 95% of existing PSI courses use some mastery learning and self-pacing, that 88% stress the written word, and that 78% use proctors. Of those responding to Boylan's survey, only 51% use lectures for motivating students. Further, Boylan found that of 303 respondents, 33% (99) use all five of the PSI features within their courses.

Advantages of the Personalized System of Instruction. The major advantage of the PSI method is that it allows learning to occur in an atmosphere that emphasizes positive outcomes. The emphasis is on making students feel good about what they have learned. Students are allowed to make mistakes and correct them, with multiple opportunities for improvement.

The PSI method is well suited for most disciplines and is particularly well suited for teaching communication. Learning how to be an effective oral communicator requires a combination of complex cognitive and psychomotor skills. The acquisition of the cognitive information necessary to be an effective communicator requires mastery of various principles and concepts. In addition, an effective communicator needs psychomotor skills that require practice, feedback, and repetition to be successful. The PSI approach provides students with immediate feedback for making corrections without penalizing them for mistakes, allows the flexibility of self-pacing, and provides students with individual help. Although it can be argued that other models of instruction include some of these features, there is empirical support showing the PSI model to be less costly and more enjoyable, efficient, and effective than traditional approaches.

Assuming all things are equal, according to Seiler (1983), the PSI method of instruction costs approximately one fourth that of a traditional method. Students rate the PSI method to be more enjoyable, more demanding, and higher in overall quality and contribution to learning than traditional approaches. On similar exams, the achievement by students in PSI versus traditional courses is higher by about 8%. Students in PSI retain about 14% more information than those in traditionally taught courses. Students rate PSI-taught courses higher in interaction and in the personal attention they receive. In addition, they receive immediate feedback, clear learning tasks, and are able to use their time more efficiently than in traditionally taught courses; a quantitative analysis comparing 75 courses taught by both traditional and PSI formats (Kulik, Kulik, & Cohen, 1979a) "PSI generally produces superior student achievement, less variations in achievement, and higher student ratings on college courses, but does not affect course withdrawal or student study time in these courses" (p. 307).

Heun, Heun, and Ratcliff (1976) stated that "Individualized instruction is, by definition and long experience of the authors, a more personalized learning system. Each learner is recognized as a unique person" (p. 188). Finally, in a comparison study between PSI-based and lecture-recitation approaches, Gray, Buerkel-Rothfuss, and Yerby (1986) found that students in the PSI-based model tend to equal or do better than the lecture-recitation format in the following four areas: (a) attitudes toward and satisfaction with the course, (b) academic achievement, (c) reduction of communication apprehension, and (d) growth in communication skills.

Disadvantages of the Personalized System of Instruction.   No method of instruction is perfect, and PSI, despite its many advantages, does have a number of disadvantages and limitations. Developing an effective PSI course is extremely time consuming, often requiring from 1 to 4 years. This may be prohibitive in some cases.

Also, there is a tremendous time commitment required of the teacher in maintaining the PSI format. That is, the teacher must be constantly updating the course to make it better (Seiler, Schuelke, & Lieb-Brilhart, 1984).

The PSI method reduces the number and type of student activities that can be effectively dealt with in performance courses. For example, in many traditionally taught communication classes, students are involved in role playing and other similar activities. In the PSI format, these must be limited because of the testing that must take place.

There is a slight tendency for students who enroll in PSI taught courses to withdraw more frequently than from other methods of instruction. In 17 of the 27 comparisons, the PSI withdrawal rate was higher. Although this is a concern, it is not a major disadvantage because the size of the withdrawals is not statistically significant (Kulik, Kulik, & Cohen 1979a).

Mastery

The term *mastery learning* refers to a large and very diverse category of instructional methods. The principal defining characteristic is the establishment of criterion levels for performance that represent "mastery" of a given skill or concept. There is frequent assessment of student progress toward meeting the mastery criterion and ample provision for corrective instruction to enable students who do not initially meet the criterion to do so on later assessments (see Block & Anderson, 1975; Bloom, 1976). The idea of mastery learning was developed by Bloom (1968) and eventually elaborated by Block (1971). Bloom (1976) included a strong emphasis on the appropriate use of the following instructional variables: cues, participation, feedback, and reinforcement. These variables, according to Slavin (1987a, 1987b), are not unique to mastery learning. The organization of time and resources to ensure that the most students are able to succeed is what separates mastery learning from other types of learning.

Slavin (1987a) described three primary forms of mastery learning:

1. The Personalized System of Instruction or the Keller Plan, which we discussed earlier and is used primarily at the postsecondary level.

2. The "continuous progress" form of mastery learning, in which students work individual units of instruction at their own rate. The continuous progress format differs from other individualized models because it uses established mastery criteria for unit tests and, for those student who are unable to master the first time, corrective activities in order to help them.

3. The most popular form of mastery learning used in elementary and secondary schools is called "group-based mastery learning" or Learning for Mastery (LFM). In this approach, the teacher presents information at the same time to the entire class. At the end of the instructional unit, a "formative test" is given to all students. A criterion, usually between 80% and 90%, is established for passing the test. Students who do not achieve the criterion level on the formative test are given corrective instruction. The corrective instruction can take the form of tutoring (either by the teacher or another student), small group instruction (where the teacher goes over the skills or concepts that students missed), or students can work on alternative activities on their own. Block and Anderson (1975) suggested that the corrective activities should be different from the original instruction. After students have completed the corrective instruction, they take another parallel formative or "summative" test. This process may be repeated if necessary. Students who complete the unit with mastery usually earn an "A" grade on the unit, regardless the number of tries it took to reach mastery.

Carroll (1963) asserted that the major index of students aptitude is *time*; that is, the time it takes students to learn—whether it is moving from ignorance to knowledge or from an inability to perform a skill to performing it. Time is often the only difference between the slower student and the student who is able to learn more quickly. Thus, Carroll has suggested that, given time, almost anything can be learned.

There are several other factors (such as the quality of instruction, student motivation, and the student's ability to understand) that enter into Carroll's formula for mastery learning. Students who have difficulty understanding instruction or do not read well often require more time to complete an instructional task. Thus, the resolution of learning problems by students usually requires: (a) more time for learning, (b) different media or materials, or (c) diagnosis to determine what deficiencies students have that are preventing them from learning. The general purpose of mastery learning is to provide materials and conditions by which most learners can be successful at most tasks.

The mastery approach requires that the teacher first delineate the instructional (or behavioral) objectives to be accomplished—that is, what exactly is the student to learn upon completion of instruction. The objectives are usually organized into units of study, each building on the competencies developed in the previous unit. Students then take criterion-referenced tests at their own pace until they master the unit. When students pass, they continue on to the next unit; if they fail, they study and take the proficiency test until they pass.

Advantages of Mastery.   Bloom has claimed that mastery learning strategies can produce outcomes that are (a) both equal (or very similar) for all students and (b) at higher levels of achievement than those of traditional approaches. Bloom (1976) found that the mastery approach could raise the achievement of 90% of the students to levels achieved by only the top 10% under nonmastery conditions. Block's findings (1971, 1974; Block & Burns, 1976) are equally optimistic about mastery learning. In a review of over 50 studies of mastery learning, Block and Burns (1976) found that:

> Mastery-taught students scored higher . . . 89 percent of the time, and significantly higher 61 percent of the time. Likewise, in comparisons of average retention test scores . . . mastery-taught students almost always score higher . . . and significantly higher 63 percent of the time. (p. 19)

Burns (1979) examined results from 157 mastery learning studies in which the learning outcome was cognitive achievement. The results: 107 studies were statistically significant in favor of mastery learning, 47 studies showed no significant differences between mastery and nonmastery, and only 3 studies showed significant differences in favor of nonmastery approaches. Finally, Hyman and Cohen (1979), after studying mastery learning over 15 years in 3,000 schools, concluded that mastery learning was consistently more effective than traditional approaches.

Disadvantages of Mastery.   Much of the criticism of mastery learning centers around the basic assumption that there is a trade-off between time an achievement. This is the basis for what Arlin (1984a, 1984b) referred to as the "time–achievement–equality" dilemma. Arlin (1984b) argued that:

> Given individual differences among students and a relationship between these differences and time needed to learn, one can reasonably argue that the more we provide equality of time to students, the more we will obtain inequality of achievement; and the more we obtain equality of achievement, the more we will have to provide inequality of time to students. (p. 66)

Muller (1973, 1976) and Cox and Dunn (1979) have criticized mastery learning because it (a) takes much of the responsibility for learning away from students, thus they may fail to learn independently; (b) it does not place a fixed amount of time for learning, thus giving students a false sense of security; (c) it holds back faster students while they wait for the slower students to catch up—unless the faster students are given additional objectives to learn; (d) it commits a large portion of the instructional resources to the slower learner; and (e) it assumes that learning must be equal among students—this assumption is difficult to defend in nonskill areas.

Cox and Dunn (1979) further described mastery learning as a "psychological trap" because the reality of factors such as time differences fall short of theoretical claims and thus often trap "unsuspecting teachers" into settling goals that are not obtainable. Finally, Muller (1976) criticized the mastery model along similar lines, referring to it as "partly boon, partly boondoggle." The "boon" is the presumption of equality of achievement across students. The "boondoggle" is the claim that mastery learning can achieve equality of time both in opportunity to learn and in time needed to learn.

Tutoring

Tutoring is one the purest forms of individualized instruction. When education was available only to the elite and wealthy, tutoring was the main method of instruction. Today, however, it is usually associated with remedial instruction. It is a method that can be used to help students of any age level. It is not unusual for the tutor to have little or no special training in education. In fact, much of tutoring that is done is done by peers or paraprofessionals. The personalized system of instruction format, for example, utilizes peers who have minimal training to serve as tutors. According to Gage and Berliner (1984), "although the specific content of tutoring determines the particulars of the process, certain general components are widely recognized: The tutor should *diagnose* and then *remedy,* all the while providing *encouragement and support*" (p.

539). In other words, the goal is to find the student's difficulty, help the student overcome the difficulty, and provide feedback along with lots of reinforcement.

Finding the Difficulty.   Before one can begin to help a student through tutoring, one must find out what the student knows and does not know. The diagnosis of the difficulty can take the form of a casual conversation in which the student describes his or her problem or difficulty. Sometimes it is easier to have the student work a problem or provide a sample of his or her work (e.g., present a speech, write an outline, or try to solve a math problem). This allows the tutor to determine where the student is having difficulty. Different students come to tutors with different problems. Some students know exactly where they are having trouble:

> Student I keep getting "affect" and "effect" confused with each other. Is there any guideline to know when to use "affect" and when "effect"?

Other students can't be as specific, but are able to point out general areas of difficulty:

> Student: I just don't understand the rules for subordination in organizing a speech. There are times when I don't seem to have any problem getting my thoughts into the proper order, but sometimes I just don't have any idea what should follow what.

Finally, some students can only vaguely describe the source of their confusion:

> Student: Speech is my problem. I just don't know how to give one.

Each of the preceding situations requires an individual response. When the student knows exactly what the difficulty is, the tutor can immediately help solve it. There is no need to waste time with further observation or diagnosis. When a student, however, can only vaguely or generally describe the problem, the tutor must spend time trying to isolate the source of the difficulty. This is usually best done by asking questions or observing the student at work at specific problems.

Help to Overcome the Difficulty.   Once the difficulty is located, corrective measures must be taken. The best way, according to Gage and Berliner (1984), is to provide students with opportunities to practice the skills that were found to be deficient. The tutor should stay with one skill until it is mastered before moving onto another.

Sometimes students have studied all the resource materials (and, thus, have a base of knowledge from which to work), but they are unable to organize the information in order to reach a correct solution. Here, the tutor can give hints or prompts that will reduce the number of possible answers and thereby aid students in organizing their thoughts. This strategy allows students to arrive at the correct answer from the information they have already learned. Some examples of this type of prompting are:

Tutor: No, communication anxiety and speech anxiety are not the same thing. Communication anxiety has something in common with speech anxiety—can you tell me what that is?

Tutor: Answering this question is dependent on remembering the definition of "perception" from the previous chapter. Can you see where that concept is relevant?

The best approach a tutor can take is to have students figure out answers for themselves. There are times when instructional materials are weak, and thus the tutor must resort to direct instruction. In this case, the tutor should take into account the three elements of effective teaching; providing instruction, requiring a response, and giving feedback. The most effective way is to present the needed information briefly, have the student respond and talk about what was presented, and let the student know when responses are correct or incorrect.

Provide Feedback and Reinforcement. The use of generous supplies of feedback and reinforcement are essential to effective tutoring. Most students who require tutoring (in the remedial sense) are those who have a history of failure—and thus school, if not already, is probably on the verge of becoming an adversive experience. The tutor's relationship to the student, as long as it is one of mutual respect and value, can give the learning environment a sense of warmth and caring. In the tutoring situation, the tutor should not compare one student to another; a student's progress should only be compared to his or her own past performances. Progress, no matter how slight, should always be presented in as positive terms as possible. Tutoring sessions should be kept reasonably short, depending on the student and the student's needs.

Advantages of Tutoring. Tutoring is one of the most personable forms of individualized instruction. It is geared to meet the needs or specific difficulties of each student. The attention given to students is generally unmatched by any other method of instruction. Bernstein (1959) reviewed over 200 articles and found that all the tutoring procedures appeared to generate positive results. The effects of tutoring, when peers are involved in the process, has been desirable for both the tutor and the student. Gage and Berliner (1984) indicate that the effects are positive in terms of cognitive objectives (e.g., scores on achievement tests) and affective objectives (e.g., self-esteem).

Cohen, Kulik, and Kulik (1982), in a meta-analysis of 65 studies examining tutoring in elementary or secondary school classrooms, found:

1. The examination performance of students who were tutored was better than those who were not tutored.
2. Tutored students express more positive attitudes toward the subject matter being taught.
3. Programs which use peer tutors also had positive effects on those children who serve as tutors.
4. In addition, the peer tutors gained a better understanding of the subject they were tutoring.

In summary, Cohen et al. (1982) concluded:

> This meta-analysis confirms some things that have been suspected about tutoring. It shows, as many commentators have suggested, that tutoring benefits both tutors and tutees on both cognitive and affective levels. In addition, it specifies the average strength of tutoring effects, and it identifies the settings and conditions where effects are strongest. (p. 247)

Finally, Vernon and Teldman (1973) found that students who have tutors produce performance that is superior to that of students who study the same material alone. Bloom (1984) indicated that the average student under tutoring outperformed 98% of the students who were not tutored.

Disadvantages of Tutoring.   There really are no disadvantages to tutoring in terms of learning. There are some disadvantages in terms of the time and cost involved. Bloom (1984) indicated that tutoring, in spite of all of its advantages, can lead to more favorable treatment of some students over others. Thus, he cautioned teachers to provide favorable conditions for learning for all students by increasing the emphasis on higher mental process learning.

Programmed Instruction and Computer-Assisted Instruction

Programmed instruction first came on the educational scene around 1954 as a new and promising approach that would cure all the ills and inade-

something), aids remedial instruction, and serves to enrich other in-
uction. Gage and Berliner (1984) suggested that CAI provides the fol-
ving advantages to programmed instruction:

1. The information concerning the individual student's responses can
stored, retrieved, and processed statistically, for review by the teacher,
most immediately, and at the end of each lesson.
2. The information concerning groups of students can be processed
atistically in the same way.
3. A single computer can handle thousands of students via telephone
es connected to terminals that may be located thousands of miles from
e computer.
4. Information concerning the latency of the student's response can be
llected. Such information tells how much time elapsed between the
esentation of a stimulus or problem and the student's response (p. 547).

CAI's greatest advantage to the teacher is that it can save time that
ight be spent on drill. Lepper and Malone (1987) found that students
nd the use of CAI to be motivating because it is usually challenging. In
ddition, students feel a sense of personal control (e.g., they are given
oices about when to continue to more difficult problems or to a new set
f materials). Kulik, Kulik, and Cohen (1979b), in a meta-analysis of
valuations of computer-based education, found that for higher education
omputers added only a small but significant contribution to achieve-
ent. It seems that its greatest strength is for drill and practice pro-
rams.

Disadvantages of Programmed Instruction and CAI. Developing effec-
ive and efficient programs is extremely difficult, very time consuming,
nd quite costly. In addition, a study by Hoffman and Waters (1982)
ound that only students who were able to quietly concentrate, pay atten-
ion to details, memorize facts, and stay on a single task until completion
enefited from computer-assisted instructional programs. In another
tudy, Pritchard (1981) suggested that students who use computers must
ave a specific learning style that includes: (a) manual dexterity, (b)
ttention to details and accuracy, (c) an aptitude for learning visually, (d)
willingness to sit still, (e) preference to work alone, and (f) strong intu-
tive and diagnostic ability.

Lawton and Gerschner (1982), in a review of articles written from 1976
to 1982, concluded: "Overall, the data appear mixed. It is noted that some
students apparently learn from computers, that some students apparently did not learn from computers. In addition, most authors were cautious when reporting results" (p. 51).

quacies of our educational system. It was B. F. Skinner (195
entitled "The Science of Learning and the Art of Teaching,"
that education was not providing adequate opportunity to
adequate reinforcement to encourage students to learn.

The philosophy behind programmed instruction is that s
learn complex ideas if they are taught in small, progressive s
reinforced immediately for each correct response or answer.
ate knowledge of the results occurs after each step or respo
dent makes. Skinner believed that being told immediately
response was correct or incorrect would be both a powerful a
ing reward for students.

The small steps or combination of steps in a programmed
format make up a "frame" in the program. The following is a
ple of programmed learning:

1. The numbered information you are now reading is
   called a FRAME. This frame is part of a larger plan
   that helps you learn quickly and easily. You have just
   finished reading Frame   .

2. Where I work, we call the larger plan a PROGRAM. A
   program is a plan for learning. Because what you are
   about to learn has been planned, we call it a

   _____.

Some programs can be less than 100 frames, whereas others
large as several thousand frames. Each frame, however, is co
three basic sections: stimulus, response, and confirmation (
Each stimulus contains small bits of information, followed by
about the information. The student studies the information in
ulus and then records or writes the answer. Then the student c
answer in the confirmation section. In this way, a continuous ex
information occurs between the student and the program.

Computer-Assisted Instruction (CAI) provides a new dimensi
grammed instruction—the use of the computer instead of a pri
It is clear that computers can individualize instruction in ways
printed program can not. The computer can provide immediate a
individualized feedback. Through diagnostic systems, the con
able to adapt instruction to meet individual student needs. Co
can be used to teach, drill, test, evaluate, and keep records of
progress.

Advantages of Programmed Instruction and CAI.   Both prog
instruction and CAI have distinct advantages in the instructional
Programmed instruction has a major value for learning skills (i.e

quacies of our educational system. It was B. F. Skinner (1954), in a paper entitled "The Science of Learning and the Art of Teaching," who claimed that education was not providing adequate opportunity to respond or adequate reinforcement to encourage students to learn.

The philosophy behind programmed instruction is that students can learn complex ideas if they are taught in small, progressive steps and are reinforced immediately for each correct response or answer. The immediate knowledge of the results occurs after each step or response the student makes. Skinner believed that being told immediately whether a response was correct or incorrect would be both a powerful and stimulating reward for students.

The small steps or combination of steps in a programmed instruction format make up a "frame" in the program. The following is a brief example of programmed learning:

1. The numbered information you are now reading is called a FRAME. This frame is part of a larger plan that helps you learn quickly and easily. You have just finished reading Frame   *1*

2. Where I work, we call the larger plan a PROGRAM. A program is a plan for learning. Because what you are about to learn has been planned, we call it a

     _____.   *program*

Some programs can be less than 100 frames, whereas others may be as large as several thousand frames. Each frame, however, is composed of three basic sections: stimulus, response, and confirmation (response). Each stimulus contains small bits of information, followed by a question about the information. The student studies the information in the stimulus and then records or writes the answer. Then the student checks the answer in the confirmation section. In this way, a continuous exchange of information occurs between the student and the program.

Computer-Assisted Instruction (CAI) provides a new dimension to programmed instruction—the use of the computer instead of a printed text. It is clear that computers can individualize instruction in ways that the printed program can not. The computer can provide immediate as well as individualized feedback. Through diagnostic systems, the computer is able to adapt instruction to meet individual student needs. Computers can be used to teach, drill, test, evaluate, and keep records of students' progress.

Advantages of Programmed Instruction and CAI.   Both programmed instruction and CAI have distinct advantages in the instructional setting. Programmed instruction has a major value for learning skills (i.e., how to do something), aids remedial instruction, and serves to enrich other instruction. Gage and Berliner (1984) suggested that CAI provides the following advantages to programmed instruction:

1. The information concerning the individual student's responses can be stored, retrieved, and processed statistically, for review by the teacher, almost immediately, and at the end of each lesson.

2. The information concerning groups of students can be processed statistically in the same way.

3. A single computer can handle thousands of students via telephone lines connected to terminals that may be located thousands of miles from the computer.

4. Information concerning the latency of the student's response can be collected. Such information tells how much time elapsed between the presentation of a stimulus or problem and the student's response (p. 547).

CAI's greatest advantage to the teacher is that it can save time that might be spent on drill. Lepper and Malone (1987) found that students find the use of CAI to be motivating because it is usually challenging. In addition, students feel a sense of personal control (e.g., they are given choices about when to continue to more difficult problems or to a new set of materials). Kulik, Kulik, and Cohen (1979b), in a meta-analysis of evaluations of computer-based education, found that for higher education computers added only a small but significant contribution to achievement. It seems that its greatest strength is for drill and practice programs.

Disadvantages of Programmed Instruction and CAI. Developing effective and efficient programs is extremely difficult, very time consuming, and quite costly. In addition, a study by Hoffman and Waters (1982) found that only students who were able to quietly concentrate, pay attention to details, memorize facts, and stay on a single task until completion benefited from computer-assisted instructional programs. In another study, Pritchard (1981) suggested that students who use computers must have a specific learning style that includes: (a) manual dexterity, (b) attention to details and accuracy, (c) an aptitude for learning visually, (d) willingness to sit still, (e) preference to work alone, and (f) strong intuitive and diagnostic ability.

Lawton and Gerschner (1982), in a review of articles written from 1976 to 1982, concluded: "Overall, the data appear mixed. It is noted that some students apparently learn from computers, that some students apparently did not learn from computers. In addition, most authors were cautious when reporting results" (p. 51).

SUMMARY

Individual instruction's main objective is to adapt instruction to the individual student. During the past several decades, individualized instruction has gained in popularity and has become an attractive alternative to traditional methods of instruction. In this chapter, the rationale for individualized instruction and its theoretical base were discussed. Eight principles of reinforcement were discussed as providing the foundation for individualized instruction.

Several of the most commonly used methods of individualized instruction were discussed. The Personalized System of Instruction (PSI), or Keller plan, is probably the most widely used individualized method of instruction. It was developed to make learning more efficient and reinforcing, and has five major features: (a) mastery, (b) self-pacing, (c) written materials, (d) proctors, and (e) lectures. The major advantage of the PSI method is that it allows learning to occur in a positive environment. It is well suited for almost any discipline; and it has been shown to be extremely cost effective and to produce higher achievement than the same course taught using a traditional method of instruction. The PSI method is, however, extremely time consuming to develop and requires a strong commitment by the instructor.

Mastery learning's main defining characteristic is its use of criterion levels for performance. The mastery approach requires frequent testing and multiple instructional strategies, and its four main characteristics are: (a) cues, (b) participation, (c) feedback, and (d) reinforcement. Mastery learning has proven to be a very successful method for increasing achievement, although the results are not completely conclusive. Its main disadvantages are: It takes much of the responsibility for learning away from students, does not place a fixed amount of time on learning, holds back the faster students, commits a large portion of the instructional resources to the slower learner, and assumes that learning is equal among most students.

Tutoring is defined as one-on-one instruction. It is often associated with remedial instruction and requires little or no training on the part of the tutor. It is the job of the tutor to diagnose the student's learning problem and then to remedy the problem by providing appropriate instruction. Tutoring requires a high degree of feedback as well as reinforcement. Tutoring is, by far, the most personable form of individualized instruction. Tutoring not only provides benefits to the student being tutored, but to the tutor as well. There are few disadvantages to tutoring except that it is time consuming and costly. It can also lead to providing some students with a disportionate amount of time as well as more favorable treatment.

Programmed instruction and computer-assisted instruction (CAI) are both based on the idea that learning should occur in small, progressive steps with lots of reinforcement for correct responses. Programmed instruction and CAI are extremely effective for teaching skills. They can also save the teacher a great amount of time by allowing students to work on their own. Programmed instruction and CAI are not easy to develop. Their major limitation is that students who have difficulty focusing on details have little success with programmed instruction or CAI.

ACKNOWLEDGMENT

This chapter was funded in part by a George Holmes Research Fellowship—University of Nebraska, Lincoln.

REFERENCES

Arlin, M. (1984a). Time variability in mastery learning. *American Educational Research Journal, 21,* 103–120.
Arlin, M. (1984b). Time, equality, and mastery learning. *Review of Educational Research, 54,* 65–86.
Bernstein, A. L. (1959). Library research: A study in remedial arithmetic. *School Science and Mathematics, 59,* 185–195.
Block, J. H. (Ed.). (1971). *Mastery learning.* New York: Holt, Rinehart & Winston.
Block, J. H. (1974). Mastery learning in the classroom: An overview of recent research. In J. H. Block (Ed.), *Schools, society, and mastery learning* (pp. 26–29). New York: Holt, Rinehart & Winston.
Block, J. H., & Anderson, L. W. (1975). *Mastery learning in classroom instruction.* New York: MacMillan.
Block, J. H., & Burns, R. B. (1976). Mastery learning. In L. S. Schulman (Ed.), *Review of research in education (Vol. 4,* pp. 3–49). Itasca, IL: F. E. Peacock.
Bloom, B. S. (1968). Learning for mastery. *Evaluation Comment. 1, 2.* Los Angeles: University of California, Center for the Study of Evaluation.
Bloom, B. S. (1976). *Human characteristics and school learning.* New York: McGraw Hill.
Bloom, B. S. (1984). The search for methods of group instruction as effective as one-to-one tutoring. *Educational Leadership, 41,* 4–17.
Boylan, H. R. (1980). PSI: A survey of users and their implementation practices. *Journal of Personalized Instruction, 4,* 40–43.
Burns, R. B. (1979). Mastery learning—Does it work? *Educational Leadership, 37,* 110–113.
Cohen, P. A., Kulik, J. A., & Kulik, C. C. (1982). Educational outcomes of tutoring: A meta-analysis of findings. *American Educational Research Journal, 19,* 237–248.
Carroll, J. B. (1963). A model of school learning. *Teachers College Record, 64,* 723–733.
Cox, W. F., Jr., & Dunn, T. G. (1979). Mastery learning: A psychological trap? *Educational Psychologist, 14,* 24–29.
Gage, N. L., & Berliner, D. C. (1984). *Educational psychology* (3rd ed.). Boston: Houghton Mifflin.

Gray, P. L., Buerkel-Rothfuss, N., & Yerby, J. (1986). A comparison between PSI-based and lecture-recitation formats of instruction in the introductory speech communication course. *Communication Education, 35,* 111–125.

Heun, L. R., Heun, R. E., & Ratcliff, L. L. (1976). Individualizing speech communication instruction. *Communication Education, 25,* 185–190.

Hoffman, J. L., & Waters, K. (1982). Some effects of student personality on success with computer-assisted instruction. *Educational Technology, 22,* 20–21.

Hyman, J. S., & Cohen, A. (1979). Learning for mastery: Ten conclusions after 15 years and 3,000 schools. *Educational Leadership, 37,* 104–109.

Keller, F. S. (1968). Good-bye teacher. *Journal of Applied Behavior Analysis, 1,* 79–89.

Keller, F. S., & Sherman, J. G. (Eds.). (1974). *Keller plan handbook.* Menlo Park, CA: W. A. Benjamin.

Kulik, J. A., Kulik, C. C., & Cohen, P. A. (1979a). A meta-analysis of outcome studies of Keller's Personalized System of Instruction, *American Psychologist, 34,* 307–318.

Kulik, J. A., Kulik, C. C., & Cohen, P. A. (1979b). Research on audiotutorial instruction. A meta-analysis of comparative studies. *Research in Higher Education, 1,* 321–341.

Kulik, J. A., Kulik, C. C., & Smith, B. B. (1976). Research on Personalized System of Instruction. *Journal of Programmed Learning and Educational Technology, 13,* 23–30.

Lawton, J., & Gerschner, V. T. (1982). A review of the literature on attitudes towards computers and computerized instruction. *Journal of Research and Development in Education, 16,* 50–55.

Lepper, M. R., & Malone, T. W. (1987). Intrinsic motivation and instructional effectiveness in computer-based education. In R. E. Snow & M. J. Farr (Eds.), *Aptitude, learning and instruction: III. Conative and affective process analyses* (pp. 255–286). Hillsdale, NJ: Lawrence Erlbaum Associates.

Muller, D. J. (1973). The mastery model and some alternative models of classroom instruction and evaluation: An analysis. *Educational Technology, 13,* 5–10.

Muller, D. J. (1976). Mastery learning: Partly boon, partly boondoggle. *Teachers College Record, 78,* 41–52.

Pritchard, W. J., Jr. (1981). Instructional computing in 2001: A scenario. *Phi Delta Kappan, 62,* 322–325.

Scott, M. D., & Young, T. J. (1976). Personalizing communication instruction. *Communication Education, 25,* 211–221.

Seiler, W. J. (1983). PSI: An attractive alternative for the basic speech communication course. *Communication Education, 32,* 15–28.

Seiler, W. J., Schuelke, L. D., & Lieb-Brilhart, B. (1984). *Communication for the contemporary classroom.* New York: Holt, Rinehart & Winston.

Sherman, J. G. (1974). *Personalized System of Instruction: Forty-one germinal papers.* Menlo Park, CA: W. A. Benjamin.

Skinner, B. F. (1954). The science of learning and the art of teaching. *Harvard Educational Review, 24,* 86–97.

Skinner, B. F. (1969). *Contingencies of reinforcement: A theoretical analysis.* New York: Appleton-Century-Crofts.

Slavin, R. E. (1987a). Mastery learning reconsidered. *Review of Educational Research, 57,* 175–214.

Slavin, R. E. (1987b). Taking the mystery out of mastery: A response to Guskey, Anderson, and Burns. *Review of Educational Research, 57,* 231–235.

Vernon, L. A., & Teldman, R. S. (1973). Learning through tutoring. *Journal of Experimental Education, 42,* 1–5.

25

Selected Active Learning Strategies

Jody D. Nyquist
Donald H. Wulff
University of Washington

Using the instructional strategies of writing, oral presentations, small groups, case studies, games, simulations, roleplays, and field study assignments requires careful instructor preparation and clear instructions to the students. Because the role of the student often changes from listener, notetaker, and occasional contributor to a discussion to that of leader, presenter, author, actor, and researcher, students must understand clearly the task and instructor expectations for their performance. The strategies described in this chapter include a variety of active learning approaches that have been successful in teaching communication content.

WRITING

Communication instructors have long used writing assignments in their courses. In spite of facing the frequently amazed questioner who queries, "You write in a speech class?", communication instructors have steadfastly upheld the unity of the two communication arts. The uses of writing in communication courses, depending on the instructors' goals, have ranged from the writing of speeches and keeping of journals of communication behavior to the making of field study notes and reports. Typically, however, the *primary* use of writing in communication classes, as in other disciplines, has been evaluative in nature (Britton, Burgess, Martin, McLeod, & Rosen, 1975). Most often, communication instructors' uses of written assignments consist of essays or term papers, essay tests, and critiques of books and articles designed to see how close the writer can come to capturing in recognizable form what the instructor has been presenting or assigning in readings. Although this is a valuable use of writing for assessment purposes, writing can be used in broader ways, according to Knoblauch and Brannon (1983), to stimulate "conceptual involvement and investigation in order to encourage the growth of students' intellectual capacities" (p. 471). This intellectual growth is a goal to be achieved and can be fostered as an instructor evaluates a finished text, comments during a revision process, or responds to ungraded student writing.

Assignments that Promote Student-Teacher Dialogue Following Writing

Assessing student understanding by the assignment of essays, essay tests, critiques of books and articles, and term papers is common in the arts and sciences as well as in the humanities and social sciences. Often in communication courses, the student writes and turns in the paper; the instructor reads, evaluates, and returns the paper. Typically, a considerable portion of a student's final grade depends on this kind of evaluation of a written product.

Although writing assignments are used frequently for this purpose, students often encounter difficulties in producing a product that meets instructor expectations. Too often, students feel as though they are engaged in a mysterious treasure hunt to find out what the instructor wants. This problem can be eliminated by explicit, carefully written instructions followed by discussions for clarification held before the assignment is undertaken. Because the aim of writing to learn is to promote intellectual growth through a dialogical relationship between the writer and the teacher/reader, the quality of the instructor's response, the commenting on student papers, becomes critical. The instructor must deal with the ideas presented primarily as a reader trying to understand the writer rather than as a judge measuring against an imaginary ideal product. Hopefully, the instructor's comments will lead students to rethink their conclusions, reconceptualize when appropriate, and experience the exchange of each other's best thinking. Unfortunately, obstacles to this process lurk on both sides; instructor comments can be terse and ambiguous, and students too often look only at a grade on a returned paper and ignore or give little time to the instructor's comments. In addition, this process leaves the instructor with only one role—evaluator of a finished text. Instructors' postwriting responses provide no opportunity to interact with the student at his or her conceptualization stage—the time when instructor comments can be most helpful.

Assignments That Promote Instructor–Student Dialogue During Writing

Composition theorists, for the last 15 years, have advocated a view of writing as process rather than finished text. This kind of writing requires, at a minimum, a four-stage process: (a) student drafting of an initial document, (b) instructor response, (c) student revision, and, finally, (d) instructor response and evaluation of a finished product. This "writing as process" view has been advocated as a means of enabling students to "write to learn."

As Knoblauch and Brannon (1983) pointed out:

> The concern is to create intellectual dialogue as a way of stimulating more learning, to use writing as a means of personal discovery but also as a means of communicating the honest extent of the writer's understanding, including difficulties, inadequacies of insight, imperfect or unproductive connections among ideas and information so that a more experienced learner can provide through reinforcing commentary some new directions for exploration. (p. 471)

Using the draft/response/revision/response process as a way of clarifying ideas and guiding student learning provides opportunity to interact with the student early in the student's thinking. The instructor can respond to analytical errors, lack of student understanding of basic concepts or philosophies, omissions of important information, and so on. More importantly, this instructor–student dialogue can encourage the pursuit of specific lines of inquiry, provide missing information, challenge and expand on students' tentative thinking, and encourage the revision process. This process—student draft, instructor response, student revision, and instructor response—allows the instructor and the student to work together to develop a better finished product based on the feedback/revision effort and enables the student to value revision as a way to enhance thinking rather than as a required rewriting, which is often viewed as a punishment for an inferior product.

Assignments That Promote Instructor–Student Dialogue Without Emphasis on Assessment

Although all writing should promote personal growth, communication instructors can employ specific writing assignments to enable students to explore various concepts without concern for assessment—in other words, to write with the primary goal being that of personal discovery. Writing assignments, not evaluated in grade form, offer a view of how students are processing information so that an instructor can identify snarls in students' thinking and make necessary adjustments in sequencing, repetition of instruction, reteaching, and so on.

This point can be illustrated with an example of a journal assignment given to a student in a course on contemporary rhetorical theory. The assignment was to compare and contrast Peter Ramus' view of rhetoric in his reformed curriculum with Francis Bacon's view of rhetoric in his *Advancement of Learning*. At the beginning of the term, before students have frameworks to apply to the text, a student's entry might look something like this:

> I'm really not sure about this "stuff." Seemingly, Ramus's purpose is to classify all knowledge into some neat and complete category system. And his scheme for dividing knowledge seems to work from what I can understand, but can we divide all knowledge into these neat little boxes? Professor Campbell's question about whether today's textbook is an example of a contemporary attempt to do that really got me to thinking. Ramus's classification system sure makes for dull reading just as many textbooks do. But how else do we make sense of knowledge? But how could one ever categorize, for that matter, all there is to know? I wish I had Ramus's level of confidence about thinking I knew the truth. Was there just simply less to know in his time? Or does this classical model of knowledge allow one to feel like the truth is knowable and can be completely classified? Somehow it seems to make for clearer thinking in some ways. But then Bacon's point is important. The illusion of completeness may be the price you pay. *Partito*— the false allure of dividing things neatly? Are classification systems sterile? But really what are techniques of insinuation? Bacon seems to argue for "ideas in progress." He never seems to finish—always more to be known. Clearly, his thinking reflects more closely that of today, but what about the core of knowledge that everyone says college students of the '80's are lacking? What is the source of our deficiency and does it have anything to do with how you think about knowledge?

Such a journal entry provides an opportunity for the instructor to respond to uncertainties, misconceptions, and confusions at an early stage in the student's thinking. Equally important, however, the response can include suggestions that will enable the student to think more deeply about the subject matter. John Campbell, Communication Professor at the University of Washington, suggested such a response to the student:

> You are on the right track in underscoring that Ramus' principal interest was in classification. When you consider the "dullness" of his system, though, you need to think about the alternative. Keep in mind those overlapping charts about the procedures of rhetoric and dialectic we passed out and discussed in class and how the students in those days were expected to know all the details of both rhetoric and dialectic by heart! Think how much

easier it would be to memorize Ramus' system. The ease with which it could be memorized was its appeal. But also consider the price of this simplification. Is there a difference between making a purely logical argument ("dialectic") and thinking a subject through from the standpoint of an audience ("rhetoric")? What is substantively lost in one's understanding of rhetoric if, on Ramus' system, "invention" is given to dialectic and rhetoric is left with only "style" and "delivery?" (Have you ever had a textbook which risked compromising its subject in an effort to make everything perfectly clear? Or, outside of the classroom have you ever encountered the use of "clarity" as a technique of distortion?) On Bacon I think you are onto something important and you could profit by carrying your thought further. How does Bacon provide a keen sense of order—but without creating the illusion of completeness?

Not only is this type of writing assignment useful in teaching rhetorical theory, but it is a powerful strategy for teaching all communication concepts. Ungraded writing assignments can be used in various ways to teach important information. Using a suggestion from Knoblauch and Brannon (1983), for example, imagine being the instructor for a basic introductory communication class with perhaps 250 students in it—clearly a difficult setting for assigning formal writing experiences. The class section might begin with a writing period in which students analyze or respond in some way to a previous day's homework assignment with a focus on identifying areas that need clarification or questions that the reading material may have raised. Following this opening exercise, students could exchange papers and respond to each other's writing, enabling students on a daily basis to be writers, readers, and respondents to peer thinking and writing over the intellectual substance of the class. The students could then orally ask questions that the instructor would answer before the day's lecture begins. Or students might work in small groups to respond in writing to part of a day's lecture during either the middle or end of the class session. Group papers require students to draft arguments, positions or explanations, read others' writing and respond, and then come to consensus about how the group's ideas can be best represented in written form. Such writing experiences can be used to establish a dialogue between instructors and students that leads to student awareness of substantive issues in the course, personal coherence or disagreement with the ideas presented, and improved levels of intellectual commitment and penetration. The instructor, in turn, gains access to students' reasoning ability, understanding of the connections students make when dealing with the course material, and areas that remain confusing and puzzling.

Becoming adept at using writing as an instructional strategy to accomplish specific goals requires careful thought and planning and cannot be covered in sufficient depth in this chapter. The articles at the end of the chapter (see SUPPLEMENTARY READING) are included as ideas for further study and classroom application. Writing, when used as a tool for learning communication content, provides a powerful method for student assimilation of information and application of communication concepts.

STUDENT ORAL PRESENTATIONS

As would be expected, student oral presentations represent one of the instructional strategies most often used by communication instructors. Clearly, classes in public speaking, interpersonal communication, oral interpretation, and debate are primarily student performance courses. To practice and exhibit mastery of the content of the course, the student must have ample opportunity to "try on" effective behaviors under supervision and be provided systematic feedback from the course instructor and members of the class.

But student oral performances are in themselves a powerful strategy for teaching knowledge of all kinds. Like writing, oral performance assignments are too often used solely for evaluation of a student's proficiency, in this case competency in speaking. A broader conception of student oral performances would enable communication instructors and teachers of other disciplines to recognize the opportunity for establishing an oral dialogical relationship with students as a vehicle for teaching any set of truths, concepts, or understandings. Such presentations enable instructors to view students' thought processes, cognitive connections, frameworks, or schema used for processing information when students must tell others, in an orderly, coherent, audience-adapted way, about new insights or knowledge.

Student individual or panel presentations, debates, readings, and role plays provide effective ways of covering curricula (students can lecture too!) in courses at all levels. In fact, it seems puzzling that so often upper division and graduate communication courses only require students to write when all in the discipline agree on the power and influence of the oral communication act.

In a rhetoric course that covers speeches of historical figures, for example, students can conduct research to enable themselves to sketch the age in which the person lived, including strong influences and societal values—in other words, the context in which the person wrote and spoke. A   presentation to classmates attempting to explain how the histor-
             on thought about specific issues of the period in which he or she
              clearly demonstrate each student's grasp of course material.
              ber responses to the presentation will further inform the in-
              ut student mastery of the subject matter.

Another example might be an upper division course in children's communication development. Such a course can be powerfully taught by assigning students to work together in groups to research, synthesize, and report to the class on various topics such as the effects of media on thinking skills of children, the effects of friendship groups on children's communication development, communication strategies that facilitate children's language development, and so on—topics the instructor may be unable to accommodate within the regular lecture schedule. (Such presentations also gain valuable "student time on task" outside class sessions in terms of research and preparation time required from the individual or groups of students as they prepare for the classroom presentation.) An additional important consideration is the desire of students to perform well in front of their peers, a motivational force not always accompanying a written assignment, which most typically is seen only by the instructor.

Debate offers another effective approach for teaching course content. Students might be asked to debate the idea of the "classical bias" and its influence on our interpretation of the medieval period in a rhetoric class, or the interpretation of Antigone in the context of being a woman during the classical period in an oral interpretation course, or the differences between Stewart and D'Angelo's (1988) and Miller and Steinberg's (1975) definitions of interpersonal communication. Obviously, the instructor must specify the rules for such debates to insure that the instructional content of the debate becomes the primary goal of all speakers. Informal debates between pairs of students who hold opposing points of view gained from the reading of course materials can motivate other students to become informed, analyze the perspectives, and form their own opinions.

Again, as with writing, the instructor must attend carefully to providing both explicit instructions for the oral assignment and content-specific oral or written feedback in response to the student presentations. When used as an instructional strategy, oral performance may or may not be evaluated for a grade. The importance of establishing an instructor–student dialogue should be a major concern. Student oral presentations provide access to the ways in which students are processing course material long before midterm or final examinations provide a formal evaluation. The instructor then has the opportunity to clarify misunderstandings and offer new ways of thinking at a formative stage of the student's mastery of the course content.

Student oral presentations covering communication material provide unique and appealing ways of promoting student commitment and mastery of material. Some communication instructors routinely use student speeches, panel discussions, debates, lectures, interviews, student readings, and role plays to teach communication content. The Sonnenschein and Whitehurst (1984) studies on the importance that critiquing plays in the mastery of information, however, suggest that students need more opportunities to listen to and critique others' presentations. Communication instructors should understand and appreciate the value of such oral presentations for teaching any kind of subject matter. Student presentations are not an abdication of the instructor's responsibilities but class time well spent for both speakers and listeners.

From basic performance courses to graduate seminars, the oral performance strategy is powerful for teaching communication content. Communication instructors should provide the leadership for the use of this instructional strategy both in their own courses and in courses taught by colleagues in other disciplines.

SMALL GROUPS

Although *small group* has been defined in a variety of ways, using small groups for instructional purposes typically requires four to six students working together to further their understanding of the course content. When learning in the classroom focuses on working together to share thoughts and ideas, the use of small groups can be an effective way to increase cooperative student-to-student communication. Groups may be used in a variety of forms and can be established on a temporary basis during one class period or on a more permanent basis for long-term course projects.

Small groups are most often used successfully when an instructor wants students to think about and develop understanding of content in particular ways. Although students can glean factual information from their small-group interaction (Hill, 1969), small groups are more commonly an opportunity for students to think critically about basic content. Presumably, in order to function most effectively in a small-group setting, students must have prior knowledge of topics to be discussed. After students have encountered the content in their assigned reading or in class lectures, an instructor may then use small groups to achieve objectives related to understanding, application, analysis, synthesis, or evaluation of the content.

At the most basic level, an instructor might use groups to help students reinforce their understanding of course content. At the beginning of a class period in a theories class, for instance, students could be asked to form groups to discuss an assigned reading about rules theory in interpersonal communication. If a general goal is to increase student understanding of this particular content, the instructor might have students in the small groups define important terms, arrive at an overall understanding of the reading, discuss major topics from the reading, apply the subject matter, and evaluate it. This process is particularly useful prior to a teacher-led class discussion, as it provides motivation for students to think about the content, participate in class discussion, and ask questions about the information they do not understand.

If, on the other hand, the instructor wants students to develop problem-solving skills as well as master the content, the students can be given a group task to solve. A description of communication difficulties between a supervisor and an employee may be presented in an organizational communication class, for example, to be worked through by group effort. Although there are a variety of specific frameworks to use to guide students in resolving the issues suggested by the events described, a common framework suggests that problem-solving groups should identify the problem, discuss its causes and effects, identify criteria that an appropriate solution must meet, propose potential solutions, apply the criteria to select the best solution, and discuss how the solution would be implemented.

When instructors plan and structure activities carefully, small groups can provide a number of advantages. For example, they can provide variation from the more traditional method of lecturing. Especially if a class becomes too "teacher-centered" or too focused on an instructor talking, small groups can provide a way for a greater number of students to be simultaneously involved in the class and to take more responsibility for their learning. In addition, working in small groups tends to increase students' motivation, partly because students enjoy the opportunity to interact with their peers but also because students care about how their peers perceive them. Furthermore, small-group discussions provide opportunities for students to compare their ideas with the ideas of their peers. Social comparison theory (Festinger, 1954; Suls & Miller, 1977) suggests that people seek to evaluate themselves against others. Hearing and expressing ideas in groups allows students to make such social comparisons. Another advantage is that if students use specific frameworks as they talk about content in their small groups, they can learn a way of thinking about content or a way of approaching problem solving. Certainly, if the instructional objectives include enhancing students' communication skills, group discussion provides opportunities to improve competency in expressing, supporting, and evaluating ideas orally. Finally, there is evidence to suggest that students retain information longer when they have an opportunity to verbalize it, particularly when they verbalize it to their peers (Webb, 1982). Bargh and Schul (1980) suggested that a student who verbalizes information to others may sometimes assume a teaching role that permits him or her "to see the issue from new perspectives, enabling him or her to see previously unthought of new relationships between the elements. It may be this building of new relationships that facilitates a better fundamental grasp of the material" (p. 595).

Despite their potential advantages, small groups can be disastrous if an instructor does not take precautions to plan and implement them carefully. Because a full elaboration of the ways small groups function is beyond the scope of this discussion, a list of additional resources is included at the end of the chapter. The following section, however, can provide a basis for further reading about some of the fundamental issues in using small groups in instruction.

Objectives

Group activities should be chosen because of the specific objectives that need to be accomplished. Specifying the outcomes of group activities is particularly important because of the potential incongruity between the goals to be accomplished through the use of small groups and the way learning is measured as a result of students' participation in small group activities. If, for example, the goal is to have students use the group process so that each student can develop an individual understanding, a set of skills, or a way of thinking, then it is appropriate to evaluate learning in the class by measuring the progress of individual students. If, on the other hand, a major goal in having students work in groups is to solve problems or generate ideas as a group, then it is incongruent to measure student learning on an individual basis. Rather, students should be evaluated on the basis of their ability to work as a group. Small groups can be used in a variety of ways in the classroom when the measurement of learning is not at issue. However, unless instructors are very specific about the goals to be achieved through the use of small groups, they may create inconsistency between the use of the method and evaluation measures in the course.

Task

A key prerequisite to students' successful participation in groups is a clearly defined task. Simply telling students to "get together and discuss" or to "solve the problem" is not adequate. At the very minimum, instructors will have to take time to create a rationale for the task, describe what students will do in their groups, and clarify expectations for the final product of each group. Having students work within an assignment or problem-solving framework (such as those previously discussed) is a helpful way to set up small-group tasks.

Student Preparation

Students are far less likely to succeed in small-group activity if they have not prepared properly. For example, if an instructor determines that a goal for students in an oral interpretation class is to generate alternative interpretations of Sylvia Plath's poem, "Daddy," it is essential that students prepare for the discussion by reading the poem carefully before they come to class, or at least two major difficulties can result. An obvious result is that students may waste valuable class time. A disadvantage of small-group activities in the classroom is that they take more time than simply "telling" students. Making sure students complete the necessary individual preparation in advance, however, can save valuable in class time. A second problem that can arise from lack of student preparation is a digression to simple "pooling of ignorance." This problem is particularly acute when using small groups to encourage critical student thought, because the instructor does not always have access to the students' thinking.

Student Roles

Active participation in small groups requires interpersonal skills that all students may not possess. Each person within a group brings to the task a variety of personality variables that create interpersonal relationships and affect the levels of participation, the satisfaction, and, ultimately, the outcomes of the group. It behooves the instructor, then, to think about the kinds of roles that emerge within small groups and ways to help groups to function with those roles. Instructors may want to talk to students about the various task, maintenance, and personal roles that group members might assume and about the stages through which a group will progress as a result of those roles. It is also helpful to clarify for students what the use of small groups requires from them in terms of preparation, participation, and debriefing.

Instructor Role

The use of small groups does not relinquish the instructor's responsibility. It does require, however, that the instructor function as a facilitator of learning rather than as a source of knowledge. As indicated earlier, the role requires thorough planning and thoughtful description of the task to be completed. In addition, it requires answering questions for specific groups and, occasionally, meeting with groups to facilitate progress toward specified outcomes. Just as important, though, the role requires summary and synthesis. Undergraduates, particularly, can be disenchanted if they do not see why their efforts are important, and simply telling them what they are supposed to have learned is not adequate. If they do not perceive the instructor "using" the information they generate in groups, students are likely to feel that they have wasted their time. They need to see direct links between the group activity and the content for which they feel they are responsible. Small-group activities must be planned, then, so there is adequate time at the end of a class period for debriefing the activity. If a single class period is inadequate, the instructor may have to get into the habit of allowing a few minutes at the beginning of each subsequent class to do the necessary summary and synthesis.

Atmosphere

The success of small groups as an instructional strategy depends, at least partially, on the atmosphere in the classroom. Typically, students are more likely to participate willingly when the instructor has established an atmosphere of trust and respect. Students then know that they can express ideas openly, that their individual ideas will be valued, and that they can receive specific reinforcement and feedback on the ideas they generate in small groups. It is essential, of course, that members of a group know each other and that they are able to arrange themselves so they can see and hear everyone else in the group with minimal distractions.

As with other strategies, a particular approach to the use of small groups can flourish only if it has been carefully selected, implemented, and debriefed. Getting students to work effectively in small groups is not an easy task, and initially failure is a real possibility. However, instructors can meet the challenges of this particular instructional method if they recognize that the use of small groups in instruction requires just as much planning and preparation as formal presentations but accomplishes slightly different objectives.

CASE STUDY METHOD

Case study, or what is referred to as the case method of instruction, has emerged as a dynamic instructional strategy offering great potential as an active learning approach for university students. Closely identified with the Harvard Business School, which has described the method as an "active, discussion-oriented learning mode, disciplined by case problems drawn from the complexity of real life" (Christensen & Hansen, 1987, p.

16), the method requires active oral participation by students led by instructors utilizing broad repertoires of facilitative behaviors. The development of the case study method has evolved from the use of initial snapshots of company problems at a given point in time presented in narrative form, which were used to trigger discussions, to what was described more recently (Christensen & Hansen, 1987) as "complex educational instruments, based on carefully designed research plans and intensive field research" (p. 26). Roland Christensen, a primary architect of the development of the case study method of instruction, which has been adopted by many professional schools including law, medicine, public affairs, and others and applied in English, political science, engineering, etcetera, suggested the following definition (Christensen & Hansen, 1987):

> A case is a partial historical, clinical study of a situation which has confronted a practicing administrator or managerial group. Presented in narrative form to encourage student involvement, it provides data—substantive and process—essential to an analysis of a specific situation, for the framing of alternative action programs, and for their implementation recognizing the complexity and ambiguity of the practical world. (p. 27)

In communication, the case study method appears to be used most often in courses in interpersonal, organizational, small-group, and instructional communication. Relevant examples include incidents of blocked or ineffectual communication within a firm or organization, teacher–student confrontations in a classroom setting, interpersonal conflicts between a supervisor and a subordinate, or the difficult deliberations of a community group attempting to prevent the construction of a high-rise apartment house. Unfortunately, the term *case study* for many communication instructors currently refers to any description of an incident that can be used for discussion purposes. These incidents range from one-paragraph, skimpy outlines of communication exchanges to sophisticated cases that may come in as many as 15 or more installments, tracing a problem over a period of time.

The most effective cases require application of particular course content and cannot be adequately solved unless the course material has been mastered. Usually, they require students to do extensive research on the problem, including determining the severity and consequences of the incident described in the case, precedents used in similar cases, possible solutions, ramifications of the adoption of various plans, and implementation considerations.

Case studies must reflect an appropriate sequencing of levels of difficulty from simple to complex. Instructors need to provide students with explicit instruction about the case study method, including how they should prepare for the discussion, what is expected of them during the discussion, and how they will be evaluated. As McKeachie (1986) pointed out:

> As in classic studies in discrimination learning in the laboratory, teachers attempting to help students learn complex discriminations and principles in problem solving need to choose initial cases in which the differences are clear and extreme before moving to more subtle, complex cases. Typically, one of the goals of the case study method is to teach students to select important factors from a tangle of less important ones that may, nevertho less, form a context to be considered. One does not learn such skills by being in perpetual confusion, but rather by success in solving more and more difficult problems. (p. 173)

In addition, the instructor will have to prepare carefully by analyzing the case in precise detail and creating questions that will elicit student responses that can be built upon to provide opportunity for the collective solving of the problem. Use of the method will require that an instructor concentrate very carefully on contributions of students and how they are advancing the thought line toward an eventual resolution of the problem based on adequate theory and proven communication principles.

Generally, instructors should begin by using a few cases in their classes and then assess student reception and conceptual achievement to guide subsequent applications. Too often, instructors announce an entire course as being a "case study course" and are driven to find or develop cases no matter what they are attempting to teach. Case study method, like any other instructional strategy, should be used only when it provides the best vehicle for attaining the goals of the unit or course.

Professors utilizing the case study method report heightened student engagement in the learning process, more effective application of problem-solving skills, and increased instructor satisfaction with the quality of the resulting classroom interaction. Difficulties with the method include the lack of available high-quality cases that demonstrate the communication principles being taught and the enormous time investment required to work through the case study process. Materials at the end of this chapter (see Supplementary Reading section) are included to assist instructors to use the case study method.

INSTRUCTIONAL GAMES, SIMULATIONS, AND ROLE PLAYS

Special kinds of interactive classroom methods include instructional games, simulations, and role plays. Instructional games are activities that require students to adhere to a specific set of rules and compete as a means of achieving prespecified objectives. Such games have been used quite widely in communication classrooms in the last two decades in activities designed to enhance skills in debate, discussion, public speaking, persuasion and intercultural, interpersonal, mass, and nonverbal communication (Dickson & Patterson, 1981; Weatherly, 1974; Weaver, 1974). Although numerous games are available for purchase and use in communication instruction (Weatherly, 1974), often instructional games are short activities developed by the instructor. For instance, if instructors want students to appreciate the importance of verbal communication in cooperative activities, they might divide the class into groups, give each group the pieces of a puzzle and ask groups to put the puzzle together without talking. The first group to complete the task wins. Depending on available resources, instructors may develop or purchase more involved games to teach complex concepts. Regardless of design, however, a game typically provides a way of achieving important course objectives, abides by a specified set of rules, and produces winners and losers (Dindia-Webb, 1979).

Simulations may differ from games inasmuch as simulations do not have to include the element of competition and the emergence of a winner. Rockler (1978) has defined a simulation as "a representation of a real-world event in a reduced and compressed form that is dynamic, safe, and efficient" (p. 288). Although there are numerous simulations available for teaching communication (Larson, 1978; Ruben & Budd, 1975), instructors can also design a variety of simulations for use in their teaching. For example, if, in an interpersonal communication class, students are to examine the kinds of disclosure that exists when people meet for the first time at a social event, the instructor might construct a situation in which class members mingle at a cocktail hour that a boss provides for all new employees. If instructors decide to design their own simulations for class use, there are several available sources that can assist in that process (Dindia-Webb, 1979; Horn, 1973; Kozma, Belle, & Williams, 1978).

Like simulations, role plays may attempt to simulate a real-life situation; however, role plays are often less structured than simulations or games. As Friedrich (1981) suggested, "Students are placed in relatively unstructured situations in which they must improvise behaviors to fit with their concepts of the roles to which they have been assigned" (p. 158). Thus, if in a course in communication education the instructor is working to increase future teachers' repertoire of ways to respond to a student who challenges a grade, one student might play the role of the teacher and another might play the role of a student who is dissatisfied with a grade on a paper. Because the goal of the role play is to increase students' repertoire of ways that the instructor might respond to the student in such a situation, the instructor might establish very clearly the roles and the situation; however, the rules governing the interaction and, especially, the specific outcomes will be left to the players based on their perceptions of the assigned roles.

When they are carefully planned and integrated into the course content, games, simulations, and role plays have a number of potential advantages. Most importantly, such activities allow instructors to achieve major course goals in novel ways. For instance, if goals are primarily cognitive, such instructional tools can help students to develop understanding or skills or to exercise critical thinking, sound reasoning, and accurate communication (Weaver, 1974). Furthermore, the methods allow the achievement of such course goals in ways that provide variation from traditional lecture or discussion methods. Also, the methods assure that students will be actively involve in the content of the course. By definition, the methods suggest that at least some students will participate by engaging in games or playing roles; however, the approaches can also be planned so that all students in the class make significant contributions to the overall outcomes. The methods are especially useful if students need the opportunity to experience a particular event/relationship or to try out skills or behaviors in a safe environment. In addition, the use of such activities offers students a unique vantage point from which to "experience emotion, reduce inhibitions, decrease resistance, permeate defenses" (Weaver, 1974, p. 302). The experience can be particularly useful when students encounter situations or play roles that force them to view a situation from a variety of perspectives. Finally, instructional games, simulations, and role plays can enhance relevance of course material as students apply it in situations often designed to take them beyond the immediate classroom. Thus, the methods have the potential to increase generalizability of course content.

Although games, simulations, and role plays are potentially advantageous instructional methods, they also have limitations. If not carefully constructed, they can be too simplistic in their representation of complex concepts or situations. In addition, no matter how hard instructors work to get them to reflect reality, such methods will always contain elements of artificiality that have to be addressed. Also, the methods often create logistical problems, particularly if they require special material or space that goes beyond the assigned classroom. Finally, because students may be involved in different ways at different levels, it is not always clear whether the learning outcomes from such activities have been the same for all students (Lederman, 1983).

Because of these potential difficulties, then, the use of games, simulations, and role plays requires careful instructor attention to the details of conducting such activities. The following discussion is designed to identify some of the major issues to consider when instructors intend to use such methods in their courses. The supplemental readings at the end of this chapter provide additional details on the use of games, simulations, and role plays as instructional tools.

Objectives

The use of games, simulations, and role plays is time consuming, in both the planning and the implementing stages. Before such tools are used in a classroom, the instructor has to determine how such an activity could be integrated into the content and find or design a game, simulation, or role play that will work. Then, during class it takes time to establish roles, rules, and guidelines and to conduct and debrief the activity. Because such activities typically take more time than traditional instructional methods, it is important to plan objectives carefully and make sure that games, simulations, or role plays are worth the time and effort for all involved.

Atmosphere

If games, simulations, and role plays are not used in an appropriate atmosphere with an appropriate degree of structure, they can result in participant embarrassment, lack of productivity, and failure to achieve desired objectives. Typically, the activities are best conducted in a supportive, participative classroom atmosphere. If appropriate, it sometimes helps for the instructor to participate in the activities. When a simulation, game, or role play only requires two participants, it is sometimes helpful to ask for volunteers or to have the entire class participate simultaneously in dyads. On occasions where students are asked to role play a scene in front of the class, risk can be reduced by asking the players to "freeze" from time to time while class members make suggestions about how the players should proceed. Thus, the players themselves do not have to be so concerned about making "mistakes," and a greater number of students can be involved in the activity.

Debriefing

In order for games, simulations, and role plays to be integrated usefully as learning activities, they must be debriefed upon completion. In the educational field, the consensus suggests that the real learning in the use of such activities comes from the debriefing process as students analyze, draw conclusions from their experience, and discuss how to modify their behavior accordingly (Dindia-Webb, 1979, p. 38).

There are a number of structured systems available for debriefing games, simulations, or role play activities (Covert, 1978; Stadsklev, 1974; Yarbrough, 1978). The EDIT system adapted by Covert (1978) suggests that students EXPERIENCE the game, simulation or role play; DESCRIBE what happened to them during the activity; INFER from the descriptions what general principles, theories, or hypotheses might be developed about communication; and then TRANSFER these principles to a usable form in their own lives. Weaver (1974) suggested that teachers and students discuss results in four areas: the awareness created of concepts and principles; the expressions of feeling brought out in the activities; the details of what happened during the interaction; and the success or failure of the exercise as a whole. Regardless of the specific approach that the instructor takes to debriefing, the basic issues concern what students learned and how that learning can be related to the content and objectives of the course. The job of the instructor, then, is to choose a structure for debriefing and to develop the questions that will assist in the debriefing process. When reasonable, debriefing should also address the strengths, limitations, and overall usefulness of the activity to provide feedback for future use.

Although games, simulations, and role plays require thorough planning and careful integration into course content, they are potentially useful instructional methods for helping students transfer learning beyond the classroom. As with any strategy, however, they must be chosen only after careful analysis of objectives, classroom constraints, and available resources.

FIELD STUDY METHODS

Field methods are used most often for collecting data for research, of course, and instructors rarely think of them as learning tools for students' use in mastering course content. In the discipline of communication, the use of field methods is typically reserved for classes focusing on methodology in qualitative, interpretive, or ethnographic research. Nevertheless, field methods can be, and have been, successfully used as a major instructional tool in communication classes.

As the name suggests, field methods are used *in situ,* in the actual setting in which a particular phenomenon of interest occurs. Philipsen (1982) suggested that the investigator who uses such methods "deliberately spends as much time as possible in the theater of observation" and "becomes personally involved with, or at least exposed to, the phenomena of interest" (p. 9). Although field researchers can use a variety of techniques to collect data, common field methods include observing, interviewing, and collecting documents.

The use of field methods as an instructional tool, then, entails getting students into a setting where they can observe, interview, and study documents to collect information about a phenomenon of interest to the class. Instructors use some variation of these methods when they ask students to conduct information-gathering interviews and synthesize the information for in-class presentation. However, when field methods are used as a more developed learning tool, an instructor usually prepares the student to be a novice researcher who will learn while simultaneously making contributions to the development of course content.

The tool is particularly potent in communication courses, because there are so many contexts in which human interaction can be observed (Wulff & Nyquist, 1988). For example, in teaching a course in adolescent communication in which a goal is to have students identify what adolescents talk about with their peers, students might study adolescents in a variety of field settings in order to identify the topics of adolescent conversation. Some class members might observe on junior high school playgrounds or in classrooms. Others might ride school buses or arrange to attend adolescent extracurricular activities. In an organizational communication class in which a major goal is to have students explain how subordinates react to innovations instigated by their supervisors, students might visit organizational settings to observe interactions and to interview supervisors and subordinates.

There are a number of reasons why one might consider using field methods to achieve the objectives for such communication courses. First, such a teaching strategy gets students actively involved in the learning process. Instead of being passive receptacles for knowledge dispensed in the classroom, students are in the field generating knowledge; and they learn to compare and contrast the content from the field with that which they are exposed to in the controlled environment of the classroom. In many instances, the learning has the potential of becoming a collaborative process in which students compare and contrast their findings and work together to understand more fully the phenomena of interest. Second, such methods provide students with a much richer sense of the phenomena being studied. In the previously mentioned adolescent communication course, for instance, college students may read a book, listen to the instructor, or even try to generate a list of topics that they think adolescents might talk about in everyday life. However, when these students study adolescents in natural settings, for example, on the playground, in the classroom, or on the school bus, the students obtain a much richer sense of adolescent communication; and they can assess whether the course content does represent the world outside the classroom. Finally, using basic field methods assists students in learning a rudimentary research process including data collection, data analysis, testing and validating hypotheses, and presenting results.

Because of the complexity of preparing students to use field methods, instructors need to plan carefully when using the approach. The following discussion identifies some of the major areas for consideration in implementing field methods as an instructional tool to enhance student learning in communication courses.

Objectives

It is important, of course, to identify the major student outcomes desired and then determine if they warrant the time spent in traveling to the field, collecting data, and conducting analyses. If a major objective of a course is to have students master a body of content that has already been clearly defined by the instructor or a textbook, then field methods may not be appropriate. If, however, major goals for the course include having students compare and contrast information from different sources or learn to analyze, synthesize, and categorize, then the instructor might want to consider the ways that field methods could be incorporated into the course.

Logistics

The biggest logistical problem in using field methods is one of matching students with appropriate field settings. Depending on the level of the college group, the instructor may be able to make assignments and let students decide issues of entry and access. However, if students need assistance finding and arranging to visit appropriate field sites, the process can be challenging, particularly if the instructor is new to the area or is teaching the course for the first time. Additionally, once students have been matched with appropriate settings, they still need information on policies and guidelines for obtaining permission to conduct studies in particular field settings. Finally, the logistics of traveling to and from a field site, observing, and interviewing take time. Consequently, the instructor frequently must balance the amount of class time required of students with the perceived value of the exercise. The course structure may have to provide students with some portion of the regularly scheduled class time each week to work in the field.

Methodology

Many undergraduates will not have been exposed to field methods. Even though some students may have conducted interviews or more formal observations, most students will not have utilized such methods as systematic ways of collecting and analyzing data and reaching conclusions. Therefore, the instructor will want to schedule time at the beginning of the course or before a specific exercise to talk very basically to the students about such topics as determining a research question, gaining access to the field as a participant or nonparticipant observer, taking field notes during interviews and observations, collecting documents, moving from field notes to tentative hypotheses, analyzing the data, and reporting the results of their work. The supplemental reading list at the end of this chapter contains references with helpful background information to assist in preparing students for the use of field methods.

New Student Roles

For the most part, students will have had very little experience in the researcher role. Furthermore, they may typically come to class expecting the instructor to be the major source of information for the subject. Consequently, the instructor will need to spend time discussing with them not only the appropriate protocol for getting into and working in the field as researchers but also the changes in the roles of instructor and student contributions to the class as a result of the research. They may need to understand that a major part of the content for a particular assignment or course is based on the data that they generate in the field and that much of the comparison, contrast, and discussion in the class will rely on tentative hypotheses and conclusions that they generate from their analyses of field notes.

New Teacher Role

When instructors use field methods as an instructional strategy, they should be prepared to assume a variety of roles, including content expert, field methods practitioner, individual consultant, and facilitator. As content experts, instructors will be responsible for providing content to which students may compare and contrast the data they generate in the field. In the role of field methods practitioner, instructors may have to assist students in deciding how to obtain data in a particular context or how to categorize and synthesize their data as a class. Instructors may assume consultant roles as they work with individual students who have particular problems analyzing their data or who have generated particularly interesting or puzzling insights about the phenomenon being studied. Finally, as facilitators, instructors will have to provide ongoing summary, analysis, and synthesis to help the students tie the information generated in the field to the important instructional objectives of the course.

Although the use of field methods as an instructional tool may require major rethinking and restructuring of the traditional ways that some of our communication courses have been taught, the value, particularly for the communication discipline, justifies the effort. As Drake (1983) suggested:

> The speech communication discipline allows for practical life experiences/contacts while completing classroom assignments. . . . Out-of-classroom practice and primary research aid students in developing self-confidence faster while, at the same time, maximizing students' interest in the subjects we teach. And professional contacts help teachers keep in touch with what is going on in communication fields. Speech communication is not/cannot be textbook and classroom bound. (p. 272)

SUMMARY

The intent of this chapter has been to provide an overview and introduction to some of the major active learning strategies used by instructors in communication. Although the approaches discussed emphasize the diversity of instructional strategies that instructors might use in their teaching, there are some common themes that have emerged consistently throughout the chapter. First, it is important to remember that course objectives determine which strategy is most appropriate for teaching a particular body of content. Therefore, to begin thinking about how to convey the content of courses, instructors should specify the learning outcomes that they wish to achieve. A second theme has been that the various strategies are ways for helping students learn. The strategies have been discussed here not as methods for evaluating students' mastery of the content, but rather as ways of helping students to master the content. Another theme has been that instructor thought and preplanning are essential to the successful use of any of the methods. The strategies require thorough planning before implementation in the classroom, including thinking about the special issues related to the procedures, the roles of instructors and students, the kinds of interactions involved, and the special logistical problems. Therefore, long before any one of these issues appears as a difficulty in the classroom, the instructor will have given special attention to it and devised appropriate ways to address it.

A final issue that has emerged consistently throughout the chapter is related to the importance of integration and evaluation. In order to use such instructional strategies successfully, the instructor must help students integrate them by showing direct links between the activities and the content being studied. Furthermore, the instructor must be continually evaluating the strategies used in terms of overall usefulness for achieving course objectives. Although this chapter cannot address more than a limited number of active learning strategies or the myriad of issues related to the use of those approaches, it can provide a starting point for serious thought about the use of active learning strategies in communication courses.

REFERENCES

Bargh, J. A., & Shul, Y. (1980). On the cognitive benefits of teaching. *Journal of Educational Psychology, 72,* 593–604.

Britton, J., Burgess, T., Martin, N., MacLeod, A., & Rosen, H. (1975). *The development of writing abilities.* London: Macmillan Education.

Christensen, C. R., & Hansen, A. J. (1987). *Teaching and the case method.* Boston, MA: Harvard Business School.

Covert, A. (1978). *Communication: People speak, Instructor's manual.* New York: McGraw-Hill.

Dickson, W. P., & Patterson, J. H. (1981). Evaluating referential communication games for teaching speaking and listening skills. *Communication Education, 30,* 11–21.

Dindia-Webb, K. (1979). *Using educational games and simulations.* Unpublished manuscript, University of Washington, Department of Speech Communication, Seattle, WA.

Drake, H. L. (1983). Classroom assignments minus the rearview mirror. *Communication Quarterly, 31,* 271–273.

Festinger, L. (1954). A theory of social comparison processes. *Human Relations, 7,* 117–140.

Friedrich, G. W. (1981). Instructional strategies in the 80's. In G. Friedrich (Ed.), *Education in the eighties: Speech communication* (pp. 155–161). Washington, DC: National Education Association.

Hill, W. F. (1969). *Learning thru discussion.* Beverly Hills, CA: Sage.

Horn, R. E. (1973). How students can make their own simulations. In D. W. Zuckerman & R. E. Horn (Eds.), *Guide to simulations/games for education and training* (pp. 439–433). Lexington, MA: Information Resources.

Knoblauch, C. H., & Brannon, L. (1983). Writing as learning through the curriculum. *College English, 45,* 465–474.

Kozma, R. B., Belle, L. W., & Williams, G. W. (1978). *Instructional techniques in higher education* (161–174). Englewood Cliffs, NJ: Educational Technology.

Larson, C. U. (1978). "Three buys"—A simulation for teaching persuasive campaigns. *Communication Education, 27,* 60–63.

Lederman, L. C. (1983). Differential learning outcomes in an instructional simulation: Exploring the relationship between designated role and perceived learning outcome. *Communication Quarterly, 31,* 266–270.

McKeachie, W. J. (1986). *Teaching tips: A guidebook for the beginning college teacher* (8th ed.). Lexington, MA: D. C. Heath.

Miller, G. R., & Steinberg, M. (1975). *Between people: A new analysis of interpersonal communication*. Chicago, IL: Science Research Associates.

Philipsen, G. (1982). The qualitative case study as a strategy in communication inquiry. *The Communicator, 12,* 4–17.

Rockler, M. J. (1978). Applying simulation/gaming. In O. Milton and Associates (Eds.), *On college teaching* (pp. 286–313). San Francisco: Jossey-Bass.

Ruben, B. D., & Budd, R. (1975). *Human communication handbook: Simulations and games*. Rochelle Park, NJ: Hayden.

Sonnenschein, S., & Whitehurst, G. (1984). Developing referential communication: A hierarchy of skills. *Child Development, 55,* 1936–1945.

Stadsklev, R. (1974). *Handbook of simulation gaming in social education.* University of Alabama: Institute of Higher Education Research and Services.

Stewart, J., & D'Angelo, G. (1988). *Together: Communicating interpersonally, Instructor's resource guide* (rev. ed.). Reading, MA: Addison-Wesley.

Suls, J. M., & Miller, R. L. (1977). *Social comparison processes.* Washington, DC: Hemisphere.

Weatherly, M. (1974). Commercially-available games for speech communication courses. *Speech Teacher, 23,* 311–319.

Weaver, R. L., II. (1974). The use of exercises and games. *Speech Teacher, 23,* 302–311.

Webb, N. M. (1982). Student interaction and learning in small groups. *Review of Educational Research, 52,* 421–445.

Wulff, D. H., & Nyquist, J. D. (1988). Using field methods as a teaching-learning tool. In J. Kurfiss (Ed.), *To improve the academy* (pp. 87–98). Still Water, OK: New Forums Press.

Yarbrough, E. (1978). *Processing skills in experiential learning methods and application.* Unpublished manuscript, University of Colorado, Denver, CO.

SUPPLEMENTARY READING

Writing

Bean, J. C., Drenk, D., & Lee, F. D. (1982). Microtheme strategies for developing cognitive skills. In C. W. Griffin (Ed.), *New directions for teaching and learning: Teaching writing in all disciplines* (pp. 27–38). San Francisco: Jossey-Bass.

Berthoff, A. E. (1981). *The making of meaning*. Montclair, NJ: Boynton/Cook.

Britton, J. (1970). *Language and learning*. New York: Penguin.

Cutliff, D. (1984). Enhancing learning: Exploiting writing. *Teaching at UNL, 5*(3), 1–3.

Emig, J. (1977). Writing as a mode of learning. *College Composition and Communication, 28,* 124.

Farris, C. (1988). *Writing to learn*. Seattle: University of Washington, Center for Instructional Development and Research.

Mc Shane, J. A. (1984). UNL faculty and writing in the disciplines. *Teaching at UNL, 5*(3), 1,4–5.

Sommers, N. (1982). Responding to student writing. *College Composition and Communication, 33*(2), 148–156.

Student Oral Performance

Staff. (1986, Fall). Berkeley launches writing and speech program. *Teaching at Berkeley,* p. 1.

Small Groups

Booth-Butterfield, M. (1986). Stifle or stimulate? The effects of communication task structure on apprehensive and non-apprehensive students. *Communication Education, 35,* 336–348.

Cooper, P. J. (1981). *Speech communication for the classroom teacher* (pp. 133–168). Dubuque, IA: Gorsuch Scarisbrick.

Cragan, J. F., & Wright, D. W. (1980). Small group communication research of the 1970's: A synthesis and critique. *Central States Speech Journal, 31,* 197–213.

D'Angelo, G., & Nyquist, J. (1973). Teaching strategies for large lecture courses: Use of multimedia and discussion groups. *The Speech Teacher, 22,* 310–317.

Hirokawa, R. Y., & Poole, M. S. (1986). *Communication and group decision-making.* Beverly Hills, CA: Sage.

Scheidel, T. M., & Crowell, L. (1979). *Discussing and deciding. A desk book for group leaders and members.* New York: Macmillan.

Schmuck, P. A., & Schmuck, R. A. (1983). *Group processes in the classroom* (4th ed.). Dubuque, IA: William C. Brown.

Winston, R. B., Jr., Bonney, W. C., Miller, T. K., & Dagley, J. C. (1988). *Promoting student development through intentionally structured groups.* San Francisco: Jossey-Bass.

Case Method

Argyris, C. (1980). Some limitations of the case method. *Academy of Management Review, 5,* 291–298.

Berger, M. (1983). In defense of the case method: A reply to Argyris. *Academy of Management Review, 8,* 329–333.

Donaldson, L., & Scannell, E. E. (1978). *Human resource development: The new trainer's guide* (pp. 81–82). Reading, MA: Addison-Wesley.

Fisher, C. F. (1978). Being there vicariously by case studies. In O. Milton and Associates (Eds.), *On college teaching* (pp. 258–285). San Francisco: Jossey-Bass.

Haskins, W. A., & Spear, S. (1985). Arbitration advocacy: A case study approach. *Communication Education, 34,* 150–155.

Kreps, G. L., & Lederman, L. C. (1985). Using the case method in organizational communication education: Developing students' insight, knowledge and creativity through experience-based learning and systematic debriefing. *Communication Education, 34,* 358–364.

Mier, D. R. (1982). From concepts to practices: Student case study work in organizational communication. *Communication Education, 31,* 151–154.

Miner, F. C. (1978). An approach for increasing participation in case discussions. *Exchange: The Organizational Behavior Teaching Journal, 3,* 41–42.

Reynolds, J. I. (1978). There is method in cases. *The Academy of Management Review, 3,* 129–133.

Romm, T., & Mahler, S. (1986). A three dimensional model for using case studies in the academic classroom. *Higher Education, 15,* 677–696.

Games, Simulations, and Role Plays

Bruneau, T. J. (1971). Using role playing in the basic college speech course. *Communication Education, 20,* 53–58.

Dickson, W. P., & Patterson, J. H. (1981). Evaluating referential communication games for teaching speaking and listening skills. *Communication Education, 30,* 11–21.
Freezel, J. D. (1982). Means-to-me: A word game without winning or losing. *Communication Education, 31,* 159–162.
Fuhrmann, B. S., & Grasha, A. F. (1983). *A practical handbook for college teachers* (pp. 239–243). Boston: Little, Brown.
Leaderman, L. C., & Ruben, B. D. (1984). Systematic assessment of communication games and simulations: An applied framework. *Communication Education, 33,* 152–158.
Seiler, W. J., Schuelke, L. D., & Lieb-Brilhart, B. (1984). *Communication for the contemporary classroom* (pp. 156–164). New York: Holt, Rinehart & Winston.

Field Study Methods

Brooks, D. M. (1980). Ethnographic analysis of instructional method. *Theory Into Practice, 19,* 144–147.
Dobbert, M. L. (1984). *Ethnographic: Theory and application for modern schools and societies.* New York: Praeger.
Fetterman, D. M. (1989). *Applied social research methods series: Vol. 17. Ethnography step by step.* Newbury Park, CA: Sage.
Goetz, J. P., & LeCompte, M. D. (1984). *Ethnography and qualitative design in educational research.* Orlando, FL: Academic Press.
Lincoln, Y. S., & Guba, E. G. (1985). *Naturalistic inquiry.* Beverly Hills, CA: Sage.
Lowman, J. (1984). *Mastering the techniques of teaching* (pp. 180–183). San Francisco: Jossey-Bass.
Miles, M. B., & Huberman, A. M. (1984). *Qualitative data analysis: A sourcebook of new methods.* Beverly Hills, CA: Sage.
Patton, M. Q. (1980). *Qualitative evaluation methods.* Beverly Hills, CA: Sage.

26

Evaluating the Process

Anita L. Vangelisti
University of Iowa

> *The evaluation of faculty is not a new phenomenon, yet it continues to elicit reactions in faculty ranging from cold apathy to heated anger.*
>
> —Arreola (1984)

For most people involved with academics, the activities, decisions, and issues associated with teacher evaluation invoke less than positive images. From a teacher's perspective, the prospect of being evaluated is often associated with anxiety about measuring up to a nebulous set of standards, obtaining an important promotion, or avoiding embarrassment in front of peers. For those who are more confident, the same event may represent a simple annoyance at having their usual teaching schedules disturbed. Administrators must deal with the design and implementation of evaluation programs, as well as the ramifications of setting those programs into action: distressed teachers, concerned parents, dissatisfied students, and, more recently, zealous attorneys (e.g., Bailey, 1986; Deneen, 1980; Eble, 1984). Students must take the time to respond to questions which, from their perspective, may have little immediate impact on their future education.

Despite such difficulties, the process of teacher evaluation is an important one. It represents not only a complex set of issues, but a powerful influence for, and on, contemporary education. This chapter addresses issues that are central to the instructional evaluation process, providing a

framework with which to describe, weigh, and improve current evaluation practices. More specifically, the chapter focuses on four questions: (a)
Why should teachers be evaluated? (b) What are the available means or
methods for evaluation? (c) What teaching activities should be the focus
of evaluation? and (d) Who should do the evaluating? Finally, criteria for
assessing the representativeness of teacher appraisals are examined, and
guidelines for evaluation are suggested.

WHY EVALUATE?

Why should educators design, implement, and act on instructional evaluations? What purposes do they serve? Some early discussions have, in
fact, suggested that teacher evaluation is a futile, if not impossible exercise (e.g., Highet, 1954, as cited in Dunkin & Biddle, 1974). However,
although educators continue to ask questions regarding the effectiveness
and importance of teacher evaluation (e.g., Huddle, 1985; McGreal,
1986), most now see the process as useful, necessary, and often even
essential to good teaching.

On a global level, teacher evaluation can be defined as a description of
how an instructor compares to a given set of implicit or explicit standards. It provides a record of what happens, instructionally, in the classroom—a record that can be used publically, by groups such as administrators and students, as well as personally, by teachers themselves. The
basic reason, then, for conducting teacher evaluations is to generate public and personal information concerning instruction.

Public Information

From a public standpoint, Lessinger (1980), Ornstein (1981), and others
have noted that the accountability provided by teacher evaluations is a
necessary precursor to the legitimization of instructional practices. In the
absence of accountability, educators leave not only their efforts but also
the fruits of those efforts open to extensive criticism. Of particular concern is a group that Seldin (1980) referred to as "outsiders"—individuals
such as parents, governmental leaders, and advocacy groups who, though
not directly involved in the process of education, have strong influence on
the direction it takes. If, as many educators claim, they need the moral
and financial support of these groups, educators are obligated to supply
evidence demonstrating that they merit such support.

In addition to a general public accountability, teacher evaluations can
provide valid, reliable information for personnel decisions. Although few
teachers look forward to the process of being evaluated, most, if not all,

would prefer promotion and tenure decisions based on relatively objective, systematic information. In this regard, when conducted and interpreted carefully, teacher evaluations can function to limit the potential subjectivity, bias, and/or discrimination that may influence such decisions.

The "public" information generated by teacher evaluations may also help students choose courses and programs of study that best accommodate their educational goals. While decisions based on this information might be tied to teacher effectiveness as reported in the evaluation, they may also be a function of students' particular preferences and learning styles (see Gorham, this volume).

Finally, as public accounts, teacher evaluations help to define criteria for research on teaching (Gage, 1972); they provide researchers with guidelines and suggest variables, processes, and events that are relevant to the study of effective instruction. Contrary to the fears of some, the explanatory purposes of educational research are not undermined by using information generated by teacher evaluations (Doyle, 1978). Indeed, when researchers utilize data from both the people doing the evaluations and the individuals being evaluated, they gain a great deal of information concerning the variables and processes that influence effective teaching. Furthermore, teachers who take an active role in the evaluative process gain the opportunity to become more effective researchers and problem solvers in their own classrooms (Friedrich, 1982), thereby bolstering their abilities to develop and test new instructional techniques.

Personal Information

Equally important as providing public information is the notion of providing teachers with personal information concerning their instructional practices: A lack of evaluation would create an informational "vacuum" for teachers. Although criteria for effective teaching might abound, the degree to which individual instructors met those criteria would remain questionable. In this sense, teacher evaluations represent a salient form of socialization—whether explicit or implicit—providing newcomers and veterans with information about what it means to be a "successful" teacher as well as what they need to do to become "successful."

The first and perhaps most common type of information provided to teachers involves the diagnosis of in-class instructional problems. Using a clinical metaphor, McDonald (1980) suggested four steps for such a diagnosis: (a) identify whether there is a problem, (b) identify the causes of the problem, (c) prescribe ways to improve the problem, and (d) assess subsequent moves toward improvement. In this way, teachers not only receive feedback with regard to behaviors or instructional techniques that need improvement, but they also are given a means by which to change. This is particularly important, because if teachers lack the knowledge necessary to make the change or do not receive feedback as to improvements resulting from their efforts, little (if any) lasting change is likely.

Another type of personal information provided to teachers is an assessment of the "nonteaching" aspects of instructors' performance. As noted by Dressel (1978), such factors might include "selection of textbooks, readings, laboratory activities, classroom activities, methods of presentation, appropriate assignments and tests" (p. 356). This information can be used both to enhance the individual instructor's course and to contribute to the development and modification of more widely applied curricula (Braskamp, Brandenburg, & Ory, 1984; Doyle, 1975).

Teacher evaluations, in short, function as an important source of information. Publically, they provide accountability to "outsiders," data on which to base personnel decisions, information to help students make appropriate academic choices, and criteria for research. Personally, they provide teachers with information about their in- and out-of-class instructional practices, furnishing a relevant comparison base for the assessment of their own behavior.

HOW DO WE EVALUATE?

At the university level, teacher evaluation is usually associated with some sort of written appraisal, whether in the form of a rating scale or a more open-ended recommendation (Seldin, 1984). Preservice teachers, on the other hand, may more frequently associate being evaluated with informal classroom "visits" from their supervisors. Whatever the form of the evaluative tool, its specificity and structure depend, to a great extent, on the type of evaluation being conducted. Most teacher evaluations fall into one of two basic category types. The first type is *diagnostic*. Diagnostic evaluations are conducted to define teachers' strengths and weaknesses—usually with the goal of improving their instructional skills. If used for general diagnostics, open-ended or free-response items might be most appropriate, because they allow for a broad range of responses. Limiting respondents' feedback to a predetermined set of behavioral or attitudinal categories prior to obtaining more descriptive information may unduly bias results toward what those designing the measures *think* ought to comprise effective teaching.

The second evaluation type is *summative*. Summative evaluations are conducted to provide information to administrators, students, or other parties, and they most often assess teachers' performance with regard to a standard set of instructional practices. When evaluators are looking for difficulties in particular areas of teaching (e.g., delivery of material, textbook selection, course organization), open-ended questions tend to generate a great deal of irrelevant information. In such cases, rating scales, designed to target behaviors and techniques of particular interest, are an appropriate choice.

Whether diagnostic or summative, teacher evaluations usually utilize one of three methods: written appraisals, interviews, or observations.

Written Appraisals

Compared to interviews and observations, written appraisals probably vary the most in terms of specificity. On one end of the continuum, written appraisals may take the form of rating scales, which require evaluators to rate the extent to which instructors conform to a particular set of qualities. On the other end are questionnaires composed of open-ended items, which require evaluators to generate their own response and sometimes even choose the focus/subject of the evaluation.

Written appraisals have the basic advantage of being easily obtained from a large number of respondents in a short period of time and, partly for that reason, "have enjoyed unrivaled status" (Dunkin & Biddle, 1974, p. 59) as an evaluation tool. Although the same type of information can be obtained through personal conferences or interviews, written appraisals are, in most all cases, more expedient. Also, the form of written appraisals is such that respondent anonymity is easily preserved. Particularly in the case of student or peer evaluations, more candid responses may be obtained in this "nameless" context.

Despite these advantages, rating scales and other structured written appraisals are relatively limited in what they assess and the detail with which they assess it. Questions are often selected without any pretesting as to relevance and, as a result, may not detect some of the more subtle differences between effective and ineffective teaching.

Interviews

Though more costly than written data, interview-based assessments give the evaluator the advantage of being able to "follow up" on information of particular interest. Inclusion of secondary or "probing" questions may be important for cases in which the nature or quality of teacher practices is being explored. Diagnosing particular instructional difficulties, for instance, may require more than a single, straightforward question (e.g., "If given the opportunity, what changes would you make in the way your instructor delivers/organizes/selects class material?"). Similarly, whether for diagnostic or research purposes, describing factors that affect teacher–student interaction or students' attitudes toward learning might require the added detail provided by interviewing.

Interviews are, however, extremely costly in terms of both time and effort. To obtain reliable, systematic data, interviewers must first be trained in data collection and recording techniques. Considering that conducting a single interview usually takes the same amount of time that collecting written questionnaires from a large group of respondents does, the time and effort may be excessive.

Observation

Like interviewing, collecting observational data allows for a great deal of flexibility on the part of the evaluator. If, midway through the observation period, some behavior or technique of particular interest is noted, the observer can include that element in the data base. "On site" or "field" research is also particularly effective for describing less obvious or more complex elements of behavior and attitudes (Babbie, 1983) that might go unreported by rating scales. Finally, observational techniques provide an account of what happens as it happens, rather than relying on retrospective data.

Observation is, however, extremely expensive and, unless tested extensively for both validity and reliability, may be less appropriate for administrative or personnel decisions than other methods, such as written appraisals. In an often-quoted statement, Gage (1972) noted:

> Observation by expert judges of teaching probably cannot be used for administrative appraisals. Observers are hard enough to ignore when they are friends or researchers, whose impressions will not affect one's standing. But when the teacher knows he is being looked over by someone whose opinion will determine his promotion or salary, his performance may depend more on his nerve than on his teaching skill. (p. 172)

Doyle (1983) added that the results of informal observation may be influenced as much by how the observation data is reported as by the data itself. This implies that teachers who happen to be assigned to an observer with poor presentation skills might receive less positive rankings than they deserve. Although such biases may not pose major problems for diagnostic evaluations, their role in summative evaluations used for personnel decisions could be professionally devastating.

WHO SHOULD EVALUATE?

Although the choice of an evaluative measure depends in part on the type of evaluation being conducted, the choice of an evaluator has the added complexity of a relationship—an association between the evaluator and the teacher that could either (a) bias results of the evaluation or (b) negatively affect the work atmosphere. In cases where the evaluator is in a position of power over the teacher, relationship issues may or may not be a problem. However, when the evaluator is of similar status (e.g., a colleague) or lower status (e.g., a student), making judgments that can affect the teacher's career may create stress for the evaluator, the teacher, and, in turn, the way they interact.

Four groups of people usually serve as teacher evaluators. They include students, colleagues, alumni, and the teachers themselves.

Students

Due, in part, to the amount of exposure they have to teachers, students, in many cases, serve as the best sources of information concerning teachers' instructional styles and course content. The status differences that are inherent to student–teacher relationships (as well as the sophistication with which many students approach the task) usually make students inappropriate observers. Written appraisals and interviews with students are more effective and are often utilized.

Regardless of the method implemented, interpretation of evaluative information collected from students should be made with caution. Although in some cases the data is less than conclusive, a number of studies have demonstrated that factors such as students' expected course grade (Centra, 1980), class size (Marsh, Overall, & Kesler, 1979), and teachers' rank (Marsh, 1980) may affect their evaluations. Because student responses to rating scales, more general written appraisals, and interviews have been found to be similar (Ory, Braskamp, & Pieper, 1980), the interpretation of any student-based evaluation should consider the possible influence of such factors.

Colleagues

Although they lack the day-to-day exposure that students have to individual instructors, colleagues such as principals, department chairs, deans, and other teachers are often used to judge a variety of in- and out-of-class instructional activities. Given time to develop observation skills and to conduct observations, for example, colleagues can make repeated classroom visits to gather information for diagnostic purposes. For more formal, personnel-related assessments, colleagues may use rating scales and open-ended written appraisals to evaluate teaching skills, course materials, and nonclass activities such as advising, service, and curriculum development.

Although collegial evaluations may not be affected by the same relational contingencies that influence student assessments, relationships between teachers and colleagues placed in an evaluative role deserve equal consideration. On one hand, *collegial relationships may affect evaluations*. In the case of observation-based assessments, for example, generalizations are often made from a small number of observations and, as a result, may be based more on relational factors or first impressions than on instructors' actual classroom behaviors. On the other hand, regardless of their validity, *evaluations may affect collegial relationships*. If taken personally, a negative evaluation might not only result in strained interaction between a teacher and an evaluator, but could, in fact, generate legal action by the teacher (e.g., Centra, 1979).

Alumni

Given the retrospective nature of their accounts, instructors' former students are usually not able to provide detailed descriptions of course structure, materials, or even teacher behaviors. They can, however, provide global assessments and comparisons of teachers' qualities to other instructors they have had. As a result, though they are probably not useful for most diagnostic evaluations, alumni evaluations can serve as one of several sources of information for personnel decisions.

Data from previous students can be collected in the form of written appraisals, telephone interviews, mail surveys, or exit interviews with graduating seniors. Written assessments, though more easily administered than interviews, often do not have as high a response rate (Babbie, 1983). However, the standardization of interviewing skills required to insure reliability across interviewers may make written responses more feasible. Regardless of the method, collecting evaluative data from alumni is an expensive process and, as a result, is usually done for small- rather than large-scale evaluations.

Self

Using teachers as their own evaluators is a practice that is becoming more popular (Seldin, 1984). Although self-appreciating biases may affect the reliability of quality-based judgments, this type of data serves a useful, and often necessary, purpose for many types of evaluation. Teachers are, for instance, probably the best reporters of the content and organization of their courses. In fact, detailed descriptions of materials such as course assignments, syllabi, class activities, and student achievement may not be obtainable from any other source. For the purposes of diagnosing problems related to class preparation (or even making personnel decisions with reference to out-of-class practices), some sort of self-evaluation may, therefore, be essential. In addition, because instructor and student ratings of global classroom variables (c.g., student involvement and teacher support) (Braskamp, Caulley, & Costin, 1979) have been found to be relatively consistent despite their potential for bias, self-evaluations can be used as supplements to evaluations made by others.

Including instructors as participants in their own evaluation provides most instructors with a sense of control and efficacy. Being told by a peer or superior that a particular area needs improvement is one, often effective, form of motivation—participating in the identification of the problem and diagnosis of its cause is another. When encouraged, for example, to watch and evaluate videotapes of their teaching, instructors can observe for themselves any difficulties they might have and, if the videotaping is conducted periodically, can note improvements over time. Similarly, the setting and accomplishing of goals for out-of-classroom change provides teachers with a sense of accomplishment that might otherwise be difficult to attain.

WHAT SHOULD BE EVALUATED?

Unfortunately, limited time and financial resources often prohibit many of the individuals who conduct teacher evaluations from focusing specifically on the improvement of teachers' instructional skills. Teacher evaluations instead are done primarily for summative purposes, to distinguish the "good" teachers from the "bad." Indeed, Doyle (1978) noted that "the practitioner's task requires knowing which criteria differentiate 'good' from 'poor' teachers. It is of little additional utility, in an immediate sense, to know why" (p. 143). Using statements such as this one as guidelines for *what* to evaluate, those who conduct teacher evaluations often use very global indices of teacher quality to determine overall effectiveness. Although pragmatically, there may be a great deal to be said for what Doyle termed the "practitioner's" approach to evaluation, limiting appraisals to the identification of "good" and "bad" teacher qualities has two, fairly serious, implications.

The first may be best illustrated by drawing a distinction between "evaluation" and "description." Many appraisals provide information that is *evaluative*. That is to say, teacher qualities are noted in terms of how well or how poorly they fit a given set of criteria. What is often lacking in these evaluations, however, is *descriptive* information. Data identifying specific teaching activities such as preparation, ability to convey knowledge of the course material, and textbook selection are not detailed. This leaves whoever is using the evaluation in a dilemma when it comes to interpretation. If, for example, an instructor is rated poorly, and there is little descriptive information available, we have no idea whether it is because of the way he or she lectures, because he or she is a tough grader, or because he or she has selected an inappropriate textbook. In short, the evaluation is virtually useless. Regardless of whether teacher appraisals are to be used for self-improvement or for decisions involving promotion, some description of what is being evaluated is necessary.

The second implication of limiting teacher appraisals to the identification of "good" and "bad" teacher qualities involves a lack of focus on the students as active, coparticipants in the learning process. The failure to evaluate how and why teachers are effective, rather than only whether they are effective (Doyle, 1978), insinuates that students are passive information receptacles (Toffler, 1974). Obviously, from a communication perspective, the instructional process involves a great deal more than the emission and absorption of information. If the evaluative process is, in part, an account of classroom happenings, failing to include some components of teacher–student interaction is a flaw.

Admittedly, incorporating an evaluative measure of teacher–student interaction into current teacher evaluations is a difficult undertaking. Although studies of classroom interaction are on the increase and the centrality of communication to the instructional process is more frequently acknowledged (Daly & Korinek, 1980; Galvin & Cooper, 1981), "it is only within the past few years that it has been possible to hope for the discovery of principles or guidelines which can be used to specify what *should* happen" between teachers and students in the classroom (Friedrich, 1982, p. 73). Even if efforts to develop and implement a tool for assessing teacher–student interaction are premature, those administering teacher evaluations should, at the very least, include an assessment of students' outcomes (i.e., student affect toward the teacher) rather than focusing only on "good" and "bad" teacher qualities. Assessing student outcomes may not capture the complexity of teacher–student interaction, but it will acknowledge and include the student as an important part of the teaching process.

EVALUATING THE EVALUATION

Validity

Regardless of which aspects of teaching are incorporated into teacher evaluations, addressing questions related to validity is vital when interpreting the appraisals. Is the evaluation an accurate representation of the teacher it is evaluating?

Response to questions such as this one can be framed in terms of three types of validity: predictive, content, and construct validity. Predictive validity deals with the degree to which the measure accurately estimates some form of external behavior (Nunnally, 1978). In the case of teacher evaluation, predictive validity typically involves the accuracy with which a particular evaluative technique can predict or distinguish the "product" of teaching: student learning, achievement, or affect. Content validity is the extent to which a measure representatively samples the substance of the area being measured. It could be, for example, that the items included on a student rating scale are irrelevant in determining teacher quality— or that one or two important components are not tapped. Dunkin and Biddle (1974), in fact, noted that items included in rating scales more often than not represent administrators' ideas about what comprises a "good" teacher rather than empirically tested variables. Finally, construct validity involves the degree to which the measure permits inferences about underlying traits (Anderson, Ball, Murphy, & Associates, 1975). If an effort is being made to measure a teacher's "enthusiasm," for example, in-class observers might note variations in the teacher's voice, the number of times he or she smiles at students, and the variety of techniques he or she uses to present class material. The evaluator concerned with construct validity would, at some point, ask questions concerning the extent to which these behaviors represent the more general construct of "enthusiasm." Could it be, for example, that an instructor might smile quite a bit and *not* be enthusiastic? Do a variety of presentation techniques have to be implemented, or is there some other aspect of presenting course material that better represents teacher "enthusiasm?"

Reliability

In addition to assessing validity, evaluators need to be concerned with issues of reliability—that is, the extent to which the measures being used in the evaluation yield similar results if implemented repeatedly. Reliability can be assessed in at least three ways. The first, internal consistency, is based on the degree to which ratings for similar items correspond to one another. For instance, an evaluator would expect to find high correlations between items measuring instructor competence, knowledge of material, and expertise in course content. If the ratings on each of these items were substantially different for the same teacher, the evaluation would not be a reliable one. The second type, interrater reliability, involves the agreement of ratings across different raters. For teacher evaluations, this type of reliability is particularly relevant when observational methods are used. If observers are not able to agree on the definition of behavioral categories and/or whether an instructor displays these behaviors, their ratings lack interrater reliability. The third and final type of reliability, test–retest, focuses on the extent to which measurements agree with one another across time or, for most teacher evaluations, at two different times during the term. This method increases the generalizability of the evaluation, because more than one assessment is made. If however, the time interval between assessments is in excess of a few days, any changes in the evaluation may be attributable to intervening variables rather than actual changes in instruction.

Cost

Although few would argue with the importance of establishing the validity and reliability of teacher evaluations, on a very pragmatic level those conducting evaluations have limited funds. School administrators and educational researcher are, as a result, restricted in their abilities to design and implement evaluation programs. It would be optimal, for example, to conduct some form of evaluation at regular intervals throughout the school year, as it would be to have a large number and variety of evaluators. The costs of achieving these two elements alone, however, are prohibitive for many programs. Not only do they require people who are willing to conduct evaluations, they also demand individuals to design the program, train the evaluators, process data collected, and put that data to use—whether it be in the form of a personnel decision, a research report, or a set of improvement-oriented goals for the instructor.

GUIDELINES FOR EVALUATION

Manatt (in an interview with McGreal, 1986) noted that "Performance appraisal is an evaluation problem; it's a research problem; it's a political problem" (p. 12). Indeed, after outlining some of the requirements for obtaining a valid, reliable account of what happens in the classroom, the appraisal of teacher performance appears, generally, to be a "problem."

Those in the positions of designing and implementing teacher appraisals face the constant dilemma of balancing evaluation goals with practical constraints tied to time, effort, and finances. Those interpreting the teacher evaluations must keep in mind potential biases and limitations of the evaluator and of the evaluative method. Those being evaluated must deal with being assessed with an often imperfect tool.

Centra (1983) summarized a number of suggestions, however, that may make the development and implementation of teacher evaluations less "problematic" for all parties involved. He recommended that: (a) multiple sources be used, (b) multiple sets of student ratings be used, (c) a sufficient number of student raters be obtained, (d) course characteristics be taken into account, (e) global ratings be stressed more than other ratings for personnel decisions, (f) diagnostic information for teaching improvement be supplemented, (g) procedures for administering the forms for student ratings be standardized, and (h) rating forms not be overused.

Although addressing each of these suggestions is probably not a feasible goal for every evaluation program, the tenor of Centra's recommendations can be captured in three general, and perhaps more easily applicable, guidelines. First, consider the purpose of the evaluation. What are the general goals of the evaluation, and what, more specifically, is the object of evaluation? Answering these questions should provide some direction as to the type of evaluative measure that would be most effectively implemented as well as who should perform the evaluation. Second, regardless of the purpose, use multiple indicators. A variety of measures will not only provide different types of information, but will serve as a means to evaluate the validity and reliability of that information. Finally, consider the specific characteristics of the course and the instructor being evaluated. Which types of evaluative techniques will most adequately assess the goals of the course and the instructor's ability to achieve those goals? Are there circumstances or previously established relationships that might mandate for or against the use of a particular evaluator?

Obviously, these and other suggestions will not eliminate all of the concerns associated with teacher evaluation. Like most forms of assessment, the assessment of teacher performance will always be subject to criticism and, thus, always subject to suggestions for improvement.

REFERENCES

Anderson, S. B., Ball, S., Murphy, R. T., & Associates (1975). *Encyclopedia of educational evaluation: Concepts and techniques for evaluating education and training programs.* San Francisco, CA: Jossey-Bass.

Arreola, R. A. (1984). Evaluation of faculty performance: Key issues. In P. Seldin (Ed.), *Changing practices in faculty evaluation* (pp. 79–85). San Francisco, CA: Jossey-Bass.

Babbie, E. (1983). *The practice of social research* (3rd ed.). Belmont, CA: Wadsworth.

Bailey, G. W. (1986). Firing a teacher? Be sure your case will hold up in court. *Executive Education, 8,* 29–31.

Braskamp, L. A., Brandenburg, D. C., & Ory, J. C. (1984). *Evaluating teaching effectiveness: A practical guide.* Beverly Hills, CA: Sage.

Braskamp, L. A., Caulley, D. N., & Costin, F. (1979). Student ratings and instructor self ratings and their relationship to student achievement. *American Educational Research Journal, 16,* 295–306.

Centra, J. A. (1070). *Determining faculty effectiveness.* San Francisco, CA: Jossey-Bass.

Centra, J. A. (1980). *Determining faculty performance.* San Francisco, CA: Jossey-Bass.

Centra, J. A. (1983). The fair use of student ratings. *Postsecondary Education Newsletter,* 1–2.

Daly, J. A., & Korinek, J. T. (1980). Instructional communication theory and research: An overview of classroom interaction. In D. Nimmo (Ed.), *Communication yearbook 4* (pp. 515–532). New Brunswick, NJ: Transaction Books.

Deneen, J. R. (1980). Legal dimensions of teacher evaluation. In D. Peterson & A. Ward (Eds.), *Due processes in teacher evaluation* (pp. 15–43). Washington, DC: University Press of America.

Doyle, K. O., Jr. (1975). *Student evaluation of instruction.* Lexington, MA: D. Heath.

Doyle, K. O., Jr. (1978). Interpreting teaching effectiveness research. *Viewpoints in Teaching and Learning, 54,* 141–153.

Doyle, K. O., Jr. (1983). *Evaluating teaching.* Lexington, MA: Lexington Books.

Dressel, P. (1978). *Handbook of academic evaluation.* San Francisco, CA: Jossey-Bass.

Dunkin, M. J., & Biddle, B. J. (1974). *The study of teaching.* Washington, DC: University Press of America.

Eble, K. E. (1984). New directions in faculty evaluation. In P. Seldin (Ed.), *Changing practices in faculty evaluation* (pp. 96–100). San Francisco, CA: Jossey-Bass.

Friedrich, G. W. (1982). Classroom interaction. In L. L. Barker (Ed.), *Communication in the classroom* (pp. 55–76). Englewood Cliffs, NJ: Prentice-Hall.

Gage, N. L. (1972). *Teacher effectiveness and teacher education: The search for a scientific basis.* Palo Alto, CA: Pacific Books.

Galvin, K. M., & Cooper, P. J. (1981). Research in communication education: Directional needs. *Central States Speech Journal, 32,* 219–226.

Highet, G. (1954). *The art of teaching.* New York: Vintage.

Huddle, G. (1985). Teacher evaluation—How important for effective schools? Eight messages from research. *National Association of Secondary School Principals Bulletin, 69,* 58–63.

Lessinger, L. N. (1980). Accountability ensures improvement. In J. W. Noll (Ed.), *Taking sides: Clashing views of controversial issues* (pp. 151–172). Guilford, CT: Duskin.

Marsh, H. W. (1980). The influence of student, course, and instructor characteristics in the evaluation of teaching. *American Educational Research Journal, 17,* 219–237.

Marsh, H. W., Overall, J. U., & Kesler, S. P. (1979). Class size, students' evaluations, and instructional effectiveness. *American Educational Research Journal, 16,* 57–70.

McDonald, F. (1980). Principles and procedures in observing classroom instruction. In D. Peterson & A. Ward (Eds.), *Due process in teacher evaluation* (pp. 89–113). Washington, DC: University Press of America.

McGreal, T. (1986). How well can we truly evaluate teachers? (interview). *The School Administrator, 43,* 10–13.

Nunnally, J. C. (1978). *Psychometric theory* (2nd ed.). New York: McGraw-Hill.

Ornstein, A. C. (1981). Accountability: Prospects for the 1980s. *School and Community, 57,* 24–25.

Ory, J. C., Braskamp, L. A., & Pieper, D. M. (1980). The congruency of student evaluative information collected by three methods. *Journal of Educational Psychology, 72,* 181–185.

Seldin, P. (1980). *Successful faculty evaluation programs.* Crugers, NY: Coventry.

Seldin, P. (1984). *Changing practices in faculty evaluation.* San Francisco, CA: Jossey-Bass.

Toffler, A. (1974). The role of the future in education. In A. Toffler (Ed.), *Learning for tomorrow* (pp. 15–23). New York: Random House.

27

Evaluating the Product

Rebecca B. Rubin
Kent State University

What is the end product of instruction? Traditionally, we view an increase in skill or knowledge as learning products in communication classes. Communication skills are typically evaluated through assessment of behavior or performance, whereas knowledge is evaluated via a written mode, usually by examination or termpaper. In both cases, evaluation serves as feedback to students on how they are progressing.

The course objectives determine whether skills or knowledge or a combination of skill and knowledge is the appropriate target for evaluation. For example, public speaking classes usually focus on both knowledge and skill in public speaking. Therefore, both knowledge and performance must be evaluated. However, communication theory classes focus on knowledge about communication rather than on skill. Sometimes the availability of a reliable and valid evaluation technique will determine the course objectives; some instructors of interpersonal communication classes measure knowledge because they perceive a lack of a valid and reliable skill measure.

This chapter examines ways of evaluating communication products in the classroom. First, I examine basic principles that guide evaluation; second, I explore common methods of evaluation of classroom performance—the use of criticism; third, I examine the ways in which we evaluate knowledge in communication classrooms; and fourth, I consider the difficult process of computing course grades.

BASIC PRINCIPLES OF EVALUATION

There are two basic approaches to evaluation used in classrooms today. *Norm-referenced measurement* compares one student's progress with that of his or her peers. With norm-referenced measurement, all students are rank ordered, and grade cut-offs are based on how well the class does. Norm-referenced methods can unduly punish low-ability students in a class of high-ability or high-achievement students and unduly reward high-ability students in a class with low ability or low-achievement students.

Criterion-referenced measurement, the preferred method, is based on absolute, objective performance standards or criteria. Evaluation closely adheres to behavioral objectives and focuses students on mastering content rather than on out-performing their peers. All students have the opportunity of doing well (or failing to do so). Criterion-referenced procedures reduce test- or evaluation-anxiety, in that students know what criteria are used to decide their grades which reduces competition among the students.

Smythe, Kibler, and Hutchings (1973) compared norm-referenced to criterion-referenced measurement in communication classes and argued that predetermined criteria are necessary in classroom teaching and evaluation. With norm-referenced criteria, standards change as a function of the group's general skill level, which is unfair to the student who happens to find himself or herself in a very high-ability group. If students are to receive grades on their communication, there must be preset standards or evaluative criteria that relate closely to the content, focus, and objectives of the course.

Whatever the approach, two further criteria of evaluation are important—validity and reliability. *Validity* refers to how accurate and comprehensive an evaluation is. Is the critique, exam, or paper really measuring learning or skill development? Content validity, one type of validity, refers to how broad-based the evaluation is. For example, does the exam cover all aspects of the text and lecture material? Does the critique sheet used in evaluation have all the categories present on which the evaluation is based?

Reliability deals with consistency and dependability. Is an instructor consistent in his or her ratings for all students? Are all speeches, papers, and essay exam answers rated using the same criteria? With objective exams, are all questions working in the same way for all students? Validity and reliability are essential aspects of any measurement, and both concepts are stressed throughout this chapter.

EVALUATION OF COMMUNICATION
PERFORMANCE

Instructors are both critics and evaluators of the communication skills they teach. In fact, evaluations that take place in the classroom are based on criticism, so whatever is said in class should be aligned with the criteria used for the evaluation. Cathcart (1981) has suggested that students learn about speaking by engaging in criticism—criticism of their own communication or that of their peers. Thus, valid criteria must be developed to guide the criticism and ultimately serve as a basis for evaluation. Post-communication criticism stimulates creative thinking and interest in the communication process, calls attention to student strengths and weaknesses, gives instructions for improvement, and motivates students to do better in the future (Smith, 1961).

It is clear from the literature that the goals or objectives of the assignment must be formulated before criticizing, evaluating, and grading communication performances. Baker (1967) suggested that an audience-centered approach be used where speech evaluation is merged with behavioral objectives. The instructor determines the specific objectives for the class and evaluates speeches on this basis. This approach places emphasis on instructor and peer evaluations for measuring achievement. Opinions vary, however, on the who, what, how, and when of speech criticism.

Who Should Give the Criticism?

There are a variety of options for providing students with feedback on their communication performance; the criticism can come from the instructor, the student, or the student's peers. *Instructors* are probably the most valid and reliable critics because of their training and experience in observation. *Students,* however, can be asked to provide criticism of their own communication, either orally in class or in writing. This is especially effective if the student has a videotape to review. Typically, self-evaluation helps students identify their goals and critical judgment skills, and it provides a means of reinforcement when they do well (Harris, 1963).

Peers can also provide helpful criticism in the classroom. Book and Simmons (1980) found that most students focus their comments on content and delivery; speakers consider negative comments to be especially helpful. In any evaluation process, the course goals and standards must be clear to student raters. Balcer (1958) argued that teachers must know where the class is going and communicate this to students. Students should evaluate each other only when they understand and accept the standards, and they should comment on content before delivery when evaluations are given in class.

But should peers give both grades and criticism? One issue in grading performance pertains to how much of the grade should be provided by the instructor and how much by the student's peer group. In one system, students' evaluations of a speech count as two thirds of the grade, and the instructor's count for one third. This system under-values the instructor's evaluation. Perhaps a variety of sources should be used for evaluation: a class observer, a panel of observers, rating objectives, posttraining evaluation conference, and exit interview. Sometimes, peer evaluators are graded on their critiques (comparing them to the instructor's) to make sure they apply criteria accurately instead of participating in a popularity contest.

Errors can occur with peer raters, however, and peer raters can be highly unreliable. They can disagree with each other and with the instructor (this would produce low interrater reliability). Student ratings are consistently higher than instructors' ratings (Wiseman & Barker, 1965) except when profanity is used in speeches, and then the ratings are lower (Bock, Butler, & Bock, 1984). Student critics who cannot adjust to the message and fear being a critic tend to give higher grades (Bock & Bock, 1984). Student critics who are "next up" to speak are also more lenient in their grading. After they're finished speaking, raters become more negative. Thus, it is NOT clear that peer evaluations are valid and reliable. The criticism given in class by peers is helpful, but their grades may not be accurate.

What Should Be Critiqued?

The communication literature is replete with criteria and rating scales for evaluating public speaking performance. Knower (1929) once proposed that rating scales increase open-mindedness in teachers and make them more accurate. In essence, rating scales force the instructor to specify the criteria before beginning the evaluation process. This basic principle has guided the discipline for the last 60 years.

Several published instruments contain standard criteria for judging public speaking performance. For example, Becker (1962) described an instrument containing three main criteria: Analysis/Content (ideas, supporting material, organization), Delivery (poise, bodily action, voice, articulation), and Language. Dedmon (1967) advocated only content and delivery. Cathcart (1981) suggested that critics should look at delivery, style, organization, proof, lines of argument, and purpose. Smith (1961) highlighted eight main sections of a speech critique: central idea, speaker preparation, main points, support, delivery, language, the introduction, and emotional appeal. Most textbooks have their own set of criteria and include similar qualities. The important point is that the qualities identified in the criticism should be those that are emphasized and taught in the class. For example, speech speed should not be critiqued or evaluated if it is not taught in the class. *Evaluating Classroom Speaking* (Bock & Bock, 1981) is a handy guide to the rating process.

How Should it be Given?

Oral or Written? The criticism/evaluation can be oral or written in nature. For example, the instructor can provide (a) oral criticism, using concrete ideas that focus on the next step to be mastered; (b) written criticism (either a checklist, rating scale, or open-ended written critique); (c) a question–answer period, which can reveal weaknesses in a speech; or (d) written evaluation, a grade based on criteria (Holtzman, 1960).

Instructors must determine which methods are most appropriate and feasible. Oral criticism should focus on growth and improvement, and it should also motivate the student to do better next time. Yet, it should be kept short and to the point. Erhart (1976) advocated three methods of orally critiquing student performance in class. With the "Tell and Sell" method, instructors inform students of their strengths and weaknesses, and then persuade them to improve; students may become hostile and defensive with this method, however. With the "Tell and Listen" method, instructors evaluate students' speeches and listen to student responses; the instructor becomes a counselor and the student is free to talk and, thus, good morale results. In the "Problem-Solving" method, the one that Erhart advocated, the student speaker evaluates the speech, and the instructor tries to lead discussion and stimulate thought.

In general, criticism should be offered by giving clear examples of the points made, and instructors should avoid lengthy discussion of moot or controversial questions. When students provide criticism of their peers, instructors should acknowledge all student criticism contributions. Brooks and Friedrich (1973) provided additional suggestions.

The criticism need not always be oral, however. Written criticism is often more useful than oral in that it is more tangible and students can save it for later reflection. Written evaluations are sometimes created by students for their peers in public speaking classes, and these are later discussed with the instructor (Hildebrandt & Stevens, 1960). Written criticism reinforces the oral criticism given in class. In one system, a combined oral/written method, critique sheets provide students with teachers' reactions, highlight important parts of speech making, and force teachers to be aware during the speech and to use predetermined categories (LaFleur, 1985). Instructors meet with students the day after the speech to review the critique sheet and view a videotaped version of the speech. In addition, a panel of four student judges (one who focuses on support-development, one on organization, one on language or style of the speaker, and one on delivery) prepare written critiques. This is a very comprehensive system of speech critiquing.

Behnke and King (1984) have computerized the speech criticism process. Their article in *Communication Education* details how to code criticism and comments, and how to construct individualized critiques for students. The authors reported that students like this system because it frees the instructor from writing during the speech (more eye contact) and the instructor can give lengthy comments and suggestions. It is useful for those who have the hardware.

Positive or Negative, General or Specific?   Research suggests that positive comments should be given during oral critiques in class (Bostrom, 1963). Criticism that focuses on one main idea designed to improve a student's ability, step by step, is more effective than providing a long list of behaviors that need to be changed (Holtzman, 1960). Positive comments enhance student attitudes about speaking, whereas negative ones diminish these attitudes. Positive comments are also appreciated more by students than negative ones. When criticism is negative, it should be atomistic and impersonal (Young, 1974).

Atomistic comments, detailed remarks that focus on specific aspects of the speech, are more helpful than holistic, general, and vague ones (Young, 1974). Impersonal comments, ones that focus on aspects of the speech rather than on the speaker, are more helpful than personal ones, especially when they are directed at aspects of delivery. This is because student speakers become defensive when they feel they are being attacked personally. Young also found that: (a) highly anxious students saw all types of criticism as more helpful than did those low in anxiety, (b) students of female instructors thought criticism was more helpful than students of male instructors, and (c) female students saw criticism as more helpful than did male students. Because Clevenger (1964) found that rating reliability was significantly higher for specific traits than for a general impression, an atomistic, detailed form might also be more reliable.

Using Rating Scales.   A variety of scales exist for turning criticism into evaluation. Simple numerical scales list the criteria for speech performance and assign numbers representing grading criteria to each. Most researchers advocate using between four and six steps. It appears that a five-point scale is ideal, especially because it conforms to the A–F grading system used in most colleges. For example, assume that content is one category for criticism and evaluation. Under content, there might be five or six specific aspects of content that are taught in the class, one of which might be organization of ideas. Using a five-point scale to critique organization of ideas, we would most likely create steps related to possible levels of achievement: Excellent, Good, Satisfactory, Poor, Unacceptable. These five steps must be clearly defined in the critic's mind so that he or she can clearly distinguish between them. "Excellent" might mean that the ideas presented were clearly organized in a distinguishable pattern (chronological, problem–cause–solution, etc.). "Good" might refer to an organization pattern that was clearly constructed but the student strayed from the pattern at one point, and so on. These five steps could be converted into a numerical system (5–1 points) or letter (A–F) system when the total grade is computed for the performance. Instructors might be interested in Oliver's (1960) system of grading criteria that distinguish between A, B, and C speeches and Gruner's (1968) translation of these criteria into behavioral objectives for the classroom.

When to Give Criticism

Opinions are mixed about when to give criticism in the classroom. Braden (1948) argued that feedback is important immediately after each speech. Dedmon (1967), however, suggested that criticism should be given at the end of the period (not after every speech), perhaps because of the possibility of overlapping.

Overlapping results when an evaluator writes a critique and rates a speaker during the speech or while the next speech is in progress. This effects immediate and delayed comprehension of information presented in speeches (lower for overlap condition) and evaluation of speeches (grade on second speech higher when overlapped) (Barker, Kibler, & Hunter, 1968). This says that a failure to listen critically inflates ratings. Therefore, instructors need to use an oral critique or some other form of lapse time between speeches (perhaps peer criticism) to allow them to complete their evaluations, or their scores will be inflated for the overlapped speaker. A computerized system of compiling criticism might be used to save time.

Evaluating Non-Speech Communication Skills

Although speeches are the primary focus of rating in the communication classroom, small group, interview, and interpersonal communication are also evaluated. Gouran and Whitehead (1971) studied group discussions and found that participants do not differ greatly from observers in their ratings. They suggested that, to increase reliability, several observers or participants be used. Sorenson and Pickett (1986) examined communication in interview settings and found that videotaped feedback was not effective, whereas peer ratings were only partially effective. Spitzberg and Hurt (1987) examined interpersonal skills using four molar clusters (interaction management, altercentrism, expressiveness, composure), each consisting of 10 molecular behaviors. This scale can be used to evaluate interpersonal skills.

Objectivity and Bias in Rating

Because of the oral nature of student presentations, rating objectivity and reliability are particularly important. In this section, I examine basic elements of objectivity, characteristics of students believed to be related to biased evaluations, characteristics of raters that lead to biased ratings, normal judgmental tendencies of raters, the importance of reliability, and ways to improve reliability through rater training.

Elements of Objective Rating.   Kelley (1965) argued that instructors need to be objective in rating. Objective rating lessens fear in communication classes, increases respect for the art of communication and the teacher, provides greater substance to knowledge and understanding by students, and enhances students' abilities and skill. According to Kelley, important elements for objective evaluation include: (a) a set of standards used for all students, (b) options in choosing speech techniques (e.g., students can choose an illustrative story, a humorous anecdote, or a profound quote to begin a speech); (c) instructions on what *not* to do; (d) criticism aimed at the next step for maximum improvement; and (e) an understanding that some principles and techniques contribute more to success than others. Kelley concluded that instructors should standardize their requirements (yet allow for individual style and personality), criticize on issues of bad choice and effect, and use an incremental system for evaluation (not just A, B, C).

Stiggins, Backlund, and Bridgeford (1985) outlined several biasing tendencies in assessing communication skills. They pointed out that: Teachers are often not trained adequately in assessment; cultural biases sometimes exist; certain characteristics of tests (ambiguous items, environment, scoring procedures) can lead to increased bias; and student evaluation anxiety can influence ratings. Other forms of bias also exist: leniency, trait error, central tendency, halo effect, logical error, rating two consecutive items alike, and comparison of a peer's performance with one's own skills. The authors argued that, although all these problems exist with rating oral performance, it is still a better alternative than a written test when assessing oral communication skills.

Characteristics of Students. Some researchers have suggested that certain characteristics of students—socioeconomic status, race, and gender—can result in biased ratings (Conville & Story, 1972; Granger, Matthews, Quay, & Verner, 1977; Natriello & Dornbusch, 1984). Low socioeconomic, Black, and male students receive lower ratings and grades than high socioeconomic, White, and female children, possibly because teachers' expectations are lower for minority students and because boys are given more academic criticism and direction in the classroom than girls. Barker (1969) also found students' and instructors' evaluations were related to their regard for the speaker and the speakers' level of academic achievement.

Other researchers have looked at degree of acquaintance and student anxiety level in relation to teacher evaluations. Henrikson (1940) found that instructors like better-known students more and judge them to be better speakers. In addition, teachers view high-apprehensive students as having lower potential for success in their future education, occupation and ability in content areas (math, English, social sciences, etc.); they also rate them higher in anxiety and lower in class participation (Smythe & Powers, 1978). Instructors must consider these student characteristics as potential sources of bias, ones they can overcome with sound standards and objective evaluations. They also need to be aware of characteristics in themselves that can lead to biased ratings and evaluations.

Characteristics of Raters. Biases specific to raters are well documented in the literature. It is clear that the validity of speech ratings can be affected by the rater's attitudes about the topic, mental dispositions about the speaker, and prior training in speech (Miller, 1964). In Bostrom's (1964) research on rater objectivity as a personality trait, openmindedness did not inflate or deflate ratings, but rigidity did. Rigid raters tended to give much lower ratings. Brooks (1957) described various types of rater errors (e.g., personal prejudice) and suggested that raters observe and record carefully. We need clear and precise behavioral objectives to reduce error in the rating context.

Research measurement literature consistently points to natural tendencies of raters or judges that lead to biased ratings (see e.g., Stiggins et al., 1985). One communication researcher examined the effect of persuasibility on leniency, halo, and trait errors and found that easy-to-persuade raters were more lenient (Bock, 1970). Leniency errors are those made when the rater gives speakers the benefit of the doubt in all close calls; halo effects are when raters view certain speakers as able to do no wrong; and trait errors are overall biases toward the speech based on some trait of the speech, such as its organization or theme. Of course, raters can be too severe or prone to making "horned effect" evaluations also. Bock and Bock (1977) found that female raters were too hard on all speakers when a male experimenter was present, and male raters were too hard on all speakers when a female experimenter was present. These results suggest that teachers can set up expectancies and confound student raters (male/female) when they evaluate speeches in class. If students give critiques before the instructor gives his or her comments, this type of bias might be eliminated.

Bias, then, can occur when communication performance is rated. Teachers and students must take steps to safeguard the objective rating process. Thompson (1944) suggested that more accurate ratings of speeches can be achieved via a panel of raters, giving raters better measuring devices, or training raters to be more skillful in their ratings.

Effects of Rater Training.   Training improves the validity and reliability of the rating process in classrooms. In one study, graduate students who were trained with videotape and instruction were more consistent raters (less variation among raters) than those without training (Bowers, 1964). Clevenger (1963) found that raters with more years of training and experience in teaching speech also had higher test–retest reliability. Through videotape, rater training can be made consistent for all raters; Gundersen (1978) provided a detailed example of how a training program can be established using videotapes of speakers.

Training students to give criticism on speeches is important because of the great probability of judgmental errors during the criticism process. Trained raters commit fewer leniency and halo errors (Bohn & Bohn, 1985). Leniency and halo errors are common when raters know that the speaker will see the results. The authors concluded that if you're going to use students' peers as raters, they should be trained. The Bohns provided a good bibliography on rating scales and raters.

Using a panel of trained student critics also helps increase the reliability of the evaluation. Without training, raters use different criteria when they evaluate a speech (Tiemens, 1965).

Tips for Criticism and Evaluation

1. Determine behavioral objectives for instruction.
2. Identify and delineate criteria to be used in evaluation; these should reflect what you teach in class.

3. Use oral criticism in addition to written after each speech; student and peer comments should come first, for they provide you with time to complete your own thoughts.

4. All students should understand the standards and scales used in the evaluation; they should be trained to make their ratings consistent.

5. Criticism should be positive and specific; focus on elements for future improvement.

6. Use a rating scale with four to six steps representing levels of achievement; students can track their own progress easily with this system.

7. Do not prejudge students based on their socioeconomic status, race, gender, level of anxiety, level of academic achievement, degree to which you know them, how much you like them, or your attitude about the topic; also, do not let on how rigidly you hold your beliefs or your own level of persuasibility influence your ratings.

EVALUATION OF COMMUNICATION KNOWLEDGE

Purposes of Testing

New instructors find it difficult to create communication exams because not only are they unsure about what questions to ask, they are unaware of the various purposes of testing. Measurements are used for diagnosis (to assess learning ability or determine initial instructional level for the class), for estimating achievement or progress (the purpose of most exams), for guiding and motivating learning (sometimes ungraded pop quizzes serve this purpose), and for research. In most classes, the purpose of testing is to measure achievement or knowledge.

We must measure what we teach. If factual knowledge is taught, use an objective test. If understanding is taught, use essay tests or papers. If self-diagnosis or awareness is what is taught, then a self-report instrument can be used. Douglas (1958) provided some helpful hints for improving measurement for various purposes.

Nunnally (1972) also provided some helpful hints on test construction. He suggested that students should be given a schedule of testing at the beginning of the course. Because college students must plan their work around a testing schedule, no pop quizzes should be given. Although unannounced tests can be used to spot-check student progress (as a result of unexpected problems in a class), they should not be used for grading purposes.

Planning the Exam

Goyer (1962), Newcombe and Robinson (1975), Nunnally (1972), and Milton and Edgerly (1976) provided the following suggestions and instructions for planning exams. First, consider the test or course objectives and the content/subject matter of the test. A valid test is one that serves its intended function. In the classroom, an exam functions to assess level of performance at a particular point in time rather than to measure a particular personality trait or predict future achievement in an area. Tests are used as teaching devices, as well. They show what information is understood and what needs further clarification.

Second, a representative sample of questions from all assigned material should be used, not questions from just one chapter or subsection of the material. The more items on the exam, the more representative the sample of questions will be (content validity). Longer tests, then, are better discriminators of the mastering of information in the testing area.

Third, plan the test items. Test items should be matched to the objectives. If knowledge of a subject is being assessed, then a written format (multiple choice, essay, matching, true–false, completion, problems, or interpretation questions) should be used. If skill is assessed, a behavioral method is most appropriate. Also, decide on the specific objectives of the exam: Are you concerned about memory of facts, or ability to understand simple or complex principles, to use principles to evaluate proposed solutions to problems or to solve problems, or to extend old principles to new ones? Tests can measure understanding, recall, memory, comprehension, and critical judgment; the questions created must be matched with the purpose.

Fourth, consider that there will be sources of error in the exam. Student performance can fluctuate because of mood, physical health, lack of sleep, and so on. Also, there will be errors due to guessing (a fill-in-the-blank question is more reliable than a multiple guess or true–false question). Scoring errors can also occur (even with machine scoring). Alternative forms of an exam (for large lecture classes) can be used to prevent cheating and to test for reliability. Be sure to give more than one or two exams during the semester/quarter so that characteristics of the student or exam will not be a major source of error in the student's overall grade.

Fifth, allow enough time for the questions during the exam. A time limit should be set up so that 90% of the students will feel that they have ample time for the test (the other 10% will never feel that they have enough time). You will need to put a limit on the number of items you use. With multiple-choice questions, allow one to two questions per minute. Ten minutes should be sufficient for essay questions requiring a one-half page answer.

Sixth, any exam, whether objective or essay, should be constructed with clear instructions. These can be clarified in class if necessary, but students who arrive late will not benefit from in-class clarification, and some students will not be listening. It is always best, therefore, to use detailed written instructions on the exam and corrections on the chalkboard. Also, pay careful attention to the physical features of the exam—spelling, punctuation, wording, clarity, and general appearance.

Seventh, keep the test results on file during the semester. It is difficult to discuss a student's answers when the test has been lost. Give the answer sheets to the students at the end of the semester, or store them for a year in the event that a student questions a grade after the class is over. Also, security must be tight around exam time or copies will disappear, sometimes without your realizing that they're gone.

Eighth, during the test, move quietly around the room to answer questions and prevent cheating. Write the time on the chalkboard occasionally if no clock exists in the room so students can budget their time. Also, the physical setting should be quiet, well-lit, and not overly crowded.

Ninth, once you create good questions, you might want to keep your exam questions for use in the future. Using separate answer sheets with test booklets solves this problem. Information about the responses to each question should be given to the student on the answer sheet, but the questions can be turned back in to the teacher. Spend time going over answers and questions in class or during office hours, but hold onto those questions. Also, when booklets are used, they can be re-used for other sections of the class, saving on copying expenses.

Constructing a good exam takes time and energy. With 30 students in a class, you break even in the time required to put together an objective exam versus the amount of time required to grade essay questions. With more than 30 students, it becomes more economical to use an objective exam (for easy scoring). If you use test booklets and separate answer sheets, a grading key can be constructed that eases grading. On the answer sheets, have students write the words "true" and "false" when T–F questions are used or have them circle a T or F (a, b, c, d, and e for multiple choice) instead of trying to decipher their handwriting.

Types of Questions

There are two basic types of questions. Recognition questions—multiple choice, true–false, and matching—give students the various answers and ask only that they recognize which one is correct. Recall questions—supply or completion, short answer, essay—require students to remember and provide the answers. Objective (non-essay) tests are more reliable than subjective essay exams, because with essays, evaluation is often based on writing ability, vocabulary, spelling, and other grammatical bases. In this section, a variety of objective and subjective questions are explained and examples of each are given.

Multiple choice (guess) items are versatile and can be used to test for facts, evaluation, application of principles, skills, and definitions. In everyday usage, however, many multiple-choice questions are ambiguous and emphasize trivial points. Multiple-choice questions consist of two main parts: the problem and the set of alternatives. The problem should point to the theme of the correct alternative answer, yet incorrect alternatives should be plausibly related to the problem (do not use joke answers), and the correct alternative should resemble in appearance the incorrect ones. With multiple choice, one alternative need not be absolutely correct, just better than the others. The correct alternatives should be randomly ordered to avoid guessing, and correct responses should be evenly distributed among the letters (we tend to put the correct answer as "c" too often).

The multiple-choice problem and alternatives should be clearly written. Avoid rote memory problems (e.g., specific numbers of things or percentages), negatively stated or double-negative items, grammatical cues that give the answer away (a, an, etc.), and superfluous detail in the problem. Each problem should be independent of every other problem. With the alternatives, do not use clues to the correct alternative (signalled by words such as "all," "always," and "never") or alternatives that overlap or include each other (a, b, a & b, all of the above; instead, have four to five clear choices). If the statement is controversial, use "According to . . . ." All in all, make sure something worthwhile is being measured. An example of a good multiple-choice question is:

EX1: Multiple choice questions should include:
      a. clues to the correct alternative
      b. alternatives that overlap each other
      c. negatively stated responses
      d. rote memory material
    *e. four or five choices

True–false items are easy to compose, yet it is difficult to create statements that are absolutely true, because not much *is* always true or false. Students have a 50% chance of guessing correctly with these, so this form of question is unreliable. Teachers and students, in their asking and answering, tend to lean towards either true or false answers, making this form of assessment even more unreliable. Many experts (e.g., Nunnally, 1972) advise against using true–false questions. However, if these statements must be used, limit the statement to a single idea, avoid specific determiners/qualifiers (all, sometimes, usually, never, always), be sure each statement is unequivocally true or false, avoid negative and double-negative statements, and use an equal number of true and false statements. Also, be sure all sentences are of about equal length (there is a tendency for longer ones to be true). An example of a good true–false question is:

EX2: True–false items are reliable forms of assessing student knowledge. (F)

Matching questions are used to cover a lot of material in a relatively small space. There is usually a list of items (should be no longer than eight) and a list of options (should be 50% longer than the list of items). All items and options should relate to the same central theme. The instructions should clearly indicate how the matching is to be performed. An example of a good set of matching items is:

EX3: On the left you'll find five different types of exam questions and on the right are some definitions. Choose one correct definition from the right-hand column for each of the exam questions on the left, and write the letter in the space provided. Each definition will be used no more than once.

_____ 1. True–false

_____ 2. Fill-in-the-blank

_____ 3. Multiple choice

_____ 4. Matching

_____ 5. Essay

a. one or two words that are supplied by the student

b. a group of answers to a question from which one correct alternative is chosen

c. a puzzle solved through clues consisting of word definitions

d. a statement that is judged for its veracity

e. a list of definitions that are related to a list of terms

f. identification of or definitions of terms given

g. a lengthy statement consisting of an answer to a question

h. a problem that is solved through computation

Supply or *completion* items (fill in the blank) eliminate the possibility of guessing and focus on naming and labeling. These items are useful when testing knowledge of simple names, dates, and facts. Authorities suggest that only one or two blank spaces be used per sentence, making sure that only one term will complete the blank. Leave only important terms blank, and place the blank space near the end of the sentence. In creating fill-in questions, avoid repeating the textbook phrasing word for word (or students will attempt to memorize the text), and avoid grammatical cues to the correct word (e.g., "a" or "an" will give clues to the first letter of the word). An example of a good fill-in question is:

EX 4: The type of test question that leaves a blank at the end of the sentence for students to complete is called _____.

Essay questions require recall and phrasing of ideas in one's own words. Be sure to limit the scope of the questions to get the size answer you expect, and ask for answers that can be given in the time you allow for each. Provide enough detail in the question to lead to a correct response, phrase the question so it reflects a high level of understanding, and avoid asking for students' personal feelings (no way to grade these).

The type of question must match the cognitive objectives of the exam, and the type of question is reflected in the explicit instructions. For example, if you want to test knowledge, you might ask students to "name and describe . . ." or if you want to test comprehension, you might ask students to "compare and contrast . . ." or "give an example of. . . ." A question that seeks to test ability to synthesize ideas might begin with "develop a theory . . ." or "create a model. . . ." If you want to test ability to analyze, you might ask "what reasons are given . . . ," and if you want to test students' evaluation skills, the question might begin with "what reasons can you see . . ." or "evaluate the reasoning given. . . ."

To increase content validity, use a larger number of short-answer items instead of a smaller number of long-answer items. Be careful, however, not to require too much writing for the time allotted for the exam. To combat the time problem, some instructors give students a choice of answering a certain number of questions, but this is poor practice. All students should be required to answer the same questions to obtain a comprehensive view of students' knowledge as opposed to how well they do on those questions they know. Open-book tests should also be avoided if you want to measure learning. An example of a good essay question is:

EX5: Name and explain three reasons why essay questions are valid indicators of achievement.

Grading Exams

An answer key makes grading of objective exams simple and quick; however, there is more to do than just grading these exams. We need to analyze objective exams to see if the exam discriminates between good and poor students (as it should), which items are too easy or too hard (examine the chance factor [50% in T–F], the range of difficulty, and then omit or rescore easy items in future use of the test), and which test items best discriminate between those who did well and those who didn't (those who do well shouldn't get the easy items wrong). Campus testing or computing centers can often compute these statistics for you if you use the mark-sensitive forms they provide

Grading essay exams (and papers) is more difficult. First, it's important that you not be biased, so remove students' names from their papers or have them provide a code that is translated at a later date. Second, there are two main ways of grading the essays—through holistic (general impression) or through analytical criteria. The analytical method is more valid and is detailed here.

First, write an ideal answer or outline the major points for use in scoring the essays, and get a colleague to do the same to make sure your answer is complete. Use reasonable expectations for grading criteria; no one will record all the information. Second, use a numerical point scale for each question and determine before reading the essays the meaning of the points. Certain items might be weighted in relation to the page-length limit for the answers. Third, total all the points and assign grades after all the individual questions are graded.

When reading the essays, don't allow factors other than knowledge (spelling, handwriting, grammar) to influence the score unless you're also teaching these; if so, create a separate grade for writing style. Score all answers to one question before going on to the next so that your standards don't shift. Fatigue can affect your use of your grading standards, so take breaks during grading. The breaks should come between questions. If possible, have a fellow instructor read your set of exams to be sure you're using your criteria consistently.

Tips for Grading

1. Consider the course objectives and functions of the test.
2. Make sure the test covers all the material covered in class and in the textbook.
3. Choose the question format most appropriate for your purpose.
4. Consider how much error is in the test.

5. Check the test length.
6. Provide clear instructions to the questions in the test booklet.
7. Have students answer questions on separate answer sheets; discuss the answers to the exam but return the answer sheets only at the end of the semester.
8. Grade essays and papers using an analytical method of evaluation.

COMPUTING COURSE GRADES

Students deserve a sensible method for combining grades from the various assignments into a grade for the course. If only objective exams are used in a class, for example, the raw scores could be combined and standards developed for final letter grades (e.g., 90% for an A, below 60% for an F). Or, if all exams are created to total 100%, they could be averaged or weighted by importance (some weight the final exam heavier than a regular exam). If only essay exams are used in a class, these grades could be averaged, and more weight could be given to longer tests (e.g., the final exam). If there is a mixture of exams or of exams and performances, a five-point scale could be used to reduce all grades to this system (4.5 − 5.0 = A; 4.0 − 4.4 = B; 3.0 − 3.9 = C; 2.0 − 2.9 = D, 1.9 or less = F). These could then be averaged and/or weighted by importance. This type of numerical grade equivalency system must be devised before the class begins and then adhered to throughout.

Again, one must keep in mind the objectives for the course in deciding how to compute these grades, and the system that will be used should be presented clearly to students in the syllabus at the beginning of the class. Students can then see what is considered most important in the class. When devising a weighting system for assignments, certain ones clearly do and should carry more weight. In the basic communication class, speeches to inform, persuade, and stimulate are usually given more weight than speeches of introduction, parliamentary procedure, impromptus, and debate. Perhaps one half of the course grade would be based on speeches, one fourth on exams, and one fourth on outlines and other written assignments.

Contract Grading

Some communication teachers have advocated using contract grading in communication classes, because they create a cooperative atmosphere instead of a competitive one. Book (1975) provided a sample contract for interpersonal communication using Bloom's taxonomy of cognitive levels, which allows for quality of work to be measured. Stelzner (1975) and Stern (1972) detailed a contract system for public speaking classes. Students declare the grade they plan to work for and the teacher gives the assignments and evaluation criteria. Wolvin and Wolvin (1975a, 1975b) described how to set up contracts in classes and give details about a contract used in technical speech communication; they argued that contracts result in greater student effort and higher grades (mainly because they can redo work until it's satisfactory). Some, however, argue that contract grading allows low-ability, highly motivated students to achieve grades higher than they should merely by exerting greater effort or devoting more time to the assignment. Contracts should be based on quality of work instead of on sheer quantity. Contract grading also requires about twice the amount of time for instructors; duplicate exams must be created, and papers are graded more than once.

How NOT to Grade

In general, students should be graded on achievement or learning, not on their class attendance, a curve, effort, work habits, character traits, personal preferences, or attitudes toward you or the class. Your evaluation of a student's attitude or personality is subjective and should not receive a grade.

Assigning grades to students and computing course averages should not be done with guilt or feelings that the grade represents the student as a person; rather, grading should be based only on what the student has done in the class during that particular semester. Instructors should keep in mind that a C is an average or normal grade, and guilt about the effect of a grade on a student's future should not inflate the instructor's grades.

Class Attendance. Is showing up for class a course requirement? Is that all you want? Or do you want active participation, thorough and on-time work, and improvement of knowledge or skill? Grades should reward that which is most important, and class attendance should be significantly less important than other objectives. It is better to deduct points for lack of attendance than to give points for attending (check your university's policy on class attendance and approved absences). If you must grade class participation, set standards and a variety of levels, and keep detailed records for each student. Students who feel they deserve higher course grades will surely confront you about the most subjective grade in the class, and that will be the participation grade. You will need to account for all your grades.

Grading on a Curve.   Students who believe that grading on a curve will improve their grades do not understand the basic principle behind the practice. These students want all their grades raised. But grading on a curve is different. A curve assumes a normal curve with a mean of 50 and a standard deviation of 10; this rarely occurs. The normal curve then determines the percentage of students in each letter grade, so there are about equal numbers of A and F students, a larger number of B and D students, and an even larger number of C students. Most classes have too few students to use this accurately, so Terwilliger (1971) has advised against it.

There are two major problems with "grading on the curve." If you have a class of highly capable students (in that all students would receive an A or B on an absolute scale), a student could fail an exam or speech with a B grade. This could have major ramifications for students' futures in that talented students would find it hard to get into graduate schools because they happened to be rank-ordered in a particular class. Obviously, classes with students who are all low in capability request grading on the curve so that students who have met the course objectives only partially will have a chance to receive an A in the class. With this system, a student's grades might be inflated, and future failure in graduate school could be easily understood. It is important to use absolute standards for evaluation, for they will help dispel claims of unfair grading practices.

Grading on a curve also sets up a competition among students in a class and affects the class attitude toward exams. If used with speeches, peer evaluation cannot be used, because students will note that their peer's success can mean their own failure. Criterion-referenced evaluation is designed to determine if students have met the course objectives and is more fair to all students.

Grading on Improvement.   Grades should not be based on improvement or progress. It is common and easy for students at low-ability levels to improve, making significant gains, whereas it is hard for those at high levels to improve as much. A better system would be to weigh more heavily later assignments; in this way, the lower skilled students would have an opportunity to improve before the more important assignments.

Grading on Effort.   According to Sussman (1975), students shouldn't think that you grade on effort or input. If they do, quality will be disregarded. Students will spend hours working on projects, as though they're punching a time-clock, yet may never achieve the quality standards that you set up. Disappointment results because of this. Perceptions of equity are based on investments or inputs and on rewards or outcomes. Teachers need to justify to students their grading systems so students see achievement of assignments, rather than investment of time, as the relevant outcome. Equity is also based on comparison with others; students compare themselves to others. A C is a normal or average grade, yet students do not want to view themselves as average.

The system advocated in this chapter, then, focuses on the necessity of having equitable standards (ones that are related to the course being taught), communicating these standards to students at the beginning of the course, and using these standards consistently for all students. This is important for evaluating all products in communication classes, whether they be speeches, group discussions, term papers, or exams. Final grades in the class should reflect the knowledge and skill called for in the course's design, and students should be given equal opportunity to demonstrate knowledge and skills in the class.

REFERENCES

Baker, E. E. (1967). Aligning speech evaluation and behavioral objectives. *Speech Teacher, 16*, 158–160.

Balcer, C. (1958). Evaluation in the speech class—Growth in desirable attitudes. *Central States Speech Journal, 9*, 13–14.

Barker, L. L. (1969). The relationship between sociometric choice and speech evaluation. *Speech Teacher, 18*, 204–207.

Barker, L. L., Kibler, R. J., & Hunter, E. C. (1968). An empirical study of overlap rating effects. *Speech Teacher, 17*, 160–166.

Becker, S. L. (1962). The rating of speeches: Scale independence. *Speech Monographs, 29*, 38–44.

Behnke, R. R., & King, P. E. (1984). Computerized speech criticism. *Communication Education, 33*, 173–177.

Bock, D. G. (1970). The effects of persuasibility on leniency, halo and trait errors in the use of speech rating scales. *Speech Teacher, 19*, 296–300.

Bock, D. G., & Bock, E. H. (1977). The effects of sex on the experimenter, expectancy inductions, and sex of the rater on leniency, halo, and trait errors in speech rating behavior. *Communication Education, 26*, 298–306.

Bock, D. G., & Bock, E. H. (1981). *Evaluating classroom speaking.* Urbana, IL: ERIC Clearinghouse on Reading and Communication Skills.

Bock, D. G., & Bock, E. H. (1984). The effects of positional stress and receiver apprehension on leniency errors in speech evaluation: A test of the rating error paradigm. *Communication Education, 33*, 337–341.

Bock, D. G., Butler, J. L. P., & Bock, E. H. (1984). The impact of sex of the speaker, sex of the rater and profanity type on language trait errors in speech evaluation: A test of the rating error paradigm. *Southern Speech Communication Journal, 49*, 177–186.

Bohn, C. A., & Bohn, E. (1985). Reliability of raters: The effects of rating errors on the speech rating process. *Communication Education, 34*, 343–351.

Book, C. (1975). Contract grading in the interpersonal communication course. *Speech Teacher, 24*, 133–138.

Book, C., & Simmons, K. W. (1980). Dimensions and perceived helpfulness of student speech criticism. *Communication Education, 29*, 135–145.

Bostrom, R. N. (1963). Classroom criticism and speech attitudes. *Central States Speech Journal, 14,* 27–32.

Bostrom, R. N. (1964). Dogmatism, rigidity, and rating behavior. *Speech Teacher, 13,* 283–287.

Bowers, J. W. (1964). Training speech raters with films. *Speech Teacher, 13,* 228–231.

Braden, W. W. (1948). Making speech criticism acceptable to the student. *Southern Speech Journal, 13,* 91–93.

Brooks, K. (1957). Some basic considerations in rating scale development: A descriptive bibliography. *Central States Speech Journal, 9,* 27–31.

Brooks, W. D., & Friedrich, G. W. (1973). *Teaching speech communication in the secondary school.* Boston: Houghton Mifflin.

Cathcart, R. S. (1981). *Post-communication: Critical analysis and evaluation* (2nd ed.). Indianapolis: Bobbs-Merrill.

Clevenger, T. (1963). Retest reliabilities of ten scales of public speaking performances. *Central States Speech Journal, 14,* 285–291.

Clevenger, T. (1964). Influence of scale complexity on the reliability of ratings of general effectiveness in public speaking. *Speech Monographs, 31,* 153–156.

Conville, R. L., & Story, R. W. (1972). Teaching to communicate: The sociolinguistic problem. *Speech Teacher, 21,* 247–254.

Dedmon, D. N. (1967). Criticizing student speeches: Philosophy and principles. *Central States Speech Journal, 18,* 276–284.

Douglas, J. (1958). The measurement of speech in the classroom. *Speech Teacher, 7,* 309–319.

Erhart, J. F. (1976). The performance appraisal interview and evaluation of student performances in speech communication courses. *Communication Education, 25,* 237–246.

Gouran, D. S., & Whitehead, J. L. (1971). An investigation of ratings of discussion statements by participants and observers. *Central States Speech Journal, 22,* 263–268.

Goyer, R. S. (1962). The construction of the "objective" examination in speech. *Southern Speech Journal, 28,* 27–35.

Granger, R. C., Mathews, M., Quay, L. C., & Verner, R. (1977). Teacher judgments of the communication effectiveness of children using different speech patterns. *Journal of Educational Psychology, 69,* 793–796.

Gruner, C. R. (1968). Behavioral objectives for the grading of classroom speeches. *Speech Teacher, 17,* 207–209.

Gundersen, D. F. (1978). Video-tape modules as a device for training speech raters. *Southern Speech Communication Journal, 43,* 395–406.

Harris, C. W. (1963). Some issues in evaluation. *Speech Teacher, 12,* 191–199.

Henrikson, E. H. (1940). The relation among knowing a person, liking a person and judging him as a speaker. *Speech Monographs, 7,* 22–25.

Hildebrandt, H. W., & Stevens, W. W. (1960). Blue book criticisms at Michigan. *Speech Teacher, 8,* 20–22.

Holtzman, P. D. (1960). Speech criticism and evaluation as communication. *Speech Teacher, 8,* 1–7.

Kelley, W. D. (1965). Objectivity in the grading and evaluation of speeches. *Speech Teacher, 14,* 54–58.

Knower, F. (1929). A suggestive study of public-speaking rating scale values. *Quarterly Journal of Speech, 15,* 30–41.

LeFleur, G. B. (1985). A special tool for offering criticism: The post-speech transcript. *Association for Communication Administration Bulletin, 54,* 63–64.

Miller, G. R. (1964). Agreement and the grounds for it: Persistent problems in speech rating. *Speech Teacher, 13,* 257–261.

Milton, O., & Edgerly, J. W. (1976). *The testing and grading of students*. New Rochelle, NY: Change.

Natriello, G., & Dornbusch, S. M. (1984). *Teacher evaluative standards and student effort*. New York: Longman.

Newcombe, P. J., & Robinson, K. F. (1975). *Teaching speech communication: Methods and materials*. New York: David McKay.

Nunnally, J. C. (1972). *Educational measurement and evaluation* (2nd ed.). New York: McGraw-Hill.

Oliver, R. T. (1960). The eternal (and infernal) problem of grades. *Speech Teacher, 8*, 8–11.

Smith, R. G. (1961). The criticism of speeches: A dialectical approach. *Speech Teacher, 10*, 59–62.

Smythe, M. J., Kibler, R. J., & Hutchings, P. W. (1973). A comparison of norm-referenced and criterion-referenced measurement with implications for communication instruction. *Speech Teacher, 22*, 1–17.

Smythe, M. J., & Powers, W. G. (1978). When trainees are apprehensive: The effect of communication apprehension on teacher expectations. *Communication Yearbook, 2*, 487–491.

Sorenson, R. L., & Pickett, T. A. (1986). A test of two teaching strategies designed to improve interview effectiveness: Rating behavior and videotaped feedback. *Communication Education, 35*, 13–22.

Spitzberg, B. H., & Hurt, H. T. (1987). The measurement of interpersonal skills in instructional contexts. *Communication Education, 36*, 28–45.

Stelzner, S. L. (1975). A case for contract grading. *Speech Teacher, 24*, 127–132.

Stern, D. A. (1972). A flow-chart approach to public speaking "On the contract plan." *Today's Speech, 20*, 25–26.

Stiggins, R. J., Backlund, P. M., & Bridgeford, N. J. (1985). Avoiding bias in the assessment of communication skills. *Communication Education, 34*, 135–141.

Sussman, L. (1975). A theoretical analysis of equity and its relationship to student evaluation. *Southern Speech Communication Journal, 40*, 321–334.

Terwilliger, J. S. (1971). *Assigning grades to students*. Glenview, IL: Scott Foresman.

Thompson, W. N. (1944). An experimental study of the accuracy of typical speech rating techniques. *Speech Monographs, 11*, 65–79.

Tiemens, R. K. (1965). Validation of informative speech ratings by retention tests. *Speech Teacher, 14*, 211–215.

Wiseman, G., & Barker, L. (1965). A study of peer group evaluation. *Southern Speech Journal, 31*, 132–138.

Wolvin, A. D., & Wolvin, D. R. (1975a). Contract grading in speech communication: Administrative implications. *Association for Communication Administration Bulletin, 13*, 43–44.

Wolvin, A. D., & Wolvin, D. R. (1975b). Contract grading in technical speech communication. *Speech Teacher, 24*, 139–142.

Young, S. (1974). Student perceptions of helpfulness in classroom speech criticism. *Speech Teacher, 23*, 222–234.

V

TACKLING SOME UNIQUE TEACHING ASSIGNMENTS

28

Directing Multiple Sections of the Basic Course

Douglas M. Trank
University of Iowa

The basic communication course is the only course within our discipline that is required by a significant number of other departments and colleges for graduation. The most recent national survey, which is consistent with earlier reports, indicates that the basic communication course is required of noncommunication majors in nearly 85% of the institutions across the country (Trank, Becker, & Hall, 1986). This unique characteristic provides healthy departmental enrollments and excellent visibility across campus, but it also places burdens on the teachers and the directors of the basic course. Although teachers in the basic course share responsibility for delivering a quality product, the ultimate responsibility for the quality of a course with several sections inevitably belongs to the director of the course.

That responsibility is often complicated by the director's status within the department. The basic course director is frequently a newly graduated and recently hired assistant professor. That person is expected to meet the normal expectations for tenure and promotion; that is, to contribute to the service and teaching needs of the department and to publish a sufficient quantity of research of sufficient quality to gain tenure and promotion within the specified time allowed. In institutions with a relatively large number of sections of the basic course, these additional responsibilities for the director can complicate what is already a demanding professional commitment. Although this chapter does not explore all of the duties and responsibilities of a basic course director, the major issues and those that frequently cause serious problems are examined. In addition, sources are identified for additional reading and research. The issues discussed are focused around the educational justification for the basic course, typical approaches to the course, problems unique to programs with multiple sections, and administrative concerns for the basic course director.

EDUCATIONAL JUSTIFICATION FOR THE
BASIC COURSE: A DUALITY OF PURPOSE

Basic course directors, if they are to be effective with all the audiences that have a vested interest, must operate from a philosophy that allows the basic course to function both as a service course and as an essential part of a student's liberal education. Unfortunately, some individuals view the term "service course" with negative connotations, as something less important than other courses within the department. It is far more productive and accurate to realize that fulfilling a duality of purpose of providing a curriculum that is a primary service to other disciplines and providing instruction that is at the core of a liberal arts education is a unique and rewarding opportunity.

Basic course directors must be concerned with the nature and purpose of instruction in the basic course. Should it focus on theory or application or some integration of the two? Should it attempt to teach the history of the discipline, the nature of human interaction, critical thinking and decision making, or should it fulfill functions more directly related to other missions of the department? Regardless of the size or the nature of the institution (or the inclination of the faculty), most basic courses in communication share these two fundamental goals: to introduce students to the discipline of communication and to meet basic communication proficiency needs (Pearson & Sorenson, 1980). It is obviously possible to design a basic course that fulfills many functions; one that meets the expectations of faculty outside the department and that satisfies the specific requirements of the communication faculty. What is critical for the effectiveness of the basic course director, however, is that the faculty within the department and the administration agree and support the position of the basic course director.

TYPICAL APPROACHES TO THE BASIC COURSE

In some institutions, the nature of the basic course is decided by colleagues and administrators outside the communication department. If, for example, the college of business and the college of education want their students to have experience and instruction in public speaking, the faculty of the department will provide a public speaking orientation if they want the course to continue as a requirement for those colleges. Although others may well have a degree of input into the nature of the basic course, the course director and the faculty in the communication department must assume the ultimate control over the course. After all, they possess the expertise in communication instruction and have a responsibility to ensure that what is being taught reflects the best theory and research available.

Communication departments typically teach the basic course through one of three standard approaches. Although it is difficult to generalize too far in describing these courses, the *interpersonal* course generally emphasizes a theoretical approach to understanding communication. The competent communicator is one who understands the nature and process of human communication. In a *public speaking* course, the competent communicator is one who can prepare and present a variety of types of messages for different purposes to different audiences. The emphasis here is on the "public" performance of students. The *combination/blend* approach shares theoretical and experiential approaches; the emphasis is broader than in either of the other courses.

Information on orientations toward the basic course, instructional methods used by various programs, and issues related to administrative concerns can be found in the results of several national surveys. They document, for example, a continued shift in the orientation of the basic course toward a public speaking approach at the expense of the interpersonal and multiple or combination approaches. Over half of the basic course programs in a 1985 survey reported a public speaking approach, a third had a combination or blend approach, and the remaining programs were split between communication theory, interpersonal, and small-group approaches (Gibson, Hanna, & Huddleston, 1985; Trank et al., 1986).

The Basic Course Committee of the Speech Communication Association and the Midwest Basic Course Directors' Conference offer annual meetings and conferences where basic course directors share information and research results specifically related to the basic course. The Central States Communication Association, Eastern Communication Association, Southern States Communication Association, and Western Speech Communication Association sponsor such conferences and meetings on a less frequent basis. Information about all of these organizations and conferences can be obtained from the Speech Communication Association. Basic course directors can discover the nature of the basic course at other institutions by attending such conferences and seeking out the results of frequent national surveys.

PROBLEMS UNIQUE TO BASIC COURSE
PROGRAMS WITH MULTIPLE SECTIONS

The basic course director must serve as the educational leader for the most critical program within most undergraduate communication departments. Major publishing companies estimate that there were approximately 1 million students enrolled in the basic course in 1980 (Ochs, 1980). A survey of a representative sample of the more than 2,000 institutions on the Speech Communication Association's mailing list reported a mean basic course enrollment of nearly 900 students each year. A liberal interpretation of this data would place the enrollment close to 2 million students each year (Trank et al., 1986).

Standardization Across Sections

Most institutions have enrollments that necessitate multiple sections of the basic course. Over three fourths of the institutions responding to a recent survey reported basic course enrollments in excess of 200 students per year, and over one fourth have enrollments in excess of 1,000 students per year (Trank et al., 1986). Multiple sections present problems not necessarily found in other instructional situations. The degree of consistency of instructional practices and content across sections is a critical issue for the basic course director. Students in Section 10 have the right to expect that the instruction they receive (their assignments and classroom activities, the goals and objectives, and the content) is very similar to that which the students in Section 356 receive. Equally important, at least in their minds, the students want to be assured that grades are distributed fairly and equally across sections. Students frequently complain that their roommate in another section did only half the work they did, or that the roommate's work was not nearly as good as theirs, yet they received a lower grade simply because they had a "tough" teacher or their roommate had an "easy" teacher. This problem is not restricted to very large programs but is likely to appear for any course that has more than one section.

Even though most faculty and students realize that absolute equality of instruction and evaluation across a large number of sections of a course is impossible, the basic course director has the responsibility to ensure some degree of consistency across sections and across semesters. Although this is accomplished to a certain extent by decisions that the director and the faculty make about the educational justification and the purpose and approach for the basic course discussed earlier, the decisions made regarding the specificity of the syllabus or course guidelines and the training of the instructors for the course are equally critical. In large institutions, the basic course is typically staffed almost entirely by graduate teaching assistants or part-time faculty. Across the nation, however, far fewer graduate students are teaching the basic course than tenured faculty, untenured full-time faculty, or even part-time faculty. Equally important, the basic course is taught by senior faculty about as frequently as it is by junior faculty and more frequently than by part-time faculty (Trank et al., 1986).

A basic course director may have difficulty enforcing a particular content, textbook, or approach on colleagues who have been teaching this course for several years or who may not want to teach at the basic course level. It may also be difficult for them to become enthused about the innovative ideas and novel approaches developed by a basic course director who has considerably less teaching and administrative experience than many of the instructors for the course. In these situations, the course director obviously needs to secure the input of colleagues before making decisions about the course. At the opposite extreme, a basic course director may be faced with a situation where half or more of the teaching assistants assigned to teach the course in the fall are coming to the campus for the first time shortly before they are expected to begin teaching. Many of them may have never taught before. In this case, the director needs to provide detailed and specific materials for the instructors and, in fact, cannot wait until these instructors have opportunities for input into the development of the course.

Weaver (1976) described a prescriptive approach for organizing the course that calls for minimal involvement from the instructors in the planning stage. This approach requires the basic course director to develop a syllabus to be used by all instructors, complete with content, activities, and exercises. The basic course director selects the textbook that will be used in the course, determines which instructional strategies are appropriate for achieving the various goals and objectives of the course, and devises strategies for achieving consistency of evaluation of student performance across sections and situations. A far less prescriptive approach requires the basic course director to determine, either alone or with the faculty, the goals and approach for the course. These goals, along with the general content (and perhaps major units of instruction), are presented in a set of general guidelines for instructors to follow. Instructors are frequently allowed a choice from a list of appropriate textbooks and are asked to make decisions about teaching strategies that work best for them in particular situations within the general guidelines. This approach works most effectively where the department has sufficient staff and resources to provide a continual advisor/supervisor function for the graduate teaching assistants who are assigned to teach the basic course. It is also used in situations where the basic course is staffed primarily or entirely by the regular full-time faculty.

It is more common, however, to find the basic course director some-where between these extremes. Regardless of the degree of control, con-sistency across sections of a large basic communication course can only be accomplished with the cooperation of all those involved in the delivery of that course. In situations where a significant number of sections of the basic course are staffed by faculty with limited teaching experience, the director must establish an ongoing instructional program in order to ensure the continuous quality and consistency of instruction. The follow-ing section examines some of the elements of such programs for profes-sional development of the instructional staff.

Professional Development Programs

Although the primary responsibility of the director is to provide quality instruction for the undergraduates enrolled in all sections of the course, there is a concomitant responsibility to help the basic course staff develop their abilities as instructors. The director needs to establish an atmo-sphere where the graduate student instructors and part-time faculty know that they are viewed as valuable members of the faculty and are given a certain degree of freedom and responsibility for what they do in the classroom. An obvious way for basic course directors to begin estab-lishing such an atmosphere is to view themselves as advisors and teach-ers rather than as supervisors and trainers.

If a relationship is established where the role of the director is to supervise, correct, and punish inappropriate behavior, it is likely that instructors will avoid the director whenever possible. If the director adopts this "overseer" role, instructors will likely withhold information about their classes for fear that their teaching will be criticized or that they will be reprimanded. Reducing opportunities for communication be-tween director and instructors decreases consistency of instruction across sections and decreases the morale of the basic course staff. Such a rela-tionship is clearly counterproductive to the goals of improving both the teaching competencies of the staff and the outcomes of instruction in the basic course.

Most large basic course programs have a preservice workshop lasting from 2 to 5 days before the beginning of the semester. Creating a suppor-tive climate at this point provides positive benefits throughout the term (Andrews 1983; Trank, 1986). In addition to providing an early oppor-tunity for developing positive interpersonal relationships among the teaching staff, the workshop is an important time to establish the goals for the course, convey the general guidelines and day-to-day chores that must be completed throughout the term, and to see to the immediate and personal needs of the teaching staff.

An increasing number of departments also conduct weekly seminars for the instructional staff throughout the term. Some continue the seminars for the entire year, and a few give graduate credit for completing the course. Topics for such seminars include the range of subjects found in this book—from establishing objectives to final evaluation and assigning grades. These seminars give the director the time and opportunity to talk about teaching strategies, classroom management, responding to and evaluating student presentations, leading discussions, attendance policies, registration, schedules, and final grade sheets. Examples of such professional development programs and considerable advice regarding the teaching and training of graduate teaching assistants and part-time staff is readily available (Andrews, 1983; Chism & Warner, 1987; Moore, 1984; Trank, 1985, 1986; Yingling, 1984).

ADMINISTRATIVE CONCERNS FOR THE BASIC COURSE DIRECTOR

The final section of this chapter deals briefly with administrative details that are critical to the effective operation of the basic course program. The problems that frequently hinder the effectiveness of the director of the basic course—budgets for new equipment, the size of general expense budget, not enough faculty, not enough secretarial help, too many students for faculty size, quality of undergraduate students—are the same problems that are perceived as the most serious for departmental executive officers (Becker & Trank, 1988). The severity and extent of these problems within any department directly affect the decisions the director makes about the instructional staff, resources, and delivery and support systems for the basic course.

Delivery and Support Systems for the Basic Course

An increasing number of departments moved to a large lecture approach to teaching the basic course a decade ago, primarily to reduce the cost-per-credit-hour of instruction. As budgets within departments held steady or declined while enrollments rose, the basic course became a logical and necessary target for exploring possible alternative instructional strategies that would save or revert a substantial portion of the departmental budget. Although the large lecture format no longer enjoys widespread popularity across the country, it remains as one of a number of alternative delivery systems.

Other alternatives also appear to be driven, at least in part, by financial reasons. Gray, Berkel-Rothfuss, and Yerby (1986) claimed that this mandate to reduce costs has forced directors and administrators to search for educational models that provide the highest number of student credit hours for the lowest investment of faculty time. The personalized system of instruction, originally defined by Keller (1968) and perhaps best exemplified by the program at the University of Nebraska (Seiler & Fuss-Reineck, 1986), is one of the better known alternative delivery systems. This is a complex system that involves student self-paced learning and the extensive use of proctors, who are usually undergraduates who have taken the course. It also necessitates a facility that can manage the ongoing multiple activities of test taking, tutoring, presenting speeches, and studying. It requires strong, organized leadership from the director of the basic course and substantial support from the administration and faculty.

The majority of basic course programs across the country continue to "deliver" the basic course in the traditional small-section format. An increasing number of these programs, however, are using undergraduate assistants or undergraduate facilitators in a variety of ways to reduce the cost of instruction (Morlan, 1985). Although using undergraduates to assist in the instruction of the basic course may provide financial benefits to the department and the college, it presents additional problems for the director in terms of supervision and evaluation of instruction and ensuring consistency across the program.

The director may also be responsible for a speaking lab, where students can get individualized help for problems ranging from speech organization to communication apprehension (Foss, 1982). More recently, scholars and instructors have become increasingly interested in problems associated with non-native speakers of English in the basic course classrooms and labs (Powell, 1987; Schliessman, 1985). As the number of foreign students in our institutions continues to increase, this issue will command additional attention from basic course directors.

Instructional Concerns in the Basic Course

Many directors have become painfully aware that, although they have responsibility for the quality of instruction in the basic course, they have little actual authority over the instructors who teach that course. In large graduate institutions where the basic course is taught primarily by graduate students, the director typically has little control over the selection process. Graduate students are recruited for their academic ability; unfortunately, impressive Graduate Record Examination scores and outstanding undergraduate grade point averages do not guarantee a high level of competence as an instructor in the classroom. Rapid turnover of graduate teaching assistants, especially in programs that hire large numbers of master's degree students, is another concern for the basic course director. It is difficult to maintain continuity in a program when a significant percentage of the teaching staff is new each year.

Even though basic course directors may have little control over who teaches the course, they are generally responsible for coordinating the evaluation of that instruction—usually through some form of written student evaluations of the course and instructors at midterm or at the end of the term. If a "cafeteria" type of evaluation system is used, it is advisable to have a common core of questions for all instructors in order to make comparisons across sections and over several semesters. The director can make more informed judgments about instructional effectiveness by visiting the instructors' classrooms, examining their class hand-outs and syllabi, and examining student folders containing the work completed during the term. Some of these evaluations, if they are to be immediately helpful for instructors, should occur well before the end of the term while there is still an opportunity to alter approaches to the class. Such evaluation ought to have two primary purposes: to reward and praise excellent instruction and to identify situations where instructors need additional help to improve classroom performance. The director must place evaluation in a positive context in order to minimize the anxiety and confusion that it creates for the instructional staff.

The director must also be concerned about the distribution of grades across the course. Because the basic course is frequently taught in small sections with considerable student–instructor interaction, grade inflation is a common concern. Grades need to convey a realistic assessment of the students' work for the semester, but they also convey a message about communicative abilities to a wider audience across and beyond the academic community. The procedure is unfair if some instructors' grades are considerably higher or lower than colleagues who are teaching the same course. The course director can provide guidance by giving the instructors the profile of grades for the course from past semesters and by providing the profile of grades for students at midterm. Those who seem unreasonably high or low can be encouraged to share a set of papers with other instructors or visit other instructors' classes and evaluate student speeches together. The role of the director here is to advise and teach.

The director also has a major responsibility regarding decisions about which instructional resources will be used in the basic course (German, 1988; Weaver, 1976). The publishing and marketing of textbooks is a major financial enterprise, and the director ought to enlist the assistance of a committee of experienced basic course instructors to select the textbooks for the course (Ochs, 1980; Trank & Shepherd, 1987). Publishing companies are providing increasingly attractive packages of ancillary instructional materials for basic communication textbooks. For some programs, the need for videotaped examples of student speeches, instructor's manuals, computerized banks of examination questions, and student workbooks are central issues in the selection of a textbook.

Procedural Concerns in the Basic Course

Finally, there are a number of concerns that affect the entire department but that are essentially the responsibility of the basic course director. Decisions about the course which need to be published in college or university catalogs, schedules of courses, and related materials are often needed 6 to 18 months ahead of time. If the basic course is required, provisions and procedures for exemption examinations need to be made. The basic course director is usually responsible for writing and administering the exemption examinations and, if students are required to give speeches, training and scheduling instructors to evaluate those presentations. If the department does not have a policy regarding plagiarism, the director ought to establish one for the basic course. The same is necessary for issues like responsible use of language, human rights, required attendance, and student appeals.

The director is also responsible for scheduling instructors into the respective sections of the basic course. In institutions where regular and part-time faculty teach the course, other teaching responsibilities may take precedence over the basic course assignment. When dealing with graduate students, the director may need to wait until their schedules of courses are complete before attempting to schedule their teaching assignments. Policies concerning absences from teaching, cooperation with research studies, and extra teaching assignments need to be clearly stated for all instructors. The director must also plan a budget and procedure for allocating additional materials such as videotapes, duplicating materials, paper, and other instructional aids.

CONCLUSION

There are obviously many responsibilities and duties for a basic course director—depending on the nature of the course and the department. The issues discussed in this chapter focused around the educational justification for the basic course, typical approaches to the course, problems unique to programs with multiple sections, and administrative concerns for the basic course director. This discussion and the following list of references provide a starting point for those who may want to learn more about the basic course or for those who suddenly discover that they are about to become a director of the basic course.

REFERENCES

Andrews, P. H. (1983). Creating a supportive climate for teacher growth: Developing graduate students as teachers. *Communication Quarterly, 31,* 259–265.

Becker, S. L., & Trank, D. M. (1988). Why are you so happy? Predictors of communication chairpersons' satisfaction. *Association for Communication Administration Bulletin, 63,* 36–43.

Chism, N. V. N., & Warner, S. B., (Eds.). (1987). *Institutional responsibilities and responses in the employment and education of teaching assistants.* Columbus, OH: The Ohio State University Center for Teaching Excellence.

Foss, K. A. (1982). Communication apprehension: Resources for the instructor. *Communication Education, 31,* 195–203.

German, K. M. (1988, February). *Coordinating the basic course: Achieving consistency without sacrificing instructional freedom.* Paper presented at the Midwest Basic Course Director's Conference, Dayton, OH.

Gibson, J. W., Hanna, M. S., & Huddleston, B. M. (1985). The basic speech course at U.S. colleges and universities: IV. *Communication Education 34,* 281–291.

Gray, P. L., Buerkel-Rothfuss, N. L., & Yerby, J. (1986). A comparison between PSI-based and lecture-recitation formats of instruction in the introductory speech communication course. *Communication Education, 35,* 111–125.

Keller, F. S. (1968). Good-bye teacher. *Journal of Applied Behavior Analysis, 1,* 79–89.

Moore, L. L. (1984, February). *Orientation for first time teaching assistants: A course approach.* Paper presented at the Midwest Basic Course Director's Conference, Youngstown, OH.

Morlan, D. B. (1985). Staffing the basic public speaking course: An evaluation of an undergraduate facilitator program. *Ohio Speech Journal, 23,* 16–24.

Ochs, D. J. (1980). An ethical perspective for selecting textbooks. *Communication Education, 29,* 298–301.

Pearson, J. C., & Sorenson, R. L. (1980). The basic speech communication course: A review of past practices and current preferences. *Resources in Education,* ED 196 088.

Powell, R. G. (1987, November). *Assessing minimal speaking proficiency of non-native speakers: Culture and the basic course.* Paper presented at the Speech Communication Association Convention, Boston, MA.

Schliessman, M. R. (1985, February). *Non-native speakers of English in the basic speech course.* Paper presented at the Midwest Basic Course Director's Conference, Indianapolis, IN.

Seiler, W. J., & Fuss-Reineck, M. (1986). Developing the Personalized System of Instruction for the basic speech communication course. *Communication Education, 35,* 126–134.

Trank, D. M. (1985). An overview of present approaches to the basic speech communication course. *Association for Communication Administration Bulletin, 52,* 86–89.

Trank, D. M. (1986). A professional development program for graduate instructors in communication and composition. *Resources in Education,* ED 277 052.

Trank, D. M., Becker, S. L., & Hall, B. (1986). Communication arts and sciences in transition. *Association for Communication Administration Bulletin, 58,* 8–20.

Trank, D. M., & Shepherd, G. J. (1987). Textbook selection criteria for a multi-section basic course taught exclusively by graduate teaching assistants. *Resources in Education,* ED 287 183.

Weaver, R. L., II (1976). Directing the basic communication course. *Communication Education, 25,* 203–210.

Yingling, J. M. (1984, February). *Training the first-time teaching assistant: An adaptation of the Friedrich/Powell program.* Paper presented at the annual Midwest Basic Course Director's Conference, Youngstown, OH.

29

Continuing Education

Virginia P. Richmond
West Virginia University

For 15 years, I have had the opportunity to work with extension graduate education in the Communication Studies Department at West Virginia University. In a very real sense, this chapter represents the many
students I have worked with in these 15 years. The students (predominantly teachers) have given me and the department an understanding of
continuing education that we might never have experienced otherwise.
Our department offered two graduate classes 16 years ago in instructional communication—today we offer a comprehensive graduate program in instructional communication throughout the state. The students,
not one of whom was required to take our classes, have made it clear that
communication is definitely worth studying and can be useful to those
who want to continue their education.

Over a decade ago, Richmond and Daly (1975) suggested that the field
of communication might strengthen its future prospects if "we are willing to adapt our programs to the needs of our society" (p. 6). The authors'
goal, seeking to establish communication curricula for the older, nontraditional student who is attempting to continue or extend his or her
education, is equally relevant today.

This perspective has been popular for decades in fields such as education, business, and agriculture. Although in the past many professionals
in the field of communication were unsure of the benefits to be accrued
through working with continuing education programs, today most leading programs in the field have a continuing education component. Thus,

417

young scholars planning careers in communication can be virtually certain that they will someday be involved in a continuing education program.

This chapter reviews characteristics of the continuing education student, examines the adult learner as a consumer, and considers what our field has to offer to continuing education students. In addition, this chapter reviews what one should know before working with continuing education students and explores the outcomes of continuing education programs.

CHARACTERISTICS OF THE
CONTINUING EDUCATION STUDENT

The most obvious characteristic that distinguishes between the continuing education student and the typical college student is the age difference—continuing education students are usually older than the typical college student. They are often beginning to pursue an education or extend their educational background after being out of school for a number of years. This age difference may or may not be an advantage for learning. The one fact that is indisputable is that the older student is just as capable of cognitive, affective, and psychomotor learning as the younger student. No matter what the "conventional wisdom" might be, you can indeed teach "old dogs new tricks"!

A second characteristic of the continuing education student is that he or she is typically employed, usually full time. Most adult learners have already chosen a career track (and are actively pursuing it) while seeking to continue their education. As a result, they attempt to adapt their school curriculum and schedule to their work schedule. For most adult learners, employment is their first priority. If the continuing education program gets in the way of the job, the continuing education program is discontinued.

A third characteristic of the continuing education student is the high probability of marriage and children. Although the trend of married couples not having children is increasing, the traditional marital model is still the norm. There may be a few DINC (Dual Income, No Children) couples in a continuing education class, but you can expect the vast majority of students to be married and have children. This, of course, places both a financial strain and, in many cases, a time strain on the student. It also impacts the amount of time students are willing or able to spend on a learning task and their perceptions of the usefulness of such tasks.

A fourth characteristic of the continuing education student is commitment to a given profession or occupation. For example, in any particular adult education class there might be students from legal, secretarial, medical, financial, and educational professions. Although some individuals in continuing education classes are seeking to change fields of employment, most are not.

A fifth characteristic of the continuing education student is an interest in knowledge for immediate use. Such students need to see meaningful application for the content the instructor is teaching *now*. Continuing education students generally are not interested in content that might be useful in the indefinite future. They want knowledge that will be useful to them in the immediate work or home environment.

Most teachers have either said or heard "you may not be able to use this content now, but in the future it will be useful to you." Although this might work with younger, more inexperienced students, it will not work with older, employed students. Such students are primarily interested in subject matter that will be helpful either for improving their interpersonal lives or for improving their work lives. If an instructor cannot demonstrate how the curricula is applicable now or in the *very* near future, then the continuing education student will conclude that the course is useless.

Adult learners ask questions such as: "How will this work in my job? What is the usefulness of this? Why are we doing this? How will this benefit me, my organization? Will I see any immediate results if I try this idea? Do you think my spouse might benefit from this course?" If an instructor of adult learners cannot answer questions like these, he or she will have to revise the curricula to adapt to the needs of the students—or there will no students left to adapt to!

A sixth characteristic of continuing education students is limited time to devote to studying for class. The instructor of adult learners must remember that members of this unique audience are already committed to meeting the demands of a job. This restricts the instructor's ability to require extensive study time. Most students need to have the majority of the course content covered in class. If the instructor insists on extensive homework between classes, he or she can count on some students not returning and others simply not doing the work.

A seventh characteristic of the continuing education student extends the sixth characteristic. In addition to having limited time for studying, the older student also has limited time for completing projects/activities outside of class. This also results from a temporal commitment to the job and family. Hence, the instructor must be sensitive to an adult learner's schedule and only require activities/projects that are of prime benefit to the student or activities that the student can complete in his or her job or home environment.

A final characteristic of continuing education students is they are among the most highly motivated students an instructor can have in class—if the content is perceived as relevant. On the other hand, if the content is not perceived as relevant, the continuing education student often simply disappears from the course. As suggested previously, most continuing education students need to see the usefulness of the content and obvious, positive results of employing the content at work or at home. If this criterion is met, the students will see the content as useful and continue in the course.

The most critical period for the retention of continuing education students is the first class meeting. The instructor must be able to demonstrate that the course will be of benefit to the different people in the class. The instructor should not suggest that the course will involve "an in-depth look at several theories related to. . . ." This introduction will "turn off" adult learners, and they will leave thinking "another typical high-level college course with very little application for me." The instructor should begin the course with an interesting exercise, presentation, or activity that illustrates the relevance of the course to each student's profession or lifestyle. As adult educators and researchers have suggested, the adult learner is a unique individual, and the program of instruction has to be "personalized" in a way that fits individual needs (Andrews, Houston, & Bryant, 1981; Warnat, 1979).

THE ADULT LEARNER—OFTEN A NAIVE CONSUMER

When older, nontraditional students search for classes to improve their home or work environment, they often overlook "speech communication" classes. Most of them do not want to give speeches, and they do not know that speech and communication classes are not necessarily the same. When informed that speech courses are available, they often think of classes such as public speaking, parlimentary procedure, and group leadership/group dynamics. The perception that public speaking is what the field of speech communication is about is still a common misconception of many continuing education students. The only referent many people have for the field is speech classes they had in high school or were required to take in college.

The general public tends to be uninformed about changes in the field of communication. Many adult learners took a public speaking class in their early college career and still think the field is primarily concerned with giving speeches. The field of communication has not done well at the task of enlightening the adult learner about the content areas available in the field. In fact, in many cases we have continued to offer traditional content areas in continuing education programs long after they have been replaced in regular campus programs.

The weakness of traditional speeches classes for many adult learners is that they never confront situations in which the content given in the class can be employed with regularity—and the potential students know this. For example, when adult learners are asked, "how often do you think you will be required to give a public speech in your occupation?", the majority of them usually respond with "never." When adult learners are asked if they would like to be better at public speaking, many indicate they would, but not at the price of having to take a public speaking class. Their rationale is that they have secured positions in which they will not be asked to give public presentations. When they were younger, they may have felt they would be required to give a public presentations. But now many of them have shaped their lives and careers around not being required to give a public speech (Richmond, 1984; Richmond & McCroskey, 1985).

The preceding paragraph is not meant to demean basic public speaking courses or to suggest that they are not useful for the right group of adult learners. Rather, the point to be made is that many adult learners are naive about what the field has to offer and think *only* in terms of the basic speech classes offered in their high school and/or college experiences.

WHAT WE CAN OFFER THE ADULT LEARNER

Many academic disciplines are not faced with the question of what they have to offer the adult learner through continuing education programs. They have already addressed the issue and have provided an extended education for the older student for many years. Our field has just recently begun to pursue expansion in this realm. Richmond and Daly (1975) suggested an "almost inexhaustible need" (p. 8) for interpersonal communication specialists to assist in adult education. They also argued that "both the society and our field will benefit" (p. 8) from providing services to adult learners such as teachers, nurses, civil service employees, police, or business and labor organizations. The expansion of continuing education programs in the field of communication has progressed rapidly at some institutions, but not at all at others. Perhaps this is because professionals in the field do not realize what the field can offer. Because people in this field are specialists in one area or another, it is perhaps difficult to see the full range of the field's potential.

While almost every area taught in regular academic programs can potentially find a place in continuing education, those mentioned here have been found to receive very positive responses from continuing education students with varied backgrounds. After students become familiar with what the field of communication has to offer, they usually suggest the following areas as most interesting and helpful: Nonverbal Communication; Improved Communication between Supervisor and Subordinate; the Impact of TV on Children; Interpersonal Relationship Development and Male/Female Communication; Parent and Child Communication/Family Communication; Communication and Aging; Overcoming Shyness; and an Overview of Human Communication.

All of these must be applied to the student's specific environment. For example, if an instructor is to teach about communication between supervisor and subordinates, he or she must adapt to the job environment with which the continuing education student is most involved. The next part of this section reviews various concepts/principles that might be taught in the continuing education classes listed before.

Nonverbal Communication is a very popular and inherently interesting class for the continuing education student. An instructor can demonstrate the differences between verbal and nonverbal messages, the impact of nonverbal communication, the functions of nonverbal communication, and then apply each category/code of nonverbal communication to the student's environment. For example, the impact of dress in the nursing profession versus the banking profession might be explored. One might also look at the impact of gestures and body movements on communication in various environments. The impact of the use of space, territoriality, and touch in the work environment are additional topics that could be explored. The overall impact of status/power and nonverbal immediacy might be discussed, and the results for the work environment examined. Presently, nonverbal communication is one of the more applicable topics for continuing education courses.

Improved Communication between Supervisor and Subordinate is a second continuing education course in high demand both in business and communication. Students can learn such concepts as flow of communication and how this impacts supervisor/subordinate relationships, the difference between a supervisor and administrator, how to predict a certain personality type's behaviors in organizations, how to determine what decision-making style a supervisor is employing, how to bring about change in an organization, what communication style a manager is employing, and how conflict and disagreement can be managed.

With the media age surrounding us, continuing education students are aware of the influence of the media in American culture. They are also concerned about the influence of media, particularly TV, on their children. An instructor in such a course might teach students the principle of gatekeeping information, the influence of ads on children and adults, the stereotyping provided by the media, what makes news and why, the prosocial and antisocial effects of the media, and the impacts of the media in the home and school environment.

For many in the North American Culture, being social and communicating with others is unrewarding and even punishing. When such people become continuing education students, they express a desire to understand why they are shy or communication apprehensive and how they might overcome shyness and apprehension. There are also adult learners who are not shy but know someone who is (e.g., friend, spouse, child, co-worker, subordinate). Both groups might take a course on overcoming shyness or communication apprehension. In such a course, the following might be taught and applied to the student's environment: effects of not communicating in a communicative society; causes of shyness; types of shy people; nature of shyness; interpersonal perceptions of shy people; impact of shyness in school, social, and work environments; and how to reduce or overcome shyness.

For many adult learners, a valuable course is an Overview of Human Communication. Given increased attention to computer literacy and the technological aspects of business, business personnel believe they have forgotten the basics of human communication and need a refresher course. In the Overview of Human Communication course, students might be taught: types of communication (such as accidental, expressive, and rhetorical) and the impacts of each within the work environment; the components of the human communication process and how communication failures occur; the functions of the communication process; and the most common misconceptions about communication and how they impact communication with others in work, social, and school environments.

In conclusion, the field of communication has a plethora of content areas that are interesting and applicable to the continuing education student. While the general communication principles remain the same, the application may vary from teacher to banker to nurse. We have the knowledge, but we have to diffuse that knowledge in an effective, instructive manner.

WORKING WITH THE CONTINUING EDUCATION STUDENT

The instructor must understand that adults participate in continuing education programs for a variety of reasons. They continue their education because they enjoy taking classes, to get away from home, to improve their interpersonal/home life, to change things at home/work, to obtain a better job, to feel good about themselves, because they simply enjoy learning, and/or because they have nothing better to do. Whatever the reason, the critical element that must be present in the course is application. The adult student must see value and usefulness for the content or he or she will simply "drop out."

If an instructor is to be successful in adult education, he or she must "personalize" the class content for the individual student. Although much of instructional time should be spent directly providing students with content, some time must be spent discussing how the concepts can be tailored to the students' concerns, problems, and environments. For example, if teaching about nonverbal communication in the work place, instructors should demonstrate how use of space, seating, color, lighting, and so on can impact the teacher–student relationship, the banker–client relationship, the nurse patient relationship, or whatever relationship is relevant to the students in the class.

The teacher of continuing education students must also know more than communication. The continuing education instructor must have a working knowledge of the world of the audience. They must be able to understand and "speak the language" of the student in order to allow the student to understand and grasp the usefulness of the concepts.

Last, the instructor of adult learners must, on many occasions, be capable of and prepared to present a "dog and pony show" that captures and keeps the students' attention. In this respect, younger and adult learners are very similar. Both want their instructor to be animated, dynamic, and interesting. In addition, the instructor needs to allow time for students to give feedback or ask questions. In conclusion, being a teacher of adult learners may be more demanding than teaching younger students. However, the outcomes of a successful continuing education experience can be worth the extra effort.

OUTCOMES OF CONTINUING EDUCATION PROGRAMS

If one has successfully implemented and taught a continuing education class (or worked with a successful continuing education program), the positive outcomes are numerous. Among the more obvious outcomes are teacher–student satisfaction with class and content, the opportunity to teach highly motivated students, and feeling that one is contributing to society in a beneficial manner. Three outcomes that are not as obvious (but are extremely important) are:

1. The students will have high levels of cognitive, affective, and behavioral learning. They are motivated to achieve, and they will achieve at high levels. They will also take the content and apply it within their organizational and personal environments.

2. The instructor will have a learning experience. Teachers learn from their students what communication concepts work in the "real world"

and what concepts do not. The effective continuing education instructor can use this student feedback to develop instructional content that will work outside the basic undergraduate classroom.

3. As a program becomes strong and produces good students, the program itself will be strengthened and expand. Students will promote the usefulness and applicability of the program to others in their organization and community. Other professional people will learn from the continuing education students that the field of communication has something to offer.

In conclusion, working with continuing education students can make the learning environment more challenging for the teacher, as well as more rewarding. The communication teacher is capable of providing useful content to the continuing education student while at the same time providing the student with a solid background in communication.

REFERENCES

Andrews, T. E., Houston, W. R., & Bryant, B. L. (1981). *Adult learners (A research study)*. Washington, DC: Association of Teacher Educators.

Richmond, V. P. (1984). Implications of quietness: Some facts and speculations. In J. A. Daly & J. C. McCroskey (Eds.), *Avoiding communication: Shyness, reticence, and communication apprehension* (pp. 145–155). Beverly Hills, CA: Sage.

Richmond, V. P., & Daly, J. A. (1975, January). Extension education: An almost inexhaustible job market for communication graduates. *ACA Bulletin, 11,* 6–8.

Richmond, V. P., & McCroskey, J. C. (1985). *Communication: Apprehension, avoidance, and effectiveness.* Scottsdale, AZ: Gorsuch Scarisbrick.

Warnat, W. I. (1979, April). A new dimension of adult learning: Inservice education. *Inservice.* Syracuse, NY: National Council of States on Inservice Education.

30

Communication in the 2-Year College

Darlyn R. Wolvin
Prince George's Community College

Andrew D. Wolvin
University of Maryland

Approximately 43% of all undergraduate students enrolled in American higher education are enrolled in 2-year institutions. These institutions are known variously as junior colleges, community colleges, technical colleges, and even some proprietary independent colleges. They can be identified essentially as institutions that offer an Associate of Arts and/or Associate of Science degree to students who complete a 2-year curriculum of, typically, 60 credit hours.

The American Association of Community and Junior Colleges estimates that in the fall, 1986, semester, 4,890,000 students were enrolled in credit courses on 2-year campuses (Palmer, personal communication 1987, September 30). It is significant to note, also, that although roughly 43% of all undergraduates are enrolled in these institutions, approximately 50% of all first-time enrollees in American higher education are enrolled in 2-year programs (Palmer, personal communication, 1987, September 30). The average college tuition figure for these 2-year students was $642 a semester (American Association of Community and Junior Colleges, 1986).

Two-year colleges were started in the early 20th century to serve an important "junior" college purpose—to provide greater access to higher education for local populations. Some of these schools emerged directly from the public school systems as extensions of (and usually governed by) the secondary schools in the jurisdiction. Other junior colleges were developed by private groups, typically a religious organization desiring a

427

Bible-based college. Still other junior colleges were established by universities to provide feeder institutions permitting students to fulfill their
first 2 years of a curriculum at a satellite campus.

The notion of the "junior" college has given way in contemporary
times, however, to a broader, more comprehensive view of most 2-year
institutions as community colleges. As community colleges, these campuses have evolved to fulfill four important functions: collegiate; career;
compensatory; and community. These functions offer an important
framework for distinguishing the institutions and for shaping the work
of a communication faculty on such a campus.

The collegiate function of a 2-year institution is to provide the foundation of a student's general education, permitting the student to take the
required courses that facilitate transfer to a 4-year institution. Upon
completion of a curriculum at a 2-year school, the transfer student is able
to move to the intended campus with most or all of the credits on his or
her transcript intact. The primary focus on these freshman and sophomore years at the 2-year college is to get the general education requirements completed so that the junior and senior years can be centered in a
major department at the 4-year school. It should be noted, however, that
many 2-year schools offer a full array of courses in a curriculum, providing a substantial base in a major program, as well as the general education courses.

Much of the collegiate, transfer curriculum in the 2-year institution
has been shaped by 4-year requirements. In most states, 2-year offerings
are directly parallel to the 4-year curriculum so that students will be able
to make direct transfer of credits. The collegiate function of the 2-year
institution has undergone some revision—particularly as enrollments in
2-year transfer programs has declined (a decline that coincides with dis-
enchantment with liberal arts and an intense focus on vocational goals
on the part of many students in higher education).

A second function is the career program of the 2-year institution. This
segment of the school is designed to provide students with solid vocational skills and certification of those skills through an Associate of Arts
or Associate of Science diploma. Students enroll in any of a number of
vocationally oriented programs on these campuses, including technical
fields, such as Fire Science and Computer Technology, and specialized
fields, such as Law Enforcement, Nursing, and Office Management.

Career programs are strong on 2-year campuses. Burgeoning enrollments and support from business and industry have encouraged administrators to put vast resources into these programs. Faculty positions
offer excellent opportunities for individuals who are specialists in a career field to share their experience and expertise with those aspiring to
enter the field. The consistent interest in vocational goals on the part of

today's students suggests that career programs will remain a strong part of the 2-year college mission.

An important third function of the 2-year institution is compensatory education. The perceived decline in American literacy has led to extensive development of programs and courses to enable high school graduates to gain basic academic skills that they missed in their prior education. Compensatory education programs are designed to offer remedial studies in such areas as writing, math, study skills, and reading. Many of the courses do not carry academic credit or are identified as compensatory in nature on a transcript. Frequently, these courses are staffed by faculty hired especially for their background in developmental education, and the administration of these programs is usually separate from the collegiate departments on the campus. Careful articulation of the objectives and the curriculum are essential to integrating the compensatory mission with the other functions of the 2-year school.

A fourth function of 2-year institutions is community education. This mission has evolved from the continuing education role assumed by colleges and universities after World War II. The community education function has played a major part in redefining many 2-year schools as community colleges—offering educational opportunities directly to a local, community-based population.

The community education program usually takes the form of special classes, workshops, and seminars offered without academic credit. A wide array of offerings may be made available to a community, including professional skills (resume writing, time management), personal skills (family dynamics, memory development), and special interests (flower arranging, wine tasting).

These four functions of the 2-year institution contribute to the uniqueness of the community/junior college and offer interesting career opportunities for the communication educator. It is helpful to consider how these functions shape the student body that one is likely to encounter on the 2-year campus.

In an earlier work (Wolvin & Wolvin, 1972), we drew a profile of the diversity of community college students from research. Our general conclusion was that, although community college students can be of any level of academic ability, they are likely to come from a family whose parents are of lower socioeconomic backgrounds and with little education beyond high school. Further, the community college student is more likely to be from an ethnic minority and be older in age than the typical 4-year college student.

A survey of public community colleges in the spring of 1986 offers additional insight into the student population. The results reveal that 36% were enrolled with the intent of transferring to 4-year institutions (the collegiate function). At the career level, 34% of the students were enrolled in order to prepare for a new occupation, and 16% were in classes to gain skills for their current occupation. Another 15% of the students were enrolled in classes to fulfill a personal interest (tapping the community function of the colleges), and 4% of the students were enrolled for the purpose of improving their English, math, or reading skills (the compensatory role; Center for the Study of Community Colleges, 1986).

This profile illustrates the heavy emphasis on the collegiate and career functions of the 2-year schools and illustrates the need for having both types of programs in a comprehensive institution. Likewise, it is interesting to consider that the average age of students enrolled in any of these credit courses is 28 years (Palmer, personal communication, 1987, September 3). Between 1969 and 1972, 2-year schools experienced a phenomenal 65% growth in adult learners and a 56% increase between 1972 and 1975 (Peterson & Associates, 1979). It should be recognized that many of these institutions have open enrollments and are charged with providing equal access to all persons in a particular community. As a result, students tend to come to the campuses with varying levels of academic ability; and many of them are not enrolled on a full-time basis because they work at full-time jobs while taking courses part-time. As Cohen and Brawer (1982) noted, "Two words sum up the students: number and variety" (p. 29).

Thus, the communication educator on the 2-year campus is likely to find a very diverse, older student population, often enrolled part-time, with varying purposes for being there. The challenge, then, is to provide a program that can meet the needs of this diverse population.

To meet the objectives of the collegiate function, the community college program ought to, minimally, provide the basic communication courses traditional in our discipline. Although the concept of "the" basic course has altered somewhat, evidence (Gibson, Hanna, & Huddleston, 1985) suggests that such a course typically takes a public speaking approach. Leininger (1987), however, discovered that the "hybrid" fundamentals course is most often the one required of students. Such a course, designed to be consistent with the communication requirements of students in 4-year institutions, is an important foundation on which to build the rest of the collegiate curriculum.

Additional courses (similar to those at the freshman and sophomore level in 4-year institutions) might include Introduction to Interpersonal Communication, Introduction to Small Group Communication, Debate, Oral Interpretation, and Listening. Many of these basic-level courses are designed to provide students with a solid foundation in theory along with communication skills in the content areas.

Institutions approach these courses in different ways. At Prince

George's Community College in Largo, Maryland, for instance, students are required to take a basic communication course that is designed to transfer to 4-year Maryland institutions. The course, offering units in intrapersonal, interpersonal, and public communication, is a "hybrid" course with a careful balance of theory and skills. Lane Community College (Oregon) offers a required Listening course of its students—a course that can transfer to other Oregon and Northwest schools that offer work in this area of communication. The transferability of courses is usually articulated carefully with faculty and administrators at the 4-year schools to ensure that students will indeed receive transfer credit for the course (Hegstrom, 1981).

Some 2-year schools also offer what is essentially a 2-year "major" in the field. Designed as a "pre-professional" degree program, Lorain County Community College in Elyria, Ohio, for instance, offers a sequence of courses for students in Theatre, Media Performance, Media Production, and Speech Communication/Rhetoric. The communication pre-professional program at Lorain highlights career opportunities for its students. As stated in the Lorain County Community College Brochure (1987): "People trained in speech communication/rhetoric can enter into the business field in such areas as public relations, personnel, labor relations, customer service, human resources, training and development, and sales; or they can pursue a career in public service as a speech writer, foreign service officer, campaign director, or fund raiser."

The career curriculum in 2-year schools parallels the transfer, collegiate curriculum in the sense that course offerings provide a basic foundation in theory and skills. The career curriculum usually is not aimed specifically at communication majors but is designed for students in any of a wide range of other career fields. Students in career curricula may be required to take a communication course that might be, again, a hybrid course offering work in intrapersonal, interpersonal, and public communication applied to career settings (see Wolvin & Corley, 1984; Wolvin & Wolvin, 1977, 1981). Other course offerings might include classes tailored to specific majors: Interpersonal Communication for Nurses; Business and Professional Speaking; Speech for the Engineer; and so on (see Doyle & Engleberg, 1981).

In a survey of state instructional offices and of community college career advisory committee members in various occupational areas, Muchmore and Galvin (1983) identified those communication skills viewed as absolutely essential (or very necessary) for the immediate entry of 2-year college students into career fields. The most important speaking skills were: (a) use words understood by others; (b) use words, pronunciation, and grammar that do not alienate others; (c) phrase questions properly in order to get accurate information; (d) explain specific requirements to others; and (e) organize messages so that others can understand them. The most important listening skills were: (a) understand directions; (b) obtain necessary factual information; (c) identify important points when given oral instructions; (d) understand accurately questions and suggestions of others; and (e) distinguish between fact and opinion. Community colleges have been urged to develop career curricula that meet these perceived communication needs in the work place.

The compensatory curriculum can (and should) be developed to parallel skill development for students in the English, math, and reading areas. Many schools find that offerings in basic oral English for nonnative speakers of English are important, particularly for schools in areas with a heavy influx of international students. Voice and articulation courses may be useful to provide remedial speech work on pronunciation and vocal clarity. Some schools couple this with listening work in the compensatory curriculum in order to enable students to build skills in both reading and listening comprehension (see Miller & Young, 1981; Strain & Wysong, 1981). The developmental program at Jefferson Community College in Louisville, Kentucky, for instance, offers a developmental speech course (entitled Individual Growth and Human Relations) for students who are (a) unsure of themselves in speaking situations; (b) hesitant to take a traditional speech course; (c) returning to school after some time and are unsure of their academic skills; or (d) below the eighth-grade level in reading and/or writing skills (Course Syllabus, 1987). To meet the individual needs of compensatory students (many of whom are non-native speakers of English), Golden West College in Huntington Beach, California, has developed courses based on skill assessments and competency-based laboratory components utilizing peer and volunteer tutoring techniques (Ratliffe & Hudson, 1986).

Although many educators decry the need for colleges to provide remedial work in basic skills, the reality is, in the words of Boyer (1987), that "far too many of today's students lack a solid academic foundation . . . and these deficiencies prove to be a serious barrier to academic progress" (p. 76). The Carnegie Foundation study on the undergraduate curriculum revealed that over 80% of institutions of higher education offer remedial courses in basic skills (Boyer, 1987).

The community curriculum is also an area that offers considerable potential for development. Special workshops and seminars in Organizational Communication, Business and Professional Speaking, Family Communication, Couple Communication, and so on are attractive offerings in community-based programs. These offerings function both as campus-based courses and as offerings taken into corporate settings as part of contracted training and development work for organizations in the community (see Strom, 1981). One well-developed community education program is that offered by Oakland Community College in Orchard Ridge, Michigan. Communication training and development in such areas as conflict resolution and management communication has been offered for such corporations as Chrysler, Michigan Bell Telephone, Mercy Health Corporation, and General Motors (Leininger, 1986).

The community curriculum tends to be the least integrated, for these programs frequently contract for the seminars and workshops with people other than the overworked faculty of the campus departments. Indeed, many of these programs operate with a director and staff who handle the programs for the entire campus, so there is little if any discipline base for the offerings. Research on the community college as a center for continuing education (Nespoli & Martorana, 1983–1984) however, supports the conclusion that "it seems clear that life-long learning and community-based activities in general are more and more becoming an accepted part of the American community college philosophy" (p. 5).

In addition to a strong curriculum aimed at meeting student needs in the four areas of collegiate, career, compensatory, and community education, many community colleges have found it productive to develop a dynamic co-curricular program that complements the curricular offerings. Most typical is the debate/forensics program, which at many schools rivals 4-year school programs in terms of both activity and funding. The national organization Phi Rho Pi provides leadership for 2-year schools in the debate/forensics area, and the annual national tournament is always well attended.

Fielding such a comprehensive curriculum in a 2-year college requires faculty prepared to address the diverse needs of students. The 2-year school is, first and foremost, a teaching institution, so the demands and the priorities are on effective teaching. Thus, rewards through salary increments and honors are based heavily on student, peer, and administrator evaluations of one's teaching performance. Although faculty at these institutions are encouraged to participate in professional activities (professional associations, research and publications, campus and community service), the rewarded focus is on one's work as a teacher.

Many of these schools offer considerable support to faculty as teachers. Because the typical semester teaching load may be 12 to 15 credit hours (with two or three or even more different course preparations), 2-year institutions offer support for the teaching function. Miami-Dade Community College in Florida, for example, has recently announced an extensive plan to hire, evaluate, and reward new faculty who are primarily devoted to the college's teaching and learning mission (Heller, 1988).

To support the teaching mission, many 2-year schools have well-equipped, well-staffed learning resource centers with up-to-date audio/visual materials and print holdings. Golden West College has the

Speech Communication Center for peer tutoring and competency-based testing. Oakland Community College (Michigan) and Prince George's Community College have elaborate video-tape laboratories. Lorain County Community College has a state-of-the-art professional television studio. Likewise, faculty in many 2-year schools are presented with opportunities for faculty development in any of a number of instructional areas such as curriculum writing, teaching styles, and evaluation techniques. In addition, many are offered travel support to attend professional meetings and conferences such as the annual Speech Communication Association convention (which has a very active community college section).

Thus, the 2-year institution offers opportunities and challenges to those who wish to be faculty members in comprehensive programs devoted to teaching diverse groups of students. As a nontraditional institution of postsecondary education, the 2-year school is often in a state of change and development, providing a dynamic atmosphere for faculty and students alike. The communication educator committed to effective teaching and creative work at the undergraduate level will find this to be a rewarding career avenue.

REFERENCES

American Association of Community and Junior Colleges (1986, Fall). *American Association of Community and Junior Colleges: Annual survey of community, technical, and junior colleges*. Washington, DC: Author.

Boyer, E. L. (1987). *College: The undergraduate experience in America*. New York: Harper & Row.

Center for the Study of Community Colleges (1986, spring). *National survey of students enrolled in credit classes*. Unpublished report.

Cohen, A. M., & Brawer, F. B. (1982). *The American community college*. San Francisco: Jossey-Bass.

Course Syllabus. (1987). *Individual growth and human relations* Louisville, KY: Jefferson Community College.

Doyle, S. L., & Engleberg, I. N. (1981). Integrating nursing majors into the group discussion and interpersonal communication courses in the community college. *Association for Communication Administration Bulletin, 35,* 68–71.

Gibson, J. W., Hanna, M. S., & Huddleston, B. M. (1985). The basic speech course at U.S. colleges and universities: IV. *Communication Education, 34,* 281–291.

Hegstrom, T. G. (1981). The Denver Conference recommendations: A status report. *Association for Communication Administration Bulletin, 35,* 62–71.

Heller, S. (1988, April 13) Miami-Dade College begins project to bolster teaching by evaluating new professors and rewarding classroom performance. *The Chronicle of Higher Education, 34,* pp. A12, A13, A18.

Leininger, J. E. (1986, April). *Speech communication education in business and industry.* Paper presented at the meeting of the Central States Speech Association convention, Cincinnati, OH.

Leininger, J. E. (1987, November). *Choosing between basic courses to meet student needs at the community college.* Paper presented at the meeting of the Speech Communication Association convention, Boston, MA.

Miller, M. B., & Young, B. (1981). A comprehensive developmental studies program which includes reading, oral and written communication, arithmetic, counseling, and tutoring. *Association for Communication Administration Bulletin, 35,* 72–75.

Muchmore, J., & Galvin, K. (1983). A report of the Task Force on Career Competencies in Oral Communication Skills for community college students seeking immediate entry into the work force. *Communication Education, 32,* 207–220. (Results of this survey have been published as a brochure, *Communication for careers,* by the Speech Communication Association.)

Nespoli, L. A., & Martorana, S. V. (1983 1984). Tensions in defining community college missions: Problem or opportunity? *Community College Review, 11,* 3–11.

Peterson, R. E., & Associates. (1979). *Lifelong learning in America.* San Francisco: Jossey-Bass.

Ratliffe, S. A., & Hudson, D. D. (1986). *A description of a student-staffed, competency-based laboratory for the assessment of interpersonal communication skills.* Unpublished manuscript, Golden West College, Huntington Beach, CA.

Strain, B., & Wysong, P. (1981). A report of developmental speech courses in selected community colleges. *Association for Communication Administration Bulletin, 35,* 76–77.

Strom, J. C. (1981). Organizational communication in the community college. *Association for Communication Administration Bulletin, 35,* 78–80.

Wolvin, A. D., & Corley, D. (1984). The technical speech communication course: A view from the field. *Association for Communication Administration Bulletin, 49,* 83–86.

Wolvin, A. D., & Wolvin, D. R. (1977). Developing the speech communication course for the technical/career student. *Association for Communication Administration Bulletin, 19,* 37–42.

Wolvin, A. D., & Wolvin, D. R. (1981). The status of the technical speech communication course in community and junior colleges. *Association for Communication Administration Bulletin, 38,* 29–31.

Wolvin, D. R., & Wolvin, A. D. (1972). The speech communication curriculum in the community college. *Today's Speech, 29,* 9–14.

31

Directing Debate and Forensics

Thomas A. Hollihan
University of Southern California

For more than 200 years, American college students have learned argumentative and speaking skills through participation in academic debate. The first debating society was established at Harvard in 1722, and by the time of the Revolutionary War, Princeton, Columbia, William and Mary, and Rutgers (Queens College) all had debating societies in place (Potter, 1954). The first intercollegiate contest occurred when Yale met Harvard at Cambridge in 1892, to debate the topic "Resolved: that a young man casting his first ballot in 1892 should vote for the nominees of the Democratic Party." Intercollegiate debates became so popular that by 1897 colleges and universities throughout the country were participating. In 1910, the first faculty debate coaches were hired to help students improve their preparation and delivery skills (Cowperthwaite & Baird, 1954).

With the hiring of the first debate coaches, one of the most demanding yet rewarding careers in communication was created. In addition to the ordinary professorial tasks of teaching classes, serving on committees, and conducting research, the college debate and forensics coach works closely with students to prepare them for competition, accompanies them to intercollegiate tournaments, serves as a critic/judge at those tournaments, and, in many cases, drives all night through inclement weather to get home in time to teach the next morning. Despite extraordinary demands, however, the rewards in coaching are also great. Forensics training challenges students to learn by stimulating their competitive instincts and, because forensics activities are so time consuming, the students who are drawn into the activity tend to be among the brightest and most motivated students on campus. It is a pleasure to teach students who want to learn and who genuinely aspire to do their best. The long hours working with students and traveling with them to tournaments also permits coaches to develop close personal relationships with students that are far more rewarding and enduring than most student–faculty relationships.

Contemporary forensics programs may offer students training and experience in policy debate, value topic debate, parliamentary debate, oratory, extemporaneous speaking, oral interpretation of literature, or a whole range of other "individual" speaking events. Some college programs elect to specialize in only one type of forensics training; others dabble in all of these activities.

This chapter attempts to offer recommendations for new forensics coaches, or for those who might someday wish to become coaches. It provides a rationale for forensics education, suggests how a new director might define the scope of his or her own program, provides a few tips on administering a forensics program (recruiting, budgeting, publicity, etc.), and finally, suggests how forensics coaches should prepare for and be evaluated for promotion and tenure.

A RATIONALE FOR A FORENSICS PROGRAM

Despite the long history of forensics activities in this nation, and the fact that hundreds of colleges and universities, thousands of high schools, and tens of thousands of students annually participate in forensics, "selling" a forensics program to one's departmental colleagues and college administrators can nonetheless be a difficult task. Building and maintaining support for your program is thus a continuing and important part of the job for any forensics director.

The benefits of forensics training are easy to document. As I have already mentioned, forensics attracts bright and motivated students to your department and to your campus. Forensics students thus tend to get good grades (despite the demands of competition—perhaps because of them), score well on standardized tests, and gain admission to good graduate and law schools. They also tend to be outgoing, highly verbal, and challenging students who will impress your colleagues and your administrators. A successful and visible forensics program attracts favorable press attention and helps recruit new students to your college or university.

Despite all these benefits, however, forensics programs are sometimes viewed as costly luxuries, and as such they are especially vulnerable during times of budget tightening. Forensics directors are continually challenged to justify their programs. I think the best strategy to follow is to argue that forensics competition provides unique laboratory experiences for gifted students. On my own campus, I have consistently argued that forensics is an "honors program," and that educational opportunities for gifted students are always more costly than those for average students. The forensics-as-laboratory argument also permits you to compare the costs of forensics education to the cost of providing laboratory education in the sciences or in engineering and, of course, by comparison forensics is a bargain. I also believe it important that you argue that forensics training is vital to the communication program. It serves gifted majors and nonmajors by providing unique educational opportunities that cannot be duplicated in the classroom. If your department offers graduate degrees, you can also argue that assigning graduate students as assistant coaches uniquely enriches their education and helps prepare them for careers in forensics. Do not characterize your program as "extracurricular"; in times of budget tightening the "extras" get cut first. Instead, characterize your forensics program as "cocurricular" and as vital to the communication program.

You should also attempt to contact forensics alumni. Unless you are starting a program on a campus that has never had forensics activities, you will likely find that you have a ready group of advocates for your program among your alumni. Undoubtedly, you will find your alumni in positions of leadership and responsibility in your community—forensics attracts and helps such people to develop. You will also find that these community leaders will speak very highly of their forensics experience, and they will be quick to come to your assistance. This may mean monetary assistance, which is obviously appreciated, but it may also mean letters of support and the use of personal contacts to help you develop and maintain your forensics program.

When justifying the cost of your forensics program, you will have to learn to present your arguments as forcefully as possible. For example, most administrators compute costs by calculating the cost per student served. Forensics programs seem very expensive when their costs are figured in this way. They seem less expensive if one calculates costs by determining the cost per round of competition. It is important to keep records of the number of tournaments your students attended, how many rounds they competed in, and how many hours they spent in preparation. Emphasizing the intensity of this learning laboratory makes your arguments on cost more convincing.

The most common complaint that is levelled against forensics programs is that they serve too few students, given their cost. I caution you against responding to this complaint by attempting to dramatically increase the size of your program. As programs become larger they demand more resources. In order to prepare students adequately for competition you will need to have other faculty or graduate assistants assigned to help you. You will need to provide more judges when you enter your students in tournaments. You will need more travel funds to get larger numbers of students to tournaments. As a result, the program may serve more students but it will also cost more money, which was, of course, what led to the need for more students—this rationale for increased size can thus become a never-ending circle. Second, it diminishes the credibility of your claims about forensics as an honors program for gifted students when your squad becomes too large. Third, the forensics director becomes much less a teacher and more an administrator and "traffic cop" charged with simply fending off entropy. Fourth, I think the most effective forensics programs, and those that offer the best experiences for their participants, are those that are small enough that the students can develop real feelings of closeness and cohesion with their peers and their instructors; on very large squads this is diminished.

How large should your squad be? That depends on your goals, the size of your budget, your proximity to tournaments, and the unique situation on your campus. The average squad is from 8 to 30 students and, if you are alone, I caution you against trying to serve more than 15 to 20 students.

A second mistake that many forensics directors make in justifying the cost of their program is to argue that they win a lot of trophies. Everyone likes winners, and a winning squad is a tremendous asset in your appeal for funds. Do not, however, make tournament victories the primary rationale for your program. Forensics is not football. The dangers in celebrating your successes too loudly should be apparent: First, not all years will be equally successful; second, administrators come to expect successes and take them for granted, thus they may take away support after a mediocre season but not reward you after a great one; and third, a program justified primarily on the basis of tournament victories trivializes forensics by sending a message to your students that you value wins more than you value the solid academic achievements that they make. Certainly your successes should be savored, and you should make certain that you promote your squad's achievements so that people on campus and in the community are aware of them, but remember that competition is the means by which you achieve your goal, not the goal itself.

DEFINING THE SCOPE OF YOUR PROGRAM

Forensics programs may give students a variety of different speaking opportunities and skills and can be primarily intramural or intercollegiate in scope, depending on the resources available to the director. Obviously, an intercollegiate program—where students must travel to tournaments and compete against students from other colleges and universities— is more costly and time consuming than an on-campus program. Such programs are more common than intramural programs, however, because they give students more speaking opportunities, permit them to be judged and critiqued by an interinstitutional faculty, and students are motivated by the competition.

As the director, you should have the primary control of the forensics program. It is important, however, to define the scope of the program in consultation with departmental colleagues, chairperson, and dean. It is much easier to maintain an effective program in an environment where your colleagues and superiors understand and support the goals that you are trying to achieve. Remember also that your program should be designed to be a part of the core curriculum in communication. As such, it is important that the entire department have input over its focus and orientation.

Define your goals by considering your own skills and resources, the skills and resources of your students, the size of the budget, and the extent of help you can expect to receive. Your squad can choose to participate in policy (NDT) debate, value topic (CEDA) debate, individual events, or all of these events, depending on your goals. The choice of which activities your squad will compete in is the first means by which you begin to establish objectives for your program.

If you are new to forensics coaching, and especially if you do not have prior experience as a competitor, I encourage you to attend some local tournaments to observe the different types of forensics activities before you decide which events to coach during your first season. Although all forensics activities provide students opportunities to practice and improve their communication skills, there are important differences in the objectives of the activities. As it has developed in recent years, policy debate emphasizes research skills and argumentative analysis a bit more than it does delivery skills. It is much easier to field competitive teams in policy debate if you have students on your squad who have prior high school or college debate experience. While CEDA debaters are also becoming very sophisticated and are using increasing amounts of evidence, CEDA debate emphasizes delivery skills more than does NDT debate, and it may be easier to field competitive young teams in CEDA than in NDT. I also encourage you to call upon other forensics coaches in your area to get their advice, because you may find that either CEDA debate or NDT debate predominates in your area and, as a consequence, you will have a difficult time finding tournaments for your students if you do not compete in that event.

You might also choose to limit your squad's participation to individual events. Obviously, individual events training emphasizes student's speaking skills rather than research or argumentative skills, but individual events training also offers students insight into the aesthetic and interpretive dimensions of communication. If you do not have debate experience yourself, you might find it very difficult to begin coaching students in debate and, in that case, individual events might be a more appropriate avenue for developing your program. My own biases are such that I prefer to see programs compete in both debate and individual events. I am convinced that both activities uniquely help develop students' abilities, but I think it important that directors develop programs that are appropriate for their particular situation.

SUGGESTIONS FOR THE
ADMINISTRATION OF YOUR PROGRAM

Before you begin your first season as a forensics director, you need to do preliminary planning. First, you need to determine what resources you have available to you for the year: How much money do you have to spend? What limitations do you face in how to spend it? Does your college supply you with transportation? What insurance or liability problems do you face? And so on. Second, you need to determine how many students will compete on the squad. If you are taking over an established program, you need to find out how many students are returning. If you are developing a new squad, you need to do some recruiting. You should decide what you take to be an optimal size for your program before you begin recruiting. You do not want to attract more students to your program than you have the resources to serve. Third, once you know how much money will be available to you and the number of students you will be serving, you can begin to project your season. This means figuring out what tournaments you will attend and how much they will cost. This is a difficult task, because you must predict how quickly your students' talent will develop.

To learn about the tournaments in your area, you will need to consult a forensics calendar. The American Forensic Association publishes a comprehensive calendar that lists tournaments in both debate and individual events. To get a copy of the calendar, you should contact the Secretary of the American Forensic Association. To find out who that person is, you can consult a recent issue of *Argumentation and Advocacy: The Journal of the American Forensic Association*. In fact, you should join the AFA, because they will help you get your program started and will send you a packet of useful materials. If you wish to compete in CEDA debate, you should also join the Cross Examination Debate Association, because they publish a calendar of all CEDA tournaments. The Secretary of the AFA will tell you how to contact CEDA officers in your area.

Once you get the calendar, you will need to plan your tentative schedule for the entire season. Try to determine what tournaments you will attend, how many students you will send to each, and what the costs will be. You must plan for transportation costs, entry fees, lodging, meals (or meal allowances), judging fees, etcetera. Always budget at least 10% more for each tournament than the minimum amount you genuinely believe you will need; your expenses on a forensics trip, like those on a vacation, are almost always more than you anticipate. There are no hard and fast rules regarding the number of tournaments you should plan to attend in a given season. My goal is usually to have students compete in three to five tournaments each semester. Experienced students will typically desire and need to attend more tournaments than will beginning students. I also try to mix the schedule so that all students attend both local tournaments and tournaments that are a bit more prestigious and farther away from home. These "reward" tournaments help to motivate students and give them something to shoot for as the season and their skills progress.

I try to schedule at least one or two tournaments during the season that virtually the entire squad attends. This helps build team unity and helps students to understand that everyone on the squad contributes to the total squad results. As your squad grows in size and quality, you can also compete for tournament sweepstakes awards, which are given for overall squad excellence.

Squad unity and good relations between forensics competitors is important to the quality of life—yours and theirs. Forensics students are competitive; they are drawn to the activity because it affords them an opportunity to compete. Challenging them to direct their competitive urges against students from other schools rather than their teammates can be a real problem and can frustrate even the most experienced coach. I tell my students that forensics is a meritocracy, and that my staff and I will always try to reward excellence. Excellence does not simply mean tournament successes, it can and should mean work effort, improvement, contributions to the total squad effort, and a positive attitude. As a coach, you should always try to be consistent in dealings with students. This is not always easy to do. You will find that you enjoy some students more than others, but you need to make an effort to clearly communicate to your students the criteria that you will use to decide who will compete at what tournaments, who will be paired with whom in debate, and so forth. If you stick with those criteria, you will have fewer problems. I also encourage you to avoid running a "star program" in which only your most gifted students get resources and attention. I am not advocating that all students should get the same amount of money spent on them, or even the same amount of time, but try to deal with all students fairly and equally so that all feel like they belong and are contributing to the squad effort.

Recruiting students is one of the most important elements in maintaining a successful and vigorous squad. Concentrate on recruiting students in your own classes and in other classes taught in your department. Make announcements at the start of each term to make sure that students are aware of the program. Go out of your way to encourage particularly bright or communicative students to become involved. Do not wait for students to find you, go out and find them. Many students are either unaware of forensics or are apprehensive about their ability to compete while also doing their classwork. You need to overcome these barriers to participation. Contact faculty in other departments. Students in Political Science or International Relations are often interested in debate. Students in Theatre are often interested in individual events. Work hard to cultivate relationships with the faculty in these departments so they will recommend their best students to you. These relationships also prove useful when it is time for you to get your students excused from classes so they can attend tournaments! Take out an advertisement or try to get a story in the school newspaper on forensics. You might also host a campus-wide demonstration debate or an individual events reading hour so that students and other faculty learn about your program.

You should also recruit students from local high schools. Attend one or two local tournaments, observe rounds, and visit with the students. Be upbeat, friendly, and positive in describing the merits of your college and your program. Do not focus only on the superstars. Often the competitors who are not the high school stars do better in college competition; they may also be easier to coach! You should also consider hosting a high school tournament on your campus—nothing is more effective in recruiting students to a college than visits to the campus. Consult with officers of the National Forensic League in your area before selecting a date for your tournament, however, so you do not conflict with other already established tournaments. If you do decide to host a tournament, there are some very useful books that you should consult to help you prepare. I especially recommend works by Zarefsky and Goodnight (1980) and Klopf and Lahman (1973).

Many forensics coaches neglect to publicize the achievements of their squad. In order to gain recognition for the program, it is important to keep your campus and community informed. Send press releases on the forensics squad to the campus and community newspapers, and perhaps even to your campus administrators. Display the awards that your squad wins in the office of the communication department. Mail a newsletter to your alumni. Remember my earlier cautions, however, and do not emphasize the number of trophies that you win to the point that they become the primary justification for your program; at the same time, keep people on your campus aware of the fact that you field competitive and successful forensics competitors. It will be more difficult for some future administrator to kill your program if you have made it visible on your campus and if it is a clearly identified part of the college or university's culture.

EVALUATING FORENSICS COACHES

The college forensics coach has an unusual job description. He or she must do all the things expected of his or her departmental colleagues while also spending many hours coaching students and traveling to tournaments. The issue of how this coaching time should be evaluated for merit reviews and promotion and tenure decisions is frequently discussed. I believe that all forensics coaches need to discuss how they will be evaluated with their chairperson and dean early in their careers, so there is no ambiguity about the criteria that will be employed.

Most colleges and universities evaluate faculty in terms of teaching, research, and service. I believe forensics coaches should be evaluated by the same general criteria as are the other faculty members in their department. Thus, if the institution values research in considerations of merit, promotion, and tenure, then the forensics coach should be expected to conduct research. The amount of research that is expected should reflect the difference in time available to the forensics coach, however, and research in argumentation and/or forensics pedagogy should be regarded favorably. I also think that forensics coaching activities should be regarded as part of the coaches' teaching performance, and that he or she should be evaluated in such a way that there is recognition that a forensics coach has far more contact hours with students than most other professors. Finally, because forensics coaches typically do things like host tournaments that are very time intensive, they should be given credit for them under service.

Different departments and institutions should be expected to establish unique criteria for evaluating their faculty. My concern is that forensics coaches understand the unique challenges that they face in such evaluations, and that they become proactively involved in working out the general criteria with which they will be evaluated in advance. I mention one final argument with regard to promotion and tenure. Forensics coaching is so demanding that very few professors elect to make it the focus of their entire career. Consequently, it is important that coaches keep reading and writing in other areas as well so that when they decide to leave the ranks of active coaching they are able to make another contribution to their department and their discipline.

CONCLUSIONS

A career in forensics coaching is unique because it gives you an opportunity to work closely with gifted students, participate in a worthwhile and challenging activity, and see the results of your teaching weekly throughout the season as students compete in tournaments. Although forensics coaches are often as competitive as their students, the forensics community is almost always a friendly and open group. Most established coaches will go out of their way to help a new or less-experienced coach develop a program. The entire forensics community is committed to increasing the number of programs and students involved. Consequently, you should always feel free to call on other coaches in your area for assistance. Hopefully, this brief chapter has provided some information that will help you get started. Good luck to you should you choose to work in forensics.

REFERENCES

Cowperthwaite, L. L., & Baird, A. C. (1954). Intercollegiate debating. In K. Wallace (Ed.), *History of speech education in America* (pp. 259–276). New York: Appleton-Century Crofts.

Klopf, D. W., & Lahman, C. P. (1973). *Coaching and directing forensics.* Skokie, IL: National Textbook.

Potter, D. (1954). The literary society. In K. Wallace (Ed.), *History of speech education in America* (pp. 238–258). New York: Appleton-Century-Crofts.

Zarefsky, D., & Goodnight, G. T. (1980). *Forensics tournaments: Planning and administration.* Skokie, IL: National Textbook.

32

Consulting

John A. Daly
University of Texas at Austin

As I started planning this chapter, I polled a number of colleagues at different schools across the country about consulting. This informal and decidedly unsystematic poll yielded some interesting reactions. One respondent, with a look of disdain on his face and clear distaste in his voice, said: "Why would any scholar want to sell his soul? The moment you start consulting is the moment you give up hope of a real academic career. If someone wants to consult, he should leave this place and get a job in some business. It's not scholarship. You're paid to do scholarship. Having someone on a faculty consult sullies all of us."

A second individual's response was markedly at odds with the first: "Consulting, huh? Boy, those guys really make money. I wish I could do more of it. I've given a few talks, but I'd like to do more. The money is great and it's easy work if you can get it. All you do is entertain, and they pay you a lot. What we need to do is find a way to get more jobs. We could all get rich!"

A third person reflected back on her years of consulting by saying: "It's the toughest work I do, but it's also the most rewarding. You deal with real people coping with real issues in the real world. You've always got to be prepared. The people you work with are paying serious money for everything you offer and they want bottom-line answers. They aren't paying for gloss. They know when you don't know your stuff. The way I judge how helpful I am is by whether I get invited back again. If I do, it isn't because I'm entertaining or fun, it's because people can see I've worked hard. I've offered my expertise and it counted in their lives."

447

Administrators of communication programs had the same reaction. One told me she didn't understand how anyone could afford to remain in the academic world without consulting—schools do not pay enough. A second brusquely said that people in his department who spend time consulting don't deserve merit raises—to him, they have given up their academic integrity, and more importantly, they are making enough "on the outside" not to worry about the paltry amounts the Department distributes for merit. Another one said that the only people in her college who were capable of successful consulting were those who were highly competent in their academic jobs. Good teachers and good researchers, she said, are also good consultants. Why? Because in the end, people hire consultants for both their acknowledged topic expertise and their palpable ability to teach that material in interesting, informative ways.

You will hear many, or all, of these comments if you ask people in a communication department about consulting. Some people think you should do it; others disdain it. Some think it an easy task, others consider it tough, demanding labor. The problem, in a nutshell, is that consulting represents an "unknown" commodity in communication. Although everyone knows what classroom teachers do and feels they have inherent value to a program, and everyone clearly understands and appreciates the role of the scholar in a department, no group, it seems, can agree on what a consultant does or even whether one trained in the academy ought to do it. The field of speech communication is different, in this regard, than most fields. Psychologists are quick to accept the notion that clinical faculty may be good teachers, good scholars, and also highly capable of working with clients on the "outside." Top notch scholars and teachers in economics, government, history, and art see nothing wrong with lending their skills to "clients," whether they be in the public or private sectors. Astronomers, physists, chemists, and biologists are not the least bit anxious about offering their learned opinions to public forums and private industry. Why this hesitation in the field of communication? Probably because many in the field are not yet confident of the status of the discipline. They think that our newly won academic respectability might be challenged and that the floodgates will open to charlatans and their chicanery if consulting were seen as a viable enterprise for the active scholar-teacher.

While it is undoubtedly impossible to disentangle all the various issues involved in consulting in a short chapter, I want to offer some personal reactions to the role of consulting in communication education. I do this by describing what consultants in communication fields do, by offering some advice on how to become a communication consultant, and by addressing some issues you'll face if you are interested in working with nonacademic groups.

Before going any further, let's focus this discussion. This chapter is aimed at those persons who want to do consulting on a part-time basis. It doesn't address the activities, roles, or issues involved in full-time consulting. Some people, after finishing a degree, decide they would rather not work in an academic environment. Nor do they want employment with a single organization. Instead, they opt to become full-time consultants offering their knowledge and skills to any buyer. While much of what is written here applies to these people, they face many issues that cannot be adequately described in a chapter of this length. Full-length books are available on this career option.

Understand also my bias from the start: Consulting is an important form of education. The setting where it takes place may not be the typical classroom; the students not the traditional 18- to 22-year-old population; the form of assessment not the customary one—there are seldom tests. But in the end, you, as a consultant, can impart vital knowledge to your listeners—knowledge that they might otherwise miss. Organizations, government agencies, businesses, and professional groups can profit from what you, as a person trained in communication, can tell them. You can offer insights, reflections, information, and reactions that can significantly affect their choices and decisions. Consulting represents as valid a form of education as that which occurs in the more traditional college education. Done well, it can have important consequences for the learner as well as for the groups the individual works for or belongs to. Moreover, working outside the environs of the academy can offer the practicing scholar-teacher many opportunities to discover important questions and consequential applications for his or her work.

WHY DO PEOPLE IN COMMUNICATION CONSULT?

Although there are as many different justifications for consulting as there are people, most reasons fall into four major categories.

First, and foremost, the field of communication has always been (and will continue to be) an applied field. Consulting represents a way of helping people communicate more effectively in their lives. It is a way of applying what knowledge we have about communication to the problems people face. We, as a discipline, purport two things: (a) that we are better than others in understanding the processes and complexities involved in communication and (b) that we are capable of helping people communicate more effectively—that there are skills people can acquire that will aid them in becoming better communicators. Our insight into communication should translate into usable, practical knowledge.

Second, consulting provides communication professionals with unique opportunities to work with people outside the normal classroom. These people may not take notes, their questions are often less theoretical than those encountered in classes, and there are seldom tests. Instead, you work with people who are listening for answers that will enhance their job performance or life satisfaction. The consultant, first and foremost, is a teacher. For many people who regularly teach college students, working with people in the nonacademic world offers a refreshing opportunity to talk with a seemingly much more varied audience. In addition, as a consultant you can affect, in substantial ways, the directions a company takes or the choices an individual makes in coping with issues. Your advice can have significant and long-lasting consequences. For many who regularly consult, the opportunity to work both within a school and outside in the nonacademic world is highly valued. Not only does one do important work, but it is fun! Do not underestimate the fun component. Many people who spend portions of their time working outside the traditional classroom will tell you that the real reason they do it is because it's fun. You are putting on a show, your mind gets challenged, and you're talking to people who, if you do a good job, will reinforce you in many ways that one seldom encounters in the traditional classroom.

Third, consulting offers the academic a "reality check." It offers the classroom teacher a chance to hear from people who aren't in school everyday. People you consult with will ask questions that hint at needed research and offer ideas that may form the corpus of later classroom lectures. They will ask "so what" questions, demand clear thinking, and wonder aloud about issues of relevance, practicality, and sensibility. They will force you, as the teacher-consultant, to directly address practical problems that need solutions. One thing that you will quickly discover is that most people are really quite smart—they've got insightful ideas, see through muddled thinking, and are quick to grasp concepts that are relevant or interesting to them.

Fourth, academicians consult because it offers them extra money above and beyond what they are paid on their regular jobs. At some schools, part of the job offer a prospective candidate receives may include a guarantee of a certain number of consulting opportunities. Most people in the field of communication do not, however, receive offers such as this. Moreover, most people who engage in part-time consulting do not make that much additional money. Money is certainly one motivator, but if money alone is what you want, consulting on a part-time basis is probably not likely to be satisfying. It requires too much work for the amount you'll take in.

WHAT KINDS OF CONSULTING
DO PEOPLE IN COMMUNICATION DO?

Every consulting job is different, but a quick survey of the sorts of work people in communication do outside of academia suggests that most consulting falls into four clusters.

Giving Talks

Many, many people in the field of communication spend some of their time giving speeches to different businesses, community groups, and professional associations. Those talks range from brief breakfast and after-dinner presentations to hour-long sessions on communication-related topics. Some of these talks are primarily informative; others, are motivational; and some, in all truth, are mostly for entertainment. Whatever the focus, the audience expects you to talk about something having to do with communication, your area of expertise. If you want to work outside of the walls of academia you should have one or two general speeches on communication well-prepared. They should be relatively short, informative, relevant, and entertaining.

Intervention Consulting

Here, an organization or group needs an expert. As a consultant, you offer your knowledge and skills to solve a particular problem the organization is experiencing. Were you an organizational communication expert, you might be asked to aid a company in communicating a major decision or change. For instance, communication consultants have helped companies cope with problems such as a serious personnel cut-back. You might also be asked to help develop a customer service program, aid in restructuring internal communication, or advise the business on new marketing techniques for products. If your expertise lies in political communication, you may find yourself working with a political candidate assessing public opinion, writing speeches, and designing an effective electoral campaign. In health communication, you may assist in developing a prevention/information campaign, counseling physicians and other health care personnel on ways to improve their communication with patients, or you may work with administrators on patient information systems. Whatever the need, the contracting entity seeks out your expertise. You know something that they need.

Personnel Training

The consultant's role in this arena is to develop and refine the communication skills of a group of people. This may include giving informative talks as well as developing workshops that teach participants those skills. In some cases, the training is highly specific (e.g., teaching new recruiters how to effectively interview job applicants, or developing selling skills in a group of beginning salespeople). In other cases, the training is designed to bolster or reinforce already existing skills (e.g., working with a group on meeting or presentation skills).

Research Consulting

An organization may request your services to discover, describe, or confirm some phenomena. You might be asked to assess the level of employee satisfaction with company communication, the impact of a particular communication modality on employee understanding of company policies (e.g., the effectiveness of written materials on company health benefits), or the effectiveness of various internal communication media in an organization. In other settings, you might be asked to evaluate consumer perceptions of product advertising, test methods to achieve greater market share for a radio station, or assess the most effective marketing technique used by salespeople for a company. In the legal arena, you might be called on as an expert witness on topics such as the reliability of eye-witness testimony, be asked to research and assist in jury selection and witness preparation, or be invited to experimentally examine the best ways of presenting a case.

ISSUES YOU NEED TO REMEMBER

Deciding to spend some time working with people in the role of a consultant requires you to reflect about a few important issues. First, and foremost, *what do you know about communication that can help others?* People hire consultants because of their expertise, because inside their group or organization they lack vital knowledge or critical skills that a consultant can provide. It's important to remember that organizations exist because they are good at what they do. They expect the same from you. One of the most common mistakes people make when they begin consulting is believing they know about every imaginable topic. They don't. Figure out where your expertise lies, and limit your consulting to that arena. Nothing is as embarrassing as purporting to be an expert at something and then having people inadvertently discover that you are not. Being the best at one thing is enough to fill your consulting calendar for years to come.

You need to stay current in your academic specialties. People who hire you want to get "the" expert in the area. If you're working with dated information, you're not going to be effective. You also need to constantly be on the lookout for things that can add to your presentations and consulting work. When you hear a humorous story, read an interesting statistic, or discover a relevant example, make sure you write it down and put it in a handy spot for later reference. You should also regularly browse business periodicals to keep informed of the newest trends in consulting. Ten years ago, customer service, as an area of training and consulting, was virtually unknown. Today (circa 1988) it is a very trendy topic.

Second, understand that any organization is spending a good deal of money on you when you act as a consultant. It's easy to forget that. The bulk of the money they are spending is not on your fee. Rather, it is the investment they are putting into your program. Work it out for yourself. Suppose some organization offers you $1,000 for a talk on improving communication skills. They bring in 60 of their executives to listen to you for 3 hours. Each of those people are paid, shall we say, on average, $25 per hour. That's $75 per person for the program or, for the 3 hours, $4,500. That amount does not include the time the company lost in work, in the availability of personnel, or in the cost of the facilities. In the end, your stipened is only about 20% of the cost to the company of your presentation. And this assumes that the organization does not need to pay for your travel or room. This means you had better do your best to give them their money's worth.

Third, preparation is key for successful consulting. *Never* assume that you can "wing it" when addressing or working with a group. In classroom teaching, there is a maxim that for every hour of classroom time, the good instructor spends 5 hours preparing. Let me suggest a corollary. When working as a consultant, double or triple that time. Preparation means working both on the content of the materials and on its presentation. To prepare a thorough outline of material you want to cover is not enough. You also need to spend time determining how best to present that material. In organizations today, audio-visual materials are often a must. People like well-done slides and overheads; people expect nicely done, complete written materials they can take home with them. Preparation also means expending time learning about the organization or person you are working with. Find their annual report or press clippings and read them carefully, take a tour of the plant and talk to employees. Do anything, in short, that will increase your familiarity. Why? Because when you do start working with the individual or organization, they will want you to address them directly. They are not paying for a "canned" talk or consulting job.

Fourth, remember that people are not listening to you because there is a test scheduled or a grade assigned. You are going to have work very hard to keep them interested and involved. Certainly, what you discuss should directly address their concerns. It is sometimes difficult for academic people to cope with the sort of information that nonacademic people desire. Often, theories, concepts, and methods academicians find fascinating are totally uninteresting to a lay audience. For the most part, people you will work with will want "bottom-line" answers that can help them solve pressing—often immediate—problems. Be prepared for numerous "so what" questions. Also be prepared to be challenged by many personal experience stories, anecdotes, and statements of "you have to be here to understand."

You will also have to be entertaining. Remember, people vote with their feet. There is nothing wrong with this. Nowhere is it written that communication professionals need to be tedious and obscure. You, as a consultant (and also, hopefully, as a teacher), need to make people want to listen. Don't misunderstand—you do not need to be a stand-up comedian. You do need to project enthusiasm, excitement, and a sense of humor when you work with groups.

Fifth, you will have to learn how to market yourself. Getting started as a consultant is tough to do. How does one go about it? The most critical thing is to let people know that you exist.

HOW DOES ONE DEVELOP CONTACTS FOR CONSULTING?

Develop Relationships With Continuing Education Programs at Your School

Most colleges and universities offer continuing education programs either independent of particular academic units or within some of those units. Business colleges often have management or executive development programs, pharmacy schools offer continuing education programs, and public affairs schools may provide public education programs. Go over to those offices and introduce yourself. Tell them what you do and ask how you might be included in programs they produce. Most continuing education offices do not pay that much—but they do offer two things: First, it is a good way to meet people who may later hire you. Impress them here, and they may seek you out for further work. Second, working in continuing education programs gives you an opportunity to try out materials in a semitraditional classroom setting. It's absolutely essential that you recognize that what works in a traditional undergraduate classroom may not work at all in the nonacademic arena. Working in a continuing education event offers you a midway point between classroom and nonclassroom to test materials, content coverage, and audience adaption.

Make Public Presentations to Community Groups

In every town or city there are many fraternal, professional, and social groups that are always looking for speakers. Most of the time, they are seeking people who can provide an interesting, informative, and perhaps entertaining talk about some topic. Most of the time, they have no money—you'll talk for free. The reason you give these talks is to develop contacts. Many of the people in an audience work in businesses or groups. Later, when they need someone with your expertise, they will remember you. Moreover, those talks give you an opportunity to try out material, to learn how to adapt information to different audiences, and most importantly, to get feedback about your presentation style.

Directly Market Yourself

Many people who want to consult spend some money and time directly marketing themselves. They may put advertisements in the phone book (in big-city Yellow Pages, for instance, there is a category called "Public Speaking Instruction"), they may call upon potential clients, and they may send out mass mailings. If you decide on this option, there are two things you need to consider. First, whatever you do, make sure that it is tastefully done. Second, make sure people in your department are aware of your efforts. Colleagues who aren't positive about consulting do not want to be surprised to see your picture in the local newspaper as working with some group. If the direct approach is not palatable to you, some indirect techniques might be useful. In some cities there are agents who try to get consultants work. Find such an agent, and let him or her market you. You might also drop hints whenever you can about your realm of expertise. Get on a local radio or television show; talk about communication, and during the conversation indicate that, in addition to your work at school, you consult. Tell your chairperson that if people call in asking for a consultant or speaker that you'd like him or her to recommend you. Get in touch with government agencies to ensure that you get every "Request for Proposals" for consulting contracts. Keep in touch, as well, with former students and alumni. Let them know that you do work for companies, individuals, and organizations. You never know when a former student might be sitting in a meeting, hearing that a consultant is needed, and think of you.

Reinforce Any Contacts You Get

When you do some work for a client, make sure your work is extraordinarily good. Make it a point to measure your success not in money alone, but in whether you get invited back to do further work. Find additional niches for your expertise in the company or organization and then offer yourself for further work in those areas. Ask people you have done work for if you might use them as a reference for other groups. Finally, and most importantly, stay in touch with people who hire you. Visit them, drop them reprints of relevant research, and so on.

CONCLUSION

In the end, the single most important thing you need to remember about getting contacts is that quality always wins out. If you develop a true expertise in an area and can communicate that expertise in an informed and interesting way, people will hear about it. Gloss without content can only go so far.

Finally, remember who you are. You are an expert in an important field that is central to humankind. You have knowledge that can be used for many different purposes. Every day, check your ethics and your values. Ethically, do not be a servant to every cause. And, if you are teaching at a college, university, junior college, or high school, remember that you are first and foremost a teacher at that institution. Do not give your students or colleagues less attention because of your desire to consult. Keep your research program going, continue your thinking, and build your teaching skills.

Effective communication is central to the success of any individual or organization. You, as a consultant, can help people and companies better themselves through your expertise in communication. Done well, consulting is a legitimate, important instructional opportunity for the scholar-teacher in the field of communication.

VI

EXPLORING IMPORTANT PROFESSIONAL ISSUES

33

Ethical Issues in Teaching

Kenneth E. Andersen
University of Illinois

During the 1980s, educational issues attracted major public attention. A number of national reports, focusing initially on elementary and secondary education, then on higher education, raised questions about the curriculum, educational quality, teacher competency, course content, and educational costs and benefits for the society and individual. Value questions and ethical issues became prominent as the ethics of government, business, and society in general were called into question. Educators were asked about their role in teaching values and instilling both ethical awareness and practices.

Not surprisingly, communication teachers are affected in many ways by the increased interest in ethical issues. The central role of communication means that many ethical decisions are tied to communication activity, including ends sought and means employed. Teachers confront efforts to remove books from libraries, ban the presentation of certain plays, and prohibit the use of certain topics and approaches to teaching. Teachers find that such matters as fair use of material, plagiarism, acceptability of language, and use of particular motivational appeals (or even topics for speeches) become sources of difficulty when students, teachers, parents, and administrators do not share common standards. Freedom of speech, rights, and responsibilities become issues in teaching, not just in the courts.

The communication classroom shares the concern of every classroom about cheating on exams, plagiarized material, fairness in grading, and ensuring responsible use of individual rights. But the teacher who deals with communication theory and practice inevitably also faces issues that arise out of the subject matter: ethical communication goals; acceptable ethical practices in treatment of content, language use, motivational appeals, and deceptive communication; policies relative to the mass media; practice of critical listening; censorship; and development of an adequate basis for making communication decisions in one's profession, community activity, and private life.

The communication teacher needs to be prepared to deal not only with ethical issues that arise in any classroom, but also with ethical issues relative to the theory and practice of communication, including assisting students in accepting responsibility for their choices within the entire range of communication activities, situations, roles, and purposes.

This chapter is designed to assist the teacher in coping with these ethical issues and value questions. The chapter examines the nature of ethics, ethical issues that arise in the classroom, ethical issues that arise in teaching communication, and methods of dealing with ethical issues.

THE NATURE OF ETHICS

Ethics, when defined as "moral philosophy," is the systematic study of value concepts such as *good, bad,* and *right,* and the application of such terms to actions, to intentions, and as descriptors of character. Ethical inquiry asks questions about principles of morality, the nature of the morally good or blameworthy. Ethics is concerned with questions as to how one ought to live and what constitutes a good life. In this sense, it is closely tied to our values, to what we esteem and value in our lives and in the lives of others: power, fairness, love, wealth, justice, honesty, freedom, knowledge, beauty.

Philosophers distinguish three kinds of ethical studies: descriptive, normative, and metaethical. *Descriptive ethics* examines the ethical practices of a particular individual, group, nation, or period. The "ethos" or "image" of a communicator is a "descriptive" judgment that someone makes of the nature or character of an individual. *Normative ethics,* sometimes called "substantive ethics," is concerned with judgments of what constitutes right or wrong, good or bad behavior, actions, and character. It is, as Norman (1983) stated, "concerned with practical questions of conduct" (p. 2). When one speaks of an ethical code, an unethical practice, or a good person, one typically is dealing with questions of normative ethics. *Metaethics* is concerned with questions of meaning (seeking to understand what we mean when we use various ethical terms) and with the logical processes involved when making ethical statements and claims.

Communication teachers find themselves making use of all three levels of ethical inquiry, for example descriptive in distinguishing standards that an audience may utilize for political speakers versus medical doctors; normative in making judgments about the ethical quality of a particular speech or speaker, or the point of view taken in reporting an event on a newscast; and metaethical in discussing the requirements for personal or professional ethics.

Philosophical inquiry serves many valuable functions: It subjects convictions and beliefs to critical scrutiny, both our own and that of others; it brings to light presuppositions and hidden assumptions; it asks questions about the ultimate worth of actions and goals. Normative ethics is not a matter merely of information, or even of knowledge (although information and knowledge are an essential base from which to proceed); normative ethics calls for judgment or wisdom.

ETHICS AND THE TEACHER

Questions that involve ethical issues arise naturally in every classroom, whatever the subject matter. Questions concerning clear communication of requirements, testing the material presented, grading standards, time for completion of major assignments, late assignments, favoritism, and the effects of bias or prejudice involve ethical practice as well as quality of teaching. Many elements of classroom management (protecting students from harassment, limiting intrusions and disruptions, accommodating a range of opinions and points of view, encouraging active participation, avoiding ridiculing or embarrassing students for "wrong answers") are important ethical goals.

Ethical issues cannot be avoided. There will be efforts to cheat on examinations. Students may copy the homework of other students in the same or other classes. Test questions may be pirated. Speakers may present material drawn almost verbatim from a recent magazine, *Cliff Notes,* or some other source given brief acknowledgment for a single direct quotation. Students may express racial prejudices, use obscene gestures, or employ sexist language. Students often bring an exaggerated concern for fairness and question many educational practices.

Such issues cannot be dealt with on a private, individual basis. Students must know what constitutes fair use of material, understand what constitutes plagiarism, and be aware of the limits of cooperative effort. A teacher should not assume that students know what constitutes plagiarism. In elementary school, my son copied items verbatim from encyclopedias and was encouraged to do so. Despite my warnings, he persisted in such practices until an English teacher assigned an F for undue reliance on outside sources. Standards had changed. Evidence from academic standards cases is persuasive. Many students do not understand the nature of plagiarism. Teachers need to be direct, clear, and firm in defining the various violations of acceptable practice and the penalties that will ensue. Teacher presentations and class discussions of specific examples are particularly helpful.

Where matters of classroom practice are concerned, wise teachers make their standards very clear. Whereas certain ethical norms are open questions that each individual must decide for oneself, and general agreement cannot be expected, on certain issues (such as plagiarism) there is a need to be quite clear that a public, exceptionless standard is mandated. Violations, however, are typically dealt with on a private basis. Typically, the teacher decides to handle the matter directly, but may turn to such existing structures as student disciplinary panels or the principal.

Numerous ethical matters are not tied directly to the classroom. Relationships with other teachers, administrators, parents, and the community pose many ethical dilemmas. When does one report the violation of school rules or standard procedures by a peer or superior? Reviewing a colleague for appointment or a merit raise or evaluating teaching effectiveness involves ethical responsibilities. In casting a play, seeking student assistance, and conducting research, there should be an assurance of informed consent and freedom from coercion. What is seen by a teacher as a means of promoting friendship and establishing good rapport may be seen as harassment by some and as favoritism by others. How accurately and precisely does a recommendation reflect one's actual judgment?

As a member of a profession, an educator is expected to adhere to responsible norms of professional conduct and can be held to those standards by the courts as well as students, parents, and administrators. Legal liabilities, contracts, social pressure, and professional preparation as well as individual conscience play an important part in guaranteeing a certain minimal standard. But if individuals as a group meet only the minimal standard, then that standard inevitably erodes to be replaced with another standard that is even less demanding.

ETHICS AND TEACHING COMMUNICATION

It is essential to understand the range of ethical issues that arise in teaching communication, whether these involve theory, practice, or criticism of the various forms, purposes, settings, and media. The remainder of the chapter highlights some areas in which ethical issues arise in teaching communication and some ways in which those issues have been resolved, and it concludes with some suggested means to enhance students' ability to deal with ethical issues in communication. Readers should be sensitive to the possible application of these ideas in their classrooms.

Nature of Ethical Issues in Communication

Potentially, ethical issues arise at any point where a choice, conscious or unconscious, is made or the perception exists that a choice could be made. Aristotle (1947) emphasized this point in his doctrine of choices as applied to communication, noting that every choice made by a speaker provides a basis for a judgment of character. It is helpful, however, to note some major areas in which ethical issues arise.

Ethical issues arise in the process of defining the nature of communication, particularly the role and functions that it serves for the individual, the group, the larger community, or humanity as a whole. Justifiable ethical positions (and defenses of ethical choices in specific cases) are derived from the role and function assigned to communication, generally, and from the specific function or form of communication being studied. Some ethical positions are grounded in the nature of the communication process itself. Thus, a dialogical approach stressing equality of all participants may yield a rather different standard than a stress on communication serving the needs of the state, whether democratic or totalitarian. The degree to which communication is to serve the individual versus the state or larger society and the priority of the goals of the one over the other have tremendous consequences for the determination of what is ethical.

A key issue concerns the locus or place of responsibility for ethical communication. Many approaches to communication place major emphasis on the source, the "originator of the communication act." Hence, many ethical standards are focused on the behavior of the source. One test of successful communication is whether it achieves the purposes or goals of the source. But if one takes a comprehensive view of communication, one knows that communication must serve also the individual receiver(s) in terms of their needs and goals. Ultimately, communication must serve the needs of or, at least, not be unduly harmful to the society. Hence, an ethic tied only to the goals and purposes of the source is almost inevitably faulty and will be rejected by other participants if it ignores their and society's interests in the communication process. Each individual plays multiple roles in the communication process over time. Is it logical that an ethic should elevate the concerns of the individual in one role over the concerns of those in every other role? Is it true that a politician functioning as a politician should be held to a different standard of "promise keeping" than that same person as salesperson, friend, or mother?

Ethical issues also arise in terms of particular mediums and settings. Does the press have a higher standard for objectivity, completeness of reporting, and accuracy than an individual speaker? Does a person in a face-to-face debate have a different standard for presentation of both sides of an issue than an individual making the only presentation on an issue to a partisan, well-informed audience? Does the standard of the overtness of presentation of erotic or pornographic material vary for print, photographs, speeches, or film? Should a nation at war restrict information flow to a greater degree than it does in peacetime? Should—must—a government allow criticism of that government? In thinking about the answers to these questions, most individuals have a sense that there are different standards to be met.

The means and instrumentalities employed within the communication process pose significant ethical issues as well. Even if the goal of a communication is sound, the means employed may be so detrimental that they corrupt the goal or achieve the goal but produce other negative consequences, such as impairing future communication. Even the most desirable goal does not legitimate every means. Historically, writers on communication have focused largely on issues of ethical content. Mary Andersen (1979) found six major categories of ethical shortcomings relevant to treatment of material: inadequate research or a failure to meet logical standards of truth; sacrificing convictions in adapting to the audience; insincerity, trying to be what one is not; withholding and suppressing relevant information; relaying false information; and using motivational materials to hinder the communication of truth.

The seventh category focused on still another area of ethical concern: the receivers' failure to listen critically, an insensitivity to ethical dimensions, and failure to respond to the content in a rational manner. Many textbooks fail to focus on questions of ethical responsibilities of readers, listeners, and consumers in the communication process, particularly consumers of the mass media. Those concerned with interpersonal and small-group communication are more likely to emphasize the active nature and the responsibilities of all participants in communication due to the immediate alteration of roles—the dual interaction that marks such communication. Ethical issues are posed by the failure of individuals to expose themselves to or respond to relevant messages. Further, the way in which individuals respond may be crucial: The receiver may depend on prejudice, stereotypes, authority figures, and blind acceptance or accept responsibility for testing and weighing communication on more relevant bases in determining a response, or some combination of the two. Many receivers do not accept the burden of responsibility for their reactions or failure to act.

Finally, specific topic areas within the study of communication may pose particular ethical issues. Cross-cultural communication, for example, involves participants in a range of ethical issues. Different practices, some of which have ethical considerations, are involved, whether in bargaining over an item for sale or in framing an international treaty. Yet, some ethical standard must be framed that permits dialogue and agreement. Even within the same culture, conflicts may arise in defining ethical practice. The guarantee of freedom of speech in the First Amendment is an unlimited source of disputes. In 1988, for example, the supreme court ruled that school newspapers are subject to a wide range of restrictions on publication, including prior restraint. The closely divided court has created a new standard of conduct for high school journalists, who, in the eyes of some supreme court jurists, have now lost Constitutionally guaranteed rights. The court has never satisfactorily defined such terms as obscenity and pornography. Yet there are increasing pressures to censor books, plays, and classroom materials on such grounds.

Methods of Resolution

How is the classroom teacher to deal with ethical issues, including the potential for conflict among the ethical views of students coming from diverse cultural, religious, and economic backgrounds? One approach to resolving ethical issues is to depend on the conscience, morality, or ethical standards of the individual teacher. However, in the absence of certainty on ethical issues, a teacher is rightly reluctant to impose personal standards on students. Students often have not tested the ethical standards they so strongly espouse. Typically, students' judgments of what is ethical will not agree. But to assert that no ethical standards apply is unreasonable. How does one proceed?

First, although there is not universal agreement on ethical standards, the lack of agreement should not be interpreted to mean that any ethical standard is as good as any other. Some standards are more defensible than others, and one task of the teacher is to assist the student in learning how to defend and test standards and to recognize strengths and weaknesses of differing views. A strategy is available for use in assessing actions for their ethicality. First, it is essential that the facts of the case be as clear and complete as possible. Often, the solution to a dispute lies in clarifying the factual basis of the matter. Many "ethical" disagreements turn out to be disagreements about factual claims. Once the facts are clear, application of various ethical standards or guidelines can be considered. The relevant ethical criteria or standards should be identified and their application justified. Often, one difficulty is that a single standard is employed when multiple standards may be relevant. Ethical codes typically contain a series of moral articles or standards ordered in terms of priority, but specific situations may require a reordering of priorities. Ethical standards are not abstract ideals, they need to be practical guides to action. Ethical standards should be tested by rational processes. But the ability of ethical standards to direct action and function as adequate justifications acceptable to others are major tests.

For more than 2,000 years, philosophers have offered, tested, and refined or discarded a wide range of views on ethics. Their thinking and the experience of societies and individuals are invaluable resources. Although most individuals have not formally studied ethics, they have been influenced by such injunctions as: treat others as you would like to be treated, seek the greatest good for the greatest number, be truthful, and avoid doing evil even if not compelled to do what is most beneficial to others. The idea of testing ethical practice from the point of view of each of the parties involved as well as the impact on society is widespread.

A number of methods, each with strengths and weaknesses, have been used to determine ethical guidelines for communication. One method is to determine the relevant ethical standards of the audience or relevant group through a process of audience analysis. If communication practices meet the standard held by those to whom the communication is addressed, it is presumably ethical. Several possible difficulties exist with this view: the analysis may be faulty; the standard may be so low that it is too defective for use; the standard may not be widely shared by the group, it may conflict with widely held standards.

A second method often used is generalizing a particular religious or moral point of view. But, there are (a) difficulties in agreeing on the proper interpretation; (b) rejection by those who do not accept that particular view; and (c) difficulty of knowing what the generalized standard dictates in a particular situation. Suppose one takes the standard of not lying as a universal prescription. How should the individual have responded when the Nazi storm troopers knocked on the door and asked, "Is X inside?" if answering truthfully would condemn an innocent individual to a concentration camp or gas chamber?

A third view is that ethical practices should flow from the nature of the political system. A democracy commits itself to an informed citizenry, creating a need for sharing information and for a free exchange of ideas. Although it seems reasonable that certain ethical responsibilities follow from living in a democracy, it is less clear that individuals do not have the right to demand the same ethical standards simply because they live in a dictatorship under a reign of terror. Are state's rights superior to those of the individual?

A fourth method for deriving ethical standards is to work from the nature of the communication process itself, a basis that I endorse (Andersen, 1983), or from the nature of humanity itself. Representative of such approaches is the stress on dialogical communication of Richard

Johannesen (1983). Many have argued that individuals have a right to respect, to fair treatment, and to information upon which to make a reasonable, informed, individual decision, simply because one is a fully functioning human being. However, what is appropriate to one communication setting or purpose may not generalize to other settings and purposes. Further, issues of what constitute human nature and the ideal "humanness" seem as problematic as agreeing upon a common ethical standard through other approaches.

A final possibility, not inconsistent with any of the preceding approaches, is to set a goal of establishing a personal ethical code consciously held and tested as a result of systematically reflecting upon and testing various approaches. This makes individuals responsible not only for coming to hold a clear view of their own ethical code, but also for a willingness to validate that code publicly, justifying it as a basis for action binding self and others until such time as the code or application is shown to be unjustified.

CLASSROOM STRATEGIES

As noted previously, teachers inevitably face ethical issues in the classroom as well as ethical issues linked to the particular subject matter. Quite spontaneously, students raise a number of ethical issues. Further, the teacher should assist students in recognizing ethical issues and their appropriate importance. The subject matter of communication courses causes a range of value questions to be addressed, although not all teachers emphasize the ethical dimension in treating those questions. In communication classes dealing with presentations to others, questions concerned with purposes, means, balance of logical and motivational elements, and fair use must receive attention. Courses that deal with communication history, with communication theory, or with regulation, criticism, and practice of communication should accord ethical considerations a proper role.

Yet, for reasons suggested earlier, including the lack of agreement on ethical standards, the ethical dimension is often given minimal attention. Such an approach is unwise. Decisions about ethics affect communication in a wide range of immediate as well as long-term ways. Omitting the ethical dimension leaves students without assistance on important issues teachers of communication are best prepared to address. Omission of the topic increases the likelihood of attacks on the teacher for failing to deal with value issues. Such attacks often come from those who believe they have *the* answer and demand that their answer become the orthodoxy of the classroom.

When and how does the teacher treat ethical issues in a course? Some ethical concerns lend themselves to integration throughout the entire course. Certain value positions and ethical presuppositions necessarily play a role throughout any course. In these instances, the ethical dimension becomes an ongoing part of the course.

In many courses, it is useful to have a unit in which ethical issues are addressed. Typically, units on ethics are offered late in the course on the grounds that substantial knowledge about the communication process is required before the significance of ethical issues can be fully seen and constructively discussed. Although ethical considerations may provide a perspective for integrating the course, it is essential that the ethical dimension be given its place throughout the course. Thus, the unit on ethics may best be seen as a final effort to rework and refine ethical issues that have surfaced throughout the course.

There are a growing number of sources devoted to communication ethics. Several of the more useful current sources are used as references or listed in the Supplementary Reading section at the end of this chapter.

Although methods and procedures will vary with teacher, subject matter, nature of the individual class, and so on, the following goals drawn from work at the Hastings Center (Rosen & Caplan, 1980) are appropriate in dealing with the ethical dimensions of communication:

- Stimulating the moral imagination: "Morality matters; it is at the core of human lives."
- Recognizing ethical issues, which involves a careful, rational effort to identify moral issues.
- Developing analytical skills to discern and weigh relevant arguments.
- Developing a sense of moral obligation and personal responsibility.
- Developing the ability to tolerate disagreement but resisting ambiguity.

CONCLUSION

Ideally, a teacher will have had a course in communication ethics, a course in moral philosophy, or have been richly exposed to the ethical dimensions of communication in the various courses completed. But preparation is not the major determinant of success in this area. The key to success in dealing with ethical issues is a sensitivity to the ethical dimension so that its presence is felt in course planning and preparation, in classroom presentations of material, in discussion, and in evaluation. Helpful resource material is readily available. Once the ethical dimension is introduced, ethical issues will pop up in the news, be brought to class by students, and appear spontaneously in the classroom. Students often enjoy the challenge of developing and justifying ethical codes for particular settings, forms, or for communication generally. Discussion of these proposed codes demonstrates that the communication process is a valuable means for exploring ethical issues while developing understanding, discouraging ambiguity, and enhancing tolerance. Whatever the means, students find their appreciation and practice of communication is better for their understanding of the nature and importance of the ethical dimension to and in communication.

REFERENCES

Andersen, K. E. (1983). *Persuasion theory and practice* (2nd ed.). Boston: American Press.

Andersen, M. K. (1979). *An analysis of the treatment of ethics in selected speech communication textbooks.* Unpublished doctoral dissertation, University of Michigan, East Lansing, MI.

Aristotle (1947). Nicomachaen ethics (W. D. Ross, Trans.). In R. McKeon (Ed.), *Introduction to Aristotle* (pp. 295–543). New York: The Modern Library.

Johannesen, R. L. (1983). *Ethics in human communication* (2nd ed.). Prospect Heights, IL: Waveland Press.

Norman, R. (1983). *The moral philosophers: An introduction to ethics.* Oxford: Clarendon Press.

Rosen, B., & Caplan, A. L. (1980). *Ethics in the undergraduate curriculum.* Hastings-on-Hudson: The Hastings Center.

SUPPLEMENTARY READING

Andersen, K. E. (1984, January). A code of ethics for speech communication. *SPECTRA,* pp. 2–3.

Bellah, R. N., Madsen, R., Smith, W. M., Swidler, A., & Tipton, S. M. (1985). *Habits of the heart.* Berkeley: University of California Press.

Bok, S. (1978). *Lying: Moral choice in public and private life.* New York: Vintage Books.

Christians, C. G., & Covert, C. L. (1980). *Teaching ethics in journalism education.* Hastings-on-Hudson: The Hastings Center.

Christians, C. G., Rotzoll, & Fackler, M. (1987). *Media ethics: Cases and moral reasoning.* New York: Longman.

Goodwin, H. E. (1983). *Groping for ethics in journalism.* Ames: University of Iowa Press.

Haiman, F. (1981). *Speech and law in a free society.* Chicago: University of Chicago.

Jaksa, J. A., & Pritchard, M. S. (1988). *Communication ethics: Methods of analysis.* Belmont: Wadsworth.

Johannesen, R. L. (1983). *Ethics in human communication* (2nd ed.). Prospect Heights: Waveland Press.

MacIntyre, A. (1981). *After virtue.* Notre Dame: University of Notre Dame Press.

Nilsen, T. R. (1974). *Ethics of speech communication* (2nd ed.). Indianapolis: Bobbs-Merrill.

34

Fitting Into the Department

James C. McCroskey
West Virginia University

Students typically see teachers as *the* power source in colleges and universities. Many new teachers, particularly graduate assistants serving as teachers for the first time, have similar perceptions. In fact, individual classroom teachers typically have comparatively little control over the environment in which they work.

Teaching is a profession that functions within complex organizations—departments, colleges, universities, university systems. Virtually all instruction that occurs in today's institutions of higher education is part of a highly coordinated educational system, one in which all of the parts are very much interrelated.

Systems are successful only to the extent that their components are successfully interrelated. Universities are composed of interrelated colleges. Colleges are composed of interrelated departments. Departments are composed of interrelated faculty members. A faculty member who thinks he or she can operate in an autonomous fashion is likely to be viewed by others as a "loose cannon." Such people are viewed as dangerous to the system, and are likely to be "thrown overboard" the first time the opportunity arises.

ACADEMIC FREEDOM

One of the most valued rights of university faculty members is "academic freedom." Unfortunately, it is also the most misunderstood. Academic freedom is the freedom of a teacher to state the truth as he or she sees it without fear of losing her or his position or otherwise being punished for the views expressed. It is the right of a teacher to speak out when he or she sees injustice in society, to support whatever political candidate or position he or she chooses, and to challenge the views of established authority. In short, this is the academic version of the right held by everyone in American society—the freedom of speech.

Unfortunately, many teachers misinterpret this right to mean that they have the freedom to teach anything in any way they please in their classrooms. Academic freedom relates to *political* issues, not to *academic* ones. Colleges are regularly forbidden to teach subject matter that is deemed more appropriate for another college. Departments are restricted from teaching content that has been assigned to another department. Within a given department, faculty are restricted from teaching content in one course that is determined to be part of a different course. Such restrictions are necessary. Otherwise, students could be subjected to the same content over and over while never having the opportunity to study things that they may need or want. Of course, anyone who has been a student knows that some needless overlap continues to exist, and some courses include materials that are of interest to no one other than the teacher teaching them. Such problems, however, are not caused by academic freedom, they are a function of one or more people ignoring or abdicating their responsibility to exercise appropriate control in the academic environment.

Control in most academic institutions of today follows a top-down path. Whoever is in control of the purse is in control of the institution. In practice, however, most control as regards individual courses is exercised at the departmental level. This occurs as a function of appropriate delegation of authority from upper levels. Every course must be approved by some unit before it can become a part of a university's curriculum, and the approval authority normally is delegated to some faculty unit—often a group of faculty members elected by their peers. Such groups frequently are known as "curriculum committees." They may exist at every level of the institution. However, because content specialists generally exist only at the departmental level, this is the level that serves the primary function of screening out inappropriate courses. This function may be performed by a departmental administrator, a faculty committee, or, particularly in smaller departments, by the faculty as a whole.

The new faculty member, then, enters a world not of his or her own making, a world full of special but not yet understood interests, a world with an unknown history, a world that is as likely to be hostile as it is to be friendly. It is a world in which the newcomer is free to say whatever he or she thinks, propose any changes he or she would like to make, and everyone else is free to support the changes, ignore the suggestions, attack them, or simply shunt the newcomer altogether. It is up to the newcomer to fit in.

DEPARTMENTAL HISTORY

If an observer looks at departments in the same field across a number of universities, regardless of the particular academic discipline, he or she most likely will be surprised at how different one department is from another. Some of the differences are obvious—size of the department, median age of the faculty, content that is emphasized, quality of the facilities, and the like. Other factors may be much less obvious but much more important to the new person's success. Near the top of that list is the manner in which the department is governed.

The manner in which a department is governed typically is a function of tradition. If one asks why a particular department is operated the way it is, the answer that usually is correct (although often not given) is because it has been operated that way for a long time. Senior faculty tend to dominate most departments and the more senior one gets, the more likely one believes the old maxim "If it isn't broken, don't fix it." Change comes only with considerable difficulty, or in the face of impending disaster, in most departments.

Tradition, then, is a driving force in most departments. The newcomer must become acquainted with that tradition as quickly as possible in order to avoid making serious errors in her or his dealings with people who have been in the department for a longer period. The first thing to determine is the basic political system. There are essentially four general systems that may be in place: autocracy, fiefdoms, democracy, and chaos.

Autocracy

An autocracy exists when one individual, usually known as a "head" or "chair," or a small group of faculty members, makes all of the major decisions and judgments in the department. In such systems, the leader(s) may or may not consult with other people prior to making decisions. The decisions may be made with individual faculty members' best interests in mind, or the interests of people may not even be taken into account.

Under the autocratic system, rank becomes very important. The "head" or "chair" is at the top, followed by the full professors, the associate professors, the assistant professors, the instructors, the doctoral assistants, the masters assistants, and so on. The value of a person's opinions is roughly equal to the rank that that person holds in the system. The opinions of new people, particularly those holding graduate assistantships, are viewed with minimum concern.

People brought up with the traditional American values for democracy often react very negatively to an autocratic system, particularly when they first enter. Their instinct is to fight, an instinct that, if not kept under control, will almost certainly result in negative consequences for the newcomer. The new person entering an autocratic system should keep in mind that it was the autocrat who decided to allow them to enter, and it is reasonable to assume that the autocrat wants to see them do well to demonstrate the wisdom of that decision.

The concept of the "benevolent" autocrat is an important one to understand. Although autocrats have the power to bring harm to the newcomer, they also have the power to provide many positive rewards. The decision of path for the autocrat to follow usually rests with the newcomer—the one who is supportive of the autocrat receives support in return. Benevolent autocrats are those who use their power to help the people under them. Few autocrats are so altruistic that they help those who choose to attack them. In large measure, then, a new person often has the choice of generating an enemy or a benevolent autocrat. Whether an autocrat is perceived as benevolent or not is a function of the relationship between the autocrat and the individual doing the perceiving.

Fiefdoms

The system of fiefdoms is a special case of autocracy. Instead of having one person (or one small collective group at the top and in control), the department is broken (either formally or informally) into smaller units that have individuals (fiefs) in charge. These individuals are nominally subordinate to a person or persons above them, but in practice do pretty much whatever they want so long as they do not stray too far into some other fief's territory. Typically fiefs are identified by titles—such as basic course director, coordinator of graduate studies, head of the division of rhetoric, and associate chair for research.

Fiefs behave mostly like other autocrats. The rule of survival is "Those that go along, get along." It is up to the new person to make peace with the various fiefs with or under whom he or she must work. Getting in trouble with a fief is tantamount to getting in trouble with the head autocrat. When pushed, the person over the fief will almost always support the fief when there is a conflict with a new person.

Within the fief system is a high sense of territoriality. Each fief has an intellectual or administrative territory over which he or she reigns. The fief approaches the new person with the basic attitude of "I've got mine. You do what you want, but don't mess with my area." Typically, there are areas within the department over which no one appears to reign. These are open to individuals to build upon, if they do so carefully.

Democracy

The idealized political system in a department is democracy. Many new teachers assume that all departments are run in a democratic manner— one person, one vote. In practice, that rarely occurs. In most departments it is recognized that some people, by nature of their background, experience, and/or rank, are "more equal" than others. The closest most departments come to democracy is a "consensus" system. Formal votes are taken only rarely, but everyone is asked for their input. If "significant opposition" to a decision emerges, that decision is not made until the opposition is dealt with. The significance of the opposition usually is determined by the status of the opposers.

Democracy is often chosen as a departmental system in revolt against an autocratic system with which people have become dissatisfied. Frequently, the outcome is the replacement of one undesirable system with another. Although democracy is not a bad system, democracy that gets completely out of control can be. It is not uncommon for a democratic system in a department to become a dictatorship of the majority. A coalition of faculty within the department simply takes over and votes down anything they do not want, even if it means trampling on the needs of the minority. Even more common is what has been called "rampant democracy." When this breaks out, people begin to complain about being "committeed" or "meetinged" to death. Some departments literally have a vote on such matters as how many paper clips to purchase or when other people will hold office hours.

For the new person who enters a department with a democratic system, the road ahead poses many pitfalls. It is critical that the new person be supported by a majority of the established people. These are the people who will determine such things as where (maybe even whether) the new person has an office, what that person will teach, when it will be taught, and, most importantly, whether the person will be retained.

Chaos

The last system is, essentially, no system. Chaos often results when a powerful person or persons leave the department. This may be the result of promotion (to dean, for example), death, retirement, or resignation.

Any relatively sudden departure of powerful people may leave a gap in the system. The time when this typically is felt most is at the beginning of a school year, exactly at the time when a new person is most likely to enter the system.

Whether the system in the past has been autocratic or democratic, specific people have been present to keep the system functioning. Only the fiefdom approach is relatively secure from the loss of a powerful person. In that system, most of the "system managers" are still in place, and only one needs to be replaced. Under conditions of chaos, tussels for power and control are likely to be common. Unless a new person has been employed specifically to replace a departed person in the same role, a new person has little chance of surviving such tussels and emerging on top. The wiser course is to avoid such battles.

Such a choice may be difficult to make, because no one may really know who is in charge. This circumstance often results when a person is appointed "interim" chair to replace a departed chair. The whole political system is, at least temporarily, "up for grabs." There may be pressure on the new person from many quarters, and too little information available to permit wise decisions.

The preceding discussion of the various departmental political systems that a new person may encounter is intended to sensitize you to the kinds of problems you may face as a new person in a department. No one of them is inherently easier to survive than another. The key to survival is to recognize what system exists and establish positive relationships with as many of the relevant decision makers in the system as possible. Always remember: The department got along without you before you came. It probably can get along quite well again if it gets rid of you.

THE BASIC COURSE

Almost all departments in academic institutions offer "basic" courses in their disciplines. New people are the ones most likely to be assigned to teach such courses. Hence, one's first experience as a faculty member in most disciplines is with the basic course.

In the communication field, it is unusual for a graduate assistant never to have any assignment with a basic course. In excess of 90% of all graduate assistants in most communication departments are involved in the teaching of the basic course. The nature of that involvement varies drastically from department to department.

Basic courses in most communication departments exist primarily to serve students who are majoring in other disciplines. They may be content or skills courses; they may center on public speaking, on interper-

sonal communication, on mass communication, on
ganizations, on rhetorical theory, on communicati
combination of those—or even something entirel'

There is no standard for what the basic course
be from department to department. Thus, it is likely that a
entering a department will be confronted with a different type of basic
course than he or she has seen or taken previously. This is particularly
problematic if the department has a relaxed approach to the course.
Sometimes the new person simply is given a text and told to teach the
course. In some cases, there is a common syllabus, in some there is not. In
some cases, the new person is not given either a text or a syllabus—he or
she is simply told to teach the course. All that is provided is the course
title and catalog description. In contrast, some departments provide a
complete package for their basic course as well as extensive training for
new people in how to teach it. In general, the degree of freedom in teaching the basic course is inversely related to the degree of assistance one is
provided for teaching the course. Generally, the more the department
values the basic course, the more assistance is provided and the less
flexibility is permitted.

How much a new teacher of the basic course is valued is partially
dependent on how much the basic course is valued by the department.
Some departments virtually live off of the basic course. For others, the
basic course is considered a necessary evil: No one wants it, but someone
has to do it. It is not unusual for departments to delegate the basic course
to one person (the basic course fief) and turn its collective head away.
Researchers may look to the basic course as the source of compliant
subjects. The university may look at it as a place to put masses of students who must take something. Other disciplines may look at the course
as a valuable contributor to their students' education, or as a source of too
many high grades. In some places, the basic course is the battle ground
for opposing intellectual forces within the department. Will the public
speaking or the interpersonal forces reign supreme? Shall we teach the
masses about the media or the postpubescents about female–male
relationships?

There are probably as many views of the basic course as there are
viewers. If there is a right and correct view, it has yet to receive the
acclamation it deserves. Nevertheless, as a new person in a department,
you are almost certain to be exposed to the "truth" about the basic course
soon after your arrival. To survive, it is best for you to go along with
whatever is the prevailing view. As a new person, your chances of introducing significant change in the department's approach to the basic
course are nil. However, if you make a significant amount of noise about
it, you might be labeled a "problem person." Problem people constantly
run into problems.

A department's curriculum is the set of courses that the department offers. But it is more than that. It is the external manifestation of the department's history and philosophy. It provides the justification for the existence of the department and the individual members of that department. It is the definition of that department both to students and to faculty members of other departments. In many ways, it *is* the department.

In many instances, a new person is employed explicitly to teach a certain course or courses in that curriculum. Even so, the new person's niche is far from guaranteed. Sometimes, one or more continuing members of the department want to take over those courses, to change them, or even to abolish them. The new person may almost immediately be put on the defensive by challenges from older department members.

It is not unnatural for a faculty member, new or not, to become possessive of a course he or she has been assigned to teach and to become defensive if that course is attacked. It is easy to forget that no faculty member "owns" any course. As teachers of courses, we are, at most, temporary custodians even if we created them. Courses belong to universities. They may be, and sometimes are, moved from one department to another, and even from one college to another.

Assumed ownership of courses causes many problems and conflicts in departments, not the least of which are problems that may be encountered by new people. A person who has taught a course in the recent past, who decided he or she did not what to teach it again, and who participated in the hiring of a new person to handle that responsibility, still may feel possessive of the course. Although all faculty members must take care to avoid undue possessiveness of courses, it is particularly important for the new faculty member to be sensitive to the causes of such responses and to avoid stimulating "ownership" reactions. One of the best ways to do this is to ask the former faculty of the course for advice. New people usually have no knowledge of the problems that have been confronted (and often solved) by their predecessors, so such advice may be extremely valuable. Even if it isn't, just being asked for it may help the other person accept the transition with less hostility. One of the worst ways to approach this new responsibility is to criticize how the course was handled previously and profess the intention to "make improvements." Such criticism will be heard as criticism of the person who taught the course before. Even if that person is no longer in the department, do not forget that friends of that person most likely still are.

One of the more difficult things for new people to deal with is having someone in charge of a course or program whom they feel has less qualifications than they possess. Almost everyone agrees that the most qualified person is the one who should be in charge. Unfortunately, far fewer people agree on what constitutes "most qualified."

The wise course for the new person is to keep his or her opinions about qualifications private. If the opinions are clearly wrong, this will avoid the embarrassment of being demonstrably wrong. If they are right, it is very likely that others will reach the same conclusions in due course. The key is "in due course," and that almost always represents more time than the new person would prefer to wait. Impatience is a fault that few new people can afford to exhibit. People who have been in systems for some time expect new people to "pay their dues" before they are granted full privileges as a member of the system. Exhibiting an unwillingness to be patient most commonly results in a longer, not a shorter, period of "dues paying" before being accepted as a true member of the system.

At some time or other, everyone in higher education must serve as a "new person" in a system. For most of us, this experience will be repeated several times over the course of our professional lives. It can be viewed as an opportunity to start afresh, accept new challenges, and make new friends, or it can be seen as knocking down barriers to doing what one really wants to do. Those who take the former view have a very good chance of being accepted into the new system and being successful in it. Those who take the latter view represent a problem waiting to happen. The new person makes the choice of which course to follow.

35

Growing As a Professional

Gerald M. Phillips
Pennsylvania State University

Mary-Linda Merriam
Wilson College

THE MATURE ACADEMIC PROFESSIONAL

This chapter discusses six major obligations of academic professionals:

- the obligation to be culturally literate,
- the obligation to be sophisticated in one's specialty,
- the obligation to do research and disseminate the results,
- the obligation to teach well,
- the obligation to serve the academic community, and
- the obligation to make sensible decisions about one's career.

Carroll Arnold once remarked that once you receive a PhD, you are permanently changed. You cannot go "home." The academic professional occupies a special place in society charged with the responsibility to consume, create, and criticize knowledge; to separate the wise from the foolish, the frivolous from the consequential, and to announce the results to students, colleagues, and the world.

Being an academic professional means more than teaching students. Teaching is crucial to society and must never be demeaned, but academic professionals must also engage in independent discovery to provide the teachables. The job of the professor is to "profess;" to declare what the truth is today and to change it whenever the data warrant.

Communication professors have a unique responsibility in the academy, for they are the guardians of the process by which knowledge is shared. Their field includes the most powerful human abilities: to speak ideas, to make collective decisions, and to share the company of other human beings. Communication professors also confront the most serious human problems: misunderstanding, conflict, exploitation, and social combat. No wonder "rhetoric is the queen of all the sciences" and the origins of the world's first universities were in its study.

MATURE CULTURAL LITERACY

Hirsch (1987) argued that all citizens must be culturally literate: sophisticated in the basic concepts that unite people in our culture. College professors are the conservators of cultural literacy. They must link past and present to influence the future. This requires more than specialized knowledge of a discipline; it means knowing the great ideas of the arts and sciences and the wisdom of the Eastern and Western worlds. There is no academic discipline that can exist out of the context of common wisdom. The mature academic professional has a good sense of where his or her discipline fits in the community of ideas.

Communication professors have a special obligation to be culturally literate. Their study, by its very nature, is interdisciplinary. It is not possible to study communication without understanding the substantive ideas about which people communicate. It is no accident that communication is not studied in totalitarian societies. Rulers who would hold their people prisoner must control their communication.

In democratic societies, communication is the fuel for the political process. Communication scholars mediate the process of analysis of old ideas and the forging of new ones. Regardless of their specific area of specialization, communication scholars must be sufficiently well read to understand the ideas about which people speak and write. The study and teaching of communication represents the prototypical synthesis of cultural literacy and specialized knowledge. Professional growth demands constant attention to both scholarship and current events. This includes knowledge of both historical and popular culture as well as the fundamentals of the arts, sciences, and humanities. Equally important is understanding of the daily life of ordinary people and sensitivity to the public issues and social concerns that confront them.

Above all, the study and teaching of human communication constrains the mature academic professional to be willing and able to revise ideas when new information or refined analysis justifies it. There is no academic so stunted as one who defends reflexively ideas that have lost both their grace and utility. Professional growth means not only possessing the means of inventing rhetoric but also the will to revise it when necessary in both teaching and research.

Cultural literacy is the basis of the academic's rhetoric; the ability to write and speak well, to listen attentively, and to read critically are the results of knowledge and experience. The ability to communicate is the bridge across the academic cultures. As communication scholars range from phonologists to philosophers, they recapitulate the arts and sciences. Communication is the only means by which knowledge can be unified into a common wisdom. It is the duty of the communication discipline to study and teach not only how to communicate, but why and how people communicate. The cultural literacy of the profession depends on sound knowledge of process combined with effective pedagogy.

CONTENT SOPHISTICATION

To avoid growing old and intellectually decadent requires content sophistication. Crackling and yellowed notes go hand in hand with intellectual stultification and error. The mature academic professional is intellectually contemporaneous and remains that way with little regard for the cost in time, money, or energy. Growth as a communication professional requires maintaining one's status as "expert."

An expert is a person who has special skill or knowledge. The professional academic is expected to be an expert on something of suitable worth. Mature professionals must keep up with new information to avoid being fooled by fads. They must avoid blind alleys and be able to discard ideas when they become obsolete or are proven false.

There are a great many areas in which communication scholars can be expert: rhetorical theory, history, and criticism; history and criticism of public address; communication theory and philosophy; organizational, small-group, interpersonal, and intrapersonal communication; public, business and professional, and ceremonial speaking; intercultural communication and comparative linguistics; speech science, linguistics, and communication disorders; telecommunication; oral interpretation and drama; freedom of speech; communication technology; and communication as it is used in various disciplines and professions. Each of these topics can be approached through various forms of research: behaviorism, experimental studies, social theory, case history, field study, philosophy, hermeneutics and exegesis, demographics, experimental studies, historiography, and more. Communication specialists must be sufficiently well informed to talk to their colleagues, whatever their field of specialization. When academics split off and talk only to their own kind, the whole discipline suffers from casuistry and scholasticism.

Academics are evaluated on their status as experts. This means they must have more valid information on a particular topic than others. What they know is judged on four criteria: it must be cogent, current, useful, and communicable. Their knowledge must be obtained regularly and steadily through a programme of reading in professional journals and scholarly books, meeting regularly with other professionals, serious inquiry and investigation, and submitting their thinking to public scrutiny and critique via publication.

Cogent means that the information an academic experiences is detailed and complex. *Current* means it is up to date. It is *useful* if the thinking of others is helped by it, and it is *communicable* when its owner has thought about it sufficiently to speak or write about it in a fashion that is intelligible and helpful to students, colleagues, or other interested parties. Mature academic professionals maintain current data bases and bibliographies. They are revisionists constantly modifying their ideas as well as those of others. Each utterance they make, whether orally or in writing, represents the most accurate and current statement possible. The true expert is not afraid to modify or recant, nor timid about attempting new ideas. The goal, of course, is to seek that singular immortality available only to academics: a notation in a future encyclopedia that says, "Dr. So-and-so once believed such-and-such, but later proved himself or herself wrong."

PUBLISH OR PERISH

In this and the following section, we discuss what we believe to be the crucial dialectic in the life of an academic professional: the balance between research and teaching. What is at stake in this decision is personal satisfaction with your career and the promise of being truly a professional academic.

Few academic professionals receive job descriptions, but virtually all receive a "faculty handbook" that explains what their institution expects of them. The consensus is that academics are evaluated on research, teaching, professional activity, and service. It is hard to evaluate teaching, and institutions vary widely in their expectations regarding it. Research, however, can be evaluated by its public results, publication. "Publish or perish" is not a canard for the mature academic professional. He or she knows how to do research and publish the results and, furthermore, knows how to integrate it into the teaching process. Not-so-successful professionals may regard publication as an onerous chore and take refuge in claims about the quality of their teaching and the demands it makes on their professional life. But, it is clear that research and teaching are counterparts essential to professional growth.

All institutions require that candidates for promotion and tenure give evidence of good teaching and research. Academic professionals can choose the kind of institution they prefer based on the emphasis it places on research and teaching. They can and should seek the institution that gives them the best opportunity to display their abilities. To choose the wrong one is to risk professional failure.

It takes time to acquire a mature conception of the relationship between research and teaching. The learning experiences required to earn a PhD are rehearsals for the life experience of the professor. Each bit of research that results in publication recapitulates the dissertation. Publication is evidence of work done. Thus, institutions justifiably assign their professionals to produce such evidence.

Publication outlets are virtually limitless. The only excuses for not publishing are failure to do research and inability to write. Neither is valid. There are 260,000 full-time academics in the United States and nearly 100,000 journals providing about a half-million publishing opportunities. These journals accept monographs, articles, reviews, research reports, commentary, history, results of experiments, think pieces, philosophical essays, and reports of classroom innovations. In addition, more than 4,000 scholarly books are published each year in addition to texts and popular articles on scholarly topics. Yet, the median number of publications for full-time academics is zero. Less than one fourth of all full time academics account for 90% of what is published. One third of all academics do not publish a single line during their entire careers.

Many academics resist the obligation to publish on the grounds that it interferes with their main mission, teaching. They argue that academic institutions should place more emphasis on teaching or that their teaching is so good that it, alone, should be taken into account in tenure and promotion decisions. However, research is crucial in determining whether an academic submits his or her ideas to the criticism of peers. The response of fellow scholars helps promotion and tenure committees decide on the value of the contribution made by each faculty member. Research is a teaching/learning process for the professional. It is "doing as I do" rather than simply "doing as I say."

Research universities argue that the best teaching is done by alert researchers who are able to bring the most current and exciting ideas to the classroom. Furthermore, remedial programs notwithstanding, the mission of a college and university is more than simply educating the young. They are repositories of knowledge and charged with the responsibility of conserving and adding to that repository. Research and teaching must be, at the least, co-equal. Those institutions in which faculties are primarily involved in research give more than lip service to quality teaching; and community colleges encourage their faculties to do research.

THE TEACHING MISSION

Teaching is an art and, as such, is extraordinarily difficult to evaluate. Should it be done based on how acceptable a teacher is to the students? Should subsequent accomplishments by students (e.g., grades in other courses or acceptance to graduate schools) be the main criterion? Some academics use teaching as a synonym for socialization with their students (as they use research as a synonym for pleasure reading). Still others use teaching as a way of winning admiration from students. Evidence of good research submitted for public scrutiny virtually guarantees objective judgment. The act of teaching generally does not enjoy this advantage.

We do not really know what makes a good teacher, although there is consensus that it is some combination of information, communication skill, and sensitivity to students' needs. Good teachers not only are appealing to students, but are sufficiently rigorous in criticism to hold students to the highest standards of knowledge. Clearly, it is more than charm or charisma (a definition of which could be charm without content). Students are entitled to more from a teacher than entertainment or demands for personal loyalty. Teaching based on out-of-date information or on ideology is not appropriate for mature academic professionals. Neither is ego-centered teaching. In fact, the quality of the content taught is the major criterion for evaluation of effective teaching.

Academic freedom makes teaching a relatively private matter between teacher and students. It receives outside evaluation only at times when decisions about retention or advancement must be made. Research, however, is always done in public view and subject to continuing evaluation. Thus, the teacher who is engaged in research and publication, in addition to teaching, is best able to maintain the balance between content and presentational style. Detachment that comes from serious concern for research responsibilities can also help in keeping a perspective and balance in relationships with students.

The closeness that is intrinsic in the communication classroom can create serious relationship problems. Because of this closeness, students are often attracted to communication teachers. During the first half of this century, the concept of *in loco parentis* helped academic institutions keep teachers and students from infringing on each others' personal rights. Today, however, it is the teacher's responsibility to maintain the proper distance from the students. Relationships between them can be productive or threatening, depending on the teacher. Young students are often very vulnerable to the influence of adults whom they admire. Mature academic professionals are careful to manage the teaching process so that it impairs neither the students' lives nor the professionals' careers.

Personal relationships between teachers and students are not unusual, nor are they always dangerous, but they must be thoughtfully and judiciously managed. The 1984 Carnegic Report (Jacobson, 1985) reports that more than 90% of faculty members enjoy contact with students outside of class. Only 24% believed contact should be restricted to classrooms and formal office hours. Teachers have enormous power over the young people in their care. An apparently harmless liaison can place a career in jeopardy and betray the trust of the student.

In situations where students have the power to evaluate their teachers, the pressure for good evaluations can create difficult problems for both. In attempting to please students, teachers can become so magnetic that students become their disciples. When this happens, the teacher assumes inordinate responsibility for what happens. Furthermore, when teachers define themselves as counselors or comrades, they also take responsibility for the outcome. It is difficult to draw the line between supportive contact and pathological transference. However, the mature academic professional is careful to protect the integrity and individuality of students and to avoid relationships that go beyond what is required to teach well. Whether the teacher's goal is to guide learning activity, provoke curiosity, stimulate originality, encourage those who fail to try again, or motivate students to aspire to greater efforts at exploration and inquiry, his or her activity must be carefully modulated to protect the privacy and integrity of everyone involved. Some teachers are tempted by the emotions that generate from contact with students and become charismatics. When this happens, one can see a decline in scholarly productivity, usually accompanied by a commensurate poor performance in the classroom. It is also important for teachers to avoid exceeding their competence. The temptation to counsel students about personal matters is very strong, but the mature academic professional knows when to defer to others with better credentials and experience.

For those who deal with graduate students, the mission is a bit more complex. Graduate study is built on intimacy (Phillips, 1979). Graduate students are actually junior colleagues. They represent the interface at which collegiality grows. The relationship between graduate students and their mentors is necessarily close because it involves collaboration in both teaching and research. Medical and law students learn a great deal through their apprenticeships, but those who seek advanced degrees literally become junior partners with their professors. The relationship presents serious moral questions about responsibility for research, supervision of teaching, joint authorship, and the maintenance of continued contact. The mature academic professional is able to enjoy the closeness of graduate study as well as use it to push forward the frontiers of knowledge through a serious and productive collaboration.

The crucial questions that affect teaching and research are matters of daily concern for mature academic professionals.

- How can a professional find an area in which to do productive research? How can he or she sustain a regular program of research and publication?
- How can a professional integrate his or her research activity into the teaching process? How can research and its related activities be made useful to students?
- How can a professional excite students without becoming a charismatic? Can professionals maintain a balance between technique and content so that they do not become performers who sacrifice serious content in order to maintain popularity?
- How can a professional enjoy relationships with students without imposing on students?
- How can a professional select an institution at which to work that will permit an appropriate balance between teaching and research?

Resolution of the practical and ethical issues inherent in these questions is crucial in the career of a mature academic professional.

THE ACADEMIC COMMUNITY

The academic community consists of faculty, administrators, and ancillary personnel working together. Each professional has an independent role to play. In addition to the local community at the particular college or university, the academic belongs to a larger community of scholars in his or her discipline, as well as to the community of scholarly professionals in general. There are obligations on every level.

The mature academic professional must be associated with the mission of their institution and must work to implement it. If they cannot do so, they are obligated to work through legitimate channels for change or to move to another institution, with whose goals they are more compatible.

Furthermore, mature professionals are responsible for acculturation of younger faculty members by providing advice, encouragement, and collaboration where possible. The mentor relationship between old and young faculty is an effective way of building lasting academic enterprises. However, it is equally important to remember that relationships in the academy are often temporary. Young faculty are free to follow their own muses. The academy does not thrive on sectarianism and disciplehood. Even in the most rigid or denominational institutions, academics must remember that their mission is the effective pursuit of truth.

To this end, academics must be "citizen soldiers." Academics cherish self-governance above all else. This can only be achieved when scholars assume responsibilities for the common good. This means committee service, housekeeping chores, and accepting responsibility for minor housekeeping and administrative chores. Without active faculty participation in governance, colleges and universities can become administrative fiefdoms in which inquiry is stifled and controversy suppressed. Faculty service to the institution is in their own interest, for they can only flourish in flourishing institutions.

The mature professional also has obligations to the profession. Membership in professional organizations is mandatory. The professional organizations support productive intellectual contact through regular meetings and maintenance of scholarly journals. They need both financial and personal support. Contact with fellow professionals is imperative to growth, for it is the most appropriate vehicle for the exchange of ideas and information.

TO THINE OWN SELF BE TRUE

The best professionals are very careful about the setting in which they do their work. Given that the two most important issues for academic professionals are (a) developing a research interest and growing with it and (b) finding an appropriate teaching style and becoming better at it, the institution at which they do it is extraordinarily influential. The best professionals have chosen their workplace with care.

The choice is difficult to make. For one thing, the right job is often not available. For another, a newly minted PhD does not always know what kind of job is best. Most academic professionals move once or twice before they make a permanent affiliation. Financial considerations are always important in job choice, but all things being equal, they are not necessarily the main consideration. If money is the sole goal, it is best sought outside the university. Very often, professionals are corrupted by their own success at private consulting and entrepreneurship.

Young PhDs are often tempted by jobs at major research institutions. Many of them discover (usually after 5 years) that they are not willing or able to assume the burden of research and publication imposed. Either they leave and literally begin a new career at another type of institution, or they are denied tenure and face even more difficulties locating a new job. It is important to make major career decisions early enough so there is an opportunity to try and revise without acquiring a sense of failure.

In general, selection of a job depends on seven major considerations:

1. Is it possible to live decently on the salary offered? Are salary and benefits comparable to those at other similar institutions? What is the policy on pay increases?

2. What are the requirements for promotion and tenure?

3. What are the policies on sabbaticals, obtaining research grants, and participating in university governance?

4. What are the expectations for research, publication, professional contact, membership in professional organizations, community service, and consulting?

5. What are the expectations for teaching evaluations, classroom contact hours, and advising/counseling of students?

6. Do the library and computer facilities meet your research needs?

7. Are colleagues compatible with your needs and interests?

It is possible to get direct information about these matters by asking interviewers or consulting local contacts and friends. Documents like the faculty handbook, benefits books, catalogues, and other official publications should be consulted, and ambiguities should be resolved during the interview process. Accurate information is essential to an intelligent choice of a position.

Most beginning faculty members have a choice of at least two or three positions. After that, moves depend on strategic job-hunting combined with reputation, references, and the support of mentors.

There is another issue as well: when or whether to leave the professoriat and enter administration. A great many talented academics are tempted to move into administration. Their professional success brings them to the attention of administrators who offer them opportunities for department headships or deanships.

But make no mistake about it: The rank of professor is the highest academic rank attainable. The is no next rung on the ladder. The job of dean or department head requires a major change both in mindset and pattern of life. Regardless of high hopes and plans, most administrators must sacrifice both research time and student contact. If you receive gratification from interacting with students or engaging in research, you will have to give it up in order to fulfill the obligations of an administrative position.

Administration is attractive, interesting, exciting, and it usually pays more than professors receive. However, the issues are very different from those in teaching, and the schedule demands are considerably more rigorous. Administrators spend a great deal of time budgeting, attending meetings, planning, and dealing with personnel issues. Academics exploring potential careers in administration must consider carefully their interest in dealing with these issues.

In the medieval university, the faculty took responsibility for administrative work. In the American university, however, the career paths have diverged. In a few major research universities, both department chairships and deanships are regarded as temporary obligations to be assumed by senior faculty members for short, specifically defined terms. In those institutions, the faculty has full authority over academic business. In most institutions, however, department headships and deanships are part of middle management. The occupants of the positions are not elected; they are selected by higher administrators, and they remain in their position as the pleasure of their superiors.

Administration as a career may look good to faculty members whose declining standard of living and increasing work loads may be depressing, but it may not be the answer. If money is the issue, it may make more sense to seek it in industry. It is useful to consider some of the professional issues confronting today's academics:

- There is no real prospect for major increases in salary for professors. Furthermore, the promotion and tenure requirements are likely to become more stringent. In fact, some institutions are attempting to do away with tenure altogether.
- Student bodies are becoming more diverse. Professors are becoming more responsible for various forms of compensatory instruction. Pressure to spend time with students is increasing without mitigating the pressure to produce research.
- Research funds are drying up. Major grants are usually available only to professors of high reputation. On the other hand, there are great many small grants available for research initiation. There are also grants available that permit faculty members to experiment for a year or so as an administrator to test their aptitude and proclivity for an administrative career.
- Demographic information indicates that available academic positions will gradually increase and hit a peak around the turn of the century. Many of the professors who started their jobs during the baby boom years are nearing retirement age. There is a small increase in the birthrate accompanied by pressure for more people to attend college. These factors will combine to increase opportunities.

To be a mature academic professional, you must choose a position that will enable you to use your talents and fulfill your goals for personal accomplishment. Those who do not find the position that suits them burn out. Those that do, experience the richness of one of the most rewarding careers available in our society.

SUMMARY

In this chapter, we have discussed the six obligations of the mature academic professional. We pointed out that cultural literacy and subject-matter sophistication are essential qualifications. We also noted the difficulty that all professionals encounter in balancing the obligations of teaching and research. Our consideration of obligations to the profession and institution culminated in a discussion of administration as an alternate career.

The mature academic professional regards his or her career as a learning experience. By raising hypotheses and testing them within the realm of possibilities, it is possible to achieve the balance of interests and skills necessary to professional success and satisfaction. Communication professors have special responsibilities because their discipline involves close contact with students in an interdisciplinary context. It simply is not possible to achieve without growing. The question is one of managing the growth to the benefit of the discipline and one's own personal and professional life.

REFERENCES

Hirsch, E. D. (1987). *Cultural literacy: What every American needs to know.* Boston: Houghton, Mifflin.

Jacobson, R. L. (1985). New Carnegie data show faculty members uneasy about the state of Academe and their own careers. *The Chronicle of Higher Education, 34*(18), p. 1.

Phillips, G. M. (1979). The peculiar intimacy of graduate study. *Communication Education, 28,* 339–345.

Author Index

Subject Index

K